Statement	Comment
SAVE [⟨name list⟩]	Used to retain values of local variables between calls.
(*)ENTRY ⟨name⟩[⟨arg. list⟩]	Not used in this text.
(*)EQUIVALENCE ⟨name list⟩	Not used in this text.
(*)BLOCK DATA ⟨name⟩	Not used in this text.

ASSIGNMENT AND PROGRAM CONTROL STATEMENTS (executable)

Statement	Comment
Assignment statement ⟨name⟩ = ⟨exp.⟩	⟨exp.⟩ may be any of the Fortran data-types depending on the type of ⟨name⟩.
STOP [tag]	[tag] is an INTEGER or CHARACTER constant.
(*)ASSIGN ⟨stmt. label⟩ TO ⟨name⟩	Not used in this text.
(*)PAUSE [tag]	Not used in this text.

FLOW-CONTROL STATEMENTS

Statement	Comment
RETURN [exp.]	Return from a subprogram. The optional [exp.] is used for alternate returns from a subroutine.
CALL ⟨subr. name⟩[⟨arg. list⟩]	Transfer of control to subroutine ⟨name⟩.
CONTINUE	Loop terminator or target of a GO TO.
GO TO ⟨stmt. label⟩	Unconditional GO TO.
GO TO (⟨stmt. label list⟩),⟨exp.⟩	Computed GO TO.
(*)GO TO ⟨assigned variable⟩	Assigned GO TO. Not used in this text.
IF(⟨arith. exp.⟩)sl_1,sl_2,sl_3	Arithmetic IF test.
IF(⟨logical exp.⟩)⟨execut. stmt.⟩	Logical IF test.
IF(⟨logical exp.⟩)THEN	Logical block IF.
ELSE	Optional ELSE block.
ELSE IF(⟨logical exp.⟩)THEN	Optional conditional block.
END IF	Block IF terminator.
DO ⟨stmt. label⟩ vn = $e_1,e_2[,e_3]$	DO loop. vn is a variable name, e_1,e_2,e_3 are expressions specifying index bounds.

FILE DIRECTIVE STATEMENTS

Statement	Comment
OPEN(⟨unit no.⟩,FILE = '⟨name⟩',[options])	Connects a file to an I/O unit.
CLOSE(⟨unit no.⟩)	Disconnects a file.
REWIND ⟨unit no.⟩	Positions a SAM file at the beginning.

Continued on back endsheets

FORTRAN 77
AND NUMERICAL METHODS
FOR ENGINEERS

FORTRAN 77 AND NUMERICAL METHODS FOR ENGINEERS

G. J. BORSE

Lehigh University

 PWS ENGINEERING • BOSTON

PWS PUBLISHERS

Prindle, Weber & Schmidt • 🐝 • Duxbury Press • ♠ • PWS Engineering • ⚙ • Breton Publishers • ⚘
20 Park Plaza • Boston, Massachusetts 02116

PWS Publishers is a division of Wadsworth, Inc.

87 88 89—10 9 8 7 6 5

Library of Congress Cataloging in Publication Data

Borse, Garold J.
    FORTRAN 77 and numerical methods for engineers.

    Includes index.
    1. Engineering—Data processing. 2. FORTRAN
(Computer program language) I. Title. II. Title:
FORTRAN Seventy-seven.
TA345.B67 1985   620'.0028'5424   85–531
ISBN 0–534–04638–X

ISBN 0-534-04638-X

Cover photograph © DEI/Phototake
Sponsoring Editor—John E. Block
Signing Representative—Winston Beauchamp
Editorial Assistants—Gabriele Bert and Suzi Sheperd
Composition: Interactive Composition Corporation
Printing and Binding: Halliday Lithograph
Cover Printing: New England Book Components

"CDC" and its computer "CDC-CYBER-730" are registered trademarks of Control Data Corporation. "DEC" and its computers "DEC-20" and "PDP-11" are registered trademarks of Digital Equipment Corporation. "IBM" and its computer "IBM-4341" are registered trademarks of International Business Machines Corporation. "TI" is the registered trademark of Texas Instruments, Inc.

The core of a beginning engineering curriculum traditionally consists of courses in calculus and physics. In the last decade a third area, Fortran programming, has gained overwhelming acceptance as one of the essential skills prerequisite to later technical studies. An enormous variety of courses have been created to satisfy this need. Most of these introductory courses have concentrated on the teaching of Fortran programming only and have left the bulk of the problem solving to later specialty courses in the various engineering disciplines. The main emphasis of these later courses is the teaching of numerical methods as they apply to each of the subfields of engineering or science. The numerical methods of these courses are essentially identical, only the example problems differ.

A number of institutions have recognized that a more efficient approach would be to include both Fortran and numerical methods in the same introductory course. This text is intended for such a course and is specifically geared to the beginning engineering and science student. The underlying premise throughout is that Fortran programming is important, not simply as a study unto itself, but as one mechanism, in addition to calculus and physics, whereby the analytical sophistication of an engineering student may be developed. Furthermore, when students are asked to solve genuinely challenging and interesting problems in engineering, their motivation increases as well as their ability in Fortran.

Engineering applications are emphasized in this text. Numerous and challenging programming assignments are used to illustrate the Fortran and numerical methods and are also useful as an introduction to the subfields of engineering. Each of the longer programming assignments is preceded by a completely solved example that may be used as a model. This will enable the student to attempt realistic and interesting problems almost immediately.

The mathematical level is appropriate for freshmen or sophomores who are currently taking a normal calculus sequence. Most of the topics considered in numerical methods are also discussed to some degree in a calculus course. The emphasis here is, however, rather different. Problems in a calculus class are often more analytical than numerical and are usually selected from fields unrelated to engineering.

The first half of the text (Chapters 1–9) is concerned with learning the elements of programming problems in Fortran 77. The emphasis is on the construction of Fortran code in a so-called structured style—that is, in terms of modular subunits. The student is encouraged to execute simple programs immediately and to continue to use the computer to solve problems, even nonassigned problems, throughout the course. There are a great many details in addition to the elements of Fortran that can best be assimilated through experience—for example, where to find the terminals to use in this course, and how to operate those terminals.

Fortran is not mathematics. There is no single, universally agreed-upon sequence of topics in its exposition. The order of topics presented here is fairly typical of a Fortran course for engineers. However, the early introduction of disk data files in Chapter 4 is rather atypical and is intended to provide access to general file-manipulation features that should be part of the longer, more complicated programs that the student will soon be constructing. The material of Chapter 7, manipulation of character variables, may be omitted without a loss of continuity if the course is concentrated. Though the mathematical level is maintained at a level appropriate to beginning engineers, new mathematical methods are kept to a minimum at this point. A few mathematical topics, such as the bisection technique for finding roots of a function or the determination of the minimum of a list of numbers or a function, are used to illustrate important programming techniques.

The numerical methods half of the text (Chapters 10–16) presents most of the popular techniques employed in engineering analysis. The idea is to incorporate the just-learned Fortran skills into useful procedures to solve a variety of mathematical problems. The running theme in this section of the text is that a fundamental test of the student's understanding of a mathematical procedure is his/her ability to meticulously and correctly translate the procedure into a working Fortran code. Traditionally, the topics of numerical methods are first encountered in the junior year or later. The treatment here was specially designed for beginning engineering students. Very few analytical derivations are used when more pictorially motivated developments would suffice. Even though there are numerous mathematical procedures that are not included here, such as eigenvalue problems or linear programming, among others, the list of topics that are present is far too extensive to comfortably fit within a typical course. Most of the material of Chapter 15, numerical solution of differential equations, though very important, may be omitted if a similar or more detailed treatment will be encountered in later courses.

Acknowledgments

When designing a new introductory course of any type, one accumulates a great many debts to individuals, from deans to teaching assistants, who freely give their time and knowledge. In the construction and evolution of a course such as the one based on this text, the list is very long indeed. Colleagues in each of the engineering disciplines helped in the construction of problems illustrating engineering analysis. The computing center at Lehigh University was continually helpful. I would like to acknowledge the special assistance of my colleagues at Lehigh, John Karakash, Curt Clump, Robert Johnson, and Stephen K. Tarby who permitted the use of a typewritten version of this text to be used in our Fortran for Engineers course.

My greatest debt is to the several thousand Lehigh engineering students who have read and used this text in its various preliminary forms and who have made innumerable suggestions for its improvement. Of course, my family, through their tolerance and encouragement, have contributed immeasurably to this work.

I am also grateful for the advice and suggestions of the many reviewers of the original manuscript, in particular:

Linda Hayes, University of Texas at Austin; Glen Williams, Texas A & M University; William Kubitz, University of Illinois; Tom Boyle, Purdue University; Philip M. Wolfe, Oklahoma State University; John B. Crittenden, Virginia Polytechnic Institute; Allen R. Cook, University of Oklahoma; Terry Feagin, University of Tennessee; Betty Barr, University of Houston; Robert Good, Widener University; Bart Childs, Texas A & M University; Richard C. Harshman, Clemson University; Walter W. Wilson, University of Texas at Arlington; Frederick Way, III, Case Western Reserve University

The help and encouragement of John Block, engineering editor at PWS Engineering, and the many contributions of John Servideo and Deborah Schneider in the production of this book are cordially acknowledged.

CONTENTS

1 THE OPERATIONS OF A COMPUTER

1.1	Introduction	1
1.2	Operation Principles of Digital Computers	4
1.3	Communicating with the Computer	9
1.4	The Mechanics of "Getting On" the Machine	11
1.5	Program Zero	20
	Problems	24

2 THE FUNDAMENTALS OF FORTRAN

2.1	Introduction	27
2.2	Constants in Fortran	28
2.3	Fortran Variables	31
2.4	Arithmetic Expressions	33
2.5	More Complicated Arithmetic Expressions	36
2.6	The Assignment Statement	39
2.7	Program Zero	41
2.8	Translating Algebra into Fortran	48
2.9	List-Directed Input and Output	50
2.10	Summary	51
	Problems	52

3 FLOW CONTROL STRUCTURES AND PROGRAM DESIGN

3.1	Introduction	55
3.2	The Use of Flowcharts and Pseudocode in Program Design	56
3.3	Decision Structures in Fortran	59
3.4	Loop Structures in Fortran	71
3.5	A Note on Good Programming Style	85
3.6	Additional Control Statements	86
	Problems	89

PROGRAMMING ASSIGNMENT I

I.1	Introduction	93
I.2	Sample Program	93
	Civil Engineering: Pressure Drop in a Fluid Flowing Through a Pipe	93
I.3	Programming Assignments	99
	Mechanical Engineering	99
	Programming Problem A: Most Cost-Efficient Steam Pipe Insulation	99

Civil Engineering	102
Programming Problem B: Oxygen Deficiency of a Polluted Stream	102

4 ELEMENTARY PROGRAMMING TECHNIQUES

4.1 Introduction	105
4.2 The Statement Function	105
4.3 Finding the Minimum and Maximum of a Set of Numbers	109
4.4 Performing a Summation	113
4.5 The Bisection Technique for Finding Roots of Equations	119
4.6 The Use of Data Files	124
Problems	135

5 ELEMENTARY FORMATTED INPUT-OUTPUT

5.1 Introduction	138
5.2 Formatted I/O Statements	139
5.3 The Format Statement	140
5.4 Elementary Input and Output of Text	148
5.5 Some Technical Points to Remember	152
Problems	156

PROGRAMMING ASSIGNMENT II

II.1 Sample Program	161
Chemical Engineering	161
Sample Program: Gas Separation	162
II.2 Programming Problems	168
Metallurgical Engineering and Materials Science	168
Programming Problem A: Carburization	169
Electrical Engineering	171
Programming Problem B: Semiconductor Diode	172
Programming Problem C: Coexistence of Liquids and Gases	174

6 DIMENSIONED VARIABLES AND DO LOOPS

6.1 Introduction	179
6.2 The DIMENSION Statement	180
6.3 Internal Storage of Arrays	187
6.4 The DO Loop	188
6.5 The Implied DO loop	194
6.6 Miscellaneous Examples of Loop Structures and Arrays	196
Problems	200

7 NON-NUMERICAL APPLICATIONS—CHARACTER VARIABLES

7.1 Review of Character Variables	203
7.2 Character Substrings	205
7.3 Intrinsic Functions Related to Character Variables	206
7.4 Character Expressions—Concatenation	208
7.5 Comparison of Character Strings	209
7.6 Sorting Algorithms	210
7.7 Plotting a Graph on the Line Printer or Terminal Screen	216
Problems	224

PROGRAMMING ASSIGNMENT III

III.1 Sample Program	228
Industrial Engineering	228
III.2 Programming Problems	235
Programming Problem A: Resonant Circuit	235
Programming Problem B: Cooling Curve for Transfer Ladle Cars	237
Programming Problem C: Compressibility Factors for Real Gases	240

8 FUNCTIONS AND SUBROUTINES

8.1 Introduction	243
8.2 Review of Statement Functions	244
8.3 Subroutine Subprograms	245
8.4 Function Subprograms	254
8.5 Example Programs Using Functions and Subroutines	256
8.6 Constructing Modular Programs	268
Problems	278

9 ADDITIONAL FORTRAN FEATURES

9.1 Additional Data Types Available in Fortran	286
9.2 Initializing Variables at Compilation Time	291
9.3 The Order of Fortran Statements	294
9.4 The DoWhile Structure in Extended Fortran	296
9.5 Additional Fortran Intrinsic Functions	298
9.6 Conclusion	298
Problems	300

PROGRAMMING ASSIGNMENT IV

IV.1 Sample Program	303

Aeronautical/Aerospace Engineering 303
Sample Program: The Range of a Rocket Trajectory 304
IV.2 Programming Problems 312
Programming Problem A: Cooling Fins on a Steam Pipe
(Mechanical Engineering) 312
Programming Problem B: Nim 315

10 TAYLOR SERIES AND NUMERICAL DIFFERENTIATION

10.1 Introduction 320
10.2 The Taylor Series 322
10.3 Numerical Differentiation 337
Problems 344

11 ROOTS OF EQUATIONS

11.1 Introduction 347
11.2 Refinement of the Bisection Method 350
11.3 Newton's Method for Root Solving 358
11.4 Rate of Convergence[1] 369
11.5 The Secant Method 371
11.6 Root-Solving Procedures for Polynomials[1] 373
11.7 Comparison of Root-Solving Methods 378
Problems 379

PROGRAMMING ASSIGNMENT V

V.1 Sample Program 383
The Determination of the Diffusion Constant 383
V.2 Programming Problems 389
Programming Problem A: Civil Engineering and Mechanics:
The Buckling of a Tall Mast 389
Programming Problem B: Mining Engineering: Depth of a
Flume 391
Programming Problem C: General Engineering: Functions
Describing Diffusion 393

12 LINEAR SIMULTANEOUS EQUATIONS—MATRICES

12.1 Introduction 396
12.2 The Notation of Matrices 397
12.3 Determinants 402

[1] Sections 11.4 and 11.6 contain somewhat more advanced material and may be omitted without a loss of continuity.

12.4 Cramer's Rule 407
12.5 The Gauss-Jordan Method of Solving Simultaneous Linear Equations 410
12.6 Matrix Inversion by the Gauss-Jordan Method 417
12.7 Relative Speed and Accuracy of the Various Matrix Algorithms 421
12.8 Iterative Techniques for Solving Simultaneous Equations 422
12.9 Miscellaneous Fortran Codes Relating to Matrices 429
Problems 432

PROGRAMMING ASSIGNMENT VI

VI.1 Sample Program 437
Civil Engineering: Fluid Flow Through a Plumbing Network 437
VI.2 Programming Problems 448
Programming Problem A: Civil Engineering: A Model of a Stress Calculation for a Bridge 448
Programming Problem B: The Currents in an Electrical Network 452

13 LEAST SQUARES CURVE FITTING

13.1 Introduction 456
13.2 The Principle of Least Squares Analysis 457
13.3 Minimum or Maximum of a Function of Two Variables 459
13.4 Minimization of the Sum of the Squared Deviations 461
13.5 Least Squares Fit of a Polynomial 466
13.6 Validity of Fit 468
13.7 The Fortran Code for a Polynomial Least Squares Curve Fit 471
13.8 An Example of a Least Squares Polynomial Fit 475
13.9 Limitations of the Least Squares Procedure 477
13.10 Cubic Spline Fits[2] 480
Problems 486

PROGRAMMING ASSIGNMENT VII

VII.1 Sample Program 490
Empirical Heat Capacities of Gases 490
VII.2 Programming Problems 494
Programming Problem A: Aerodynamics: Free Fall in Air 494
Programming Problem B: Record Times for the Mile Run 499

[2] Section 13.10 contains somewhat more advanced material and may be omitted without a loss of continuity.

14 NUMERICAL INTEGRATION

14.1 Introduction 502
14.2 The Trapezoidal Rule 504
14.3 Simpson's Rule Approximation for an Integral 508
14.4 Beyond Simpson's Rule 514
14.5 Romberg Integration 515
14.6 Beyond Romberg 522
14.7 What If the Integration Interval Is Infinite? 527
14.8 Singularities in the Integrand 530
14.9 Double Integrals 531
14.10 Conclusion 534
Problems 534

PROGRAMMING ASSIGNMENT VIII

VIII.1 Sample Program 537
    Mechanical Engineering: Conductive Heat Losses 537
VIII.2 Programming Problems 546
    Programming Problem A: Mechanical/Aeronautical Engineering:
      The Shear Face on an Airplane Wing 546
    Programming Problem B: Curve Fitting with Legendre
      Polynomials 549

15 NUMERICAL SOLUTIONS TO DIFFERENTIAL EQUATIONS

15.1 Introduction 552
15.2 The Meaning of a Differential Equation 553
15.3 A Note on Computational Errors: A Question of
    Trade-offs 557
15.4 Euler's Method 559
15.5 Improvements to Euler's Method 562
15.6 The Method of Runge-Kutta 569
15.7 Predictor-Corrector Methods 573
15.8 Second-Order Differential Equations 574
15.9 Boundary-Value Problems 583
15.10 Conclusion 584
Problems 584

16 ERROR ANALYSIS

16.1 Introduction 588
16.2 A Review of Definitions Relating to Error Analysis 589
16.3 Types of Error 592
16.4 Round-Off Errors 593
16.5 Approximation Errors: Discretization and Truncation 602

16.6 Experimental Errors   **604**
16.7 Conclusion   **608**

APPENDIX SUMMARY OF FORTRAN STATEMENTS AND GRAMMAR RULES

A.1 Procedure Statements   **610**
A.2 Specification Statements   **612**
A.3 Assignment and Program Control Statements   **617**
A.4 Flow-Control Statements   **619**
A.5 Fortran File Directive Statements   **624**
A.6 Input/Output Statements   **626**

REFERENCES   **628**

ANSWERS AND SOLUTIONS TO ODD-NUMBERED PROBLEMS   **630**

INDEX   **652**

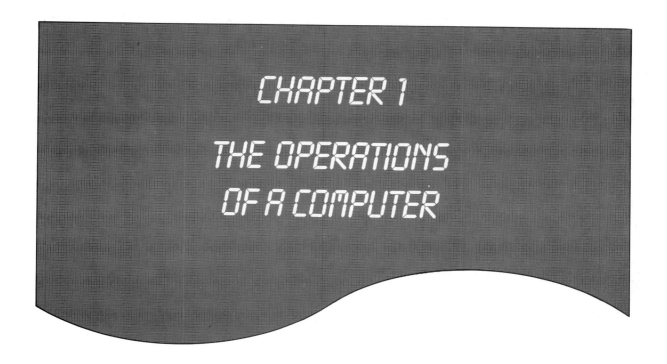

CHAPTER 1

THE OPERATIONS OF A COMPUTER

1.1 INTRODUCTION

The last century was the golden age of applied mathematics. A rather large fraction of the great minds of that era were interested in the solution of problems in the area of engineering and physical sciences. Men like Laplace, Gauss, Bessel, and others determined what problems could be solved and specified the form of the solutions in elegant mathematical analyses. These men shaped the course of this century far more than we realize. The method of approaching almost any problem in engineering is due to the mathematics developed more than 100 years ago. However, there is a revolution in applied mathematics going on right now, all around us, and it will most certainly affect the future in unforeseen but dramatic ways. Of course, I'm talking about the effect of computers on engineering mathematics. Problems that were impossible to solve by hand are now often trivial. Problems that previously required ingenious approximations and "tricks" are now solved with no approximations and no tricks, but on large computers. Problems that most thought were not worth the effort are now solved anyway.[1] The era of computers has come upon us so quickly and the capabilities of the machines

---

[1] Not long ago, π was computed to an accuracy of tens of thousands of digits.

are presently advancing so rapidly that mathematical techniques specially suited to large computers are currently being developed. These methods are generally not suitable for an elementary text. The numerical procedures discussed in this text were originally developed for hand calculations and have been adapted for use on large computers.

The uses of large computers can be divided into two classes:

1. Numerical computation
2. Information and data storage, retrieval, processing, and synthesis

The first classification is, of course, the reason for the invention of modern computers. However, it is the second classification that is experiencing the most rapid growth and already dominates all aspects of computer technology. For example, the billing and record keeping of all large companies are handled by computers. Most large newspapers use computers to edit the text so that the words fit neatly in columns. There are programs that can match a patient's symptoms to a list of diseases and assist in medical diagnosis. The evaluation of huge amounts of data is now universally done by machines. In fact, it was the Bureau of the Census that was among the first to make use of the early computers. And, of course, we are all aware of the enormous popularity of video games and other uses of small personal computers.

Today, the number and type of applications of computers in all aspects of a community are obviously too vast to attempt to catalog. Moreover, the growth in their use is expanding at an ever-increasing rate.

The variety of uses of computers in society is limited only by the number of people trained in their programming and who are simultaneously expert in some discipline of potential application.

In this text we shall concern ourself almost exclusively with numerical computation. There is an important reason for this. The first two years of an engineering or science program in college are among the most crucial periods in your career. You will be taking physics and calculus along with this programming course. The individual goals of each of these courses are to acquaint you with the important and useful topics that will ultimately become the basis upon which other engineering disciplines will build. Viewed collectively, however, these courses have an even more important function, that is, to develop an analytical sophistication. Each course is intended to reinforce the other and the total is then greater than the sum of its parts. The best programming of a problem is done by someone who understands the physical principles of the problem and the mathematics involved.

The first half of this text is concerned with developing fluency in the programming language called Fortran. There is a large variety of programming languages in addition to Fortran, and each has its hard core of enthusiastic supporters claiming superiority in some aspect of its use or its ease of learning. Many linguists contend that all human languages are of roughly the same difficulty when being learned as the first language, and I feel the same can be said of programming languages. As for the relative utility of programming languages, the analogy with spoken languages is again useful. It can be argued that French, for example, is more exact than English, or more poetic, or superior in some other sense. Regardless of the validity of arguments of this type, the essential point is that English is the international language of science and engineering, and every scientist or engineer, anywhere in the world, must have at least a reading knowledge of English. The same is true of Fortran. Regardless of its relative merit as compared with other programming languages, it is the universally accepted scientific programming language, and the overwhelming majority of scientific and engineering computer programs, both in the United States and elsewhere, are written in Fortran.

Since it was introduced in the mid-fifties, there have been many attempts to correct some of the failings and limitations of Fortran, which were generally perceived to be

1. Inadequate ability to read, write, and manipulate textual-type data.
2. Awkward program flow control commands that resulted in needlessly complex programs.
3. Limited ability to handle a variety of data-base types. The only way to store large blocks of data in Fortran is via a subscripted array like x_i. (We will encounter arrays in Chapter 6.) Newer languages are more versatile in this regard.
4. The lack of recursive-type procedures. Programs or subprograms in Fortran are not allowed to "call" themselves, while many numerical problems are most succinctly expressed in terms of a recursive-type relation as we shall see.

The introduction of the latest version of Fortran, Fortran 77, addresses the first two shortcomings rather nicely. The situations in which the latter two limitations become serious handicaps are ordinarily quite advanced, and by the time you encounter such problems you will, I hope, be fluent in at least one or two other computer languages and will be able to choose the one that best suits the overall situation.

Fortran is relatively easy to learn, much easier than, say, German or Spanish. However, it is essential for efficient and accurate programming to understand that the Fortran language is more than simply a mode of communication between humans and computers; it is a set of instructions for a series of operations of the computer. If you were to prescribe for a friend a set of procedures to follow to solve a mathematics problem,[2] a certain amount of ambiguity in the instructions can be tolerated. Depending on the sophistication of the person carrying out the instructions, grammatical errors or trivial assumptions will be overlooked and your friend will interpret what you intended. A computer is unable to do this and all instructions to the computer must be absolutely precise and complete. A misplaced comma will very likely cause the computer to not recognize or to misinterpret the instruction. Thus, it is important that we have at least a minimum understanding of what is going on inside the computer.

---

[2] A recipe for the solution of a problem is more formally called an *algorithm*.

1.2 OPERATION PRINCIPLES OF DIGITAL COMPUTERS

1.2.1 Binary Representation of Numbers and Information

The actual internal operations of a computer are not, in principle, very profound. Several centuries ago it was realized that since a switch has two states, open or closed, it can be used to represent the numbers 0 and 1. A large collection of switches may then be used to represent or store a great many 0s and 1s. Next, ordinary numbers (base ten) can be rewritten in terms of strictly 0s and 1s (i.e., base two) and then be represented by combinations of open and closed switches. For example, the 372 is base ten, which means:

$$372 = 3(10^2) + 7(10^1) + 2(10^0)$$

and can also be written as:

$$372 = 1(256) + 0(128) + 1(64) + 1(32) + 1(16)$$
$$+ 0(8) + 1(4) + 0(2) + 0(1)$$
$$= 1(2^8) + 0(2^7) + 1(2^6) + 1(2^5) + 1(2^4)$$
$$+ 0(2^3) + 1(2^2) + 0(2^1) + 0(2^0)$$

or

$$(372)_{10} = (101110100)_2$$

Thus, nine switches would be required to represent the number 372.

In addition to storing numbers, other forms of data can be converted to a binary code (i.e., written in terms of 1s and 0s) and stored and processed in a computer. For example, each of the letters of the alphabet can be assigned a coded sequence of 1s and 0s and ultimately words and sentences constructed and manipulated. The information content of a photograph can be (approximately) replaced by a dot matrix with the location, color, and density of each dot allocated a binary code and the resolution of the photograph may then be computer-enhanced or the entire contents of the picture transmitted to another site by phone lines or satellite relay.

1.2.2 Main Memory

Originally the actual elements that played the role of switches in a computer were electrical-mechanical relays. They were physically rather large, consumed significant electrical power, and were very noisy. Over the past several decades advances in microelectronics have resulted in the replacement of actual switches by small transistor circuits called *flip-flops*. Each flip-flop circuit can be in only one of two states, on (representing 1) and off

(0). The state of each circuit can be sensed (information read from) or altered (stored into). Additionally, in the last two decades methods have been developed that permit the placement of several thousand discrete circuits on a single wafer or chip. The result is called a *very large scale integrated circuit* (VLSIC) although the size is actually about 1 centimeter square. (See Figure 1-1.) These technological advances have made possible modern computers that are much faster, more reliable, and considerably cheaper than those of an earlier generation.

The main memory of a large computer consists of a few million such storage elements for 1s and 0s (called *bits*). The bits are arranged in groups of eight (called *bytes*) in which may be stored the binary code for a letter,

Figure 1-1 The central section of a 64K memory chip magnified about 400 times. The actual size of the entire chip is about 1/4 inch on a side. The access time for this chip is about 20×10^{-9} seconds, and information is discharged in units of 16 bits at a time. The paired "L"-shaped patterns arrayed in each corner of the square are the memory cells. (*Courtesy of IBM*)

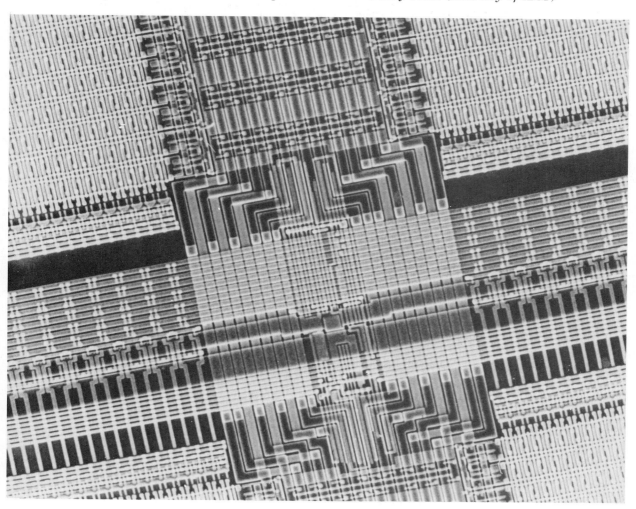

digit, special symbol such as a comma, or a control symbol such as a carriage return. The unit of information that is transferred to and from the main memory is called a *word*. A computer word may consist of from 4 to 16 bits for microcomputers like many of the popular personal computers; 12 to 32 bits for larger, so-called minicomputers; or 32 to 64 bits or more for large computers.

The details concerning the nature of a computer's main memory are usually of little consequence to a programmer except for the following two features that will be repeatedly referred to throughout this text.

1. Associated with each element or memory cell in main memory are two items:

The contents of the memory cell. A unit of data or some type of instruction written in a binary-coded form.
The address of the memory cell. The cells can be thought of as boxes in a row, each box labeled by its position in the row.

2. The size of each memory cell, i.e., a computer word, is finite. This means that for each number used in a computation only a finite number of digits can be stored. Thus numbers represented by nonterminating binary expressions must be truncated before they can be stored in main memory. Incidentally, this refers to nonterminating fractional numbers expressed in base two not base ten. For example, $(0.1)_{10}$ is a nonterminating fraction in base two. (See Problem 1-1.) The length of a computer word will then limit the accuracy of the numerical computations and is an important characteristic of each computer.

The access time (the time required to read the information stored in a particular address) is of critical importance in the operation of the computer. A large computer can ordinarily add two numbers in less time than it takes to find them in main memory. The access time for a large semiconductor main memory consisting of 500,000 computer words is typically 5×10^{-7} seconds.[3] Memory of this type is called *random access memory* (RAM) meaning that the access time for all addresses is roughly the same. The information on a RAM unit is not stored sequentially, but for the time being we will find it simpler to think of all the information as being stored in order. The main memory of a large computer will typically have a storage capacity for 100,000 or more computer words.

In addition to main memory, there are several other possibilities for storing large amounts of data. These are called *secondary memory* and usually consist of magnetic tape or magnetic disk devices, although data can also be stored on cards or paper tape. The data in secondary memory are not

---

[3] Even this incredibly short time can be reduced somewhat by temporarily storing the recently used data and instructions in a smaller, even faster memory device called *cache memory*. The idea is that the recently used items are likely to be used again shortly, and if so they can be more quickly accessed if grouped together.

directly accessible but must first be transferred to main memory for processing. Secondary memory storage is considerably less expensive than main memory, but the price is paid in significantly longer access times on the order of milliseconds or more.

1.2.3 The Central Processing Unit

The part of the computer that performs the operations on the data using the instructions stored in main memory is called the *central processing unit* (CPU). It is responsible for two distinctly different functions:

1. The CPU must monitor and control the entire system consisting of all the devices to get information in and out of the computer (I/O) and control the associated traffic of information flow between the various elements of the computer.
2. The CPU processes the binary-coded instructions transmitted to it from main memory.

The CPU may thus be thought of as two submodules to perform these operations. The *control unit* will execute the necessary control functions, whereas the data and instruction processing unit will be responsible for executing the elementary commands of a program. These consist primarily in performing the operations of arithmetic as well as the ability to compare two data items. This unit is thus called the *arithmetic-logic unit* (ALU). (See Figure 1-2.)

   The control unit is responsible for fetching the next instruction and the address of the required data items from memory and temporarily storing them in local fast memory registers. The instructions are retrieved from

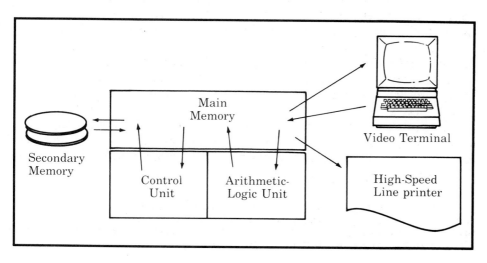

Figure 1-2
Block diagram of the functions of a computer.

memory in the order that they are stored in the program and the required data items are then likewise fetched from memory. The two data items are then transmitted to the ALU along with an instruction to add, subtract, compare, etc. The control unit is then responsible for moving the result back to main memory.

Recall that all of the items processed by the CPU, data and instructions, are written in a binary-coded fashion. This is the only form of communication that is directly understandable to a computer. Programs written in this manner are called machine language or microcode programs. Fortunately, it is unlikely that you will ever have to concern yourself with microcode programs.

1.2.4 Input/Output Devices

Two common and rather embarrassing errors in computer programming are to instruct the computer to execute some operation on data items that were never stored in memory, and to complete a computation and forget to print the result. The mechanism for getting data and the instructions for processing that data into the computer and then to have the results displayed in a useful form are obviously an important concern. The most common input devices include video terminals, punched card readers, and magnetic tape and magnetic disk reading devices. The results generated by the computer can then be displayed on the same video terminal, printed on a high-speed line printer, written on magnetic tape or disk, or punched on cards. We will be primarily concerned with input via the terminal and output at the terminal or on a line printer. Somewhat later (in Chapter 4) we will make use of the magnetic disk which will be described in more detail at that time.

All of the machinery comprising the CPU, the main and secondary memory units, and the various input/output devices are called computer *hardware*. The set of coded instructions or programs available on the computer is called *software*.

1.2.5 The Computing Speed of a Large Computer

In summary, then, what a computer is doing is rather trivial. It is simply manipulating 1s and 0s, nothing more. Its claim to fame rests on the fact that it can do the elementary operations on hundreds of thousands of stored numbers at an absolutely incredible speed. A typical time to add two 60-bit numbers (about 14 decimal digits) is about one-millionth of a second. To appreciate the enormous consequences of this fact, consider that it would take you about 10 seconds to add two 12-digit numbers, and there is a fair possibility that you would make a mistake. The computer adds the two numbers seven orders of magnitude faster, with the likelihood of an error being extremely small. Not only that, if you were highly paid to do this operation (perhaps because you are very accurate in addition and can do hundreds of thousands of these additions without becoming bored, in short have many of the attributes of a computer) and get say $10 per hour, this represents about three cents per addition. The large computer works at typically $500 per hour or 1.3×10^{-7} cents per addition. Thus the machine not only is faster by a factor of about 10^7, but cheaper by roughly the same factor. This is the main reason for all the excitement about computers. The tremendous advances in computing have taken place in a period of about 30 years. Consider for a moment the analogy with the advances over the years in transportation. For untold centuries, humans were limited by the fact that getting around meant walking, which meant about 5 mph. The discovery of the horse revolutionized civilization but was only a change of from 5 to about 20 mph, not even a factor of 10. Modern automobiles, which have a top legal speed of 55, represent a tremendous advancement (one factor of 10) and airplanes that travel at about 500 mph are a further advancement (two factors of 10). All of this in about one century. However, imagine what the consequences would be if the achievements in transportation could match those in computing (increase in speed by 10^7, decrease in cost by 10^{-7}, in 30 years). You could travel from New York to Los Angeles in less than 1 sec and the total cost of your car would be less than 1 cent. Clearly then, such dramatic changes in the field of computational mathematics will have very profound effects on society.

1.3   COMMUNICATING WITH THE COMPUTER

In the early days of computing, programming a computer to do calculations was extremely tedious. The difficulty was that the programmer was forced to communicate with the machine on its own terms. If a program required the product of two numbers represented by the symbols A and B, the programmer would have to code binary instructions to accomplish the following operations:

> Recall number A from address X
> > Transfer to arithmetic unit
> Recall number B from address Y
> > Transfer to arithmetic unit
> Multiply the two numbers
> > Transfer the result to address Z
> Etc.

All of this just to multiply two numbers. Also the machine language code written in this fashion would work only on the machine for which it was originally intended and no others. This meant that the use of the computer was limited to only those brave souls who had mastered this monotonous skill. The first significant step in broadening the pool of potential computer users occurred in 1955 at IBM when the first version of Fortran was developed. The idea was, once and for all, to write a program in machine language that would take a set of instructions written in a form resembling ordinary algebra and translate these instructions into all the transfer-here–store-there instructions required by the computer. Thus a statement like

$$X = 7.0 * A + 3.0 * B$$

which, of course,[4] represents

$$x = 7a + 3b$$

would be read off a punched card. A program permanently residing in the computer would then translate this into terms understandable to the machine, that is, the binary instructions for the operations:

Fetch the number in the location allotted to symbol A
    Transfer it to the arithmetic unit
    Multiply by 7.0
    Temporarily store the result
Fetch the number in the location allotted to symbol B
    Transfer it to the arithmetic unit
    Multiply by 3.0
Add the result to the previously stored multiplication
Store the result in a location allotted to symbol X

The program that does the translation of the Fortran equation into machine language is called the *compiler*. The set of instructions written in Fortran is called the *source* code and the machine language translation is called the *object* code. Since machine code is written to conform to the specific features of an individual computer, an object code program will run only on the machine for which it was intended. The expression that is to be translated is, on the other hand, universal. That is,

$$X = C - D$$

would look the same in any program run on any machine. Fortran compilers were the first to appear and are still among the most common in use. Programs written in Fortran closely resemble ordinary algebra plus some simple English key words. (Fortran stands for FORmula TRANslator.) It is one of many so-called higher computer languages (i.e., above machine language)

---

[4] The instructions to the computer to carry out the operations of multiplication and division are effected by the symbols * (asterisk, as in 7.0 * A) and / (slash, as in B/2.). Two side-by-side asterisks, **, are used to designate the operation of exponentiation as in X**2, which represents x^2. A complete description of how a sequence of arithmetic instructions is written in Fortran will be discussed in the next chapter.

and has undergone several revisions. The form used in this book is Fortran 77.

Since the introduction of Fortran, numerous other programming languages have been developed and each of those listed below can very likely be compiled on every large computer in the world.

Common Higher-Level Computer Languages

ALGOL
Pascal
PL/I $\Big\}$ General-purpose languages
C
APL

COBOL Designed for applications in business
BASIC   A simplified language, similar to Fortran, and commonly used on microcomputers

The universal nature of these programming languages has resulted in very rapid growth in computer usage and also in collaboration between individuals working on different machines.

1.4 THE MECHANICS OF "GETTING ON" THE MACHINE

There are two modes of communication with a computer, *batch processing* and *interactive time sharing*. Batch processing generally refers to the execution of computer programs that have been previously punched on a deck of computer cards or that have been stored in a file on magnetic tape or disk. The instructions encoded on the cards or in the files will be carried out in sequence by the computer and ordinarily, once the computing job begins, the programmer cannot correct or alter the program until the job has passed through the machine. The programmer then checks the printed output for errors, corrects them, and resubmits the program. Thus batch processing is basically a "hands-off" computing mode.

Conversely, interactive computing is "hands-on" computing. The program is composed, edited, executed, and corrected at a video terminal connected to the computer. Both forms of computing have certain advantages; batch processing allows you to see the entire printed listing of the program and perhaps to make thoughtful changes at your leisure, whereas the terminal allows you to see only 20 lines or so at a time and program surgery at a terminal frequently tends to be somewhat hectic. In addition, the execution cost of a program run in a batch mode is considerably lower than the cost of the same job run interactively. In spite of these points, the last few years have seen a tremendous growth in interactive computing and consequent reduction in demands for batch processing. Card punches have all but disappeared from college campuses. Clearly this is due to the increased ease of

---

computing via conveniently located terminals as compared with the repeated visits one was forced to make to the computing center in the past, lugging along boxes of computer cards. It is assumed throughout this text that you will be communicating with the computer by means of a cathode-ray tube (CRT) terminal. The response of the computer will usually be on the terminal screen, although computed results may also be sent to a high-speed line printer.

1.4.1 Interactive Processing

Interactive processing, also called time-sharing on large multiuser computers, allows you to monitor your program as it compiles and executes and to correct errors or alter the program immediately. The program is typed in at a terminal, the appropriate system commands are entered to execute the program, and the output is displayed on the terminal screen. The terminal may be wired directly to the computer or may use an audio link by means of a telephone. You may also have the computer produce a printed copy of the program and its results. There is a wide variety of terminals in use today, and the operational procedures for running Fortran programs vary considerably from one computer to the next; thus only general instructions can be given here. For the detailed instructions appropriate to your site you should obtain an "Interactive Computing User's Guide" or its equivalent from your computing center.

To execute a Fortran program at the terminal there are three levels of procedures that must be learned.

1. The system protocol or job control language (JCL) defined by your computing center. This will include a set of instructions for accessing the computer through your terminal and for having the computer translate (compile) the Fortran code into machine language object code, executing the program, saving the program, and getting results printed on a line printer. None of these instructions are Fortran and the precise forms of the JCL commands differ considerably from site to site. We will, however, discuss the general structure of some elementary JCL commands shortly.
2. Program composition and editing. In addition to translating and executing your Fortran program, the computer can be used to assist you in writing and correcting the program. Many computing centers provide a program that is accessed by entering a particular JCL command like EDIT or some variation that takes you into the next layer of commands called editing commands. These again are site-specific and at least a few of the elementary editing commands must be learned before you can enter and execute a Fortran program.
3. The third layer of procedures is the Fortran program itself.

1.4.2 The Format of Fortran Lines

When entering Fortran code at the terminal some general rules must be followed regarding the postitioning of various types of information on each line. The characteristics of a Fortran line are shown in Figure 1-3. The entire line is 80 columns wide. The Fortran statement must appear in columns 7 to 72. The compiler ignores blank columns, so the Fortran statements may appear anywhere in this field. Columns 1 to 5 are available for supplying an identifying statement number to a particular line of Fortran. Thus an instruction like

```
731        STOP
```

will result in termination of the program's execution. This Fortran statement can be referenced by means of its statement number, 731. Again blanks are ignored and the 731 could appear anywhere in the statement number field (columns 1 to 5). Column 6 is called the *continuation field*. If a Fortran statement is too long to fit on a single line it may be continued on the next line by including any symbol other than 0 in column 6. I would suggest using either a plus sign(+) or a dollar sign ($) to indicate that a line is a continuation of a previous line. The maximum length of a single Fortran expression is 20 lines (one line plus 19 continued lines). A line that is a continuation of a previous line may not have a statement number.

From the discussion thus far we would conclude that all of the Fortran statements at the top of page 14 would be translated identically.

Figure 1-3 The placement of information on a Fortran line.

```
Column
No.
              1              2              3              4              7              8
1....67..0...........0...........0..........0..         ..0.2..........0
         C
         O
Stmnt.   N       Fortran
         T                                                          Identification
No.      I          Statements
         N
         U            Appear  in
         A                                                          Field
         T               Columns
         I                                                          73-80
         O            7 <==> 72
         N
```

```
                  1              2
1....67..0..........0...
731        STOP
7 31         ST        OP

731      S
         +T
         +O
         +P
```

Columns 73 to 80 on the Fortran line are called the *identification field*. Anything that is entered in this part of the line is ignored by the compiler but does appear on the listing of the program supplied by the compiler. Usually the identification field is used to add sequencing numbers to the Fortran lines, which are useful in reassembling a card deck that has been accidentally dropped. They are rarely used in interactive programming.

If a C or an asterisk($*$) appears in column 1, the entire contents of the line are ignored by the compiler; but, as with the identification field, the information contained on the line is included with the listing. These lines are called *comment* lines and they constitute a very important part of a program's documentation. They are used to explain to someone reading the program what each element of the program is attempting to do. Even if you are the only one who will ever read a particular program, it is still a good idea to amply sprinkle comment lines throughout your program. Few tasks are more frustrating than trying to understand the operation of an undocumented code that you wrote six months ago. Some installations of Fortran permit the use of either lower- or uppercase letters within a program. If this is the case on your computer, I suggest that your comment lines be entered in normal lowercase English and that the Fortran be in uppercase only. An example of a possible use of comment lines is shown in Figure 1-4.

1.4.3 Logging On

The general form of the steps necessary to initiate a program at a terminal are as follows:

1. Log on to the machine. You will have to supply your name, a password, and perhaps additional information.
2. Enter the job control statements that specify that you will be writing a Fortran program. The Fortran code to follow will be stored on what is called a *file,* which has to be given a name.
3. Type in the Fortran program (See Section 1.4.4.)
4. Enter the job control statements that instruct the computer to compile and execute the program. If during execution the program is to read data,

Figure 1–4 An example of the use of comment lines.

```
                1           2           3           4           5
  1234567      0           0           0           0           0
  - - - - - - - - - - - - - - - - - - - - - - - - - - - - - - - - - - - - - -
           PROGRAM ZERO
  C
  C   THIS IS A DEMONSTRATION PROGRAM THAT ILLUSTRATES THE
  C   VARIOUS ARITHMETIC OPERATIONS IN FORTRAN AND SOME OF
  C   THE ODD FEATURES OF INTEGER AND REAL (FLOATING POINT)
  C   ARITHMETIC ON THE COMPUTER.   IT IS ALSO AN EXERCISE
  C   IN LEARNING THE NECESSARY PROCEDURES TO ENTER AND
  C   EXECUTE A FORTRAN PROGRAM INTERACTIVELY.
  C      PROGRAMMED BY
  C
  C
  C           ****************
  C           *              *
  C           * JOE STUDENT  *
  C           * ROOM 6C      *
  C           * NORTH QUAD   *
  C           *              *
  C           ****************
  C
  C   THE INPUT VARIABLES -- A,B -- ARE ASSIGNED VALUES BY
  C   ENTERING THE NUMBERS, SEPARATED BY A COMMA, UPON
  C   EXECUTION OF THE READ STATEMENT IN THE PROGRAM.
  C
           READ *, A, B
```

the program will stop and wait for you to enter the data at the terminal. If there were either compilation or execution time errors, you can correct them and try again.

5. If all was successful, instruct the computer to produce a printed copy of both the program and its output.

In summary, before you commence writing Fortran programs you must learn the appropriate commands to handle the above steps. You should make a short list of these instructions for easy reference when you are working at a terminal. In addition, you should determine what some of the "panic" buttons are for your computer. That is, how to stop the program if it seems stuck in an endless loop, how to save a program for another try on another day. On many computers, simply entering the word "HELP" will call up a short tutorial session that may lessen some of your confusion. Also, do not be afraid of inadvertently entering some instuctions that will cause the machine to grind to a halt. For the novice, this is next to impossible to do.

1.4.4 Using an Editor Program To Enter the Fortran Code

The original versions of Fortran assumed that the code would be entered on cards. The Fortran statements would then be correctly positioned on each card and the entire card deck assembled and submitted. Even though the Fortran statements entered at a terminal are identical to the statements submitted on cards and each line on the screen can be viewed as a single card, the physical properties of terminals have resulted in a need to alter somewhat the rules described in Section 1.4.2 for a Fortran line. The description that follows gives some general characteristics of the use of an editor program to construct Fortran code. You should determine the specific features available in the editing program available on your computer.

Line Numbers

Each line of the Fortran code is assigned a sequencing line number. These line numbers usually begin at 100 and increase in equal steps of 10 or 100 to allow for later insertion of new lines between the old ones. Depending upon the operating system for the computer, these numbers may be displayed automatically for you, or you may have to type them in yourself. It is important to understand that these line numbers are *not* part of the Fortran program and will be useful primarily in editing the code later.

```
Line      Column  No.
                  1        2        3        4        5
          1234567 0        0        0        0        0
          - - - - - - - - - - - - - - - - - - - - - - - - - - - - - - - -
00100  C     A COMMENT LINE
00110           A = 3.5
00120     651   X = 3.0 + A
00130  *     Another comment line
00140           Y = 2./X
00150           PRINT *,X,Y
```

Line 120 of the Fortran code bears the statement label 651. Elsewhere in the program this statement may be referenced by using this number. Statement numbers are most often used to designate particular Fortran statements as targets of various branchings in the program. Since the line numbers are not part of the Fortran program, they may not be referenced in the Fortran code itself.

A line may be inserted between line 120 and 130 for example by entering

```
00125     731   Z = A + X
```

or line 110 may be deleted by simply entering the line number again followed by a blank line (line number, RETURN). Of course line 110 could be altered by simply retyping the line number followed by the corrected Fortran statement.

Automatic Positioning of Fortran Code

The second major difference is a result of the difficulty in determining exactly at which column the terminal cursor is currently positioned. With some editing programs the TAB key on the terminal keyboard is used to move the cursor directly to column 7, whereas other editing programs will automatically reposition the information entered so that it satisfies the format rules of a valid Fortran line. The Fortran statements and their statement numbers are repositioned according to the following rules:

1. If the column immediately after the line number contains an asterisk, the entire line is interpreted as a comment. (An alternative is a C followed by a blank space.)
2. If the first column is not a C or an asterisk, then the line is interpreted as a Fortran statement. If a line begins with a number, it is viewed as a statement number which will then be followed by a blank and some Fortran statement. A line number followed by a blank space and any letter is interpreted as a Fortran statement without a statement number.
3. If the first column after the line number contains a plus sign,[5] it is considered to be a continuation of the previous Fortran statement line.

```
00100C    A COMMENT LINE
00110 A = 3.5
00120 651 X = 3.0 + A
00130*    Another comment line
00140 Y = 2./X
00150 PRINT *,X,
00160+ Y
```

If we next instruct the computer to list the Fortran code, we find that all the lines have been correctly sequenced by line number and that the Fortran has been automatically positioned to satisfy the rules we learned for the correct formatting of Fortran lines. (Section 1.4.2).

Correcting and Executing the Fortran Program

Typing errors are easily corrected at the terminal by backspacing or deleting before a RETURN is entered or by simply replacing the entire line. When you are somewhat more experienced, you will learn more powerful program editing procedures; but for now the simple ones will suffice.

Even though we have not yet started the study of the Fortran language, I am sure you are anxious to try your hand at submitting and executing a

---

[5] Some editor programs use a dollar sign for this purpose.

simple program. Once you have determined the required log-on procedures, you should attempt to execute the simple programs below. I am sure that you will have no difficulty in reading and understanding the Fortran code.

1. Simple arithmetic

```
Column No.
           1              2              3
1....567..0..........0..........0...
         A = 2.5
         B = 3.5
         C = A + B
         PRINT *,A,B,C
         STOP
         END
```

The PRINT statement[6] instructs the computer to display the numbers A,B,C, which will then appear on the terminal screen.

2. Printing text

```
           1              2              3
1....567..0..........0..........0...
         A = 100.0
         B = A*A
         PRINT *,A,' SQUARED EQUALS ',B
         STOP
         END
```

The three items to be printed are separated by commas and in this case include the two-word phrase, SQUARED EQUALS, which must be enclosed in apostrophes. The symbols between the apostrophes are printed "as is," including blanks.

3. An infinite loop

```
           1              2              3
1....567..0..........0..........0..
C THIS PROGRAM CONTAINS AN INFINITE LOOP
         X = 100.
    12   PRINT *,' X = ',X
         X = X*X
         GO TO 12
         END
```

---

[6] The mechanism in Fortran for having a program display results obtained at any particular point in that program is quite easy. The word PRINT followed by an asterisk and a comma,

PRINT *,

simply precedes the list of variables or constants to be printed or displayed on the terminal

This program will first print the current value of X, i.e., 100., then replace the current value of X with the value of X squared. The GO TO 12 statement is a Fortran transfer statement that causes the program to branch directly to the Fortran line that bears the statement label 12. The GO TO statement will be discussed in more detail in Section 3.4.1, but for now its meaning is rather transparent and you should have no trouble in understanding the effects of GO TO statements. In this instance, the effect is to branch back to the print statement and continue with the calculation from that point. There is no way out of this loop and the values of X will grow without limit. Of course, there is a limit to the size of the numbers that can be stored in the computer and the program will terminate when this number is exceeded. This will also generate an error message on the terminal screen.

4. Reading data

```
         1               2          3
1....67..0...........0...........0...
     PRINT *,'INPUT X AND Y, SEPARATED BY A COMMA'
     READ *,X,Y
     Z = X * Y
     W = X/Y
     PRINT *,X,' TIMES ',Y,' EQUALS ',Z
     PRINT *,X,' DIVIDED BY ',Y,' EQUALS ',W
     STOP
     END
```

This program will execute the first PRINT statement and the program will then pause at the READ statement and wait for you to enter the values of X and Y at the terminal. The program will then resume after the values are entered (after the carriage return).

1.4.5 A Typical Terminal Session

In Figure 1-5 is the complete dialogue required with the computer to execute one of the above problems. This program was run on a CDC CYBER 730 computer and except for the Fortran itself you should expect all of the JCL and edit commands to differ from those on your computer. The general structure of the commands will be similar, however. In Figure 1-5 the output from the computer is in capital letters, while the response to the computer is in lowercase.

---

screen. These are in turn separated by commas. Upon execution of this line of the program, the *values* associated with the quantities in the list will be displayed. This manner of printing results will be discussed in more detail in Section 2.9.

Figure 1-5 An example of a dialogue with the computer while at a terminal.

```
LEHIGH UNIVERSITY CY170-730.
USER NAME: borse               〈The response of the computer is in capital letters.
PASSWORD:                         My response is in lowercase.〉


/senator                       〈The editor program on my computer is called
SENATOR VER 2.7 (84/05/09)        senator.〉
*system,fortran                〈The program will be written in Fortran.〉
*new,test                      〈And will be stored on a file called TEST.〉
*input
INPUT LINES

100    a = 100.0
110    b = a*a
120    print *,a,'squared equals ',b
130    stop
140    end

*list
                               〈When the program is listed the editor will position
    100       A = 100.0            the Fortran correctly.〉
    110       B = A*A
    120       PRINT *,A,'SQUARED EQUALS ',B
    130       STOP
    140       END

*run
                               〈This is the local instruction to execute the
                                  program.〉

 TEST        15:25      FORTRAN

 100.SQUARED EQUALS 10000.
*logout                        〈Here are the results of the program.〉
```

1.5 PROGRAM ZERO

As a somewhat more demanding test of your abilities to execute a program, you should attempt to run the program listed in Figure 1-6 on your computer. Enter the Fortran code exactly as it appears, execute the program, and in addition obtain a printed listing of the program and its output. This program is more complicated than those described earlier and I do not expect

Figure 1-6 A program to demonstrate arithmetic operations.

```
Column Number
            1           2          3          4          5
1234567     0           0          0          0          0
- - - - - - - - - - - - - - - - - - - - - - - - - - - - - - - - - - -
        PROGRAM ZERO
        REAL A,B,C,D,E,F,G,H,P,Q,R,S,T,U,V
        INTEGER IA,IB,IC
        PRINT *,'INPUT VALUES FOR A,B SEPARATED BY A COMMA'
        READ *,A,B
        C = A + B
        D = A - B
        E = A/B
        F = A*B
        G = C*D/(E*F) + (B/A)**2 - 1.
C INTENTIONAL MIXED MODE FOLLOWS (6 LINES)
        IA = A
        IB = B
        IC = IA**IB
        H = IC
        P = LOG(H)/IB
        Q = EXP(P) - IA
        R = A/G
        S = B/Q
        V = 0.0
        PRINT *,'INPUT VALUES A = ',A,' B  =  ',B
        PRINT *,'COMPUTED VALUES G = ',G,' Q = ',Q
        PRINT *,'R = ',R,' S = ',S
        T = 1./V
        PRINT *,'THE RESULT OF 1 DIVIDED BY 0 IS ',T
        U = A*T
        STOP
        END
```

you to be able to completely understand the Fortran. We will go over the code, line by line, in the next chapter.

If you spot typing errors after you have the computer list the Fortran code, these should be corrected before you attempt to execute the program. If undetected typing errors remain, the computer will likely indicate these as errors in Fortran grammar and will give you some indication of the location and nature of the error. You should then have no trouble in correcting them.

You will notice that near the end of this code is a statement involving division by zero. Obviously this is going to cause problems during the execution of this program. Do not try to correct this line; let us just see what happens. If you find that this program will not execute at all, remove the line U = A*T and try again.

1.5.1 Error Diagnostics

Once you have typed the entire program in Figure 1-6 and have submitted the code for compilation and execution, the computer will first attempt to translate the Fortran into machine language. If there are typing errors, the compiler will endeavor to diagnose the nature of the error. For example, if the line C = A + B were typed C = A # B, the output would indicate:

```
                              C = A # B
FATAL ERROR    *****   ILLEGAL USE OF OPERATOR   --   A #
```

This indicates that the compiler was unsuccessful in translating this statement. The symbol # is not an allowed symbol in Fortran.[7] This error has resulted in a line of code that does not satisfy the rigid rules of Fortran grammar that we will begin to learn shortly and results in a *compilation* time error. No object code is generated and there can be no attempt at execution.

But beware. Frequently, typing errors will result in a Fortran line that is grammatically correct but that has a meaning significantly different from that intended. For example, leaving out the addition operator in the line C = A + B results in C = A B, which is the same as C = AB. Since there has been no value assigned to a variable named AB, the value assigned to C will be meaningless and will likely cause the program to "die" during execution. (See Problem 1-8.)

Frequently the messages supplied by the compiler when a compilation error is encountered are extremely cryptic and they may not be readily understandable to the novice. In such cases you can consult the reference manual that describes the features of the Fortran compiler in use on your computer or seek help from your instructor. (These manuals are usually available in the computing center.) Ordinarily, merely knowing in which line the error is located is sufficient information to find a simple typing error.

Elimination of errors in programs is called *debugging,* and the correction of compilation time errors is the first and easiest stage of debugging a program. After you have all the Fortran corrected so that it now satisfies the grammar rules, the compilation of the Fortran can be completed and the program may then begin execution. However, the program may still die

---

[7]The only symbols allowed in Fortran are the letters of the alphabet, the integers, plus the special characters:

+	plus	.	period	,	comma
−	minus	'	apostrophe	=	equals
/	slash	(	left parenthesis	)	right parenthesis
$	dollar	*	asterisk		
:	colon				

during execution, for example, by division by zero. An error such as this is called an *execution* time error. The second stage of program debugging then consists of eliminating all execution time errors. These are usually much more difficult to find and correct. Most modern compilers have available special commands that will attempt to trace back an execution time error such as division by zero. These debugging programs will locate the general region of a program in which the error occurred and will print the values of the variables in the program at the time of the error. You should familiarize yourself with the instructions necessary to implement these features.

After these hurdles are passed and the program runs to completion, the final and most difficult phase of debugging a program begins; that is, to verify the validity of the results. For example, even a perfect Fortran code will not produce valid answers if the results depend on the value of π and π was incorrectly entered as PI = 3.4416. All three phases of program debugging will be dealt with in due course.

1.5.2 Additional Information Supplied by the Compiler

The example listing in Figure 1-7 is for a successful compilation and execution of program zero. The output was then sent to a line printer. The printed output you receive from your computing center may look quite different, but the overall features should be similar. First is a complete listing of the Fortran program you submitted. This is called the SOURCE code. The compiler will generally add sequenced line numbers off to the left and will insert error diagnositcs if required. Next comes the output of the compiler program, giving some details concerning the translation of the Fortran code. This is called the load map and may include such things as a list of all variables used in the program and all library functions required by your program (such as EXP). Additional information usually contained in a load map is the size of the program and the time for compilation.

Following the load map is the computed output of program zero. We will go over this in Chapter 2. The last item on a listing is usually the dayfile, which includes several bookkeeping items such as the time and date of program execution, a list of job control commands executed, central processor time (CP) used, main memory requirements, and of course the cost of the job. In addition, if execution time errors are encountered, they are listed here.

Figure 1-7 An example of the printed output of an interactive program.

```
1              PROGRAM ZERO
2              REAL A,B,C,D,E,F,G,H,P,Q,R,S,T,U,V
3              INTEGER IA,IB,IC
4              PRINT *,'INPUT VALUES FOR A,B SEPARATED BY A COMMA'
5              READ *,A,B
```

Continued

```
6              C = A + B
7              D = A - B
8              E = A/B
9              F = A * B
10             G = C * D/(E * F) + (B/A)**2 - 1.
11    C = INTENTIONAL MIXED MODE FOLLOWS (6 LINES)
12             IA = A
13             IB = B
14             IC = IA**IB
15             H = IC
16             P = LOG(H)/IB
17             Q = EXP(P) - IA
18             R = A/G
19             S = B/Q
20             V = 0.0
21             PRINT *,'INPUT VALUES A = ',A,' B = ',B
22             PRINT *,'COMPUTED VALUES G = ',G,' Q = ',Q
23             PRINT *,'R = ',R,'S = ',S
24             T = 1./V
25             PRINT *,'THE RESULT OF 1 DIVIDED BY 0 IS ',T
26             U = A*T
27             STOP
28             END
```

⟨A listing of the program⟩

⟨A Site-Dependent LOAD MAP
usually appears here⟩

```
INPUT VALUES FOR A,B SEPARATED BY A COMMA
INPUT VALUES A = 7. B = 13.
COMPUTED VALUES G = -1.42108547152E-14 Q = 0.
R = -4.92581209243E+14S = R
THE RESULT OF 1 DIVIDED BY 0 IS R
```

⟨This is the output of the program.⟩

PROBLEMS

1. Rewrite the following base-ten numbers in binary (base two).

    a. 11   **d.** 2.5 ⟨use $.5 = 2^{-1}$⟩

    b. 33   **e.** 12.625

    c. 100   **f.** 0.1 ⟨this will be a continuing fraction⟩

2. Rewrite the following base-two numbers as base ten.

    a. 1011.0

    b. 110011.0

c. 0.11

d. 100000000.00001

3. Perform the following base-two arithmetic operations and verify by converting the problem to base ten.

    a. 1011   **b.** 1010

    <u>+ 11</u>   <u>− 11</u>

4. Convert the following base-ten arithmetic to binary and compute the result in binary arithmetic. Verify your answers with a base-ten calculation.

    a. $3 + 3 + 3$ (or 3×3)

    b. 11×33

    c. 10×0.1

5. As a rare example of the utility of binary arithmetic that is not related to digital computers, consider the following description of the ancient oriental game of Nim: One player places any number of markers on the table arranged in rows. Any number of rows and any number of counters per row are allowed. The two players then alternately remove counters from the arrangement, taking any positive number from any *one* row. Either player may begin. The one removing the last counter is the winner. If you go first and if the initial arrangement is not a trivial one, you should be able to win almost every time. Consider the initial arrangement

$$X\ X\ X\ X \quad (4)$$
$$X\ X\ X \quad (3)$$
$$X \quad (1)$$

The game-winning strategy is most easily explained by writing the number in each row in base two.

$$X\ X\ X\ X \quad (100)$$
$$X\ X\ X \quad (011)$$
$$X \quad (001)$$

The correct next move is to remove enough counters from some row so that the base-two numbers of those remaining add up to even numbers when each column is added (base ten) separately. Thus the correct first move is to remove two markers from row one to obtain

$$X\ X \quad (0\ \ 1\ \ 0)$$
$$X\ X\ X \quad (0\ \ 1\ \ 1)$$
$$X \quad \underline{(0\ \ 0\ \ 1)}$$
$$\text{even-even}$$

Explain the reasoning behind the winning strategy for the simpler case of just two rows with any number in either row.

6. Explain the significance of the following columns on a Fortran statement line:
   a. column 1
   b. column 6
   c. columns 73 to 80
   How is a blank interpreted when it appears in columns 1 to 5?, column 6?, columns 7 to 72?

7. To answer the following questions you will have to consult the documentation supplied by your computing center that explains the necessary procedures for interactive computing.
   a. Explain the procedures for logging on at a terminal.
   b. What commands are necessary in order to initiate the writing of a Fortran program at the terminal? (e.g., How do you create a Fortran file? How is it sequenced? How do you position the Fortran statements to begin in column 7?)
   c. How do you erase a line, backspace or delete a character, insert a line, end the program at a terminal?
   d. How is the Fortran program then saved, executed, compiled? How do you get your results printed? How do you terminate the terminal session?

8. The following short program contains several grammatical errors. Enter and run the program as is. What error diagnostics are supplied by the compiler? Use these clues to correct the Fortran as best you can and try again. Were there any obvious errors that were missed by the compiler?

```
PROGRAM OPPS
PRINT *,'ENTER VALUES FOR A,B,C SEPARATED BY COMMAS'
READ *, A, B C
D = 2A + BC
E = D/-A
B = F
PRINT *,'A=',A,' B=,B,' C=',C
+' D=',D,' E=',E,' F=',F
STOP
END
```

9. Determine the answers to the following for your computing environment:
   a. What is the size of the central memory of your computer?
   b. What is the length of a computer word in bits? What is the corresponding number of decimal digits?
   c. Where are the public access terminals that are connected to this machine and what are the hours that they are available?
   d. Where is the reference manual for the Fortran compiler located?

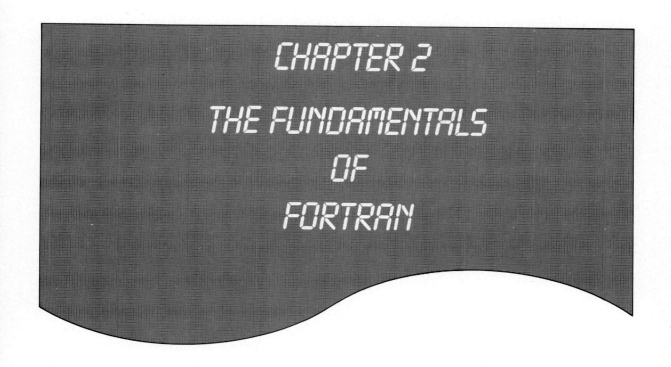

CHAPTER 2
THE FUNDAMENTALS
OF
FORTRAN

2.1 INTRODUCTION

The data types that can be processed by a Fortran program come in a variety of forms. The two most commonly used forms for numerical values are called *INTEGER* type and *REAL* type, while textual items (symbols) are of type *CHARACTER*. There are a few additional data types available and these will be described in Chapter 6. The three data types given above will be sufficient for most programs.

The arithmetic involving the numbers used in Fortran differs in many ways from the arithmetic you have previously used. Moreover, in the majority of cases in which a seemingly valid program gives incorrect results, the wrong answers are the result of the odd features of computer arithmetic. The purpose of this chapter is to enable you to translate algebraic expressions into Fortran code so that the computer will evaluate the expressions in precisely the manner intended.

2.2 CONSTANTS IN FORTRAN

A Fortran constant is a fixed quantity that may be either numerical or a specified collection of symbols. The numerical constants that we will use will be either of type INTEGER or of type REAL.

2.2.1 INTEGER Constants

An integer constant in Fortran is any number that does not possess a decimal point. It can be positive, negative, or zero. If it is positive, the plus sign can be omitted. For example:

```
+3
-17
999999999
```

Note that embedded commas are not permitted (e.g., 999,999,999), but since Fortran ignores blanks, large numbers could be written in groups of three digits as 999 999 999.

The computer stores each of these numbers in main memory in a computer word of from 8 to 64 bits in length. The largest allowed integer depends upon the word length, which varies from machine to machine but is, of course, finite in every case. Some examples of the maximum allowable integers for a variety of computers are listed in Table 2-1.

The finite nature of the number set in computer arithmetic has some odd consequences, as we shall see shortly.

2.2.2 REAL Constants

The numbers most often used in computation are numbers with decimal points. Numbers with a decimal point are called REAL.[1] These numbers can be written either with or without an exponent.

1. Reals without exponents. Again, if the number is positive the plus sign may be omitted.

---

[1] A somewhat older terminology calls numbers with a decimal point *floating-point* numbers, while numbers without a decimal point are called *fixed-point* numbers. Of course, the Fortran definition of the word "REAL" is somewhat different from and should not be confused with mathematical terminology wherein "real" is used to characterize all numbers that are not complex or imaginary.

Table 2-1 Maximum number of decimal digits permitted for integers for selected computers.

Type of Computer	Maximum Number of Decimal Digits
CDC-CYBER	14
IBM-4341	10
PDP-11	11
DEC-20	8
Typical Computer	10

Valid

    3,   ⟨*This is not the same as integer 3*⟩
    -3,14159259

Invalid

    999,888,0   ⟨*Again, embedded commas are not allowed.*⟩

2. Reals with exponents. The exponent consists of the letter E followed by a positive or negative integer and corresponds to the power of ten used when the number is written in scientific notation. If the integer exponent is positive, the plus sign may be omitted. The base of the number, that part of the number that precedes the exponent, should contain a decimal point.

Valid

    1234,56E-3   ⟨*This is the same as 1234.56 × 10^{-3}; that is, 1.23456.*⟩
    0,123456E+1
    1,E10

Invalid

    123,45E-5,5   ⟨*A decimal point is not allowed in the exponent.*⟩
    123E+45   ⟨*The base should have a decimal point.*⟩
    123,E-456   ⟨*On most computers the exponent is limited to two digits. See below.*⟩

Once again the maximum allowable real number is determined by the word length of the particular computer. For example, on a computer with an exceptionally long word length of 64 bits, the limits are

$$10^{-294} \quad \text{to} \quad 10^{+322}$$

while on most other 32-bit machines the limits are typically

$$10^{-78} \quad \text{to} \quad 10^{+75}$$

Of course, you should determine what the precise limitations on the size of integers and reals are for your computer. (See Problem 2-1.)

2.2.3 CHARACTER-Type Constants

A CHARACTER-type constant is a string of any of the allowed symbols in Fortran (see footnote 7 in Chapter 1) that are enclosed in apostrophes. The string of characters is stored in memory exactly as it appears, with blanks included. The minimum number of symbols in a character constant is one, while the maximum is at least several thousand and depends on your local compiler. We will use character constants primarily to label the output of the program using the PRINT statement.

Examples of valid character constants:

```
'NOW IS THE TIME FOR ALL GOOD ...'
'X = '
' '         (a single blank space)
'4.2'       (the symbols for four–decimal point–two,
                not the numerical value)
```

Examples of incorrect character constants:

```
NOW IS THE TIME    (apostrophes missing)
'END OF RUN''      (too many terminating apostrophes²)
```

The values of constants are printed in a Fortran program by means of the PRINT statement. The form of the PRINT statement is[3]

```
PRINT *,     (a list of constants or variables separated by commas)
```

This is an *executable* Fortran statement. All Fortran lines can be classified as either executable or nonexecutable. An executable Fortran line will ordinarily call for some action on the part of the computer, while nonexecutable Fortran lines will be used to preset various attributes in a program such as declaring which variables are of type INTEGER and which are of type REAL. (Type-declaration statements are covered in the next section.) Most nonexecutable statements are positioned at the very beginning of the program and are followed by the main body of the program, which consists of executable statements. The PRINT statement may be placed anywhere among the executable statements and may be used to display the values of integer, real, or character constants or variables that have been assigned values. For example, the three types of constants are all present in the

---

[2] If the character constant itself contains an apostrophe, the single apostrophe in the string is represented by two consecutive apostrophes in the character constant. Thus the expression ⟨don't quit⟩ would be written as a character constant as

```
'DON''T QUIT'
```

[3] In many of the examples of Fortran statements that will be given in this text, the correct form of the Fortran expression will be given in capital letters and a description of the remainder of the Fortran statement will be in lowercase and enclosed in angle brackets ⟨. . .⟩.

statement

```
PRINT *,100,'SQUARED IS ',1.E4
```

The output that results from this statement is:

```
100SQUARED IS 1.0E+04
```

The PRINT statement will be explained in more detail in Section 2.9.

2.3   FORTRAN VARIABLES

As in ordinary algebra, quantities may be associated with symbols or variable names and these may then be symbolically manipulated according to the rules of arithmetic. Each variable name identifies an address in memory, and whenever the variable name is referenced, the current value in that location is used in its place. Variable names in Fortran must satisfy two rules:

1. The variable name may be any combination of letters or numbers, but must begin with a letter. No special symbols are allowed in a variable name.
2. The number of symbols in a variable name is limited to six or fewer.

   Variable names may be declared as containing a constant of type CHARACTER, REAL, or INTEGER.

2.3.1   Default Typing of Variable Names

Unless the Fortran code explicitly states otherwise (see the next section), the type of the number that is associated with a given variable name is determined by the following default typing rule:

All variable names that begin with the letters

I   J   K   L   M   N

refer to integers. All others refer to reals.

A few examples are listed in Table 2-2.

Table 2-2 Examples of valid and invalid Fortran variable names

INTEGER Names			REAL Names		
Valid	I K27B INTGR KOUNT		Valid	X XK57 ANSWER	
Invalid	X K-8 INTEGER	⟨real⟩ ⟨only letters and numerals allowed⟩ ⟨too many characters⟩	Invalid	IDIOT ENGINEER	⟨integer⟩ ⟨too many characters⟩

2.3.2 Explicit Typing of Variable Names

A sound procedure in every Fortran program is to invent variable names that have a clear meaning when the code is read. For example, if your program is concerned with printing the current date, you will need INTEGER variable names to store the values of the month, day, and year. You could use IM, ID, IY; but the meaning of the Fortran code would be much more transparent if you used instead MONTH, DAY, YEAR. However, the variables DAY and YEAR would be default-typed as real and thus could not be used to store integer values. The method provided in Fortran to override default typing is called *explicit variable typing* and involves using the following Fortran statements.

REAL   ⟨list of variable names⟩
INTEGER   ⟨list of variable names⟩

These statements are called *specification statements* and should appear at the top of the Fortran code. They are nonexecutable statements in that they do not call for any action by the computer. The variables in the list are any valid Fortran names and are separated by commas. Of course, a variable name declared to be type REAL cannot also be declared to be type INTEGER. Attempts to do so will result in a compilation time error.

Examples:

REAL COST,LENGTH,MASS
INTEGER DAY,YEAR,MONTH

The REAL and INTEGER statements can be in either order and one or both may be absent from the program. All variables that are not explicitly typed will follow the default-typing rule.

To avoid confusion, it is generally suggested that *all* variables that appear in a program be explicitly typed. This suggestion is often relaxed somewhat for simple variable names that are always used for the same function such as a subscript or counter (I or J), variables in an equation such as X, or common fixed constants such as PI.

Default typing can be used only for REAL and INTEGER variable names. To declare a variable to be of type CHARACTER an additional statement is required. This statement is slightly more complicated since the length of the character string that is to be stored in the variable must also be specified. The form of the CHARACTER specification statement is

```
CHARACTER name₁*<sl₁>,name₂*<sl₂>,...
```

where $name_1$, $name_2$, etc. are the names of the variables and $\langle sl_1 \rangle, \langle sl_2 \rangle, \ldots$ are positive integers corresponding to the length of the string stored in the corresponding name. For example,

```
CHARACTER NAME*10,STREET 12
```

If all of the variables in the CHARACTER statement are to be of the same length, the statement can be shortened by attaching the common string length to the word CHARACTER, as, for example,

```
CHARACTER*10 NAME,STREET,CITY
```

The two forms of the CHARACTER statement can be combined. For example, in the statement

```
CHARACTER*10 NAME, STREET*12, CITY
```

the variables NAME and CITY are of length 10 while STREET is of length 12.

2.4 ARITHMETIC EXPRESSIONS

An arithmetic expression in Fortran is an instruction to perform one or more arithmetic operations on constants or variables that have previously been assigned values. An expression can be quite simple, as A + B, or complicated, extending over several lines. The expression is evaluated and the entire expression is replaced by that value. The operations that are to be carried out in the expression are determined by the operators that it contains and by the sequence in which they appear.

2.4.1 Arithmetic Operators

The ordinary operations of arithmetic are effected in Fortran by means of the following symbols:

+	Addition
−	Subtraction
*	Multiplication
/	Division
**	Exponentiation

The symbols for multiplication, division, and exponentiation were chosen because they are available on every typewriter. Also, the exponentiation operator is defined to be a single symbol.

The rules for constructing arithmetic expressions are fairly simple:

1. No two operation symbols may occur side by side.
2. The multiplication, division, and exponentiation operators must appear in conjunction with two numbers or variables, e.g.,

```
A * B    D / 2.0    F ** 2
```

while the addition and subtraction operators may appear with a pair of numbers or variables,

```
A + B        D - 2.0
```

or with a single variable or number, as in negation.

```
+A     -B     -7.0
```

Note that in Fortran

1. Multiplication can never be implied as it often is in ordinary algebra. Thus, $a(b + c)$ must be written as A * (B + C), not A(B + C).
2. The rule about side-by-side operators must be carefully adhered to, even in cases where there appears to be no ambiguity. For example,

Incorrect Fortran	Valid Fortran	Algebraic Expression
X**−2	X**(−2)	x^{-2}
A * −3.0	A * (−3.0) or −3.0 * A	$-3a$

the entries in the first column will result in compilation time errors.
3. Note that, just as in ordinary algebra, terms may be grouped by using parentheses. The expression within a pair of parentheses is then evaluated before any operations outside the parentheses are executed.

2.4.2 Integer Arithmetic

Arithmetic expressions involving only integers will always result in a number that is an integer. This is especially important to remember when the expression involves division. If the division of two integers is not itself an integer, the computer automatically truncates the decimal fraction.

```
6/2 = 3   6/3 = 2   6/4 = 1   6/5 = 1   6/6 = 1   6/7 = 0
```

Because of this odd feature, integers should never be used in arithmetic expressions in which physical quantities are computed. They should be used exclusively as counters or indices.

2.4.3 Real Arithmetic

The actual computation in a Fortran program is done with real numbers and variables. The result of any arithmetic expression containing real numbers is a real number and so the above problem with integers does not occur.

```
6./2. = 3.      6./3. = 2.      6./4. = 1.5
6./5. = 1.2     6./6. = 1.      6./7. = 0.857142...
```

However, real arithmetic has pecularities all its own that are a consequence of the finite word length of the computer. For example,

$$1./3. = 0.333333333\ldots$$

where ... means that the decimal expression repeats indefinitely. The decimal answer stored in the computer, however, cannot repeat indefinitely but is limited by the number of significant figures in a computer word. A typical size for a computer word is about ten significant figures, so in real arithmetic

$$1./3. = 0.333333333 \qquad \langle no \ldots \rangle$$

or, put another way, the result of 1./3. is slightly less than one-third. Thus

$$3.*(1./3.) - 1. \neq 0.0$$

while

$$2.*(1./2.) - 1. = 0.0$$

Of course, the numbers stored in the computer are stored in a base two notation. Thus, in base two

$$1/2 = (0.100000000\ldots)_2$$

$$1/3 = (0.010101010\ldots)_2$$

and thus

$$[2(1/2) - 1]_{10} = (10. \times 0.1 - 1.0)_2$$

$$= 1. - 1. = 0.0$$

$$[3(1/3) - 1]_{10} = (11. \times 0.0101010101 - 1.0)_2$$

$$= 0.1111111111 - 1.0$$

$$= -0.0000000001$$

This is true on most computing devices. (Try it on your pocket calculator.)

2.5   MORE COMPLICATED ARITHMETIC EXPRESSIONS

2.5.1   Hierarchy of Operations

The sequence in which the computer processes a series of mixed arithmetic operations is determined by a set of rules that have been formulated to remove potential ambiguities. The understanding of these rules is an essential element in the ability to readily read and program code in Fortran. This ordered sequence or hierarchy is listed below

The order in which the arithmetic operations in an expression are executed.

First: Clear all parentheses (innermost first).
Second: **
          Perform exponentiation.
Third: * or /
          Perform multiplication and/or division (equal priority).
Fourth: + or −
          Perform addition and/or subtraction (equal priority).

These rules are effected by successive scans of the expression, looking for each of the above in turn from *left* to *right*.[4] Some examples follow.

1. A + B + C is evaluated as $\underbrace{\underbrace{(A + B)}_{\text{first}} + C}_{\text{second}}$

---

[4] Unfortunately, successive exponentiation is an exception to the left-to-right rule. Fortran 77 compilers are written so as to evaluate A**B**C as A**(B**C)—i.e., right to left. For operations of this type it is always best to avoid confusion and include parentheses to force the sequence of operations to be what you intended.

2. $4 * 3/2 \rightarrow 12/2 \rightarrow 6$
but
$3/2 * 4 \rightarrow 1 * 4 \rightarrow 4$
3. $2.**3 - 1. \rightarrow 8. - 1. \rightarrow 7.0$

Consider how the machine would process an expression like

$$A**B/C + D*E*(F-G)$$

Assume that the variables A through G have been previously assigned the values

Variable	A	B	C	D	E	F	G
Value	2.0	3.0	4.0	5.0	6.0	7.0	8.0

The first scan is to clear all parentheses and thus the first operation is to evaluate $(F - G)$ and temporarily store the result in say R_1. $\langle(7. - 8.) = -1. = R_1\rangle$. The expression now reads

$$A**B/C + D*E*R_1 \qquad \langle R_1 = -1.0\rangle$$

The next scan looks for exponentiation, replacing $A**B$ with the temporarily stored value R_2 $(2.**3. = 8. = R_2)$. So that we next have

$$R_2/C + D*E*R_1 \qquad \langle R_2 = 8.0\rangle$$

The third scan carries out all the multiplication or division found, proceeding left to right

$$R_2/C = R_3 \qquad \langle 8./4. = 2. = R_3\rangle$$
$$D*E = R_4 \qquad \langle 5. \times 6. = 30. = R_4\rangle$$
$$R_4*R_1 = R_5 \qquad \langle 30. \times (-1.) = -30. = R_5\rangle$$

and we are left with

$$R_3 + R_5$$

The final scan executes all addition or subtraction proceeding left to right to obtain the final value of the expression

$$R_6 = (2. + (-30.)) = -28.0$$

Of course, additional parentheses could be inserted to alter the order of operations and perhaps the result. You should verify that the slightly changed expression

$$A**B/(C + D) * (E*(F - G))$$

has the value −5.333333333. A beginners' rule is, **When in doubt, always add parentheses.**

2.5.2 Mixed-Mode Expressions

All of the arithmetic expressions we have seen thus far have been carefully constructed to contain only elementary operations between the same types of numbers, integers added to integers, reals times reals, etc. The reason for this is that the ALU of the computer is set up to execute the operations of arithmetic or comparison *only* between numbers of the same type. It does not know how to multiply a real number times an integer. To carry out such an operation, the numbers must be first converted to the same type.

All modern compilers are written to handle an arithmetic operation between two numbers of different types by first converting the numbers to the same type and then carrying out the operation. To accomplish this in an unambiguous manner, levels of dominance are assigned to the number types REAL and INTEGER, with reals having dominance over integers. Thus an expression like

```
3.0*I
```

is evaluated by first converting the integer I to a real number and then multiplying by 3.0. The result of the operation is then real. An expression such as this is called a *mixed-mode expression.*

Mixed-mode expressions often cause considerable confusion among both beginning and more experienced programmers. This is especially true when the expression involves division. The presence or absence of a decimal point can dramatically alter the result.

Mixed-mode expression	is evaluated to be
1. + 1/2	1. $\langle 1/2 \to 0 \rangle$
1 + 1./2	1.5 $\langle 1./2 \to 1./2. \to .5$
	$1 + .5 \to 1. + .5 \to 1.5 \rangle$

Mixed-mode expressions can serve very useful functions in programming; however, they should be avoided by beginners. Numerical computations should involve reals only, with integers being used primarily as counters. If you do find it necessary to use mixed-mode expressions, I suggest that, for a while, every Fortran statement you write that employs mixed-mode arithmetic be preceded by a comment line like

```
C  INTENTIONAL MIXED MODE FOLLOWS
```

which will serve both as a reminder and as an announcement to others.

2.6 THE ASSIGNMENT STATEMENT

The assignment operator = in Fortran bears a striking resemblance to the equal sign in ordinary algebra, but they have significantly different meanings. A Fortran expression like

```
X = 14. - 4.**.5
```

is a set of instructions to the computer to complete the arithmetic computation on the right and *to assign* that value to a variable called X. An important feature of higher computer languages like Fortran is that this statement will automatically determine and remember a storage location in main memory for this number. Subsequent access to this number is had by simply using the variable name, as in

```
Y = X**3
```

Since what was stored in X is 12.0 (i.e., 14. − 2.), the value stored in Y is 1728.0. With this understanding of what the = operator does, Fortran statements like

```
I = I + 1
X = X + 0.1
```

make sense, whereas in algebra they would be nonsense. That is, in Fortran the statement I = I + 1 means: Take the value already assigned to I, add 1 to it, and store the result in the location allotted to I.

2.6.1 Character Assignment Statements

Variables that have previously been declared as type CHARACTER may be assigned "values" by means of the assignment operator =. Of course, the value of a character variable is not numerical but is a string of symbols. For example,

```
CHARACTER NAME*6,STREET*6,CITY*7
NAME = 'MILLER'
STREET = 'E.MAIN'
CITY = 'CHICAGO'
```

In each case the character constant on the right of the assignment operator is assigned to the variable name on the left. Previously defined character variables may also appear on the right of the expression, as

```
NAME = 'MILLER'
STREET = NAME
CITY = 'CHICAGO'
```

The variables NAME and STREET now contain the same string of characters.

If the lengths of the string on the right of the expression are not the same as the specified length of the variable, the expression is altered to fit the length of the variable. If the expression is longer than the length of the variable, the expression is first truncated from the right until the lengths match.

```
CHARACTER NAME*6
NAME = 'WILLIAMS'        ⟨stored in NAME is the string |W|I|L|L|I|A|⟩
```

If the expression is shorter than the length of the variable, it is padded with blanks on the right.

```
NAME = 'DOE'      ⟨stored in NAME is the string |D|O|E|_ |_|_|⟩
```

2.6.2 Mixed-Mode Replacement

Next consider the consequences of statements like

```
I = 14./3.          ⟨the number stored in I is 4⟩
N = 3.*(1./3.) - 1.   ⟨the number stored in N is 0⟩
R = 4/3              ⟨the number stored in R is 1.0⟩
```

In each case, the expression on the right of = is first evaluated as either a real or integer value and then the assignment is made to the variable on the left, which here requires the mode of the result (i.e., integer or real) be converted. Thus 14./3. = 4.66666667 and the assignment to I automatically converts this to an integer by truncating the decimal part. The above statements are an illustration of what is called *mode conversion,* i.e., an integer (or real) is converted automatically into a real (or integer) by the assignment operator. The reason for this is that the number stored in the address allocated to I, for example, must be an integer and so the number must be converted to integer before it can be written in location I. One of the most common errors made by novice Fortran programmers is that of unintentional mode conversion, caused by using integer variable names for quantities that were intended to be real numbers. However, mode conversion can be an extremely useful feature of Fortran if used with care. As with mixed-mode expressions, I would strongly suggest that while you are learning Fortran every statement you write that employs mode conversion be preceded by a comment line like

```
C  INTENTIONAL MODE CONVERSION FOLLOWS
```

It should be obvious to you that expressions or assignment statements that mix character variables or constants with numerical values will always result in compilation errors. Thus, the code below

```
CHARACTER NAME*5
REAL X,C
X = 2.0
NAME = 'JONES'
B = X + NAME    ⟨Error—character and other type values may not be
                             mixed in an arithmetic operation.⟩
C = NAME        ⟨Error—character values cannot be converted to real.⟩
```

will result in two fatal compilation time errors.

2.7 PROGRAM ZERO

Fortran, like any skill, is best learned by doing and so it is probably best at this point to forestall any further exposition of rules and features and to carefully go over the program you executed earlier, program zero. You should have the complete output with you. The listing of the program given in Figure 1-6 is reproduced at the top of page 42.

The first Fortran statement in the program is

```
PROGRAM ZERO
```

which simply gives this program a name of ZERO. This line is optional; if it is omitted, the compiler will assign a name. The next two lines of Fortran code

```
REAL A,B,C,D,E,F,G,H,P,Q,R,S,T,U,V
INTEGER IA,IB,IC
```

explicitly type the variables as either real or integer. If these two lines were omitted, the variables would have been default-typed exactly the same. However, it is usually good practice to explicitly type all variables that appear in a program.

The first executable statement in the program appears next.

```
PRINT *,'INPUT VALUES FOR A,B SEPARATED BY A COMMA'
```

This phrase will then be printed on the terminal screen and serves as a

Figure 1–6 A program to demonstrate arithmetic operations.

Column Number

```
              1          2          3          4          5
1234567       0          0          0          0          0
- - - - - - - - - - - - - - - - - - - - - - - - - - - - - -
       PROGRAM ZERO
       REAL A,B,C,D,E,F,G,H,P,Q,R,S,T,U,V
       INTEGER IA,IB,IC
       PRINT *,'INPUT VALUES FOR A,B SEPARATED BY A COMMA'
       READ *,A,B
       C = A + B
       D = A - B
       E = A/B
       F = A * B
       G = C * D/(E * F) + (B/A)**2 - 1.
C INTENTIONAL MIXED MODE FOLLOWS (6 LINES)
       IA = A
       IB = B
       IC = IA**IB
       H = IC
       P = LOG(H)/IB
       Q = EXP(P) - IA
       R = A/G
       S = B/Q
       V = 0.0
       PRINT *,'INPUT VALUES A = ',A,' B  =  ',B
       PRINT *,'COMPUTED VALUES G = ',G,' Q = ',Q
       PRINT *,'R = ',R,' S = ',S
       T = 1./V
       PRINT *,'THE RESULT OF 1 DIVIDED BY 0 IS ',T
       U = A*T
       STOP
       END
```

prompt for the READ statement that follows:

```
READ *,A,B
```

This is an instruction to read the values that will then be assigned to the variables A and B from a file called INPUT. When the program is run interactively at a terminal this will cause the program to pause and wait for you to enter the numbers. The values entered are separated by a comma and, since A and B are associated with REAL values, should contain a decimal point. Note, if we had neglected to insert the previous PRINT statement, the program would still stop at the READ and we could easily be confused as to why. Inserting this form of a prompt before each READ statement is essential if the program is to be run at a terminal. The READ * statement is an example of list-directed input and is discussed in more detail in Section 2.9.

The next PRINT statement,

```
PRINT *,'INPUT VALUES A = ',A,' B = ',B
```

is called an *echo print* and is an important part of every program. The echo print is a verification of the read statement. Typing errors when entering numbers are very common and this form of safeguard can save you considerable time in attempting to understand why an apparently valid program gives incorrect results.

When the program is executed assume that the following were entered as input:

$$7.0, \quad 13.0 \qquad \langle followed \; by \; a \; RETURN \rangle$$

After execution of the READ line in the code, the variables A and B contain the values 7.0 and 13.0, respectively. Also, it is important that the type of the numbers entered as data (real or integer) agree with the type of the variable name in the READ statement.

The next four statements,

```
C = A + B
D = A - B
E = A/B
F = A*B
```

are trivial examples of real arithmetic operations and assignments. Notice that from what we know about the assignment operator, statements like,

```
A - B = D
 -D = B - A
```

would not make sense in Fortran although they would be perfectly valid in algebra.

The next statement is a bit more complicated.

```
G = C*D/(E*F) + (B/A)**2 - 1.
```

To untangle this, we need to use the hierarchy rules and successively scan the statement from left to right. Rewriting this expression in algebra, it would look like:

$$g = \frac{cd}{ef} + \left(\frac{b}{a}\right)^2 - 1$$

But recall

$$c = a + b$$

$$d = a - b$$

$$e = \frac{a}{b}$$

$$f = ab$$

so

$$g = \frac{(a + b)(a - b)}{a^2} + \left(\frac{b^2}{a^2}\right) - 1$$

$$= \frac{a^2 - b^2}{a^2} + \left(\frac{b}{a}\right)^2 - 1$$

$$= 1 - \left(\frac{b}{a}\right)^2 + \left(\frac{b}{a}\right)^2 - 1$$

$$= 0.0$$

Thus the value assigned to g is zero regardless of the values of a or b.

The statement IC = IA**IB appears simple enough but is deserving of a few moments consideration. To execute the exponentiation operation, the computer calls up a special program that is stored in main memory whose assignment is to take an integer base (IA) and raise it to an integer power (IB). The procedure used to calculate IA**IB is simply to multiply IA times IA, IB − 1 times, and if IB is negative, invert the result. Clearly, IA and/or IB may be either positive or negative.

The exponentiation in a previous statement, (B/A)**2, is of a different sort (real base, integer exponent) and a different subprogram is required to process the operation. Once again, to execute the exponentiation, if the exponent is INTEGER, the subprogram simply multiplies the base times itself the required number of times. The base and/or the exponent may be positive or negative. However, an operation like

$$(B / A) * * 2 . 3$$

requires special care. The subprogram that calculates this quantity must use logarithms, and since the logarithm of a negative number is undefined in our number system (it is actually an imaginary number), we must take care that the base is always positive. For example,

(−3.)**3	works	gives −27.
(−3.)**(−3)	works	gives −1./27.
(−3.)**(−3.)	will not work	

If the exponent is real—the base must be positive.

You have perhaps noticed that we have been cavalierly mixing modes without including the appropriate comment lines. The reason for this is that exponentiation is an exception to the previously stated mixed-mode rule. From the explanation given for the execution of the operation

$$X**7 \qquad \langle real\ base,\ integer\ exponent \rangle$$

we can see that at no time are two quantities of differing mode involved in an elementary arithmetic operation (addition, subraction, multiplication, division). In fact, whenever possible, exponentiation should be of the form

$$X**I$$

rather than

$$X**R$$

since the former is much faster and safer.

The next several lines in the program employ intentional mixed-mode arithmetic or replacement.

```
C INTENTIONAL MIXED MODE FOLLOWS (6 LINES)

      H = IC
      P = LOG(H)/IB
      Q = EXP(P) - IA
```

We have no difficulty in predicting the result of the statement H = IC; however, the next two statements are probably confusing. They both make use of what are called *intrinsic functions*. That is, subprograms stored in main memory that can be used by a Fortran program to calculate several common mathematical functions. Thus, LOG(X) computes the natural logarithm of X and EXP(X) computes e^x. For both of these intrinsic functions, the argument (X) should be real. The operation of these functions is very similar to those in your pocket calculator when you push the appropriate key. (e.g. $\ln(x)$ or e^x). These are but two of a long list of intrinsic functions available to Fortran programs. A few of the more commonly used functions are listed in Table 2-3.

Returning to the assignment statements for P and Q; once the $\ln(h)$ and e^p have been calculated, the rest of the statements involve authentic mixed-mode arithmetic, which should be avoided. However, in this instance we can easily figure out how the machine handles it. As mentioned earlier, before the division and subtraction operations are executed, both numbers involved [i.e., LOG(H) and IB], are converted to the dominant mode, in this case real. Now to see the effect of all these statements, let us rewrite them in algebraic notation.

$$h = i_c = (i_a)^{i_b}$$

Table 2-3 Some of the intrinsic functions available in Fortran.

FORTRAN	Algebra	Description	Argument	Result	Example
LOG(X)	$\ln(x)$	Natural log	Real	Real	Y = LOG(3.1)
EXP(X)	e^x	$e = 2.71828\ldots$	Real	Real	P = EXP(1.5)
SQRT(X)	$\sqrt{x}$	Square root	Real	Real	R = SQRT(4./6.)
SIN(X)	$\sin(x)$	Trigonometric sine	Real ⟨radians⟩	Real	S = SIN(3.14)
COS(X)	$\cos(x)$	Trigonometric cosine	Real ⟨radians⟩	Real	T = COS(0.)
ABS(X)	$|x|$	Absolute value	Real	Real positive	W = ABS(−5.5)
ACOS(X)	$\cos^{-1}(x)$	Inverse cosine, if $x = \cos(\theta)$ then $\theta = \cos^{-1}(x)$	Real	Real ⟨radians⟩	PI = ACOS(−1.)

$$p = \frac{\ln(h)}{i_b} = \frac{\ln[(i_a)^{i_b}]}{i_b}$$

$$= \frac{i_b \ln(i_a)}{i_b} = \ln(i_a) \qquad \langle\textit{Note: } \ln(x^y) = y \ln(x)\rangle$$

$$q = e^p - i_a$$

$$= e^{\ln(i_a)} - i_a$$

$$= i_a - i_a = 0.0 \qquad \langle\textit{Note: } e^{\ln(x)} = x\rangle$$

Thus, q is zero regardless of the values of i_a and i_b. Also recall that we determined that g is identically zero as well.

The next two assignment statements then do forbidden things:

```
R = A/G
S = B/Q
```

To see the results of the calculation thus far, the program next prints the current values of some of the variables.

```
PRINT *,'COMPUTED VALUES G = ',G,' Q = ',Q
PRINT *,'R = ',R,' S = ',S
```

We expect the computed values for both G and Q to be 0 and thus the values for R and S will be undefined (i.e., infinity). On your job run find the numbers printed for G and Q. The results are perhaps something like

```
INPUT VALUES A = 7.00000  B = 13.0000
COMPUTED VALUES G = -2.8422E-14  Q = -1.1366E-13
R = -2.4629E+14  S = -1.1437E+14
```

Both G and Q are very small numbers, but not zero. Why not? The answer once again is due to the fact that the machine, when working with real numbers only carries about ten significant figures, so

$$B/A = 13.0/7.0 = 1.8571428571428 . . .$$

Thus the statements we thought were errors (division by zero) were not caught by the machine. The computer does, however, catch division by precisely zero, as in the later statement

$$T = 1./V \quad \langle \text{V has been assigned the value } 0.0 \rangle$$

This is genuinely bad. However, the computer assumes you know what you are doing and dutifully assigns positive indefinite (i.e., + infinity) to T. If you attempt to print T, some compilers will print an "R" (meaning indefinite) or some other symbol; others will terminate the program at this point with an execution time error. If your program has made it this far, it will not get past the next statement:

$$U = A*T$$

At this point the machine is forced to conclude that all the faith it had in you was not well founded. You do not know what you are doing. Since no definite value has been assigned to T, this operation cannot be processed. The program dies at this point, not at the point where division by zero occurred but where an attempt was made to use the result of division by zero. This is an illustration of a common execution time error. When a program dies by an execution time error, the computer will inform you of the mode of the program's death and the approximate location of the error. In this example, the fatal execution time error is in the statement U = A * T.

The last two lines of the code are essential to the execution of a Fortran program. The statement

$$STOP$$

will cause termination of the program. This is an *executable* statement because it calls for some action on the part of the computer. Other examples of executable statements that we have seen so far are the simple arithmetic assignment statements.

The last line in the program,

$$END$$

is also executable and can be used to terminate the program. However, the principal use of END statements is as a marker to inform the compiler where the program ends and where to stop the translation into machine language. It is suggested that you use the END statement only for this purpose. Every Fortran program or subprogram must have END as its last line.

2.8 TRANSLATING ALGEBRA INTO FORTRAN

In order to develop a facility in the use of the hierarchy rules, you should next translate several moderately complicated algebraic expressions into Fortran and vice versa. A few examples follow:

1. Translate the following into Fortran (a) using parentheses and (b) totally without parentheses.

$$x = \frac{rP}{1 + (1 + r)^{-n}}$$

a. `X = R*P/(1. + ((1. + R)**(-N)))`
b. `TERM = 1. + R`
   `TERM = TERM**N`
   `BOTTOM = 1. + 1./TERM`
   `X = R*P/BOTTOM`

2. Write a single algebraic formula for the following Fortran statements.

```
TERM1 = C + 1.
TERM1 = A*B/TERM1
TERM2 = 1. + R
TERM2 = TERM2**N
TERM2 = TERM2 - 1.
TERM2 = TERM2/R
T = X*TERM1 - P/TERM2
```

Transcribing this line by line into algebraic notation, we obtain

$$t_1 = c + 1$$

$$t_1 = ab/(c + 1)$$

$$t_2 = 1 + r$$

$$t_2 = (1 + r)^n$$

$$t_2 = (1 + r)^n - 1$$

$$t_2 = \frac{(1 + r)^n - 1}{r}$$

Thus the final result can be written as

$$t = \frac{ab}{1+c}x - \frac{rP}{(1+r)^n - 1}$$

3. The velocity of very small water waves is given by the formula

$$v = \sqrt{\frac{2\pi t}{\lambda d} + \frac{g\lambda}{2\pi}}$$

where t is the surface tension (N/m), d is water density (kg/m³), g is the gravitational acceleration (m/sec²), and λ the wavelength (m) of the wave. The computed velocity will be in meters per second.

Write a complete program to read t and λ from a terminal and compute the wave velocity. The density d and the gravitational constant g should be assigned values of 1000. and 9.8, respectively, in the program.

You should have no difficulty in writing this program. Your result should resemble the code given below:

```
PROGRAM WAVES
D = 1000.
G = 9.8
PI = 3.14159265
READ *,T,WAVLTH
V = 2.*PI*T/(WAVLTH*D) + G*WAVLTH/2./PI
V = SQRT(V)
PRINT *,V
STOP
END
```

Note:

Since the variable names were not explicitly typed as INTEGER or REAL, using the names L or LAMBDA for the wavelength would have been incorrect and might have resulted in errors.
Unlike most pocket calculators, the computer has no stored value for π. A somewhat more accurate assignment is obtained by

```
PI = ACOS(-1.)
```

The successive divisions at the end of the sixth line of code are equivalent to

```
G*WAVLTH/(2.*PI)
```

2.9 LIST-DIRECTED INPUT AND OUTPUT

The Fortran programs we have seen up to this point have made use of list-directed input statements of the form

    READ *,   ⟨a list of variables⟩

The values entered at the terminal must agree in number and in type with the variable names in the READ statement. The values should be separated by commas.[5] For example, the statement

    READ *,X,IA,Y,KOUNT

when used to enter the following values

    5.72,4,3.E6 ,10002

is equivalent to the assignments,

    X   = 5.72
    IA   = 4
    Y   = 3000000.
    KOUNT = 10002

If the data were entered as

    5.72, 4,   ⟨CR⟩
      3.E6 ,10002

where ⟨CR⟩ stands for carriage return, exactly the same assignments would be made. The input

    5.72, , ,10002

would read zero(0) for IA and zero(0.0) for Y.
The list-directed read statement in the form

    READ *,   ⟨variable list⟩

can also be used to read values for variables of type CHARACTER, provided the character strings that are read in are enclosed in apostrophes.

------

[5] You may alternatively separate the numbers by blanks, but this is not recommended.

The list-directed output statement

```
PRINT *,    ⟨a list of variables, arithmetic expressions,
                or character strings⟩
```

operates in a similar fashion, with the additional features that arithmetic expressions may be included in the list and also strings of characters may be printed if enclosed by apostrophes. A few examples are listed in Table 2-4. The ability to print character strings as well as numerical values can be used to facilitate data input at a terminal. As suggested earlier, including an explanatory PRINT before each READ will eliminate a great many mistaken variable assignments. An additional reminder: It is a good idea to immediately print the values just read to verify they are indeed what you intended. This is called an echo print. For example, the water wave velocity problem in the previous section would be incomplete without the addition of the PRINT/READ lines:

```
PRINT *, 'ENTER T(SURFACE TENSION) AND THE WAVELENGTH'
READ *,T,WAVLTH
PRINT *,'T = ',T,'WAVELENGTH = ',WAVLTH
```

Table 2-4 Examples of list-directed output.

Fortran	Output
X = 5.	
Y = 8.	
I = 6	
J = 12	
PRINT *,X,Y,I,J	5.0000 8.0000 6 12
PRINT *,Y/X,I+J	1.6000 18
PRINT *,I+SQRT(X/Y)	6.79057
PRINT *,'X = ',X,'I-J =',I-J	X = 5.0000 I-J = -6

2.10 SUMMARY

As a review of some of the concepts covered in this chapter, Table 2-5 lists several common examples of incorrect transcriptions of algebra into Fortran along with the corrected versions.

Table 2-5 Common errors in translating algebra into Fortran.

Algebra	Incorrect Fortran	Correct Fortran	Comments
$a(b + c)$	A(B + C)	A*(B + C)	
$2a + 4$	2*A + 4	2.*A + 4.	Legal but mixed mode not appropriate for beginners
a^{n+1}	A**N + 1	A**(N + 1)	
$a^{(1/n)}$	A**(1/N)	A**(1./N)	Legal; however (1/N) is likely zero (integer arithmetic)
$\dfrac{ab}{cd}$	A*B/C*D	A*B/(C*D) or A*B/C/D	
$(-x)^n$	−X**N	(−X)**N	In Fortran 77 exponentiation precedes negation. −X**N is the same as −(X**N)
$x = 3. \times 10^6$	X = 3.*10.**6	X = 3.E+6	Note the correct version requires no arithmetic operations

PROBLEMS

1. What are the limits for numerical values on your computer? That is, find out what the maximum number of digits are for an integer, for a real number.
   a. Evaluate $[(\sqrt{2}.)^2 - 2.]$ directly on your computer (or calculator) and from the result determine the number of significant figures in a computer word.
   b. Execute the following code on your computer

   ```
         I = 1000
   1     PRINT *,I
         I = I*10
         GO TO 1
         END
   ```

   and from the results determine the maximum allowable integer. (You cannot use your calculator for this part; calculators do not have integer arithmetic.)

2. From the definition of the assignment operator, explain why the following Fortran statements are in error.

a. `3, = K`
b. `A + B = C` ⟨*Assume that A and B have been assigned values.*⟩
c. `X = 1,0`
   `X = Y`
   `PRINT *,X,Y`

3. For every computer the following arithmetic is true:

$$1000, + EPS = 1000,$$

provided EPS is chosen small enough.
   a. If the maximum number of digits on your computer is six, what is the largest value of EPS for which the above is true?
   b. If EPS = 0.0001, what is the result of

$$EPS + EPS + EPS + \cdots + EPS \qquad ⟨100\ million\ terms⟩$$

   c. Is this the same as 100 million times EPS? (i.e., 1.E8 * EPS)

4. Identify any **compilation** errors in the following. If none write "OK."
   a. `REAL IJKLMN`   **f.** `INTEGER X`
   b. `INTEGER REAL`   `X = 17`
      `REAL INTEGER`   `REAL Y`
   c. `INTEGER*5 X,Y`   `Y = 4,`
   d. `REAL X,Y,Z`   **g.** `CHARACTER TWO*2,ZERO*0`
      `INTEGER IX,Y`   **h.** `N = 7`
   e. `INTEGER IX,IY`   `M = 6`
      `REAL IX IY`   `CHARACTER NAME*N,SEX*M`
                              i. `INTEGER X, REAL Y`

5. Identify the **compilation** errors in the following. If none, write "OK."
   a. `X = 1,000,001,2`   **g.** `I = 7,/7,1`
   b. `Y = -1,73E-6,2`   **h.** `S = X**-2,`
   c. `Z = 61E-06`   **i.** `U = (-3,)**,5`
   d. `W = 7`   **j.** `V = 16,/2,/2,/2,/2,`
   e. `R = 2,E2`   **k.** `A = I`
   f. `6XA = 12,`   **l.** `X = X`

6. Determine the output of the following programs.
   a. `I = 2`   **b.** `R = 0,07`
      `J = 3`   `P = 2000,`
      `K = I + J`   `N = 20`
      `L = K + I`   `T = 1, + R`
      `I = I + L + 1`   `T = T**N`
      `L = K/J`   `X = R*P/T`
      `PRINT *,I,J,K,L`   `PRINT *,P,R,N,X`
      `STOP`   `STOP`
      `END`   `END`

```
c.  I = 2                        d.      X = 1.
    J = 3                     1       Y = 1. + X
    K = 4                             Z = X/Y
    L = I**J                          W = (Y + X)*(Y - X)/Y/Y
    M = I**(-J)                       W = W + Z**2 - 1.
    N = (J**I)**K                     C = SQRT(W)
    NN = J**(I*K)                     PRINT *,C
    MM = J**(I**K)                    X = X + 1.
    PRINT *,L,M,N,NN,MM               GO TO 1
    STOP                              END
    END
```

7. Assuming mixed-mode arithmetic is, for the moment, acceptable, determine the value of the following arithmetic expressions:

   a. `1 + 1./.5`   **e.** `28/3/2/3`   **i.** `9.**1./2.`
   b. `5*4/5`   **f.** `28/3/2./3`   **j.** `3.**9**.5`
   c. `4/5*5`   **g.** `28/(3/2)/3`   **k.** `27/3**3`
   d. `4./5*5`   **h.** `4/1+1`

8. Translate the following algebraic expressions into Fortran expressions. Use Fortran intrinsic functions where indicated.

   a. $\sin[\cos^{-1}(\beta)]$ **e.** $\tan^2(x/\pi + y)$
   b. $e^{\alpha+\beta} - \sin(\alpha - \beta)$ **f.** $\cos^{-1}(x + |\ln(y)|)$
   c. $\dfrac{1}{|a + b|}c + d$ **g.** $\left(\dfrac{x}{y}\right)^{n+1}$
   d. $\dfrac{x/y + \pi}{\pi - y/x}$

9. The following translations of algebra into Fortran are incorrect. Rewrite the correct Fortran expressions.

   a. $\dfrac{xy}{z + 1}$ $\rightarrow$ `XY/Z+1`

   b. x^{n+1} $\rightarrow$ `X**N+1`
   c. $x^{1/2}$ $\rightarrow$ `X**1./2.`
   d. $\cos^{-1}(|\ln(x)|)$ $\rightarrow$ `ACOS(LOG(ABS(X))`
   e. $(x^a)^b$ $\rightarrow$ `X**A**B`

10. The equation for the height of a falling object is

$$y = y_0 + v_0 t - (g/2)t^2$$

where y_0 is the starting height at $t = 0$, v_0 is the starting velocity, and g is the gravitational acceleration (9.8 m/sec^2). Write a program to read y_0, v_0, and a value of y that is less than y_0 and return a value of t that satisfies this equation. (You will have to use the quadratic formula.)

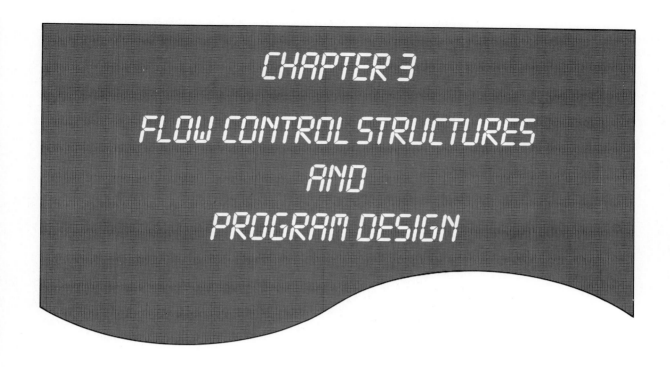

CHAPTER 3
FLOW CONTROL STRUCTURES
AND
PROGRAM DESIGN

3.1 INTRODUCTION

A program normally proceeds from one statement to the next. Fortran flow control structures may be used to alter this in a number of ways, such as

Decision structures: Compare the values of two quantities and, based on the result, branch to a variety of points in the program.
Loop structures: Return to a previous statement and repeat the calculation using different numbers.

It is mainly this ability to follow diverse paths through a code that makes the computer the useful computational tool that it is. If the program only requires one straight-through pass, it is merely duplicating the operation of a simple calculator and in almost all cases it would be more efficient to do the calculations by hand on your calculator.

In this chapter we will discuss a few of the control statements available in Fortran that make it possible to create interesting repetitive programs. In addition, since these programs will execute via numerous alternate paths, the structure of the program's flow can be quite complicated and so some systematic procedures for designing efficient programs will be discussed.

The step-by-step recipe for the solution of a problem is called an *algorithm,* and the design of clear, concise, and effective algorithms is the keystone of computer programming. Once an algorithm has been designed, the construction of a Fortran code to implement the algorithm is usually straightforward. There are a variety of mechanisms for preparing computational algorithms. The two most common schemes presently in use are called *flowcharts* and *pseudocode.*

3.2 THE USE OF FLOWCHARTS AND PSEUDOCODE IN PROGRAM DESIGN

The construction of programs that employ complicated branchings requires significantly more forethought than was indicated in the program examples to this point. Frequently both the reading and the writing of such code can create considerable confusion in even the best of programmers. The difficulty is that in such a project you can no longer trace the computation straight down from the first line to the END statement, but are forced to consider two or more possible alternatives simultaneously. Facing similar problems in, say, developing a complicated essay, you would resort to an outline. The outline of a Fortran program has been standardized and is called a flowchart. Before you begin to write any moderately complicated program, some sort of flowchart is essential as a guide to the construction of the code. Flowcharts themselves are not always easy to read and are often difficult to alter, especially if the program is quite long; and their popularity among professional programmers and engineers has diminished considerably in recent times. An alternative to flowcharts will be discussed in Section 3.2.2. Nonetheless, preparing a neat flowchart is an excellent means of accurately organizing your thoughts on a computational algorithm. Additionally, the flowchart can be an important part of a program's documentation and is especially useful if you intend to discuss your code with colleagues or your instructor. It is usually much easier to read someone else's flowchart than their Fortran.

3.2.1 Flowcharts

A flowchart is a method of diagramming the logic of an algorithm using a standardized set of symbols to indicate the various elements of the program. The most common symbols that are used in flowcharts are shown in Table 3-1. In a complete flowchart, short messages are ordinarily written within each symbol to explain the current activity.

Symbol	Meaning
Input/Output (parallelogram)	data are read in or results are printed out either via batch processing or at a terminal
Annotation (box with dashed line)	a box containing explanatory remarks
Process (rectangle)	a collection of statements that performs some sort of computation or operation
Terminal (rounded rectangle)	the beginning or end of a program or subprogram
Decision (diamond)	the branching to alternate paths on the basis of an IF test
(connector circle)	a connector, a point where several flow lines merge

Table 3-1 Symbols used in flowcharting fortran programs.

A flowchart should have one *start* and one or more *stops*. The logical flow of the algorithm is from top to bottom, and alternative paths are indicated by flow lines with arrowheads to indicate the direction of the calculation. Flow lines may cross, but the merging of two or more computational paths at a point in a program is indicated by means of the connector symbol (circle) which may also include the statement number of the junction point of the lines in the program.

As an example of a flowchart representation of a simple program, consider the problem of computing the wages for a worker who has worked a given number of hours this week and who is paid at a rate of PAYRAT in dollars per hour for the first 40 hours and at a higher rate of OVTRAT in dollars per hour for time exceeding 40 hours. The flowchart for this rather simple problem is shown in Figure 3-1. The key element of the algorithm is the decision structure represented by the diamond-shaped symbol. At this point, the program is expected to compare the value read for hours worked with the number 40. If the hours are more than 40, a calculation of the

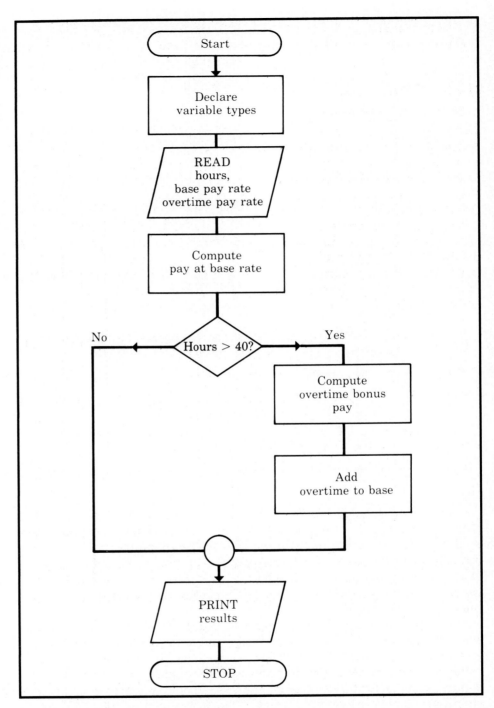

Figure 3-1
Illustration of a
flowchart for a
simple program.

overtime pay is executed and this result is added to the base pay; otherwise
the program skips the overtime computation. The Fortran implementation
of decision structures is by means of the IF(. . .)THEN statements which
will be discussed in Section 3.3.

More complicated flowcharts will be illustrated in subsequent examples, but first we will consider a competing method of outlining an algorithm.

3.2.2 Pseudocode Outlines of Computational Algorithms

Before a program can be written, the problem to be solved must be mapped out and some form of outline constructed. One procedure for doing this is the flowchart described above. However, a great many scientists and engineers who write complicated programs feel that the flowchart is too formal and artificial a device for a preliminary draft and resort instead to a highly informal procedure called pseudocode. The idea is to describe the operation of the program using a simplified mix of Fortran and English. Since pseudo-code is a response to the rigidity of flowcharts, there are very few rules. Basically you write out the operation of the program using minimal English, capitalizing Fortran phrases, using one separate line for each distinct segment of the code. It is also a good idea to indent subsegments as in an ordinary outline. A pseudocode outline of the salary problem follows:

>   READ in hours worked, base pay rate, and overtime rate
>   Echo PRINT
>
>   compute pay using base rate
>   PAY = PAYRAT*HOURS
>
>   IF Hours worked > 40 THEN
>   multiply excess of 40 by overtime bonus rate
>   (HOURS − 40)*(OVTRAT − PAYRAT)
>   add to base pay
>   ELSE
>   skip overtime computation
>
>   PRINT pay
>   STOP

In this form of the outline, the decision structure in the program is indicated by the English words IF and ELSE. This is very close to the form of the actual Fortran implementation of the algorithm as described in the next section.

3.3 DECISION STRUCTURES IN FORTRAN

In addition to the elementary arithmetic operations, the ALU in the computer is designed to compare two items and execute instructions based on that comparison. In the most elementary type of comparison, the two items are either the same or not the same. In order to facilitate the construction of comparison tests that are easy to read and understand, a new form of expression, in addition to arithmetic and character expressions, has been added to Fortran. This is called the *logical expression* and it constitutes the central ingredient in decision structures. Logical expressions are employed in logical IF tests and logical block IF structures. The logical IF test is a short form of the logical block IF structure and will be discussed in Section 3.6.1.

3.3.1 The Logical Block IF Structure

The Fortran structure which is the keystone of all decision procedures is the logical block IF structure which is of the following form.

IF(〈logical expression〉)THEN

> Set or block of Fortran statements that will be executed only if the logical expression is evaluated as TRUE.

END IF

If the logical expression is TRUE—
The block of Fortran statements is executed.
If the logical expression is FALSE—
The block of statements is ignored and the program proceeds to the next statement after the END IF.

The IF(. . .)THEN occupies one line and the Fortran statements that constitute the execution block appear on subsequent lines. The block of statements to be executed conditionally *must* be followed by the statement END IF. The END IF statement *should not* have a statement number. Also, for every IF(. . .)THEN there must be a corresponding END IF. To improve the readability of the code, the block of Fortran statements is usually indented with respect to the IF(. . .)THEN and the END IF.

Logical Expressions The action of the IF statement of course depends on the definition of the logical expression. A logical expression is built up from combinations of one or more *relational expressions* of the form

$$a_1 \text{ op } a_2$$

where a_1, a_2 are arithmetic expressions, variables, constants, or character strings; in short, things that have values that can be compared. By "op" is meant a "relational logic operator" belonging to the following set:

Relational logic operator	Meaning
.EQ.	Equal to
.NE.	Not equal to
.GT.	Greater than
.GE.	Greater than or equal to
.LT.	Less than
.LE.	Less than or equal to

Note: The periods are part of the operator and must always be present. A relational expression must have a value[1] of ⟨true⟩ or ⟨false⟩. The simplest logical expression consists of a single relational expression like

```
12 .GT. 6        This has a value of ⟨true⟩.
```

A logical expression may then be incorporated in an IF block structure, for example,

```
IF(TEMP .GT. 450.)THEN
     PRINT *,'STEAM TEMPERATURE DANGEROUSLY HIGH'
     STOP
END IF
```

More complex logical expressions can be built up by combining two or more relational expressions by means of the following combinational operators:

Combinational logic operator	Meaning	
.OR.	Or	
.AND.	And	
.NOT.	Not	(Changes a value ⟨true⟩ into a value ⟨false⟩ and vice-versa)

The evaluation of logical expressions is fairly transparent, as can be seen from the following examples.

1. If the variable SIZE has previously been assigned the value 12.0, then the expression

---

[1]In addition to the data types REAL, INTEGER, and CHARACTER, Fortran permits values of type LOGICAL. Logical variables may only have a value of .TRUE. or .FALSE. (Again, the periods are part of the expression.) The Fortran values are indicated in the text as ⟨true⟩, ⟨false⟩. LOGICAL variables are described in more detail in Section 9.1.3.

$$(\text{SIZE .LT. 100.0})$$

Has a value of ⟨true⟩.

2. All arithmetic operations are processed before the logical expression is evaluated. Thus

$$(\text{SIZE .LT. 10. * SQRT(100.)})$$

has the same value as the previous expression.

3. Parentheses may be added for clarity or to alter the value of the expression.

$$((\text{SIZE - 6.) .LT. (10. * SQRT(100.) - 6.)})$$

4. Logical subexpressions may be combined by using the operators .AND. and .OR. and are then evaluated according to the following rules.

$$⟨\text{true}⟩ \text{ .AND. } ⟨\text{true}⟩ = ⟨\text{true}⟩$$

$$⟨\text{true}⟩ \text{ .AND. } ⟨\text{false}⟩ = ⟨\text{false}⟩$$

That is, the entire expression is ⟨false⟩ if either side of the .AND. is ⟨false⟩.

$$⟨\text{true}⟩ \text{ .OR. } ⟨\text{false}⟩ = ⟨\text{true}⟩$$

$$⟨\text{false}⟩ \text{ .OR. } ⟨\text{false}⟩ = ⟨\text{false}⟩$$

The entire expression is ⟨true⟩ if either side of the .OR. is ⟨true⟩. For example, if the variables A and B have values 2. and 8., respectively, then

`(A .GT. 6. .AND. 2. * B .LT. 20.)`	*Is evaluated as* ⟨*false*⟩ *.AND.* ⟨*true*⟩ *which is then* ⟨*false*⟩
`(A * B .EQ. 0. .OR. A .LT. 10.)`	*Is evaluated as* ⟨*false*⟩ *.OR.* ⟨*true*⟩ *which is then* ⟨*true*⟩

A New Hierarchy Rule The processing of complicated logical expressions can lead to ambiguities, and so an additional hierarchy rule is required over those used in ordinary arithmetic (see Section 2.5.1). It reads

A logical expression is evaluated by first processing all arithmetic expressions according to the hierarchy rules pertaining to arithmetic expressions. Then the logic operators are processed scanning from left to right. The subexpressions are combined (the .AND. .OR. operators processed) from left to right with the .AND.'s processed before the .OR.'s.

Consider the meaning of the following rather complicated logical statement:

```
(I .EQ. 10 .OR. X .LT. 1. .AND. Z .GE. 0.0)
```

This could also be written as

```
((I .EQ. 10) .OR. (X .LT. 1.) .AND. (Z .GE. 0.0))
```

and has the same meaning as

```
((I .EQ. 10) .OR. ((X .LT. 1.) .AND. (Z .GE. 0.0)))
```

That is, .AND. is done before .OR. If the values assigned to the variables are

$$I = 10$$
$$X = 0.$$
$$Z = -1.$$

The expression reads

$$(\langle\text{true}\rangle \text{ .OR. } (\langle\text{true}\rangle \text{ .AND. } \langle\text{false}\rangle))$$

Since $\langle\text{true}\rangle$ .AND. $\langle\text{false}\rangle$ = $\langle\text{false}\rangle$, this expression is equivalent to

$$(\langle\text{true}\rangle \text{ .OR. } \langle\text{false}\rangle)$$

which has a value of $\langle\text{true}\rangle$. The expression forcing .OR. before .AND. has a quite different meaning.

```
( ((I .EQ. 10) .OR. (X .LT. 1.)) .AND. (Z .GE. 0.) )
```

Using the same values for the variables, this is equivalent to

$$((\langle\text{true}\rangle \text{ .OR. } \langle\text{true}\rangle) \text{ .AND. } \langle\text{false}\rangle)$$

or

$$(\langle\text{true}\rangle \text{ .AND. } \langle\text{false}\rangle)$$

and in this case the expression has a value of $\langle\text{false}\rangle$.

A Few Potential Pitfalls   There are several very common errors made when using a logical IF test.

1. *Never* test for equality of reals obtained from computation. The reason is of course due to the approximate nature of the arithmetic operations involving finite word length representations of real numbers. For example, if

```
A = 2.
B = (SQRT(2.)**2)
IF(A .EQ. B)THEN
     STOP
END IF
```

the test will possibly fail since B may have been assigned the value 1.99999999.

2. If it is necessary to test whether a quantity is smaller than some very small number, say EPS, the form of the test should never be

```
IF(X .LT. EPS)THEN        ⟨Incorrect test for smallness⟩
```

but rather

```
IF(ABS(X) .LT. EPS)THEN
```

The point being that X might possibly be negative, and any negative number, regardless of size, would satisfy the first IF test. The comparison of the two reals, A and B, should then possibly read

```
IF(ABS(A - B) .LT. EPS)THEN
```

There are several other forms of IF statements which will be discussed in Section 3.6. However, all of the additional features they present can be duplicated by combinations of block IF structures and, more importantly, these alternate forms of the IF test date from earlier versions of Fortran and are partly responsible for generating Fortran code that is difficult to read and even more difficult to change or correct. Whenever possible, the decision structures in a program should employ the IF(. . .)THEN statements.

3.3.2 Examples of IF(. . .)THEN–END IF Structures

A very important part of any program is the error diagnostic. As we shall see in Section 3.4.3, a great many programs are designed to monitor the behavior of some function, and if the computation proceeds as anticipated, print the result. If problems develop during the calculation, the program should be written so that it will flag the error and take some action. For example,

```
IF(VOLTGE .GT. 125. .OR. VOLTGE .LT. 105.)THEN
     PRINT *,'DANGER WARNING'
     PRINT *,'VOLTAGE OUTSIDE ACCEPTABLE LIMITS'
     STOP
END IF
```

Note that this test could not be written as

```
IF(VOLTGE .GT. 125. .OR. .LT. 105.)THEN     ⟨Incorrect⟩
```

Since the logical expression has two operators side by side (.OR. .LT.) the statement will lead to a compilation time error. An analogous statement that will not lead to compilation errors but which is also incorrect is to write the test for I = 0 or I = 10 as

```
IF(I .EQ. 0 .OR. 10)THEN     ⟨Incorrect⟩
```

Both sides of the .OR. operator must have a value of either ⟨true⟩ or ⟨false⟩ and in this case the value of the expression on the right is 10.[2]

Another example is to simply flag the errant condition and continue.

```
REAL BALANC ,WITHDR
INTEGER FLAG
FLAG = 1
IF(BALANC - WITHDR .LT. 0.0)THEN
      FLAG = 0
      WITHDR = 0.0
END IF
  . . .          . . .
  . . .          . . .
IF(FLAG .EQ. 0)THEN
      PRINT *,'INSUFFICIENT FUNDS'
      STOP
END IF
```

The Fortran code for the calculation of overtime pay discussed in Section 3.2.1 may now be constructed by using the IF block as

```
PROGRAM PAY
REAL PAY ,PAYRAT ,OVTRAT ,OVRTYM ,HOURS
READ * ,HOURS ,PAYRAT ,OVTRAT
*
*                              FIRST COMPUTE THE PAY BASED ON
*                              THE BASE HOURLY PAY RATE
*
PAY = PAYRAT * HOURS
*                              IF MORE THAN 40 HOURS , COMPUTE
*                              OVERTIME BONUS AT HIGHER RATE FOR
*                              EXCESS HOURS
```

Continued

---

[2] The results of this statement are unpredictable. Some compilers will check one side of an .OR. and if it is ⟨true⟩ ignore the other side. (If either side is ⟨true⟩, the expression is ⟨true⟩.) A similar operation will occur if either side of an .AND. is ⟨false⟩.

```
*
      IF(HOURS .GT. 40.0)THEN
          OVRTYM = (HOURS - 40.) * (OVTRAT - PAYRAT)
*
*                              ADD OVERTIME PAY TO BASE PAY
*
          PAY = PAY + OVRTYM
      END IF
      PRINT *,'HOURS WORKED = ',HOURS
      PRINT *,'BASE PAY RATE = ',PAYRAT
      PRINT *,'OVERTIME PAY RATE = ',OVTRAT
      PRINT *, 'PAY = ',PAY,'DOLLARS'
      PRINT *,'OF WHICH ',OVRTYM,'DOLLARS WAS OVERTIME PAY'
      STOP
      END
```

Note the similarity between the actual Fortran and the pseudocode version of the program.

The block IF could also be used to convert a number in radian measure to an angle θ between 0 and 360°. The number must first be scaled so that it is between 0 and 2π by subtracting integer multiples of 2π.

```
      REAL THETA,RADIAN,PI
      INTEGER MULTPL
      PI = ACOS(-1.)
      READ *,RADIAN
*
*                              MULTPL IS THE INTEGER NUMBER
*                              OF 2 PI MULTIPLES IN RADIANS.
*                              THIS STATEMENT INVOLVES MIXED-
*                              MODE REPLACEMENT.
*
      MULTPL = RADIAN/(2. * PI)
      IF(MULTPL .GT. 0)THEN
*
*                              THIS STATEMENT EMPLOYS MIXED-
*                              MODE ARITHMETIC.
*
          RADIAN = RADIAN - MULTPL * 2. * PI
      END IF
      THETA = RADIAN * 360.0/(2. * PI)
      PRINT *,RADIAN,'RADIANS = ',THETA,'DEGREES'
      STOP
      END
```

3.3.3 The IF(. . .)THEN–ELSE Structure

Frequently an algorithm will have two computational branches as a result of a logical IF test. If the condition is ⟨true⟩, a complete block of statements is to be executed, while if ⟨false⟩, an alternate set of statements is to be executed. You could easily accomplish this using two block IF structures. However, an additional option in the block IF structure enables you to construct a code that is easier to read and, more importantly, ties together the two related branches into one structure. This is the ELSE statement, which is placed between the IF(. . .)THEN and END IF.

IF(logical expression)THEN
　　Block of statements to be executed only if the expression is
　　⟨true⟩
ELSE
　　Block of statements to be executed only if the expression is
　　⟨false⟩
END IF

As with the END IF, the ELSE statement occupies a line all by itself and it should not have a statement number.

Consider the problem of writing an algorithm to find the smallest-magnitude real root (if any) of the quadratic equation

$$ax^2 + bx + c$$

The nature of the roots depends on the value of the discriminant, $\Delta = b^2 - 4ac$

If	Then
$\Delta > 0$	two real and distinct roots

$$x_+ = \frac{1}{2a}(-b + \Delta^{1/2})$$

$$x_- = \frac{1}{2a}(-b - \Delta^{1/2})$$

$\Delta = 0$　　　two real roots, both identical

$$x_+ = x_- = -\frac{b}{2a}$$

$$\Delta < 0 \qquad \text{two complex and distinct roots}$$

$$x_+ = \frac{1}{2a}[-b + i(-\Delta)^{1/2}]$$
$$\qquad\qquad\qquad\qquad\qquad i = (-1)^{1/2}$$
$$x_- = \frac{1}{2a}[-b - i(-\Delta)^{1/2}]$$

If it is desired to compute the smallest-*magnitude* real root of a quadratic with coefficients a, b, c, the program will have to first compute the discriminant Δ. If Δ is negative, the program will print a message (complex roots) and stop. If Δ is not negative (including the case $\Delta = 0$) the smallest-magnitude real root is

$$\frac{1}{2a}(-b + \Delta^{1/2}) \qquad \textit{if b is positive}$$

$$\frac{1}{2a}(-b - \Delta^{1/2}) \qquad \textit{if b is negative}$$

The flowchart for this problem is given in Figure 3-2 and the Fortran program is given in Figure 3-3. In this code there are two nested IF blocks. The inner IF block is completely contained within the outer IF block, and for each IF(. . .)THEN there is one corresponding END IF. IF blocks may be nested in this manner, one inside the other, but they must never overlap.

```
IF(A .LT. 0.)THEN
        ...
        ...
        IF(B .GT. 0.)THEN
                ...
                ...
        END IF
                ...
                ...
        END IF
```

In spite of the suggestive indentations, the first END IF is paired with the inner IF block and thus the code will not execute in the manner that was probably intended.

The algorithm used to determine the roots of a quadratic has three natural branches depending on the value of the discriminant $b^2 - 4ac$, and even though the program will correctly handle the third possibility, that of $\Delta = 0$, to avoid confusion, it is best to use a decision structure better suited to a situation with more than two alternatives. There is a further option available in the block IF structure that is designed to handle multiple paths as the result of an IF test: the ELSE IF structure.

Figure 3-2 The flowchart for the smallest-magnitude real root of a quadratic.

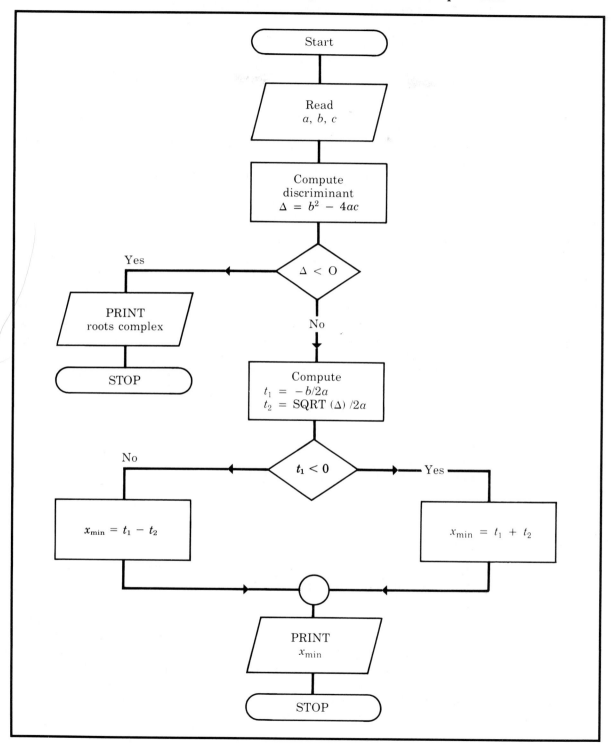

Figure 3-3 The Fortran program to compute the smallest-magnitude real root of a quadratic.

```
PROGRAM QUAD
REAL A,B,C,DISCR,T1,T2,XMIN
READ *,A,B,C
DISCR = B * B - 4. * A * C
IF(DISCR .LT. 0.)THEN
     PRINT *,'BOTH ROOTS ARE COMPLEX'
     STOP
ELSE
*
*                            DEFINE THE TWO TERMS T1 AND T2
*
     DENOM = 2.*A
     T1 = -B/DENOM
     T2 = SQRT(DISCR)/DENOM
     IF(B.GE.0.)THEN
          XMIN = T1 + T2
     ELSE
          XMIN = T1 - T2
     END IF
*
END IF
PRINT *,'SMALLEST-MAGNITUDE REAL ROOT = ',XMIN
STOP
END
```

3.3.4 The ELSE IF Statement

Frequently the possible branches of a computational algorithm are more numerous than the two permitted in a true-false test. To accommodate these cases the ELSE IF structure is used and is best explained by an example. The code for the roots of the quadratic may be written using this structure in the following way:

```
READ(*,*)A,B,C
DELTA = B * B - 4. * A * C
IF(DELTA .GT. 0.)THEN
          • • •
          • • •
          • • •
ELSE IF(DELTA .EQ. 0.)THEN
          • • •
          • • •
          • • •
ELSE
```

```
  · · ·
  · · ·        ⟨These statements are executed
  · · ·          only if both IF tests fail.⟩
  · · ·
END IF
```

Notice that the ELSE IF(...)THEN is *not* paired with an END IF. Also, as with the simple ELSE, the ELSE IF(...)THEN occupies a single line by itself. An unlimited number of ELSE IFs may be placed within the block IF structure.

As a second example of nested block IFs with multiple alternatives, consider the problem of determining whether three lengths, a, b, c, can form a triangle, and if so, whether the triangle is isosceles or equilateral.

Three lengths a, b, c can form a triangle if

$$|a - b| < c < a + b$$

The triangle is isosceles if

$$a = b \quad \text{or} \quad a = c \quad \text{or} \quad b = c$$

The triangle is equilateral if

$$a = b \quad \text{and} \quad a = c \quad \text{and} \quad b = c$$

The program for this problem will have to make multiple comparisons and account for several possibilities. The flowchart for the solution is shown in Figure 3-4 and the Fortran program is given in Figure 3-5.

3.4 LOOP STRUCTURES IN FORTRAN

Perhaps the most common and useful computational structure in programming is the loop structure, wherein a block of statements is executed and the block is then simply repeated with some of the parameters changed. The formal construction for operations of this type is a loop structure, called a *DoWhile* loop structure. The characteristics of a DoWhile loop are

1. An entry point (the top) labeled as DoWhile(...)
2. An execution block. The body of the loop containing the block of Fortran statements to be conditionally repeated.
3. A normal exit point (the bottom) labeled as EndDo.
4. Optional abnormal exit points (jump out of the loop from within)
5. Loop control specifications. Conditions on a parameter that determine when the cycling of the loop is to be terminated. The conditions are placed in the parentheses in the DoWhile entry point labels.

Figure 3-4 A flowchart for determining whether a triangle is isosceles or equilateral.

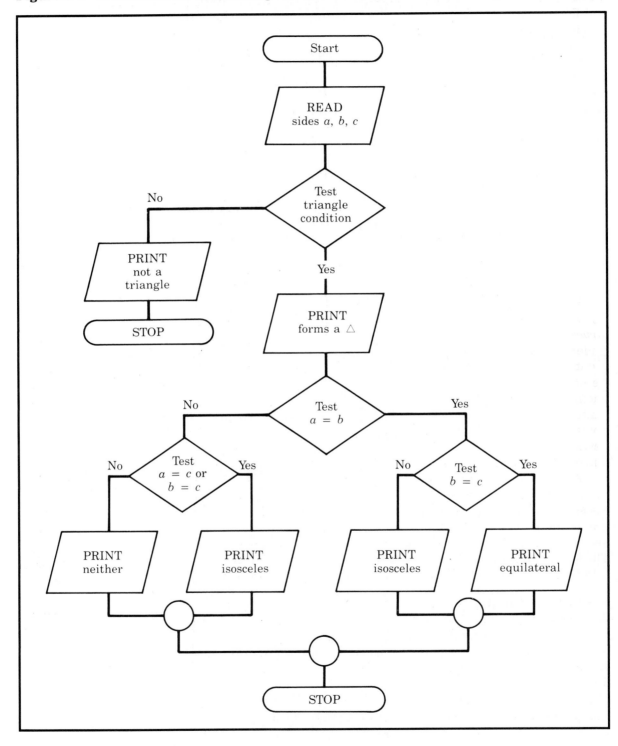

Figure 3-5 A program to determine if a triangle is isosceles or equilateral.

```
READ *,A,B,C
IF(ABS(A - B) .LE. C .AND. C .LE. A + B)THEN
      PRINT *,'SIDES ',A,B,C,' DO FORM A TRIANGLE'
      IF(A .EQ. B)THEN
            PRINT *,'THAT IS ISOSCELES'
            IF(B .EQ. C)THEN
                  PRINT *,'AND EQUILATERAL'
            END IF
      ELSE IF(A .EQ. C .OR. B .EQ. C)THEN
            PRINT *, 'THAT IS ISOSCELES'
      ELSE
            PRINT *,'THAT IS NOT ISOSCELES OR EQUILATERAL'
      END IF
ELSE
      PRINT *,'SIDES ',A,B,C,'DO NOT FORM A TRIANGLE'
END IF
```

I must point out at the very beginning of the discussion that at present *Fortran 77 does not contain specific DoWhile or EndDo statements for constructing loop structures.* However, the loop structures are more easily understood when expressed in terms of constructions analogous to the statements used in decision structures, and for this reason these statements have become more or less standard in pseudocode outlines of a program even though they *do not exist* as actual Fortran statements. Fortunately, it is quite easy to combine existing Fortran statements to accomplish the objectives of the missing statements. Future revisions of Fortran will almost certainly add the DoWhile and the EndDo to the vocabulary. A flowchart of the operation of the loop structure is shown in Figure 3-6.

As an example of a problem employing loop structures, consider the task of reading a list of student exam scores and simply counting the number who passed (score $\geq$ 60). The program could be arranged in a DoWhile structure as

```
NPASS = 0
DoWhile (<there is input left>)
   <Test: Any more input? If so, proceed; if not, quit>
   READ *,SCORE
   IF(SCORE .GE. 60.)THEN
       NPASS = NPASS + 1
   END IF
EndDo <Return to top of execution block.>
```

The only significant difference between the two structures shown in Figure 3.6 is the placement of the test for completion of the loop.

Figure 3-6 Loop structures in Fortran.

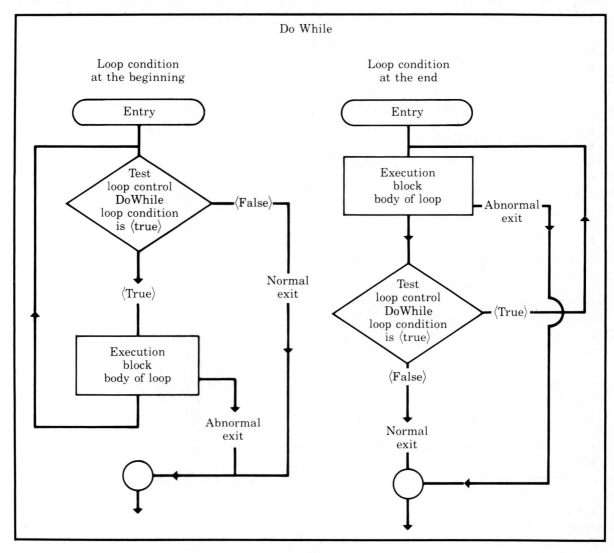

The above examples are, of course, not valid Fortran programs but are merely pseudocode versions of the algorithm, as discussed in Section 3.2.2. The construction of loop structures using valid Fortran statements is the subject of the next section.

3.4.1 Fortran Implementation of DoWhile Structures

The basic ingredients of a loop structure are the test for completion and the instruction to return to the top of the execution block. The test for completion will of course consist of an IF(. . .)THEN test. The Fortran statement that accomplishes a return to the top of the execution block is called an *unconditional GO TO*.

The Unconditional GO TO   The form of the unconditional GO TO statement is

$$GO\ TO\ \langle statement\ label \rangle$$

where ⟨statement label⟩ is the statement number of an executable statement. The effect of this statement is to transfer control of the program to the statement bearing the indicated statement number, which may be any executable statement in the program, coming either before or after the GO TO. For example,

```
      NPASS = 0
1     READ *,SCORE
          IF(SCORE .GT. 100.)THEN
              PRINT *,'ERROR ON INPUT - SCORE TOO LARGE'
              GO TO 99
          END IF
          IF(SCORE .GE. 60.)THEN
              NPASS = NPASS + 1
          END IF

          IF(SCORE .GE. 0.0)THEN
              GO TO 1
          END IF
*
      PRINT *,'NUMBER WHO PASSED = ',NPASS
99    STOP
      END
```

This program has an abnormal exit if a score larger than 100 is entered and will continue to cycle back to the READ statement until a negative score is entered by the user.

> *Caution:* The unconditional GO TO is the statement that is primarily responsible for Fortran code that resembles spaghetti: numerous unrestrained branchings up and down in a program that result in code that is unreadable and unalterable. You should be extremely conservative in the use of this statement.

The CONTINUE Statement   The CONTINUE statement in Fortran is an executable statement that performs no operation and is used primarily as a marker for the end of a loop or as the target of a GO TO. The form of the CONTINUE statement is

⟨*statement label*⟩   CONTINUE

The CONTINUE statement should have a statement number label. Since Fortran 77 does not have an EndDo statement in its vocabulary, this statement is used in its place. An example of its use in a DoWhile structure is given below.

```
      NPASS = 0
   1  READ *,SCORE
      IF(SCORE .LT. 0.0)THEN        i.e., DoWhile
                                    score is ≥ 0
         GO TO 12
      END IF
         ...            ...
         ...            ...
      GO TO 1
  12  CONTINUE                      This plays the
                                    role of EndDo.
*
      PRINT *,'NUMBER PASSED = ',NPASS
         ...          ...
  99  STOP
      END
```

3.4.2   Examples of Loop Structures—The Repetitive Program

Very frequently we will want to design a program that executes a calculation for a given set of parameter values and then simply repeats the calculation with a slightly modified set of values, and so on. The loop control is often accomplished by means of a counter that is incremented after each calculation,

```
      IRUN = 1
   1  READ *, <set of input data>

         perform calculation
         PRINT *, <results> ,IRUN

      IRUN = IRUN + 1
```

```
   IF(IRUN .LE. 10)THEN
        GO TO 1
   ELSE
        STOP
   END IF
```

This code will execute ten independent calculations.

An alternative, when you are uncertain of how many calculations are required, is to use a so-called trailer data line,

```
1 READ *,ITEST, <list of the rest of the input data>

   IF(ITEST .LT. 0)THEN
        STOP
   ELSE
            perform calculations
            PRINT *, <results>
        GO TO 1
   END IF
```

This code will continue to loop until a negative integer is entered on the last line of data.

As a final example of a loop structure, consider the situation where it is desired to examine the results of a calculation for a variety of values of a single parameter over a limited range. For example, the temperature dependence of the speed of sound in air is given approximately by the expression

$$v = 331\left(1 + \frac{T}{273}\right)^{1/2} \quad (\text{m/sec})$$

where T is expressed in °C. If we are interested in obtaining values for the sound velocity for temperatures in the range $20° \text{ C} \le T \le 35° \text{ C}$ in steps of $1° \text{ C}$, the Fortran code would be

```
   T = 20.
   DT = 1.
10 V = 331. * SQRT(1. + T/273.)
   PRINT *,'FOR T = ',T,' THE SOUND SPEED IS ',V
   T = T + DT
   IF(T .LT. 36.0)THEN
        GO TO 10
   ELSE
        PRINT *,'CALCULATION COMPLETE -- JOB TERMINATED'
        STOP
   END IF
   END
```

Example Program—Auto Loans When buying a new car some of us must borrow money. If the amount of money borrowed is P, at a yearly interest rate of R for Y years, and the payments are monthly, then the amount of the monthly payment, PAYMNT, is given by

$$\text{PAYMNT} = rP \frac{1}{1 - (1 + r)^{-n}}$$

where r is the monthly interest rate ($r = R/12$) and n is the total number of installments ($n = 12Y$).

The problem is to write a program to calculate PAYMNT and the total cost of the loan for all the possible combinations of

$$Y = 2, 2\tfrac{1}{2}, 3, 3\tfrac{1}{2}, 4 \text{ years}$$

$$R = 10, 11, \ldots, 18\%$$

with $P = \$9500$. The flowchart for this program is given in Figure 3-7. This program requires that two independent loops, one for the values of R and one for the values of Y, be nested, one completely inside the other. For each value of Y, the term of the loan, a complete cycle of interest rates is executed. The R loop is called an *inner loop* and the Y loop is the *outer loop*. As with nested block IF structures, nested loops must never overlap. The complete Fortran program is given in Figure 3-8. Notice that the output from the example program is not particularly neat or orderly. It is difficult to produce tables using the PRINT * statement. However, vertical spacing can be achieved by inserting blank lines in the output by printing a blank, i.e., PRINT *, ' ' .

3.4.3 Examples of Loop Structures—The Iterative Program

You may be familiar with a method, resembling long division, of calculating the square root of a number. It is very awkward and tedious. However, if you have a calculator available to handle ordinary division, there is an alternative procedure devised by Isaac Newton that is an excellent example of an iterative calculational method.

Newton's algorithm for the calculation of square roots is: If x_0 is a guess for the value of the square root of a number C, then an improved value is x_1, where

$$x_1 = \frac{1}{2}\left(x_0 + \frac{C}{x_0}\right)$$

The idea is to read a number C whose square root is to be computed, guess the square root x_0, and improve the guess with Newton's algorithm. If the improved guess x_1 is still not accurate enough (i.e., $x_1^2 - C$ is not small), the value is again improved by a further application of the algorithm. This

Figure 3-7 A flowchart for calculation of auto loan payments. This program has two nested loops.

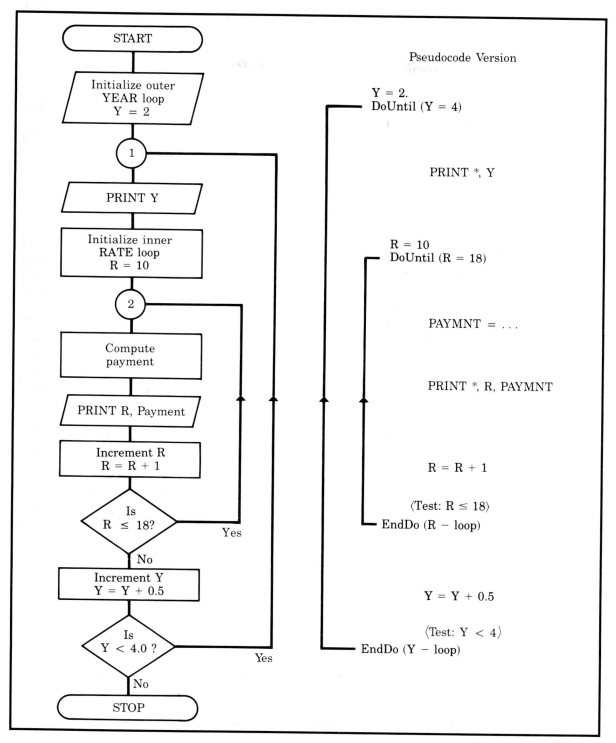

Pseudocode Version

Y = 2.
DoUntil (Y = 4)

PRINT *, Y

R = 10
DoUntil (R = 18)

PAYMNT = . . .

PRINT *, R, PAYMNT

R = R + 1

⟨Test: R ≤ 18⟩
EndDo (R − loop)

Y = Y + 0.5

⟨Test: Y < 4⟩
EndDo (Y − loop)

Figure 3-8 The Fortran code and results for the auto loan program.

```
      PROGRAM CARS
* ---
* ---  THIS PROGRAM WILL COMPUTE THE AMOUNT OF THE MONTHLY
* ---  PAYMENT FOR AN AUTO LOAN FOR LOANS OF 2 THROUGH 4
* ---  YEARS IN HALF-YEAR STEPS AND FOR INTEREST RATES FROM
* ---  10 TO 18 PERCENT. THE PROGRAM ILLUSTRATES NESTED
* ---  LOOPS.
* ---
* VARIABLES
* ---
      REAL P,YMAX,R,XY
      INTEGER N,RMIN,RMAX,RATE
* ---
* ---  P     -  PRINCIPAL, THE AMOUNT OF THE LOAN - INPUT
* ---  YMAX  -  MAXIMUM LENGTH OF THE LOAN IN YEARS - INPUT
* ---  RMIN  -  STARTING VALUE OF THE INTEREST RATE
* ---                 IN PERCENT - INPUT
* ---  RMAX  -  MAXIMUM INTEREST RATE - INPUT
* ---  Y     -  CURRENT VALUE OF LOAN LENGTH IN YEARS
* ---  RATE  -  CURRENT VALUE OF THE INTEREST RATE
* ---  R     -  CURRENT VALUE OF THE INTEREST RATE
* ---                 PER MONTH EXPRESSED AS A DECIMAL
* ---  X     -  THE COMPUTED VALUE OF THE MONTHLY PAYMENT
* ---  N     -  THE NUMBER OF PAYMENTS (12 * YEARS)
* ---
*------------------------------------------------------------
* INITIALIZATION
* ---
* ---  READ IN THE PRINCIPAL AND THE LIMITS ON THE INTEREST
* ---  RATES AND THE LENGTH OF THE CALCULATION. ECHO PRINT.
* ---
      PRINT *,' '
      PRINT *,'ENTER PRINCIPLE'
      READ *,P
      PRINT *,'ENTER THE MAXIMUM LENGTH OF THE LOAN'
      READ *,YMAX
      PRINT *,'ENTER MINIMUM, MAXIMUM INTEREST RATES(PERCENT)'
      READ *,RMIN,RMAX
      PRINT *,' '
* ---
* ---  PRINT THE OVERALL HEADINGS FOR EACH SET OF
* ---  CALCULATIONS (I.E., ONE FOR EACH VALUE OF Y)
* ---
      PRINT *,'THE PRINCIPAL OF THE LOAN IS ',P,' DOLLARS'
      PRINT *,' '
      PRINT *,'    THE CALCULATION LIMITS ARE'
      PRINT *,'       YEARS - FROM 2 TO ',YMAX,' YEARS'
      PRINT *,'       INTEREST - FROM ',RMIN,' TO ',RMAX,' PERCENT
      PRINT *,' '
```

```
ENTER PRINCIPAL  9500.00
ENTER THE MAXIMUM LENGTH OF THE LOAN 4.0
ENTER MINIMUM, MAXIMUM INTEREST RATES(PERCENT)  10,18

THE PRINCIPAL OF THE LOAN IS 9500. DOLLARS

   THE CALCULATION LIMITS ARE
      YEARS - FROM 2. TO 4. YEARS
      INTEREST - FROM 10 TO 18 PERCENT

THE RESULTS FOR A LOAN OF 2. YEARS ARE
```

INTEREST RATE	NUMBER OF PAYMENTS	PAYMENT (DOLLARS)	TOTAL COST OF LOAN
10	24	438.3768002065	1021.043204956
11	24	442.7744462867	1126.587108808
12	24	447.1979861211	1232.751666905
13	24	451.6473145904	1339.535555171
14	24	456.1223910498	1446.937385195
15	24	460.6231564459	1554.955754702
16	24	465.1495499172	1663.589198013
17	24	469.7015088122	1772.836211492
18	24	474.2789687103	1882.695249047

```
THE RESULTS FOR A LOAN OF 2.5 YEARS ARE
```

INTEREST RATE	NUMBER OF PAYMENTS	PAYMENT (DOLLARS)	TOTAL COST OF LOAN
10	30	359.2083366108	1276.251898323
11	30	363.6416066668	1409.248200004
12	30	368.1070755506	1543.212266518
13	30	372.6047178087	1678.141534262
14	30	377.1344443752	1814.033331256
15	30	381.6961626159	1950.884878478
16	30	386.2897763744	2088.693291232
17	30	390.9151860176	2227.455580529
18	30	395.5722884845	2367.168654536

```
THE RESULTS FOR A LOAN OF 3. YEARS ARE
```

INTEREST RATE	NUMBER OF PAYMENTS	PAYMENT (DOLLARS)	TOTAL COST OF LOAN
10	36	306.5382783415	1535.378020295
11	36	311.0178126115	1696.641254013
12	36	315.5359432221	1859.293955996
13	36	320.0925440313	2023.331585128
14	36	324.6874827013	2188.749377248
15	36	329.3206207897	2355.542348431
16	36	333.9918138453	2523.705298443
17	36	338.700911504	2693.232814145
18	36	343.4477575912	2864.119273283

THE RESULTS FOR A LOAN OF 3.5 YEARS ARE

INTEREST RATE	NUMBER OF PAYMENTS	PAYMENT (DOLLARS)	TOTAL COST OF LOAN
10	42	269.0097837627	1798.410918035
11	42	273.5416838825	1988.750723064
12	42	278.1184473382	2180.974788204
13	42	282.7398947456	2375.075579313
14	42	287.4058370092	2571.045154387
15	42	292.11607496	2768.875170833
16	42	296.8704022155	2968.55689305
17	42	301.6686000047	3170.081200199
18	42	306.5104427214	3373.438594298

THE RESULTS FOR A LOAN OF 4. YEARS ARE

INTEREST RATE	NUMBER OF PAYMENTS	PAYMENT (DOLLARS)	TOTAL COST OF LOAN
10	48	240.9445426301	2065.338046247
11	48	245.5324648088	2285.558310823
12	48	250.1714366033	2508.22895696
13	48	254.8612109908	2733.33812756
14	48	259.601526703	2960.873281744
15	48	264.3921085315	3190.82120951
16	48	269.2326676455	3423.168046983
17	48	274.1229019203	3657.899292174
18	48	279.0624962775	3894.999821321

CALCULATION COMPLETED

```fortran
* - - -     NEXT PRINT THE TABLE HEADINGS
* - - -
      Y = 2.0
      PRINT *,' '
      PRINT *,' '
    1 PRINT *,'THE RESULTS FOR A LOAN OF ',Y,' YEARS ARE'
      PRINT *,' '
      PRINT *,'     INTEREST     NUMBER OF       PAYMENT      TOTAL COST'
      PRINT *,'       RATE       PAYMENTS       (DOLLARS)      OF LOAN'
* - - - ------------------------------------------------------------
* COMPUTATION
* - - -
* - - -     THE CURRENT MONTHLY INTEREST RATE IS COMPUTED
* - - -
      RATE = RMIN
      N = 12. * Y
* - - -
* - - -     THE TOP OF THE INNER LOOP
* - - -
    2 R = RATE/100./12.
      TOP = R * P
      BOT = 1. - (1. + R)**(-N)
      X = TOP/BOT
* - - -
* - - -     PRINT THE CURRENT TABLE ENTRY
* - - -
      PRINT *,'    ',RATE,'     ',N,'     ',X,'     ',
     +         N*X - P
* - - -
* - - -     INCREMENT RATE AND IF STILL WITHIN LIMITS LOOP
* - - -     BACK TO TOP OF THE INNER LOOP, ELSE PROCEED TO
* - - -     NEXT CALCULATION
* - - -
      RATE = RATE + 1.
      IF(RATE .LE. RMAX)THEN
         GO TO 2
* - - -
* - - -     AT THE END OF THE RATE LOOP, INCREMENT THE YEAR
* - - -     VARIABLE AND TEST FOR COMPLETION OF THE CALCULATION.
* - - -
      ELSE
         Y = Y + 0.5
         IF(Y .GT. YMAX)THEN
            PRINT *,' '
            PRINT *,' CALCULATION COMPLETED'
            STOP
         ELSE
            GO TO 1
         END IF
      END IF
* - - -
      END
```

process is continued until the computed value for x_1 is sufficiently accurate, or until the program exceeds its maximum cycle limit which is supplied by the programmer.

All iterative programs should have built-in checks for potential problems, such as

1. The algorithm is diverging. That is, successive answers are getting worse, not better.
2. The convergence is too slow. After a prescribed maximum number of iterations, satisfactory accuracy has not been attained.

The pseudocode outline of a program to implement Newton's method is given below,

```
READ in number whose square root is wanted (C)
Echo PRINT
Determine initial guess for square root (X)
      ⟨initial guess is (C + 1)/2⟩
Initialize iterations counter (ITER)
    Using Newton's algorithm, improve the guess by the replacement
      [X ← 0.5 * (X + C/X)]
    Increment the iterations counter by one
      Check for excessive number of iterations
        ⟨IF(ITER > 100) quit and print
          failure statement⟩
    Check for convergence: is |C − X * X| small?
      IF yes → success, quit and PRINT results
      IF no →  has not yet converged, return to improvement statement
    Success path: PRINT results
    Failure path: PRINT diagnostic
```

A flowchart version of the program is given in Figure 3-9 and the complete Fortran code is illustrated in Figure 3-10. In preliminary versions of this program the prudent programmer would have the program print the latest value of X in each iteration to see how the calculation is progressing. A failure to converge to an answer could be caused by an incorrect algorithm or by using too small a value for the convergence criterion. For example, if your machine only retains eight digits in a computer word, a test for success of the form

```
IF(ABS(C - X * X)) .LT. 1.E - 12)THEN
```

would be inappropriate and would always fail if C is larger than 0.001. If the number entered is 200., the output from this program is

```
ENTER NUMBER WHOSE SQUARE ROOT IS WANTED
200.
THE SQUARE ROOT OF 200.0000 IS 14.14214
THE NUMBER OF ITERATIONS WAS     6
```

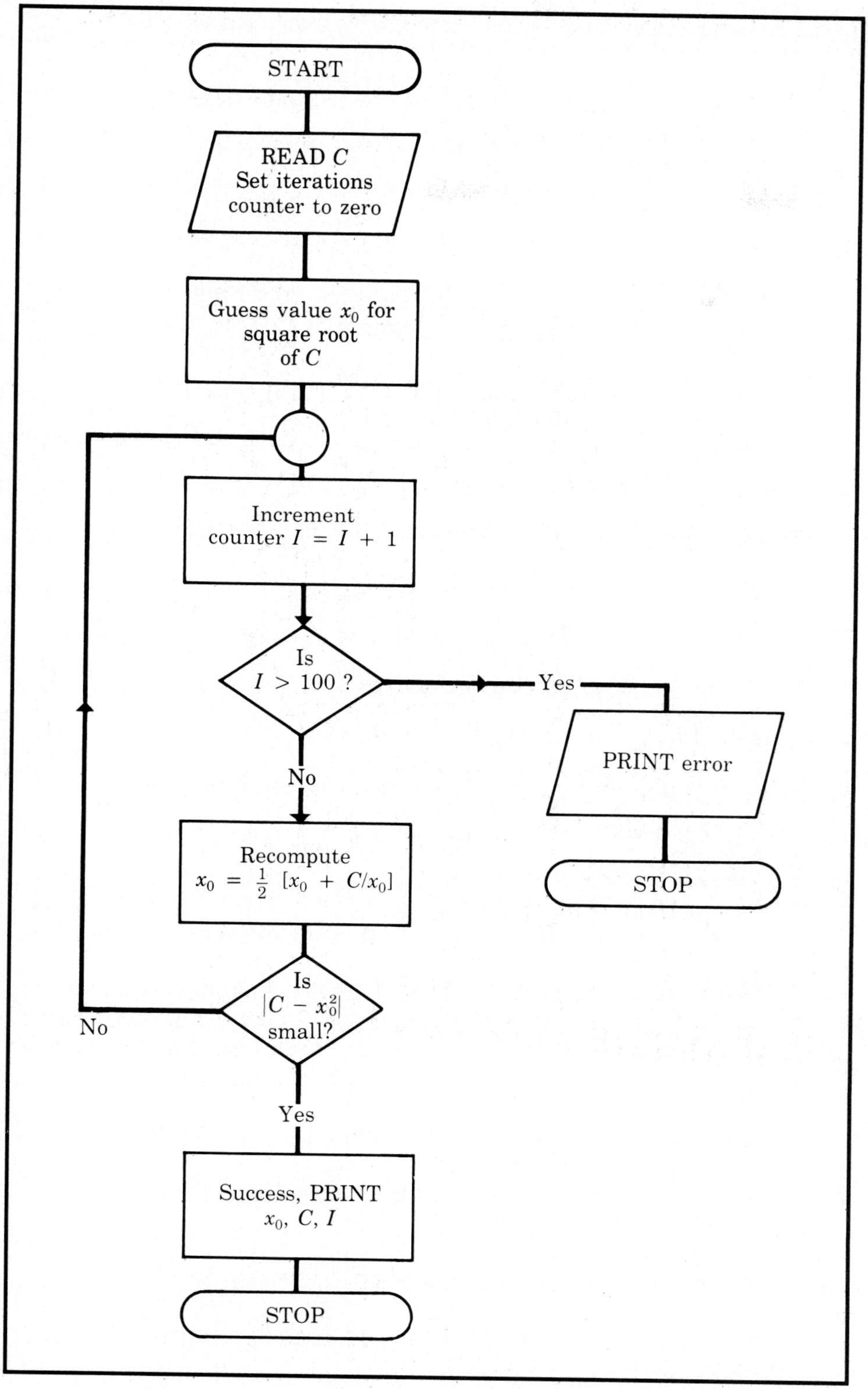

Figure 3-9
Flowchart for square roots via Newton's algorithm.

Figure 3-10 The Fortran code for calculating square roots via Newton's algorithm.

```
      PROGRAM SQROOT
C --DEMONSTRATION PROGRAM ILLUSTRATING NEWTON'S ITERATIVE
C --ALGORITHM FOR COMPUTING SQUARE ROOTS
C --         XNEW = 0.5 * (XOLD + C/XOLD)
C --------------------------------------------------------
C VARIABLES
      REAL X, C
      INTEGER I
C                         C -- THE NUMBER WHOSE SQUARE ROOT
C                            IS DESIRED (INPUT)
C                         X -- THE SUCCESSIVE VALUES OF THE
C                            SQUARE ROOT OF C
C                         I -- ITERATIONS COUNTER
C --------------------------------------------------------
C  INITIALIZATION
C
      PRINT *,'ENTER NUMBER WHOSE SQUARE ROOT IS WANTED'
      READ *,C
      I = 0
C                         FOR AN INITIAL GUESS FOR SQRT(C)
C                         WE TRY SIMPLY (C + 1)/2
      X = (C+1.)/2.
C --------------------------------------------------------
C   COMPUTATION ALGORITHM
C
C                         IMPROVE THE GUESS AND INCREMENT I
C
   1  X = .5 * (X + C/X)
      I = I + 1
C                         TEST FOR EXCESSIVE ITERATIONS
C
      IF(I .GT. 100)THEN
         PRINT *,'NOT CONVERGING IN 100 STEPS'
         STOP
C                         TEST FOR CONVERGENCE BASED ON ABSOLUTE
C                         DIFFERENCE BETWEEN X * X AND C
C
      ELSE IF(ABS(X * X - C) .LT. 1.E-6)THEN
C
C                         SUCCESS - PRINT RESULTS
C
         PRINT *,'THE SQUARE ROOT OF ',C,' IS ',X
         PRINT *,'THE NUMBER OF ITERATIONS WAS ',I
         STOP
C                         CURRENT VALUE OF X IS NOT ACCURATE
```

Figure 3-10 *Continued*

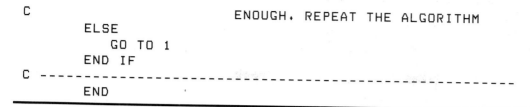

```
C                          ENOUGH, REPEAT THE ALGORITHM
        ELSE
             GO TO 1
        END IF
C  - - - - - - - - - - - - - - - - - - - - - - - - - - - - - - - - - - - -
        END
```

3.5   A NOTE ON GOOD PROGRAMMING STYLE

Every so often, one reads in the newspapers accounts of individuals who have been recorded as dead by the Social Security Administration and who show up one day, in person, requesting the error be corrected and are told that the mistake is irreparable, the computer code has no entry for "resurrected." These stories are examples of poorly documented computer programs, assembled piecemeal over many years by numerous individuals. These codes are often a mysterious black box to those who use them and are almost impossible to modify. This is a serious problem everywhere computers are used. It cannot be stressed too strongly that the programs you write must be understandable, now and anytime in the future, to any potential user.

I have already suggested inserting comment lines throughout your code to explain the operation of your program. There are several additional steps you can take to improve a program's readability.

1. Segment the program into a sequence of blocks or modules. For example,

Variable dictionary:	A list of all the variables in the program and an explanation of their meaning (perhaps including units).
Initialization block:	A segment of the program where the constants are assigned values and the data are read in.
Computation block:	Contains the body of algorithms used in obtaining the numerical results.
Success path:	After a successful completion of the program it branches to here and the results are printed.
Failure path:	If problems are encountered during execution, the program branches here and some form of diagnostic message is printed.

2. Explicitly declare each variable in the program to be either INTEGER, REAL, or CHARACTER.
3. Echo print all numbers read in to verify accurate assignments. This usually means that a corresponding PRINT statement should immediately follow each READ statement. This is often relaxed somewhat provided that *every* value read is eventually printed somewhere later in the program.
4. Before you begin writing the program, outline it by means of a simplified flowchart or pseudocode description. After the program has been tested and successfully executed, prepare a detailed flowchart as part of the documentation for the program.
5. The fundamental commandment of structured programming is: Spend more time on the design of the program *before* you begin to write the code. You may think you can sit down at a terminal and compose a program, and often you can. But 90 percent of the time you will end up frustrated. Write out the program first, in block form, using either a flowchart or pseudocode. Include ample comments in the program and liberally add error diagnostics.

3.6 ADDITIONAL CONTROL STATEMENTS

As promised, several of the alternative forms of the Fortran control statements are described in this section.

3.6.1 The Logical IF Test

Frequently the block of statements that is to be executed as a result of a single option IF(. . .)THEN—END IF structure will consist of a single executable Fortran statement. For example,

```
IF(ITER .GT. 100)THEN
        GO TO 99
END IF
```

Fortran permits simple block IFs of this type to be written as a single line with the executable Fortran statement following the IF test, as

```
IF(<logical expression>)   <an executable Fortran statement>
```

If the logical expression is evaluated as ⟨true⟩, the Fortran statement is executed.

If the logical expression is evaluated as ⟨false⟩, the Fortran statement is ignored and the program proceeds to the next line of code.

The Fortran statement can be almost any of the executable statements that we have encountered, such as READ, PRINT, assignment, GO TO, STOP. It cannot, however, be another IF-type statement (or a DO statement, which will be discussed in Chapter 6).

It is usually acceptable to replace single option–single statement block IF structures by a one-line logical IF statement. However, if you find your program contains numerous statements of the form

```
IF(...)GO TO
```

you are probably creating a code that contains excessive branchings. Structured programming means that you should, whenever possible, be constructing all computational algorithms out of the basic decision and loop structures discussed in this chapter. If the logical IF statement is part of one of these larger structures, it is acceptable; if not, it is likely that it violates the normal style considerations of structured programming.

3.6.2 The Computed GO TO Statement

The form of the computed GO TO statement is

$$\text{GO TO } (k_1, k_2, k_3, \ldots, k_n), \text{Iexp}$$

where $k_1, k_2, \ldots, k_n$ are statement numbers of existing executable statements and Iexp is an integer, integer variable, or integer arithmetic expression. This statement transfers control to one of the statements in the parentheses depending on the value of Iexp. If

Iexp $= 1$	*the program branches to statement k_1*
Iexp $= 2$	*the program branches to statement k_2*
...	...
Iexp $= n$	*the program branches to statement k_n*
Iexp $> n$	*no transfer is made, the next statement is executed*
Iexp < 1	*no transfer is made, the next statement is executed*

For example,

```
K = 15
I = 6
GO TO (4,83,15,1,9,15,6),K/I + 1
```

has the same effect as GO TO 15. The comma after the parenthesis is optional.

3.6.3 The Arithmetic IF Statement

The form of the arithmetic IF statement is

$$IF(exp)k_-, k_0, k_+$$

where k_-, k_0, k_+ are statement numbers of executable statements existing somewhere in the program, and exp is an integer or real constant, variable, or expression. The arithmetic IF transfers control to one of the three statement labels depending upon the value of exp.

If exp < 0.0 *the program branches to statement k_-*

If exp $= 0.0$ *the program branches to statement k_0*

If exp > 0.0 *the program branches to statement k_+*

For example,

```
X = 2.
IF(X**2 - 3.)17,35,108     (transfer is made to statement 108)
```

But beware of the following improper code,

```
X = 2.
Y = SQRT(X)
Z = Y**2 - X
IF(Z)7,8,9
```

will probably cause a transfer to statement 7, not statement 8. This is of course the recurring problem of approximate arithmetic when using real numbers.

In the earliest versions of Fortran the arithmetic IF statement was the only comparison statement available, and as a consequence many of the "old-timers" use it almost exclusively. In modern usage it has been replaced by IF(. . .)THEN structures or the logical IF test.

1. Identify the compilation errors in the following. If none write OK.

```
a. IF(A .EQ. 5)
      THEN STOP
   END IF


b. IF(A .LT. 5.)THEN
        A = 5.
   ELSE
        A = 5.
   END IF


c. IF(I .GT. 10 .AND. X .LT. 1.)THEN
        X = X/2.
        I = I + 1
   ELSE IF(I .LE. 10 .OR. X .GE. 1.)THEN
        X = 2. * X
        I = I - 1
   ELSE
        PRINT *,'HOW DID WE GET HERE'
   END IF
```

2. The following code will print how many of the values A, B, C match. By simply indenting portions, rewrite the code in a more readable form.

```
    IF(A .EQ. B)THEN
 →IF(B .EQ. C)THEN
 →→PRINT *,'ALL THREE MATCH'
 →ELSE
 →→PRINT *,'TWO MATCH'
 →END IF
    ELSE IF (B .EQ. C .OR. C .EQ. A)THEN
 →PRINT *,'TWO MATCH'
    ELSE
 →PRINT *,'NONE MATCH'
    END IF
```

3. Identify the errors in the following. If none, write OK.

```
a. GO TO END
b. GO TO (5,4,3,2,1),INDEX
c. GO TO (5,5,5,5,2),INDEX
d. IF(A = 0.)STOP
e. IF(X .AND. Y .EQ. 1.5)GO TO 5
```

```
    f. IF(C .LT. 5. .AND. C .GT. 5.)C = 5.
    g. IF(A .EQ. 0.)A .EQ. 0.
    h. IF(I .LT. 10)IF(I .EQ. 6)GO TO 9
    i. IF(GE .GE. LE)PRINT *,GE,LE
    j. IF(EQ)1,5,3
    k. IF(SQRT(B**2 - 4. * A * C))2,2,3
```

4. Write a program that will read a person's age and print the word TEEN-AGER if $13 \leq AGE \leq 19$ or the word RETIRED if $AGE \geq 65$.

5. Determine whether the following logical expressions are ⟨true⟩ or ⟨false⟩. Use the following values for the variables.

$$
\begin{aligned}
I &= 2 \\
K &= 4 \\
X &= -2. \\
Y &= 1.0
\end{aligned}
$$

```
    a.(I**4 .EQ. 2 * K .AND. K/I .EQ. I * I .OR. Y .GT. X)
    b. (I .GT. K .AND. Y .GT. X .OR. K - I * I .EQ. 0)
    c. ((I .GT. K) .AND. (Y .GT. X .OR. K - I * I .EQ. 0))
```

6. Write a pseudocode description of the program in Figure 3-2.

7. Write a program that will determine whether an integer is even or odd.

8. Write a program that will print the squares of all odd integers less than 50.

9. Write a program that will determine whether
   a. Four sides that are read in could form a polygon. *Note:* if the sides are labeled a, b, c, d, the conditions that must be satisfied are

   $$
   \begin{aligned}
   a &\leq b + c + d \\
   b &\leq a + b + c \\
   c &\leq a + b + d \\
   d &\leq a + b + c
   \end{aligned}
   $$

   b. If a polygon can be formed, whether the polygon could be a rectangle or a square.

10. An algorithm to compute the inverse of a number C without using any division is

    $$x_{new} = x_{old}(2 - Cx_{old})$$

    provided that the initial guess for the inverse (x_{old}) is chosen such that $(2 - Cx_{old})$ is not negative.
    a. Write a complete flowchart to

    - Read a positive number C.
    - Specify an initial guess for the inverse of C.

- Check that $(2 - Cx)$ is not negative. If it is negative, reduce x and try again.
- Set an iteration counter to zero.
- Improve the guess for the inverse and increment the counter.
- Test for success by determining if $|1. - Cx| < 1 \times 10^{-8}$.
- Test for excessive iterations.
- Print C and x if successful.

b. Write and execute a Fortran program corresponding to your flowchart. Also carry out the calculation on your pocket calculator for a variety of numbers.

11. A nonlinear equation can sometimes be solved by an iterative procedure called *the method of successive substitutions*, provided the equation can be written in the form

$$x = f(x)$$

The procedure is to guess a value for the solution, say x_{old}, and compute a new value for the solution via

$$x_{new} = f(x_{old})$$

This is continued until the difference between successive values of x are smaller than some prescribed small number or until it is clear that the procedure is diverging. (That is successive x's differ by more than some prescribed large number.) Write a complete program to solve for a root of the following functions (i.e. find an x such that $f(x) = 0.0$). The program should have safeguards to handle a diverging solution.

a. $F(x) = \dfrac{x}{3} - e^{-x^2}$

First write the equation, $F(x) = 0$ as $x = [\ln (3/x)]^{1/2}$ and then try writing it as $x = 3e^{-x^2}$. The root is near $x = 1.0$

b. $g(x) = x^{10} + 5x^3 - 7$

First write the equation $g(x) = 0$ as $x = (7 - 5x^3)^{1/10}$ and then try writing it as $x = ((7 - x^{10})/5)^{1/3}$. The root is near $x = 1.0$

c. $h(x) = a_0 + a_1 x + a_2 x^2$

The values a_0, a_1, a_2 should be read in.

12. The commission earned by a used-car salesman is determined by the following rules:

If the amount of the sale is less than $200 there is no commission.
If the amount of the sale is between $200 and $2500, the commission is 10 percent of the sale.
If the amount of the sale is greater than $2500, then the commission is $250 plus 12 percent of the amount above $2500.

The amount of the sale is the price of the car sold less the value of any trade-in. Write a complete program which reads in the value of the sale, the value of the trade-in, and calculates the commission.

13. Write a program to determine whether an integer N, where $100 < N < 10{,}000$, is a prime number. The number N is to be read in and your program should be as efficient as you can make it. *Note:* An integer N is divisible by an integer I if

$$(N/I * I) .EQ. N$$

Do you understand why? Also, you only need to test whether N is divisible by numbers I from $I = 2$ to $I = N^{1/2}$.

PROGRAMMING ASSIGNMENT I

I.1 INTRODUCTION

To learn Fortran, you must write programs. The short programming exercises in the problem sections after each chapter are meant to illustrate specific elements of Fortran; but to really develop skill in Fortran programming, you must construct more complicated programs. A moderately long program is usually much more challenging than several short programs. There are eight major programming assignments in this text. Each is designed so that it can be completed in a week or so and is sufficiently challenging to be interesting.

In addition, these programming assignments will be used to familiarize you with some of the methods of engineering analysis associated with the subfields of engineering. Each branch of engineering uses the computer to solve a variety of problems, many of which can be understood by a novice and can provide a good illustration of the ideas used in that area of engineering. Each of the programming assignments is constructed in such a way that the understanding of the background material concerning engineering concepts is not essential to the problem's solution. Also, each major programming assignment will begin with a sample problem similar to the assignment. The sample problem is completely solved and can be used as a model for constructing your programs.

I.2 SAMPLE PROGRAM

Civil Engineering: Pressure Drop in a Fluid Flowing Through a Pipe

Background: When an incompressible fluid is pumped at a steady rate through a pipe from point 1 to point 2, the pressure drop is given by

$$dP = P_1 - P_2$$
$$= \rho(gh + W)$$

where W is the energy lost per kilogram due to internal friction in the fluid and with the pipe walls. The fluid density is ρ and the gravitational acceleration is g. All units are SI (i.e., mks). The expression for the energy loss is

$$W = \frac{4fv^2L}{D}$$

where L = pipe length (m)

$\quad\quad D$ = pipe diameter (m)

$\quad\quad v$ = velocity of fluid flow (m/sec)

$\quad\quad f$ = friction factor

$\quad\quad Q$ = fluid flow rate (m^3/sec)

For smooth pipes the friction factor f depends only on the Reynold's number R.

$$R = \frac{\rho v D}{\mu}$$

where μ is viscosity of the fluid.

$\quad\quad$ If $(R < 2000)$, the flow is laminar and $f = 8/R$

$\quad\quad$ If $(R > 2000)$, the flow is turbulent and $f = .0395R^{-1/4}$

Problem: Write a program to do the following:

1. Initialize a counter for each run as IRUN = 1
2. Read D, h, ρ, μ, and echo print with labels along with the run number (IRUN).
3. Read Q_{start} and L_{start} and print.
   a. Let $Q = Q_{start}$
   b. Let $L = L_{start}$
      (1) From the values of L, D, and Q determine v (and print).
      (2) Compute R, determine f (print)
      (3) Determine W and dP (print)
      (4) Increment $L = L + L_{start}$ and if L is less than three times L_{start}, return to (1) and repeat the calculation, otherwise
   c. Increment $Q = Q + 0.5Q_{start}$ and if Q is less than two times Q_{start}, return to (b) and repeat the calculation, otherwise
4. Increment IRUN = IRUN + 1 and if IRUN < 3 return to the READ statements and repeat the entire calculation for a different set of parameter values, otherwise STOP.

The output of the program should be neat. Suggested data follows:

Run No.	$\rho(kg/m^3)$	$\mu(kg/m\text{-}sec)$	h	D	Q_{start}	L_{start}
1	1500.	0.03	3.0	0.02	0.01	30.0
2	1500.	0.03	3.0	0.60	0.25	100.0
3	1500.	0.001	25.0	0.60	2.50	100.0

Sample Program Solution The Fortran program for this problem is given below.

```
          PROGRAM FLUID
*--
*--     This program computes the pressure drop for a fluid flowing
*--     through a pipe, The flow is either laminar or turbulent,
*--     depending on the Reynold's number,
*-------------------------------------------------------------------
* Variables
*
        REAL DENSITY,VISCOS,HEIGHT,DIAM,FRICT,L,LSTRT,Q,QSTRT,R,W,VEL,
     +      DP
        INTEGER IRUN
*--
*--            IRUN      -  Run Number
*--            DENSITY   -  Fluid density (Kg/m**3)
*--            VISCOS    -  Fluid viscosity (Kg/m-sec)
*--            DIAM      -  Pipe Diameter (m)
*--            HEIGHT    -  Distance fluid is pumped above original
*--                         position
*--            LSTRT     -  Length of pipe for first calculation (m)
*--            QSTRT     -  Flow rate in first calculation
*--            L         -  Current pipe length
*--            Q         -  Current flow rate
*--            VEL       -  Velocity of flowing fluid
*--            FRICT     -  Pipe friction factor (dimensionless)
*--            W         -  Energy loss/Kg due to friction
*--            R         -  Reynold's number
*--            DP        -  Pressure drop
*-------------------------------------------------------------------
* Initialization
*--
        PI = ACOS(-1.)
        IRUN = 1
    1   PRINT *,'RUN NUMBER = ',IRUN
            PRINT *,'  '
            PRINT *,'ENTER DIAMETER,HEIGHT,DENSITY,VISCOSITY'
            READ *,DIAM,HEIGHT,DENSTY,VISCOS
```

Continued

```
               PRINT *,'DENSITY = ',DENSTY,'  VISCOSITY = ',VISCOS,
     +                  '   DIAMETER = ',DIAM,'  HEIGHT = ',HEIGHT
               PRINT *,'ENTER QSTART AND LSTART'
               READ *,QSTRT,LSTRT
               PRINT *,'Q-START = ',QSTRT,' AND L-START = ',LSTRT
               PRINT *,'  '
*-----------------------------------------------------------------------
*-----------------------------------------------------------------------
* Calculation
               Q = QSTRT
    2          PRINT *,'  '
               PRINT *,'  '
               PRINT *,'  THIS CALCULATION IS FOR A FLOW RATE = ',Q
               L = LSTART
*--
*--            The velocity of flow is determined from
*--            Q and DIAM
*--
               VEL = Q/(PI * .25 * DIAM**2)
*--
*--                 Next compute the Reynold's number
*--                 and the friction factor
*--
               R = DENSTY * VEL * DIAM/VISCOS
               IF(R .LT. 2000.)THEN
                       FRICT = 8./R
               ELSE
                       FRICT = 0.395/R**.25
               END IF
               PRINT *,'        VELOCITY = ',VEL
               PRINT *,'   FRICTION FAC. = ',FRICT
               PRINT *,'    REYNOLDS NO. = ',R
               PRINT *,'  '
*--
*--                 Compute the energy loss (W) and
*--                 the pressure drop (DP). Also print
*--                 table heading for L loop.
*--
               PRINT *,'  '
               PRINT *,'  PIPE      ENERGY       PRESSURE'
               PRINT *,'  LENGTH    LOSS/KG         DROP'
    3          W = 4. * FRICT * VEL**2 * L/DIAM
               DP = DENSTY * (9.8 * HEIGHT + W)
*--
*--                 Print intermediate results
*--
```

```
                              PRINT *,'  ',L,'     ',W,'     ',DP
*--
*--                                           Increment the pipe length
*--                                           and loop back
*--                                           to stmt. 3
*--

                              L = L + LSTRT
                       IF(L .LT. 4. * LSTRT)GO TO 3
*--
*--                                           We have completed the calculations for
*--                                           all the desired lengths. Next increment
*--                                           the flow rate and loop back to statement
*--                                           2 to repeat the calculation.
*--

                              Q = Q + .5 * QSTRT
                       IF(Q .LT. 2.*QSTRT)GO TO 2
*--
*--                                           This calculation is complete. Next loop
*--                                           back to stmt 1 for the next data set.
*--

                       IRUN = IRUN + 1
              IF(IRUN .LE. 3)THEN
                       GO TO 1
              ELSE
                       PRINT *,'CALCULATION COMPLETED -- JOB TERMINATED'
                       STOP
              END IF
              END
```

The output from this program is

```
RUN NUMBER = 1

ENTER DIAMETER,HEIGHT,DENSITY,VISCOSITY
0.02,  3.0,   1500.0,  0.03
DENSITY = 1500.000  VISCOSITY = 3.00000E-02 DIAMETER = 2.00000E-02   HEIGHT = 3.0000
ENTER QSTRT AND LSTRT
0.01,  30.0
Q-START = 1.00000E-02   AND L-START = 30.00000

  THIS CALCULATION IS FOR A FLOW RATE = 1.00000E-02
       VELOCITY = 31.83099
   FRICTION FAC. = 2.9572263E-02
     REYNOLDS NO. = 31830.99
```

```
    PIPE          ENERGY        PRESSURE
   LENGTH        LOSS/KG          DROP
  30.00000      179777.8     2.6971080E+08
  60.00000      359555.6     5.3937750E+08
  90.00000      539333.4     8.0904421E+08
    THIS CALCULATION IS FOR A FLOW RATE = 1.5000000E-02
           VELOCITY = 47.74648
     FRICTION FAC. = 2.6721556E-02
      REYNOLDS NO. = 47746.48

     PIPE           ENERGY        PRESSURE
    LENGTH         LOSS/KG          DROP
   30.00000       365507.1     5.4830470E+08
   60.00000       731014.1     1.0965653E+09
   90.00000       1096521.     1.6448259E+09
 RUN NUMBER = 2

ENTER DIAMETER,HEIGHT,DENSITY,VISCOSITY

         <etc. Output continues for two more runs>

CALCULATION COMPLETED -- JOB TERMINATED
```

You should note that there are three nested loops in this program.

The Fortran code is made somewhat more readable by indenting each layer of loop.

The output from this program is not particularly readable or attractive. This will be corrected in Chapter 5 when we discuss formatted output.

I.3 PROGRAMMING PROBLEMS

Mechanical Engineering

Generally speaking, mechanical engineers are concerned with machines or systems that produce energy or its application. The spectrum of technological activities that carries the banner of mechanical engineering is probably broader than any other engineering field. The field can be roughly subdivided into:

Power:
: The design of power-generating machines and systems such as boiler-turbine engines for generating electricity, solar power, heating systems, and heat exchangers.

Design:
: Innovative design of machine parts or components from the most intricate and small to the gigantic. For example, mechanical engineers work alongside electrical engineers to design automatic control systems such as robots.

Automotive:
: Design and testing of transportation vehicles and the machines to manufacture them.

Heating, Ventilation, Air Conditioning, and Refrigeration:
: Design of systems to control our environment both indoors and out, pollution control.

The mechanical engineer usually has a thorough background in subjects like thermodynamics, heat transfer, statics and dynamics, and fluid mechanics.

Programming Problem A: Most Cost-Efficient Steam Pipe Insulation

When deciding on the amount of insulation to be installed on a long steam supply line (see Figure I-1), the amount of money to be saved from lower fuel bills must be compared with the initial insulation purchase and installation costs; that is, excessive insulation can be just as wasteful as too little. This problem will allow you to determine the thickness of the insulation that will give the greatest savings for the least cost. The heat flow through the insulation is given by

$$Q_1 = 2\pi kL \, \frac{(T_a - T_b)}{\ln(b/a)} \qquad \text{(watt)} \qquad\qquad \textbf{(I.1)}$$

While the heat transfer from the insulation to the air is given approximately by

$$Q_2 = 2\pi bF(T_b - T_{\text{air}})L \qquad \text{(watt)} \qquad\qquad \textbf{(I.2)}$$

Figure I-1
Insulated Steam
Pipe

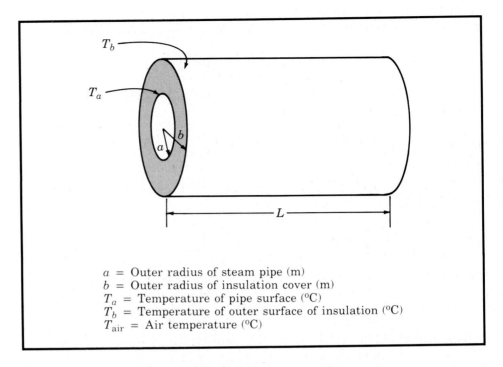

a = Outer radius of steam pipe (m)
b = Outer radius of insulation cover (m)
T_a = Temperature of pipe surface (°C)
T_b = Temperature of outer surface of insulation (°C)
T_{air} = Air temperature (°C)

where   k = Thermal conductivity of the insulation
      = 0.1 watt/(m °C)

    F = Convection coefficient for the air-insulation interface
      = 3.0 watt/(m² °C)

In a steady-state situation $Q_1 = Q_2$, so that T_b can be eliminated from Equations (I.1) and (I.2), and by combining the two equations we obtain

(I.3)
$$Q = \left[\frac{2\pi bkFL}{k + b\mathrm{F}\,\ln(b/a)} \right] (T_a - T_{air})$$

(Verify that this is true.)
    Now for the costs. The pipe insulation costs $325.00 per cubic meter ($C_{vol} = 325.0$) and the installation costs amount to $1.50 per meter of pipe ($C_L = 1.50$), independent of thickness. The cost of heat is 0.4 cents per kilowatt-hour or $1.11 × 10⁻⁹ per watt-sec ($C_{heat} = 1.11 \times 10^{-9}$). Assuming a pipe of length L, the volume of the insulation used is $\pi(b^2 - a^2)L$ and the total insulation cost is

(I.4)
$$C_{insul} = \pi(b^2 - a^2)LC_{vol} + LC_L$$

To obtain the amount of fuel savings we need the difference between the heat loss with no insulation, i.e.,

(I.5)
$$Q_3 = 2\pi aF(T_a - T_{air})L$$

and the heat loss with insulation [Equation (I.3)], i.e., $dQ = Q_3 - Q$, or

$$dQ = Q_3\left[1 - \frac{b/a}{1 + (bF/k)\ln(b/a)}\right] \qquad \textbf{(I.6)}$$

(Verify this equation.)

The fuel savings then over a 5-year period (1.578×10^8 sec) is then

$$C_2 = dQ(1.578 \times 10^8)C_{\text{heat}} \qquad \textbf{(I.7)}$$

The outer radius of the pipe is 5 cm ($a = 0.05$) and insulation is available in thicknesses t ranging from 1 to 10 cm in 1-cm steps (i.e., $b = a + t, t = 1, 2, \ldots, 10$ cm). For air temperatures of $T_{\text{air}} = -10°$ C and $+10°$ C, determine the most cost-effective thicknesses of insulation.

Details

Write a program that will

1. Read the REAL variables

A	- pipe radius	= 0.05 m
L	- pipe length	= 500.0 m
TP	- pipe temperature	= 150.0° C
TAIR	- air temperature	= −10.0° C
RK	- conductivity constant	= 0.10 watt/(m °C)
RF	- convection constant	= 3.0 watt/(m² °C)
CVOL	- cost per volume of insulation	= $325.0
CL	- cost per meter for installation	= $1.50
CH	- cost per kilowatt-hour for heat	= $0.004

and echo print them all with labels.

2. Read the air temperature and print table headings of the form

```
FOR RUN NUMBER xxx
THE AIR TEMPERATURE IS xxx (OC)

AND THE RESULTS OF THE COST-EFFECTIVENESS
COMPUTATIONS ARE

THICKNESS        INSULATION        SAVINGS OVER
 (METERS)           COST            FIVE YEARS
```

3. Start with the insulation thickness, T = 0.01 and calculate the total cost of insulation [Equation (I.4)], and the dollar savings over 5 years [Equation (I.7)]. Print these quantities as one line in the table. (Be sure to convert CH to cost per watt-second.)
4. Increment the thickness by 0.01 (T = T + 0.01), and if T is less than or equal to 0.10 GO TO step 3 and repeat the calculation. [IF(T .LE. 0.10)GO TO. . . .]
5. When T > 0.10 the above IF test fails and the program should then GO TO step 2 and read a second value for the air temperature (+10.00° C). The remaining parameters stay the same.
6. Add a run counter (IRUN) to the program that is incremented after each complete set of calculations. The program should STOP if IRUN > 2.
7. By inspecting the printed output from your program, determine the most cost-effective insulation thickness for each of the two air temperatures. Indicate this optimum thickness in pencil on your output. Include a flowchart with your program.

Civil Engineering

The field of civil engineering is primarily concerned with large-scale structures and systems used by a community. A civil engineer designs, constructs, and operates bridges, dams, tunnels, buildings, airports, roads, and other large-scale public works. Civil engineers are also responsible for the effects on society and the environment of these large-scale systems. Thus, civil engineers are involved in water resources, flood control, waste disposal, and overall urban planning. The field can be subdivided into

Structures:	Design, construction, and operation of large-scale edifices such as dams, buildings, and roads. The properties of materials, geology, soil mechanics, and statics and dynamics are important elements of the background training. For example, how tall a building can be constructed before it will buckle under its own weight is a question involving all of these subjects.
Urban Planning:	Planning, design, and construction of transportation systems (roads, railroads, river development, airports) and general land use. Surveying and mapmaking are necessary skills.
Sanitation:	Waste treatment, water supply, and sewage systems. Fluid mechanics, hydrology, pollution control, irrigation, and economics are important considerations.

Programming Problem B: Oxygen Deficiency of a Polluted Stream

The determination of the variation with time of the dissolved oxygen in a polluted stream is important in water resources engineering. Organic matter in sewage decomposes through chemical and bacterial action. In this process, free oxygen is consumed and the sewage is deoxygenated. A standard procedure for determining the rate of deoxygenation of sewage involves diluting a sewage sample with water containing a known amount of dissolved oxygen and measuring the loss in oxygen after the mixture has been maintained at a temperature of 20° C for a period of 20 days. This loss is called the first-stage biochemical oxygen demand (B_{20}). The subscript refers to the temperature. For any temperature T, the first-stage demand B_T can be computed from

$$B_T = B_{20}(0.02T + 0.6)$$ (I.8)

As mentioned, when sewage is discharged into a stream, oxygen is consumed in the decomposition of organic matter. At the same time, oxygen is absorbed from the air. However, deoxygenation and reoxygenation take place, in general, at different rates. Usually, reoxygenation lags behind deoxygenation, the dissolved oxygen decreases with time, reaches a minimum, and then increases. As the dissolved oxygen is at a minimum, the oxygen deficit is at a maximum.

The oxygen deficit of the polluted stream may be computed from

$$D(t) = \frac{K_d B_T}{K_r - K_d}(e^{-K_d t} - e^{-K_r t}) + D_0 e^{-K_r t}$$ (I.9)

where $D(t)$ = Oxygen deficit of the stream at time t (mg/L)

   K_d = Coefficient of deoxygenation

   K_r = Coefficient of reoxygenation

   D_0 = Initial oxygen deficit (mg/L)

   B_T = First-stage biochemical oxygen demand of steam at temperature T (mg/L)

   t = Elapsed time in days (when $t = 0$, $D(t) = D_0$)

The constants K_r and D_0 are known and tabulated for this stream; however, K_d depends on the amount and type of sewage dumped into the stream. If $K_d(20)$ is the measured coefficient of deoxygenation at 20° C, then the value at a temperature T is given by

$$K_d(T) = K_d(20)(1.047)^{T-20}$$ (I.10)

Furthermore, The first-stage biochemical oxygen demand of the mixture of stream plus pollutants is given by

$$B_{20} = [(B_{20,\text{upstream}})Q_s + (B_{20,\text{sewage}})Q_{\text{sewage}}]/Q$$ (I.11)

where $B_{20,\,upstream}$ = First-stage biochemical oxygen demand of stream above point at which the sewage is discharged

$B_{20,\,sewage}$ = First-stage biochemical demand of sewage

Q_s = Flow rate of the stream

Q_{sewage} = flow rate of the sewage

Q = Net flow rate of sewage plus stream

$= Q_s + Q_{sewage}$

Thus using Equations (I.11) and (I.8) we can calculate B_T for the stream at the temperature T.

Details

Write a Fortran program that will

1. For each case, read in and echo print the parameters listed in Table I-1.
2. For each case compute the oxygen deficit $D(t)$, starting at $t = 0$ days and continuing in time steps of 0.1 days until the oxygen deficit reaches a maximum and then decreases. That is, stop if the current value is less than the previous one.
3. Print out the results for the three separate cases. In your printout each case is to be identified as CASE1, CASE2, etc. Where appropriate, include units in your labels. Avoid excessive recalculations.

Table I-1 Input parameters for pollution problem.

Case no.	Q_{stream} (L/sec)	Q_{sewage} (L/sec)	D_0 (mg/L)	$K_d(20)$	K_r	$B_{20,stream}$ (mg/L)	$B_{20,sewage}$ (mg/L)	T (°C)
1	1500	150.0	1.3	0.23	0.50	0.8	145.0	17.6
2	2000	150.0	1.3	0.23	0.50	0.8	145.0	17.6
3	1500	150.0	1.3	0.23	0.50	0.8	145.0	21.1

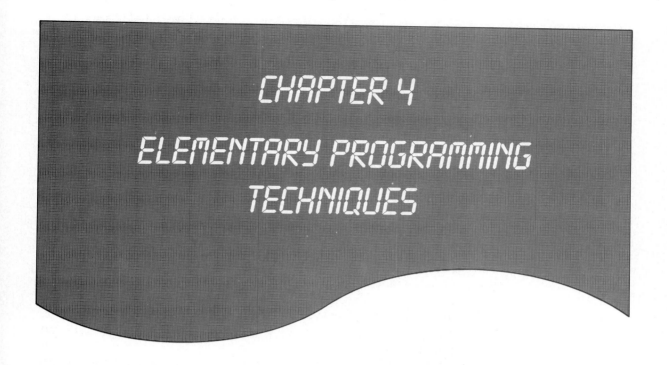

CHAPTER 4
ELEMENTARY PROGRAMMING TECHNIQUES

4.1 INTRODUCTION

With the introduction of the flow control structures to our Fortran vocabulary, a vast array of problems become amenable to our analysis. It is the purpose of this chapter to concentrate on a few elementary techniques that form the basis for a great many computational algorithms. Additionally, as your programs become more elaborate, they will be called upon to read large amounts of data and evaluate complicated algebraic expressions. For this reason, the use of data files and statement functions will also be described here.

4.2 THE STATEMENT FUNCTION

4.2.1 Definition

The form of the Fortran statement defining a statement function is

FNC(A,B,X) = Any algebraic combination, including intrinsic functions, of
the variables A, B, X, and constants

The name of the function (here FNC) may be any valid Fortran name. It is strongly suggested that any and all variables appearing on the right side of the replacement operator should also appear as one of the variables in the argument list (here, A,B,X), although this is not required.

Two examples follow:

1. $f(x) = 35x^2 - \sin(\pi x) - \sqrt{x}$ would be written as a statement function

```
FNC(X) = 35.0 * X * X - SIN(3.14159 * X) - SQRT(X)
```

2. The function for $x^3 + ax^2 + bx + c$ could be written

```
CUBE(A,B,C,X) = X**3 + A * X**2 + B * X + C
```

The type of the value returned by the function is determined by the type of the name of the function. Thus with default typing, F(X) would be REAL and N(X) would be INTEGER. The function name can also be explicitly typed by including it in a prior type statement.

> *Important:* **A statement function definition is not considered an executable statement and it must appear before the first executable statement and after the type declarations (i.e., INTEGER, REAL, and CHARACTER).**

4.2.2 Use of the Statement Function

The definition of the statement function given above allows us almost limitless possibilities for constructing our own set of intrinsic-like functions in addition to those listed in Table 2-3. Statement functions are often used to reduce long and complicated program statements and make the code easier to read. This in turn makes the program much less prone to error. A statement function is used, or *referenced*, in precisely the same manner that intrinsic functions are referenced. After the function has been introduced in the defining line, the name of the function, along with its argument list, can be used in any arithmetic expression or executable Fortran statement.

For example, when the need arises in a program to calculate the square root of a number, we could insert the line defining a statement function called SQROOT that employs one iteration of Newton's algorithm to compute $\sqrt{C}$ using an initial guess X0 (see Section 3.4.2).

```
SQROOT(C,X0) = 0.5 * (X0 + C/X0)      (statement function
                                       definition)
```

The code using this function to obtain a rough value for $\sqrt{7}$. then might be

```
X = SQROOT(7.,2.)
```

or a better value would be

```
X = SQROOT(7.,2.)
X = SQROOT(7.,X)
```

or

```
X=SQROOT(7.,SQROOT(7.,SQROOT(7.,2.)))
```

Of course a much simpler and more accurate approach would be to use the intrinsic function SQRT(C), which, incidentally, also uses Newton's algorithm.

When the compiler encounters a Fortran name followed immediately by a parenthesis, as in

```
SQROOT(C,XO)
```

a search is initiated for the definition of the name SQROOT. The compiler has been written to recognize that a "name–left parenthesis" structure like FA(C + D) *does not* imply multiplication but instead that the name FA must have a special meaning. To determine precisely what is represented by FA, the compiler looks at the beginning of the program to see if this name has been defined as a statement function. If so, a value is computed for FA as defined by the code in the statement function and is returned to the line in the program that contained the reference to FA. The program then continues from that point. If FA is not found at the top of the program, a search of the library is made, and if a function named FA is found, it is linked with the main program and that function is used whenever the name is referenced. If the function is not found among the intrinsic functions an execution time error results.

Notice, this implies that if we had named our square root function SQRT[1], the program would use that function and not the intrinsic function, since it finds ours first. Obviously, to minimize confusion you should try to avoid defining functions with names identical to intrinsic functions.

---

[1]A word of caution: In some installations of Fortran 77 it is forbidden to define statement functions that have the same name as existing intrinsic functions; and in all circumstances it is flagrantly poor programming style.

4.2.3 The Argument List

The variable names that appear in the definition of a statement function are called *dummy* arguments, meaning that they are not to be thought of as representing numerical quantities in the same sense as ordinary Fortran variable names. That is, instead of designating a location in memory for a numerical value, a dummy argument name merely reserves a position in the arithmetic procedure defined in the statement function. Only later, when the statement function is referenced in the program, will an actual numerical value be inserted in the function expression. This is analogous to the ordinary symbolic manipulation of variable names in algebra.

When the function is referenced, the names, numbers, or arithmetic expressions that appear in the arguments list are called *actual* arguments, implying that they are then expected to have numerical values at that point in the program. Consider the following code:

```
F(A,B) = (A**2 - B**2) * PI
PI = ACOS(-1.)
X = F(3.,2.)                    Output
Y = F(X + 1.,X)
PRINT *,'X= ',X,' Y= ',Y        X=15.7080  Y=101.8376
                                (i.e., x = 5π, y = 10π² + π)
PRINT *,'A= ',A,' B= ',B        Output is unpredictable
```

The variables A and B were never *assigned* values in this program. The statement function definition merely defines a procedure for symbolically manipulating the variables in its argument list. Thus, in the first reference, the value of F will be determined after replacing the symbols A by 3.0 and B by 2.0. Notice that at this point in the program PI has been assigned a value and since it will not be changed it need not appear in the argument list. The value used for PI will be whatever value currently resides in that memory location. In the second reference to F, the arithmetic expressions in the argument list are first evaluated before the function expression is actually used.

In summary, actual arguments represent numbers that are transferred to the dummy arguments in the statement function definition. The transfer is determined by the *position* in the argument list, not by the name of the variable. That is, in the example above, the value associated with B is whatever number appears in the second position when the function F is referenced. In addition, the argument list in any reference to a statement function must agree in *number* and *type* with the argument list in the function's definition. In our example this means that any reference to function F must have two numbers, variable names, or expressions representing numbers in the argument list and both must be of type REAL. We will return to considerations regarding dummy and actual arguments in Section 8.3.2.

4.3 FINDING THE MINIMUM AND MAXIMUM OF A SET OF NUMBERS

A very common and useful programming procedure is a code that will scan a list of numbers and determine the minimum and/or the maximum number in the list. The basic algorithm simply mimics the steps you or I would follow in scanning a list of numbers. Starting at the top of the list we define the current maximum to be the first number. We then check the next element in the list. If this number is larger than the current maximum, it becomes the current maximum and we discard the earlier value. If not, the current maximum is still valid and we proceed to the next number in the list. The Fortran code to accomplish this would be

```
      READ * ,X
      XMAX=X
  1   READ * ,X
*--
*--                     COMPARE CURRENT X AND XMAX
*--                     IF NEED BE REDEFINE XMAX
*--
      IF(X .GT. XMAX)XMAX = X
      IF(X .LT. 0.)THEN
*--
*--                     END OF LIST MARKED WITH
*--                     NEGATIVE VALUE OF X
*--
         PRINT *, 'MAXIMUM VALUE = ',XMAX
         STOP
      ELSE
         GO TO 1
      END IF
      END
```

The most important statement in the program is the IF test where the current maximum (XMAX) is compared with the most recently read value of X. If X is greater than the current maximum, the current maximum is redefined.

This method can also be used to find the maximum or minimum of a function of a single variable x over some interval, $a < x < b$. A program to accomplish this is illustrated in the following example.

4.3.1 Example—Minimizing the Costs

In an automobile manufacturing plant, door handles are made in large lots, placed in storage, and used as required in assembling the cars. A common problem is the determination of the most economical lot size x. The following parameters enter into the considerations.

w = work days per year	= 242	days/yr
s = setup cost to produce one lot of door handles	= 947.0	dollars/lot
u = usage rate (door handles/day)	= 190.0	no./day
m = material + labor costs per door handle	= 2.05	dollars
a = annual storage costs	= 9.65	dollars/yr

Thus the number of lots used per year is

$$\frac{w\,(\text{day/yr})u\,(\text{no./day})}{x\,(\text{no./lot})} = \frac{wu}{x}\,(\text{lots/yr})$$

and so the yearly equipment setup cost is

$$\frac{swu}{x} \quad (\text{dollars/yr})$$

The storage costs increase with the size of a lot and the annual cost is ax. Finally, the annual production cost is given by

$$umw \quad (\text{dollars/yr})$$

Adding all the costs we obtain the following expression

$$c(x) = \frac{swu}{x} + umw + ax$$

We next turn to the computer to find the minimum of this expression as a function of the lot size x. The procedure will be built around the algorithm given earlier for finding the minimum and/or maximum of a list of numbers.

The Fortran program to determine the lot size that results in a minimum overall cost would be constructed along the following lines:

Pseudocode description of optimum lot size code.

Type all variables as they are encountered in writing the code
  REAL X, W, S, U, M, A, COST, CC, CZERO
  INTEGER STEP

Statement function for costs
  COST(X) = . . .

Initialize:
   X—starting *x* value
   STEP—step counter
   CZERO—current minimum
        [start with COST(X)]

DoWhile (costs are still decreasing)

1   Increment X → X + 10.
             STEP → STEP + 1

         Compare COST (new X) with COST (previous X)
             If latest COST is less, THEN
                     proceed to next STEP
                     GO TO 1
             ELSE
                     We have found the minimum, print the results for X,
                     COST (X) and STOP
             END IF

END

The results of a Fortran program constructed from this pseudocode outline
are shown in Figure 4-1.

Figure 4-1   The output of a program that computes the optimum lot size.

```
INPUT WORK DAYS/YR AND USAGE RATE 242., 190.
INPUT COSTS FOR SETUP, MATERIAL, AND STORAGE 947.0, 2.05, 9.65


   A COMPUTATION OF THE OPTIMUM LOT SIZE


            INPUT PARAMETERS
                  WORK DAYS/YEAR      --    242.
                  USAGE RATE PER DAY  --    190.
                  SETUP               -- 947.00 DOLLARS
                  MATERIAL-LABOR      --    2.05 DOLLARS/ITEM
                  ANNUAL STORAGE      --    9.65 DOLLARS/ITEM



      THE OPTIMUM LOT SIZE IS   2120.0

      ANNUAL COSTS FOR THIS LOT SIZE ARE 135256.10 DOLLARS
```

4.3.2 A Reconsideration of the Optimum Lot Size Problem

The previous program is an example of one of the most common errors in programming: Computing without first carefully thinking the problem through. Even though the program finds a valid estimate of the optimum lot size, and does so with relative ease, the calculation can be greatly improved in both speed and accuracy with the introduction of more intelligence into the algorithm. The expression obtained for the cost was a simple function of the lot size and is graphed in Figure 4-2.

At the lot size corresponding to the minimum cost, the curve has a tangent line that has zero slope; i.e., it is horizontal. Since the slope of the tangent line at a point is equal to the derivative, we have as the requirement for the minimum point on the curve

$$\frac{dc(x)}{dx} = 0 = swu\,\frac{d}{dx}\left(\frac{1}{x}\right) + 0 + a\,\frac{d(x)}{dx}$$

$$= a - \frac{swu}{x^2} \qquad \left(\frac{d}{dx}x^{-1} = -x^{-2}\right)$$

Solving this equation for x yields the optimum lot size x_{best}

Figure 4-2 Annual production costs (c) as a function of lot size (x).

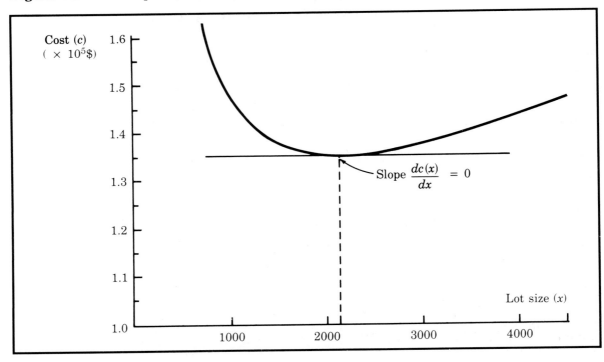

$$x_{\text{best}} = \left(\frac{swu}{a}\right)^{1/2} = 2124.202 \rightarrow 2124 \qquad \langle \textit{truncated to an integer} \rangle$$

with no need for a computer at all. This example illustrates the fundamental tenet of all of numerical analysis on a computer: Intelligence is more important than computing power. It is not at all rare to replace a computer program that costs thousands of dollars per run with an improved version that obtains more accurate results for only pennies. This is done by programmers experienced in the analysis of the problem as well as in writing Fortran code.

4.4 PERFORMING A SUMMATION

Perhaps the single most useful task a computer is called upon to handle is to quickly perform a summation. The ability to transcribe the algebraic equations for summations in Fortran code is an absolutely essential element in developing programming skills.

4.4.1 The Structure of the Summation Algorithm

If we represent the current value of the sum as SUM and the current value of an individual term in the sum as TERM, then the Fortran code for executing a summation consists of four parts.

1. *Initialize*[2] the variables SUM, TERM, and a counter, say K.

```
SUM = 0.0
K = 1
TERM = ...
```

2. *Summation* by the replacement

```
SUM = SUM + TERM
```

---

[2]Some installations of Fortran preset all memory locations to zero before the program begins, but most do not. If a variable that has not been assigned a value within a program is used in an arithmetic expression, the results will be unpredictable. Thus a fundamental commandment of Fortran is: *All* variables that are used in a program *must* have been assigned values earlier within that same program.

---

3. *Increment* the counter and *redefine* TERM

```
K = K + 1
TERM = ...
```

4. *Test* for completion and loop

```
IF(K .LT. KMAX)GO TO ...
```

or

```
IF(ABS(TERM) .LT. EPS)GO TO
```

4.4.2 Examples of Summations

In Figure 4-3 the Fortran code is illustrated that will compute the sum of the squares of the integers from 1 to 100 (called ISUM) and the sum of the square roots of the integers from 1 to 100 (called XSUM). The algebraic notation for these quantities is

$$i_{sum} = \sum_{i=1}^{100} i^2 = 1^2 + 2^2 + 3^2 + \cdots + 100^2$$

$$x_{sum} = \sum_{x=1}^{100} \sqrt{x} = \sqrt{1} + \sqrt{2} + \sqrt{3} + \cdots + \sqrt{100}$$

Figure 4-3 Fortran program for summations.

```
      PROGRAM SUMS
*  ---
*  --- THIS PROGRAM PERFORMS TWO SUMMATIONS, ONE USING REAL ARITH-
*  --- METIC, THE OTHER INTEGER ARITHMETIC. THERE ARE 100 TERMS IN
*  --- EACH SUM.
*-------------------------------------------------------------------
* INITIALIZATION
*
      REAL X,XSUM,XTERM
      INTEGER I,ISUM,ITERM,COUNT

      COUNT = 0
      X = 0.0
      I = 0
      XSUM = 0.0
      ISUM = 0
*
   1  XTERM = SQRT(X)
      ITERM = I * I
*-------------------------------------------------------------------
*           SUMMATION CONSISTS IN THE REPLACEMENT
*                     SUM => SUM + TERM
*
      XSUM = XSUM + XTERM
      ISUM = ISUM + ITERM
*
*           INCREMENT COUNTER, X AND I
```

```
*
         COUNT = COUNT + 1
         X = X + 1.0
         I = I + 1
*
*
             TEST FOR COMPLETION
*
      IF(COUNT .LE. 100)THEN
           GO TO 1
      ELSE
*
*
             THE LOOP HAS BEEN EXECUTED 100 TIMES,
*
             PRINT THE RESULTS


         PRINT *,' '
         PRINT *,'THE SUM OF THE SQUARE ROOTS OF THE INTEGERS'
         PRINT *,'FROM ONE TO ONE HUNDRED IS'
         PRINT *,'                         ',XSUM
         PRINT *,' '
         PRINT *,'THE SUM OF THE SQUARES OF THE INTEGERS'
         PRINT *,'FROM ONE TO ONE HUNDRED IS'
         PRINT *,'                         ',ISUM
         PRINT *,' '

      END IF

      STOP
      END


      THE SUM OF THE SQUARE ROOTS OF THE INTEGERS
      FROM ONE TO ONE HUNDRED IS
                     671.4629471032

      THE SUM OF THE SQUARES OF THE INTEGERS
      FROM ONE TO ONE HUNDRED IS
                     338350
```

4.4.3 Infinite Summations

A great many functions in mathematics are represented in a form involving the summation of an infinite number of terms. For example, the series expansion for the exponential function can be found in any book of mathematical tables.

$$e^x = 1 + x + \frac{x^2}{2!} + \frac{x^3}{3!} + \cdots + \frac{x^n}{n!} + \cdots = \sum_{n=0}^{\infty} \frac{x^n}{n!} \qquad (4.1)$$

where $n!$ (n factorial) means

$$n! = n(n - 1)(n - 2) \ldots 2 \times 1$$

That is $2! = 2$, $3! = 6$, etc. Also, $0!$ is defined to be unity. Equation (4.1) is exact only if an infinite number of terms are included in the summation. However, you will notice that eventually the terms in the sum will become extremely small (i.e., $n!$ will be very large) and we may be justified in terminating the summation when this is the case. (The tricky question of deciding whether dropping an infinite number of small quantities is justified is left for you to ponder for now and will be considered in more detail in Chapter 10.)

The relation between successive terms in this sum can be expressed in terms of their ratio,

(4.2)
$$R = \frac{(\text{term})_{n+1}}{(\text{term})_n} = \frac{x^{n+1}}{(n+1)!} \frac{n!}{x^n} = x \frac{n!}{(n+1)!}$$

Since $(n+1)! = (n+1)n!$, this can be simplified to

(4.3)
$$R = \frac{x}{n+1}$$

This ratio approaches zero as $n \to \infty$ for *any* finite value of x. The key step in the algorithm to compute the sum is then the line that calculates the *next* term in the series by using Equations (4.2) and (4.3).

(4.4)
```
TERM => TERM * RATIO = TERM * (X/(N + 1.))
```

The Fortran code to calculate e^x for a specific x by summing the series expansion until the absolute value of a term is less than 10^{-6} is given in Figure 4-4. However, I should warn you that this program will have difficulty obtaining accurate results if x is large and negative. (See Problem 4-4.)

As a final example, consider the problem of finding both the maxima and minima and performing a summation in the same program. Specifically, the problem is:

Given a list containing the following information on each line: (a) a student ID number (e.g., Social Security number) and (b) a final exam score, the task is to write a program to compute the average exam score, the minimum score, the maximum score, and the ID numbers of the corresponding students. The program is given in Figure 4-5.

This program will not handle tie scores. You should attempt to modify the program to cover the situation of a few students tying for the best or worst scores. You will note that the program will very quickly get very complicated.

Figure 4-4 The Fortran code to evaluate e^x.

```
      PROGRAM ETOX
* ---
* --- THIS CODE EVALUATES THE SERIES EXPANSION FOR EXP(X). THE
* --- SUMMATION IS TERMINATED WHEN ABS(TERM) .LT. 1.E-6. EACH
* --- TERM IS RELATED TO THE PREVIOUS TERM IN THE SUMMATION BY
* ---
* ---            TERM-(N + 1) = TERM-(N) * RATIO
* ---
* --- WHERE RATIO IS AN ALGEBRAIC EXPRESSION FOR THE RATIO OF
* --- TERMS.
*-----------------------------------------------------------------
* VARIABLES
* ---
      REAL X,TERM,SUM,RATIO
      INTEGER I
*-----------------------------------------------------------------
* INITIALIZATION
* ---
      PRINT *,' '
      PRINT *,'ENTER VALUE OF X'
      READ *,X
* ---
      I = 0
      SUM = 0.0
      TERM = 1.0
* ---
* ---        NOTE: THE TERMS ARE LABELED BY THE POWER OF X. THUS
* ---              THE ZERO-TH TERM (X**0 => 1) IS 1 AND THE I = 1
* ---              TERM IS X.
*-----------------------------------------------------------------
* SUMMATION
* ---
    1 SUM = SUM + TERM
* ---
*-----------------------------------------------------------------
* REDEFINE TERM
* ---
      RATIO = X/(I+1.0)
      TERM = TERM * RATIO
*-----------------------------------------------------------------
* INCREMENT I AND TEST FOR TERMINATION OF SUMMATION
* ---
      I = I + 1
      IF(I .GT. 100)THEN
* ---
* ---            FAILURE PATH--EXCESSIVE NUMBER OF TERMS
* ---
        PRINT *,'PROGRAM FAILED--TERMS NOT SMALL AFTER 100 TERMS'
        STOP
* ---
      ELSE IF(ABS(TERM) .GT. 1.E-6)THEN
* ---
* ---            SERIES NOT YET CONVERGED, PROCEED TO NEXT TERM
```

Continued

```
              GO TO 1
*  ---
        ELSE
*  ---
*  ---                       THIS IS THE SUCCESS PATH
*  ---
          PRINT *,'THE COMPUTED VALUE OF EXP(',X,') IS ',SUM
          PRINT *,'THE NUMBER OF TERMS INCLUDED WAS N = ',I
*  ---
        END IF
*  ---
        STOP
        END


    ENTER VALUE OF X 1,0
    THE COMPUTED VALUE OF EXP(1.) IS 2.718281525573
    THE NUMBER OF TERMS INCLUDED WAS N = 10
```

Figure 4-5 A program to compute the best, worst, and average exam scores.

```
    PROGRAM EXAMS
*--
*-- This program will read a set of student ID's and exam scores
*-- entered at the terminal. The list is scanned for the minimum
*-- and maximum scores. The ID of the students with these scores
*-- are then printed. Also the scores are summed and an average
*-- computed.
*------------------------------------------------------------------
* Variables
*--
        REAL AVG
        INTEGER EXAM,BEST,WORST,SUM,IDBEST,IDWRST,ID,N
*--
*--         ID      - Current student ID
*--         EXAM    - Current exam score
*--         BEST    - The maximum exam score
*--         WORST   - The lowest exam score
*--         IDBEST  - The ID of student with best exam
*--         IDWRST  - The ID of student with worst exam
*--         SUM     - Sum of all exam scores
*--         N       - The total number of exams
*--         AVG     - The average of all exams
*------------------------------------------------------------------
* Initialization
*--
        SUM = 0.0
        N = 0
        BEST = 0
        WORST = 100
*--
*--         Note, we start with impossible values for best/worst
*--
    1   READ *,ID,EXAM
```

```
*--
*--             The End-of-data is marked with a negative ID
*--
              IF(ID .LT. 0)GO TO 99
*-------------------------------------------------------------------
* Summation
*--
              SUM = SUM + EXAM
              N = N + 1
*-------------------------------------------------------------------
* Determine the maximum and minimum exam score
*--
              IF(EXAM .LT. WORST)THEN
                    WORST = EXAM
                    IDWRST = ID
              END IF
              IF(EXAM .GT. BEST)THEN
                    BEST = EXAM
                    IDBEST = ID
              END IF
*--
*--             Return to read next data line
*--
        GO TO 1
*-------------------------------------------------------------------
* Output section
*--
  99    AVG = SUM/N
*--
*--          (Note the use of intentional mixed-mode arithmetic)
*--
        PRINT *,'THE AVERAGE OF THE ',N,' EXAMS IS ',AVG
        PRINT *,' '
        PRINT *,'STUDENT ID = ',IDBEST,' HAD THE HIGHEST SCORE OF ',BEST
        PRINT *,'STUDENT ID = ',IDWRST,' HAD THE LOWEST SCORE OF ',WORST
*--
        STOP
        END
```

4.5   THE BISECTION TECHNIQUE FOR FINDING ROOTS OF EQUATIONS

A very common feature found in almost every program concerned with numerical analysis is to have the computer repeatedly monitor some property of a function and to take some action when a particular condition is satisfied. A rather nice example of this is found in the determination of the roots of an equation by the bisection method.

4.5.1 Roots of Equations

Engineering and scientific problems very often require the calculation of the roots of a function or equation for their solution. That is, it is required to find a value of x, such that $f(x) = 0$. The function may be a polynomial like

$$p(x) = x^7 - 5x^5 + 6x^4 - 2x^2 + 1 = 0$$

or a more complicated expression involving transcendental functions,

$$t(x) = e^{-x} - \sin\left(\tfrac{1}{2}\pi x\right) = 0$$

The problem could be

Since the polynomial is of degree 7, find all seven roots of $p(x)$.
If the polynomial $p(x)$ has less than seven real roots, find only the real roots or only the positive real roots.
The second equation, $t(x) = 0$, has an infinite number of positive roots. So perhaps we need only the first five, or only the first.
Given an approximate value for a root, find a more precise value.

For the moment, we will concentrate on the last, least ambitious project.

As with any program, we begin by gathering as much information as we can before we make any attempt at constructing a Fortran code. In functional analysis this almost always means you should attempt a rough sketch of the function under consideration. The second equation above can be written as

$$e^{-x} = \sin\left(\tfrac{1}{2}\pi x\right)$$

A root of the equation then corresponds to any value of x such that the left side and the right side are equal. If the left and right sides are plotted independently, the roots of the original equation then are given by the points of intersection of the two curves (see Figure 4-6). From the sketch we see that the roots are approximately

$$\text{Roots} = 0.4, 1.9, \ldots$$

and since the sine oscillates there will be an infinite number of positive roots. We will concentrate first on improving the estimate of the first root near 0.4. We begin by establishing a procedure, or algorithm, that is based on the most obvious method of attack when using a pocket calculator. That is, we begin at some value of x just before the root (say 0.3) and step along the x axis, carefully watching the magnitude and particularly the sign of the function.

Figure 4.6 The intersection of e^{-x} and $\sin(\frac{1}{2}\pi x)$.

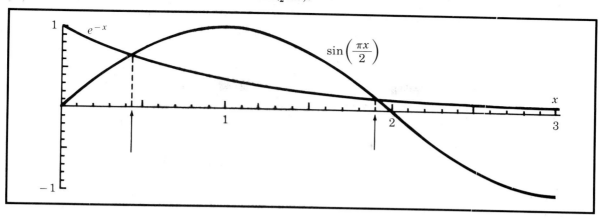

Step	x	e^{-x}	$\sin(\frac{1}{2}\pi x)$	$f(x) = e^{-x} - \sin(\frac{1}{2}\pi x)$
0	0.3	0.741	0.454	0.287
1	0.4	0.670	0.588	+0.082
2	0.5	0.606	0.707	−0.101

The function has changed sign between 0.4 and 0.5, indicating a root and that we have stepped too far. We therefore
1. backup one step
2. reduce the step size by half, and continue

Step	x	e^{-x}	$\sin(\frac{1}{2}\pi x)$	$f(x) = e^{-x} - \sin(\frac{1}{2}\pi x)$
3	0.45	0.638	0.649	−0.012
4	0.425	0.654	0.619	+0.0347
5	0.4375	0.6456	0.6344	+0.01126
6	0.44365	0.6417	0.6418	−0.00014
⋮				

The key element in the procedure is the monitoring of the *sign* of the function. When the sign changes, we take specific action to refine the estimate of the root. This will also form the key element of the computer code.

You should try this rather unsophisticated root-solving method on some simple equation. For example,

$$f(\alpha) = \sin(\alpha) - \frac{\alpha}{3} = 0 \qquad (\alpha \text{ is in radians})$$

This equation may be written as

$$\sin(\alpha) = \frac{\alpha}{3}$$

Again plotting left and right sides independently (see Figure 4-7), we see that the first positive root is near 2.2. The answer you should get for the root is

$$\alpha = 2.2788626602$$

4.5.2 The Bisection Method

The root-solving procedure illustrated in the previous section is quite suitable for hand calculations; however, a slight modification will make it somewhat more "systematic" and easier to adapt to computer coding.

Suppose we already know that there is a root between $x = a$ and $x = b$. That is, the function changes sign in this interval. For simplicity I will assume that there is only one root between $x = a$ and $x = b$, and that the function $f(x)$ is continuous in this interval. The function might then resemble the sketch in Figure 4-8. If I next define $x_1 = a$ and $x_3 = b$ as the left and right ends of the interval, and $x_2 = 0.5(x_1 + x_3)$ as the midpoint, consider the question: In which half-interval does the function cross the axis? In the drawing, the crossing is on the right, so I *replace* the full interval by the right half-interval,

$$x_1 \to x_2$$
$$x_3 \to x_3$$
$$x_2 = 0.5(x_1 + x_3)$$

and ask the question again. After determining a second time whether the left half or the right half contains the root, the interval is once more replaced by either the left or right half-interval. This is continued until we narrow in

Figure 4-7

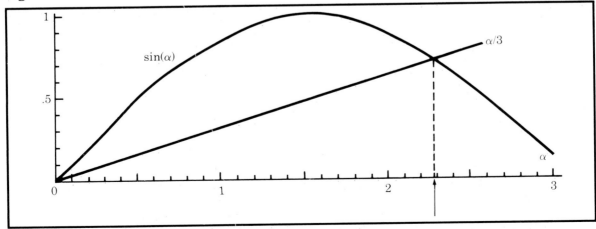

Figure 4-8

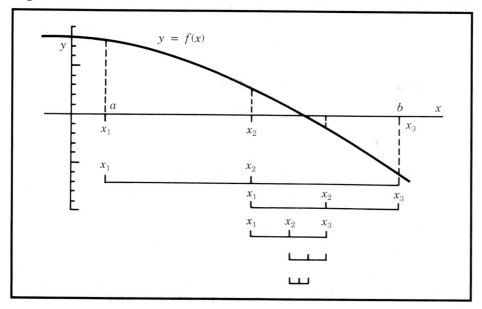

on the root to within some previously assigned accuracy. Each step halves the interval, and so after n iterations, the size of the interval containing the root will be $(b - a)/2^n$. If we are required to find a root to within a tolerance δ; i.e., $|x - \text{root}| < \delta$, the number of iterations n required can be determined from

$$\frac{(b - a)}{2^n} < \delta$$

For example, the initial search interval in the example of Section 4.5 was $(b - a) = 0.1$. If the root was required to an accuracy of $\delta = 10^{-5}$, then

$$\frac{0.1}{2^n} < 10^{-5} \quad \text{or} \quad 2^n > 10^4$$

So

$$n > \frac{\log(10^4)}{\log(2)} > 13$$

The only element of the bisection method that has been omitted is how the computer is to determine which half of the interval contains the axis crossing. To that end, consider the product of the function evaluated at the left end, $f_1 = f(x_1)$, and the function evaluated at the midpoint, $f_2 = f(x_2)$.

IF	THEN
1. $f_1 f_2 > 0.$	f_1 and f_2 are *both* positive or *both* negative. In either case there is no crossing between x_1 and x_2.
2. $f_1 f_2 < 0.$	$f(x)$ has changed sign between x_1 and x_2 and thus the root is in the left half.

The program to compute the root of an equation by this procedure is given in Figure 4-9. This program illustrates most of the ideas of this chapter and should be carefully studied. You will notice the following features:

1. In each iteration after the first, there is only *one* function evaluation. It would be highly inefficient to reevaluate $f(x_1)$, $f(x_2)$, and $f(x_3)$ for each iteration since two of them are already known. If the function were extremely complicated, this could be a serious problem. A great deal of computer time is wasted every day by careless programs that contain unnecessary function evaluations.
2. The program contains several checks for potential problems along with diagnostic messages (e.g., excessive iterations, no root in interval, etc.) even though the programmer may think these possibilities are remote. Generally, the more of these checks a program contains, the better. They only take a few minutes to add to a code and they can save you hours of debugging time.
3. The criterion for success is based on the size of the interval. Thus, even if the function were not close to zero at this point, x is changing very little and continuing would not substantially improve the accuracy of the root.

One final comment: This method is an example of a so-called brute force method, that is it possesses a minimum of finesse. It is an excellent example of Fortran techniques, but much more powerful and clever procedures will be found when we discuss numerical analysis.

4.6 THE USE OF DATA FILES

It is very likely that the programs you will be writing in the future will be designed to execute at a terminal and will require numerous variables to be assigned values by reading data. Every time the program is executed at the terminal, the data will have to be reentered and correctly positioned. During the debugging stage of a program's development, this can be an extremely annoying interruption to your work. It is possible in Fortran to set up a *data file* that contains all of the input lines that are to be read by the program and

Figure 4-9 The Fortran program for the bisection algorithm.

```
      PROGRAM BISEC
*--
*-- The interval a < x < b is Known to contain a root of f(x). The
*-- estimate of the root is successively improved by finding in
*-- which half of the interval the root lies and then replacing
*-- the original interval by that half.
*-------------------------------------------------------------------
* Variables
*--
      REAL X1,X2,X3,F1,F2,F3,A,B,EPS,D,DO
      INTEGER I,IMAX
*--
*--      X1,X3,X2 - The left, right, and midpoint of the
*--                 current interval.
*--      F1,F3,F2 - The function evaluated at these points
*--      A,B,DO   - The left and right ends of the original
*--                 interval and its width (b-a).
*--      EPS      - Convergence criterion based on the size
*--                 of the current interval
*--      D        - The width of the current interval (x3-x1)
*--      IMAX     - Maximum number of iterations
*--      I        - Current iteration counter
*-------------------------------------------------------------------
* Statement function for the function f(x)
*--
      F(X) = EXP(-X) - SIN(PI * X/2.)
*--
*--                     (Or any other function)
*-------------------------------------------------------------------
* Initialization
*--
      PI = ACOS(-1.)
      PRINT *,'ENTER LIMITS OF ORIGINAL SEARCH INTERVAL-A,B'
      READ *,A,B
      PRINT *,'ENTER CONVERGENCE CRITERION AND MAX ITERATIONS'
      READ *,EPS,IMAX
      PRINT *,' THE ORIGINAL SEARCH INTERVAL IS FROM ',A,' TO ',B
      PRINT *,' THE CONVERGENCE CRITERION IS FOR INTERVAL < ',EPS
      PRINT *,' THE MAXIMUM NUMBER OF ITERATIONS ALLOWED IS ',IMAX
*--
      X1 = A
      X3 = B
      F1 = F(X1)
      F3 = F(X3)
      I  = 0
      DO = (B - A)
      D  = 1.0
*--
*--      First verify that there is indeed a root in the interval
*--
```

Continued

```
              IF(F1 * F3 .GT. 0.0)THEN
                      PRINT *,'NO ROOT IN ORIGINAL INTERVAL'
                      STOP
              END IF
*--
   1    X2 = (X1 + X3)/2.
        F2 = F(X2)
*-------------------------------------------------------------
*                       Convergence test
*--
              IF(D .LT. EPS)THEN
                      PRINT *,' A ROOT AT X = ',X2' WAS FOUND'
                      PRINT *,' IN ',I,' ITERATIONS'
                      PRINT *,' THE VALUE OF THE FUNCTION IS ',F2
                      STOP
              ELSE IF(I .GT. IMAX)THEN
*--
*--                 Failure path - excessive iterations
*--
                      PRINT *,'FAILURE--NO CONVERGENCE IN ',I,' STEPS'
                      STOP
              END IF
*--
*--                 Check for crossing in left half
*--
              IF(F1 * F2 .LT. 0.)THEN
                      D = (X2 - X1)/D0
                      F3 = F2
                      X3 = X2
*--
*--                       Or in the right half
*--
              ELSE IF(F2 * F3 .LT. 0.)THEN
                      D = (X3 - X2)/D0
                      F1 = F2
                      X1 = X2
*--
*--               If no crossing in either half,
*--               either f(x2) = 0.0 or an error
*--
              ELSE IF(F2 .EQ. 0.0)THEN
                      PRINT *,'F(',X2,') IS IDENTICALLY ZERO'
                      PRINT *,' FOUND IN ',I,'STEPS'
                      STOP
              ELSE
                      PRINT *,'THE CURRENT INTERVAL ',X1,' TO ',X3
                      PRINT *,'DOES NOT CONTAIN A ROOT, THE'
                      PRINT *,'CODE FOR F(X) IS PROBABLY WRONG'
                      STOP
              END IF
*--
*--               Increment interations counter and repeat
*--
        I = I + 1
        GO TO 1
*-------------------------------------------------------------
     END
```

then instruct the program to read data from this file during execution. In addition, you could have the program write all or some of the results to a data file (distinct from output) and after execution of the program view some of the results on the terminal screen, and if it looks OK, send the results file to the line printer. Manipulation of data files is a rather advanced topic in Fortran and so I will only sketch some of the more elementary applications.

4.6.1 The "Long" Form of Fortran I/O Statements

The standard Fortran form of statements that read data into the machine or write numbers or text is

READ(i, j) ⟨list of input variables⟩

WRITE(i, j) ⟨list of output values, variables, or expressions⟩

The first symbol (i) in the parentheses is an integer constant that refers to a device or file. That is, $i = 3$, for example, may designate the card reader, or a paper tape reader, or the line printer, or any of several other I/O devices. The specific identification numbers of each of the I/O devices varies from one computing center to another. You must determine the particular number code for I/O devices at your computing center. An alternative procedure of assigning your own numbers to each will be discussed in Section 4.6.2.

The second item in the parentheses (j) is an integer constant that refers to an *existing format statement* in the Fortran code that bears that statement number. Format statements are used, for example, to specify the position of printed numbers on an output line and will be described in the next chapter. For now it is sufficient to know that if the format label (j) is replaced with an asterisk (*), the READ or WRITE statement will be executed using a list-directed form of I/O; that is, the same form we are accustomed to when using the statements ⟨READ *,⟩ and ⟨PRINT *,⟩.

Following the parentheses is a list of those variables (separated by commas) to be read in or printed out. These statements would then be translated into English as:

Read (write), using device i, according to format number j, the variables . . . .

And the statements

```
READ(13,*)A,C,MAX
WRITE(13,*)A,C,MAX
```

would be interpreted as

Read(write), using I/O unit 13, by list-directed input (or output), the variables.
. . .

The most common, though not universal, assignments are

$i = 5$ means card reader ⟨using file named INPUT⟩

$i = 6$ means line printer ⟨using file named OUTPUT⟩

I should point out that when a program is run interactively at a terminal, the normal I/O devices—the card reader and the line printer— are usually replaced by the terminal. That is, unless you specifically instruct the machine otherwise, any command to WRITE on the line printer will be diverted so that the output will appear on the terminal screen (and will *not* be printed). Likewise, instructions to READ data will be diverted to the terminal where you will be expected to enter the data.

The form of the READ and WRITE statements given above is valid in all versions of FORTRAN and is usually the preferred form. A somewhat shorter form is also available, namely

READ *j*,   ⟨*list of input variables*⟩

PRINT *j*,   ⟨*list of output variables*⟩

In this form it is assumed that printed output will go to the line printer and that data will be read from the card reader. (Again, all I/O to the line printer or from the card reader when working interactively at a terminal is diverted to the terminal.) These statements then read

Read (or print) according to format *j*, the variables . . . .

Replacing the format specification *j* by an asterisk in these statements results in the list-directed I/O statements that we have been using to this point. These forms are also available in all versions of Fortran but, as we shall see, are somewhat less flexible. Entering an extended data list at the terminal can be rather tedious and in these cases we will need a procedure whereby our programs can read data from a list already stored in memory. This can easily be done using the long form.

Finally, make careful note of the punctuation in the example I/O statements below

```
READ 7,A,B,C,M          No comma after READ
PRINT 52,IZ,DELTA
WRITE(6,33)X,DX         No comma after (6,33)
READ(5,111)TEMP
```

Of course, 7, 52, 33, 111 refer to existing format statements in the program. The list-directed versions of these same statements would be

```
READ *,A,B,C,M
PRINT *,IZ,DELTA
```

```
WRITE(6,*)X,DX
READ(5,*)TEMP
```

In summary, when using either the WRITE (. . .) or the long form of the READ(. . .) statement, the first number in the parentheses always refers to the associated I/O device or unit. The most common identifications are UNIT = 5 for input(card reader) and UNIT = 6 for output(line printer), and of course both input and output files are connected directly to the terminal if you are working interactively. Since these number identifications are not universal, you should have determined the unit numbers for files input and output used by your computing center.

Finally, if you are unaware of the correct unit numbers, Fortran provides an out. If the unit number is replaced by '*', all READ(*, . . .) commands are directed to file input and all WRITE(*, . . .) commands to file output. Thus the statements

```
READ(*,*)X,Y,Z
WRITE(*,*)X,Y,Z
```

read and write using files input and output respectively (the first *) by means of list-directed I/O (the second *).

4.6.2   The OPEN Statement—Naming Data Files

The procedure in Fortran for linking with a program files other than the normal input and output files is via the OPEN statement. These files are normally written to or read from the secondary magnetic disk memory connected to the computer.

Disk Files As mentioned in Section 1.2, there are two types of memory in a computer: main memory (or fast memory) and secondary memory (slower). Data files are always stored in secondary memory. In order to visualize the structure of data files it is useful to have some familiarity with the operation of two secondary memory devices, magnetic tape and magnetic disk.

One of the first devices used to store large amounts of data was magnetic tape. On the tape, each line of data or code is called a record and the information is copied onto the tape sequentially. The end of the data or program is then marked with an END OF FILE mark. These files are called SAM (*s*equential *a*ccess *m*ethod) files, and the information contained on these files can only be read in the same order in which it was written. This can be inefficient when huge data files are being used and manipulated. A second type of file is available in Fortran which makes use of the properties of a magnetic disk.

The magnetic disk, like magnetic tape, stores information compactly in terms of magnetized bits. The physical structure is quite similar to a phonograph record and the information is read from the disk by an access arm. The information recorded on the disk can be placed in a random order with each line (or record) assigned a sequencing record number. Such files are called DAM (*d*irect *a*ccess *m*ethod) files. We will not use DAM files in this text but you should be aware of their existence.

It is also possible to write SAM files on the disk, using the disk much like a magnetic tape. To do this you must inform the computer that the file you wish to create or use is a disk file and is of type sequential access. This is done in Fortran with the OPEN statement.

The Form of the OPEN Statement   The OPEN statement in Fortran is used to connect a disk file to a program and to define various attributes of the file. Some of the common disk file specifications that are prescribed in an OPEN statement are

1. To associate an existing disk file with a UNIT number. For example, the data for your program could be assigned to UNIT = 11. Then all READ(11, . . .) statements will read from this file. Or the output could be stored on UNIT = 12. Then WRITE(12, . . .) will place the results on a disk file which can be later printed at the line printer.
2. To associate a ⟨NAME⟩ of the file that is to be opened with the UNIT number. Thus the data file for your program could already reside on the disk and have a name like 'MYDATA'.
3. To define whether the file is type SAM or DAM.
4. To specify whether blanks in the file are to be interpreted as zeros or as blanks.
5. To specify whether the file already exists in the system (like a data file) or is to be a new file (e.g., results).

The form of the OPEN statement to accomplish all this is

```
      OPEN(UNIT = u,ERR = sl,FILE = flname,
     +      STATUS = stat,ACCESS = acc,BLANK = blnk)
```

where   u is an integer and specifies the unit of the file to be opened.

sl is a statement number of an executable statement to which the program will branch if there is an error encountered while opening the file. (Perhaps the data file is not present in the system.) The ERR = sl field is optional.

flname is a name (six or fewer characters, starts with a letter) that identifies the file. Since this is ordinarily a character expression it must be enclosed by apostrophes—for example, 'MYDATA'.

stat is a character expression that specifies whether the file already exists or is to be created. The valid values are

'OLD'   File ⟨flname⟩ already exists in the system
Note, the apostrophes must be included.
'NEW'   The file does not yet exist in the system.

The STATUS = stat field is also optional and if it is omitted the value of stat is UNKNOWN.

acc is a character expression that specifies whether the file is of sequential or direct-access type. The valid values of acc are

'SEQUENTIAL'   file ⟨flname⟩ is SAM
'DIRECT'   file ⟨flname⟩ is DAM

The ACCESS = acc specification is optional and if it is omitted the file is assumed to be of SEQUENTIAL type.

blnk is a character expression used to specify whether blanks are to be interpreted as zeros or blanks. It may have the following values.

'ZERO'   All blanks, other than leading blanks are treated as zeros.
'NULL'   Blanks appearing in numerically formatted lines are ignored, except that a line of all blanks is treated as zero.

The default value is BLANK = 'NULL'.

The expression UNIT = 9 may be shortened to simply

```
OPEN(9,FILE = 'MYDATA')
```

which, because of the default assignments is the same as

```
OPEN(UNIT = 9,FILE = 'MYDATA',STATUS = 'UNKNOWN',
+       ACCESS = 'SEQUENTIAL', BLANK = 'NULL')
```

Notice the name of the file is a character expression and must be enclosed by apostrophes.

Most of the time we will be using a simplified form of the above statement like

```
OPEN(UNIT = 9,FILE = 'MYDATA')
```

The OPEN statement is an executable Fortran statement.

4.6.3 The REWIND and CLOSE Statements

When using a disk data file it is always a good idea after opening the file to make sure that the computer is positioned at the beginning of the file. (It likely will be but it won't hurt to make sure.) This is done with the REWIND statement in Fortran, which is of the form

$$REWIND \quad \langle unit\ number \rangle$$

Another common application of this command is to read a large amount of data from a data file, execute the calculation, change a parameter or two, and reread the same data file after first rewinding the data file. The RE-WIND statement is an executable Fortran statement.

After you are finished with a file, the file may be disconnected from your program with the CLOSE statement. The specification options for the CLOSE statement are very similar to those for the OPEN statement. Thus, after reading data from the data file OPENed above you could close the file with

$$CLOSE(9,FILE = 'MYDATA')$$

Closing a file is not required, as all files are automatically closed when execution of the program is completed.

Note, you should never attempt to OPEN, CLOSE, or REWIND the files INPUT and OUTPUT for obvious reasons.

4.6.4 Creating a Data File

The steps involved in creating a data file at the terminal are similar to those you used in setting up a Fortran program. The specific computer instructions are quite system-dependent but basically they will involve

1. Log-on
2. CREATE a file (or some similar instruction). You will have to name the file and perhaps specify
   a. That the file is 'NEW'.
   b. The type of the file is "data" (as opposed to "Fortran")
3. After the file is created you may have to instruct the computer to save the file on the disk.

The following file was entered and saved as a data file with the name GRADES. The information on each line consists of a student's ID number(Social Security number), class (1 = freshman, 2 = sophomore, etc.), college(1 = Arts and Science, 2 = Business, 3 = Engineering, 4 = Education, 5 = Architecture), hour quiz grades(3), homework, and final exam.

```
column              1       2       3
        1234567890 . . . . . 0 . . . . . . 0 . . . .
        123456789, 2,3,71,65,82,80,77
        123456790, 2,1,95,92,91,30,85
        375409441, 3,1,66,50,59,66,62
        348223917, 2,5,77,75,80,86,83
        482230914, 1,1,91,96,93,88,94
        263471257, 2,2,71,65,80,80,72
        342287418, 2,3,82,89,91,75,84
        458334185, 2,3,61,68,60,42,57
        672261774, 2,4,71,80,77,65,73
        254661789, 2,3,82,71,88,56,71
        355429874, 3,2,66,75,77,67,82
        124567821, 2,3,45,60,62,21,51
        375446851, 2,3,91,86,94,92,91
        265443197, 2,1,71,65,66,61,69
        −999
```

The program ASSIGN (Figure 4-10) reads the file GRADES (several times), computes a final score (the sum of the quizzes plus homework plus three times final exam) for each student. It rereads the file once for each college and lists the students in that college and his or her final grade. Note rereading the data file in this manner is extremely inefficient. We will

Figure 4-10   Fortran program for computing student grades.

```
      PROGRAM ASSIGN
*
      CHARACTER GRADE*1
      INTEGER ID,CLASS,COLLGE,Q1,Q2,Q3,HW,EXAM,TOTAL,K
*
      OPEN(2,FILE = 'GRADES',ERR=99)
*
      K = 1
    1 REWIND(2)
        WRITE(*,*)'RESULTS FOR STUDENTS IN COLLGE = ',K
    2         READ(2,*)ID,CLASS,COLLGE,Q1,Q2,Q3,HW,EXAM
              IF(ID .LT. 0)THEN
                  K = K + 1
                  IF(K .LE. 5)THEN
                      GO TO 1
                  ELSE
                      PRINT *,'END OF ALL GRADE ASSIGNMENTS'
                      STOP
                  END IF
```

Continued

Figure 4-10 *Continued*

```
              END IF
*--
*--                    COMPUTE STUDENT LETTER GRADE
*--
              TOTAL = Q1 + Q2 + Q3 + HW + 3 * EXAM
              IF(TOTAL .GE. 600)THEN
                  GRADE = 'A'
              ELSE IF(TOTAL .GE. 540)THEN
                  GRADE = 'B'
              ELSE IF(TOTAL .GE. 475)THEN
                  GRADE = 'C'
              ELSE IF(TOTAL .GE. 410)THEN
                  GRADE = 'D'
              ELSE
                  GRADE = 'F'
              END IF
*
              IF(COLLGE .EQ. K)THEN
                  WRITE(*,*)'STUDENT-',ID,' GRADE = ',GRADE
              ELSE
                  GO TO 2
              END IF
*
   99 PRINT *,'ERROR IN OPENING FILE GRADES'
      STOP
      END
```

discover more efficient methods for problems of this type in Chapter 6. A pseuodocode outline of the program follows.

```
    PROGRAM ASSIGN
    OPEN data file
    For class K = 1 (freshmen)
  1   REWIND data file
      PRINT headings for college K
  2   READ student data line
              End-of-data marked by negative ID
              IF End-of-data THEN
                  Increment class, K = K + 1
                  IF class ≤ 5 THEN
                      GO TO rewind data, statement 1
                  ELSE
                      terminate program
                  END IF
              END IF
      Compute student letter grade
      IF student in class K THEN
          PRINT student grade
      ELSE
          return to READ next student line, statement 2
      END IF
```

Notice that in addition to the inefficient rereading of the data file, this program recomputes each student's grade several times unnecessarily. How would you change the code to correct this?

1. Write statement functions for the following:
   a. $f(x) = 3x^2 + x - 1$
   b. $g(z) = ax^2 + bx + c$
   c. $h(x) = e^{-ax} + \ln(\sin(\pi x))$
   d. index $= 3i + 2j$

2. A data file with the name of GRADES contains the results of an examination. The data on each line includes: (1) student ID, (2) exam score. The last data line has a negative ID number. Write a complete program to read the data file and
   a. Write the IDs and exam scores of students who have failed (score < 60) as they are encountered.
   b. Count the total number of exams and the number of each grade A to F assigned according to

$$F < 60 \le D < 70 \le C < 80 \le B < 90 \le A$$

   c. Determine the IDs of the students with the maximum and minimum score.
   d. Determine the average of the exam.
   e. Determine the class grade point average (GPA) on the A $= 4.0$, F $= 0.0$ basis.

3. Write programs to evaluate the following, terminating the sums when the absolute value of a term is less than 10^{-6}. (*Note:* Problem 3(f) is an infinite product and must be handled somewhat differently.)

   a. $\dfrac{1}{1^2} + \dfrac{1}{2^2} + \dfrac{1}{3^2} + \cdots + \dfrac{1}{n^2} + \cdots \qquad \left(= \dfrac{\pi^2}{6} \right)$

   b. $1 - \dfrac{1}{3} + \dfrac{1}{5} - \dfrac{1}{7} + \cdots \qquad \left(= \dfrac{\pi}{4} \right)$

   c. $1 + \dfrac{1}{2} + \dfrac{1}{4} + \dfrac{1}{8} + \cdots + \dfrac{1}{2^k} + \cdots \qquad (= 2)$

   d. $\dfrac{1}{4} + \dfrac{1}{16} + \dfrac{1}{64} + \cdots + \dfrac{1}{4^k} + \cdots \qquad \left(= \dfrac{1}{3} \right)$

   e. $1 + \dfrac{1}{2!} + \dfrac{1}{3!} + \dfrac{1}{4!} + \cdots + \dfrac{1}{n!} + \cdots \qquad (= e)$

   f. $\left[\dfrac{2(2)}{1(3)} \right] \left[\dfrac{4(4)}{3(5)} \right] \left[\dfrac{6(6)}{5(9)} \right] \cdots \left[\dfrac{(2n)(2n)}{(2n - 1)(2n + 1)} \right] \cdots \qquad \left(= \dfrac{\pi}{2} \right)$

4. The Fortran program to sum the series for e^x given in Figure 4-4 is not an acceptable method to evaluate e^x when the magnitude of x is large. If x is large and positive, successive terms in the series will continue to grow until n, the order of the term, is greater than x, and a great many terms will have to be included to obtain an accurate result. For x large and negative, the situation is much worse. Not only will a great many large initial terms have to be accumulated, but since the result is nearly zero (e.g., $e^{-10} \sim 0.000045$) the near cancellation of large terms will introduce considerable round-off error. Rewrite the program to read a value of x and if x is larger than 10 in magnitude, first scale to a value between 0 and 1. Once the series is evaluated, e^x is then scaled back up. Test the program for $x = +50$ and $x = -50$.

5. The golden mean of antiquity is defined to be a solution of the equation

$$r = \frac{1}{1 + r}$$

Solve this equation iteratively—i.e.,

$$r_{new} = \frac{1}{1 + r_{old}}$$

Start with $r = 1.0$. Also, show analytically that the limit of the iterative solution is $r = (\sqrt{5} - 1)/2$.

6. Using a pocket calculator and the bisection technique, solve for the smallest positive roots of the following functions. Find the root accurate to five significant figures.
   a. $f(x) = x^2 + 2x - 15$ (initial interval $2.8 < x < 3.1$; answer = 3.0)
   b. $g(x) = \sin(x) \sinh(x) + 1$ (elliptic gear equation, $\sinh(x) = (e^x - e^{-x})/2$; initial interval $1.0 < x < 4.0$; x is in radians)
   c. Predict the number of steps needed to obtain the answer to the specified accuracy in both problems.

7. Write a program that
   a. Creates a data file of 101 lines, the first line contains values for dt, v_x, and v_y and the numbers on successive lines are the values of t_i, x_i, y_i, where

$$x_i = v_x t_i$$

$$y_i = v_y t_i - (g/2)t_i^2$$

$$t_i = i\, dt \qquad \text{for } i = 1 \text{ to } 100$$

and

$$v_x = 10.5 \qquad v_y = 51.0 \qquad dt = 0.1 \qquad g = 9.8$$

   b. Write a program that reads and prints the data file.

8. Write a program that will read a file called ROSTER. The first line of the file contains the total number of data lines that follow. On each of the subsequent lines is a student's ID number and the number of credits earned to date. If the number of credits is 130 or more, the student has graduated, so rewrite the entire file deleting these students.

9. Construct a program to find a maximum of a function $f(x)$. Do this by starting at x_0 with a step size Δx. Evaluate $f_1 = f(x_0)$, $f_2 = f(x_0 + \Delta x)$. If $f_1 < f_2$, continue, otherwise reduce Δx by half and repeat the comparison.

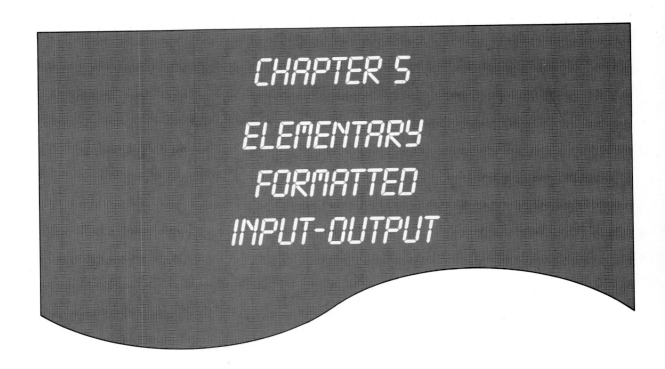

CHAPTER 5

ELEMENTARY FORMATTED INPUT-OUTPUT

5.1   INTRODUCTION

We have already seen a few simple examples of getting numbers in and out of the computer in Section 2.9. In almost every case, it is preferable to have the computer print the results in the form of tables with appropriate headings and some explanatory text. This necessitates a large number of editing decisions. Before the results are printed or the data file is read, the following questions must be addressed:

In what form are the numbers to be printed?
  Integers?
  Reals without exponents?
  Reals with exponents?
  How many significant figures are to be printed?
Where will the numbers appear on the page or where are the numbers to be found on an input data line?
What text appears with the numbers, table headings, etc.?

All of these decisions are made in the form of FORMAT statements, and clearly all of this arranging of output (and input) can take considerable time.

138

Formatting the input and output is the most tedious aspect of programming, but it is not terribly difficult to understand, and if you have spent a lot of time and effort in getting some intricate code to execute efficiently and correctly, it is certainly worth some additional time arranging the output in a neat, clear, and pleasing form.

5.2 FORMATTED I/O STATEMENTS

To this point, all of the I/O statements that we have used have been written in terms of the list-directed I/O option available in Fortran 77. This was effected by using an asterisk (*) in either the PRINT/WRITE or READ statements. The various forms of I/O statements employed thus far are

READ *,⟨input list⟩	*Simply separate numbers by commas. The values are read from file INPUT.*
READ(34,*)⟨input list⟩	*Same as above except the numbers are read from file opened with number 34.*
READ(*,*)⟨input list⟩	*The first asterisk means that the numbers are read from the file INPUT. This form is identical to READ *,⟨list⟩.*
PRINT *,⟨output list⟩	*List-directed output to file OUTPUT.*
WRITE(42,*)⟨output list⟩	*List-directed output to file opened with number 42.*
WRITE(*,*)⟨output list⟩	*The first asterisk means that the numbers will be written to the file OUTPUT. This form is identical to PRINT *,⟨list⟩.*

Each of the I/O statements listed above can be used to write or read information according to specific editing instructions that are included in a FORMAT statement. The asterisk that designates list-directed I/O is simply replaced by the statement number of the associated format statement. (Format statements are described in the next section.) Thus

	Means
READ 88,⟨input list⟩	*Read from file INPUT according to format number 88 the values for ....*
WRITE(2,2)⟨output list⟩	*Write to file number 2, according to format number 2 the values ....*

5.3 THE FORMAT STATEMENT

The form of a Format statement is:

$$j \qquad \text{FORMAT}(\text{spec}_1, \text{spec}_2, \text{spec}_3, \ldots)$$

The integer j is a unique statement number and of course the word FORMAT begins in column 7 or later. Inside the parentheses is a list of formatting specifications separated by commas (or slashes, /, see Section 5.3.2) relating to the numbers, variables, or characters that are to be read in or printed out by the relevant READ or WRITE statement. The FORMAT statement is a *nonexecutable* statement and it may appear anywhere in the program, either before or after the associated READ/WRITE statement.

5.3.1   Format Specifications—Numerical Descriptors

The F Format(Floating-Point or Real Numbers Without Exponent)

The form of the F format specification is

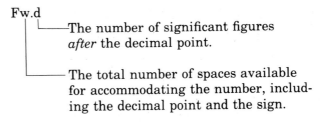

Fw.d
└── The number of significant figures *after* the decimal point.

└── The total number of spaces available for accommodating the number, including the decimal point and the sign.

For example,

```
         READ(5,66)X,Y
66       FORMAT(F10,3,F5,1)
```

If $X = 271.736$ and $Y = 3.1$, the data line or input line at the terminal would be

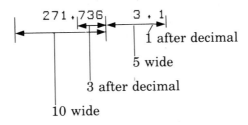

```
          1                 2               3             4
1234567890 . . . . . . . . . 0 . . . . . . . 0 . . . . . . . . 0
```

271.736   3.1
                1 after decimal
           5 wide
      3 after decimal
10 wide

and the same numbers printed with

```
            WRITE(6,13)X,Y
    13   FORMAT(F7.2,F6.2)
```

would result in

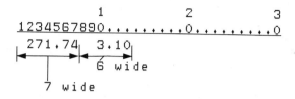

Some Technical Points to Remember Regarding Formatted I/O

When printing either on the line printer or on the terminal screen, the first column of each line may not be displayed. Many computer systems use the first column of an output line for vertically positioning the output (carriage control). This will be described in Section 5.5.1. For the present, each line of output should skip over column 1.

When REAL numbers are printed, the values displayed are *rounded*, not truncated. In the above example, the value printed for X was 271.74. The number stored in memory for X is still 271.736, however.

Ordinarily when reading data the machine will read a blank space as a blank, i.e., it is ignored. However some installations have set up the read statement so that a blank is interpreted as a *zero*. Thus the above input line would actually be read as

000271.7360003.1

and the same values would be assigned to X and Y. However, if the first number is accidentally misplaced so that it spills over into the field of the second number, as

```
            1            2          3
    1234567890.........0.........0
        271.736  3.1
```

which is the same as

```
          1              2          3
1234567890.........0.........0
0000271.73603.1
```

then X would be read as 271.73 and Y as 603.1, significantly different from what was intended. Most computers that are used for interactive computing read a blank as a blank, and in this case the assignments would be X = 271.73 and Y = 63.1, which is still wrong. For this reason it is essential that you verify that each value read in has resulted in the intended assignment. You should *always echo print* values read in. Moreover, whenever possible a list-directed READ is safer and easier to use than a formatted read.

If the number entered in a READ command fits in the prescribed width (w), and the number has a decimal point, then the placement of the decimal point overrides the d specification in the FORMAT statement. Thus the first number below

```
          1              2          3
1234567890.........0.........0
271.73600      3.1
```

is entered as an F10.5 and the original format was F10.3. This number would be read correctly and the assignment for X would again be 271.736.

If the numerical value being read does not contain a decimal point, the d specification in the F format will act as a negative power-of-10 scaling factor. Thus if the number 1234 were entered with an F5.2 format, the value stored would be

$$1234. \times 10^{-2} = 12.34 \qquad d = 2$$

It is suggested that you always include a decimal point when entering real numbers.

The I Format (Integers)

The form of the I format specification is

Iw

└──── Total width of the field

For example,

```
                    READ(5,21)N
          21    FORMAT(I9)
```

If the value to be assigned to N is 23, then the data line or terminal input line would look like

```
              1              2              3
     1234567890.........0..........0
              23
```

Of course, there can be no decimal point anywhere in an integer field. Notice, if the number were misplaced in the field as

```
              1              2              3
     1234567890.........0..........0
          23
```

the number would still be read as 23 if blanks are ignored and as 230000 if a blank is read as a zero.

Attempts to read or print numbers by means of a format that conflicts with the type of the number will result in errors. For example, printing the integer M using an F-type format will cause an incorrect value to be printed. Other examples of I/O errors resulting from a mismatch of format and number type are listed below.

Variable type	If READ with format	Result
INTEGER	F	Value assigned will be incorrect
REAL	I	Execution time error—decimal point in I field
	If WRITE with format	
INTEGER	F	An output error may result. (The program will continue.)
REAL	I	An output error will result. (The program will continue.)

When printing either real or integer values some care must be exercised to ensure that the field width (w) is sufficiently large to accommodate the anticipated size of the numbers printed. If the field width is too small, the computer will instead fill the field with asterisks. For example, an attempt to print X = 123.45 and K = 1234 with formats F5.3 and I3, respectively, will result in output that resembles that below,

```
*****
 ***      * Indicates field-width overflow
```

The E Format (Floating-Point or Real Numbers with Exponent)

The form of the E format specification is

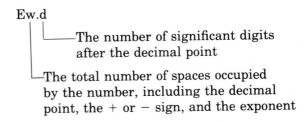

A typical real number with exponent is

```
-0.12345E-05
```

which occupies twelve spaces (w) and has five digits (d) following the decimal point. In addition to the mantissa digits (12345), seven spaces are required for the leading sign (1), leading zero (1), decimal point (1), E (1), exponent sign (1), exponent power (2). Thus when using E formats, $w \geq d + 7$. For example,

```
      READ(5,22)X,Y
 22   FORMAT(E14.5,E10.2)
```

If $X = 2.71736E+02$ and $Y = 31.0E-11$, the values entered would appear as

```
            1           2           3
  1234567890.........0.........0
     2.71736E+02 31.00E-11
```

An important point to keep in mind when reading numbers with an E format is that the exponent *must* be placed at the extreme right of the field and of course the numbers must fit within the specified field width. If the format specification were

```
 22   FORMAT(E13.5,E10.2)
```

the above line would assign

$$X = 2.71736E+0 = 2.71736 \times 10^0 = 2.71736$$
$$Y = 2\ 31.00E-1 = 23.1 \quad \langle \text{or } 2031.00E-1 \text{ if a blank}$$
$$\text{is interpreted as a zero} \rangle$$

which are incorrect assignments. As with F format, if a decimal point is included with the number, it overrides the d specification of the format. Thus, if the above numbers were read with either of the formats below, correct assignments would still result.

```
22   FORMAT(E14.7,E10.3)
22   FORMAT(E14.0,E10.0)
```

Writing numbers with the latter format would result in only the exponent being printed.

In summary, you should remember the following points concerning the Ew.d format:

For output especially, $w \geq d + 7$. For input the decimal point included in the number overrides the d specification of the format.

For input, the exponent field must be right-adjusted, i.e. positioned to the extreme right of the field.

The mantissa (the fractional part of the number) should contain a decimal point.[1]

For input, the exponent should contain no more than two digits.

If the E field is missing on input, the E format is used as if it were an F format. So, if the number entered contains a decimal point, it will be correctly read and stored. For example, the number 12.34, read with a format E10.3, would be stored as 12.34.

5.3.2   Format Specifications—Position Descriptors

The X Format (Skip a Space)

The form of The X format specification is

nX
|
|———— Number of spaces to be skipped

---

[1]As with the F format, the decimal point is optional when reading real numbers. If the decimal point is omitted, the d specification in the format Ew.d will act as a negative power-of-ten scaling factor. Thus, reading the number 1234E+4 with a format E9.2 would result in the value

$$(1234.E+4) \times 10^{-2} = 0.1234E+6 \quad d = 2$$

being stored.

For example,

```
         I=12
         J=34
         K=56
         WRITE (6,6)I,J,K
    6    FORMAT(1X,I2,9X,I2,5X,I2)
```

would result in

```
                   1           2           3
       1234567890.........0.........0
        12          34       56
```

Recall, we are avoiding the printing of numbers in column 1 for the moment.

The Slash (/) Format (Skip to Next Line)

An example of the slash format is

```
         WRITE(6,5)I,J,K
    5    FORMAT(1X,I2/2X,I2///3X,I2)
```

These statements would result in

```
                   1           2
       1234567890.........0
        12
         34

         56
```

Note that

Multiple line skips cannot be specified as n/. To skip five lines and begin on the sixth, you could use //////. An alternative is discussed in the next section.

The line skip specification need not be separated from other format specifications by commas. In fact, format specifications may be separated by either commas or slashes. However, you may find it easier to read the format statement by explicitly separating off the slashes by commas. Thus format 5 above could also be written as

```
    5    FORMAT(1X,I2,/,2X,I2,///,3X,I2)
```

Immediately following a slash, the position of the format specification is in column 1, the carriage control position for printed output.

The T Format (Tab)

You can have the printed output (or input) skip to a particular position on the line in much the same way you use a tab key on a typewriter by means of the T format. This format has the forms

Tn Tab to column number n moving either right or left

TRn Skip forward (tab right) by n positions, measured from the current position.

TLn Skip backward (tab left) by n positions, measured from the current position. If n is greater than the current column number, it will position in column 1.

These forms are particularly useful in constructing tables. For example,

```
      READ *,X,Y,Z
      WRITE(6,10)
      WRITE(6,11)X,Y,Z
 10   FORMAT(2X,'OUTPUT TABLE')
 11   FORMAT(T15,'VALUES',//,T17,F3.1,//,T17,F3.1,TL6,
     +  F3.1)
```

with input of X = 1.0, Y = 2.0, and Z = 3.0, will result in

```
      OUTPUT TABLE
            VALUES
             1.0
          3.02.0
```

5.3.3 Repeatable Format Specifications

With the exception of the slash and T formats, each of the formats discussed thus far may be repeated by preceding the format specification by a multiplying integer factor. That is,

```
      3F5.2
```

is the same as

```
      F5.2,F5.2,F5.2
```

It is also possible to have multiples of combinations of format specifications by enclosing groups in parentheses and preceding the parentheses by a multiplicative factor. For example,

```
      WRITE(6,33)X,IA,A,IB,B,IC,C
 33   FORMAT(5(/),3X,F10.5,3(/,3X,I2,2X,F5.2))
```

will print a total of nine lines.

5.4   ELEMENTARY INPUT AND OUTPUT OF TEXT

5.4.1   Introduction

The output of most programs will consist of more than just numbers. Tables will have labels and most computed results will require some identification and explanation. The printing of text (also called Hollerith or character strings) is quite simple in Fortran 77. More elaborate procedures for handling character strings will be addressed in Chapter 7, but for the moment the elementary methods outlined below will be sufficient for most applications.

5.4.2   The Apostrophe as a String Delimiter

Up to this point, textual material and character strings have been printed by using the list-directed output statement

```
      PRINT *, <character strings and/or variables>
```

in which the character strings are enclosed in apostrophes. A character string constant can also be included in a FORMAT statement and the procedure is similar: the string is simply enclosed in apostrophes and separated from other format specifications by commas or slashes. The string may contain any of the valid symbols in Fortran (see page 22) and will be printed exactly as it appears, including blanks. For example,

```
        IDAY=11
        IYEAR=86
        WRITE(6,11)IDAY,IYEAR
11      FORMAT(5X,'TODAY IS SEPT.',I2,',  19',I2)
```

First string
14 characters

Second string
4 characters
(includes the
comma)

will produce the output

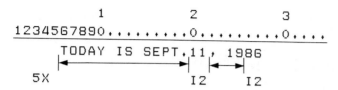

Also, the statements

```
        WRITE(6,12)
12      FORMAT(10X,60('*'))
```

will result in a line of 60 asterisks.

As a somewhat more complicated example, the statements below will produce a table of temperature and resistance values. Obviously, some care was used in designing the FORMAT statement so that the column headings and numerical values are properly aligned and centered.

```
    WRITE(6,13)T1,R1,T2,R1,T3,R3
13  FORMAT(5X,'A TABLE OF ELECTRICAL RESISTANCE',
   +              ' VS.TEMPERATURE',
   +//,9X,'TEMPERATURE       RESISTANCE',/,
   +   9X,'  (DEG-C)          (OHMS)',/,
   +3(10X,F10.3,5X,F10.1,/))
```

Assuming that the variables have been assigned values, these statements would produce the following output:

```
A TABLE OF ELECTRICAL RESISTANCE VS. TEMPERATURE

    TEMPERATURE       RESISTANCE
      (DEG-C)           (OHMS)
      124.300          10344.3
       93.200          10113.7
       21.700           9958.4
```

If the string itself contains an apostrophe, it can be printed by typing two consecutive apostrophes.

```
      PRINT 14
14    FORMAT(2X,'DON''T FORGET TODAY''S ASSIGNMENT')
```

results in

```
DON'T FORGET TODAY'S ASSIGNMENT
```

Note, on some printing devices, the apostrophe is represented as ↑ .

5.4.3   Replacing the * with Format Specifications

Unless the formatting of a PRINT or WRITE statement is quite complicated, it is usually more convenient to use the list-directed form of the output statements, i.e., PRINT *, or WRITE(6, *), especially for preliminary results. However, there are frequently situations that fall somewhere between simple and complicated. For example, if you wished to print A = 5.0 and B = 3.0 on separate lines and centered on the page, this could easily be done with a FORMAT statement or you may simply replace the '*' with the required format specification. That is,

```
      PRINT 11, A,IA
      WRITE(6,11)B,IB
11    FORMAT(25X,F5.2,/,27X,I2)
```

could be replaced by

```
      PRINT '(25X,F5.2,/,27X,I2)',A,IA
      WRITE(6,'(25X,F5.2,/,27X,I2)')B,IB
```

or

```
      PRINT '(2(25X,F5.2,/,27X,I2))',A,IA,B,IB
```

Notice, when replacing the asterisk with format specifications, they must be enclosed in parentheses and delimited fore and aft by apostrophes. Thus, if the format specifications themselves contain an apostrophe, an error will result. To print labels in addition to numbers using this option, a slightly different approach is required and is explained in the next section.

5.4.4   The A Format for Printing Text

The A Format

A variable that is of type CHARACTER is printed by means of the alphanumeric format specification, Aw, where w is the length of the character

---

expression to be printed. For example, to print a character variable of length 24, the format specification would be

```
      CHARACTER PHRASE*24
      PHRASE = 'CHARACTER VARIABLE OF LENGTH 24'
      WRITE(6,21)PHRASE
   21 FORMAT(5X,A24)
```

Fortran-77 also permits a very convenient variation of the above A format specification. In place of 'A24' in the format statement we could simply use 'A' and the computer will count the length of the variable and allot the proper number of spaces.

```
      CHARACTER NAME*10,STATE*2
      NAME = 'ANDERSON  '
      STATE = 'PA'
      WRITE(6,22)NAME,STATE
   22 FORMAT(2X,'MR. ',A,' LIVES IN ',A)
```

In summary, the form of the A format specification is

$$Aw \quad \text{or} \quad A$$

And it is used to print character-type variables or expressions. Next consider how labels might be printed with the list-directed form.

The Form PRINT '(A)',⟨character string⟩

Text may be printed using list-directed output by employing the A format in place of the ∗.

```
      CHARACTER STAR*1
      STAR = '*'
      PRINT '(A)',STAR
```

Note that the format specification must be enclosed in parentheses. An even more concise procedure is

```
      PRINT '(A)','*'
```

Variations on this particular form are quite easy to construct and can make the chore of obtaining intermediate results from a program almost painless.

```
      PRINT '(5X,A,I2,A,F6.2)','THE LOAD ON BEAM NO. ',I2,
     +    ' IS ',LOAD
      WRITE(6,'(5X,A,E9.2,A)')'THE FLOW RATE IS ',FLOW,
     +      'CUBIC METER/SEC'
```

Input of Character Variables

If a variable has been designated as type CHARACTER, it may be assigned a value by means of assignment statements as in the previous examples, or by reading input data using the A format. Thus if the code below is used to read data entered at a terminal, an entire line of 80 characters will be stored in the variable LINE.

```
CHARACTER LINE*80
READ '(A)', LINE
```

Note that ⟨READ *, LINE⟩ will only work if the character string to be assigned to the variable LINE is enclosed in apostrophes. This is not required with the A format. Also, if the length of the character string being read is less than 80 characters, the rest of variable LINE is filled-in with blanks. The significant characters are left adjusted.

From the discussion thus far it should be apparent that facility in using character variables for manipulating text is an important and useful part of overall Fortran 77 fluency. However, it is not a skill that comes easily, but requires considerable practice. Character string manipulation is a feature that was added to Fortran to broaden the usefulness of the language to applications in fields outside its historical base of science and engineering. Alphabetizing a list or an inventory search is done using character variables. As important as these uses may be, our primary concern as engineers is plain old "number crunching," and so more detailed explanations of character variable features in Fortran 77 will be postponed to Chapter 7.

5.5 SOME TECHNICAL POINTS TO REMEMBER

5.5.1 Carriage Control

All of the programs and examples thus far have avoided printing in column 1. The reason for this is that Fortran uses the character placed in column 1 of each line as a vertical spacing or carriage-control command. This character is not printed. Carriage-control commands apply particularly to printed output, they do not generally affect the output at a terminal. The four characters that are used for vertical spacing are listed in Table 5-1. The list-directed forms of output (PRINT *, ⟨list ⟩) always insert a blank at the beginning of each line to ensure single spacing. The program below illustrates some uses of carriage control. In particular, notice the use of the tab format and how Mr. Smith's score is given a commendation. In addition, the program terminates by comparing each name read with the character string 'END OF SET'.

```
      PROGRAM SCORES
      CHARACTER NAME*10
      PRINT '(A)','1'     〈Ejects to next page〉
      PRINT '(1X,A,/,T5,A,T20,A)',
     +'RESULTS OF FINAL EXAM','NAME','SCORE'
*
*                          CONTINUE TO READ NAMES UNTIL
*                          THE PHRASE 'END OF SET' IS READ
*
    1     READ(5,'(A10,F4.0)')NAME,SCORE
          PRINT '(T2,A10,T20,F4.0)',NAME,SCORE
          IF(SCORE .EQ. 100)THEN
              PRINT '(A1,T30,A)','+','EXCELLENT'
          END IF
          IF(NAME .EQ. 'END OF SET')THEN
              STOP
          ELSE
              GO TO 1
          END IF
*
      END
```

Input	Output

```
JONES,A.    63.     RESULTS OF FINAL EXAM
ADAMS,J.    71.        NAME              SCORE
SMITH,C.   100.        JONES,A           63.
BROWN,B.    82.        ADAMS,J.          71.
END OF SET             SMITH,C.         100.   EXCELLENT
                       BROWN,B.          82.
                       END OF SET       ****
```

Table 5-1 Vertical spacing control characters.

Character	Effect
Blank	Space down one line then print
0	Space down two lines then print
1	Advance to first line of next page
+	No advance before printing; allows overprinting

5.5.2 What If the Computer Runs Out of Format?

If the number of elements to be printed or read by a READ/WRITE/PRINT statement exceeds the number allotted in the associated FORMAT statement, the computer will always complete the entire command by reusing the same FORMAT statement, each time starting a new line. Thus

```
          WRITE(6,17)A,B,C,D,E,F,G
     17   FORMAT(1X,2F5.1)
```

will result in three lines with two numbers and a fourth with the single value associated with G. After printing A and B, the WRITE statement runs out of format and continues to print the elements in the list until the list is exhausted. Notice in the final line the entire format is only partially used. The situation for READ statements is similar. For example, suppose the following input data file is stored on the disk and named DATA3.

```
                        Input file
        column          1          2
              1234567890.........0
                1.0 2.0 3.0 4.0
                5.0 6.0 7.0 8.0
                9.0 10. 11. 12.
                -1.
```

and is read and printed by the following code.

```
          OPEN(37,FILE = 'DATA3')
          REWIND 37
     1    READ(37,'(3F4.0)')A,B,C,D
          PRINT *,A,B,C,D
          IF(A .NE. -1.)GO TO 1
```

The result will be

```
                                      ⟨The value 4.0 was missed.
1.000  2.000  3.000  5.000            The READ ran out of format
9.000  10.00  11.00  -1.00            and went on to the next line.⟩
```

and the program will fatally terminate by reading the end of the file. The clever use of -1.0 as a flag for the end of the data was missed by the computer by assigning it to D rather than A. Apparently the READ format was intended to be '(4F4.0)'.

If the format specifications themselves contain parentheses, the situation is somewhat more complicated. The rule is

> If the computer runs out of format, it scans the format
> specifications *right to left* and reuses the first paired set of
> parentheses it encounters, or its multiple.

Thus, assuming the variables A to G have been assigned the values 1.0 to 7.0, respectively,

```
      PRINT 77,A,B,C,D,E,F,G
  77  FORMAT(X,'THE RESULTS ARE ',/,X,20(*),/,
    +            2(1X,(2F3.0)))
```

results in

```
          THE RESULTS ARE
          *******************
            1.02.0 3.04.0
            5.06.0 7.0
```

The recycled specification was 2(1X,(2F3.0)).

5.5.3   Additional Features of READ/WRITE Statements

Very frequently a data file will consist of an unknown number of lines and the program will read some data, compute results, return to the READ statement, and repeat the calculation until the data file is exhausted. However, if the READ statement is used beyond the last data line an execution time error is generated. This has been avoided in previous examples by placing a trailer data line at the end of the file and after each READ checking for a known flag (See program SCORES on page 153 and the program on page 154.)

As we have seen, this procedure is not always successful. A preferred option is available in the READ statement.

$$\text{READ(unit, format, ERR} = sl_1, \text{END} = sl_2)$$

The option ERR $= sl_1$ directs the computer to statement number sl_1 if an error was encountered during the read (e.g., a real number with an integer format). The option END $= sl_2$ causes a transfer to statement number sl_2 only if an END OF FILE is encountered. An example follows:

```
      READ(5,11,ERR=100,END=99)X,Y
      READ(*,11,END=99)A,B
```

```
        READ(*,*,END=99)I,J
    11 FORMAT(1X,2F5.0)
        PRINT *,'X= ',X,' Y= ',Y,
                  'A= ',A,' B= ',B,
                  'I= ',I,' J= ',J,
        STOP
    99 PRINT *,'END OF DATA'
        STOP
   100 PRINT *,'I/O ERROR'
        STOP
        END
```

The ERR = sl option may also be included in WRITE statements.

PROBLEMS

1. Formatted READ and WRITE
   a. Give two methods of specifying the input device as INPUT (i.e., default to the terminal for data input) in a READ statement.
   b. Give two methods of testing for the end of a data file.
   c. Using only one line of Fortran, print e^π with an F9.6 format.
   d. If your program has a FORMAT statement that is never used, will the computer detect this and inform you of a possible error? (Try it and see.)
   e. Which of the following format specifications can be repeated by preceding by a multiplying integer? (F,T,E,/,I,X,A,')
   f. Give an example of when replacing the word READ by WRITE in a correct Fortran statement will result in a compilation time error.
   g. Can you GO TO a FORMAT statement?
2. Identify the errors, if any, in the following:
   a. READ(*)X,Y   d. READ(5,5)FIVE
   b. PRINT *,X,Y,Z   e. READ *,X + Y
   c. WRITE (6,*)X + Y   f. READ(5,6),X,Y
3. Locate any errors in the following. If none write OK.
   a.   READ(5,1)X,IX,Y,IY   d.   READ(5,4)X,Y,IX,IY
      1 FORMAT(2X,F6.6,I5,2F4.1)   4 FORMAT(150X,2F9.3,2I10)
   b.   READ(*,2)X,Y,IX,IY   e.   READ(5,5)X,Y,Z,W
      2 FORMAT(2X,2(F5.1,1X,I5))   5 FORMAT(1X,F3.0,4(1X,F7.1))
   c.   READ(*,3)X,Y,Z,W   f.   READ(5,6)X,Y,IX,IY
      3 FORMAT(2X,3F7.1)   6 FORMAT(2E9.6,2I9)
4. Identify the errors, if any, in the following FORMAT statements assuming an appropriate READ statement of the form READ(*,10)(list of variables).

a. `10 FORMAT(I1,F3.0,I1,F3.0)`
b. `10 FORMAT(2X,I1,2X,F3.0,2X,F3.0,2X,I1)`
c. `10 FORMAT(1X,2(I2,F3.1,I1))`
d. `10 FORMAT(2X,I6,F6.7,I2,F3.2)`
e. `10 FORMAT (5X,I10,F7.2E+02,I4,F3.0)`
f. `10 FORMAT(T5,I5,E8.1,I4,E4.0)`
g. `10 FORMAT(1X,'I=',I2,'X=',F3.0,'J=',I4,'Y=',F6.2)`
h. `10 FORMAT(T20,I5,TR10,I5,TL10,F5.1,TR10,F5.1)`
i. `10 FORMAT(//,2(I5,2/,F4.2))`
j. `10 FORMAT(1X,(I1,F3.1,I1))`

5. Identify the errors, if any, in the following formatted WRITE statements and their associated FORMAT statements.

a.   `WRITE(*,10)X,Y,X+Y`
    `10 FORMAT(F5.0)`
b.   `WRITE(6,11)X,X**2,X**3,EXP(X)`
    `11 FORMAT(4E9.1)`
c.   `WRITE(6,12)X,I,Y,J`
    `12 FORMAT(1X,2('R=',E8.1,'K=',I10))`
d.   `WRITE(*,13)A,B,C,D,E`
    `13 FORMAT(5X,F5.1,TL5,F5.1)`
e.   `WRITE(*,15) 'A=',A,'B=',B`
    `15 FORMAT(5X,A2,F3.1,/,5X,A,F3.1)`
f.   `WRITE(6,16)A,B,IA,IB`
    `16 FORMAT('0',F3.1,'+',F3.1,/,'+',2I4)`
g.   `WRITE(6,17)A,'B=',B`
    `17 FORMAT(5X,'A=',A2,2F5.0)`
h.   `PRINT 18,A,B`
    `18 FORMAT('1','A=',F5.0,'B=',F5.0,'C=',F5.0)`

6. Using the assignments X = 2., Y = 3., Z = 1./3., I = 2, J = 3, K = 4, determine the output of the following WRITE statements. Indicate blanks as ƀ.

a.   `WRITE(6,1)X,Y,Z`
    `1 FORMAT(2X,F3.1,2X,F2.0,2X,F7.4)`
b.   `WRITE(6,2)X,Y,Z`
    `2 FORMAT(/,2X,F7.5,2(/,1X,F6.3,/))`
c.   `WRITE(*,3)X,I,K,J,Y,Z`
    `3 FORMAT(5X,F2.0,'*',I2,'=',I2,/,5X,I1,'/',F3.1,'=',F7.6)`
d.   `WRITE(*,4)Y*Z,Y,J,J,J,J`
    `4 FORMAT(/,4X,F9.6,'/',F2.0,'= ',5I1)`
e.   `WRITE(*,5)K,J,I`
    `5 FORMAT(T12,I1,TL2,I1,TL3,I1)`
f.   `WRITE(*,6)I,J,K`
    `6 FORMAT(T2,I1,T5,I1,T7,I1)`
g.   `WRITE(*,7)I,J,K`
    `7 FORMAT(T2,I1,TR5,I1,TR7,I1)`
h.   `WRITE(*,8)I,J,K`
    `8 FORMAT(1X,I1)`

i.
```
      WRITE(*,9)X,Y,Z
    9 FORMAT(2X,E7.0,1X,E9.2,1X,E12.5)
```
7. What is the output from the following, assuming the assignments, X = 1.0, Y = 2.0, Z = 1./3., I = 2, J = 3. Indicate blanks as ƀ.
a.
```
      PRINT '(F4.0,2X,F4.2,F2.1,2I5)',X,Y,Z,I,J
```
b.
```
      WRITE(*,10)X,Y,I,J
   10 FORMAT(T5,2E9.1,/,2I1)
```
c.
```
      WRITE(*,11)X,I,Y,J,Z
   11 FORMAT(2X,E9.1,I5)
```
d.
```
      WRITE(*,'(F5.1,A4)')X,' = X'
```
e.
```
      WRITE(*,12)X,Y,Z
   12 FORMAT(/,F5.0)
```
f.
```
      WRITE(6,13)I,X
   13 FORMAT(1X,F5.0,I5)
```
g.
```
      WRITE(*,'(F4.1,A3,I4)')X,'***',I,Y,'---',J
```
h.
```
      WRITE(*,14)Z,1./Z,1./Z*Z-1.
   14 FORMAT(5X,3E10.3)
```
8. Determine the output from the following. Use the assignments: I = 2, J = 3, K = 4, X = 4., Y = 5., Z = 1./6.
a.
```
   WRITE(*,1)
 1 FORMAT(5X,3(4('*'),2X))
```
b.
```
   WRITE(*,2)I,J,K
 2 FORMAT(2X,'I=',I1,/,2X,'AND J=',I1,/,2X,'AND K=')
```
c.
```
   WRITE(*,3)I,J,Z
 3 FORMAT(/,2X,'1/(',I1,'*',I1,') =',F9.6)
```
d.
```
   WRITE(*,4)X,Y,X+Y,1./Z
 4 FORMAT(1X,'X=',F4.1,'Y=',F4.1,/,
  +       1X,'X+Y=',F4.1,'1/Z=',F4.1)
```
e.
```
   WRITE(*,'(1X,3F3.0,3I2)')X,Y,Z,I,J,K
```
f.
```
   WRITE(*,'(1X,A,I1,A,I1)')'I = ',I,'AND K = ',K
```
g.
```
   WRITE(*,'(1X,F5.1,/,1X,I2)')X,I,Y,J,Z,K
```
h.
```
   WRITE(*,'(A)')'CANDY IS DANDY BUT LIQUOR IS . . . '
```
i.
```
   WRITE(*,5)X,Y,K,X*Y,X*Y*K
 5 FORMAT(///,5X,'DIMENSIONS OF ROOM',//,5X,
  +       'LENGTH= ',F5.1,2X,'WIDTH= ',F5.1,'HEIGHT= ',I3,//,
  +       3X,'SURFACE AREA = ',F12.7,//,9X,
  +          'VOLUME = ',E10.2)
```
j.
```
   WRITE(*,6)
 6 FORMAT(30X,70('X')/6(2X,'*',2X),3(T31,70('X')/),
  +       3X,5(2X,'*',2X)///6(2X,'*',2X)//T31,70('X')/,
  +       3X,5(2X,'*',2X),3(T31,70('X')/),6(2X,'*',2X)///,
  +       3X,5(2X'*',2X)//,
  +       30X,70('X')/6(2X,'*',2X),3(T31,70('X')/),
  +       3X,5(2X,'*',2X)///6(2X,'*',2X)//,
  +       3(4(100('X')/)//////),4(100('X')/))
```
9. Write a single line of Fortran that will:
   a. Print the variables X, Y, X + Y on separate lines.

b. Print 'X = ',X and 'Y = ',Y on separate lines.

10. Write a program to compute the height, $y = -9.8t^2 + 5t$ (m), and the velocity, $v = -9.8t + 5$ (m/sec), for a falling object for time $t = 0$ to $t = 10$ sec in steps of 0.2 sec. The results should be displayed in a neat table with column headings, including units. The numerical results should be centered in the columns and a counter printed for each time value.

11. Write a program to read and print the name of a metal and its melting temperature in the form of a table with column headings, including units. In addition, if the melting temperature is greater than 1400° C, print TOO HIGH on the same line, if less than 600° C, print TOO LOW on the same line. Use the carriage-control characters.

12. Write a program to read a data file stored on disk and named CLASS which has a student's last name (A10), gender (M or F, A1), hometown (A10), and class (I1) on each line. The program is to count the number of:

a. Male juniors and seniors from Boston

b. All females from Cincinnati

c. Freshmen from Chicago

In addition, the program should print the names of all students from Detroit, with their name preceded by either Mr. or Miss.

13. Write a program to print, with appropriate headings, the integers from 1 to 100. If the number is a perfect square or perfect cube, print on the same line a statement like

```
27    IS THE CUBE OF    3
```

Use the carriage-control character +.

14. Write a program to read and print a Fortran program devoid of all comment lines. The program is to be read from a data file.

15. Design format statements to handle the following:

a. Print a "block" letter; for example,

```
MM          MM
MMM         MMM
MM M      M MM
MM   M   M   MM
MM    M M    MM
MMMM    M    MMMM
```

b. With one format, print a table heading for (i, x_i, y_i) plus positions for five entrees in the table.

c. Ask the terminal user if he or she wishes to compute the SUM. If the answer is YES, instruct the user to enter ten values, one at a time, in a specified format. The program should then add the stored numbers and use a single format to print the ten numbers (F9.4) and their SUM (E12.4) in the form

```
                    ENTREES
                         XX.XXXX
                        XXX.XXXX
                           . . . . .
                          X.XXXX
                        - - - - - - - -
          TOTAL  =        X.XXXXE+XX
```

d. Read the time of day expressed as the total number of minutes past midnight and print the time in the form XX:XXAM (or PM).

PROGRAMMING ASSIGNMENT II

II.1 SAMPLE PROGRAM

Chemical Engineering

Chemical engineering is the application of the knowledge or techniques of science, particularly chemistry, to industry. The chemical engineer is responsible for the design and operation of large-scale manufacturing plants for all those materials that undergo chemical changes in their production. These include all the new and improved products that have so profoundly affected society, such as petrochemicals, rubbers and polymers, new metal alloys, industrial and fine chemicals, foods, paints, detergents, cements, pesticides, industrial gases, and medicines. In addition, chemical engineers play important roles in pollution abatement and the management of existing energy resources.

The field has grown to be so broad, it is difficult to classify the activities of a chemical engineer. A rough subdivision is into engineers concerned primarily with large-scale production systems or chemical processing or with smaller-scale or molecular systems.

Chemical Processing Concerns all aspects of the design and operation of large chemical processing plants. Example are

Petrochemicals: The distillation and refinement of fuels such as gasoline, synthetic natural gas, coal liquefaction and gasification, and the production of the infinite variety of products from petroleum from cosmetics to pharmaceuticals.

Synthetic Materials: The process of polymerization, a joining of simpler molecules into large complex molecules, is responsible for a great many modern materials such as nylon, silicon, synthetic rubbers, polystyrene, and a great variety of plastics and synthetic fibers.

Food and Biochemical Engineering: The manufacture of packaged food, improved food additives, sterilization, and the utilization of industrial bacteria, fungi, and yeasts in processes like fermentation.

Unit Operations: The analysis of the transport of heat or fluid such as the pumping of chemicals through a pipeline or the transfer of heat between substances. Also, the effect of heat transfer on chemical reactions such as oxidation, chlorination, etc.

Cryogenic Engineering: The design of plants operating at temperatures near absolute zero.

Electrochemical Engineering: The use of electricity to alter chemical reactions such as electroplating or the design of batteries or energy cells.

Pollution Control: A rapidly growing field which seeks to monitor and reduce the harmful effects of chemical processing on the environment. Topics of concern are waste water control, air pollution abatement, and the economics of pollution control.

Molecular Systems   Application of laboratory techniques to large-scale processes. Examples are

Biochemical Engineering: Application of enzymes, bacteria, etc. to improve large-scale chemical processes.

Polymer Synthesis: Molecular basis for polymer properties and the chemical synthesis of new polymers adapted for large-scale production.

Research and development in all areas of chemical processing.

Preparation for a career in chemical engineering requires a thorough background in physics, chemistry, and mathematics, and a knowledge of thermodynamics, and physical, analytic, and organic chemistry. Though extensively trained in chemistry, chemical engineers differ from chemists in that their main concern is the adaptation of laboratory techniques to large-scale manufacturing plants.

Sample Program: Gas Separation

A very important problem in chemical engineering is the separation of a gas mixture into its constituents by means of selective absorption of gases in liquids based on differences in absorption rates of the gases. For example, it is desired to separate a gas containing (percentages by moles) hydrogen (65%), methane (18%), ethane (14%), and propane (3%) by bringing the gas into contact with an oil. After each pass the gas is assumed to be in equilibrium with the oil. Each pass is called a *plate* and a series of plates will constitute a packed tower. The equation defining the properties of a set of plates is

$$E = 1 - \frac{A - 1}{A^{n+1} - 1} \qquad \text{(II.1)}$$

where E = Desired absorption efficiency for a particular chemical
A = Absorption factor for a particular chemical (see below)
n = The number of plates

Of course, the liquid will absorb only as much of each gas required to reach a phase equilibrium, which depends upon a variety of thermodynamic properties. An empirical expression for the absorption factor is

$$A = \frac{1}{k}\frac{L}{G} \qquad \text{(II.2)}$$

where L = mole/sec of flowing liquid
G = mole/sec of flowing gas
k = experimentally determined equilibrium vaporization constant which is equal to the ratio of the equilibrium concentrations of the particular chemicals in the supply gas to that of the liquid and is dependent on pressure, temperature, and the types of gas and liquid.

Since A is not really constant, an effective value is used.

$$A = A_e = [A_b(A_t + 1) + \tfrac{1}{4}]^{1/2} - \tfrac{1}{2} \qquad \text{(II.3)}$$

where $A_b(A_t)$ is the absorption constant appropriate for conditions at the bottom (top) of the process.

Problem

For the given gas-oil combination, it is desired to have an absorption efficiency E for ethane. If the following conditions hold

Constituent	k	
	Bottom	Top
Ethane	1.470	1.439
Methane	9.500	8.000
Propane	0.510	0.480
Gas Flow	55.00	52.00
Oil Flow	95.00	98.00

1. Use the bisection algorithm to solve Equation (II.1) for n, the number of plates required for $E = 0.9, 0.92, \ldots, 0.98$. The number of plates should then be rounded to an integer.
2. For each value of n (integer), determined above, print the resulting absorption efficiencies for methane and propane.

Sample Program Solution

The program to solve this problem is given in Figure II-1 and the output of the program is given in Figure II-2.

Figure II-1 Fortran code for sample program two.

```
      PROGRAM DISTIL
*--
*-- THIS PROBLEM DETERMINES THE NUMBER OF THEORETICAL ABSORPTION
*-- PLATES REQUIRED TO ACHIEVE A GIVEN ABSORPTION EFFICIENCY FOR
*-- ETHANE GAS FLOWING THROUGH OIL. THE PROBLEM IS SOLVED FOR
*-- EFFICIENCIES E = 0.90 THROUGH 0.98 IN STEPS OF 0.02. ONCE
*-- THE NUMBER OF PLATES IS DETERMINED, THE ABSORPTION EFFICIENCY
*-- FOR PROPANE AND METHANE IS COMPUTED. AN EFFECTIVE ABSORPTION
*-- FACTOR A IS COMPUTED FOR EACH GAS FROM THE PROPERTIES AT THE
*-- TOP AND BOTTOM OF THE COLUMN.
*---------------------------------------------------------------
* VARIABLES
*
      REAL EETH,EMTH,EPRP,KETHT,KETHB,KMTHT,KMTHB,KPRPT,KPRPB,
     +             AETHT,AETHB,AMTHT,AMTHB,APRPT,APRPB,
     +             GFLOWT,GFLOWB,LFLOWT,LFLOWB,
     +             N,A,N1,N2,N3,F1,F2,F3,AT,AB,E
*
      INTEGER I,PLATES
*                   IN THE VARIABLE LIST
*                    ETH => ETHANE, MTH => METHANE, PRP => PROPANE
*                    LAST LETTER T => TOP, B => BOTTOM
*
*                   E***  --  ABSORPTION EFFICIENCY
*                   K**** --  EXPERIMENTAL VAPORIZATION CONST.
*                   A**** --  ABSORPTION FACTOR
*                   GFLOW*--  GAS FLOW RATE
*                   LFLOW*--  OIL (LIQUID) FLOW RATE
*                   N     --  COMPUTED NUMBER OF PLATES
*                   PLATES--  NUMBER OF PLATES (INTEGER)
*---------------------------------------------------------------
* STATEMENT FUNCTION FOR EFFECTIVE ABSORPTION FACTOR
*
      A(AT,AB) = SQRT(AB * (AT + 1.) + 0.25) - .5
*---------------------------------------------------------------
* STATEMENT FUNCTION FOR EQ. 1.
*
      F(N,E,AT,AB) = E - 1. + (A(AT,AB) - 1.)/(A(AT,AB)**N - 1.)
*---------------------------------------------------------------
* INITIALIZATION
```

```
*
          OPEN(9,FILE='GASDAT')
          REWIND 9
          READ(9,10) GFLOWT,GFLOWB,LFLOWT,LFLOWB,
         +            KETHT,KETHB,KMTHT,KMTHB,KPRPT,KPRPB
*
          AETHT = LFLOWT/KETHT/GFLOWT
          AETHB = LFLOWB/KETHB/GFLOWB
          X1 = 2.0
          X3 = 20.0
          EPS = 1.E-3
          IMAX = 25
          DO = (X3 - X1)
*
*                    PRINT OUT INPUT PARAMETERS AND TABLE HEADINGS
*
          WRITE(*,11)X1,X3,EPS,IMAX
          WRITE(*,12)GFLOWT,LFLOWT,KETHT,KMTHT,KPRPT,
         +            GFLOWB,LFLOWB,KETHB,KMTHB,KPRPB
          WRITE(*,13)
*
*                    START OF THE E - LOOP
*
          EETH = 0.9
*          -----------------------------------------------------------
   1 N1 = X1
          N3 = X3
          F1 = F(N1,EETH,AETHT,AETHB)
          F3 = F(N3,EETH,AETHT,AETHB)
          D = 1.
*                    -----------------------------------------------------
*                    THE BISECTION CODE TO FIND THE ROOT OF F(N)
*                    IS THE SAME AS FIG. 4.9
*
          IF(F1*F3 .GT. 0.)THEN
              WRITE(*,20)N1,N2
              STOP
          END IF
*
   2 N2 = (N1 + N3)/2.
          F2 = F(N2,EETH,AETHT,AETHB)
          IF(D .LT. EPS)THEN
              GO TO 3
*
*                    STMT 3 IS THE SUCCESS PATH
*
*         ELSE IF(I.GT. IMAX)THEN
              WRITE(*,*)'--ERROR-- EXCESSIVE ITERATIONS = ',I
              STOP
          END IF
*
          IF(F1*F2 .LT. 0.)THEN
              D = (N3 - N2)/DO
              F3 = F2
              N3 = N2
          ELSE IF(F2*F3 .LT. 0.)THEN
```

Continued

```
                  D = (N2 - N1)/D0
                  N1 = N2
                  F1 = F2
              ELSE IF(F2 .EQ. 0.)THEN
                  GO TO 3
              ELSE
                  WRITE(*,22)I,N1,N3
                  STOP
              END IF
*
          I = I + 1
          GO TO 2
*                     -----------------------------------------------------------
*
*
*                  SUCCESS PATH - PLATES IS THE NEAREST INTEGER
*                                 TO THE ROOT N2
*
      3 PLATES = N2
        II = N2 - 0.5
        IF(II .EQ. PLATES)PLATES = PLATES + 1
*
*                  PRINT THE RESULTS FOR ETHANE
*
        WRITE(*,23)EETH,PLATES
*
*                  COMPUTE AND PRINT THE RESULTS FOR METHANE AND
*                  PROPANE.
*
* METHANE------------------------------
        AMTHT = LFLOWT/KMTHT/GFLOWT
        AMTHB = LFLOWB/KMTHB/GFLOWB
        AMTH = A(AMTHT,AMTHB)
        EMTH = 1. - (AMTH - 1.)/(AMTH**PLATES - 1.)
        WRITE(*,24)EMTH
*
* PROPANE------------------------------
        APRPT = LFLOWT/KPRPT/GFLOWT
        APRPB = LFLOWB/KPRPB/GFLOWB
        APRP = A(APRPT,APRPB)
        EPRP = 1. - (APRP - 1.)/(APRP**PLATES - 1.)
        WRITE(*,25)EPRP
*
*                  INCREMENT E AND REPEAT
*
        EETH = EETH + 0.02
        IF(EETH .LE. 0.98)GO TO 1
        STOP
*-----------------------------------------------------------------
* FORMATS
*
     10 FORMAT(10F5.2)
     11 FORMAT(///,10X,'THE BISECTION ALGORITHM PARAMETERS ARE',//,
       +          10X,'INTERVAL: FROM ',F6.2,' TO ',F6.2,//,
       +          10X,'EPS = ',E7.1,' IMAX = ',I4)
*
     12 FORMAT(///,5X,'INPUT PARAMETERS',//,43X,'ABSORPTION',//,
```

Continued

```
    +      10X,'    GAS        OIL                  CONSTANTS',/,
    +      10X,'    FLOW       FLOW      ETHANE    METHANE     PROPANE'
    +      ,/,2X,'TOP',5X,5(2X,F7,3,1X)
    +      ,/,2X,'BOTTOM',2X,5(2X,F7,3,1X))
*
   13 FORMAT(///,20X,'COMPUTER RESULTS',//,
    + T10,'ABSORPTION',T25,'REQUIRED',T45,'ABSORPTION',/,
    + T10,'EFFICIENCY',T25,'NUMBER',  T45,'EFFICIENCY',/,
    + T10,' (INPUT) ',T25,'  OF  ',  T45,'(COMPUTED)',/,
    + T10,'  ETHANE',T25,'PLATES',T40,'  METHANE    PROPANE',//,
    + T10,50(1H-))
*
   20 FORMAT(2X,'--ERROR-- NO ROOT IN INTERVAL ',2F8,4)
   22 FORMAT(2X,'--ERROR-- AFTER ',I4,' ITERATIONS',/,15X,
    +        'NO ROOT IN SUB-INTERVAL ',2F8,4)
   23 FORMAT(11X,F8,6,T26,I3)
   24 FORMAT(1H ,T40,F8,6)
   25 FORMAT(1H ,T52,E8,2)
*
      END
```

Figure II-2 Output from the Sample Program

```
      THE BISECTION ALGORITHM PARAMETERS ARE

      INTERVAL: FROM   2.00 TO  20.00
      EPS =   .1E-02 IMAX =    25


 INPUT PARAMETERS
                                       ABSORPTION
           GAS        OIL              CONSTANTS
           FLOW       FLOW     ETHANE   METHANE    PROPANE
 TOP       52.000     98.000    1.439    8.000      .480
 BOTTOM    55.000     95.000    1.470    9.500      .510



                      COMPUTER RESULTS

          ABSORPTION        REQUIRED         ABSORPTION
          EFFICIENCY        NUMBER           EFFICIENCY
           (INPUT)            OF             (COMPUTED)
           ETHANE           PLATES        METHANE   PROPANE
          ------------------------------------------------
            .900000            6            .188912   .28E-13
            .920000            7            .188942   .28E-13
            .940000            8            .188947   .28E-13
            .960000            9            .188948   .28E-13
            .980000           12            .188949   .28E-13
```

II.2 PROGRAMMING PROBLEMS

Metallurgical Engineering and Materials Science

Advances in many areas of engineering in the twentieth century have been made possible to a large extent by discoveries of new materials and a better understanding of properties of existing materials. Knowledge of the physical and chemical principles determining the electrical properties of exotic materials called semiconductors have resulted in the fantastic progress in the field of solid-state devices, from the transistor to the integrated circuit chip to large computers. Better understanding of the origins of metallic properties such as hardness, strength, ductility, corrosiveness, and others have led to improved design of automobiles, aircraft, spacecraft, and all types of machinery. The field is basically subdivided into metals and nonmetals, although there is often considerable overlap of interests and activities.

Materials Science: The behavior and properties of materials, both metals and nonmetals, from both microscopic and macroscopic perspectives.

Ceramics: Noncrystalline materials, such as glass, that are nonmetallic and which require high temperatures in their processing. Ceramics can be made brittle or flexible, hard or soft, stronger than steel, and to have a variety of chemical properties.

Polymers: Structural and physical properties of organic, inorganic, and natural polymers that are useful in engineering applications.

Materials Fabrication, Processing, and Treatment: All aspects of the manufacture of ceramics, metals, and polymer synthesis, from the growth of crystals and fibers to metal forming.

Corrosion: Reaction mechanism and thermodynamics of corrosion of metals in the atmosphere or submerged under water or chemicals whether standing or under stress.

Stress-Strain, Fatigue-Fracture of Engineering Materials: Physical properties governing the deformation and fracture of materials, their improvement and use in construction and design.

Metallurgical Engineering: The branch of engineering that is responsible for the production of metals and metal alloys, from the discovery of ore deposits to the fabrication of the refined metal into useful products. Metallurgical engineers are important in every step in the production of metal from metal ore.

Mining Engineering: Usually a separate branch of engineering; however, the concerns of the mining engineer and the metallurgist frequently overlap in the processes of extraction of metals from metal ores and the refinement into usable products. Extraction metallurgy makes use of physical and chemical reactions to optimize metal production.

Metals Fabrication: Metal forming into products such as cans, wires, and tubes, casting and joining of metals—for example, by welding.

Physical Metallurgy: Analysis of stress-strain, fatigue-fracture characteristics of metals and metal alloys to prevent engineering component failures.

Programming Problem A: Carburization

Introduction

To improve the hardness characteristics of steel, carbon is added to the steel in a controlled manner by a process called *carburizing,* which involves the gradual diffusing into the steel of atoms of carbon applied at the metal surface. For example, if a rod of pure iron is welded to a similar rod containing 1% carbon, the carbon content of the pure end is found to vary with time and position down the rod in a manner indicated in Figure II-3. At $t = 0$ the concentration of carbon in the right half is zero, while at some later time it is found that the concentration in the enriched half has been depleted near the boundary and carbon atoms have migrated into the pure end. After an infinite amount of time the distribution of carbon will be uniform throughout. The rate of the transport of the carbon atoms at a point x in the bar is found to be proportional to the negative of the slope of the concentration curve at that point, zero at the extreme ends, and large positive near the middle.

Figure II-3   Diffusion of carbon between rods of differing composition.

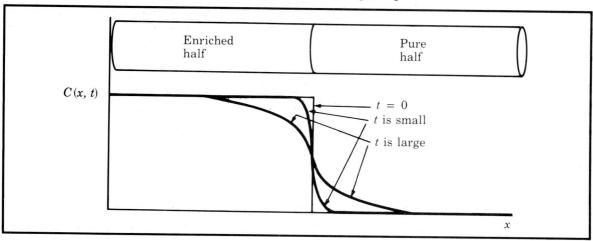

(II.4)
$$F = -D \frac{dC(x,t)}{dx}$$

where F is the volume concentration of atoms migrating per second, $C(x,t)$ is the concentration of carbon atoms at position x and time t, and the proportionality constant D is called the diffusion constant. It can be shown that combining this equation with the constraint that the total number of carbon atoms remain constant leads to the following expression for $C(x,t)$:

(II.5)
$$C(x,t) = \frac{C_0}{2}\left[1 - \frac{2}{\sqrt{\pi}} \int_0^{x/2Dt} e^{-y^2} dy \right]$$

where C_0 is the initial concentration at $x = 0$ and the integral is the area under the curve e^{-y^2} from zero to $y = x/(2Dt)$. This integral is called the error function and is defined as

(II.6)
$$\text{Erf}(\alpha) = \frac{2}{\sqrt{\pi}} \int_0^{\alpha} e^{-y^2} dy$$

This integral cannot be evaluated in terms of elementary functions but occurs so frequently in engineering analysis that it has been extensively tabulated and even included as an intrinsic function in Fortran on some systems. If your local computer supports this function, the Fortran to compute Erf(3.6) would simply be

```
A=ERF(3.6)
```

The diffusion process is found to be extremely temperature dependent and this can be taken into account in the diffusion constant by expressing it as

(II.7)
$$D = D(T) = D_0 e^{-q/RT}$$

where D_0 is constant, q is called the activation energy and is constant, R is the ideal gas constant (8.31 J/molK). The units of D are m^2/sec. Thus once the constants D_0, R, q, C_0, and the temperature T have been specified, the concentration $C(x,t)$ can be determined for any value of x or t.

Problem Specifics

It is desired to allow the diffusion to take place until the average concentration in the right half reaches C_r, then disconnect the two halves and heat the right half until the concentration smooths out to a uniform concentration which would equal C_r.

The average concentration across the right half could be expressed as

$$C_{avg}(t) = [C(0,t) + C(\Delta x, t) + C(2\Delta x, t) + \cdots + C(L,t)]\frac{1}{n+1} \quad \textbf{(II.8)}$$

$$= \frac{1}{n+1}\sum_{i=0}^{n} C(i\Delta x, t)$$

where $\Delta x = L/n$.

Write a program with statement functions for Equations (II.5) and (II.7) that reads the parameters in Table II-2. The program should:

1. Have statement functions for Equations (II.5), (II.7), and (II.8)

$$D(TEMP) = \ldots$$

$$C(X, T) = \ldots$$

$$F(T) = C_{avg}(t) - C_r$$

where $C_{avg}(t)$ is computed using Equation (II.8) with $n = 5$.

2. Define the initial search interval to be 10 to 50 days (these must then be converted to seconds in the program) and use the bisection method to find the root of $F(t)$. Use IMAX = 30, EPS = 1.E−4 in the bisection algorithm. Print all parameters and the computed diffusion time with appropriate labels.

Table II-2 Input parameters for the carburizing problem.

C_0	= 0.25	(%)	= Initial end concentration
D_0	= 2.40×10^{-5}	m³/sec	= Diffusion parameter
q	= 0.74×10^5	J	= Activation energy
T	= 1300	K	= Temperature
L	= 0.2	m	= Length of bar
C_r	= 0.030	(%)	= Desired average final concentration

Electrical Engineering

Electrical engineering deals with the application of the principles of electricity and electromagnetism to the manufacture of all forms of machines and devices that either make use of electricity or produce electrical energy. The field, the largest of all engineering fields, has evolved from its beginning in the mid-1800s with a concern for the generation of electrical energy, to its present very broad boundaries encompassing solid-state devices such as transistors, communication, and computers, and robotics.

Power: The generation of electrical energy in large fossil-fuel, nuclear, solar, or hydroelectric plants, or the efficient utilization of electrical energy by means of motors or illumination devices. Also important are the transmission and distribution of electrical energy through overhead lines, microwaves, light pipes, and superconducting lines.

Solid-State Electronics: In conjunction with modern physics and material science, exotic semiconducting materials are being developed and used to construct microcircuitry which is used in monitoring and controlling the operations of all manner of present-day devices from video games to assembly-line robots. The improved reliability, rapidly shrinking size, and reduced power requirements of modern miniaturized electrical components have created limitless opportunities for applications.

Communications: Design and construction of equipment used in transmission of information via electricity or electromagnetic waves (radio, light, microwaves, etc.). The use of the laser for communication is a topic of modern concern, while antenna characteristics and radar are somewhat older.

Computers and Robotics: While electronics deals with the principles associated with the functions of miniaturized components, the computer engineer is concerned with designing the complex circuitry that interweaves the components into a computer. Microprocessors, or small computers, are designed to constantly monitor and control the operations of a particular piece of equipment such as a lathe or an autopilot.

Programming Problem B: Semiconductor Diode

In a simple resistor, the current i that flows through the resistor is to a good approximation proportional to the voltage V that is applied to the resistor. This is represented schematically as

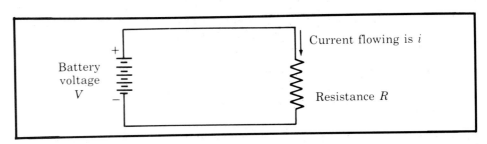

$$i = \left(\frac{1}{R}\right)V \qquad \text{Ohm's law}$$

The proportionality constant is $(1/R)$, where R is the resistance (in ohms) of the resistor. The units of current are amperes and of voltage are volts. The current flows from the positive pole of the battery through the resistor and returns to the negative pole. Current is conserved, i.e., the current leaving the battery is equal to that returning.

The relation between current and voltage is not nearly so simple in solid-state devices. In a semiconductor diode the relationship is

$$i = I_s(e^{\lambda V} - 1) \tag{II.9}$$

where I_s = reverse saturation current (amperes)
λ = diode characteristic (volts^{-1})

Both of these quantities vary from one diode to the next. Note that the diode has the property that current flows readily in only one direction as is shown in Figure II-4.

Problem Specifics

For the combination of diodes in Figure II-5 the following equations apply:

$$i = i_1 + i_2 \tag{II.10}$$
$$i_1 = I_{s1}(e^{\lambda_1 V} - 1) \tag{II.11}$$
$$i_2 = I_{s2}(e^{-\lambda_2 V} - 1) \tag{II.12}$$

Thus, in this circuit the relationship between current and voltage is

$$i = I_{s1}(e^{\lambda_1 V} - 1) + I_{s2}(e^{-\lambda_2 V} - 1) \tag{II.13}$$

1. Write a program to read in the two sets of diode parameters and a desired current I_0 and print with appropriate labels.

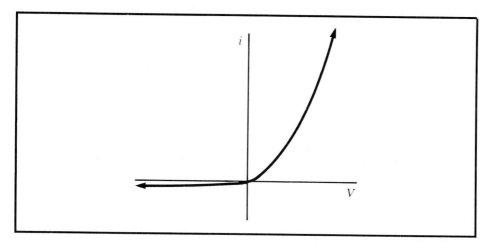

Figure II-4
Current vs. voltage for a typical diode.

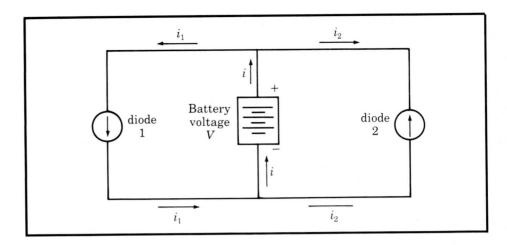

Figure II-5 A circuit diagram for a simple two-diode circuit.

2. For each value of current $i = 0.1I_0, 0.2I_0, \ldots, I_0$ determine the necessary applied voltage V by using the bisection algorithm. For *each* value of the current i, you must first determine the initial search interval before you start the bisection code. Do this by evaluating the statement function based upon Equation (II.13) at $V = 0$ and then at steps of size $\Delta V = 0.01$ until the function changes sign. Use this last interval as the initial search interval.

3. Print the results in the form of a table for each set of parameters (see Table II-3) and plot i vs. V on a piece of graph paper.

Table II-3 Input parameters for diode problem.

Set	I_{s1}	I_{s2}	λ_1	λ_2	I_0
1	0.01	0.10	38.10	41.00	0.60
2	0.03	0.05	40.00	40.00	0.30

Programming Problem C: Coexistence of Liquids and Gases

Introduction

The chemical engineer deals continually with chemical and physical interactions between gases and liquids, and it is essential that he or she have some form of approximate mathematical description of the properties of a substance as it undergoes a transition from gas to liquid phases and back. In elementary chemistry you are introduced to the ideal gas equation of state, which for 1 mole of gas may be written

(II.14)
$$P = \frac{RT}{V}$$

where P = pressure (n/m²)
V = volume of 1 mole (m³)
T = temperature (K)
R = ideal gas constant = 8.317 J/mole K

This equation is adequate for low pressures and high temperatures where the liquid state is not present. In fact the ideal gas law assumes that the substance remains a gas even down to a temperature of absolute zero. Over the years there have been hundreds of suggestions as to how to modify the ideal gas equation to incorporate the possibility of a gas condensing into a liquid. One of the earliest and still one of the best is the Van der Waal's equation of state for an imperfect gas, which may be written in a simplified form as

$$p = \frac{8t/3}{(v - \frac{1}{3})} - \frac{3}{v^2} = 0 \tag{II.15}$$

where p, v, t are scaled pressure, volume, and temperature; i.e.,

$$p = \frac{P}{P_c} \qquad v = \frac{V}{V_c} \qquad t = \frac{T}{T_c}$$

and P_c, V_c, T_c are the values of the pressure, volume, and temperature at the critical point—i.e., the unique value of P, V, and T at which equal masses of the vapor phase and the liquid phase have the same density. These critical point values are extensively tabulated for most substances. The Van der Waal's equation of state is sketched for three temperatures in Figure II-6. As

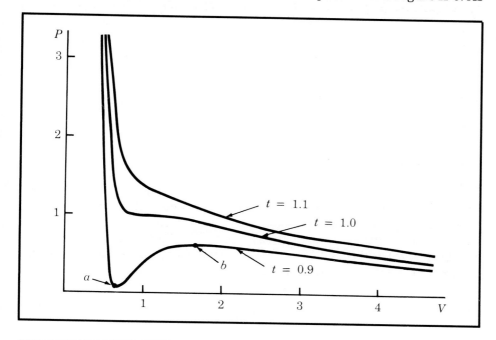

Figure II-6 Plot of Van der Waal's equation of state.

the temperature is reduced below the critical point temperature ($t = T/T_c < 1$), the gradual development of a hill and valley in the pv curve will be interpreted as a transition from gas to liquid. There is, however, a difficulty: the slope of the curve from point a to point b on the graph is positive,

$$\frac{\Delta p}{\Delta v} > 0 \qquad \text{between points } a \text{ and } b$$

Thus if the pressure is *increased*, $p \rightarrow p + \Delta p$, the volume is predicted to *increase*, $v \rightarrow v + \Delta v$. This is clearly unphysical and must be corrected. If p_a and p_b are the pressures at the points a and b, respectively, the procedure is to replace the unphysical part of the curve (where the slope is positive) with a horizontal straight line as shown in Figure II-7. Along this line the substance can change its volume with the pressure remaining constant by changing from gas to liquid or liquid to gas. The straight line is chosen in such a way that the area under the line is equal to the area under the curve it replaces, namely $\int p \, dv$. That is, in Figure II-7 the area labeled I below the line is equal to the area above the line, II. This is a rather complicated condition to satisfy, so, for now, we will simply estimate the position of the line as follows: The points a and b on the Van der Waal's curve which correspond to a local minimum and maximum of the function are determined by a procedure explained below. The line is then drawn through the point c, which is specified by assuming that

Figure II-7 Coexistence of liquid-gas phases on a Van der Waal's plot.

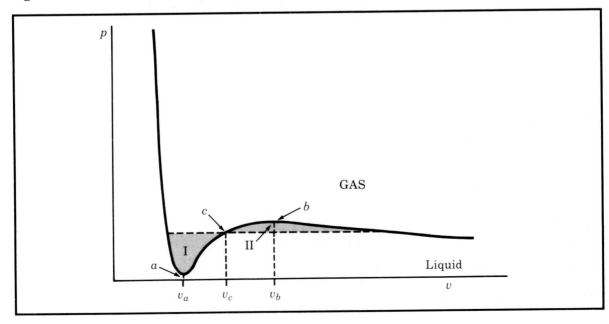

$$v_c = \tfrac{1}{2}(v_a + v_b)$$

Once v_c is known, p_c can be obtained from the Van der Waal's equation (II.15). This value for p_c is a prediction for the pressure required to condense the gas into a liquid at the given temperature.

Note that the slope of the tangent line to the curve at points a and b is zero, that is, the tangent is horizontal. So

$$\frac{dp(v)}{dv} = 0 \tag{II.16}$$

$$= -\frac{8t/3}{(v - \frac{1}{3})^2} + \frac{6}{v^3}$$

which may be rewritten as

$$f(v) = v^3 - C_2 v^2 + C_1 v - C_0 \tag{II.17}$$

where

$$C_2 = \frac{9}{4t} \qquad C_1 = \frac{3}{2t} \qquad C_0 = \frac{1}{4t} \tag{II.18}$$

Equation (II.17) has three positive real roots, $v = r_1, r_2, r_3$. The smallest, say r_1, will turn out to have a value less than $\frac{1}{3}$ and thus corresponds to a nonphysical region. [From Equation (II.15), we see that if $v < \frac{1}{3}$, the pressure is negative.] Discarding this root, the points a and b in Figure II-7 then correspond to the roots $v_a = r_2$, $v_b = r_2$. Once v_a and v_b are known, the predicted condensation pressure at this temperature is $p_c = p(v_c)$, where $v_c = (v_a + v_b)/2$.

Problem Specifics

Write a program to do the following:

1. Read in the critical point values for the first substance in Table II-4 and the value of the temperature to be used. Print with appropriate headings.

Table II-4 Input parameters for liquid-gas coexistence problem.

Substance	T_c (K)	P_c (Pa)	V_c (m^3/mole)	T (K) (given)
Carbon dioxide (CO_2)	304.26	7.40×10^6	2.02×10^{-5}	280.0
Benzene (C_6H_6)	561.66	4.83×10^6	2.37×10^{-5}	500.0
Nitrogen	126.06	3.39×10^6	4.36×10^{-6}	108.00
Water (H_2O)	647.56	22.0×10^6	7.21×10^{-6}	550.00

2. Use the bisection algorithm to find a root of Equation (II.17). Since $f(v = 0)$ is negative, you should step along the v axis in steps of 0.05 until $f(v)$ changes sign to find the initial bisection search interval. Then find this root to a tolerance $\delta = 10^{-8}$.

3. Next, on a separate piece of paper, verify that if r is a root of Equation (II.17), we may write

(II.19)
$$
\begin{aligned}
f(v) &= v^3 - C_2 v^2 + C_1 v - C_0 \\
&= (v - r)[v^2 - (C_2 - r)v + (C_1 - C_2 r + r^2)] \\
&= 0
\end{aligned}
$$

(Try multiplying this expression out.) Thus once a root of the cubic equation is obtained via the bisection algorithm, the remaining two roots can be found by applying the quadratic formula to the second term in Equation (II.19).

4. Use statement functions for Equations (II.15) and (II.17). Make sure your program has safeguards for potential problems like excessive iterations, complex roots, etc. Print out the limits of the liquid-gas coexistence region for this substance at the given temperature.

5. Repeat for the remaining substances in Table II-4.

6. The variables in the problem are all scaled (i.e., divided by the critical point values). Your printed results should not be scaled, but rather values with the appropriate units. Note that the units of pressure in SI are called Pascals (Pa) ($1 \text{ Pa} = 1 \text{ N/m}^2$) These can be related to the more familiar units of atmospheres by

$$
1 \text{ N/m}^2 = 1 \text{ Pa} = 9.87 \times 10^{-6} \text{ atmospheres}
$$

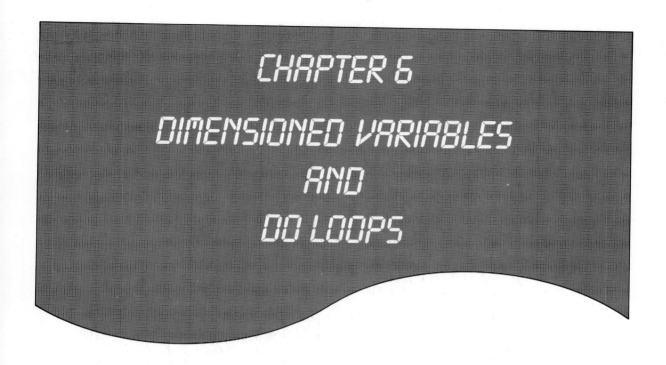

CHAPTER 6

DIMENSIONED VARIABLES

AND

DO LOOPS

6.1 INTRODUCTION

The Fortran described thus far can be used to solve a great many types of problems. However, there is as yet an entire class of problems that is not easily handled without introducing some new Fortran features. For example, if we wish to alter the program in Section 4.4.3 that computed the average of a list of exam scores to calculate in addition the deviation from the average, we face a formidable problem. The data set will have to be scanned twice, once to obtain the average score, and then again to compute the deviations of each score from this average. However, the individual scores were never stored. A single variable was used for the current value of the exam score and was repeatedly updated with each READ. Thus to alter the program we will have to assign each score as it is read to a separate variable which then can be reused in the second calculation. If 400 students took the examination, the READ statement might then appear

```
READ(*,*)STU1,STU2,STU3, ... ,STU400
```

It will probably take longer to type this single READ statement than it took to enter the entire previous program.

The algebraic notation for this problem suggests a remedy.

$$\text{avg} = \frac{1}{n} \sum g_i$$

The set of exam scores is represented by the variable g_i, and individual scores of each student are distinguished from each other by the subscript i. Subscripted variables are introduced into Fortran by means of the DIMENSION statement.

6.2 THE DIMENSION STATEMENT

As we saw in Chapter 1, the Fortran feature most responsible for the success of Fortran and other higher-level computer languages is the method of automatically assigning an address to variable names. Whenever the compiler encounters a new variable name it associates the name with a location in memory. The contents of that memory location are then accessible by simply using the variable name. Each variable is allotted one word of memory.

It is also possible to instruct the compiler to reserve more than one memory word to a variable, say an entire block of words. Each word in this block would have the same variable name, but of course the address of each word would be different, analogous to a subscripted variable. The Fortran instruction to accomplish this is the DIMENSION statement. The form of the DIMENSION statement is

DIMENSION A(subscript),X(subscript₁,subscript₂),NUMBR(subscript₁)

The names A, X, and NUMBR could be any valid integer, real, or character Fortran names. Any number of variables, separated by commas, may be listed after DIMENSION. The quantities in the parentheses specify the range of the subscript associated with the variable. A subscripted variable in Fortran may have up to seven subscripts. The simplest form for specifying the subscript range merely uses the number of words to be reserved for a particular variable.

```
DIMENSION INDEX(50),STU(400,4)
```

The integer variable INDEX occupies 50 words of memory. The first element of the block is accessed by INDEX(1) and the last by INDEX(50). The number appearing in the parentheses in this form *must* be a *positive integer*. The real variable STU occupies 1600 words of memory (i.e., STU_{ij}, $i = 1–400, j = 1–4$). Variable names may never appear in the specification for the subscript range in a Fortran program. The compiler must know, prior to the program's execution, how much space to reserve for each variable.

The DIMENSION statement is a nonexecutable statement and should be placed before any executable statement.

Subscripted variables in Fortran are called *arrays*. As mentioned, the individual elements of an array are accessed by specifying the subscript or index.

```
X(3) = 13.4 + EXP(-5.2 * T)
```

or

```
A = X(16) + 4. * Y(4)**2
```

or

```
I = 12
RADIUS = SQRT(X(3*I - 2)**2 + Y(3*I - 2)**2)
```

When referencing an array element, the index may be any integer expression. All of the elements of an array are of the same data type, which is specified by the name of the array.

6.2.1 Combining Type and DIMENSION Statements

Type declarations and DIMENSION statements may be combined as follows:

```
REAL KLASS
DIMENSION KLASS(50)
```

has exactly the same effect as

```
REAL KLASS(50)
```

The combining of type INTEGER or CHARACTER declarations with a DIMENSION statement is similar.

`REAL X,JUNIOR`	*is the*	`REAL X(50),JUNIOR(20)`
`INTEGER C`	*same*	`INTEGER C(512)`
`CHARACTER NAME*8`	*as*	`CHARACTER NAME(100)*8`
`DIMENSION X(50),`		
`+    JUNIOR(20),`		
`+    C(512),NAME(100)`		

I suggested earlier that *all* variables that appear in a program be type-declared at the beginning of the program. Applying this to dimensioned variables as well means that the shorter combined form of a dimension declaration is preferred. That is, modern programming style demands that the word DIMENSION not appear in your program. The Fortran DIMENSION statement was introduced in this chapter only to facilitate your understanding of the concept of arrays, and all subsequent program examples will employ the preferred combination of type and DIMENSION statements to declare a variable to be an array.

6.2.2 Example Program for the All-University GPA

Again assuming we have a data file containing the grade point average (GPA) of all 8000 students in the university with each line of the file containing the following information:

1. Student's name (A10)
2. ID (I9)
3. College (I1) (1 = arts and science, 2 = engineering, 3 = education,
                4 = architecture, 5 = business, 6 = nursing,
                7 = night, 8 = other)
4. Class (I1)   (1 = freshman, 2 = sophomore,
                3 = junior, 4 = senior)
5. Sex (A1)   (M = male, F = female)
6. Current GPA (F4.2)
7. Last semester's GPA (F4.2)
8. Credit hours attempted thus far (F6.2)

The code to compute the average GPA would be

```
PROGRAM AVERAGE
REAL SUM,STU(8000),XN,GPA
INTEGER I

OPEN(8,FILE='GRADES')
REWIND(8)

I = 1
SUM = 0.0

1   READ(8,10,END=2)STU(I)
10  FORMAT(22X,F4.2)

    SUM = SUM + STU(I)
```

```
          I = I + 1
          GO TO 1

    2  XN = I - 1
       GPA = SUM/XN
       WRITE(*,*)'THE ALL-UNIVERSITY GPA =  ',GPA
       STOP
       END
```

If we also need to compute the standard deviation, given by the expression

$$\sigma^2 = \frac{1}{n-1} \sum_i |s_i - s_{avg}|^2$$

a second pass through the list of students will be required. This could be accomplished by inserting the following code in the above program just before the STOP.

```
       I = 1
       DEV = 0.
    3  DEV = DEV + (STU(I) - GPA)**2
          I = I + 1
          IF(I .LE. XN)GO TO 3
       DEV = SQRT(DEV/(XN - 1.))
       WRITE(*,*)'AND THE AVERAGE DEVIATION IS ',DEV
```

The index for the array STU must not be zero or negative and must not exceed the limit specified in the DIMENSION statement, 8000. If the index is outside the proscribed range (here 1–8000), most compilers will print an execution time error message, but many will not. In those cases the computer may simply use some element stored in memory near the location of the variable. For example, STU(8007) would access the memory location seven words beyond the end of the block called STU. This location may contain a number, or a format, or some executable instruction, and the result will be unpredictable. This type of error, since it is often extremely difficult to track down, is one of the most grievous that a programmer can make. If your computer does not check whether the subscript is within the limits given in the DIMENSION statement, you must always do so yourself. Thus the program above should contain a check of the form

```
   IF(I .GT. 8000)THEN
          WRITE(*,*)'INDEX OUT OF RANGE, I = ',I
          STOP
   END IF
```

The previous program could be easily adapted to compute the individual averages and deviations for each class, for each college, etc. To accomplish this we could separately dimension four arrays to hold the grades for freshmen, sophomores, juniors, and seniors.

```
REAL FRSH(2000),SOPH(2000),JUNR(2000),SENR(2000)
```

Or we could accommodate all four classes in a single variable STU(I,J), where I (from 1 to 2000) identifies a student in a class, and J (from 1 to 4) identifies the class. There will now be four separate averages and four counts of the total number in a class. Thus we will need two addtional arrays, GPA(4) and N(4). The algebraic statement of the problem is

$$c_k = \frac{1}{n_k} \sum_{i=1}^{n} g_{ik} \qquad \text{Class averages for each } k = 1 \text{ to } 4$$

$$t = \frac{1}{4} \sum_{k=1}^{4} c_k \qquad \text{Average of the four averages}$$

The program to accomplish this is shown in Figure 6-1.

This program could be adapted further to calculate the averages classified not only by class, but by gender as well. For example, the average of junior women. In this case the array STU would be dimensioned as STU(1000,4,2), the last index designating male or female. You should have no trouble in constructing the code to handle this case and so it will not be given here.

6.2.3 Upper and Lower Subscript Bounds in a DIMENSION Statement

The simplest form of the DIMENSION statement

```
DIMENSION X(10),K(6,4)
```

or the equivalent form

```
REAL X(10)
INTEGER K(6,4)
```

allow for an index range on the variable x_i from $i = 1$ to $i = 10$, and the range of the two indices of the variable k_{mn} from 1 to 6 and 1 to 4, respectively. Frequently it is desirable to have the index assume negative values or zero. This is permitted in Fortran, provided the compiler is informed of the precise range of the index when the variable is first allotted space in a type or DIMENSION statement.

$$\text{REAL A}(I_{lower}:I_{upper})$$

Figure 6-1 A program to compute individual class averages.

```
* PROGRAM AVERAGE
*--
*--   THIS PROGRAM READS THE DATA FILE <GRADES> AND COMPUTES THE
*--   AVERAGE GRADE BY CLASS (FRESHMAN, SOPHOMORE, ETC.) AND THE
*--   STANDARD DEVIATION FOR EACH CLASS.
*------------------------------------------------------------------
* VARIABLES
*--
      REAL SUM(4),STU(1000,4),STDEV(4),GPA(4),DELTA,AVE
      INTEGER I,N(4)
      CHARACTER*9 CLASS(4)
*--
*            STU(I,K)   --   CURRENT GPA OF STUDENT I IN CLASS K
*            SUM(K)     --   SUM OF ALL GPA'S IN CLASS K
*            GPA(K)     --   AVERAGE GPA FOR CLASS K
*            STDEV(K)   --   STANDARD DEVIATION FROM THE AVERAGE
*                            FOR CLASS K
*            N(K)       --   NUMBER OF STUDENTS IN CLASS K
*            AVE        --   ALL UNIVERSITY AVERAGE GPA
*            DELTA      --   AVERAGE OF THE FOUR STANDARD DEVIA-
*                            TIONS
*            XXX        --   TEMPORARY VALUE FOR CURRENT STUDENT
*                            GPA
*------------------------------------------------------------------
* INITIALIZATION
*--
      CLASS(1) = 'FRESHMAN'
      CLASS(2) = 'SOPHOMORE'
      CLASS(3) = 'JUNIOR   '
      CLASS(4) = 'SENIOR   '
      N(1) = 0
      N(2) = 0
      N(3) = 0
      N(4) = 0
      AVE = 0.0
      DELTA = 0.0
      OPEN (UNIT=66,FILE='GRADES')
      REWIND 66
*------------------------------------------------------------------
*--
*--               READ THE GRADES FILE AND COUNT THE NUMBER
*--               IN EACH CLASS
*--
    1 READ(66,10,END=99)K,XXX
          N(K) = N(K) + 1
          STU(N(K),K) = XXX
          GO TO 1
*------------------------------------------------------------------
*--
*--               FOR CLASS K = 1 TO 4, SUM STU(I,K) FROM
*--               I = 1 TO N(K)
*--
   99 K = 0
    2 K = K + 1
      IF(K .LE. 4)THEN
         SUM(K) = 0
         I = 0
    3    I = I + 1
         IF(I .LE. N(K))THEN
            SUM(K) = SUM(K) + STU(I,K)
```

Continued

```
                GO TO 3
           ELSE
*--
*--
*--                THE SUM OVER I IS COMPLETE, COMPUTE GPA(K)
*--
               GPA(K) = SUM(K)/N(K)
           END IF
           AVE = AVE + GPA(K)
*--
*--                RETURN TO START OF LOOP AND SUM NEXT CLASS
*--
           GO TO 2
        ELSE
*--
*--                ALL CLASSES HAVE BEEN SUMMED
*--                COMPUTE GRAND AVERAGE
*--
           AVE = AVE/4.
        END IF
*---------------------------------------------------------------
*--                RESCAN THE ENTIRE LIST TO COMPUTE THE STANDARD
*--                DEVIATIONS FOR EACH CLASS
*--
        K = 0
    4   K = K + 1
        IF(K .LE. 4)THEN
           STDEV(K) = 0.0
           I = 0
    5      I = I + 1
           IF(I .LE. N(K))THEN
               STDEV(K) = STDEV(K) + (STU(I,K) - GPA(K))**2
               GO TO 5
           ELSE
               STDEV(K) = SQRT(STDEV(K)/(N(K) - 1.))
           END IF
           DELTA = DELTA + STDEV(K)
           GO TO 4
        ELSE
           DELTA = DELTA/4.
        END IF
*---------------------------------------------------------------
*-- PRINT RESULTS
*--
        K = 0
        NTOT = 0
        WRITE(*,11)
    6   K = K + 1
        IF(K .LE. 4)THEN
           NTOT = NTOT + N(K)
           WRITE(*,12)CLASS(K),N(K),GPA(K),STDEV(K)
           GO TO 6
        ELSE
           WRITE(*,12)'TOTALS',NTOT,AVE,DELTA
           STOP
        END IF
*---------------------------------------------------------------
*--FORMATS
*--
   10 FORMAT(20X,I1,1X,F4.2)
   11 FORMAT(///,10X,'    RESULTS -- ALL UNIVERSITY GPA',//,
      +      T20,'NUMBER',/,
      +      T5,'CLASS',T20,' OF',T30,'AVERAGE',T40,'AVERAGE',
      +      T20,'STUDENTS',T30,' GPA',T40,'STD. DEV.',//,45('-'))
*--
   12 FORMAT(T5,A9,T23,I4,T33,F5.2,T42,F7.4)
      END
```

where I_{lower} is the lower limit of the index range and I_{upper} the upper limit. Thus,

```
REAL PROFIT(1963:1984)
```

would allot 22 words of memory ($I_{upper} - I_{lower} + 1$) to the variable PROFIT. Other examples are

```
REAL X(0:20),TIME(-50:50)
INTEGER B(1:10)    ⟨This is the same as B(10).⟩
```

6.3   INTERNAL STORAGE OF ARRAYS

After a program has been compiled, the entire program is stored sequentially in memory. That is, variables, FORMAT statements, arithmetic instructions, etc. are assigned addresses in a string. Thus, we can imagine an array B(5) to be stored as

$$
\begin{vmatrix} B_1 \\ B_2 \\ B_3 \\ B_4 \\ B_5 \end{vmatrix}
$$

An array with two subscripts is usually visualized as a two-dimensional rectangular block; i.e., B(2,4) would be pictured as

$$
\begin{array}{cccc} b_{11} & b_{12} & b_{13} & b_{14} \\ b_{21} & b_{22} & b_{23} & b_{24} \end{array}
$$

where the first index characterizes the row and the second the column in the block. But since the computer must store all arrays in a string, the array is actually stored as

$$
\begin{array}{c} b_{11} \\ b_{21} \\ b_{12} \\ b_{22} \\ b_{13} \\ b_{23} \\ b_{14} \\ b_{24} \end{array}
$$

That is, the first index increments first.

If an array is dimensioned as $X(k_1, k_2)$, then $X(i_1, i_2)$, with $i_1 \leq k_1$, $i_2 \leq k_2$, is the nth element in the block, where

$$n = i_1 + (i_2 - 1)k_1$$

Thus if two arrays are dimensioned as X(10,10) and Y(11,9), then X(3,7) is the 63rd element of X, while Y(3,7) is the 69th element of Y. This has important consequences in connection with the input and output of arrays. The Fortran statement

```
WRITE(*,*)B      ⟨B was dimensioned as B(2,4)⟩
```

will print *all* of the variables with the name B, i.e., eight elements. The order in which the elements are printed is the same as the order in which the elements are stored in memory—i.e., the same as the string given above. Similarly, a statement like

```
READ(*,*)B
```

will read eight numbers and store them in the sequence given.

However, a Fortran statement like

```
B = 35,      ⟨Error if B has been dimensioned⟩
```

will result in a compilation time error. Since a unique memory location has not been specified to the left of the assignment operator, the statement cannot be executed. Similarly, the arithmetic operations in the statement

```
Z = 2, * B + 4,0      ⟨Error if B has been dimensioned⟩
```

will likewise result in a compilation time error. No unique value has been specified to be used in place of the symbol B.

In short, in all I/O operations the appearance of an array name only, without specifying the indices, causes the entire contents of the array to be used. In other Fortran statements the use of the variable name only will cause an execution time error.

6.4 THE DO LOOP

The primary goal of structured programming is to construct code that is easy to read and that employs logic that is easy to follow. This usually translates into a total banishment of GO TO statements. The block IF structures of Section 3.4 are a major step in this direction. Yet there remain cases for which GO TOs are unavoidable: namely any algorithm that involves looping.

```
        I = 1
        SUM = 0.0
      1 SUM = SUM + X(I)
        I = I + 1
        IF(I .LT. IMAX)GO TO 1
```

Frequently the loop will consist of a *known* number of cycles (IMAX) which is monitored by a loop index (I). The arithmetic in each cycle will often involve subscripted variables identified by the loop index X(I). A special structure in Fortran to handle situations like this without employing GO TOs is the DO loop.

6.4.1   The Structure of the DO loop

The DO loop structure is a block of statements with an entry point (the top) and a normal exit point (the bottom). The beginning line of a DO loop has the general form

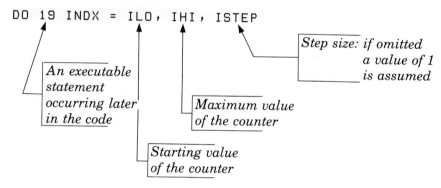

All Fortran statements beginning with the DO statement down to and including the DO terminator (here statement 19) are executed first with the index INDX = ILO. The loop is then repeated with INDX = ILO + ISTEP, etc. until the maximum value is reached. The terminal statement of the DO loop must be an executable statement, but it cannot be any of the following:

```
        GO TO      (unconditional)
        IF         (arithmetic)
        ELSE
        ELSE IF
        STOP
        END
        DO
```

If the terminator is a logical IF, it must not contain a DO, another IF (block or logical), ELSE, ELSE IF, END, or END IF. Rather than attempt to remember these rules, we reintroduce a Fortran statement whose primary purpose is to serve as the terminator of DO loops. This is the CONTINUE statement, which has the simple form

$$\langle\text{stmt number}\rangle\ \texttt{CONTINUE}$$

The CONTINUE statement is defined to be an executable (though do-nothing) statement.

The index range parameters, ILO, IHI, and ISTEP, may be either integer or real constants, variables, or expressions. The indexing variable INDEX may also be integer or real, however it is suggested that whenever possible integer values be used exclusively. The DO-loop structure has a built-in test for completion of the loop.[1] After completion of the DO loop, the index parameter retains its most recent value. A few examples are given in Table 6-1.

Table 6-1
Examples of DO statements.

DO statement	No. of cycles executed	Value of index after loop	Comments
`DO 44 I = 1,5`	5	6	
`DO 73 K = 5,1`	0(or 1)	5	
`DO 73 K = 5,1,-1`	5	0	Negative steps
`DO 11 M = 1,9,3`	3	10	
`DO 15 X = 1.0,4.0,0.8`	4	4.2	
`DO 15 M = 1.0,4.0,0.8`	None (execution time error—zero step not allowed)	Undefined	The loop limits are first converted to the type of M, so this is the same as DO 15 M = 1,4,0
`DO 91 R = SQRT(2.),5.`	4	$4. + \sqrt{2}.$	

6.4.2 Examples of DO Loops

Several of the previous programs that have employed a loop structure may now be rewritten using a DO loop.

1. Summations

```
SUM = 0.0
DO 1 I = 1,N
     SUM = SUM + X(I)
1    CONTINUE
```

---

[1] The test for completion may be at the beginning or at the end of the loop, depending on the local installation of Fortran. Thus on some machines, a DO loop is always executed at least once, while on other computers the same loop may be executed zero times. See the second example in Table 6-1.

2. Zero-fill an array

```
REAL X(50),Y(50)
DO 3 I = 1,50
    X(I) = 0.0
    Y(I) = 0.0
3   CONTINUE
```

3. Factorials, $n! = n(n - 1)(n - 2) \ldots 2 \times 1$

```
INTEGER N,FACT
READ(*,*)N
FACT = N
DO 1 I = N - 1,1,-1
    FACT = FACT * I
1   CONTINUE
```

6.4.3 Abnormal Exits from a DO loop

Frequently, you may wish to terminate a loop structure before the total number of cycles are executed. This is usually done with a logical IF and a GO TO; such a situation arises in iterative calculations. For example, in searching for the first positive root of a function of x, $f(x)$, you might start at $x = 0.0$ and proceed along the x axis in steps of 0.1 and monitor the relative sign of two successive values of $f(x)$. If you are fairly sure that the root is less than, say, $x = 15$, the code would be

```
PROGRAM ROOT
F(X) =                        〈Statement function for f(x)〉
X = 0.0
DX = 0.1
F1 = F(X)

DO 1 I = 1,150
    X = X + DX
    F2 = F(X)
    IF(F1 * F2 .LE. 0.0)THEN
                             〈Leave the loop
        GO TO 99             before it completes 150 cycles〉
    ELSE
        F1 = F2
    END IF
1 CONTINUE
```

```
      WRITE(*,*)'NO ROOT'          ⟨No root found in 150
      STOP                          steps, print and stop⟩
  99  X3 = X
      X1 = X - DX                  ⟨An axis crossing was
      F1 = F(X1)                    found before x = 15,
      F3 = F2                       so start bisection from
      X2 = .5 * (X1 + X3)          here⟩
          ⟨etc.⟩
```

When exiting a DO loop before completion, the value of the index parameter is the last value assigned. You should never branch from outside a DO loop to statements within a DO loop. The counter will most likely not have an assigned value. In addition, the DO loop index and the limits should not be redefined within the loop.[2]

To improve the readability of DO loops it is suggested that the body of the loop be indented in a manner similar to block IF statements.

6.4.4 Nested DO loops

When one DO loop is entirely contained within another DO loop, the grouping is called a *DO loop nesting*. Nesting of DO loops to any depth is permitted, provided each inner loop is entirely within the range of the next-level outer loop. Basically this means DO loops may never overlap. An inner loop and an outer loop may, however, share a terminal statement. A few examples of allowable nestings are shown in Figure 6-2. For each cycle of an outer loop, the inner loops are completely executed. Thus

```
        DO 2 I = 0,9
            DO 2 J = 0,9
                WRITE(*,'(5X,I2)')J + 10*I
      2 CONTINUE
```

will print the integers from 0 to 99 in order.

The program on page 185 may be rewritten using nested DO loops as follows:

---

[2] The potential number of cycles of the DO loop is ordinarily computed by the compiler at the very beginning of the loop from the index range parameters in the DO statement. And, except for abnormal exits from the loop, that many cycles are executed *even if* the index and index range parameters are changed within the loop.

```
   ...                           ⟨n_k = the number per class;
   ...                             STU_ik = individual student
 STNDEV = 0.0                      GPA's (read in)⟩
 GPA = 0.0
 DO 3 K = 1,4
     AVE(K) = 0.0
     DO 1 I = 1,N(K)
         AVE(K) = AVE(K) + STU(I,K)
1    CONTINUE
     AVE(K) = AVE(K)/N(K)
     DEV(K) = 0.0
     DO 2 I = 1,N(K)
        DEV(K) = DEV(K) + (AVE(K) - STU(I,K))**2
2    CONTINUE
     DEV(K) = DEV(K)/(N(K)-1)
     DEV(K) = SQRT(DEV(K))

     GPA = GPA + AVE(K)
     STNDEV = STNDEV + DEV(K)
3 CONTINUE
 GPA = GPA/4.


 STNDEV = STNDEV/4.
```

$$\left\langle a_k = \frac{1}{n_k} \sum_{i=1}^{n} STU_{ik} \right\rangle$$

$$\left\langle \sigma_k^2 = \frac{1}{n_k - 1} \sum_{i=1}^{r} (a_k - STU_{ik})^2 \right\rangle$$

$$\left\langle GPA = \frac{1}{4} \sum_{k=1}^{4} a_k \right\rangle$$

$$\left\langle \sigma_{\text{ave}} = \frac{1}{4} \sum_{k=1}^{4} \sigma_k \right\rangle$$

Figure 6-2
Examples of nested DO loops.

6.4 THE DO LOOP 193

6.5 THE IMPLIED DO LOOP

A special form of DO loop is available exclusively for I/O: the implied DO loop. The form of the implied DO loop for input is

```
READ( ) (<list of variables> , INDX = ILO,IHI,ISTEP)
```

and for output is

```
WRITE( ) (<list of variables> , INDX = ILO,IHI,ISTEP)
PRINT sl,(<list of variables> , INDX = ILO,IHI,ISTEP)
```

In either case, the list of variables is read or printed first with the index, INDX = ILO, then again with INDX = ILO + ISTEP, etc., until the loop is completed. The rules concerning the index and range parameters are the same as those of an ordinary DO loop. Note, the loop is enclosed in parentheses and the index specifications are separated from the I/O list by a comma. For example,

```
WRITE(*,'(1X,6F5.2)') (X(I),I=4,9)
```

has exactly the same effect as

```
WRITE(*,'(1X,6F5.2)')X(4),X(5),X(6),X(7),X(8),X(9)
```

and is distinctly different from

```
        DO 1 I = 4,9
            WRITE(*,'(1X,6F5.2)')X(I)
      1 CONTINUE
```

The first two examples print all six numbers on a single line, while the last will result in six lines of output from six separate WRITEs. An implied READ is interpreted as a *single* READ of a repeated list of variables rather than a repeated READ. Similar considerations apply to WRITE/PRINT statements. Thus,

```
        REAL X(50)
        PRINT *,(X(I),I=1,50)
```

is the same as

```
        REAL X(50)
        PRINT *,X
```

More than one variable may be included in the I/O list.

```
   REAL X(6)
   DO 1 R = 1.,6.
       I = R
 1     X(I) = R
   PRINT *,(X(J),2*J,J = 3,5)        ⟨3.000 6  4.000 8  5.000 10⟩

   WRITE(*,11)(X(I),X(I + 1),I = 1,5,2)   ⟨1. 2.00
11 FORMAT(1X,F3.0,2X,F4.2)                  3. 4.00
                                            5. 6.00⟩
   WRITE(*,'(5F4.1)')(X(3),I = 1,4)    ⟨3.0  3.0  3.0  3.0⟩
```

Implied DO loops are also useful for reading data, as illustrated in the following:

```
   REAL X(50),Y(50)
10 FORMAT(10F5.1)
11 FORMAT( 2F5.1)

   READ(*,11)(X(I),Y(I),I=1,50)     ⟨Requires 50 lines of
                                     input, 2 numbers per
                                     line⟩

   READ(*,10)(X(I),Y(I),I=1,50)     ⟨Requires 10 lines of
                                     input, 5 pairs x_i, y_i
                                     per line⟩

   DO 1 I = 1,50                     ⟨Requires 50 lines of
       READ(*,10)X(I),Y(I)           input, 2 numbers per
 1 CONTINUE                          line⟩

   READ 10,X,Y                       ⟨Requires 10 lines of
                                     input, first 5 lines
                                     for Xs, last 5 for Ys⟩
```

Implied DO loops may also be nested as illustrated in the following example.

```
        REAL A(4,5)
     10 FORMAT(5F6.2)
        WRITE(*,10)((A(I,J),J = 1,5),I = 1,4)
```

*Inner
loop*

*Outer
loop*

will print the elements of A in the arrangement

a_{ij}				
i \ j	1	2	3	4	5
---	---	---	---	---	---
1	a_{11}	a_{12}	a_{13}	a_{14}	a_{15}
2	a_{21}	a_{22}	a_{23}	a_{24}	a_{25}
3	a_{31}	a_{32}	a_{33}	a_{34}	a_{35}
4	a_{41}	a_{42}	a_{43}	a_{44}	a_{45}

6.6 MISCELLANEOUS EXAMPLES OF LOOP STRUCTURES AND ARRAYS

6.6.1 Infinite Series

In any book of mathematical tables you can find examples of series representations of various common functions. One such series that we have already encountered in Section 4.4.3 is

$$e^x = 1 + x + \frac{x^2}{2!} + \frac{x^3}{3!} + \cdot \cdot \cdot + \frac{x^n}{n!} + \cdot \cdot \cdot$$

If you attempt to sum this series by computing the individual terms as

```
TERM = X**N/FACTN
```

where FACTN is $n!$ and is evaluated on page 191, you may get the correct answer, but the program would be extremely inefficient. The evaluation of a single term would require exponentiation, which is relatively slow, and the use of a DO loop to compute $n!$. If a large number of terms is required to obtain an accurate result, serious problems involving computation time (i.e., money!) may result, even leading to failure of the code due to round-off error. Frequently, when a series expansion involves factorials, it is more efficient to relate successive terms by means of their ratio, as was done in Section 4.4.3. For the series above we would once again obtain

$$R = \frac{(\text{term})_{n+1}}{(\text{term})_n} = \frac{x}{n + 1}$$

The code to sum the series without using DO loops was given in Section 4.4.3. Rewriting this code using a DO loop yields the following:

```
      READ(*,*)X
      SUM = 1.
      TERM = X
      DO 2 I = 1,1000
          SUM = SUM + TERM
          IF(ABS(TERM) .LT. 1.E-6)THEN
              WRITE(*,*)'EXP(',X,') = ',SUM
              STOP
          ELSE
              TERM = TERM * X/(I + 1.0)
          END IF
    2 CONTINUE
      WRITE(*,*)'DID NOT CONVERGE AFTER 1000 TERMS'
      STOP
```

This procedure for summing an infinite series, either with a DO loop or without, is a very important computational technique. You should attempt to code the following series expansions.

1. The $\sin(x)$

$$\sin(x) = x - \frac{x^3}{3!} + \frac{x^5}{5!} - \frac{x^7}{7!} + \cdots \qquad \text{only odd terms}$$

where you should verify that

$$(\text{term})_{n+2} = (\text{term})_n \times \left[-\frac{x^2}{(n+1)(n+2)} \right]$$

and SUM and TERM should be initialized as

$$\begin{aligned} \text{SUM} &= 0.0 \\ \text{TERM} &= X \end{aligned}$$

2. The $\cos(x)$

$$\cos(x) = 1 - \frac{x^2}{2!} + \frac{x^4}{4!} - \frac{x^6}{6!} + \cdots \qquad \text{only even terms}$$

where

$$(\text{term})_{n+2} = (\text{term})_n \times \left[-\frac{x^2}{(n+1)(n+2)} \right]$$

3. The natural logarithm, $\ln(1 + x)$

$$\ln(1 + x) = x - \frac{x^2}{2} + \frac{x^3}{3} - \frac{x^4}{4} + \cdots \qquad \text{for } |x| \leq 1$$

where

$$(\text{term})_{n+1} = (\text{term})_n \left(-x \frac{n}{n+1} \right)$$

4. The binomial expansion

$$(1 + x)^p = 1 + px + \frac{p(p-1)}{2!} x^2 + \frac{p(p-1)(p-2)}{3!} x^3$$

$$+ \cdots + \binom{p}{n} x^n + \cdots$$

where the notation $\binom{p}{n}$ is called the combinatorial and is defined as

$$\binom{p}{n} = \frac{p!}{n!(p-n)!}$$

For example,

$$\binom{p}{2} = \frac{p!}{2(p-2)!} = \frac{p(p-1)}{2}$$

The ratio of successive terms in the expansion may then be evaluated as

$$R = (\text{term})_{n+1}/(\text{term})_n$$

$$= \frac{\binom{p}{n+1} x^{n+1}}{\binom{p}{n} x^n}$$

$$= \frac{p!}{(n+1)!(p-n-1)!} \frac{n!(p-n)!}{p!} x$$

and since

$$\frac{n!}{(n+1)!} = \frac{1}{n+1}$$

and

$$\frac{(p-n)!}{(p-n-1)!} = \frac{(p-n)(p-n-1)!}{(p-n-1)!} = (p-n)$$

we obtain

$$(\text{term})_{n+1} = \left(x \frac{p-n}{n+1} \right)(\text{term})_n$$

For example, using $p = 4$ we obtain from the above:

$$\binom{4}{0} = 1 \quad \binom{4}{1} = 4 \quad \binom{4}{2} = 6 \quad \binom{4}{3} = 4 \quad \binom{4}{4} = 1 \quad \binom{4}{5} = 0$$

so

$$(1 + x)^4 = 1 + 4x + 6x^2 + 4x^3 + x^4$$

If p is a positive integer, the infinite series terminates and the expression reduces to a polynomial. However, if p is not a positive integer, the binomial expansion results in an infinite number of terms.[3] What are the expansions for $p = -1$?, for $p = \frac{1}{2}$?

6.6.2 Maximum/Minimum of an Array

In Section 4.3 I described a simple method for finding the largest or smallest element of a list of numbers. This procedure can be easily adapted to finding the minimum and/or maximum element of an array. However, we are frequently interested in finding not only what the maximum element is, but where it is—that is, which element in the array is the largest (or smallest). This is accomplished by using what is called a *pointer,* in the following manner.

```
       REAL X(100)
       XMAX = X(1)
       IMAX = 1
       DO 1 I = 2,100
           IF(X(I) .GT. XMAX)THEN
                   XMAX = X(I)
                   IMAX = I
           END IF
1 CONTINUE
       WRITE(*,*)'THE LARGEST ELEMENT IS THE I = ',IMAX,
      +    ' ELEMENT'
       WRITE(*,*)'WHICH HAS A VALUE OF',X(IMAX)
       STOP
       END
```

---

[3] The factorial for half-integers has not been defined, so the combinatorial expression cannot be used. However, the equation for the ratio of successive terms remains valid. For example,

$$(1 + x)^{-1} = 1 + (-1)x + \frac{(-1)(-2)}{2} x^2 + \frac{(-1)(-2)(-3)}{6} x^3 + \cdots$$

so that

$$R = (\text{term})_{n+1}/(\text{term})_n = x \frac{(-1 - n)}{(n + 1)} = -x$$

The position of the largest element of an array with more than one index is found in a similar manner.

6.6.3 Printing Two-Dimensional Arrays

We saw in Section 6.5 that a two-dimensional array is usually pictured as a rectangular block of numbers labeled by rows and columns. Such a grouping is also called a *matrix* and will be discussed in depth in Chapter 12. When printing such an object, the output should also include the row and column labels. The Fortran to do this is not difficult, but occasionally takes some trial and error to get everything lined up correctly. The code below will print a square 8 by 8 array with F6.2 formats.

```
      REAL B(8,8)
      WRITE(*,11)(I,I = 1,8)
      DO 1 IROW = 1,8
         WRITE(*,12)IROW,(B(IROW,ICOL),ICOL = 1,8)
    1 CONTINUE
   11 FORMAT(5X,8(3X,I1,3X))
   12 FORMAT(2X,I1,2X,8(F6.2,1X))
      ...
```

PROBLEMS

1. Find any errors in the following. If none write OK.
   a. DIMENSION A(50),B(5,000)
   b. DIMENSION A(9,9,9,9,9,9,9)
   c. M = 5
      N = 3
      DIMENSION X(M,N)
   d. DIMENSION INTEGER I(50), REAL X(25)
   e. DIMENSION A(5,5,5,5)
   f. DIMENSION A(B(5))
   g. DIMENSION A(5)(1:2)
   h. REAL A(6,6),B(2,2,0:1)
   i. CHARACTER*4 FOUR(−4:4)
   j. INTEGER A(0:0)
   k. CHARACTER*2 REAL(4)
   l. INTEGER REAL(2:3)
   m. INTEGER X(−5:−7)
2. Write a program to count the number of times each vowel is used in a text of several hundred lines. The text is contained on a data file. Store all the counters in a single array.

3. Starting with a function of two variables, for example,

$$z = f(x, y) = e^{x-y}\sin(5x)\cos(2y)$$

for

$$0 \leq x \leq 2 \qquad 0 \leq y \leq 2$$

a. Write a Fortran program employing DO loops to compute and store a square grid (21 by 21) of values of Z(I,J) for equally spaced values of x and y within the specified range.

b. Determine the maximum and minimum of the array Z. Copy the array Z into an integer array IZ(0:20,0:20) defined by

```
IZ(I,J) = 10*(Z(I,J) - ZMIN)/(ZMAX - ZMIN)
```

c. Print the array IZ as a 20 by 20 square block of integers. Interpret the result.

4. Write a segment of a Fortran program that determines and prints which element of a two-dimensional array A(50,50) is largest. That is, the output should be something like

```
THE LARGEST ELEMENT IS IN ROW III, COLUMN III
```

5. Redo the solutions to Problem 4.3, using DO loops.

6. To determine whether an integer k is a prime number or not you must test whether k is divisible by all primes less than $\sqrt{k}$. To do this you must have a table of primes. Write a program to determine and print the first 100 prime numbers. A pseudocode outline of the program is given below.

INTEGER p_i, $i = 1,100$
$p_1 = 2$, $p_2 = 3$
For $m = 2,100$
    let $k = p_m + 2$
    test whether k is divisible by $p_1, p_2, \ldots, p_m$
      if yes → increment k by 2 and retest
      if no → $p_{m+1} = k$

The test to determine whether a number is evenly divisible by another number is given in Problem 3.13.

7. Translate the following into Fortran using DO loops:

a. $s = \displaystyle\sum_{i=1}^{10} a_i x_i$

b. For all $i = 1,10$

$$t_i = \sum_{j=1}^{10} a_{ij} x_j$$

c. For all $i, j = 1,10$

$$c_{ij} = \sum_{k=1}^{10} a_{ik} b_{kj}$$

8. Write a segment of a Fortran program that:

a. Interchanges the entire rows K and J of a square array Z(10, 10).

b. Scans column K of the array, determines the row containing the largest element, and then interchanges this row with the first row of the array.

9. Determine the output from the following:

```
INTEGER K(0:4,0:4)
DO 1 I = 0,4
    DO 1 J = 0,4
        K(I,J) = 10 * I + J
1 CONTINUE
```

a.
```
    WRITE(*,1)(K(0,J),J=1,4)
    1 FORMAT(1X,10I2)
```
b.
```
    WRITE(*,2)((K(I,J),J=1,4),I=1,4)
    2 FORMAT(2X,5I3)
```
c.
```
    WRITE(*,3)(I,I=0,4),(M,(K(M,J),J=0,4),M=0,4)
    3 FORMAT (5X,5(2X,I1,2X),/,
              5(2X,I1,2X,5(2X,I2,1X),/))
```
d.
```
    WRITE(*,4)((K(I,J),J=I,4),I=0,4)
    4 FORMAT(2X,5I3)
```
e.
```
    WRITE(*,5)((K(I,J),I=4,0,-1),J=0,4)
    5 FORMAT(2X,5I3)
```
f.
```
    DO 3 I=0,4
        WRITE(*,6)(K(I,J),J=I,4)
    3 CONTINUE
    6 FORMAT(2X,5I4)
```
g.
```
    DO 4 I=0,4
        WRITE(*,7)(K(I,J),J=4,I,-1)
    4 CONTINUE
    7 FORMAT(20X,5(I3,TL8))
```

CHAPTER 7
NON-NUMERICAL APPLICATIONS— CHARACTER VARIABLES

7.1   REVIEW OF CHARACTER VARIABLES

Non-numerical applications of computers like graphics or word processing
are the areas of computer science experiencing the most rapid growth. And
even though an engineer will be using a computer primarily to solve mathematical problems or analyze numerical data, the character manipulation
abilities of the computer will frequently be found to be quite useful. This
chapter deals with applications of character variables in a variety of situations, such as sorting a list of names, or plotting a graph on the printer or
terminal screen.

First, let us review the properties of character-type variables introduced
in Section 2.2.3. A variable is defined to be of type CHARACTER with a
length of ⟨integer⟩ characters by a statement

```
CHARACTER [name]*<integer>
```

or

```
CHARACTER*<integer> [name₁], [name₂], ...
```

For example,

```
CHARACTER*5 METAL,OXIDE,ACID(6)      ⟨all have length five⟩
CHARACTER GAS(0:5)*8, SYMBOL(6)*1    ⟨Each of the six ele-
                                      ments of GAS is of
                                      length eight⟩
```

These variables may then be assigned "values," which must be a sequence of characters.

Assignment statement	Value stored				
METAL = 'STEEL'	S	T	E	E	L
OXIDE = 'AL3O2'	A	L	3	O	2
ACID(1) = 'H2CO3'	H	2	C	O	3
ACID(2) = 'H2S'	H	2	S		

The remainder of the word is filled with blanks.

GAS(0) = 'NEON'	N	E	O	N				
SYMBOL(2) = 'CL'	C							

The value is truncated from the right until it fits the length of the variable.

SYMBOL(1) = GAS(0) | N |

GAS(1) = SYMBOL(2) | C | | | | | | | |

and may be compared in IF tests

Comparison	Value of comparison
IF(METAL .EQ. 'STEEL')	⟨true⟩
IF(METAL .EQ. 'STEAL')	⟨false⟩
IF('NEON' .EQ. GAS(0))	⟨true⟩

⟨The shorter variable ⟨'NEON'⟩ is extended with blanks to the same length as the longer variable before the comparison.⟩

IF(SYMBOL(2) .EQ. 'CL') ⟨false⟩   ⟨Compares |C | | with |C|L|⟩

The input and output of character variables is accomplished with the A format.

```
        WRITE(*,12)METAL
     12 FORMAT(5X,A5)
```

or

```
     12 FORMAT(5X,A)
```

As a reminder: Character variables contain coded values for symbols and can never be used in any arithmetic expressions.

```
     CHARACTER M*5
     INTEGER N
     N  =  3 + 4          ⟨N contains the numerical value 7⟩
     M  = '3 + 4 '        ⟨M contains the symbols '3 + 4'⟩
```

7.2   CHARACTER SUBSTRINGS

The result of an assignment statement involving a character variable is to store in the variable a set of symbols in a so-called string. A character string may be any length from one to several thousand characters. Clearly, it will frequently be necessary to access parts of a long string. The parts of a complete string are called substrings, and the form of a reference to a character substring is shown in Figure 7-1.

$$\text{CHNAME}(p_l : p_r)$$

where   CHNAME   is the name of the character variable.

p_l is an integer or integer expression designating the position of the first or leftmost character in the substring. If omitted, a value of 1 is assumed.

p_r is an integer or integer expression designating the position of the last or rightmost character in the substring. If omitted, the last position in the string is used.

If the entire string is of length n characters, then $1 \le p_l \le p_r \le n$.

Figure 7-1
Character substring reference.

For example, if a character variable ABCS is defined as

```
CHARACTER ABCS*26
ABCS = 'ABCDEFGHIJKLMNOPQRSTUVWXYZ'
```

then references to substrings might be

Substring reference	Value
ABCS(1:2)	'AB'
ABCS(3:6)	'CDEF'
ABCS(:4)	'ABCD'
ABCS(20:)	'TUVWXYZ'
ABCS(4:4)	'D'
ABCS(:)	same as ABCS—i.e., entire string

If the character variable itself is a dimensioned array, then substrings of each array element may be referenced in a similar manner. First a particular element in the array is given, followed by the specification of the substring in that element. For example,

```
CHARACTER NAME(6)*8, ADDRESS(0:5)*25, A*2
NAME(2) = 'JONES'
ADDRESS(0) = '1442 STATE, BOSTON, MA'
```

A = NAME(2)(2:3) ⟨A is assigned the value of the second and third characters in the second element of the array NAME⟩

ADDRESS(0)(6:10) = 'MAIN' ⟨STATE is replaced by MAIN. Note, MAIN is extended by a blank.⟩

Just as with an array, you must be very careful that the substring specifications are within the bounds of the complete character string. If p_1 is less than 1 or p_r is greater than the length of the string, an execution error will result.

7.3 INTRINSIC FUNCTIONS RELATED TO CHARACTER VARIABLES

Many of the applications of character variables involve searching a string for a particular substring and then performing a replacement. There are several Fortran intrinsic functions that have been designed to help in the coding of such tasks.

7.3.1 The Length of a String—Function LEN

The Fortran function LEN simply returns the length of the character string that is the argument of the function.

```
LEN(string)
```

Some examples are

```
CHARACTER A*4,B*5
INTEGER I,K,M,N
A = '1234'
B = 'NAME'
I = LEN(A)                 ⟨value assigned to I is 4⟩
K = LEN(B)                 ⟨value assigned to K is 5,
                           the value stored in B is
                           |N|A|M|E| |⟩
M = LEN(A(2:4))            ⟨value assigned to M is 3,
                           the length of the substring
                           is (4 − 2) + 1⟩
N = LEN(A)/LEN('ABC')      ⟨LEN('ABC') is 3, so N is
                           assigned the value 1⟩
```

7.3.2 The Location of a Substring—Function INDEX

The Fortran function

```
INDEX(string,substring)
```

will return the position of the substring within the string. Both entrees in the argument list must be of type CHARACTER. If the second character string in the argument list occurs as a substring in the first, the result is an integer corresponding to the starting position of the substring within the first named string. If a match is not found, including the case where the substring is larger than the string, the value returned is zero. If there is more than one match within the string, only the starting position of the first occurrence is given. For example,

```
CHARACTER ABCS*26,A*1,B*2
ABCS = 'ABCDEFGHIJKLMNOPQRSTUVWXYZ'
A = 'A'
B = 'B'               ⟨note, stored in B is |B| |⟩
I = INDEX(ABCS,A)     ⟨value assigned to I is 1⟩
J = INDEX(ABCS,'C')   ⟨value assigned to J is 3⟩
```

```
K = INDEX(ABCS,'DEF')        ⟨value assigned to K is 4⟩
L = INDEX(ABCS,B)            ⟨value assigned to L is 0,
                               the substring |B| | is not
                               contained in ABCS⟩
ABCS(INDEX(ABCS,'P'):INDEX(ABCS,'R'))='**********'
                             ⟨the positions P through R
                              are replaced with asterisks.
                              Note the string on the right
                              is truncated⟩
```

7.4 CHARACTER EXPRESSIONS—CONCATENATION

The only character string operation provided in Fortran is called *concatenation,* which means joining together. If S_1 and S_2 are two character strings of length n_1 and n_2, respectively, then the concatenation of S_1 and S_2 is effected by the operator // (two slashes, interpreted as a single symbol). Thus

$$S_1//S_2$$

has a value of a string of length $n_1 + n_2$, consisting of the two individual strings joined into one. For example,

```
CHARACTER*10 NAME1,NAME2
NAME1 = 'JOHN SMITH'
NAME2 = NAME1(6:)//','//NAME(:4)
```

Successive concatenations proceed from left to right, so

```
NAME2 => | S | M | I | T | H | , | J | O | H | N |
```

The code to read a list of names in the form first name, middle initial, last name and store them, last name first, would then be

```
      CHARACTER*30 XX,NAME(100)
      INTEGER PERIOD,LAST,I

      I = 1
  1   READ(*,'(A)',END=99)XX
      PERIOD = INDEX(XX,'.')        ⟨Finds the location of the period after
                                      the middle initial⟩
      LAST = INDEX(XX,'  ') - 1     ⟨The end of the name is the occurrence of
                                      two successive blanks⟩
      NAME(I) = XX(PERIOD+2:LAST)//','//XX(:PERIOD)
      I = I + 1
      IF(I .LT. 100) GO TO 1
  99  CONTINUE
      ...
      ...
```

The binary code for symbols 'A', 'B', . . . , 'Z' has been set up so that the value of 'A' is less than the value of 'B', is less than the value of 'C', etc. Furthermore, the value of a blank is less than the value of 'A'. Thus character strings may be compared in logical IF tests. A few examples are given below

IF test	**Value of argument**	
IF('A' .LE. 'G')	⟨true⟩	
IF('AA' .LT. 'A ')	⟨false⟩	blank < 'A' so
		$\lfloor A \mid A \rfloor > \lfloor A \mid \ \rfloor$
IF('ABCDE' .LT.'ABCDZ')	⟨true⟩	

Once again, if the character variables being compared are of unequal length, the shorter variable is extended by adding blanks to the right before the comparison.

Unfortunately, the ordering of the remaining characters in Fortran is not standard and will vary from site to site. There is a Fortran intrinsic function that will tell you what ordering of characters is employed at your computing center: the function CHAR(I). The range of I values is also system-dependent and may take some experimenting on your part to determine. On my computer the allowed range of I is from 0 to 63 and the function CHAR(I) returns a single character for each I in this range. Thus CHAR(0) on my computer has a value of   , i.e., ⟨blank space⟩, meaning that this character has the smallest binary value of all the allowed Fortran symbols. Printing out all the remaining 63 allowed Fortran symbols by means of this function then establishes their relative ordering

```
      DO 1 I = 1,63
      WRITE(*,'(2X,I2,2X,A)')I,CHAR(I)
    1 CONTINUE
```

and, for my computer, gives the following result:

I	CHAR(I)										
1	!	12	'	25	9	38	F	51	S
2	' '	13	-	26	:	39	G	52	T
3	#	14	.	27	;	40	H	53	U
4	$	15	/	28	<	41	I	54	V
There is no		16	0	29	=	42	J	55	W
symbol defined		17	1	30	>	43	K	56	X
for I = 5		18	2	31	?	44	L	57	Y
6	&	19	3	32	@	45	M	58	Z
7	'	20	4	33	A	46	N	59	[
8	(	21	5	34	B	47	O	60	\
9	)	22	6	35	C	48	P	61	]
10	*	23	7	36	D	49	Q	62	^
11	+	24	8	37	E	50	R	63	_

You might wish to try this on your machine.

The inverse of the function CHAR is the intrinsic function ICHAR( ). The argument is a *single* character and the function returns the local sequencing number associated with that character on your computer. Thus, from the list given above, the value of ICHAR('A') on my computer is the integer 33.

In Section 4.3 we discussed a procedure for finding the minimum or maximum of a list of numbers by repeatedly comparing pairs of numbers using an IF test. Since character variables may also be compared in an IF test, the same ideas may be used to alphabetize a list of names. The procedure is simply to scan the list of names and find the name with the minimum "value," for example, AARDVARK, and put this name at the top of the list. The remainder of the list is then scanned once more for the minimum in the remaining list of names, and this name is placed in the second position, and so on. This is an example of what is called sorting and is described more completely in the next section.

7.6   SORTING ALGORITHMS

The arranging of the elements of a list or set into some sort of ordered sequence is called *sorting* and the most common example is the alphabetizing of a list of names. In principle, the basic ideas involved in sorting are rather trivial, as we have seen; however, the difficulty increases dramatically with the size of the list being sorted, roughly speaking increasing with the square of the size of the list. So while one algorithm may be quite suitable to sort the names of the students in a university (about 10,000 names), it might be next to useless in sorting the names in the New York City phone book (about 3,000,000 names or 300^2 times more difficult). To a professional programmer, writing program code which will be used perhaps thousands of times, obviously efficiency of code is extremely important and the programmer will spend many hours or days rewriting a perfectly good code to optimize the speed and minimize the memory requirements of the program. However, for most of the rest of us such meticulous care would not be cost-effective. For programs that will only be executed a few times and from which we want an answer quickly, it would be foolish to spend an extra week reducing the run time from 73 seconds to 47 seconds. (Of course, a reduction of run time from 73 hours to 47 hours would be a different matter.) For this reason, only the simplest sorting algorithms will be discussed here, neither of which would be suitable for excessively long lists for which extremely sophisticated procedures have been devised.

7.6.1 The Selection Sort

The *selection sort* algorithm (also called *exchange sort*) is the most obvious method of arranging a list and was described at the end of the previous section.

Find the *minimum* of the list of n elements.
Place this element on top.
Find the *minimum* of the remaining list of $n - 1$ elements.
Place this element next.
Continue until the remaining list contains only one element.

The Fortran to accomplish a selection sort is given in Figure 7-2. After the first pass through the outer loop, NAME(1) = overall minimum in the list, after the second pass NAME(2) = second smallest value, etc. Also, notice that when the two values, MIN and NAME(I) were exchanged, three lines of code and the use of a temporary variable, TEMP, were required. If we had used simply

```
NAME(I) = MIN
MIN = NAME(I)
```

both variables would have been assigned the same value, namely MIN.
During execution of the program, a total of

$$(n - 1) + (n - 2) + (n - 3) + \cdots + 2 + 1 = \tfrac{1}{2}n(n - 1)$$

comparisons are made and, assuming a random initial ordering, the number of interchanges should be somewhat less than half the number of comparisons.

There are two further considerations concerning the selection sort algorithm: First, even if the original list were already in order, exactly the same number of comparison tests would have to be made, although of course there would be no replacements. Second, if the original, unsorted list consisted of not just names but contained additional information as well, such as addresses, ID numbers, and bank balances, during each exchange all of these items would have to be interchanged as well. This could seriously affect the efficiency of the algorithm. These shortcomings of the selection sort are addressed in the next two sections.

Figure 7-2 The Fortran code for a selection sort alphabetization.

```
*    SELECTION SORT PROGRAM
*
     PROGRAM SELECT
*
     CHARACTER*20 NAME(1000),MIN,TEMP
     INTEGER I,N,TOP

     READ(*,'(A20)',END=99)(NAME(I),I=1,1000)
99   N = I - 1

     DO 2 TOP = 1,N
         MIN = NAME(TOP)
         DO 1 I = TOP + 1,N

             IF(NAME(I) .LT. MIN)THEN
                 TEMP = NAME(I)
                 NAME(I) = MIN
                 MIN = TEMP

             END IF

1        CONTINUE
         NAME(TOP) = MIN
2    CONTINUE
```

TOP is the number of the first element in the remaining list.

If the current name is less than the current minimum, we redefine the minimum by switching positions.

The minimum is now placed at the top of the remaining list.

7.6.2 The Bubble Sort

Another simple sorting algorithm, the bubble sort, is especially useful when the original list is partially sorted to begin with. The idea in the bubble sort algorithm is illustrated in the sequence below.

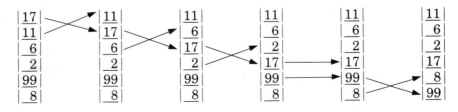

1. Compare the first two elements (17 and 11) and if out of order exchange.

2. Compare the next pair (now 17 and 6) and if out of order, exchange.

3. Continue this through the entire list. Notice that after the first pass the largest element in the list (99) has "bubbled" down to the bottom.

4. In the second pass through the list only compare the remaining elements, since the largest element is already in the proper position. The arrangement of the numbers after the second pass will be

$$\begin{array}{|c|}\hline 6 \\ \hline 2 \\ \hline 11 \\ \hline 8 \\ \hline 17 \\ \hline 99 \\ \hline \end{array}$$

The Fortran code to accomplish a bubble sort is given in Figure 7-3. The purpose of the variable FLAG is to signal when the entire list has been

Figure 7-3 The Fortran code for a bubble sort.

```
*
*  THE BUBBLE SORT
*
       CHARACTER FLAG*3
       INTEGER I,N,J
       REAL A(1000)

       READ(*,'(F10.5)',END=99)(A(I),I=1,1000)
  99   N = I - 1
*
       DO 2 I = N,2,-1                    I is the bottom element in
                                          the current comparison set.
           FLAG = 'OFF'
           DO 1 J = 1,I - 1               Compare successive pairs
                                          of the remaining set.
               IF(A(J) .GT. A(J + 1))THEN
                   TEMP = A(J)            If out of order, exchange.
                   A(J) = A(J + 1)
                   A(J + 1) = TEMP
                   FLAG = 'ON'
               END IF
  1        CONTINUE
           IF(FLAG .EQ. 'OFF')THEN        If there were no exchanges
               GO TO 3                    at all in this pass, the
           END IF                         list is sorted. So ter-
                                          minate the sort.
  2    CONTINUE
  3    CONTINUE
           ...
```

compared and *no exchanges* have been required. If this is the case, the list is already in order and the sorting can stop.

7.6.3 Sorting with a Pointer

As mentioned above, a sorting problem is frequently complicated by the fact that associated with each name in a list are many other additional items. Each time two names are switched positions in the list, all the corresponding data must be exchanged as well. In such cases it is much more convenient to simply keep track of the rearrangements by means of an indexing array, called a *pointer*. The idea is to leave the original list, NAME(I), intact, while the alphabetic order of the elements is determined and stored in INDX(K). Thus the first name in the sorted list would be given by NAME(INDX(1)). Perhaps AARDVARK is the twelfth name in the original list and AARON is the seventh, so the result of the sorting would give:

```
INDX(1) = 12
INDX(2) =  7
NAME(INDX(1)) => 'AARDVARK'
NAME(INDX(2)) => 'AARON'
      etc.
```

Either the exchange sort or the bubble sort can be rewritten using a pointing index array. The code for the exchange sort with a pointer is given in Figure 7-4.

The output from this code for a sample list of 10 names is given below:

I	ORIGINAL LIST	SORTED LIST	ORIGINAL POSITION
1	ZEKE	ALICE	7
2	WILL	CARL	8
3	FRANK	CAROL	9
4	PAUL	DON	6
5	KEN	FRANK	3
6	DON	KEN	5
7	ALICE	PAUL	4
8	CARL	WILL	2
9	CAROL	ZEKE	1
10	ZELDA	ZELDA	10

To print out all the data associated with each name with the names in

```
* EXCHANGE SORT WITH A POINTER ARRAY
*
      CHARACTER*5 NAME(1000),MIN
      INTEGER INDX(1000),I,N,TOP,TEMP
*
      READ(*,'(A)',END=99)(NAME(I),I=1,1000)
   99 N = I - 1

      DO 1 I = 1,1000                          Initialize the pointer
         INDX(I) = I                           array to the order 1, 2, . . .
    1 CONTINUE
*
      DO 3 TOP = 1,N - 1                        INDX(TOP) refers to the
                                                name at the top of the re-
                                                maining unsorted list, i.e.,
                                                NAME(INDX(1)) = ⟨first
         MIN = NAME(INDX(TOP))                  name⟩. Initialize MIN to
                                                be the top name.
         DO 2 I = TOP,N

            IF(NAME(INDX(I)) .LT. MIN)THEN
               TEMP = INDX(I)                   If a smaller value is
               INDX(I) = INDX(TOP)              found, redefine pointer;
               INDX(TOP) = TEMP                 i.e., INDX(TOP) and the
               MIN = NAME(INDX(TOP))            value of MIN.
            END IF

    2      CONTINUE
    3 CONTINUE

      WRITE(*,11)
      WRITE(*,12)(I,NAME(I),NAME(INDX(I)),INDX(I),I = 1,N)
      STOP

   11 FORMAT(//,5X,'ORIGINAL SORTED ORIGINAL',/,
     +       2X,'I',4X,'LIST',5X,'LIST',3X,'POSITION',/)
   12 FORMAT(1X,I2,3X,A5,4X,A5,6X,I2)

      END
```

Figure 7-4 The
Fortran code for
a selection sort
with a pointer.

alphabetical order, we need only the information contained in the pointer
array.

```
      • • •
      DO 37 I = 1,N
         K = INDX(I)
         WRITE(*,14)NAME(K),ADDRESS(K),ID(K), • • •
   37 CONTINUE
      • • •
```

7.7 PLOTTING A GRAPH ON THE LINE PRINTER OR TERMINAL SCREEN

7.7.1 Plotting with a Typewriter

As with any problem, plotting a graph on the terminal screen requires that we first carefully analyze the steps involved in plotting a graph on ordinary graph paper and attempt to construct an algorithm understandable to the computer. Plotting a graph consists of the following steps:

1. Generate a table of number pairs, $(x_i, y_i, \text{ for } i = 1,n)$

i	x_i	y_i
1	0.0	0.0
2	2.0	32.0
3	3.0	72.0
. . .	. . .	. . .
. . .	. . .	. . .

These numbers may represent experimental data, say position vs. time for a falling object, or may be generated from a particular functional relation between x and y as $y(x) = 8x^2$. Once the data set is complete we can begin to represent the set by points on a graph.

2. Determine the range of both x_i and y_i. This will require a determination of both the minimum and maximum values of x and y in the data set and then

$$(\text{Range})_x = (x_{max} - x_{min})$$
$$(\text{Range})_y = (y_{max} - y_{min})$$

These values are then used for scaling the x and y axes. That is, adjusting the scales of the axes so that the graph fits neatly on the graph paper. This is the most difficult aspect of plotting and I will return to the details in Section 8-5.

3. Step through the points and graph them one by one. You might not think that such a trivial step is worth mentioning. However, graphing a function in this manner is one of the surest ways to appreciate the meaning of the term "function." Since this is so critical to further understanding of mathematics, it warrants possibly insulting your intelligence. Thus, for each value of x_i (the independent variable) there is a corresponding y_i (the dependent variable). Or, for each value of i there is a pair (x_i, y_i).

Since a typewriter or line printer executes one horizontal line at a time, then proceeds to the next line, stepping along the x axis and graphing y values will mean that the graph will have to be constructed moving down the page, not across.

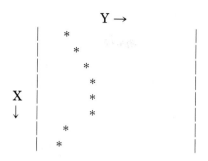

When one line is displayed, 80 or so characters will be printed (depending on the length of the y axis) for a particular value of x (say $x = 1.22$). *All* of these characters will be blanks except one. The position corresponding to $y(x = 1.22)$ will contain some symbol—e.g., an asterisk. To determine the proper placement of the asterisk, consider the following:

Suppose we have a function $y = f(x)$ and wish to graph the function y vs. x for $x = 0$ to $x = 5$. Thus $(\text{Range})_x = 5 - 0 = 5$. We also need the range in y values. We might determine the following:

$$y_{max} = 16.38$$

$$y_{min} = -7.21$$

so

$$(\text{Range})_y = 16.38 - (-7.21) = 23.59$$

Next, if at $x = 3.0$, $y(3.0) = 12.2$, where in the horizontal line is the asterisk to be placed? If the y axis is to be 81 columns wide, we could first define

$$\text{Ratio} = \frac{y(3) - y_{min}}{y_{max} - y_{min}}$$

Notice that ratio is between 0.0 and 1.0. The appropriate column for the asterisk is

$$IY = 80. * RATIO$$

For the particular choice of numbers above, $y(3) = 12.2$, we obtain

```
RATIO = .82281
IY = 66
```

The Fortran code to execute this single line of the graph might then be:

```
CHARACTER*1 LINE(0:80),HIT,MISS
INTEGER IY,I
REAL X(0:80),Y(0:80)
    ...
    ...
X(27) = 3.0
Y(27) = 12.2
    ...
    ...
YMAX = 16.38
YMIN = -7.21
    ...
    ...
RATIO = (Y(27) - YMIN)/(YMAX - YMIN)
IY = 80.0 * RATIO
HIT = '*'
MISS = ' '
DO 13 I = 0,80
     LINE(I) = MISS     Initialize the entire line to be blanks.
13 CONTINUE
     LINE(IY) = HIT           Place a * in column IY.
     WRITE(*,'(2X,81A1)')(LINE(I),I = 0,80)
```

The idea then for graphing the complete set of values x_i, y_i, is to use this algorithm repeatedly for each line of the graph. The complete Fortran code is illustrated in Figure 7-5. The output from this program for the function

$$f(x) = \sin^2\left(\pi\frac{x}{10}\right) \qquad 0 \le x \le 10$$

is shown in Figure 7-6.

7.7.2 Contour Plots

To represent a function of two variables on a graph, a contour plot is often used. You have probably seen contour maps that give the elevation of the land above sea level as closed paths drawn on a normal map. If x represents the east-west position on the map (longitude) and y represents the north-south position (latitude), then the elevation of any point of land can be written as a function of x and y: elevation = $E(x, y)$. If we next connect all those points with an elevation of 100 feet, we would get a curve of constant (100 feet) elevation. This is then repeated for elevations of 200 feet, 300 feet,

Figure 7-5 The Fortran code to graph a function at the terminal.

```
      PROGRAM PLOT
      CHARACTER*1 LINE(0:60)
      REAL X(0:25),Y(0:25),YMAX,YMIN,XHI,XLO,XSTEP,F,Z,

      F(Z) = ...                              A statement function for
                                              f(x); note I have used Z,
                                              since X is a dimensioned
                                              variable.

      N = 25
      READ(*,*)XLO,XHI                        The limits on the x's
      XSTEP = (XHI - XLO)/(N - 1.)
      DO 1 I = 0,N
          X(I) = I * XSTEP                    Fill in the table of xᵢ, yᵢ.
          Y(I) = F(X(I))
    1 CONTINUE

      YMAX = Y(0)                             Determine the min/max
      YMIN = Y(0)                             y values.
      DO 2 I = 1,N
          IF(Y(I) .LT. YMIN)YMIN = Y(I)
          IF(Y(I) .GT. YMAX)YMAX = Y(I)
    2 CONTINUE
      SCALE = YMAX - YMIN

      DO 3 I = 0,60
          LINE(I) = ' '                       Initialize the line to be
    3 CONTINUE                                all blanks.

      WRITE(*,12)
      DO 4 IX = 0,25                          Step through the x values.
          ISTAR = (Y(IX) - YMIN)/SCALE * 60.  ISTAR is the position of
          LINE(ISTAR) = '*'                   the asterisk in the line.
          WRITE(*,11)X(IX),Y(IX)(LINE(I),I = 0,60)
          LINE(ISTAR) = ' '                   Blank out the star to
    4 CONTINUE                                set up for next line.

      STOP
   11 FORMAT(1X,2F6.2,')',61A1,')')
   12 FORMAT(4X,'X',5X,'Y ',63('-'))
      END
```

etc. This is shown in Figure 7-7. The idea can be applied to any function of
two variables.

1. Given a function of two variables, $z = f(x, y)$, with known limits on x and
   y such that $a \leq x \leq b, c \leq y \leq d$, compute a two-dimensional table of z

Figure 7-6 A printer plot of $f(x) = \sin^2\left(\pi\dfrac{x}{10}\right)$.

```
INPUT XLO,XHI  0., 12.5
    X     Y  ---------------------------------------------------------------
 0.00  0.00)*                                                              )
  .50   .02)  *                                                            )
 1.00   .10)        *                                                      )
 1.50   .21)            *                                                  )
 2.00   .35)                  *                                            )
 2.50   .50)                       *                                       )
 3.00   .65)                            *                                  )
 3.50   .79)                                 *                             )
 4.00   .90)                                      *                        )
 4.50   .98)                                          *  )
 5.00  1.00)                                             * )
 5.50   .98)                                          *  )
 6.00   .90)                                      *                        )
 6.50   .79)                                 *                             )
 7.00   .65)                            *                                  )
 7.50   .50)                       *                                       )
 8.00   .35)                  *                                            )
 8.50   .21)            *                                                  )
 9.00   .10)        *                                                      )
 9.50   .02)  *                                                            )
10.00   .00)*                                                              )
10.50   .02)  *                                                            )
11.00   .10)        *                                                      )
11.50   .21)            *                                                  )
12.00   .35)                  *                                            )
12.50   .50)                       *                                       )
       ---------------------------------------------------------------
```

Figure 7-7 A contour map.

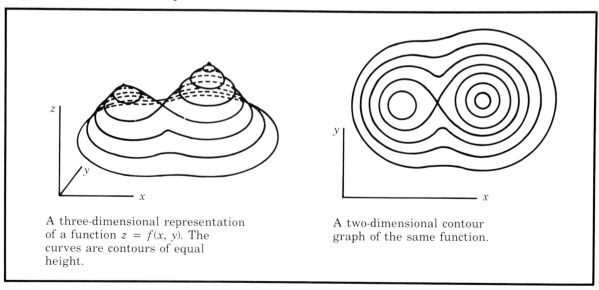

A three-dimensional representation of a function $z = f(x, y)$. The curves are contours of equal height.

A two-dimensional contour graph of the same function.

values for all combinations of x_i, $i = 1$, n_x and y_j, $j = 1$, n_y in this range. That is Z(I, J).

2. Compute the overall maximum and minimum values of Z(I, J) and thus determine the range of z values.

3. Print out a square array of symbols corresponding to the values of Z(I, J) defined in the following manner:

a. Let $(\text{Range})_z = z_{max} - z_{min}$

b. Replace Z(I, J) → 50 * (Z(I, J) − ZMIN)/(Range)$_z$. All the z values are now between 0.0 and 50.0.

c. Construct an integer array IZ(I, J) = Z(I, J).

d. For those points (I, J) that have an IZ(I, J) that is divisible by 5, assign a symbol from '0', '1', . . . , to '9', by the relation

```
        CONTUR(I,J)  =  NUMBER(IZ(I,J)/5)
```

where   NUMBER(0) = '0'

NUMBER(1) = '1'

NUMBER(2) = '2'

. . .   . . .

NUMBER(9) = '9'

e. If IZ(I, J) does not divide evenly by five, assign a blank.

```
    IF(IZ(I,J)/5 * 5 .NE. IZ(I,J))CONTUR(I,J) = '  '
```

The Fortran code for such a program is illustrated in Figure 7-8 and the output for the function

$$z = f(x, y) = \sin^2\left(\pi\frac{x}{5}\right) \sinh\left(\pi\frac{y}{5}\right)$$

is given in Figure 7-9.

Figure 7-8 Fortran code for a contour plot of a two-dimensional function.

```
      PROGRAM SQUARE
*--
*--   WILL PRODUCE A 20 BY 20 CONTOUR PLOT OF THE FUNCTION F(X,Y)
*--   FOR XMIN < X < XMAX, YMIN < Y < YMAX. THE MIN/MAX VALUES
*--   FOR THE FUNCTION ARE DETERMINED AND THE COUNTOURS ARE REP-
*--   RESENTED BY INTEGERS, 0 FOR MINIMUM, 9 FOR MAXIMUM.
*-----------------------------------------------------------------
*  VARIABLES
```

Continued

```
      CHARACTER*1 NUMBER(0:9),CONTUR(20,20),BLANK
      REAL X,Y,XMIN,XMAX,YMIN,YMAX,ZMIN,ZMAX,RANGEZ,
     +     Z(20,20)
      INTEGER IZ(20,20)
*
*           Z(I,J)        - CONTAINS THE VALUES OF THE FUNCTION
*                           FOR X,Y VALUES ON THE GRID.
*           IZ(I,J)       - CONTAINS THE VALUES OF Z SCALED TO
*                           THE RANGE 0-50 AND TRUNCATED.
*           CONTUR(I,J) - CONTAINS A SYMBOL '0' THROUGH '9'
*                           OR A BLANK AT EACH GRID POINT.
*-------------------------------------------------------------
* STATEMENT FUNCTION FOR F(X,Y)
*
      F(X,Y) = ((SIN(3.1415926*X/5.))**2)*SINH(3.1415926*Y/5.)
*-------------------------------------------------------------
* INITIALIZATION
*
      NUMBER(0) = '0'
      NUMBER(1) = '1'
      NUMBER(2) = '2'
      NUMBER(3) = '3'
      NUMBER(4) = '4'
      NUMBER(5) = '5'
      NUMBER(6) = '6'
      NUMBER(7) = '7'
      NUMBER(8) = '8'
      NUMBER(9) = '9'
*
*                        THIS COULD BE SHORTENED WITH A
*                        DO LOOP AND THE FUNCTION CHAR( ).
*
      BLANK = ' '
      PRINT *,'INPUT LIMITS ON THE X AXIS'
      READ *,XMIN,XMAX
      PRINT *,'INPUT LIMITS ON THE Y AXIS'
      READ *,YMIN,YMAX
      DX = (XMAX - XMIN)/19.
      DY = (YMAX - YMIN)/19.
*
*                        THERE ARE 20 POINTS BUT ONLY 19
*                        STEPS. NEXT FILL IN Z ARRAY.
*-------------------------------------------------------------
*
      Y = YMIN
      DO 2 IY = 1,20
```

```
            X = XMIN
            DO 1 IX = 1,20
                Z(IX,IY) = F(X,Y)
                X = X + DX
      1     CONTINUE
            Y = Y + DY
     2 CONTINUE
*
*                                FIND MIN/MAX OF Z VALUES.
*
       ZMAX = Z(1,1)
       ZMIN = Z(1,1)
       DO 3 IX = 1,20
       DO 3 IY = 1,20
          IF(Z(IX,IY) .LT. ZMIN)ZMIN = Z(IX,IY)
          IF(Z(IX,IY) .GT. ZMAX)ZMAX = Z(IX,IY)
     3 CONTINUE
*
*                                SCALE THE Z'S TO BE BETWEEN 0-50 AND
*                                CONSTRUCT THE CONTUR ARRAY.
*
       RANGEZ = (ZMAX - ZMIN)
       DO 4 IX = 1,20
       DO 4 IY = 1,20
          TEMP = (Z(IX,IY) - ZMIN)/RANGEZ * 50.0
          IZ(IX,IY) = TEMP
*
*                                SET CONTUR = BLANK UNLESS IZ IS
*                                DIVISIBLE BY 5.
*
          CONTUR(IX,IY) = BLANK
          IF(IZ(IX,IY)/5 * 5 .EQ. IZ(IX,IY))THEN
             CONTUR(IX,IY) = NUMBER(IZ(IX,IY)/5)
          END IF
     4 CONTINUE
*------------------------------------------------------------------
* PRINT THE CONTOUR PLOT
*
       WRITE(*,8)XMIN,XMAX
       WRITE(*,9)YMIN
       WRITE(*,'(2X,62A1)')('*',I=1,62)
       DO 6 I = 1,20
          WRITE(*,10)'*',(CONTUR(J,I),J = 1,20),'*'
```

Continued

```
      6 CONTINUE
        WRITE(*,'(2X,62A1)')('*',I = 1,62)
        WRITE(*,9)YMAX
        STOP
*
      8 FORMAT(///,2X,F4.1,25X,'X',25X,F4.1)
      9 FORMAT(1X,'Y = ',F4.1)
     10 FORMAT(2X,A1,20(1X,A1,1X),A1)
        END
```

Figure 7-9 Contour plot of $f(x, y) = \sin^2\left(\pi\dfrac{x}{5}\right)\sinh\left(\pi\dfrac{y}{5}\right)$.

```
-1.0                                 X                                2.0
Y = -2.0
  **************************************************************
  *     5                  7   7           6         4                1       0 *
  *                        7   7           6     5         3                  *
  *          6             7   7                     4                        *
  *          6             7   7                    5                   2 *
  *                        7   7              6                      3 *
  *      6                 7   7                   5                      *
  *      6            7    7   7              6         5          4 *
  * 6                 7    7   7                        5              *
  *                   7    7   7   7              6              5 *
  *                   7    7   7   7                   6              *
  *                   7    7   7   7                        6   6      *
  *              7    7    7   7   7   7                              *
  *         7   7   7    7   7   7   7   7   7                        *
  * 7   7   7   7   7    7   7   7   7   7   7   7   7   7   7   7   7 *
  *         7   7   7    7   7   7   7   7   7                        *
  *              7   7   7   7   7   7   7                      8   8 *
  *                   7    7   7   7   7              8   8          *
  *                   7    7   7   7   7                   8          9 *
  *                        7   7   7   7         8            9      *
  * 8                      7   7   7   7                              *
  **************************************************************
Y = 1.0
```

PROBLEMS

1. What is the output from the following:

```
CHARACTER*5 B,C,D(0:3),E(-2:2)
CHARACTER F*1,G*2,A*1
```

```
A = 'A'
C = A
F = C
B = '12345'
G = B(4:)
E(-1)(3:4) = B(2:3)
E(-1) = A
D(0)(:) = B(:)
E(-2) = A//G//B(:2)
E(0) = B(5:5)//B(4:4)//B(3:3)//B(2:2)//B(1:1)
E(1) = A//B
```

a. `WRITE(*,'(1X,A)')A`

b. `WRITE(*,'(1X,A)')B`

c. `WRITE(*,'(1X,A)')C`

d. `WRITE(*,'(1X,A)')F`

e. `WRITE(*,'(1X,A)')G`

f. `WRITE(*,'(1X,A)')E(-1)`

g. `WRITE(*,'(1X,A)')D(0)`

h. `WRITE(*,'(1X,A)')E(-2)`

i. `WRITE(*,'(1X,A)')(E(0)(I:I),`
`        +                I = 5,1,-1)`

j. `WRITE(*,'(1X,A)')E(1)`

k. `WRITE(*,'(1X,A)')B//B`

2. Write a program to read a character string ending with a period and print the string in reverse order. Assume the length of the string is less than 80 characters.

3. Design a program that will read a paragraph consisting of less than 25 lines and count the number of words. Assume that each line is 80 characters long, each line ends with two blank spaces, sentences end with a period followed by a single blank space, and no words are hyphenated. Also, the paragraph has fewer than 25 sentences and the first line is not indented.

4. Write a program to read a document of unknown length and everywhere replace the word "under" with "below." Watch out for compound words.

5. Write the code to read the phone book for the name 'JONES, JAMES' who lives on JENNINGS Street and prints out the phone number. The phone number in the listing is always in the form XXX-XXXX.

6. Execute the program on page 209 and determine the ordering of the Fortran symbols on your computer.

7. Rewrite the selection sort program to arrange the set in *decreasing* order.

8. Rewrite the selection sort program to also count the number of duplicate values in the list.

9. In the version of the bubble sort algorithm given in section 7.6.2, the largest element of the array "bubbles" down to the bottom of the array after one pass. Rewrite the algorithm so that the smallest element of the remaining list will "bubble" up to the top of the list.

10. Let each digit of a huge integer (less than 200 digits) be stored, right-adjusted, in the integer array, L(200). Write the Fortran code to accomplish the following:

   a. Form a copy of this number in the character array DIGIT (200)*1.

Each element of DIGIT is a numerical symbol from "0" to "9" in place of the numerical values, 0 to 9, stored in L.

b. Since the number is originally right-adjusted, it will likely contain a great many leading zeros. Replace all the leading zeros in DIGIT by blanks.

c. If all of the digits of L are multiplied by an integer k, it would be useful to incorporate the normal arithmetic concept of carrying into the multiplication. Thus if

L_5	L_4	L_3	L_2	L_1
0	6	7	1	5

is multiplied by 5, the elements of L would be

L_5	L_4	L_3	L_2	L_1
0	30	35	5	25

which we would prefer to write as

L_5	L_4	L_3	L_2	L_1
0	0	5	5	5
+ 3	3	0	2	0
3	3	5	7	5

By considering several numerical examples, show that the code below accomplishes the task of carrying.

```
NTERMS = 200
ICARRY = 0
DO 1 I = 1,NTERMS
    L(I) = L(I) * K + ICARRY
    ICARRY = L(I)/10
    L(I) = L(I) - 10 * ICARRY
1 CONTINUE
```

d. Construct a program to compute 75! *exactly*. This number has more than 100 digits.

11. Rewrite the bubble sort program to include a pointer array. The original list should be left intact. Test your program on a sample list.

12. Alter the plotting program to include a border of asterisks around the graph. Also print four y values along the y axis along with equally spaced tic marks. For example,

In addition, along the x axis, print a value of x only every tenth line.

13. Alter the plotting program to graph two functions simultaneously, using different symbols. Note you will have to determine an overall minimum/maximum.

14. Execute contour plots for the following functions:

   a. $f(x, y) = \sin(x^2 + y^2)$ $-1 \leq x \leq 1$
   $$-1 \leq y \leq 1$$

   b. $g(x, y) = e^{-xy}$ $-1 \leq x \leq 1$
   $$-1 \leq y \leq 1$$

   c. $h(x, y) = (x - 1)^2 + 2(y - 1)^2$ $0 \leq x \leq 2$
   $$0 \leq y \leq 2$$

15. To produce a graph with the x axis horizontal and the y axis vertical, a different procedure must be employed. Once again a table of (x_i, y_i) is first obtained and the range of the x and y values determined. This time the entire plot will be stored in the character array

   ```
   CHARACTER PAGE(0:60,0:50)*1
   ```

   After initializing the entire array as all blanks, step through the tabulated values and determine the positioning of the points on the page by

   $$I_x = 60 \frac{(x_i - x_{min})}{(\text{Range})_x}$$

   $$I_y = 50 \frac{(y_i - y_{min})}{(\text{Range})_y}$$

   and assign a symbol, say *, to this point,

   ```
   PAGE(IX,IY) = '*'
   ```

   Finally the array PAGE is printed

   ```
   DO 7 IY = 50,0,-1
         WRITE(*,'(2X,61A1)')(PAGE(IX,IY)IX = 0,60)
   7 CONTINUE
   ```

   Follow this procedure to obtain a graph of $y = e^{-x/3} \sin(\pi x/2)$ for $0 \leq x \leq 4$.

PROGRAMMING ASSIGNMENT III

The programming problems in this section are meant to illustrate the material covered to this point in the text, particularly Chapters 6 and 7. These programs are quite demanding and will require a considerable amount of your time. I suggest that you start early and allow ample time for debugging the programs. In addition, you should attempt to structure the programs in block form as suggested in Section 3.5. The programs should contain safeguards with diagnostic PRINT statements to handle any potential problems. A carefully constructed, neat code may take somewhat longer to design, but it pays dividends when problems arise. Of course, as your programs grow longer and more complex, the role of the flowchart or its alternatives becomes more critical. Again, you will find that the effort that you put into a clear outline of the workings of a proposed program will be time well spent.

III.1 SAMPLE PROGRAM

Industrial Engineering

Each of the traditional engineering disciplines (civil, mechanical, electrical, chemical, and metallurgical/mining) relies on a particular area of natural science for its foundation. Industrial engineering, however, seeks to incorporate the knowledge of the social sciences into designing improvements in the overall human-machine systems. The industrial engineer has responsibility for design, installation, and evaluation of not merely machines or systems but also for their interfacing with people to effect an overall productivity improvement. This may involve an understanding of human behavioral characteristics and their effect on the design of machines or the workplace, or on demands and services from outside from customers or clients. The industrial engineer will draw heavily on knowledge in economics, business management, and finance, as well as in the natural sciences. The areas of specialization of the industrial engineer may be classified as

Operations Research: The application of analytical techniques and mathematical models to phenomena such as inventory control, simulation, decision theory, and queuing theory to optimize the total systems necessary for the production of goods.

Management or Administrative Engineering: The increasingly complex interplay of management and production skills in modern industrial operations have resulted in a need for technically trained managers. They will evaluate and plan all manner of corporate ventures, interact with labor, engineering departments, and subcontractors. In addition, a management engineer may participate in the financial operations of a company, drawing on knowledge in economics, business management, and law.

Manufacturing and Production Engineers: Before a product is produced, the complete manufacturing process must be designed and set-up to optimize the economics involved and the final quality of the item. This requires a broad knowledge of process design, plant lay-outs, tool design, robotics, and man-machine interactions.

Information Systems: The use of computers to gather and analyze data for decision making, planning, and to improve man-machine activity.

In a recent survey by the American Institute of Industrial Engineers the following list includes the most common responsibilities of those industrial engineers that responded.

Facilities planning and design
Methods engineering
Work systems design
Production engineering
Management information and control systems
Organization analysis and design
Work measurement
Wage administration
Quality control
Project management
Cost control
Inventory control
Energy conservation
Computerized process control
Product packaging, handling, and testing
Tool and equipment selection
Production control
Product improvement studies
Preventive maintenance programs
Safety programs
Training programs

Sample Program: Minimizing Repair Costs

A large manufacturing plant has many identical machines, all of which are subject to failure at random times. Repairmen are hired to patrol and service the machines. The determination of the appropriate number of repairmen to hire is dependent on the following considerations:

1. Good repairmen are expensive. Assume an hourly wage of W (dollars/hr). The number of repairmen is R.
2. A repairman can work on only one machine at a time, so several down machines may have to wait for repair resulting in a productivity loss to the company. We will assume the loss per machine while it is inoperative is L (dollars/hr).
3. Too many repairmen will reduce the number of malfunctioning machines but may result in excessive idle time for these workers.

In addition we will make the following assumptions regarding the servicing of these machines.

1. The failure rate is known and is characterized by the average time between failures for an individual machine.

$$\lambda = \text{failures per machine per unit time (no./hr)}$$

$$1/\lambda = \text{time between failures per machine (hr)}$$

2. The average repair time is known and is characterized by

$$\mu = \text{repairs per hour per repairman (no./hr)}$$

$$1/\mu = \text{average repair time per machine (hr)}$$

The quantity

$$\rho = \frac{\lambda}{\mu}$$

is called the *traffic intensity* and $1/\rho$ represents roughly the number of machines that one repairman can handle [(time between machine failures)/(repair time per machine)].

The basic problem is to minimize the cost of the wages to the repairmen plus the downtime costs of inoperative machines; i.e.,

(III.1) $$\text{Cost}(R) = WR + \langle N_d \rangle L$$

where $\langle N_d \rangle$ is the average number of inoperative machines at any one time. This will of course depend on how many repairmen (R) are hired. The main complexity of this problem is in calculating $\langle N_d \rangle$.

Let us assume that the likelihood that all machines are working can be represented by a number P_0 between 0 and 1 with $P_0 \sim 0$ representing a very small possibility that all are working and $P_0 \sim 1$ representing near certainty that all are working. Thus P_0 is the probability that zero machines are down.

Similarly, P_1 is the probability that only one machine is down, P_n the probability that n machines are down. The following result may then be obtained from queuing theory to relate these probabilities:
If $n < R$

$$P_{n+1} = \rho\left(\frac{N - n}{n + 1}\right)P_n \tag{III.2}$$

If $R \le n < N$

$$P_{n+1} = \rho\left(\frac{N - n}{R}\right)P_n$$

where N is the total number of machines. For example if $N = 50$ and $R = 5$, then

$$P_1 = 50\rho P_0$$

$$P_2 = \frac{49}{2}\rho P_1 = 49(25)\rho^2 P_0$$

$$P_3 = \frac{48}{3}\rho P_2 = 16(49)(25)\rho^3 P_0$$

$$\cdots \quad \cdots$$

$$P_6 = \frac{45}{6}\rho P_5 = 105938\rho^6 P_0$$

Thus every P_n can be related to P_0.

Finally, P_0 is determined from the condition

$$\sum_{n=0}^{N} P_n = 1 \tag{III.3}$$

Since each P_n is proportional to P_0, this is accomplished by

First setting $P_0 = 1$
Computing all the P_n on this basis
Evaluating the sum in Equation (III.3)
Rescale each of the P_n by replacing P_n by P_n/sum

The average number of down machines may then be expressed as

$$\langle N_d \rangle = \sum_{n=0}^{N} nP_n \tag{III.4}$$

That is, the number down times the likelihood of that many down, summed over all possibilities.

Once this expression is computed, Equation (III.1) may be evaluated for a variety of values of R and the value that results in a minimum cost determined.

Problem Specifics

Write a program to accomplish the following:

1. Read the values of N, R_{max}, λ, μ, W, and L for the first case (fast, expensive repairmen and good, reliable machines). Print with appropriate headings. Use character variables for "fast, expensive" and "good, reliable."
2. For $R = 1$ to R_{max}, execute the following calculation:
   a. For $n = 1$ to N, compute and store the values of P_n assuming a value of 1 for P_0.
   b. Sum all the P_n (including P_0) and then rescale so that the sum of all the P_n is now 1.
   c. Compute the average number of down machines, $\langle N_d \rangle$, from Equation (III.4) and store in an array DOWN(R,ICASE) where ICASE is the case number.
   d. Compute and store the total repair costs for this case and for this number of repairmen in a similar array.
3. Determine and print the results for the minimum repair costs for this case.
4. Repeat for the three subsequent cases.
5. Produce two "printer plots" for repair costs and average number of down machines with all four cases plotted simultaneously on each plot. Use different symbols for each case.

The Fortran code for this problem is shown in Figure III-1 and the output from the program is shown in Figure III-2.

Table III-1 Input parameters for repair costs problem.

Case, i	Repairmen	Machine	No. of machines, N	Maximum No. of repairmen R_{max}	Failure rate, λ	Repair rate, μ	Repairman wages, W	Loss per machine, λ
1	fast, expensive	good, reliable	65	15	0.03	0.66	16.0	250.0
2	fast, expensive	poor, cheap	70	15	0.04	0.66	16.0	215.0
3	slow, cheap	good, reliable	65	15	0.03	0.58	11.0	250.0
4	slow, cheap	poor, cheap	70	15	0.04	0.58	11.0	215.0

Figure III-1 The Fortran code for the minimum repairs cost problem.

```fortran
      PROGRAM REPAIR

*--
*-- Computes the optimum number of repairmen to be hired
*-- to service a large number of machines that break
*-- down randomly. Several situations are considered
*-- and the overall best case is found.
*--
* Variables
*--
      CHARACTER*4 MEN,MACHINE
      INTEGER N,RMAX,ROPT(4),IC,IBEST,R,NCASE
      REAL  FRATE,RRATE,W,LOSS,CSTMIN(4),RHO,P(0:75),
     +      DOWN(15,4),COST(15,4),SUM,CBEST

*--   IC       -- Case number (1 to 4)
*--   N        -- Number of machines
*--   RMAX     -- Maximum number of repairmen
*--   R        -- Current number of repairmen
*--   NCASE    -- Total number of cases considered
*--   FRATE    -- Failure rate of the machines
*--   RRATE    -- Repair rate of the repairmen
*--   RHO      -- Traffic intensity (Frate/Rrate)
*--   W        -- Repairmen's hourly wage
*--   LOSS     -- Down time loss per machine
*--   MEN      -- Type of repairmen (fast - slow)
*--   MACHINE  -- Type of machine (good - poor)
*--   P(K)     -- Probability that K machines are down
*--   DOWN(R,I)-- Avg. no. down for case I and R
*--               repairmen
*--   COST(R,I)-- Total cost for the same conditions
*--   CSTMIN(I)-- Minimum cost for case I
*--   ROPT(I)  -- Optimum no. of repairmen for case I
*--   IBEST    -- The optimum case number
*--   SUM      -- Sum of the P(K)
*--   CBEST    -- Overall minimum cost
*--
* Initialization
*--
      OPEN(UNIT=36,FILE='RPRCST')
      REWIND 36

*--
*--   Print table headings
*--
      WRITE(*,21)
      IC = 1
    1 READ(36,*,END=10)MEN,MACHNE,N,RMAX,FRATE,RRATE,
     +      W,LOSS
      WRITE(*,22)      MEN,MACHNE,N,RMAX,FRATE,RRATE,
     +      W,LOSS

      RHO = FRATE/RRATE

*--
* Computation
*--
*--   Determine the probabilities (unscaled) for
*--   R = 1 to Rmax.
*--
      DO 4 R = 1,RMAX
         P(0) = 1.0
         SUM = 0.0
         DO 2 I = 0,N - 1
            IF(I.LT.R)THEN
               P(I + 1) = RHO*(N - I)/(I + 1.)*P(I)
            ELSE
               P(I + 1) = RHO*(N - I)/R*P(I)
            END IF
            SUM = SUM + P(I + 1)
    2    CONTINUE

*--
*--   Next scale the P's and determine the avg.
*--   number down.
*--
         DOWN(R,IC) = 0.0
         DO 3 I = 0,N
            P(I) = P(I)/SUM
            DOWN(R,IC) = DOWN(R,IC) + I*P(I)
    3    CONTINUE

*--
*--   Once the average down is known, compute costs.
*--
         COST(R,IC) = W*R + DOWN(R,IC)*LOSS
    4 CONTINUE

*--
*--   Find the minimum costs and no. of
*--   repairmen for this case.
*--
      CSTMIN(IC) = COST(1,IC)
      ROPT(IC) = 1
      DO 5 R = 1,RMAX
         IF(COST(R,IC).LT.CSTMIN(IC))THEN
            CSTMIN(IC) = COST(R,IC)
            ROPT(IC)   = R
         END IF
    5 CONTINUE

*--
*--   This case is complete, return and read next
*--   data set.
*--
```

Continued

```
*--
      IC = IC + 1
      GO TO 1
*--
*--   All cases considered, determine optimum case.
*--
10    NCASE = IC - 1
      IBEST = 1
      CBEST = CSTMIN(1)
      DO 11 IC = 2,NCASE
      IF(CSTMIN(IC) .LT. CBEST)IBEST = IC
11    CONTINUE
*--
* Print final results
*--
      WRITE(*,23)
      DO 12 IC = 1,NCASE
      WRITE(*,24)IC,ROPT(IC),CSTMIN(IC)
      IF(IC .EQ. IBEST)THEN
      WRITE(*,25)'OPTIMUM SITUATION'
      END IF
12    CONTINUE
      STOP
*--
* Formats
*--

21    FORMAT(///,13X,'RESULTS OF THE REPAIR COST ',
     +               'PROBLEM',//,
     +       5X,'INPUT PARAMETERS',//,
     +       6X,'NUMBER',T31,'MAX',//,
     +       7X,'OF',5X,'TYPE',3X,'NUMBER',4X,'OF',T57,
     +               'DOWN',//,
     +       6X,'REPAIR',9X,'OF',8X,'REPAIR FAIL REPAIR'
     +               ,'WORKER TIME',//,
     +       ' CASE  MEN   MACHINE MACHINE  MEN    RATE  ',
     +               'RATE    WAGES  LOSS',//,
     +       1X,60('-'))
22    FORMAT(3X,I1,2(3X,A4),5X,I2,6X,I2,3(2X,F5.2),
     +       2X,F5.1)
23    FORMAT(/,5X,'COMPUTED RESULTS',//,
     +       T20,'OPTIMUM',T32,'OPTIMUM',//,
     +       T20,'NUMBER ',T32,' COSTS ',//,
     +       11X,'CASE',T22,'OF',T31,'FOR THIS',//,
     +       10X,'NUMBER  REPAIRMEN',5X,'CASE',//,
     +       10X,6('-'),2X,9('-'),3X,8('-'))
24    FORMAT(12X,I1,9X,I2,6X,F8.2)
25    FORMAT('-',T40,A)

      END
```

Figure III-2 The output from the minimum repair costs problem.

```
                 RESULTS OF THE REPAIR COSTS PROBLEM

     INPUT PARAMETERS
           NUMBER                         MAX
           OF       TYPE    NUMBER         OF                        DOWN
           REPAIR-  OF      OF             REPAIR-  FAIL   REPAIR  WORKER   TIME
     CASE  MEN      MACHINE MACHINE        MEN      RATE   RATE    WAGES    LOSS
     ----------------------------------------------------------------------------
       1   FAST     GOOD    65             15       .03    .66     16.00   250.0
       2   FAST     POOR    70             15       .04    .66     16.00   215.0
       3   SLOW     GOOD    65             15       .03    .58     11.00   250.0
       4   SLOW     POOR    70             15       .04    .58     11.00   215.0

     COMPUTED RESULTS

                          OPTIMUM      OPTIMUM
                          NUMBER       COSTS
               CASE       OF           FOR THIS
               NUMBER     REPAIRMEN    CASE
               ------     ---------    --------
                 1            6         815.77   OPTIMUM SITUATION
                 2            8         996.84
                 3            7         883.84
                 4            9        1076.65

     STOP
```

Programming Problem A: Resonant Circuit

A common problem in electrical engineering is the design of a tuning circuit to select radio waves with a particular frequency from the thousands always present as background noise. This is accomplished by means of a resonant circuit which will only sustain frequencies in a narrow band, $f_0 \pm \Delta f$, on both sides of the desired frequency f_0. Since I suspect that you may be more familiar with mechanical than electrical oscillations, I'll first describe the problem in terms of an analogous mechanical system consisting of a spring, weight, driving force, and damping fluid as illustrated in Figure III-3.

In introductory physics you determined the natural frequency of a spring as

$$f_0 = \frac{1}{2\pi}\left(\frac{k}{m}\right)^{1/2} \tag{III.5}$$

The mass, if displaced and released, will oscillate with this frequency. Next, if the top of the spring is forced up and down with a different frequency, $f \neq f_0$, the mass and the driving force will be out-of-phase. Occasionally, when the mass is moving up, the driving force will be moving down and the net result is that there will be no net motion of the mass. However, if the driving frequency is adjusted so that $f = f_0$, the two oscillations are in-phase so that the motion of the weight is reinforced with every oscillation, resulting in very large amplitude oscillations. Thus this system will sustain an input frequency $f = f_0$ and no others, and by varying the spring stiffness or the weight, we can tune this system to a variety of frequencies.

If the oscillations take place in a fluid such as air, water, oil, or molasses,

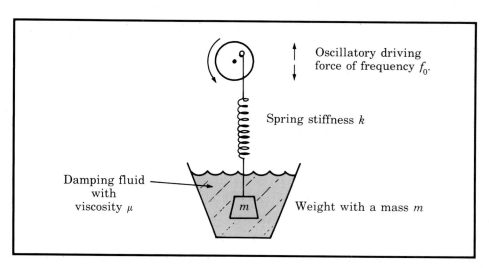

Figure III-3 A mechanical system to demonstrate resonant vibrations.

the analysis is a bit more complicated. The most important new feature is that the system will now sustain frequencies in a band of half-width Δf about f_0. The half-width is given by

(III.6)
$$\Delta f = \frac{1}{4\pi}\frac{\mu}{m}$$

where μ is the viscosity of the fluid. Thus the more viscous the fluid, the less selective the system is in discriminating the tuned frequency.

The mechanical system has a precise analogy with an electrical circuit. The role of the spring is played by a capacitor, a device for storing charge; the viscous force is represented by a resistor which dissipates energy; and the inertia or weight is represented by a coil which resists abrupt changes in the current. The equivalent circuit is shown in Figure III-4.

Figure III-4   A resonant electric circuit.

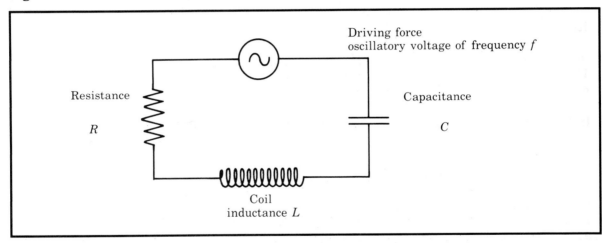

The correspondence between the mechanical and the electrical components is

Viscosity $\quad\mu \leftrightarrow\quad$ resistance R

Spring stiffness $k \leftrightarrow\quad$ (capacitance)$^{-1}$, $1/C$

Mass $\qquad\quad m \leftrightarrow\quad$ inductance L

Thus from Equation (III.5) the natural frequency of the circuit would be

(III.7)
$$f_0 = \frac{1}{2\pi}\left[\frac{1}{LC}\right]^{1/2}$$

and the half-width or selectivity of the circuit is

$$\Delta f = \frac{1}{4\pi} \frac{L}{R} \tag{III.8}$$

Furthermore, the amplitude of the oscillations (the voltage across the resistor) can be expressed as a function of the driving frequency as

$$V_r(f) = V_0 \left[1 + \frac{(f^2 - f_0^2)^2}{f^2 \Delta f^2} \right]^{-1/2} \tag{III.9}$$

where f_0 and Δf are given by Equations (III.5) and (III.6).

A good tuner will be selective enough (small Δf) so two signals at slightly different frequencies can be distinguished. However, if it is too selective you may have difficulty in finding the station. The actual tuning is done by varying the capacitance.

Problem Specifics

Write a program to

1. Read the inductance L of a coil and the driving voltage V_0. (Use $L = 10^{-5}$, $V_0 = 10$.)
   a. Compute the capacitance C required for a frequency of $f_0 = 710{,}000$ hertz (Hz).
   b. Compute the resistance necessary for half-widths of

$$\Delta f = \frac{f_0}{5}, \frac{f_0}{20}, \frac{f_0}{80}$$

   c. Print all the above with appropriate labels.
2. Produce three simultaneous printer plots of $V_r(f)$ for the three resistances above. The plot should extend from 500,000 Hz to 1,000,000 Hz along the f axis. Use different symbols for each curve.
3. In addition, the program should determine the actual selectivity of the circuit and compare it with the quantity Δf. To obtain a value for the actual half-width at half-maximum, your program should scan the computed values of V_r and determine the values of f on the left and right of f_0 that minimize $|V_r(f) - \frac{1}{2}V_0|$. The actual half-width is then $\frac{1}{2}[f_{right} - f_{left}]$.

Programming Problem B: Cooling Curve for Transfer Ladle Cars

The transfer of molten pig iron from a blast furnace to the steelmaking facilities is a seemingly simple procedure. The molten iron is placed in an elongated tilting ladle railroad car as pictured in Figure III-5. If the distance

Figure III-5
Sketch of a
150-ton transfer
ladle car.

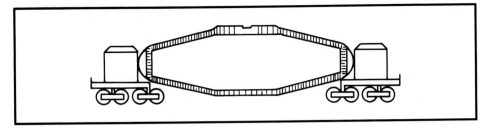

to be transferred is considerable or if for other reasons the molten iron will remain in the ladle car, it is very important that the cooling rate of the car and its contents be continually monitored. If the molten iron begins to solidify in the transfer car, you can imagine the resulting problems.

The purpose of this problem is to estimate and plot the temperature of the molten iron vs. time based on two assumptions:

1. The heat (Q) flowing out from the iron through the car walls (J/sec = watts) is equal to the heat transferred from the car surface to the air by convection and radiation.

(III.10)
$$Q_{cond} = Q_{conv} + Q_{rad}$$

The conduction term depends upon the geometry of the ladle car. If we approximate the car as a cylinder of length L, outer radius a, and wall thickness δ, and if the car material has a heat conductivity k, the heat flow Q_{cond} can then be expressed approximately as

(III.11)
$$Q_{cond} = k\frac{A_\lambda}{\delta}[T(t) - T_s]$$

where A_λ is the log-mean area involved in the heat conduction, $T(t)$ is the temperature of the molten iron at time t, and T_s is temperature of the outside surface of the car.

The log-mean area A_λ is expressed in terms of the areas of the outside cylinder surface ($A_O = 2\pi aL$) and the inside surface ($A_i = 2\pi(a - \delta)L$) as

(III.12)
$$A_\lambda = \frac{A_0 - A_i}{\ln (A_0/A_i)}$$

which can be written as

(III.13)
$$A_\lambda = -\frac{2\pi\delta L}{\ln (1 - \delta/a)}$$

(Note: The logarithm is negative so A_λ is positive.)

2. If the temperature of the surrounding air is T_a, the heat loss from the car to the air is

(III.14)
$$Q_{conv} + Q_{rad} = h_c A_\lambda (T_s - T_a)^{5/4} + \sigma\epsilon A_\lambda (T_s^4 - T_a^4)$$

where h_c = coefficient for convective heat transfer from a cylinder

σ = coefficient for radiative heat transfer, Stefan-Boltzman constant

ϵ = emissivity of the car's surface

Thus Equation (III.10) may be written

$$T(t) = T_s - \frac{a}{k \ln(1 - \delta/a)}[h_c(T_s - T_a)^{5/4} + \sigma\epsilon(T_s^4 - T_a^4)] \qquad \textbf{(III.15)}$$

Knowing the temperature of the iron at a time t, $T(t)$, and the air temperature T_a, we will use this equation to determine the temperature of the car surface, T_s.

The rate of heat loss by the molten iron is related to its temperature through its specific heat C by

$$Q_{cond} = \frac{\Delta Q}{\Delta t} = -mC\frac{\Delta T}{\Delta t} \qquad \textbf{(III.16)}$$

$$= -mC\frac{T(t + \Delta t) - T(t)}{\Delta t}$$

where m is the mass of the molten iron and C its specific heat. This equation may be written

$$T(t + \Delta t) = T(t) - \frac{\Delta t Q_{cond}}{mC} \qquad \textbf{(III.17)}$$

This equation will be used to compute T at a later time $t + \Delta t$, knowing $T(t)$ and Q_{cond}.

The basic procedure is thus

1. Start at $t = 0$
   a. Knowing $T(t)$ and T_a, use the bisection algorithm to solve Equation (III.15) for T_s
   b. Use Equation (III.11) to compute Q_{cond}
   c. Use Equation (III.17) to compute T at the next time step—i.e., $T(t + \Delta t)$
2. Increment $t \to t + \Delta t$ and repeat
3. Printer-plot the results of $T(t)$ vs. t

Problem Specifics

The input parameters for this problem are listed in Table III-2. These should be stored in a data file which will be read by your program. The calculation should proceed as follows:

1. Read all the input data from a data file and neatly print them.
2. For the initial calculation ($t = 0$) of T_s use the interval

$$T_a < T_s < T(0)$$

   while for all subsequent steps use an interval based on the previous calculation. For example, if T_s is the latest computed surface temperature, the next computed value should be only slightly lower. Thus a reasonable interval to use for the next calculation might be $T_s - \frac{1}{25}(T_s - T_a) \leftrightarrow T_s$.
3. For the first-case initial temperature compute the 76 temperature values for the 75 time steps and store in an array T(0:75, 2).
4. Repeat for the second-case initial temperature.
5. Print a table of the results for the two initial temperatures.
6. Determine the maximum and minimum elements of the array T.
7. Produce a printer plot of both temperature vs. time results simultaneously, extending from $T = T_{min}$ to T_{max} and from $t = 0$ to $t = t_{max}$ seconds.
8. All internal values of temperature are in kelvin but all your printed values should be in degrees Celsuis ($K - 273 = °C$). Likewise, the internal time is in seconds while the output should be in hours.
9. Indent DO loops and IF blocks, segment the code into blocks.

Table III-2   Input parameters for the cooling curve problem.

a	= 1.50	= outer radius of ladle car (m)
L	= 8.00	= length of ladle car (m)
δ	= 0.50	= thickness of car walls (m)
k	= 4.20	= heat conductivity of walls (W/K-m)
h_c	= 1.70	= heat convection coefficient for a cylinder (W/K-m)
ε	= 0.80	= emissivity of ladle car surface
m	= 1.35E5	= mass of molten iron (kg)
C	= 1172.	= effective specific heat of molten iron (J/kg-K)
T_a	= 298	= air temperature (K)
σ	= 5.67E-9	= radiative heat coefficient
Δt	= 1200	= time step (sec)
t_{max}	= 9.0E4	= maximum time (sec), i.e., 25 hr
T_{solid}	= 1430.	= solidification temperature of molten iron (K)
eps	= 10^{-3}	= convergence criterion for bisection (K)
I_{max}	= 40	= maximum number of iterations in bisection algorithm
$T(0)$	= case 1	= initial temperature of molten iron (K)
	1800.0	
	case 2	
	1700.0	

Programming Problem C: Compressibility Factors for Real Gases

As I indicated in Programming Assignment II-C, the understanding of the properties of real gases in contrast to ideal gases is of great importance to chemical engineers. There have been numerous attempts to formulate equations of state for a substance that would incorporate both liquid and gaseous phases. A rather accurate summary of the experimental properties of imperfect gases is contained in the Beattie-Bridgeman equation, which can be written as

$$P = \frac{RT(1 - \varepsilon)}{v^2}(v + B) - \frac{A}{v^2} \qquad \textbf{(III.18)}$$

where P = pressure (Pa)

T = temperature (K)

v = molar volume (m^3/mol)

R = ideal gas constant = 8.317 J/mol-K

A = $A_0(1 - a/v)$

B = $B_0(1 - b/v)$

ε = c/vT^3

and $A_0, B_0, a, b,$ and c are the five experimental parameters in the equation that depend upon the specific gas in question.

A quantity of frequent use in chemical engineering problems is the compressibility of a gas defined as

$$Z = \frac{Pv}{RT} \qquad \textbf{(III.19)}$$

which for an ideal gas would be constant and equal to one. For a real gas this quantity is then a measure of the deviation of the real gas from ideal gas properties and is useful in isolating thermodynamic regions where the ideal gas may or may not be used. That is, when $Z \sim 1$ we would expect minimal error if the ideal gas equation is used in our calculations in place of the more complicated expressions. The purpose of this problem is to generate a plot of Z vs. P which can then be used in this manner.

Problem Specifics

Your program should do the following:

1. Read the Beattie-Bridgeman parameters for a particular gas from Table III-3 and print with appropriate labels. Use character variables for the name of the gas.
2. Do separate calculations for each of the temperatures $T_c/2$, T_c, and $2T_c$ using statement functions for Equations (III.18) and (III.19), fill in the values of an array $Z(0:60)$ with values of the compressibility factor for 61 equally spaced values of v between $\frac{1}{2}$ and $3v_c$. Do the same for an array PRESS(0:60) using Equation (III.18).
3. We next wish to plot Z vs. P, not v, while our data at this point consist of

a table of Z and P vs. v values. These data must first be rearranged into a table of Z vs. P values. To accomplish this you will have to execute a pointer sort on the array PRESS for each of the three temperatures. When this is completed the data will consist of three sets of $(Z_i, P_i, i = 0.60)$ values. Note the P values will be in order but *will not* be equally spaced.

4. Since the P values are not equally spaced it is somewhat difficult to produce a printer plot; instead you will have to make use of the automatic pen-and-ink plotting routines available to you. Unfortunately, the instructions on the use of these routines vary considerably from site to site. Often all that is required, once the two arrays that form the x-y axes of the plot are filled, is a CALL to a special plotting machine inserted in the code. For example,

```
CALL PLOTER(X,Y,N,<x title>,<y title>,<graph title>,NG)
```

where X, Y   *are the arrays containing the data to be plotted*

          N   *is the number of points in a single plot*

        ⟨x title⟩, ⟨y title⟩ *are character expressions labeling the x and y axes*

        ⟨graph title⟩ *is a character expression labeling the overall graph*

        NG   *is the number of plots on this set of axes (e.g., one for each temperature)*

Determine the necessary Fortran commands to execute multiple graphs on a special pen-and-ink graphics device.

Table III-3
Beattie-Bridgeman parameters for some common gases

Gas	v_c (m³ × 10⁻⁵)	T_c (K)	A_0 (×10⁻¹)	B_0 (×10⁻⁶)	a (×10⁻⁶)	b (×10⁻⁶)	c (×10⁰)
Air	80.00	132.5	1.320	46.1	19.30	−10.99	43.35
O_2	37.21	154.4	1.510	46.26	25.60	4.210	47.96
CO_2	95.65	304.3	5.074	104.7	71.36	72.35	660.
H_2	64.52	33.26	0.200	20.96	−5.06	−43.58	.507
Ammonia	72.34	405.6	2.424	34.15	170.4	191.1	4769.

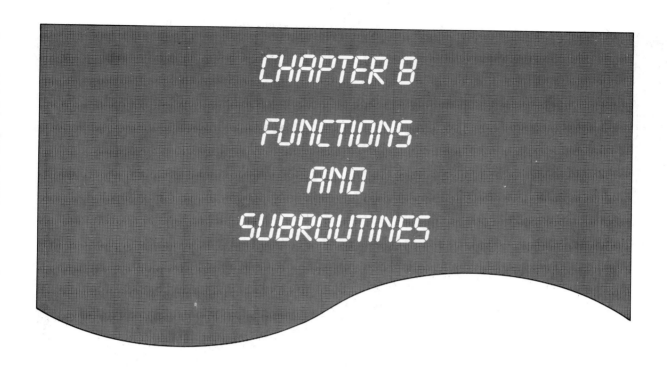

CHAPTER 8

FUNCTIONS

AND

SUBROUTINES

8.1 INTRODUCTION

In the not-too-distant future, in subsequent engineering courses or in your career, you will be solving problems by using the computer, and these problems will very likely be much more complicated and involve much longer Fortran code than we have encountered thus far. As an example, suppose you wanted to

Compute a very complicated function, $y = f(x)$
Obtain a rough sketch of the function on the line printer
Find the zeros of the function by bisection
If all of the above went well, graph the function on an automatic
pen-and-ink graphics device.

If you do this more than once in a lifetime, it would be a waste of effort and time to recode and retype those elements of the program that remain basically unchanged from your earlier programs. Fortran allows the segmentation of a long program into subprogram blocks that are compiled separately. These blocks are called statement functions, functions, and subroutines.

Statement functions have been discussed in Section 4.2. In this chapter I will discuss primarily Fortran functions and subroutines. Each of these subprogram types may be used as elements of a larger program and later reused in other codes performing similar tasks. For example, we shall shortly construct a subroutine that will graph a function, any function, on the line printer. This code may then be stored on cards, on a disk, or on magnetic tape. Anytime in later programs you wish to have a quick plot of some function, you simply call up this subroutine. Obviously this is an extremely convenient feature of Fortran, and indeed, subprograms are a fundamental element of almost all relatively long Fortran programs. The ability to use previously tested code instead of reprogramming the same ideas also frees us from the frustration and agony of making the same dumb errors twice.

Repeatedly I have stressed the importance of top-down programming; constructing a program in a block pattern with each block or segment being to some extent independent from the others. Subprograms permit a further layer of blocks or modules that will be quite useful in building a program up from parts that can be separately tested.

8.2   REVIEW OF STATEMENT FUNCTIONS

Before we begin the description of subroutines and functions, I will quickly review the properties of statement functions. You will recall that the rules relating to statement functions were concerned with their definition and use.

Definition

1. A statement function definition must precede the first executable statement and must follow all type or dimension declaration statements in a program.
2. All variables in the statement function expression should appear in the argument list of the function. For example,

```
FNC(A,B,T) = A + B*SIN(T)
```

Use

1. The statement function is called up by simply using the function name followed by its argument list in any arithmetic expression or Fortran statement.
2. When using the function, the variables or numbers appearing in the argument list must agree as to type (INTEGER, REAL, CHARACTER) with the variable names in the function definition.
3. The order or sequence of the variables in the argument list is critical.

An example follows:

```
X = 2.
A = 3.
B = 4.
W = A/FNC(A,B,X)                    ⟨X not T is used in the
                                    reference to the function.⟩
Y = 3./FNC(3.,4.,2. * A - B)        ⟨Y has the same value as W.⟩
```

8.3 SUBROUTINE SUBPROGRAMS

Frequently the operations that we wish the program to execute are too extensive to be represented by a statement function and yet too distracting to the logical flow of the program to include in the body of an otherwise clear algorithm. For example, if in the middle of a program we find that we need the smallest four positive roots of a function $f(x)$, it would be very helpful if we could simply instruct the computer to

Go off to the side, compute the smallest roots of the function $f(x)$, and when they have been found, return and we will continue from there.

The mechanism for doing this in Fortran is the subroutine. A Fortran subroutine is a complete subprogram that is compiled separately from the main program and will appear after the END statement in the main program. As with statement functions, the rules for subroutines relate to their definition and use.

8.3.1 Defining and Referencing a Subroutine

Definition: A Fortran subroutine is a self-contained subprogram that can be initiated in a main program or in other subroutines or functions. The subroutine is compiled separately from the main program and all other subprograms, and the beginning and end of this compilation unit are delimited by a special header line at the beginning and closed with an END statement. The form of the first line of a subroutine is

```
SUBROUTINE    name(argument list)
```

The name of the subroutine may be any valid Fortran variable name; however, since it will designate a procedure, not a variable, it cannot be assigned a value or used within the body of the subroutine. In short, the subroutine *will not* return a value for "name." All computed quantities are passed to and returned from the subroutine via the argument list.

It is not required that a subroutine have an argument list, although most will. The parameters in the argument list of a subroutine definition are called "dummy" arguments, meaning that they will be assigned specific values only when the subroutine has been called by some other program unit. For example, the subroutine LENGTH below computes the length of a vector in the first quadrant. If the vector is not in the first quadrant, the length is assigned a value of -1.0. When the subroutine is compiled the variable names X, Y, L have not yet been assigned values and are dummy arguments.

```
SUBROUTINE LENGTH(X,Y,L)
REAL X,Y,L
IF(X .LT. 0. .OR. Y .LT. 0.)THEN
     L = -1.0
ELSE
     L = SQRT(X * X + Y * Y)
END IF
RETURN
END
```

Subroutines usually contain at least one RETURN statement. When this statement is encountered, the operation of the program transfers back to the line from which the subroutine was called and continues from that point. The END statement is of course used to mark the end of a compilation unit and is not used to terminate the operations of the subroutine.

All variables and statement numbers defined within a subroutine are only locally defined and will not conflict with variable names or statement numbers used in the main program or other subprograms. This is important as it would detract considerably from a subroutine's portability if we had to eliminate such potential conflicts every time a subroutine was used in a large program. The only communication of the calling program with the subroutine is by means of the argument list, which can be thought of as the only "window" in the structure.

Referencing Subroutines

A subroutine is accessed by means of a CALL statement

```
CALL name(argument list)
```

where the "name" agrees with the name in the subroutine definition and the variable names in the argument list agree in number and by type (REAL, INTEGER, CHARACTER) with the dummy arguments in the defining argument list. The number of variable names in the argument list of the subroutine CALL must agree with the number of arguments in the subroutine definition or an execution error will result. Ordinarily, when a subroutine is called, the computation proceeds from the first line of the subroutine until a RETURN or STOP statement is encountered. For example, a program employing the simple subroutine above is

```
PROGRAM VECTOR
REAL RX,RY,R
READ *,RX,RY

CALL LENGTH(RX,RY,R)

IF(R .LT. 0.)THEN
      PRINT *,'VECTOR NOT IN FIRST QUADRANT'
ELSE
      PRINT *,'THE LENGTH OF THE VECTOR IS ',R
END IF
STOP
```

The parameters are transferred to and returned from the subroutine by position in the argument list. Thus, if the values read for RX and RY were 5.0 and 12.0, the values assigned to X and Y within the subroutine would be 5.0 and 12.0 and the subroutine would compute a value of 13.0 for the length L. (See the code below.) When the subroutine returns to the main program, this value is then assigned to the variable R. That is, the input to the subroutine is 5.0, 12.0 (assigned to RX, RY) and the output is 13.0 (assigned to R). I emphasize that the things passed back and forth between the main program and the subroutine are numerical values, not variable names (at least not yet).

```
PROGRAM VECTOR
REAL X,Y,L
X = 5.0              ⟨In the main program, X has
L = 12.0             a value of 5.0 and L is 12.⟩

CALL LENGTH(L,X,Y)   ⟨A value of 13.0 is computed
                     by LENGTH and assigned to Y.⟩
   ...
   ...
END
SUBROUTINE LENGTH(X,Y,L)
REAL X,Y,L
                     ⟨Within subroutine LENGTH,
   ...               X has a value of 12.0, Y a
   ...               value of 5.0, and L is computed
                     to be 13.0.⟩
RETURN
END
```

A subroutine may not directly or indirectly call itself.

8.3.2 Protecting Dummy Arguments

When a subroutine is referenced by a CALL statement, the input variables in the argument list are assumed to have been assigned numerical values, and after the CALL the output variables will also have numerical values. These variables are called *actual* arguments, and the assignments to the dummy arguments in the subroutine definition are made by position in the argument list when the subroutine is entered *and* when it is exited. This can result in unintentional changes in the input variables. For example, a subroutine is given in Figure 8-1 which will compute the root of a function $f(x)$ by using the bisection algorithm of Section 4.5. The function F(X) must be included elsewhere in the code as a separate Fortran FUNCTION subprogram (to be discussed in Section 8.4). The root of the function is known to be in the interval $x_1 \le$ root $\le x_3$. The input to this subroutine is the interval X1, X3, the convergence criterion, EPS, and the maximum number of iterations, IMAX, and the output is the actual number of iterations I, and the answer, ROOT. However, even though X1 and X3 are input to the code, their values change within the subroutine and therefore when a RETURN is executed the actual variables in their position in the CALL will be assigned the final values of X1, X3. Thus if the reference to BISEC in the main program were

```
A = 4.0
B = 6.0
IMAX = 25
EPS = 1.E-6
CALL BISEC(A,B,EPS,IMAX,I,ANS)
PRINT *,A,B,I,ANS
```

the values of A and B would have been altered by the subroutine and the original size of the search interval has been lost. To avoid this, the following safeguard is recommended:

Protect Dummy Input Arguments: Within a subroutine, all dummy input variables should be replaced by locally defined variables. Dummy input variables should never appear to the left of =.
    Thus subroutine BISEC should be amended as

```
SUBROUTINE BISEC(A,B,EPS,IMAX,I,ROOT)
    ...                          ...
                                 ...
    X1 = A              The input variables A, B are
    X2 = B              protected and will retain the
       ...              same values before and after
       ...              the execution of BISEC.
    END
```

248 FUNCTIONS AND SUBROUTINES

Lest you think this is unduly scrupulous programming, I have one more example; this time not protecting dummy variables will lead to very star-

Figure 8-1 A subroutine for roots of a function by bisection.

```
      SUBROUTINE BISEC(A,B,EPS,IMAX,I,ROOT)
*--
*--   A ROOT OF THE FUNCTION F(X) IS FOUND BY SUCCESSIVE
*--   INTERVAL HALVING. THE FUNCTION MUST BE A FUNCTION OF A
*--   SINGLE VARIABLE. THE CODE IS SIMILAR TO THAT OF FIGURE 4-9.
*--   IF AN ERROR IS ENCOUNTERED A DIAGNOSTIC IS PRINTED, THE ROOT
*--   IS ASSIGNED THE VALUE 1.E99 AND THE SUBROUTINE RETURNS.
*-------------------------------------------------------------------
* VARIABLES
*
      REAL A,B,EPS,ROOT,X1,X2,X3,F1,F2,F3,D,DO
      INTEGER I,IMAX
*
*                 A,B        --  THE ORIGINAL SEARCH INTERVAL
*                 X1,X3,X2-- THE LEFT, RIGHT, AND MIDPOINT OF
*                            THE CURRENT INTERVAL SEGMENT
*                 F1,F3,F2-- THE FUNCTION EVALUATED AT THESE X'S
*                 D          --  THE RATIO OF THE CURRENT INTERVAL
*                            TO THAT OF THE ORIGINAL INTERVAL
*                 ROOT       --  THE ROOT OF THE FUNCTION (OUTPUT)
*                 I          --  ITERATION COUNTER
*                 IMAX       --  MAXIMUM NUMBER OF ITERATIONS
*                 EPS        --  CONVERGENCE CRITERION BASED ON D
*-------------------------------------------------------------------
* INITIALIZATION
*
      X1 = A
      X3 = B
      F1 = F(X1)
      F3 = F(X3)
      I  = 0
      D  = 1.0
*
*                             VERIFY THAT THERE IS A ROOT
*                             WITHIN THE ORIGINAL INTERVAL
*
      IF(F1 * F3 .GT. 0.)THEN
         WRITE(*,10)A,B
         ROOT = 1.E99
         RETURN
      END IF
```

Continued

```
*
*                                   THE INTERVAL IS HALVED AND EACH SIDE
*                                   IS CHECKED FOR THE POSITION OF ROOT
*
    1 X2 = (X1 + X3)/2.
      F2 = F(X2)
*
*                                   CONVERGENCE TESTS
*
      IF(D .LT. EPS)THEN
         ROOT = X2
         RETURN
      ELSE IF(I .GT. IMAX)THEN
*
*                                   FAILURE EXCESSIVE ITERATIONS
*
         WRITE(*,11)I,X2,F2
         ROOT = 1.E99
         RETURN
      END IF
*
*                                   CHECK FOR CROSSING ON THE LEFT
*
      IF(F1 * F2 .LT. 0.0)THEN
         D = (X2 - X1)/(B - A)
         F3 = F2
         X3 = X2
*
*                                   OR ON THE RIGHT
*
      ELSE IF(F2 * F3 .LT. 0.0)THEN
         D = (X3 - X2)/(B - A)
         F1 = F2
         X1 = X2
*
*                                   IF CROSSING IS IN NEITHER HALF
*                                   EITHER F2 = 0.0 OR AN ERROR.
*
      ELSE IF(F2 .EQ. 0.0)THEN
         ROOT = X2
         RETURN
      ELSE
         WRITE(*,12)I,X1,X3
         ROOT = 1.E99
         RETURN
      END IF
*
```

```
*
*
      I = I + 1
      GO TO 1
*--------------------------------------------------------------------
*FORMATS
*
   10 FORMAT(//,5X,'----ERROR----',/,10X,'FROM BISEC',/,
     +      10X,'THE INTERVAL ',F8.4,' TO ',F8.4,/,
     +      10X,'DOES NOT CONTAIN A ROOT')
*
   11 FORMAT(//,5X,'----ERROR----',/,10X,'FROM BISEC',/,
     +      10X,'EXCESSIVE ITERATIONS, I = ',I5,/,
     +      10X,'LAST VALUE WAS F(',F9.5,') = ',E9.2)
*
   12 FORMAT(//,5X,'----ERROR----',/,10X,'FROM BISEC',/,
     +      10X,'THE SUB-INTERVAL ',F8.4,' TO ',F8.4,/,
     +      10X,'DOES NOT CONTAIN A ROOT')
      END
```

tling results. You should execute the simple Fortran program in Figure 8-2. The output from this program will probably be

$$1 + 1.0 = 3.0$$

The error in the code is rather subtle. The first value in the CALL statement (1.) is probably intended as input, but in the subroutine this value is changed (to 2.) and upon the return to the main program the value 2. is assigned to the first position in the CALL argument list. The net effect is that in this instance the *constant* 1.0 has been overwritten with the value 2.0. Thereafter, everywhere in the code where we have used 1.0 the computer will use a value 2.0. This could obviously cause considerable confusion. It is, however, easily avoided by following the suggestion for protecting dummy input variables.

```
PROGRAM GRIEF
CALL NONO(1.,X)
PRINT *, '1 + ', X, ' = ', 1. + X
STOP
END
SUBROUTINE NONO(A,B)
B = 1.
A = 2.
RETURN
END
```

Figure 8-2 An example of a subroutine overwriting a constant.

8.3.3 Arrays as Elements of an Argument List

An entire array can be transferred to or from a subroutine by simply including the name of the array in the calling and defining the subroutine argument list. Of course, the array must be dimensioned in the main (or calling) program. The array must likewise be dimensioned in the subroutine as well. The purpose of this secondary dimensioning is *not* to allot memory space to the array, but merely to inform the subroutine that this variable is an array, already dimensioned elsewhere. For this reason the size of the array as dimensioned in the subroutine may be any value that is less than or equal to the actual dimension size in the main program, or may even be variable. The following examples are correct illustrations of this.

```
PROGRAM XXX
 REAL A(11),B(50),
+ C(-2:7),D(10,10)
```

`CALL XX(A)`	`SUBROUTINE XX(R)`
	`REAL R(10)`
$a_1 \longleftrightarrow r_1$	`...`
$a_{10} \longleftrightarrow r_{10}$	`...`
	`END`
`CALL YY(B)`	`SUBROUTINE YY(S)`
	`REAL S(-20:29)`
$b_1 \longleftrightarrow s_{-20}$	`...`
$b_{50} \longleftrightarrow s_{29}$	`...`
	`END`

```
N = 3
CALL ZZ(D,N)                  SUBROUTINE ZZ(T,I)
                              REAL T(I,I)    I must be
        d₁₁ ←→ t₁₁                          less than
        d₉₁ ←→ t₃₃                ...       or equal
                                  ...       to 10.
                              END
```

`CALL ZZ(D,N)`   `SUBROUTINE ZZ(T,I)`
`REAL T(I,I)` *I* must be less than or equal to 10.

$d_{11} \longleftrightarrow t_{11}$
$d_{91} \longleftrightarrow t_{33}$

```
CALL WW(A,C,M)                SUBROUTINE WW(U,V,J)
                              REAL V(1)      legal but
                                             not recom-
                                             mended
                              REAL U(-J:J)   J must be
        a₁ ←→ u₋ⱼ                            less than
                                  ...        or equal
                                  ...        to 5.
END                           END
```

`REAL U(-J:J)` *J* must be less than or equal to 5.

$a_1 \longleftrightarrow u_{-j}$

In this program

The element	in the subroutine	has the same value as the	element	in the program.
R(9)	XX		A(9)	
S(-20)	YY		B(1)	
S(0)	YY		B(21)	
T(1,1)	ZZ		D(1,1)	
T(3,3)	ZZ		D(9,1)	
V(5)	WW		C(2)	
U(5)	WW		A(11)	

Of course any dummy variables in the defining argument list that refer to the dimension size of an array must be integers.

When the array being transferred has two or more subscripts, special care must be used in the secondary dimensioning. For example, if the array A were dimensioned in the main program as

```
PROGRAM MANE
REAL A(3,3)
CALL ALPHA(A,2)
```

the elements are stored in the sequence (see Section 6.3)

$$a_{11} \quad a_{21} \quad a_{31} \quad a_{12} \quad a_{22} \quad a_{32} \quad a_{13} \quad a_{23} \quad a_{33}$$

If the array elements are transferred to a subroutine with a dummy variable for the size of the array, as

```
SUBROUTINE ALPHA(X,N)
REAL X(N,N)
```

the elements of the dummy variable X would be (for N = 2)

$$x_{11} \quad x_{21} \quad x_{12} \quad x_{22}$$

and the correspondence would be

$$x_{11} \leftrightarrow a_{11}$$
$$x_{21} \leftrightarrow a_{21}$$
$$x_{12} \leftrightarrow a_{31}$$
$$x_{22} \leftrightarrow a_{12}$$

Since it is usually the case that the indices are desired to match, the arrays should be dimensioned as the *same* size in both the main program and the subroutine. This could be accomplished in the subroutine with an additional index as

```
SUBROUTINE ALPHA(X,NA,NL)
REAL X(NA,NA)
DO 55 I = 1,NL
DO 54 J = 1,NL
      X(I,J) =  ...
```

where NA is the actual dimension size of the array as specified in the main program and NL is the local size of the array as used in the subroutine.

In the following statements

```
PROGRAM ALPHA
REAL A(25)
CALL BETA(X,Y,A(25))
      ...
      ...
END
```

only the twenty-fifth element of the array A is transferred to the subroutine and not the entire contents of the array as may have been intended. (Note: A reference like A(25) would not be permitted within the argument list of the subroutine definition.)

8.4 FUNCTION SUBPROGRAMS

Another form of Fortran subprogram is the external function, which combines the features of the statement function and the subroutine. Like a subroutine, it is a complete subprogram, separately compiled from the main program and other subprograms. The rules for passing information to and from the function via the argument list are the same as for subroutines. Like a statement function, it is referenced by simply using the function name followed by its argument list in any Fortran arithmetic expression or statement. Fortran functions are used most often when a single value is to be computed and returned to the calling program. The principal differences between functions and subroutines are a consequence of the fact that a function returns a value associated with its name and the subroutine does not. The name of a function is important, the name of a subroutine is usually not. The rules relating to the definition and use of a Fortran function are

1. The header line for a function is one of the following

```
FUNCTION  name(argument list)
REAL FUNCTION  name(argument list)
```

```
INTEGER FUNCTION name(argument list)
CHARACTER FUNCTION name(argument list)
```

The data type of the value returned through the function name depends on the data type of the name. I would recommend that you use the default typing (I through N for integers, rest real) in selecting function names.

```
FUNCTION KOUNT(A,B,C)     Returns an integer   KOUNT
FUNCTION BGGST(X,N)       Returns a real       BGGST
```

2. Since the function is expected to return a value associated with the name, it is crucial that before any RETURN is encountered in the body of the function subprogram, an assignment statement of the form

```
NAME = ...
```

be present.

3. Whereas a subroutine is not required to have an argument list, a function subprogram must have an argument list (which may be empty). That is, the compiler has been programmed to recognize that a name followed by a left parenthesis represents something other than a simple variable.

Referencing a Function

A Fortran function is accessed by its name, not with CALL, in precisely the same manner as statement functions.

As a simple example, consider the program in Figure 8-3, which reads a set of numbers from a data file and scales the numbers by dividing each number by the largest number in the set. A function BGGST is used to determine the maximum element. In this program you will note that in the function BGGST a variable BIG is used to keep track of the maximum element and only after the entire search is completed is the assignment BGGST = BIG made. The reason for this is that you must be very cautious when using the function name while inside the function. As a general rule, the function name should never appear to the right of the assignment operator (=) inside the function. A statement like . . . = BGGST could be interpreted as the function calling itself which is not allowed in Fortran.

Also, every cycle of the DO loop in the main program recomputes the maximum element of the array (and in addition each time changes the set X). Even if this would give the correct result, it is a serious error. Needlessly recomputing a function can waste considerable computer time. The loop should be rewritten as

```
XMAX = BGGST(X,N)
DO 2 I = 1,N
    X(I) = X(I)/XMAX
2 CONTINUE
```

Figure 8-3 Use
of a function to
incorrectly scale
a list of numbers.

```
PROGRAM SCALES
REAL X(100)
OPEN(37,FILE='XDATA')
REWIND(37)
READ(37,'(F9.5)',END=1)(X(I),I=1,100)
1  N = I - 1
DO 2 I = 1,N
    X(I) = X(I)/BGGST(X,N)
2  CONTINUE
WRITE(*,'(1X,5F9.6)')(X(I),I=1,N)
STOP
END
```

```
FUNCTION BGGST(A,M)
REAL A(M),BIG
BIG = A(1)
DO 1 I = 2,M
    IF(A(I) .GT. BIG)BIG = A(I)
1  CONTINUE
BGGST = BIG
RETURN
END
```

Even though functions may return values in addition to their name by
means of the argument list in precisely the same manner as subroutines,
this should be avoided. If the subprogram is to return one value, use a
function; if it is to return more than one value, use a subroutine. Using a
function structure when a subroutine would be more appropriate results in
a very confusing logical flow to a program.

Finally, none of the dummy arguments in the argument list of a function
should be altered within the body of the function. This suggestion is most
easily adhered to if you agree to never use variables in the argument list as
output from a function. Also, just as with the arguments in a subroutine
argument list, function variable names should always be protected by introducing local replacements.

8.5 EXAMPLE PROGRAMS USING FUNCTIONS AND SUBROUTINES

In addition to the example programs in this section, essentially all of the
procedures discussed to this point would profit by recasting in a modular
form using functions and subroutines. The algorithms for roots of a function

by bisection, sorting an array, computing the minimum/maximum and average of an array, etc. should be rewritten in a structured style. Furthermore, you may find it useful when constructing a program to employ subroutines for reading extensive data lists and for printing elaborate tables. In the future your main programs may consist of little else than CALLs to subroutines to read data, print output, and execute the computations.

8.5.1 Fractions

You certainly remember, perhaps with some pain, the rules for adding fractions and reducing them to simplest form by dividing both numerator and denominator by common factors. To add a large number of fractions exactly, i.e., to express the answer as a fraction rather than a decimal, usually involves a considerable amount of tedious arithmetic. Thus the evaluation of

$$1 + \frac{1}{2} + \frac{1}{3} + \frac{1}{4} + \ldots + \frac{1}{25}$$

is easily done on a pocket calculator if the numbers are expressed as decimals. (The answer is 3.815958177...). If you attempt to add the fractions exactly you will see that the problem quickly becomes hopelessly complicated. But hopelessly complicated and terribly tedious arithmetic is the computer's strong suit. To code this problem we will have to construct the following main and subprograms:

Function IGCF(ITOP, IBOT): An integer function that determines the greatest common factor contained in both the numerator, ITOP, and the denominator, IBOT, of a given fraction

Subroutine ADD(IA, IB, IC): A subroutine to add two fractions, IA, IB, and return the result as a fraction, IC. The fractions are represented as two-element arrays, the numerator of IA is IA(1) and the denominator is IA(2). Thus

$$\frac{a_1}{a_2} + \frac{b_1}{b_2} = \frac{c_1}{c_2}$$

where $c_1 = a_1 b_2 + a_2 b_1$ and $c_2 = a_2 b_2$

The fraction is then reduced to lowest terms by using the function IGCF

Program series: A program that will sum the series by repeatedly calling the subroutine ADD

The main program is quite similar to an ordinary summation and is given in Figure 8-4. The subroutine to add two fractions and reduce the result to lowest terms is fairly simple and is given in Figure 8-5.

The algorithm to determine the greatest common factor in two integers was developed by Euclid and consists of dividing the first integer (the larger, P) by the second (the smaller, Q) and determining the remainder R. If the remainder is not zero, the pair (P, Q) is replaced by the pair (Q, R) and the

Figure 8-4 The main program to add a series of fractions.

```
      PROGRAM SERIES
      INTEGER SUM(2),TERM(2),K(2),LIMIT
*
*                         ALL THE ARRAYS REPRESENT FRACTIONS,
*                         THE FIRST POSITION IS THE NUMERATOR
*                         THE SECOND IS THE DENOMINATOR
*                         THE SUM IS FROM 1 TO 1/LIMIT.
*
*     READ *,LIMIT
*                         INITIALIZE THE SUM = 0/1
      SUM(1) = 0
      SUM(2) = 1
*
      DO 1 I = 1,LIMIT
*
*                         ASSIGN A VALUE TO TERM
*
         TERM(1) = 1
         TERM(2) = I
*
*                         ADD SUM + TERM AND CONVERT THE RESULT
*                         TO LOWEST TERMS. THE RESULT IS IN K
*
         CALL ADD(SUM,TERM,K)
*
*                         REPLACEMENT, SUM = SUM + TERM
*
         SUM(1) = K(1)
         SUM(2) = K(2)
    1 CONTINUE
      WRITE(*,2)LIMIT,SUM
      STOP
*
    2 FORMAT(5X,'THE SUM OF FRACTIONS 1/N FOR N = 1 TO ',I3,//,
     +        20X,'IS',//,
     +        15X,I12,/,15X,12('-'),/15X,I12)
      END
```

```
      SUBROUTINE ADD(A,B,C)
      INTEGER A(2),B(2),C(2),ID
      C(1) = A(1) * B(2) + A(2) * B(1)
      C(2) = A(2) * B(2)
*
*                     The greatest common factor in
*                     C(1), C(2) is obtained from the
*                     function IGCF.
*
      ID = IGCF(C(1),C(2))
      C(1) = C(1)/ID
      C(2) = C(2)/ID
      RETURN
      END
```

Figure 8-5
A subroutine to add two fractions.

process repeated. If the remainder is zero, the greatest common factor (GCF) is the last value of Q. For example, starting with $P = 221$, $Q = 91$, Euclid's algorithm yields

P	Q	R
221	91	39
91	39	13
39	13	0

So the GCF is 13. The function to execute this algorithm is then shown in Figure 8-6. By the way, the result of the problem with LIMIT = 25 is

$$\frac{34052522467}{8923714800}$$

Of course, problems involving integer arithmetic are not often very useful in engineering applications; however, the structure of this program illustrates several features of functions and subroutines and should be thoroughly understood before you attempt to code your own subprograms. There are several series involving fractions in the problem section of this chapter and you are invited to attempt to compute answers to these problems as fractions in lowest terms.

8.5.2 The Function ROUNDR

In Chapter 7 I outlined the procedures that are followed when graphing a function. One crucial step was omitted. If the range of the x values that are

Figure 8-6
A function to
compute the
greatest common
factor.

```
       FUNCTION IGCF(ITOP,IBOT)
*
*                         In order not to destroy the
*                         dummy variables ITOP, IBOT,
*                         we introduce local variables.
*
       IA = ITOP
       IB = IBOT
*
*                         IR is the remainder, note the
*                         use of integer arithmetic.
*
   1   IR = IA - IA/IB * IB
       IF(IR .EQ. 0)THEN
             IGCF = IB
             RETURN
       ELSE
             IA = IB
             IB = IR
       END IF
       GO TO 1
       END
```

to be plotted is, say, -13.63 to $+8.77$, you would naturally set the x axis from -15 to $+10$. That is, the minimum and maximum values are rounded up in magnitude. The function that accomplishes this is given in Figure 8-7. It is somewhat tricky, but you should be able to follow the algorithm. The function ROUNDR is used primarily in constructing axes for a printer plot, as in the next example.

8.5.3 A Subroutine for Printer Plots

We are now in a position to assemble a modular program to execute a printer plot of an arbitrary function $f(x)$. The code will consist of several parts:

Main Program: The main program will compute a list of values, $(x_i, y_i, i = 0, 40)$ to be graphed by calling a function subprogram F(X). For this example it is assumed that the x values are equally spaced between zero and XMAX. The main program then calls the subroutine PLOT, which will graph the tabulated values.

Figure 8-7 A Fortran function to round an arbitrary number.

```
        FUNCTION ROUNDR(Q)
*
* Roundr will round the real number Q up in magnitude so that
* the result will have the first two digits divisible by 5, e.g,
* 771.3 becomes 800, and -0.08341 becomes -0.085.
*
        A = Q
*
                        The input dummy variable Q
*                       is protected. If Q < 0 use -Q.
*
        IF(A .LT. 0.)A = -A
*
        B = LOG10(A)
        IB = B
        B = B - IB
*
*
*                       If B is pos, it is the mantissa, and
*                       IB is the characteristic; e.g, if
*                       Q = 15,log(15) = 1.1761, IB = 1, B = 0.1761.
*                       If B is neg, we express the log as
*                       0.XXXX-1.0, So
*
        IF(B .LT. 0.)THEN
           B = B + 1.
           IB = IB - 1
        END IF
*
*
*                       If Q = 0.8, IB = 0, B = -0.0969 are
*                       replaced by B = 0.9031, IB = -1,
*                       i.e, log(0.8) = 0.9031 - 1.
*
        C = 10.**B
*
*
*                       C is the number Q without its sign
*                       or exponent.
*
        IC = 2.*C + 1.
*
*                       This line does the actual rounding;
*                       next reattach the correct power of 10.
*
        R = IC/2. * 10.**IB
        IF(Q .LT. 0.)R = -R
        ROUNDR = R
        RETURN
        END
```

SUBROUTINE PLOT (X,Y,N):   The subroutine will then:

1. Determine the range of y values (y_{min}, y_{max}) by calling a subroutine MIN-MAX.
2. Round the minimum and maximum values of y to produce a y axis with whole numbers at the beginning and end.
3. Print the y axis horizontally with y values and tic marks.
4. Step through the x values, one by one, and print a horizontal line of all blanks except a * in the corresponding column for $y(x_i)$.
5. The code will also print an x value for every tenth line and the graph will have a border on all four sides.

FUNCTION F(X):   A function subprogram for the function we wish to graph. The function may require more information in its argument list.

SUBROUTINE MINMAX: A subroutine to scan a single subscripted array A of size N and return the minimum AMIN and the maximum AMAX of the values in the array.

FUNCTION ROUNDR: A function to round values up to magnitude and used to establish the limits of the axes. (See Figure 8-7.)

The code to handle all this is shown in Figure 8-8.

The function chosen for the graph represents damped harmonic motion, such as the gradual shrinking of the amplitude of a pendulum (small damping) or the removal of almost all "bounce" on a bumpy road in a car with good shock absorbers (large damping). The mathematical function describing such motion is the product of a decaying exponential and a periodic function such as a cosine.

$$(8.1) \qquad y(t) = e^{-\alpha t}\cos(\beta t)$$

where $y(t)$ represents the amplitude of the oscillations at time t, α is the decay constant, and $\beta/(2\pi)$ is the oscillation frequency. The parameters α, β are related to physical quantities by

$$(8.2) \qquad \alpha = \frac{\gamma}{2m}$$

$$(8.3) \qquad \beta = \left(\frac{k}{m} - \frac{\gamma^2}{4m^2}\right)^{1/2}$$

where m = mass (kg)

k = restoring spring force constant (N/m)

γ = damping or viscosity coefficient (N-sec/m)

The output from this program is shown in Figure 8-9.

Figure 8-8 A Fortran program to printer plot a function.

```
        PROGRAM MAINE
*--
*--     THE MAIN PROGRAM COMPUTES A TABLE OF X(), Y() VALUES BY
*--     CALLING THE FUNCTION F(X). AFTER THE TABLE IS COMPLETED,
*--     THE SUBROUTINE PLOT IS USED TO OBTAIN A LINE PRINTER
*--     SKETCH OF THE COMPUTED VALUES.
*-----------------------------------------------------------------
* VARIABLES
*
        REAL X(0:50),Y(0:50)
*
*--               COMPUTE THE TABLE
*--
        X(0) = -10.
        DX = 0.4
        Y(0) = F(X(0))
        DO 1 I = 1,50
           X(I) = X(I - 1) + DX
           Y(I) = F(X(I))
      1 CONTINUE
*--
*--               CALL PLOT TO EXECUTE A PRINTER PLOT
*--
        CALL PLOT(X,Y,50)
*--
*--
        STOP
        END
*-----------------------------------------------------------------
        FUNCTION F(X)
*--
        F = ...
*--
        RETURN
        END
*-----------------------------------------------------------------
        SUBROUTINE PLOT(X,Y,N)
*--
*--     THIS SUBROUTINE WILL SKETCH THE TABULATED VALUES IN THE
*--     ARRAYS X(),Y(). IT IS ASSUMED THAT THE X VALUES ARE
*--     EQUALLY SPACED FROM A = X(0) TO B = X(N). THE RESULTS WILL
*--     BE DISPLAYED ON THE TERMINAL SCREEN OR ON THE LINE
*--     PRINTER. THE GRAPH WILL BE N LINES LONG (X) AND 60
*--     COLUMNS WIDE (Y).
*-----------------------------------------------------------------
```

Continued

8.5 EXAMPLE PROGRAMS USING FUNCTIONS AND SUBROUTINES 263

```
* VARIABLES
*
      REAL A,B,X(O:N),Y(O:N),YMAX,YMIN,XSTEP,RNGY
      INTEGER N,ISTEP,STRCOL
      CHARACTER*1 LINE(O:60),BLANK,STAR
*
*                    A,B       --   THE LIMITS OF THE X AXIS(INPUT)
*                    YMIN,     --   THE MIN/MAX VALUES OF THE
*                      YMAX         COMPUTED Y VALUES
*                    XSTEP     --   THE STEP SIZE ALONG THE X AXIS
*                    N         --   THE NUMBER OF STEPS ALONG X
*                    X(),Y()   --   ARRAYS FOR STORING THE COMPUTED
*                                   VALUES FOR X AND Y
*                    LINE()    --   THE ARRAY CONTAINING THE SYMBOLS TO
*                                   BE PRINTED FOR ONE VALUE OF X
*                    ISTEP     --   THE CURRENT STEP IN THE PLOT
*                    STRCOL    --   THE COLUMN NUMBER TO POSITION THE
*                                   STAR FOR THIS LINE
*                    RNGY      --   THE RANGE OF THE ROUNDED Y VALUES
*                    BLANK     --   CONTAINS ONE BLANK CHARACTER
*                    STAR      --   CONTAINS THE SYMBOL *
*-----------------------------------------------------------------
* INITIALIZATION
*
      BLANK = ' '
      STAR = '*'
      DO 1 I = 0,60
          LINE(I) = BLANK
    1 CONTINUE
*
      A = X(0)
      B = X(N)
      XSTEP = (B - A)/N
*-----------------------------------------------------------------
*
*                    DETERMINE THE MIN/MAX VALUES OF Y()
*
      CALL MINMAX(Y,N + 1,YMIN,YMAX)
*
*                    NEXT SCALE THE AXES BY ROUNDING THE VALUES
*                    (IF BOTH YMIN AND YMAX ARE THE SAME SIGN,
*                    ONLY ROUND THE LARGER.)
*
      IF(YMAX * YMIN .LT. 0.)THEN
          YMAX = ROUNDR(YMAX)
```

Continued

```
            YMIN = ROUNDR(YMIN)
      ELSE IF(YMAX .GT. 0.)THEN
            YMAX = ROUNDR(YMAX)
            YMIN = 0.0
      ELSE
            YMIN = ROUNDR(YMIN)
            YMAX = 0.0
      END IF
*--------------------------------------------------------------------
* PRINT THE GRAPH
*
*                      FIRST PRINT THE INPUT DATA ALONG THE Y AXIS
*                      INCLUDING TIC MARKS
*
      RNGY = YMAX - YMIN
      WRITE(*,10)(YMIN + RNGY/3.*I,I = 0,3)
*
*                      NEXT STEP ALONG THE X AXIS PRINTING THE CON-
*                      TENTS OF LINE() AT EACH STEP. POSITION THE
*                      STAR AT THE PROPER COLUMN EACH STEP AND EVERY
*                      TENTH STEP PRINT AN X VALUE AS WELL.
*
      DO 3 ISTEP = 0,N
         STRCOL = (Y(ISTEP) - YMIN)/RNGY * 60.
         LINE(STRCOL) = STAR
         IF(ISTEP/10 * 10 .EQ. ISTEP)THEN
            WRITE(*,11)X(ISTEP),(LINE(K),K=0,60)
         ELSE
            WRITE(*,12)(LINE(K),K=0,60)
         END IF
*
*                      AFTER LINE() IS PRINTED, IT IS AGAIN SET
*                      EQUAL TO ALL BLANKS
*
         LINE(STRCOL) = BLANK
*
    3 CONTINUE
*
*                      PRINT A BOTTOM BORDER ON THE GRAPH
*
      WRITE(*,13)
      RETURN
*--------------------------------------------------------------------
* FORMATS
*
```

Continued

```
   10 FORMAT(///,20X,'A PLOT OF Y VS. X',//,25X,'Y(X)',/,
     +         3X,F7.3,3(13X,F7.3),/,
     +         7X,'+',3(19X,'+'),//,
     +         6X,63('+'))
*
   11 FORMAT(F7.3,61A1,'*')
   12 FORMAT(6X,'*',61A1,'*')
   13 FORMAT(6X,63('*'),//,7X,'+',3(19X,'+'))
*
      END
*---------------------------------------------------------------
      SUBROUTINE MINMAX(A,N,AMIN,AMAX)
*--
*-- MINMAX DETERMINES THE MINIMUM (AMIN) AND THE MAXIMUM (AMAX)
*-- OF THE ARRAY A() WHICH CONTAINS N ELEMENTS.
*---------------------------------------------------------------
*
      REAL A(N),AMIN,AMAX
*
      AMIN = A(1)
      AMAX = A(1)
      DO 1 I = 2,N
        IF(A(I) .LT. AMIN)AMIN = A(I)
        IF(A(I) .GT. AMAX)AMAX = A(I)
    1 CONTINUE
      RETURN
      END
*---------------------------------------------------------------
      FUNCTION ROUNDR(Q)
*--
*--   See Figure 8-7
*--
      END
*---------------------------------------------------------------
*
```

Figure 8-9 A printer plot of damped harmonic motion.

```
INPUT X LIMITS OF PLOT (A,B) 0.0001, 10.0
ENTER SPRING STIFFNESS, MASS, VISCOSITY 25.0, 10.0, 5.0


            A PLOT OF DAMPED HARMONIC MOTION

   SPRING STIFFNESS    =   25.0000 N/M
```

```
   OBJECTS MASS        =   10.0000 KG
   VISCOSITY COEF.     =    5.0000 N-SEC/M

 COMPUTED QUANTITIES
    DECAY CNST.(ALPHA)  =   .250E+00  /SEC
    FREQUENCY (BETA)    =   .156E+01  /SEC

    -.650              -.100            .450            1.000
      +                  +               +                +
      ***********************************************************
 .000 *                                                    *  *
      *                                              *         *
      *                                        *               *
      *                                   *                     *
      *                             *                           *
      *                        *                                *
      *                   *                                      *
      * *                                                        *
      * *                                                        *
      *   *                                                      *
2.500 *      *                                                   *
      *          *                                               *
      *                *                                         *
      *                     *                                    *
      *                        *                                 *
      *                            *                             *
      *                              *                           *
      *                                *                         *
      *                             *                            *
      *                         *                                *
5.000 *                       *                                  *
      *                   *                                      *
      *               *                                         *
      *             *                                           *
      *            *                                            *
      *             *                                           *
      *                *                                        *
      *                   *                                     *
      *                     *                                   *
7.500 *                       *                                 *
      *                        *                                *
      *                        *                                *
      *                        *                                *
      *                       *                                 *
      *                    *                                    *
      *                  *                                      *
      *                *                                        *
      *              *                                          *
      *             *                                           *
10.000*            *                                            *
      ***********************************************************
      +                  +               +                +
       STOP
```

8.6 CONSTRUCTING MODULAR PROGRAMS

8.6.1 The EXTERNAL and INTRINSIC Statements

The subroutine in the previous section could be restructured to be somewhat more modular by having the subroutine PLOT graph an *arbitrary* function from x_1 to x_2. Thus, if we wanted to graph $\sin(x)$ from 0 to 2π we could simply insert the following lines anywhere we wish:

```
X1 = 0.0
X2 = 2. * 3.1415926
CALL PLOT(X1,X2,SIN)
```

Or to graph a more complicated function called, say, BESSEL(X), where BESSEL is a function subprogram included elsewhere in the complete code, the command would be

```
CALL PLOT(2.5,12.3,BESSEL)
```

However, you should have noticed that we are using the argument list of a subroutine in a manner significantly different from all previous examples. Up to this point we have transferred either ordinary variables or dimensioned arrays by means of the argument list. These are things with numerical values. The transfer considered here is the transfer of a *name*. In the above call to PLOT the function names SIN or BESSEL appear, while in the body of the subroutine a dummy name like FNC is used.

```
SUBROUTINE PLOT(A,B,FNC)
REAL X(50), Y(50)
CHARACTER*1 LINE(66)
   . . .          . . .
F1 = FNC(A)
F3 = FNC(B)
   . . .          . . .
   . . .          . . .
RETURN
END
```

There is no function called FNC and in all the statements in PLOT that refer to this function, the computer must be instructed to replace the name FNC with SIN or BESSEL or some other existing function subprogram.

This is accomplished in Fortran by means of the EXTERNAL and INTRINSIC statements, which have a form

```
EXTERNAL name1, name2,...

INTRINSIC name3, name4,...
```

where $name_1$, $name_2$, ... are names of functions that are not called directly, but which appear in the argument list of referenced subroutines or functions. The EXTERNAL statement is used to identify a name as that of a user-written function subprogram that appears elsewhere in the code, while the INTRINSIC statement identifies a name as a library function.

The EXTERNAL and INTRINSIC statements are required only in the program unit that makes indirect reference to the function through the argument list of a referenced subprogram. It is *not* required in the subprogram that makes a *direct* reference to the function. Thus, in the above example, the statements

```
EXTERNAL BESSEL
INTRINSIC SIN
```

would be required in the main program that calls PLOT (which in turn calls SIN and BESSEL), but would not be needed in PLOT itself. The point is this: the compiler must be instructed that in the call to PLOT in the main program, the name BESSEL *is not* a variable but the name of an entire function. Since the function BESSEL is defined "externally" to the main program, the compiler has no way of determining this, unless we specify that BESSEL is a function name defined elsewhere. Naturally then, this does not apply to statement functions which are defined internally. Statement function names can never be included in an EXTERNAL or INTRINSIC statement. The EXTERNAL and INTRINSIC statements are nonexecutable and must appear before the first executable statement. Subroutine names may also be declared EXTERNAL.

A sketch of the complete code to graph the functions SIN and BESSEL is given in Figure 8-10.

8.6.2 An Example Program Illustrating EXTERNAL Statements

The theory of probability is concerned with describing the results of measurements that contain a degree of randomness and has applications in a variety of fields. For example, suppose that you wish to determine whether investing in a gas station on the new interstate is a good idea. The most important factor in the decision is of course the volume of traffic passing the station. The traffic flow can be characterized by λ, the average number of cars that pass per minute in the daylight hours. To aid in your decision, you set up some expensive electronic equipment to measure how many cars pass in each minute during the day. When you return in a few days, you find a problem. The electronics could not keep up with the counting when the flow was extremely heavy. Whenever 60 or more cars pass per minute, the counting apparatus malfunctions and effectively registers "tilt." This is found to occur in 20 percent of the measurements. Is all lost? No, but to unravel the results may take a bit of work and will require a few assumptions.

Figure 8-10
Outline of the
code to execute
printer plots.

```
PROGRAM XXX
REAL A,B,C,D
EXTERNAL BESSEL
INTRINSIC SIN

READ *,A,B,C,D
CALL PLOT(A,B,SIN)
CALL PLOT(C,D,BESSEL)
    ...          ...
    ...          ...
END
```

plotting intervals, $a - b$, $c - d$

```
SUBROUTINE PLOT(X1,X2,FNC)
REAL X(50),Y(50)
CHARACTER*1 LINE(66),BLANK,STAR

DX = (X2 - X1)/49.
DO 37 I = 1,50
    X(I) = (I - 1.) * DX
    Y(I) = FNC(X(I))
37  CONTINUE
CALL MINMAX(Y,50,YMIN,YMAX)
TOP = ROUNDR(YMAX)
    ...          ...
    ...          ...
RETURN
END
```

*PLOT will printer-
plot an arbitrary
function which has
the dummy name
FNC. When it is
called, the replace-
ment FNC $\to$ SIN or
BESSEL is made.*

```
FUNCTION BESSEL(S)
BESSEL = ...
RETURN
END
```

```
SUBROUTINE MINMAX(A,N,AMIN,AMAX)
    ...          ...
RETURN
END
```

```
FUNCTION ROUNDR(Q)
    ...          ...
ROUNDR = ...
RETURN
END
```

First of all, probability theory says that if λ is the average number of events (i.e., cars passing) in an interval, the probability of k events in a given interval is given approximately by the Poisson function:

$$P_k(\lambda) = \frac{\lambda^k e^{-\lambda}}{k!} \qquad (8.4)$$

Where $P_k \sim 1$ implies near certainty that k cars will pass in any given minute.

Now, your faulty measurements tell you that the probability of 60 *or more* cars per minute is 20 percent, in other words

$$0.2 = \sum_{k=60}^{\infty} P_k(\lambda) \qquad (8.5)$$

This equation must be solved for the average λ.

To evaluate the infinite sum, we once again determine the ratio of successive terms

$$\text{Ratio} = \frac{P_{k+1}(\lambda)}{P_k(\lambda)} = \frac{\lambda^{k+1}e^{-\lambda}}{(k+1)!} \frac{k!}{\lambda^k e^{-\lambda}} = \frac{\lambda}{k+1} \qquad (8.6)$$

Also, since the summation begins at $k = 60$, the value of 60! must be evaluated first. We will express Equation (8.5) as a function called TILT(x), i.e.,

$$\text{Tilt}(x) = \sum_{k=60}^{\infty} P_k(x) - 0.2 \qquad (8.7)$$

The Fortran code for this function is given in Figure 8-11.

The program to solve the problem must determine the root of Equation (8.7) and is given in Figure 8-12. The setup for this program would have the main program first, followed by the subprograms in any order. I would suggest that they be ordered in relation to the sequence that they are called. That is PLOT calls MINMAX and should precede it in the listing.

The result of the calculation is

```
AVERAGE NUMBER OF CARS/MINUTE = 53.403
PROBABILITY OF THIS MANY CARS/MIN = 0.05463
PROBABILITY OF ZERO CARS/MIN = 0.64E-23
```

8.6.3 The SAVE Statement

Occasionally, when a subprogram is called more than once, we may wish to make use of a *locally* defined variable that was computed in an earlier call. Ordinarily, all values associated with variable names within a subprogram

Figure 8-11
The Fortran
code for the func-
tion in Equation
(8.7).

```
        FUNCTION TILT(X)
*
*                       Be careful with X = 0. Since
*                       0.**K is zero, set TILT(0.) = -0.2.
*
        IF(X .EQ. 0.)THEN
            TILT = -0.2
            RETURN
        END IF
*
        K = 60
*                       The sum begins at K = 60, we need
*                       to compute 60-factorial to start.
*
        FACT60 = 1.
        DO 1 I = 1,K
          FACT60 = FACT60 * I
    1   CONTINUE
*
*                       Sum from K = 60 until terms are
*                       smaller than 1.E-6.
*
        TERM = X**60/FACT60
        SUM = 0.
        DO 2 I = 1,100
          SUM = SUM + TERM
          IF(ABS(TERM) .LT. 1.E-6)THEN
                TILT = EXP(-X) * SUM - 0.2
                RETURN
          ELSE
                RATIO = X/(I + 1.)
                TERM = TERM * RATIO
          END IF
    2   CONTINUE
*
*       PRINT *,'SUM NOT CONVERGING, X = ',X
        STOP
        END
```

that are not also in the argument list are lost after leaving the subprogram.
To preserve the value associated with a variable from one use of a subprogram to the next, the SAVE statement is inserted before the first executable statement in the subprogram. The form of the SAVE statement is

$$\text{SAVE } name_1, name_2, \ldots$$

For example, in the previous section, the function TILT computes 60!

Figure 8-12 The code to find the average number of cars passing per second.

```
        PROGRAM CARS
*--
*--    BASED ON THE INFORMATION THAT THE PROBABILITY OF 60 OR MORE
*--    CARS PASSING PER MINUTE IS 20 PERCENT, THE AVERAGE NUMBER OF
*--    CARS PASSING PER MINUTE IS ESTIMATED BY ASSUMING A POISSON
*--    DISTRIBUTION AND SOLVING THE EQUATION
*--
*--                SUM( P(K,AVE) ) = 0.20
*--
*--    WHERE THE SUM IS FROM 60 TO INFINITY AND AVE IS THE ROOT OF
*--    THE EQUATION. TO AVOID THE INFINITE SUM, THE EQUATION IS RE-
*--    WRITTEN AS
*--
*--        TILT(AVE) = 0.20 - SUM( P(K,AVE) )
*--
*--    WHERE THE SUM IS NOW FROM 0 TO 59.
*-----------------------------------------------------------------
* VARIABLES
*
        REAL A,B,EPS,AVE
        INTEGER IMAX,IAVE
*
*               A,B        --  LEFT AND RIGHT ENDS OF THE SEARCH
*                              INTERVAL.
*               EPS        --  CONVERGENCE CRITERION FOR BISEC
*               IMAX       --  MAXIMUM NO. OF ITERATIONS IN BISEC
*               AVE        --  THE ROOT OF THE EQ. RETURNED
*                              BY BISEC
*               IAVE       --  THE ROOT TRUNCATED TO AN INTEGER
*-----------------------------------------------------------------
* DECLARE THE FUNCTION TILT AS EXTERNAL
*
        EXTERNAL TILT
*-----------------------------------------------------------------
* INITIALIZATION
*
        A = 25.
        B = 60.
        IMAX = 50
        EPS = 1.E-6
*-----------------------------------------------------------------
* COMPUTATION
*
                THE ONLY FUNCTION OF THE MAIN PROGRAM IS TO
*               CALL BISEC TO FIND THE ROOT OF TILT.
```

Continued

```
*
      CALL BISEC(A,B,EPS,IMAX,I,AVE,TILT)
*-----------------------------------------------------------------
* OUTPUT
*                     AND PRINT THE RESULTS
*
      IAVE = AVE
      WRITE(*,10)AVE
      WRITE(*,11)P(IAVE,AVE)
      WRITE(*,12)P(0,AVE)
*-----------------------------------------------------------------
* FORMATS
*
   10 FORMAT(10X,'AVERAGE NUMBER OF CARS/MINUTE   = ',F7.3)
   11 FORMAT(10X,'PROBABILITY OF THIS MANY CARS/MIN = ',F7.5)
   12 FORMAT(10X,'PROBABILITY OF ZERO CARS/MINUTE  = ',1E9.2)
      END
*-----------------------------------------------------------------
      FUNCTION P(K,X)
*--
*--   P(K,X) IS THE POISSON DISTRIBUTION WHICH GIVES THE APPROX.
*--   PROBABILITY THAT K EVENTS OCCUR IN A TIME INTERVAL IF THE
*--   AVERAGE IN THAT INTERVAL IS KNOWN TO BE X.
*-----------------------------------------------------------------
* VARIABLES
*
      REAL X,FACT,P
      INTEGER K,I
*                 X      --   THE AVERAGE NUMBER OF EVENTS/INTERVAL
*                 K      --   EVENTS PER TIME INTERVAL
*                 FACT   --   K - FACTORIAL
*                 I      --   A COUNTER
*-----------------------------------------------------------------
*
*                 THE CASE K = 0 MUST BE HANDLED SEPARATELY
*
      IF(K .EQ. 0)THEN
         P = EXP(-X)
      RETURN
      END IF
*-----------------------------------------------------------------
      FACT = 1.
      DO 1 I = K,1,-1
         FACT = FACT * I
    1 CONTINUE
      P = X**K * EXP(-X)/FACT
      RETURN
      END
```

```
        SUBROUTINE BISEC(A,B,EPS,IMAX,I,ROOT,F)
            ...              ...
            SEE FIGURE 8-1
            NOTE:  A DUMMY FUNCTION NAME HAS BEEN ADDED TO THE
                   ASSIGNMENT LIST.
            ...          ...
        END
```

```
        FUNCTION TILT(X)
            ...          ...
            SEE FIGURE 8-11
            ...              ...
        END
```

every time the function is referenced, which may be hundreds of times. This could be remedied by inserting a flag in the function which is undefined the first time the function is called and is defined and saved after the initial call.

```
        FUNCTION TILT(X)
        SAVE FLAG,FACT60
*                          The variable FLAG has not yet
*                          been defined and it is very
*                          unlikely that it has the value
*                          of 1357.1.
        IF(FLAG .NE. 1357.1)THEN
                           Compute FACT60 = 60!
                           Assign FLAG = 1357.1
        END IF
```

Note that there is never a need to explicitly SAVE variables in the argument list of a subprogram, and attempts to do so will result in compilation time errors. SAVEd variables may, however, appear as actual arguments in the argument list of a subprogram that is called *from* the current subprogram.

   If the SAVE statement appears without a list of variables, then *all* the locally defined variables in the subprogram are saved from one call to the next.

8.6.4   A Note on Floating-Point Overflow

If you attempt to execute the program CARS of Figure 8-12, there is a good chance, depending on the word length characteristic of your machine, that the program will fail. The Fortran code itself is perfectly valid; however, the function TILT requires the calculation of very large factorials, (e.g.,

$60! = 8.32 \times 10^{81}$) and these may easily exceed the capacity of a typical computer. The maximum real number on a computer, of course, depends on the word length of the machine and a typical maximum real number might be 9.0×10^{99}. If a computed number exceeds this maximum, the result is an execution time error called *floating-point overflow* and the correction of the problem can often be extremely difficult. Often the only recourse is to rewrite the entire code so as to avoid the problem if possible. This usually requires considerable ingenuity. In the present problem, however, the correction is rather easy. Recall that

$$\text{Tilt}(x) = \sum_{k=60}^{\infty} P_k(x) - 0.2$$

and note that

$$\sum_{k=0}^{\infty} P_k(x) = 1 \tag{8.8}$$

Equation (8.8) is a statement that the sum of the probabilities of all possibilities must be one. (It is a certainty that either zero cars or some cars pass in 1 minute.) Combining these two equations, we obtain

$$\text{Tilt}(x) = \left[\sum_{k=0}^{\infty} P_k(x) - \sum_{k=0}^{59} P_k(x) \right] - 0.2 \tag{8.9}$$

$$= 0.8 - \sum_{k=0}^{59} P_k(x)$$

and thus the function Tilt may be rewritten without any infinite summations. Once again, a careful analysis of the problem before a Fortran code is attempted can frequently reduce enormously the time spent in later patching up a poorly thought out and casually constructed program.

8.6.5 The COMMON Statement

Up to now, the only communication that subroutines and functions have had with each other and with the main program is via the variables that appear in their argument lists. There is one additional mechanism for transferring information, called COMMON blocks. The idea is to reserve special blocks of memory that may be accessed by one or more program units. The form of the statement that assigns variables to these blocks is

COMMON/blockname/variable$_1$, variable$_2$, . . .

or

$$\text{COMMON variable}_1, \text{variable}_2, \ldots$$

In the first example, called *labeled* COMMON, a block of memory is assigned a name, "blockname," which is any valid Fortran name and is set off by slashes. The list of variables contained in this block then follows, separated by commas. The variables may be a mix of integers, reals, and arrays, but the list may not contain any function names. Additionally, if any of the variable names in the block is of type CHARACTER, *all* the variable names in the block must be of type CHARACTER.

The second example is called *blank* COMMON and the only difference is that the reserved block of memory has been left unnamed. Examples of COMMON statements follow:

```
COMMON/ABLOCK/X,Y,J,K
COMMON/BBLK/A(50),C,D/CBLC/F(35)   ⟨BBLK is 52 memory words,
                                     followed by block CBLC,
                                     35 memory words.⟩
COMMON/W/W                          ⟨Block W is one word and
                                     contains the variable W.⟩
```

In this text I will use labeled COMMON blocks exclusively. ⟵
The rules pertaining to COMMON statements are

1. A pair of slashes is used to separate the name given to a group of variables, all stored together in a block.
2. A COMMON statement is nonexecutable and must appear before the first executable statement.
3. A similar Fortran line, with the *same* block name, must appear in both the program units that share the use of some or all the variables in the block.
4. The assignment of values to variables in the block proceeds in the same manner as for argument lists: i.e., values are assigned by position in the list, not by variable name.
5. If a variable is in a COMMON block, it *cannot* simultaneously be in an argument list. This is because such an arrangement would require two distinct memory addresses for the same variable. For example,

```
        SUBROUTINE PROD(X,Y,N)
        COMMON/AAA/X                    ⟨Incorrect⟩
```

6. A DIMENSION declaration may be combined with COMMON statements, for example,

```
        DIMENSION X(50),Y(25)
        COMMON/CCCC/X,Y
```

has the same effect as

```
COMMON/CCCC/X(50),Y(25)
```

You will have no difficulty in understanding COMMON statements if you recognize that they are simply a replacement for an argument list. Thus,

```
PROGRAM MANE                              PROGRAM MANE
READ *,D,E,F                              COMMON/COEF/D,E,F
Z = 2.                                    READ *,D,E,F
T = F(D,E,F,Z)                            Z = 2.
                                          T = F(Z)
STOP                                      STOP
END                                       END


FUNCTION F(A,B,C,X)          and          FUNCTION F(X)
F = A * X**2 + B * X + C                   COMMON/COEF/A,B,C
RETURN                                     F = A * X**2 + B * X + C
END                                       RETURN
                                          END
```

are essentially interchangeable.

COMMON blocks are most often employed in two very frequently occurring situations in Fortran:

Eliminating Long Argument Lists: If a subprogram is referenced many times and if the argument list of the subprogram is quite long, it is very easy to make errors. The order of the variables or their type may be entered incorrectly, or some accidentally omitted. In these cases it is suggested that most or all of the variables be passed through a COMMON block. This also makes the program somewhat easier to read.

Matching the Argument List to a Dummy Function: Frequently a subprogram module will make reference to a function of a *single* variable, F(X), while the particular function in question requires several parameters in addition to X. The only recourse is to pass the additional parameters through a COMMON block. Thus if we wished to PLOT the function F above, the first representation would not be suitable.

PROBLEMS

1. Write a short program segment that reads two positive numbers corresponding to the x, y coordinates of a point in the first quadrant and by using subroutine LENGTH of Section 8.3.1 determines whether the point lies between the two circles of radii 1. and 3.

2. Properties of subroutines:
   a. Write a subroutine that does something useful and has no argument list at all.
   b. A subroutine will compile without a RETURN statement. Construct a subroutine that again does something useful and does not have a RETURN statement.
   c. Is it possible to do the following from a subroutine?
      i. Stop
      ii. Call a different subroutine
      iii. Call a different subroutine and from the second subroutine return directly to the main program
      iv. Print output
      v. Read data
3. Redo the above problem applied to function subprograms.
4. Write a subroutine that takes two real variables (A, B) and returns the values interchanged—i.e. (B, A).
5. Write the code for a subroutine that evaluates the "product" of two arrays A(N,N) and B(N,N) defined by the equation

$$C_{ij} = \sum_{k=1}^{n} A_{ik} B_{kj} \qquad \text{for all } i, j = 1 \text{ to } n$$

The arrays have been dimensioned in the main program to be N by N, but the subroutine should accommodate any square array of size M ≤ N.
6. Rewrite the code for a pointer sort found in Chapter 7 as a subroutine which is to take a list of N items stored in an array A(N) and return the sequencing index array INDX(N).
7. University records for all students are stored on a file called STUDAT as follows:

Last name (begins in col. 1)	Format	(A10)
First and middle initial		(A2)
Student ID		(I9)
Class (1-freshman, 4-senior)		(I1)
Sex (M or F)		(A1)
SAT(Verbal)		(I3)
SAT(Math)		(I3)
College(A+S = 1, Engr = 2, Bus = 3,		
Educ = 4)		(I1)
Current GPA		(F4.2)
Last semester GPA		(F4.2)

   a. Write a subroutine called INPUT which will read the file, store and return the information in appropriately named arrays, and prints the total number of students. The name of the file should be passed to the subroutine through its argument list. You can assume that there are less than 8,000 students in the university.

b. Write a main program that then:
  i. Counts the number of students in each college.
  ii. Counts the number of females in each college with SAT(Math) $\geq$ 600 and prints the result.
  iii. Produces an alphabetical list of all students and prints the list including all the related information. You can assume you have available a subroutine to execute a pointer sort that returns the array INDX.
  iv. Produce an alphabetical list of males in A+S college who expect to graduate next year but who are currently on probation (current GPA $\leq$ 1.8). The quickest way to proceed is to find all such students, copy the list into a separate array (including a separate indexing array) and then call for a pointer sort.

8. A rather famous infinite series for early computations of π is

$$\frac{\pi}{6} = \frac{1}{2} + \frac{1}{2} \cdot \frac{1}{3 \cdot 2^3} + \frac{1 \cdot 3}{2 \cdot 4} \cdot \frac{1}{5 \cdot 2^5} + \frac{1 \cdot 3 \cdot 5}{2 \cdot 4 \cdot 6} \cdot \frac{1}{7} \cdot \frac{1}{2^7} + \cdots$$

This series converges quite rapidly. Determine an expression for the general term in the series and for the ratio of successive terms. Write a program to add the first P terms as *fractions* reduced to lowest terms to obtain an accurate fractional approximation to π.

9. The two linear equations in two unknowns x, y

$$ax + by = e$$
$$cx + dy = f$$

are easily solved by writing the first as

$$x = \frac{e - by}{a}$$

and substituting this into the second equation and solving for y. The result is

$$x = \frac{ed - fb}{ad - bc} \qquad y = \frac{af - ec}{ad - bc}$$

Write a program that will read *fractions* for the constants a, b, c, d, e, f (i.e., IA(1), IA(2), the numerator and denominator of a, etc.) and will obtain the solutions for x and y expressed as a fraction in lowest terms. Use FUNCTION IGCF and write two subroutines MINUS and MULTP to subtract and multiply two arbitrary fractions and return the result as a fraction.

10. Write a subroutine CHANGE that will determine the appropriate change to be returned when an amount PAY is submitted for an item that has a price COST. Assume that PAY is less than $100 and that there are no $2 bills. The subroutine should return

$$(I10D,I5D,I1D,I25C,I10C,I5C,I1C)$$

where I10D is the number of $10 bills, I25C is the number of $0.25 coins, etc. to be returned. The subroutine should, of course, minimize the amount of small change returned.

11. Rewrite function ROUNDR to round an arbitrary real number *down*. Thus if $Q = 0.16731$, then ROUNDR(Q) = 0.15.

12. Rewrite the PLOT program (Figure 8-8) as a subroutine that will graph an arbitrary function FNC(X) in 50 steps from X = A to X = B.

13. Find any errors in the following:

a. `SUBROUTINE AB(X,I + 1,EPS,ANSWER)`
b. `CALL CD(X,I + 1,EPS,ANS)`
c. `FUNCTION EF(X,A(12),I)`
d. `Z = GH(Y,A(3),K)`
e. `FUNCTION SUM(X,Y)`
   `Z = X + Y`
   `RETURN`
   `END`
f. `SUBROUTINE DIFF(X,Y)`
   `DIFF = X - Y`
   `RETURN`
   `END`

14. All of the student data is contained on the file described in Problem 8.7. Also, the pointer array INDX(I) has been determined that arranges all the names in alphabetical order (i.e., NAME(INDX(1)) is the first name in the alphabetized list). Write a subroutine that (a) reads a complete set of information for a new student and adds it to the end of the data file (you will have to rewrite the entire file to a new data file); (b) puts the new student's name in the correct alphabetical position. (You only need change the array INDX.)

15. Polynomial evaluation
a. Write a function to evaluate a polynomial POLY(X,N,C) for a particular value of x. The polynomial is of degree n and the coefficients are supplied in c_n. Thus

$$\text{Poly}(x) = c_n x^n + c_{n-1} x^{n-1} + \cdots + c_2 x^2 + c_1 x^1 + c_0$$

$$= \sum_{i=0}^{n} c_i x^i$$

b. Rewrite the function POLY so that *no exponentiation* is employed. For example

$$c_2x^2 + c_1x + c_0 = [(c_2x + c_1)x + c_0]$$

For n large, this method of evaluating a polynomial is far more efficient.

16. The combinatorial function is

$$C(n, p) = \frac{n!}{(n - p)! \, p!}$$

Write a function subprogram to compute all the $C(n, i)$'s for $i = 1$ to p. Note: Your function should *not* compute any factorials. Instead, express $C(n,p)$ as an extended product, where

$$C(n, i + 1) = (\text{Ratio}) \times [C(n, i)] \qquad \text{for } i = 1, p$$

Start with $C(n, 1) = n$, compute $C(n, 2)$, etc. up to $C(n, p)$. Surprisingly it is about as efficient to compute all $C(n, i)$ in this manner as it is to compute a single combinatorial using factorials.

17. Write a function subprogram that returns the cube root of a real number x. (**Note:** x can be negative.)

18. A vector $\mathbf{a} = [a_x, a_y, a_z]$ can be represented by an array A(I), I = 1,3; i.e., $[a_1, a_2, a_3]$. The dot product of two vectors is a number defined by

$$\mathbf{a} \cdot \mathbf{b} = a_1 b_1 + a_2 b_2 + a_3 b_3$$

And the cross product is a *vector* whose components are defined by

$$\mathbf{c} = \mathbf{a} \times \mathbf{b}$$
$$c_1 = a_2 b_3 - a_3 b_2$$
$$c_2 = a_3 b_1 - a_1 b_3$$
$$c_3 = a_1 b_2 - a_2 b_1$$

Write a function for the dot product and a subroutine for the cross product of two vectors. Write a main program that tests whether the identity

$$(\mathbf{a} \times \mathbf{b}) \cdot (\mathbf{c} \times \mathbf{d}) = (\mathbf{a} \cdot \mathbf{c})(\mathbf{b} \cdot \mathbf{d}) - (\mathbf{a} \cdot \mathbf{d})(\mathbf{b} \cdot \mathbf{c})$$

is correct for values of $\mathbf{a}, \mathbf{b}, \mathbf{c}, \mathbf{d}$ that are read in.

19. A point on a sphere can be characterized by two angles, the polar angle α, and the azimuthal angle β as shown on Figure 8-13. These angles are related to the longitude and latitude as follows:

$$\alpha = 90° - \text{latitude (if north)}$$

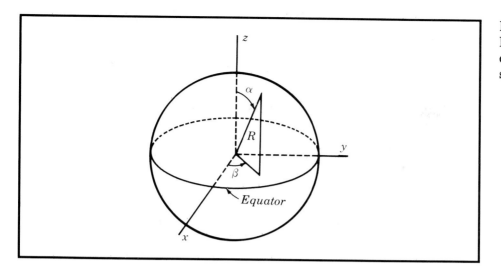

Figure 8-13
Polar coordinates of a point on a sphere.

$$\alpha = 90° + \text{latitude (if south)}$$

$$\beta = \text{longitude (if west)}$$

$$\beta = 360° - \text{longitude (if east)}$$

Furthermore, if the angular separation between two points on the sphere is θ_{12}, then the expression for the cosine of this angle is

$$\cos(\theta_{12}) = \cos(\alpha_1)\cos(\alpha_2) + \sin(\alpha_1)\sin(\alpha_2)\cos(\beta_2 - \beta_1)$$

and once the angle θ_{12} is determined, the surface distance between the two points is given by $d = \theta_{12}R$, where R is the radius of the sphere.

a. Write a subroutine subprogram that will convert the coordinates of a point on the earth given in terms of longitude and latitude in degrees into coordinates in terms of the angles (α, β) in radians. The input angles should be in the form:

Latitude: if north (e.g., XX°XX′N) use → +XX.XX

                    south (e.g., XX°XX′S) use → −XX.XX

Longitude: if west (e.g., XX°XX′W) use → +XX.XX

                    east (e.g., XX°XX′E) use → −XX.XX

b. Write a function subprogram that will return the surface distance between two points on the earth whose coordinates are given in terms of the pairs of angles (α_1, β_1), (α_2, β_2). The radius of the earth is 3958.89 miles.

c. Use these subprograms to determine which two cities in the following list have the largest surface separation.

	Latitude	Longitude
Chicago	41°49'N	87°37'W
Los Angeles	35°12'N	118°02'W
Montreal	45°30'N	73°35'W
London	51°30'N	0°07'W
Rio de Janeiro	22°50'S	43°20'W
Melbourne	35°52'S	145°08'E
Vladivostok	43°06'N	131°47'E
Johannesburg	26°08'S	27°54'E

20. True or false? Explain!

    a. The name of a COMMON block must not be the same as that of any variable in the list.

    b. To use a COMMON block in a subroutine, the block must also appear in the main program.

    c. Two COMMON blocks can appear on the same line, i.e., COMMON/AA/X,Y,Z/GG/D,E,F

    d. The variables X, Y in the two COMMON blocks

```
COMMON/SS/W(3:12),T,II,Y,R(7)
COMMON/SS/U(-1:5),MM(6),X,SS,B,C,D,E,F
```

    have the same value.

    e. All variables in a COMMON block must be of the same type.

21. You have at your disposal a subroutine

```
SUBROUTINE ROOT(A,ANSWER,F)
```

that will find a root of a function of a single variable $f(x)$ when an initial guess (A) is given for the root. The root is returned as ANSWER. You also have a function subprogram,

```
FUNCTION XINTGL(A,B,FNC)
```

which computes the definite integral of fnc(t) from $t = $ A to $t = $ B; i.e.,

$$XINTGL(A,B,FNC) = \int_a^b fnc(t)\ dt$$

(Don't panic—You do not need to understand integration to do this problem.) Write a program that will find the root of the equation

$$g(x) = 5e^{-2x^2} - \sin\left(\frac{\pi x}{2}\right) + \int_0^x (4t^2 - 5)e^{-t^2}\ dt$$

starting with an initial guess of $x_1 = 1.0$. (Notice that the variable is x and it appears in the limits of the integral.)

22. Consider the program below:

```
PROGRAM XXX
COMMON/B/B(9,9),D,E,F
READ *,B
READ *,D,E,F
E = E/2. - 1.
D = -G(E)
F = B(9,9)
PRINT *,D,E,F
STOP
END
FUNCTION G(B)
COMMON/B/D(8,8),E(20)
E(17) = 9.
F = B - E(20)
G = 7.*F
B = -7.
RETURN
END
```

Reads 81 zeros
Reads 0.0, 4.0, 6.0

What values are printed?

CHAPTER 9
ADDITIONAL FORTRAN
FEATURES

There are several advanced features in Fortran that have not been discussed to this point, some very specialized that we can, for now, do without; others that are more frequently encountered and which you may find useful. These are described in this chapter. For a more complete compendium, see the Appendix.

9.1 ADDITIONAL DATA TYPES AVAILABLE IN FORTRAN

The majority of programs only require the three data types that we have encountered thus far: integer, real, and character. In special situations these may not be suitable or sufficient for the solution of the problem at hand. Three additional data types are available in Fortran for use in more advanced programming problems. They are *double-precision, complex,* and *logical* variable types.

9.1.1 Type DOUBLE PRECISION

As you are aware, the real number computations done by a computer are only approximate arithmetic due to the finite length of a computer word. A computer will carry anywhere from 8 to 14 significant digits for each real variable. As we will see in Chapter 16, every arithmetic operation then involves some round-off error, a loss of significant digits. Most of the time this does not cause problems, but there are situations where round-off error can invalidate a calculation. If the number you want is $C = A - B$ and A and B are very nearly equal, say $A = 1.0000032$, $B = 1.0000031$, both with eight significant figures. Then $C = 1.E-7$ with only *one* significant figure. In cases like this, Fortan allows you to double the number of significant digits allotted to a particular variable by reserving two computer words to that variable. This is then a new type of variable in addition to the three we have seen: real, integer, character. The form of the type statement for these variables is

$$\text{DOUBLE PRECISION } name_1, name_2, \dots$$

which like other type statements is nonexecutable and must appear before the first executable statement.

Double-precision constants with an exponent use the letter D to designate the exponent part of the number in place of the letter E that is used for this purpose when writing real numbers. That is, the number $3.5D+06$ is type DOUBLE PRECISION, while $3.5E+6$ is type REAL or single precision.

Similarly, when printing or reading double-precision numbers, the E format should be replaced by a D format (i.e., $E7.1 \rightarrow D7.1$). The D format instructs the computer to expect a number that occupies two words of memory. In all other respects the D format is the same as the E format. Double-precision numbers may be read or written using F or E formats without execution time errors but a loss of accuracy may result. Arithmetic expressions involving reals and double-precision numbers or integers and double-precision numbers are now a new form of mixed-mode arithmetic and special care must be exercised when you use them. Double-precision variables are defined to have "dominance" over reals, which in turn have dominance over integers. (See Section 2.2.2.)

```
PROGRAM MIXMOD
INTEGER I
REAL      R
DOUBLE PRECISION DP1,DP2,DP3

I = 5
R = 4.2
DP1 = 6.3
DP2 = 2.D+2      ⟨D replaces E in the exponent on double
                   precision constants.⟩

DP3 = DP1/R      ⟨R is converted to double precision before
                   dividing, the result is DP3 = 0.15D+1⟩

I = DP2/DP1      ⟨The result of DP2/DP1, .3125D+2 is
                   truncated to I = 31⟩
```

Double-precision variables should only be invoked when absolutely necessary since the computer executes double-precision arithmetic at a much slower rate than ordinary real arithmetic. (It is more than a factor of 2 slower.)

Function subprograms may also be "typed" as double precision:

```
DOUBLE PRECISION FUNCTION A(X)
```

In addition, all of the commonly used library functions like SIN(X), EXP(X), LOG(X) that accept real values for input will accept double precision values as input. The value returned by these functions will then be double-precision. This is *not* the case with a user-written subprogram. If a double-precision value is used in the argument of a type REAL function, the value returned to the referencing program will be real, not double-precision, unless the function has been explicitly typed as a double-precision function.

9.1.2 Type COMPLEX

In algebra you learned that a generalization of the ordinary set of real numbers is the set of complex numbers written in the form

$$a + ib$$

where i is used to designate the square root of -1 ($i = \sqrt{-1}$), a is called the *real* part and b the *imaginary* part of the number. Note that both a and b are themselves ordinary real numbers. Complex numbers occur frequently in scientific and engineering applications and the common arithmetic operations of addition, subtraction, and multiplication can be generalized to include complex numbers.

$$
\begin{array}{cc}
(a_1 + ib_1) & (a_1 + ib_1) \\
+\ (a_2 + ib_2) & -\ (a_2 + ib_2) \\
\hline
(a_1 + a_2) + i(b_1 + b_2) & (a_1 - a_2) + i(b_1 - b_2)
\end{array}
$$

$$(a_1 + ib_1)(a_2 + ib_2) = (a_1 a_2 + i^2 b_1 b_2) + i(a_1 b_2 + a_2 b_1)$$
$$= (a_1 a_2 - b_1 b_2) + i(a_1 b_2 + a_2 b_1)$$

Arithmetic operations can also be effected between complex numbers in Fortran. First, variable names that will be used to store complex numbers are declared as complex with a type statement of the form

COMPLEX   ⟨*list of variable and/or array names*⟩

Next, complex constants are written in Fortran in terms of two real numbers, the real and imaginary parts *enclosed in parentheses* and separated by a comma. Some examples are

```
COMPLEX Z,ROOT,S,T
Z = (3,0,4,0)              i.e., z = 3 + 4i
S = (0,0,2,0)                  s = 2i
T = S * Z                      t = 2i(3 + 4i) = -8 + 6i
ROOT = SQRT((-4,,0,))      Notice, if the argument of SQRT is
                           complex, the result is likewise,
                           root = 2i, i.e. (0., 2.)
```

When a complex number is read using a list-directed READ statement, the form entered must include the enclosing parentheses and the comma separating the real and imaginary parts. Similarly, when a complex number is printed using a list-directed output statement, the form displayed will include parentheses and a separating comma.

```
COMPLEX A,B
READ *,A,B              Enter (4., 5.), (1., 0.)
PRINT *,'A*A = ',A*A    Output is A*A = (-9.0, 40.0)
```

Formatted READ and WRITE statements may also be used to input and output complex numbers provided *two* real-number fields are provided for each complex number.

Mixed-mode arithmetic operations combining complex numbers and real- or integer-type numbers is permitted with the expression evaluated by assigning complex numbers dominance over reals. That is, the result of $2. * (-2., 3.) + 2$ is a complex number whose value is $(-2., 6.)$. However, complex and double-precision numbers may never appear in the same arithmetic operation. Attempts to do so will result in a compilation time error.

It is quite interesting that many of the common numerical techniques developed with real-number arithmetic in mind remain valid when the number set is generalized to include complex numbers. For example, Newton's method for finding square roots may be generalized to obtain complex results by simply typing the relevant variables as complex.

9.1.3 Type LOGICAL

The result of a logical relation of the form (2.**2 .EQ. 4.) must be a value of either ⟨true⟩ or ⟨false⟩. The Fortran data type that is used to store these values is the type LOGICAL. A variable name may be declared to be of type LOGICAL with a type statement of the form

```
LOGICAL    ⟨list of variables and/or arrays⟩
```

Variable names declared in this manner are permitted to contain *only* LOGICAL constants. There are only two logical constants,

```
.TRUE.        .FALSE.
```

The periods at the beginning and end of the word are part of the constant.

```
LOGICAL TEST
TEST = .TRUE.
IF(2**2 .EQ. 4 .AND. TEST)THEN     ⟨true⟩ .and. ⟨true⟩ → ⟨true⟩
```

In addition to the logical combinatorial operators .AND. and .OR., there are two more operators that you may find useful. These are

.EQV.   *Equivalent*
.NEQV.   *Not equivalent*

which may be used to compare two logical variables, constants, or expressions to determine whether or not they have the same value. Thus if *both* sides of .EQV. are the same, either ⟨true⟩ or ⟨false⟩, the entire expression is ⟨true⟩, otherwise it is ⟨false⟩.

```
((4 .LT. 0) .EQV. (1 .GE. 5))   →   ⟨true⟩
```

To my mind the use of LOGICAL variables and constants is rather artificial and unnecessary in most programs and I recommend that you avoid employing them.

9.1.4 IMPLICIT Type Statements

Explicit typing of variable names is achieved by means of the six type statements: REAL, INTEGER, CHARACTER, DOUBLE PRECISION, COMPLEX, and LOGICAL. In addition Fortran automatically will implicitly type variable names, unless instructed otherwise, as

Names that begin
with the letters
I through N   → type INTEGER

All others   → type REAL

The Fortran IMPLICIT statement allows you to alter this. The form of the statement is

IMPLICIT ⟨type⟩ $(a_1\text{-}a_2)$

where a_1, a_2 are single letters, and ⟨type⟩ can be any of the six Fortran number types. This statement then forces all variable names that begin with the letters a_1 through a_2 to be of the specified data type. Thus,

```
IMPLICIT REAL (A-Z)
```

will cause all variables, unless otherwise explicitly typed, to be real. The IMPLICIT statement is, of course, nonexecutable and must precede all executable statements. More significantly, it affects only those statements that come after it and so should be the very first line after the PROGRAM line.

A very common programming error is simply misspelling or mistyping a variable name. Usually, then, the misspelled variable will not have been assigned a value, and when it is used in an arithmetic expression an execution time error will result. These errors are sometimes very difficult to trace. Using the IMPLICIT statement you can construct a trick to detect misspellings immediately at compilation time. The idea is to implicitly type all variables as CHARACTER*1 at the start of the code, and explicitly type all variables that appear later. If any variables are found in the program that have not been explicitly typed (i.e., misspellings) they will be of type CHARACTER and therefore arithmetic expressions involving these variables will be illegal.

```
PROGRAM SPELL
IMPLICIT CHARACTER*1 (A-Z)
REAL X(50),Y(50)
INTEGER LOW,HI,I
X(1) = 0.0
DO 1 I = 1,50
    X(I) = I*(HI - LO)/49.
    Y(I) = F(X(I))
1 CONTINUE
```

The variable LOW is misspelled as LO in the DO loop. Since LO is implicitly typed as character, this statement will result in a compilation time error.

9.2 INITIALIZING VARIABLES AT COMPILATION TIME

Up to this point, values are stored in memory locations assigned to variable names only during execution of the program by either an assignment statement (X = . . .) or by a READ statement (READ *,X). There are, however, situations when it is wasteful or distracting to use valuable execution time to assign values. Setting a large array to all zeros or initializing PI = 3.1415926 are but two examples of occasions of when it would be useful to have values already stored in memory *before* the program begins execution. Most programs require the initialization of numerous constants before the computation can commence. These assignments differ in nature from the initialization of the variables of the problem, which will be changed from one run to the next by reading input data. Each Fortran assignment or READ statement is, of course, an executable statement and will add to the execution time of the program. If the assignments occur in a subprogram that is referenced hundreds of times, this can accumulate to a significant cost. Fortran provides two mechanisms for assigning values to variable names *during compilation*. These are the DATA and the PARAMETER statements.

9.2.1 The DATA Statement

The form of a DATA statement is

$$\text{DATA } \langle \text{namelist} \rangle / \langle \text{valuelist} \rangle /$$

where ⟨namelist⟩ is a list of Fortran variables to be initially assigned a corresponding value in the ⟨valuelist⟩. Of course, the values in the ⟨valuelist⟩ must agree by type to the corresponding name.

```
DATA PI,ILOW,IHI/3.1415926,0,50/
```

Note that the names and the values are separated by commas and that the ⟨valuelist⟩ is enclosed by slashes.

Also, the constants in the ⟨valuelist⟩ can be repeated by including an unsigned nonzero integer as a replication factor. This is very useful in "zeroing" an array.

```
REAL A(10,10)
DATA A/100*0./
```

In addition, implied DO loops may be used in the ⟨namelist⟩ to specify portions of an array.

```
REAL B(50)
DATA (B(I),I = 1,49,2),(B(J),J = 2,50,2)/25*0.,25*1./
```

Thus, the elements of B are 0., 1., 0., 1., . . . If you had wanted to assign the odd elements of B the value $-1.$, you could try $25*(-1.)$ in the ⟨valuelist⟩; however, standard Fortran 77 does not permit parentheses in a ⟨valuelist⟩ and, depending on the local version of Fortran installed on your machine, it may or may not work. A more contrived version that makes use of the PARAMETER statement is described in the next section.

A variable may not appear twice in the same or different DATA statements, and function names may not appear at all. Also, any variables in *blank* COMMON may not be initialized by a DATA statement. (Variables in labeled COMMON are, however, permitted.) Finally, the number of variables in the ⟨namelist⟩ must match the number of values in the ⟨valuelist⟩.

The rules pertaining to the initialization of character variables are similar to those for ordinary assignment statements:

If the length of the character variable in the ⟨namelist⟩ is longer than the corresponding character string in the ⟨valuelist⟩, the right end of the character variable is filled with blanks.

If the length of the character variable in the ⟨namelist⟩ is shorter than the corresponding character string in the ⟨valuelist⟩, the additional symbols to the right are ignored.

```
CHARACTER WORD1*6,WORD2*3
DATA WORD1,WORD2/'BIG','BIGGER'/
```

WORD1   *contains* | B | I | G | | | |

WORD2   *contains* | B | I | G |

9.2.2 The PARAMETER Statement

Occasionally a Fortran variable is to be assigned a value and it is intended that this value *never* be altered. An example is PI = 3.1415926. All variables defined in Fortran, whether they are initialized by an assignment statement, a READ statement, or a DATA statement can be reassigned a different value later in the code. All, that is, except variables initialized by means of the PARAMETER statement. The use of the PARAMETER statement is rather like that of the DATA statement, except for two important distinctions: First, once a variable name has been assigned a value in a PARAMETER statement, the compiler will not permit the value of that variable to be altered thereafter in the program. Second, variable names initialized in a PARAMETER statement are formally called *named constants,* meaning that they may then be used in place of ordinary numerical constants in all subsequent Fortran statements except format edit specifications or as designations for statement numbers. The form of the PARAMETER statement is

```
PARAMETER (name₁=value₁,name₂=value₂,...)
```

where name$_1$, name$_2$, . . . are Fortran variable names and value$_1$, value$_2$, . . . are the values they are to be permanently assigned. These values may be constants, constant expressions, or character strings. For example:

```
INTEGER SIZE,EXIT,INFILE
PARAMETER (PI=3.1415926, INFILE=12, SIZE=20, EXIT=99)

REAL A(SIZE,SIZE)              ⟨This is now a valid dimension
                                statement.⟩

OPEN(INFILE,FILE='DATA3')
REWIND INFILE
READ(INFILE,*,END=EXIT)        ⟨Error, the use of EXIT is
                                incorrect. You cannot use a
                                name in place of a statement
                                number.⟩
```

Using a PARAMETER statement to assign a value to the various array sizes at the beginning of a program is one of several useful applications. If the array sizes need to be changed in subsequent runs of the program, only a single line of the code need be changed.

More exotic applications can be constructed by using character strings as elements of a PARAMETER statement:

```
CHARACTER LIST*11
REAL X(50)
PARAMETER (LIST = '(1X,10F6.2)')
READLIST,X                          (Note: This is equivalent
                                     to READ '(1X,10F6.2)',X)
```

In addition to permanently fixing the value of Fortran variable names, an important feature of PARAMETER constants is that they may then be used in subsequent DATA statements. Thus, the attempt to assign −1. to elements of the array B(I) in the previous section may now be accomplished as follows:

```
REAL XX,B(50)
INTEGER TOP
PARAMETER (XX = -1.0,TOP = 25)
DATA (B(I),I = 1,2*TOP-1,2),(B(I),J = 2,2*TOP,2)
+      /TOP*XX , TOP*1.0/
```

The imaginative use of PARAMETER and DATA statements is a distinctive feature of modern programming style.

9.3 THE ORDER OF FORTRAN STATEMENTS

Numerous new Fortran statements have been introduced in this chapter and you may be uncertain regarding the relative ordering of the various types of executable and nonexecutable statements. The correct arrangement is indicated in Table 9-1. Within each group, the various statements of the same classification may appear in any order, but the groups must be arranged as shown. Statements that can appear anywhere within more than one group are indicated in vertical columns that overlap two or more groups. For example, FORMAT statements may appear anywhere after the PROGRAM line.

The following points regarding statement ordering are worth repeating:

Table 9-1 The ordering of the various types of Fortran statements

Fortran statements			
PROGRAM/SUBROUTINE/FUNCTION			
IMPLICIT	PARAMETER	FORMAT	Comments
INTEGER REAL *Type* CHARACTER *specifications* DOUBLE PRECISION			
DIMENSION COMMON *Specification* EXTERNAL *statements* INTRINSIC LOGICAL			
STATEMENT FUNCTIONS			

Assignment Statements
DO
CONTINUE
IF
ELSE
ELSE IF   DATA
END IF
GO TO
CALL
RETURN
STOP
OPEN
CLOSE
REWIND
READ
WRITE
PRINT			

END			

Comment lines can appear anywhere in a program. Those that are placed after an END statement will be listed with the next program unit.

FORMAT statements can appear anywhere within a program or subprogram.

The END statement is the last statement of a program unit.

Generally, specification statements precede executable statements.

The arrangement of statements within the specification grouping is:

PARAMETER statements can appear anywhere in the group, but must be placed before any reference to variables they define.

Variable names should be type-declared prior to being assigned values in a PARAMETER statement.

IMPLICIT statements *must* precede *all* other specification statements (except PARAMETER).

Statement functions must appear after the specification statements and before the first executable statement. When there is more than one statement function, the ordering must be such that each function references only those placed above it.

DATA statements can be placed anywhere after the specification statements and before, after, or among the statement functions. The recommended placement is after the specifications and before all statement functions.

9.4 THE DoWhile STRUCTURE IN EXTENDED FORTRAN

In Section 3.4 the construction of Fortran loops was described in terms of a DoWhile-EndDo structure. At that time you were advised that present versions of Standard Fortran 77 do not support explicit DO WHILE and END DO statements. However, a great many local installations of Fortran 77 do permit these statements and you should determine whether your computing center is one of these. A version of Fortran 77 that allows for DO WHILE statements is usually called *extended Fortran*. Any program that employs one or more loops will benefit from a rewrite using the new loop control statements.

The form of the Extended Fortran DO WHILE statement is

```
DO [statement number] WHILE(logical expression)
```

The statement number is enclosed in brackets to indicate that it is optional. The brackets do not appear in the actual Fortran statement. If a statement number is included, it specifies the loop-terminating statement, which may be any of the allowed executable statements used to terminate a normal DO loop, or it may be an END DO statement. (See below.) The logical expression within the parentheses is tested at the beginning of each cycle of the loop, including the first. If the expression is evaluated as ⟨true⟩ the body of the loop is executed, otherwise control is transferred to the statement following the loop terminator.

The preferred terminus of a DO WHILE structure is the END DO statement, which has the form

```
END DO
```

An END DO statement *must* be used to terminate a DO or a DO WHILE if
the optional terminal statement number has been *omitted*. An END DO may
have a statement number. A few examples are

$$I_{sum} = \sum_{i=1}^{100} i$$

```
I = 0
ISUM = 0
DO WHILE (I .LT. 100)
     ISUM = ISUM + 1
     I = I + 1
END DO
```

$$e^x = \sum_{n=1}^{\infty} \frac{1}{n!} x^n$$

```
READ *,X
N = 1
SUM = 0.
TERM = X
DO WHILE (ABS(TERM) .LT. 1.E-6)
     SUM = SUM + TERM
     TERM = TERM * X/(N + 1.)
     I = I + 1
     IF(I .GT. 100)THEN
          PRINT *,'NOT CONVERGING'
          STOP
     ENDIF
END DO
```

The DO WHILE structure can be used with or without an END DO statement:

```
READ *,C
X = 0.5 * (C + 1.)
I = 0
DO 99 WHILE (ABS(X * X - C)) .GT. 1.E-6)⟨Newton's
     X = 0.5 * (X + C/X)                 algorithm for
     I = I + 1                           square roots⟩
     IF(I .GE. 50)THEN
          PRINT *,'NOT CONVERGING'
          STOP
     END IF
99 CONTINUE                          ⟨or 99 END DO⟩
```

Note that most of the structured features of Fortran 77 reduce the need for statement number labels and as a result make possible the writing of code that is to a large extent readable in a continuous path from beginning to end. Generally, associating statement numbers with Fortran statements is done to provide alternative paths through the program which in turn can make the program difficult to decipher. Except for FORMAT statements, with the introduction of the DO WHILE and END DO statements into the language there is little compelling reason for using statement numbers *at all.*

9.5   ADDITIONAL FORTRAN INTRINSIC FUNCTIONS

The most commonly used intrinsic functions in scientific and engineering applications were introduced in Section 2.7. There are numerous other intrinsic function available in Fortran and several of these are listed in Tables 9-2 and 9-3.

Most Fortran mathematical intrinsic functions come in a variety of forms depending upon the data type of the argument. For example, DSQRT(D) can be used if the argument is double-precision and the computed result will then also be double-precision. Similarly, CSQRT(C) can be used if the argument is a complex number and the result will be of type COMPLEX. However, a very convenient alternative to choosing the function to fit the type of its argument is to use the *generic* function names that are provided in Fortran. For example, the generic name for computing a square root is SQRT(X). If the argument is real, the result returned is likewise real; if the argument is double-precision, the result returned is double-precision, etc. The specific function names (DSQRT, CSQRT, etc.) have been retained in Fortran to provide compatibility with earlier versions, and I suggest that your programs employ generic function names exclusively, when possible. In Tables 9-2 and 9-3 the symbol I is used to denote an integer argument, X for real, D for double-precision, C for complex, CH for character, and L for logical.

9.6   CONCLUSION

We have now covered all of the elements of Fortran 77 grammar necessary to construct programs to solve almost any problem that is amenable to solution by a computer. There are a few additional Fortran statements that have not been discussed and which are described in the Appendix. Also there are thousands of subtle points that have been glossed over or even purposely

Table 9-2 Fortran mathematical intrinsic functions.

Function name	Description	Argument	Result
SQRT(X)	$\sqrt{x}$ square root, generic	Real Double precision Complex	Real Double precision Complex
EXP(X)	e^x exponential, generic	Real Double precision Complex	Real Double precision Complex
LOG(X)	$\ln(x)$ natural logarithm, generic	Real Double precision Complex	Real Double precision Complex
LOG10(X)	$\log_{10}(x)$ base-10 logarithm, generic	Real Double precision	Real Double precision
ABS(X)	$\|x\|$ absolute value, generic; for complex argument returns $(x^2 + y^2)^{1/2}$	Integer Real Double precision Complex	Integer Real Double precision Real
SIN(X) COS(X) TAN(X)	Trigonometric functions sine, cosine, tangent argument is radians	Real Double precision Complex (sin, cos, only)	Real Double precision Complex (sin, cos, only)
ASIN(X) ACOS(X) ATAN(X)	Inverse trigonometric functions: $\sin^{-1}(x)$, $\cos^{-1}(x)$ $\tan^{-1}(x)$ result in radians; if $x = \tan(\theta)$ then $\theta = \tan^{-1}(x)$	Real Double precision	Real Double precision
SINH(X) COSH(X) TANH(X)	Hyperbolic functions: $\sinh(x) = (e^x - e^{-x})/2$; $\cosh(x) = (e^x + e^{-x})/2$; $\tanh(x) = \sinh(x)/\cosh(x)$	Real Double precision	Real Double precision
MOD(X,Y)	Remainder of division of x by y	Real Double precision	Real Double precision
MAX(X$_1$,X$_2$, ...)	Maximum element of the list x_1, x_2, ...	Real Double precision	Real Double precision
MIN(X$_1$,X$_2$, ...)	Minimum element of the list x_1, x_2, ...	Real Double precision	Real Double precision

disguised or ignored. You do not learn programming or anything else by first memorizing myriad details. These will come naturally with time and experience. You must first develop confidence in your ability to solve complicated problems with what you already know. The analogy with languages is very apt. The best way to become fluent in a language is not to spend great effort in learning a vocabulary by memorization, but rather to begin communicating as soon as you can with the small vocabulary you currently have.

An important responsibility of an instructor is to see to it that the student does not fall into a variety of bad habits that may not appear serious

Table 9-3 Fortran intrinsic functions for converting data types.

Function name	Description	Argument	Result
REAL(X)	Converts argument to real	Real	Real
		Integer	Real
		Double Precision	Real
		Complex	Real
CMPLX(X)	Converts argument to complex	Real	Complex
		Integer	Complex
		Double Precision	Complex
		Complex	Complex
INT(X)	Converts argument to integer by truncation	Real	Integer
		Integer	Integer
		Double precision	Integer
		Complex	Integer
NINT(X)	Round x to nearest integer	Real	Integer
		Double precision	Integer
LEN(CH)	Return length of character string CH	Character	Integer
INDEX(CH$_1$,CH$_2$)	Position of substring CH$_2$ within string CH$_1$	Character	Integer
ICHAR(CH)	Position of the single character CH in the system established sequence	Character	Integer
CHAR(I)	The single character in the ith position of the collating sequence for character symbols	Integer	Character

now but will be difficult to break later. Structured programming was devised to aid in the logical construction of programs, and you should try to segment and "layer" even the simplest of codes. In addition, your programs should contain every manner of internal checks for potential errors that you can devise. By now, you are well aware that some execution time errors are extremely difficult to track down and in such cases helpful clues supplied by the programmer would be greatly appreciated.

The problem now is to use the Fortran developed to this point and to attempt to dovetail it with the mathematics, science, and engineering that you have already seen or will soon see. Once that is accomplished, you will be quite fluent in the mathematical analysis of engineering and science problems.

PROBLEMS

1. True or False? Explain!
   a. Any PARAMETER statement must precede all type statements.
   b. Variables typed as real may also be typed as double precision in the same program unit.

c. Variables implicitly typed as integer may also be typed as real in the same program unit.

d. Variables initialized in a DATA statement may not be altered in the same program unit.

e. Character variables may not be initialized via a DATA statement, a PARAMETER statement must be used instead.

f. Complex variables may not appear in a DATA statement.

2. Use a DATA statement to initialize a square 10 by 10 array, A(I, J), in the following manner.

$$
\begin{aligned}
a_{ij} &= +1 && \text{for } j > i && \text{above the main diagonal} \\
a_{ii} &= 0 && && \text{along the main diagonal} \\
a_{ij} &= -1 && \text{for } j < i && \text{below the main diagonal}
\end{aligned}
$$

You will also need a PARAMETER statement (for the -1's), and several nested implied DO loops in the DATA statement.

3. Rewrite the Fortran code in Section 3.4.3 for Newton's method for finding the square roots of numbers to find the square root of a complex number. Test the program by evaluating the square roots of a negative real number and of an arbitrary complex number. Verify your answer by comparing the square of the result with the test number. (Note: For a test for "smallness" of a complex number c use

```
IF((ABS(C)) .LT. 1.E-6)THEN
```

That is, the sum of the squares of the real plus imaginary parts determines the "size" of the complex number.)

4. Write a Fortran program to use the method of successive substitutions (see Problem 3.10) to find a complex root of a function. Test the program by finding a root of

$$f(x) = x^3 - 4x^2 + 6x - 4 = 0 \qquad \text{Exact roots} = 1 + i, 1 - i, +2$$

Hint: Write the equation as $x = \frac{1}{2}[x^3 + 6x - 4]^{1/2}$ and start with $x_0 = (1.0, 0.5)$.

5. Determine the output of the following program

```
PROGRAM ANDOR
LOGICAL A,B,C,D,E
A = .FALSE.
C = .TRUE.
DO 1 I = -1,1
   B = I .GT. 0
   D = B .AND. (A .OR. C)
   E = B .AND. A .OR. C
   IF(D .NEQV. E)THEN
```

```
                PRINT *,'THE ORDER OF AND/OR MAKES'
                PRINT *,'A DIFFERENCE FOR '
                PRINT *,B,',AND,',A,',OR,',C
          END IF
      1   CONTINUE
```

6. Division of complex numbers can be defined in terms of the multiplicative inverse of the number, which can be obtained in the following manner:

$$c = a + ib \quad \text{(a, b are known)}$$

$$c^{-1} = \alpha + i\beta \quad \text{(α, β are to be determined)}$$

$$c(c^{-1}) = 1 = (a + ib)(\alpha + i\beta)$$

$$= (a\alpha - b\beta) + i(a\beta + b\alpha) = 1 + 0i$$

So

$$b\alpha + a\beta = 0$$

$$a\alpha - b\beta = 1$$

a. Solve these equations for (α, β) in terms of (a, b) to obtain:

$$\alpha = \frac{a}{a^2 + b^2} \qquad \beta = \frac{-b}{a^2 + b^2}$$

b. Test these equations directly on the computer by executing a program to read two complex numbers, X, Y and evaluate and print X/X, X/Y, Y/X, (X/Y)*(Y/X).

7. Determine any compilation errors in the following. If none write OK.

a. `PARAMETER (PI = ACOS(-1.))`

b. `PARAMETER (M = 2)`
`OPEN (M,FILE = 'DATA')`

c. `PARAMETER (N = 44)`
`GO TO N`

d. `PARAMETER (N = 4)`
`REAL A(N)`
`DATA (A(I),I = 1,N)/N*3./`

e. `PARAMETER (N = 4)`
`INTEGER A(N)`
`DATA (A(I),I = 1,N)/N*N/`

f. `CHARACTER NAME*3,STUDENT*12`
`PARAMETER (NAME = '(A)')`
`READNAME,STUDENT`

PROGRAMMING ASSIGNMENT IV

The goal of this programming assignment is to construct moderately complicated programs in modular form, employing numerous subprograms, and to illustrate the use of DATA, IMPLICIT, SAVE, and PARAMETER statements.

IV.1   SAMPLE PROGRAM

Aeronautical/Aerospace Engineering

Among the youngest of the engineering disciplines, aeronautical/aerospace engineering is concerned with all aspects of the design, production, testing, and utilizing of vehicles or devices that fly in air (aeronautical) or in space (aerospace); from hang gliders to the space shuttle. Since the science and engineering principles involved are so broad-based, the aeroengineer will usually specialize in a subarea which may overlap with other engineering fields such as mechanical, metallurgical/materials, chemical, civil, or electrical engineering. Such subareas are

Aerodynamics: The study of the flight characteristics of various structures or configurations. Typical considerations are the drag and lift associated with airplane design, or the onset of turbulent flow. A knowledge of fluid dynamics is essential. Additionally, the modeling and testing of all forms of aircraft is part of this discipline.

Structural Design: The design, production, and testing of aircraft and spacecraft to withstand the wide range of inflight demands expected of these vehicles. In addition, similar problems involving other types of vehicles, such as underwater vessels, are in the province of the structural engineer.

Propulsion Systems: The design of internal combustion, jet, and liquid- and solid-fuel rocket engines and their coordination in the overall design of the vehicle. Rocket engines, especially, require innovative engineering to accommodate the extreme temperatures of storing, mixing, and burning fuels such as liquid oxygen.

Instrumentation and Guidance: The aerospace industry has been a leader in developing and utilizing solid-state electronics in the form of microprocessors to monitor and adjust the operations of hundreds of air- and spacecraft functions. This field makes use of the expertise of both electrical and aeroengineers.

Navigation: The computation of orbits within and outside the atmosphere, and the determination of the orientation of a vehicle with respect to points on the earth or in space.

Sample Program: The Range of a Rocket Trajectory

The trajectory that maximizes the range of a rocket is obviously a topic of importance to the aerospace engineer. In general the problem is quite complex, but, as always, by making some simplifying assumptions, we can reduce the problem to one that is amenable to a computer solution and use the results to suggest the desirable characteristics of rocket engines.

The major assumptions we will make are (1) to neglect air resistance, (2) to assume that the earth is flat (or equivalently that the trajectory is of short range), and (3) that the inclination of the thrust of the rocket is held fixed with respect to the horizontal. Furthermore, we wish to compare two types of rocket engines:

Constant Thrust: Characterized by rapid burn rates, usually solid fuel, not suitable for manned flight, as the acceleration on board increases with time without limit. It is called constant thrust as the output of the engine is constant until the fuel is expended.

Constant Acceleration: Characterized by slower burn rates and use of liquid fuels. The ratio of the thrust output of the engine to the current total mass (spacecraft plus fuel) is held constant. As the rocket burns fuel and becomes lighter, the thrust is correspondingly reduced.

The force diagram for the rocket in flight is shown Figure IV-1. In the figure,

T = thrust of the engine (N)

θ = fixed angle of inclination of T with respect to the horizontal

m = current mass of the spacecraft plus unexpended fuel

g = gravitational acceleration (m/sec^2) assumed constant.

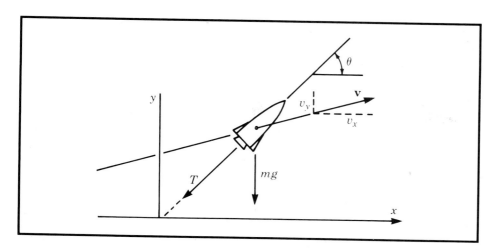

Figure IV-1
Force diagram for
a rocket in flight.

Newton's equations $(F = ma)$ can be written down and solved for this problem, and for strictly vertical flight $(\theta = \pi/2)$, this problem is often analyzed in introductory physics. For motion in both the x and y directions, the analysis is more complicated but straightforward.[1]

The results depend on the following parameters:

v_e = exhaust velocity of the propellant relative to the spaceship

g = gravitational acceleration (value at the earth's surface; i.e., 9.8 m/sec^2)

M_0 = original mass (including fuel) of the rocket

Ω = ratio of the mass of the fuel to the total mass

β = burn rate of the rocket engines (kg/sec)

b = ratio of the burn rate to the original mass (β/M_0)

θ = angle the thrust makes with the horizontal

t_c = burn time for the engines, time to use up all the fuel

t_{hit} = total flight time, the time that the rocket hits the earth's surface

$\begin{matrix} x(t) \\ y(t) \end{matrix}$ = the x and y positions of the rocket as a function of time

x_c, y_c = the x and y positions at the time of cutoff of the engines.

The properties of the trajectories associated with each type of rocket engine are given in Table IV-1.

In this problem you will compute a table of values of $x(t)$, $y(t)$, for $t = 0$ to t_{hit} for each of the two rocket characteristics given in Table IV-2. If you have available to you a pen-and-ink graphics device, you should also plot $y(t)$

---

[1] See Angelo Miele, *Flight Mechanics*, vol. 1, Addison-Wesley, Reading, Mass., 1962.

vs. $x(t)$ for both rockets simultaneously and indicate the point of engine cutoff for each engine on the graph.

Problem Specifics

Your program should

1. Read the rocket engine parameters from Table IV-2.
2. Determine the value of Q for each engine.

Table IV-1
Trajectory characteristics for two rocket types.

Constant thrust	Constant acceleration
Before Cutoff $$\begin{aligned} v_x(t) &= [v_e \cos(\theta)][-\ln(1 - bt)] \\ v_y(t) &= [v_e \sin(\theta)][-\ln(1 - bt)] - gt \\ x(t) &= [v_e \cos(\theta)]f(b, t) \\ y(t) &= [v_e \sin(\theta)]f(b, t) - gt^2/2 \end{aligned}$$ where $$f(b, t) = t + \frac{1}{b}(1 - bt)\ln(1 - bt)$$ The cutoff occurs at a time t_c defined by $$bt_c = \Omega$$ *After Cutoff* $$\begin{aligned} x(t) &= x_c + v_x(t_c)t \\ y(t) &= y_c + v_y(t_c)t - gt^2/2 \end{aligned}$$ where $x_c, y_c, v_x(t_c), v_y(t_c)$ are the position and velocity at cutoff. The optimum angle θ is determined from the root of $$Q\sigma^3 - (\sigma^2 - \tfrac{1}{2}) = 0$$ where $\sigma = \sin(\theta)$, and $$Q = [-\Omega + \ln(1 - \Omega)[\ln(1 - \Omega)]^2]\frac{g}{bv_e}$$ The rocket hits the ground at $t = t_{\text{hit}}$, the positive root of $$y(t = t_{\text{hit}}) = 0$$	$$\begin{aligned} &= [v_e \cos(\theta)]bt \\ &= [v_e \sin(\theta)]bt - gt \\ &= [v_e \cos(\theta)](bt^2)/2 \\ &= [v_e \sin(\theta)]bt^2/2 - gt^2/2 \end{aligned}$$ $$= -\ln(1 - \Omega)$$ $$\begin{aligned} &= x_c + v_x(t_c)t \\ &= y_c + v_y(t_c)t - gt^2/2 \end{aligned}$$ $$= \frac{1}{2}\frac{g}{bv_e}$$

Table IV-2
Characteristic parameters for two types of rocket engines.

	v_e [exhaust velocity (m/sec^2)]	M_0 [original total mass (kg)]	Ω [fuel to total mass ratio]	β [burn rate (kg/sec)]
Constant thrust	5000	30,000	0.6	550
Constant acceleration	3000	65,000	0.5	900

3. Solve the cubic equation for $\sigma = \sin(\theta)$ to obtain the optimum angle for maximum range. Do not use the bisection algorithm for this simple equation. Instead, write a function subprogram that starts with a guess for σ ($\frac{1}{2} < \sigma < 1$.) and employs successive substitutions to obtain the root. That is, first write the cubic as

$$\sigma = (Q\sigma^3 - \tfrac{1}{2})^{1/2}$$

Use your guess for σ in the expression on the right and compute a new value for σ. Repeat this until successive values change by less than 1.E−5%. The function should contain appropriate error diagnostics.

4. Compute the cutoff time for each engine.

5. Compute the positions and velocities of the rockets at the time of cutoff.

6. Solve the quadratic equation for $y(t)$ to determine the value of t_{hit}. Also use this value to determine the range (i.e., $x(t = t_{hit})$ for each engine. Use a subroutine.

7. Using the larger of the t_{hit} values, divide the time interval into fifty steps and compute a table of $x(t)$, $y(t)$ values. (Note: If the computed value of y is negative, replace with zero.)

8. Print all the results in a neat table.

9. If you have access to an automatic graphics plotting device, graph both trajectories on the same graph and indicate on the graph the position at time of cutoff for each rocket.

Your program should have the following subprograms:

FUNCTION CUBRT(Q,X)   *Solves the cubic equation by successive substitution. The maximum number of iterations should be 50.*

SUBROUTINE QUAD(THIT)   *Returns the positive root of the equation $y(t) = 0$. The rest of the parameters should be passed through labeled COMMON.*

FUNCTION X(T,TC,TYPE)   *Computes $x(t)$ for $t \le t_{cutoff}$, or for $t > t_{cutoff}$ and for the two types of engines [TYPE = 'CT' (constant thrust), or 'CA' (constant acceleration)]. Also similar functions for $y(t)$, and the velocity components.*

FUNCTION F(BT)   *This function will be used by $x(t < t_c)$ and $y(t < t_c)$ for type 'CT'.*

Whenever possible, use the argument list for independent variables and common blocks for parameters.

The solution for this problem is given in Figures IV-2 and IV-3.

Figure IV-2 The Fortran code for the rocket trajectory program.

```fortran
      PROGRAM ROCKET
*--
*--  THIS PROGRAM WILL COMPUTE THE FEATURES OF THE TRAJECTORIES
*--  OF TWO TYPES OF ROCKET ENGINES: 1-CONSTANT THRUST,2-CONSTANT
*--  ACCELERATION. THE ROCKET CUTOFF TIME AND POSITION ARE COM-
*--  PUTED AND THE OVERALL RANGE OF EACH ROCKET IS DETERMINED.
*--  ADDITIONALLY THE COMPLETE TRAJECTORIES OF BOTH ROCKETS ARE
*--  DETERMINED AND PLOTTED ON AN AUTOMATIC PEN AND INK PLOTTING
*--  DEVICE. THE MAJOR ASSUMPTIONS MADE WERE THAT THE INCLINATION
*--  ANGLE OF THE ROCKET TO THE HORIZONTAL WAS FIXED AND THAT AIR
*--  RESISTANCE COULD BE NEGLECTED.
*-----------------------------------------------------------------
* VARIABLES
*
      REAL VEX,MZERO,FRATIO,BURNRT,OPANGL(2),TCUT,
     + Q,SIGMA,LN,OMEGA,VXCUT,VYCUT,XCUT,YCUT,
     + G,THIT(2),TLIMIT,B,RANGE(2),VCUT
      REAL X(0:50,2),Y(0:50,2),X1(51),X2(51)
      INTEGER TYPE
      CHARACTER NAME*12
      COMMON/PARAM/B(2),VEX(2),VCUT(2),XCUT(2),YCUT(2),TCUT(2),G,
     + VXCUT(2),VYCUT(2)
*
*     INPUT PARAMETERS
*
*        VEX()    --  VELOCITY OF EXHAUST FOR EACH
*                     ROCKET TYPE
*        MZERO    --  ORIGINAL ROCKET MASS INCL. FUEL
*        FRATIO   --  RATIO OF FUEL TO TOTAL MASS
*                     FOR EACH TYPE ENGINE
*        BURNRT   --  BURN RATE OF EACH ROCKET ENGINE
*        NAME     --  IDENTIFYING NAME OF ENGINE TYPE
*
*     INTERMEDIATE COMPUTED QUANTITIES
*
*        B()      --  RATIO OF BURN RATE TO MZERO
*        Q        --  PARAMETER IN EQ FOR OPTIMUM
*                     ANGLE
*        SIGMA    --  SINE OF OPTIMUM ANGLE
*        LN       --  LOG(1 - FRATIO)
*        FACTR    --  TEMPORARY CONSTANTS USED
*        VFACTR       IN EQUATIONS
*        XFACTR
*        DISCR
*        T, DT    --  TIME AND TIME STEP
*        TYPE     --  EQUALS 1 OR 2 FOR TWO TYPES OF
*                     ROCKET ENGINES
*
*     COMPUTED RESULTS
*

*                     COMPUTE POSITION AND VELOCITY AT CUTOFF
*
      VXCUT(TYPE) = VEX(TYPE)*COS(OPANGL(TYPE))*VFACTR
      VYCUT(TYPE) = VEX(TYPE)*SIN(OPANGL(TYPE))*VFACTR -
     +              G*TCUT(TYPE)
      VCUT(TYPE) = SQRT(VXCUT(TYPE)**2 + VYCUT(TYPE)**2)
      XCUT(TYPE) = VEX(TYPE)*COS(OPANGL(TYPE))*XFACTR
      YCUT(TYPE) = VEX(TYPE)*SIN(OPANGL(TYPE))*XFACTR -
     +              G*(TCUT(TYPE))**2/2.
*
*                     COMPUTE TIME OF HIT AND RANGE
*
      DISCR = VYCUT(TYPE)**2 + 2. *G*YCUT(TYPE)
      THIT(TYPE) = (VYCUT(TYPE) + SQRT(DISCR))/G
      RANGE(TYPE) = DIS(TYPE,THIT(TYPE),1,OPANGL(TYPE))
    1 CONTINUE
*
*                     PRINT THE RESULTS FOR BOTH ROCKET ENGINES
*                     (THE OPTIMUM ANGLE IS PRINTED IN DEGREES)
*
      WRITE(*,13)(OPANGL(K)*360./2./PI,TCUT(K),XCUT(K),
     + YCUT(K),VCUT(K),THIT(K),RANGE(K),K = 1,2)
*
*                     COMPUTE THE TWO ROCKET TRAJECTORIES IN 50
*                     STEPS FROM T = 0. TO T = TLIMIT (THE LARGER
*                     OF THE TWO FLIGHT TIMES)
*
      IF(THIT(1) .GT. THIT(2))THEN
        TLIMIT = THIT(1)
      ELSE
        TLIMIT = THIT(2)
      END IF
      DT = TLIMIT/50.
*
      T = 0.0
*
*                     THE POSITIONS ARE COMPUTED IN THE FUNCTION
*                     DIS(), 1 FOR X, 2 FOR Y, IF A COMPUTED
*                     VALUE FOR Y IS NEGATIVE, SET Y = 0.0.
*
      DO 3 I = 0,50
      DO 2 TYPE = 1,2
        X(I,TYPE) = DIS(TYPE,T,1,OPANGL(TYPE))
        Y(I,TYPE) = DIS(TYPE,T,2,OPANGL(TYPE))
        IF(Y(I,TYPE) .LT. 0.)THEN
          Y(I,TYPE) = 0.0
        END IF
    2 CONTINUE
```

```
*       OPANGL() --    ANGLE THE ENGINE MAKES WITH THE
*                      HORIZONTAL (COMPUTED FOR MAXIMUM
*                      RANGE)
*       VXCUT()  --    POSITIONS AND VELOCITIES AT THE
*       VYCUT()  --    TIME OF CUTOFF
*       VCUT()
*       XCUT()
*       YCUT()
*       TCUT()   --    TIME OF CUTOFF
*       THIT()   --    TIME ROCKET STRIKES THE EARTH
*       TLIMIT   --    THE LARGER OF THE TWO THIT'S
*       RANGE()  --    THE RANGE OF EACH TRAJECTORY
*       X(),Y()  --    THE COORDINATES OF EACH
*                      TRAJECTORY
*
* --------------------------------------------------------
* INITIALIZATION AND COMPUTATION
*
      G = 9.8
      PI = ACOS(-1.)
      OPEN(UNIT = 1,FILE = 'ROKDAT')
      REWIND 1
      WRITE(*,11)
      DO 1 TYPE = 1,2
      READ(1,10)VEX(TYPE),MZERO,FRATIO,BURNRT,NAME
      WRITE(*,12)NAME,VEX(TYPE),MZERO,FRATIO,BURNRT
      LN = LOG(1. - FRATIO)
      B(TYPE) = BURNRT/MZERO
*
*              COMPUTE THE OPTIMUM THRUST ANGLE
*
      IF(TYPE .EQ. 1)THEN
         FACTOR = -(FRATIO + LN)/LN**2
      ELSE
         FACTOR = 0.5
      END IF
*
      Q = FACTOR * G/B(TYPE)/VEX(TYPE)
      SIGMA = CUBRT(Q,.75)
      OPANGL(TYPE) = ASIN(SIGMA)
*
*              COMPUTE THE TIME OF CUTOFF
*
      IF(TYPE .EQ. 1)THEN
         TCUT(TYPE) = FRATIO/B(TYPE)
         VFACTR = -LOG(1. - B(TYPE)*TCUT(TYPE))
         XFACTR = F(B(TYPE),TCUT(TYPE))
      ELSE
         TCUT(TYPE) = -LN/B(TYPE)
         VFACTR = B(TYPE) * TCUT(TYPE)
         XFACTR = 0.5 * B(TYPE) * (TCUT(TYPE)**2)
      END IF
```

```
      T = T + DT
    3 CONTINUE
*
*              PRINT THE COORDINATES OF BOTH TRAJECTORIES
*
      WRITE(*,14)
      DO 6 K = 0,50
      WRITE(*,15)(X(K,TYPE),Y(K,TYPE),TYPE = 1,2)
    6 CONTINUE
*
* ************************************************************
*    INSERT HERE THE CODE NECESSARY TO GRAPH THE
*    TRAJECTORIES OF AN AUTOMATIC PEN AND INK PLOTTER.
* ************************************************************
*
      STOP
* FORMATS
*
   10 FORMAT(2F6.0,F3.0,F4.0,A12)
   11 FORMAT(10X, 'A COMPARISON OF THE PERFORMANCES',//,
     +       10X,'OF TWO ROCKET ENGINES',///,
     +        5X,'INPUT PARAMETERS',//,
     +       32X,'ORIGINAL FUEL TO',//,
     +       22X,'EXHAUST    TOTAL     TOTAL    BURN',//,
     +       21X,'VELOCITY   MASS      MASS     RATE',//,
     +       23X,'(M/S)      (KG)      RATIO    (KG/S)')
   12 FORMAT(7X,'CONSTANT',//,7X,A12,T23,F8.2,2X,F8.2,
     +       4X,F4.1,3X,F8.2)
   13 FORMAT(///,10X,'RESULTS OF THE CALCULATION',///,
     +       T29,'X',T39,'Y',/,
     +    4X,' OPTIMUM     TIME      POSITION  POSITION  VELOCITY',
     +    ',      TIME      OF        AT        AT        AT',
     +    4X,' THRUST    OF',/,
     +    4X,' ANGLE     CUTOFF    CUTOFF    CUTOFF    CUTOFF',
     +    ',      FLIGHT    FLIGHT',/,
     +    4X,' (DEG)     (SEC)     (M)       (M)       (M/S)',
     +    ',      (S)',/,/,
     +    1X,'CT',4X,F6.2,6(1X,E9.2),/,
     +    1X,'CA',4X,F6.2,6(1X,E9.2))
   14 FORMAT(//,5X,'THE TRAJECTORIES OF THE TWO ROCKETS',///,
     +    T10,'CONSTANT',T45,'CONSTANT',/,
     +    T10,'THRUST',T45,'ACCELERATION',///,
     +    T9,'X',T20,'Y',T49,'X',T60,'Y',//)
*
```

Continued

Figure IV-2 Continued

```fortran
15 FORMATS(T5,2(1X,E9.2,1X),T45,2(1X,E9.2,1X))
   END
*----------------------------------------------------------------
   FUNCTION DIS(I,T,IXY,THETA)
*----------------------------------------------------------------
*-- THIS FUNCTION WILL COMPUTE THE X (IXY = 1) OR Y (IXY = 2)
*-- COORDINATES OF THE ROCKET'S TRAJECTORY FOR THE CASES OF
*--       T <  T-CUTOFF
*--       T >  T-CUTOFF
*--       I =  ROCKET TYPE 1 OR 2
*----------------------------------------------------------------
   COMMON/PARAM/B(2),VEX(2),VCUT(2),XCUT(2),YCUT(2),
  +             TCUT(2),G,VXCUT(2),VYCUT(2)
*
   IF(T .LT. TCUT(I))THEN
*
     IF(I .EQ. 1)THEN
       FACTR = F(B(I),T)
     ELSE
       FACTR = B(I) * T**2/2.
     END IF
*
     FACTR = FACTR*VEX(I)
     IF(IXY .EQ. 1)THEN
       DIS = FACTR*COS(THETA)
       RETURN
     ELSE
       DIS = FACTR*SIN(THETA) - G*T**2/2.
       RETURN
     END IF
*
   ELSE
     IF(IXY .EQ. 1)THEN
       DIS = VXCUT(I)*T + XCUT(I)
       RETURN
     ELSE
       DIS = VYCUT(I)*T + YCUT(I) - G*T**2/2.
       RETURN
     END IF
   END IF
   END
*----------------------------------------------------------------
   FUNCTION F(B,T)
*----------------------------------------------------------------
*-- THIS FUNCTION IS USED IN COMPUTING THE TRAJECTORIES OF A
*-- CONSTANT THRUST ROCKET.
*----------------------------------------------------------------
   F = T + (1. - B * T) * LOG(1. - B*T)/B
   RETURN
   END
*----------------------------------------------------------------
   FUNCTION CUBRT(Q,X)
*----------------------------------------------------------------
*-- CUBRT SOLVES FOR THE ROOT OF THE EQUATION
*--
*--       X = SQRT(Q * X**3 + .5)
*--
*-- BY SUCCESSIVE SUBSTITIONS
*----------------------------------------------------------------
   I = 0
 1 TEST = SQRT(Q * X**3 + 0.5)
   I = I + 1
   IF(I .GT. 50)THEN
     PRINT *,'EXCESSIVE ITERATIONS IN CUBRT (MORE THAN 50)'
     PRINT *,'RUN TERMINATED'
     STOP
   ELSE IF(ABS(X - TEST) .GT. 1.E-5)THEN
     X = TEST
     GO TO 1
   ELSE
     CUBRT = TEST
     RETURN
   END IF
   END
```

A COMPARISON OF THE PERFORMANCES
OF TWO ROCKET ENGINES

Figure IV-3
The output from
the rocket
trajectory
program.

INPUT PARAMETERS

	EXHAUST VELOCITY (M/S)	ORIGINAL TOTAL MASS (KG)	FUEL TO TOTAL MASS RATIO	BURN RATE (KG/S)
CONSTANT THRUST	5000.00	30000.00	.6	950.00
CONSTANT ACCELERATION	3500.00	65000.00	.5	500.00

RESULTS OF THE CALCULATION

	OPTIMUM THRUST ANGLE (DEG)	TIME OF CUTOFF (SEC)	X POSITION AT CUTOFF (M)	Y POSITION AT CUTOFF (M)	VELOCITY AT CUTOFF (M/S)	TIME OF FLIGHT (S)	RANGE OF FLIGHT (M)
CT	45.48	.19E+02	.26E+05	.25E+05	.45E+04	.64E+03	.21E+07
CA	49.63	.90E+02	.71E+05	.43E+05	.18E+04	.23E+03	.44E+06
CA	OPTIMUM	.90E+02	POSITION	POSITION	VELOCITY	.23E+03	.44E+06

THE TRAJECTORIES OF THE TWO ROCKETS

CONSTANT THRUST		CONSTANT ACCELERATION	
X	Y	X	Y
0.	0.	0.	0.
.11E+05	.99E+04	.14E+04	.87E+03
.11E+06	.10E+06	.57E+04	.35E+04
.15E+06	.14E+06	.13E+05	.78E+04
.19E+06	.17E+06	.23E+05	.14E+05
.23E+06	.20E+06	.35E+05	.22E+05
.27E+06	.23E+06	.51E+05	.31E+05
.31E+06	.26E+06	.69E+05	.43E+05
.35E+06	.29E+06	.23E+06	.91E+05
.39E+06	.31E+06	.25E+06	.90E+05
.43E+06	.34E+06	.27E+06	.87E+05
.48E+06	.36E+06	.29E+06	.83E+05
.52E+06	.38E+06	.31E+06	.77E+05
.56E+06	.40E+06	.33E+06	.69E+05
.60E+06	.42E+06	.35E+06	.60E+05
.64E+06	.43E+06	.37E+06	.49E+05
.68E+06	.45E+06	.39E+06	.37E+05
.72E+06	.46E+06	.41E+06	.23E+05
.76E+06	.47E+06	.43E+06	.73E+04
.80E+06	.48E+06	.45E+06	0.
.84E+06	.49E+06	.47E+06	0.
.88E+06	.50E+06	.49E+06	0.
.93E+06	.50E+06	.51E+06	0.
.97E+06	.51E+06	.53E+06	0.
.10E+07	.51E+06	.55E+06	0.

Continued

CONSTANT THRUST		CONSTANT ACCELERATION	
.10E+07	.51E+06	.57E+06	0.
.11E+07	.51E+06	.59E+06	0.
.11E+07	.50E+06	.61E+06	0.
.12E+07	.50E+06	.63E+06	0.
.12E+07	.49E+06	.65E+06	0.
.13E+07	.49E+06	.67E+06	0.
.13E+07	.48E+06	.69E+06	0
.13E+07	.47E+06	.71E+06	0.
.14E+07	.45E+06	.73E+06	0.
.14E+07	.44E+06	.75E+06	0.
.15E+07	.42E+06	.77E+06	0.
.15E+07	.41E+06	.79E+06	0.
.15E+07	.39E+06	.81E+06	0.
.16E+07	.37E+06	.83E+06	0.
.16E+07	.35E+06	.85E+06	0.
.17E+07	.32E+06	.87E+06	0.
.17E+07	.30E+06	.89E+06	0.
.17E+07	.27E+06	.91E+06	0.
.18E+07	.24E+06	.93E+06	0.
.18E+07	.21E+06	.95E+06	0.
.19E+07	.18E+06	.97E+06	0.
.19E+07	.15E+06	.99E+06	0.
.19E+07	.11E+06	.10E+07	0.
.20E+07	.77E+05	.10E+07	0.
.20E+07	.39E+05	.11E+07	0.
.21E+07	0.	.11E+07	0.

IV.2 PROGRAMMING PROBLEMS

Programming Problem A: Cooling Fins on a Steam Pipe (Mechanical Engineering)

The heat from a steam pipe is more effectively transferred to its surroundings by the addition of metal radiator fins. The fins are heated by the pipe, and because of their large surface area can efficiently transfer heat by radiation and convection to the surrounding air. To simplify the analysis, I have assumed that the steam pipe is square and that the fin is rectangular, as shown in Figure IV-4.

The first step in determining the heat transfer is to compute the temperature distribution $T(x, y)$ across the area of the fin. This is ordinarily a rather complex mathematical problem, requiring sophisticated techniques. However, the algorithm for a numerical solution is quite transparent and is based on some simple ideas concerning temperature and heat flow.

A fundamental property of heat flow is that of diffusion. A hot or a cold spot will smooth or average out in time and the final temperature distribution will be the smoothest possible distribution consistent with the con-

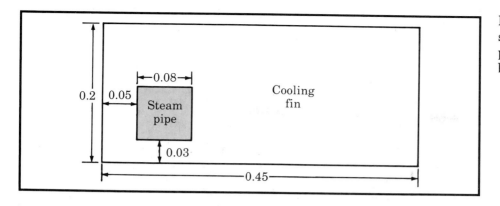

Figure IV-4 A square steam pipe surrounded by a radiator fin.

straints of the problem. For example, if a metal bar has one end in ice water (0 °C) and the other end in boiling water (100 °C), and the rest of the bar insulated, the final temperature distribution will be a simple linear decrease across the length of the bar. (See Figure IV-5.)

Another way of stating this idea of smoothing is that the temperature at any point will ultimately be equal to the *average* of the temperatures of its immediate surroundings. This algorithm can be easily adapted to our fin problem. First we superimpose a two-dimensional grid over the fin and pipe and require that the initial guess for the temperature at each point on the fin, T_{ij}, be replaced by the average of the temperatures of its four nearest neighboring points. (See Figure IV-6.)

$$T_{ij,\text{new}} \rightarrow \tfrac{1}{4}(T_{i+1,j} + T_{i,j+1} + T_{i-1,j} + T_{i,j-1}) \qquad \textbf{(IV.1)}$$

This replacement is done for all the points on the fin and is repeated until there is very little change from one pass to the next. The same algorithm can be used to find the temperature distribution on an airplane wing or on a thin semiconductor element of a transistor.

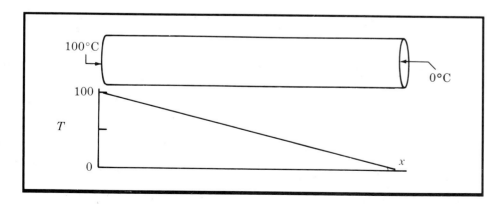

Figure IV-5 Equilibrium temperature distribution in a bar.

Figure IV-6 A grid superimposed on the fin pipe problem.

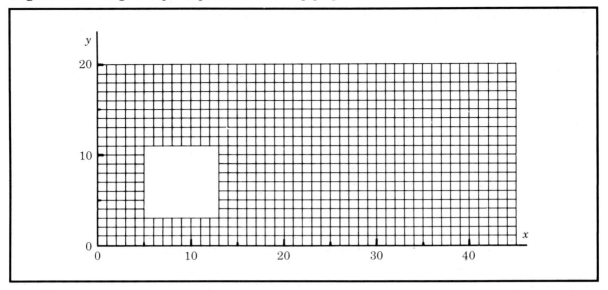

Program Specifics

Write a program to solve for the temperature distribution on the radiator fin and to execute a contour printer plot. (Also see Section 7.7.2.)

The value of the temperature at the edges of the fin and inside the pipe should be initialized via a DATA statement.

For all *interior* fin grid points, start with an initial guess of TOLD(I, J) = 50.

Compute

$$\Delta = \frac{1}{N} \sum_{ij} |T_{ij,\text{new}} - T_{ij,\text{old}}|$$

where N is the total number of interior points. If this quantity is greater than 10^{-2}, repeat the calculation.

Check for excessive iterations and other problems.

Once the equilibrium temperature distribution has been obtained, call a subroutine to execute the contour plot. (See below.)

A sketch of the subroutine for the contour printer plot is:

Using a DATA statement, initialize an array GRID of type CHARACTER*1

$$\text{GRID}_{ij} = \text{'*'} \qquad \textit{around the edge of the fin}$$
$$\text{GRID}_{ij} = \text{'X'} \qquad \textit{inside the pipe}$$

Initialize a CHARACTER*1 array, LETTER(0:27) as

```
(LETTER(I),I=0,27,3)/'A','B', ... ,'H','I'/
```

and all other elements of LETTER are blank (i.e., ' ').
For all interior points, assign the elements of GRID to one of the
  elements of LETTER by

```
IJ = 27*(T(I,J) - TMIN)/(TMAX - TMIN)
```
                               ⟨Note: IJ is between 0 and 27.⟩
```
GRID(I,J) = LETTER(IJ)
```

Print the GRID
Repeat the calculation with the bottom edge of the fin in ice water.

Programming Problem B: Nim

Perhaps it is appropriate at this point to take some time out from engineering programs and to write a program strictly for fun—well, not exclusively for fun. In the event you decide to leave engineering, you could possibly make your fortune writing computer games. As a first step along such a
path, you are invited to write an interactive program to play (and win!) the
game of Nim (Problem 1.5).[2]
  The game consists of placing any number of counters (say less than 10)
in any number of rows (say less than 6) and each of the players then alternately removing any nonzero number of counters from any one row. The
player removing the last counter is the winner. The winning strategy can be
found in Chapter 1. A sketch of the program, which will consist of numerous
calls to subroutines, is given in Figure IV-7.
  The output from your program should consist of the complete dialogue
between the computer and the player for one play of the game.
  One conclusion you can reach from this programming assignment is that
the actual algorithm in a computer game is almost always a minor part of
the complete code. The dominant part of the code is concerned with input and
output.

Programming Problem C: Optimum Depth of a
Fluidized-Bed Reactor (Chemical Engineering)

A fluidized-bed chemical reactor is a structure that is used extensively in
chemical engineering to provide more uniform contact for chemical reac-

---

[2] In 1939, Professor E. U. Condon designed and constructed a rudimentary computer that
would play the game of Nim. This device was exhibited at the World's Fair and was one of the
many technological highlights of the fair.

Figure IV-7 A pseudocode outline of the Nim program.

```
PROGRAM NIM

CALL INTRO        Displays instructions to the player, asks for how
                  many rows and how many counters in each row, checks
                  for zeros and negatives, and asks "who goes first":
                  FLAG = 1 for player's move, = 0 for computer's move.

CALL DISPLA       Prints the current arrangement of X's by rows.

MOVEP = 0
MOVEC = 0

1 CONTINUE

IF(FLAG .EQ. 1)THEN
        Ask player for move
        CALL ALTER        ALTER rearranges the number of Xs in each row accordingly

        IF(the move has resulted in a potential win)THEN
                PRINT congratulatory message
        ELSE
                PRINT derogatory message No. MOVEP
        END IF
        MOVEP = MOVEP + 1
        FLAG = 0
ELSE
        IF(MOVEP .EQ. 1)Print derogatory message
                              indicating bad choice
        CALL MYMOVE          MYMOVE computes the optimum move according to the
                             winning strategy. If a winning move is not possible,
                             execute a stalling move.

        CALL ALTER
        FLAG = 1
        MOVEC = MOVEC + 1
END IF
CALL DISPLA
CALL ENDGAM                  ENDGAM determines whether the game
                             has ended (FINIS = 1) and the
                             winner (player = 1, computer = 0)
IF(FINIS .EQ. 1)THEN
        IF(winner = 1) Print incredulous remark and STOP
        If(winner = 0) Print nasty comment and STOP
END IF
GO TO 1
END
```

tions such as catalytic cracking in petroleum processing or heat transfer in combustion operations. A fluidized reactor contains a bed of granular material through which a fluid is flowing at a rate sufficiently high to suspend the material (akin to "quicksand" conditions). An important design concern is to provide sufficient height of reactor to prevent the loss of the bed particles. In addition, an operating constraint is to keep the rate of fluid flow through the reactor sufficient to suspend the material but not enough to "flush" the material out of the reactor. The reactor is sketched in Figure IV-8.

Once the fluid is flowing in the reactor, the total height of the fluid plus material increases to the expanded height H_e, which is given by the expression

$$H_e = H_0(1 + f) \sum_{i=1}^{n} \left[\frac{p_i}{(1 - \varepsilon_i)} \right] \tag{IV.2}$$

where H_0 = static (unexpanded) bed height (m)
$\quad\quad f$ = void fraction of the unexpanded bed
$\quad\quad p_i$ = fraction of bed particles with diameter d_i (m)
$\quad\quad \varepsilon_i$ = porosity or void fraction of the expanded bed part that is made up of particles of size d_i

The individual void fractions ε_i for the expanded bed for particles of size d_i can be found from

$$\frac{\varepsilon_i^3}{(1 - \varepsilon_i)} = F(q, d_i) \tag{IV.3}$$

where $F(q, d_i)$ is a function that depends on the flow rate q and the particle size d_i, and is given by

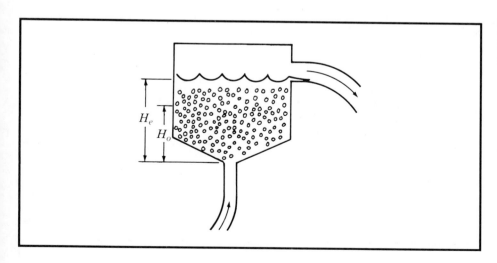

Figure IV-8   A fluidized-bed chemical reactor.

(IV.4)
$$F(q, d_i) = \frac{180}{g} \frac{\mu}{(\rho_s - \rho)} \frac{q}{d_i^2}$$

where g = gravitational acceleration, 9.8 m/sec^2
μ = fluid viscosity (N − sec/m^2)
ρ_s = particle density (kg/m^3)
ρ = fluid density (kg/m^3)
q = reactor bed flow rate (m/sec)

The cubic equation for the void fractions can be written as

(IV.5)
$$\varepsilon = F^{1/3}(1 - \varepsilon)^{1/3}$$

This equation is solved for a particular value of q and d_i by guessing a value for ε_i, inserting it into the expression on the right, and computing a new value for ε_i. If the new value is sufficiently close to the guess, a solution has been found; if not, the new value is inserted into the right and the process continued until successive values differ less than some small quantity. This process is known as successive substitutions.[3] For a given flow rate q, the

---

[3] The method of successive substitutions does not always work. If we are attempting to find the root of an equation written in the form

$$x = f(x)$$

in an iterative manner—i.e.,

$$x_{k+1} = f(x_k)$$

and if the unknown root is designated by α, [i.e., $\alpha = f(\alpha)$], we begin by assuming that x_k is near α

$$x_k = \alpha + \delta_k$$

and that each successive iteration is an improvement ($|\delta_{k+1}| < |\delta_k|$).
But if δ_k is small, then the derivative of $f(x)$ is approximately

$$f'(\alpha) = \frac{f(\alpha + \delta_k) - f(\alpha)}{\delta_k} = \frac{f(\alpha + \delta_k)}{\delta_k} - \frac{\alpha}{\delta_k}$$

or

$$\alpha + \delta_{k+1} = f(\alpha + \delta_k) = \alpha + f'(\alpha) \delta_k$$

Thus for the procedure to converge ($|\delta_{k+1}| < |\delta_k|$), the magnitude of the derivative of $f(x)$ near the root *must* be less than 1. For this reason, successive substitutions applied to the equation,

$$x^3 - \frac{1 - x}{8} = 0$$

written in the form

$$x = \frac{1}{2}(1 - x)^{1/3}$$

Static height H_0	Static void fraction f	Particle density ρ_s	Size distribution ($i = 1, 4$) p_i	Particle size ($i = 1, 4$) $d_i(10^{-3}$ m)
4.5	0.45	2666.	0.256	2.0
			0.350	8.4
			0.295	4.0
			0.099	1.3

Table IV-3
Static-bed reactor parameters.

void fractions ε_i for each of the constituent particles in the bed can be obtained by this means. Once all the ε_i's have been computed, the sum in Equation (IV.2) can be evaluated and the bed height H_e determined.

Problem Specifics

There are particles of identical material but of four different sizes in the static bed. The static-bed reactor characteristics are given in Table IV-3. The properties of the fluid flowing through the reactor are:

$$\mu = \text{viscosity} = 8.13 \times 10^{-3}$$
$$\rho = \text{density} = 1000$$

Your program should:

1. Initialize the bed characteristics via a DATA statement.
2. Read the fluid parameters
3. Print all the parameters neatly
4. For $q = 0.004$ to 0.012 in steps of 0.001, do the following:
   a. For each of the particle sizes d_i, solve the cubic equation, [Equation (IV.3)] for ε_i by successive substitutions. This should be done in a function subprogram that calls $F(q, d_i)$ [Equation (IV.4)]. The maximum number of iterations should be 40 and the convergence criterion on the fractional change in ϵ_i is 10^{-4}.
   b. Once all the ε_i's have been determined, evaluate the summation in Equation (IV.2) to obtain H_e.

5. Print a table of H_e and q.

Your program should have ample error diagnostics.

---

will work; while

$$x = 1 - 8x^3$$

will not. (The root is near 0.418).

CHAPTER 10

TAYLOR SERIES AND NUMERICAL DIFFERENTIATION

10.1 INTRODUCTION

In the mathematics courses you have taken to date, almost all of the problems that you have faced had solutions that could be expressed in terms of relatively simple algebraic expressions. These so-called closed-form solutions may have involved combinations of trigonometric functions, radicals, exponentials, or logarithms. But regardless of how complicated the answer, I am sure you felt more comfortable with them than with a numerical result expressed, for example, as

$$\int_0^5 e^{-x^2}\,dx$$

This integral cannot be expressed in terms of simpler functions, and we somehow have the feeling that this result is less satisfactory than, say, $\sqrt{7}$. Of course both expressions represent well-defined numbers, but to compare them to other numbers we have yet to carry out some numerical operations (push the $\sqrt{}$ key on a calculator, or numerically estimate the area under the curve e^{-x^2} from $x = 0$ to $x = 5$). Numerical analysis is the study of procedures whereby approximate answers are obtained for problems that do not have a closed-form solution or whose closed-form solution is too complicated to be useful. The vast majority of real problems fall in this category.

In calculus it is important that you develop a facility to reason abstractly, and so numerical results are ordinarily not stressed in favor of expressions involving symbolic variables. Yet in actual engineering and scientific applications, a numerical answer is almost always the best you can hope for. Real problems rarely have neat and tidy answers in terms of simple functions.

Numerical analysis is now acknowledged as an essential tool for all engineers, as important as any other skill. Even the engineer who relies on code written by someone else to solve problems must be well versed in numerical methods to appreciate the limitations and range of the "canned" routines used. The most important quality of a result, more important than the result itself, is the estimate of its validity.

A course in numerical methods has traditionally been a junior- or senior-level mathematics course for scientists and engineers. The reasons for this are not at all compelling. The primary reason is that physics needs calculus, so calculus must come first in the mathematics curriculum. Ordinarily beginning students take only one mathematics course at a time and so other noncalculus topics must be postponed. The impression is then given that since topics like linear algebra or matrices or series expansions appear in junior and senior courses, they are "advanced" topics and thus more difficult than calculus, when just the opposite is true. Of course, since these topics are presented to an audience of advanced students they are presented in a much more sophisticated manner than is absolutely necessary. The treatment we present here was designed for a student who has had one semester of calculus or who is now taking a first calculus course. However, most of the topics will be discussed here long before they appear in your calculus text.

As was mentioned in the introduction to Chapter 1, modern computers are revolutionizing the way we do mathematics, and it is very important that the beginning mathematics curriculum both recognize this and adjust to it. Some topics in mathematics are very well suited to learning through machine computation. In fact topics like elementary differential equations, definite integrals, series, matrices, curve fitting, and interpolation are perhaps *best* learned by the process of meticulously coding the appropriate algorithms and by discovering the limitations of a particular numerical method. Translating an algorithm into a working program is, as you are well aware, a very stringent test of the depth of your understanding of the algorithm.

It is hoped that the student will use this text to learn mathematics via computers to supplement what he or she learns in calculus and science. You should try to incorporate the Fortran and the mathematics. We will insist that the mathematics is not understood unless you are able to code it for the computer.

A great many of the numerical methods we will discuss are but variations on a single theme:

It is frequently desired to effect a complicated mathematical operation on a complicated function. The problem is rendered tractable by approximating it by a somewhat simpler operation on a decidedly simpler function over a limited range. Typically a function will be replaced by a straight line or a parabola for points in the region of interest.

The procedure for approximating a function by simpler functions is based on the theory of Taylor series expansions.

10.2 THE TAYLOR SERIES

10.2.1 The Meaning of a Taylor Series

You are familiar with the notation for trigonometric functions

$$\sin(x), \ \cos(\theta), \ \tan(\beta), \ \text{etc.}$$

or with logarithms and exponentials,

$$\log(x), \ \ln(y), \ e^z$$

If you had to tell the computer what these things mean, could you do it? You might start off by recognizing that each is a *function* or mapping. That is, given any x you can determine something called $\sin(x)$ or $\ln(x)$. The "meaning" then of $\sin(x)$ is contained in the algorithm for its computation. Which is? Well, one way of computing $\sin(x)$ is based on its series expansion, which we saw in Section 4.4.3. Namely

(10.1)
$$\sin(x) = x - \frac{x^3}{3!} + \frac{x^5}{5!} - \frac{x^7}{7!} + \ \cdot \ \cdot \ \cdot$$

Notice that since this is an *identity* (true for all x) the expression on the right is more than just equal to $\sin(x)$, it *is* $\sin(x)$. Any other method of calculating $\sin(x)$ must be equivalent to this series. Now to answer the difficult question of where this series came from. We begin with the derivative of a power of x

$$\frac{d(x^n)}{dx} = nx^{n-1}$$

Furthermore I will use the notation

$$\frac{df(x)}{dx}\bigg|_0$$

to mean the value of the derivative at $x = 0$ (i.e., first differentiate, then set $x = 0$). Next we differentiate the entire series for $\sin(x)$ with respect to x once and set $x = 0$. We obtain

$$\frac{d\,[\sin(x)]}{dx}\bigg|_0 = 1 - \frac{3x^2}{3!}\bigg|_0 + \frac{5x^4}{5!}\bigg|_0 - \cdots = 1 \qquad (10.2)$$

Continuing, we can further differentiate the entire series again and set $x = 0$ to obtain

$$\frac{d^2\sin(x)}{dx^2}\bigg|_0 = 0 - \frac{6x}{3!}\bigg|_0 + \frac{20x^3}{5!}\bigg|_0 - \frac{42x^5}{7!}\bigg|_0 + \cdots = 0 \qquad (10.3)$$

Since $6/3! = 1$, it is clear that the third derivative evaluated at $x = 0$ will be -1. We could keep this up forever, or at least until we have found a pattern. The result would be

$$\frac{d^n[\sin(x)]}{dx^n}\bigg|_0 = 0 \qquad \text{if } n \text{ is even} \qquad (10.4)$$
$$= (-1)^{(n-1)/2} \qquad \text{if } n \text{ is odd}$$

Assuming that differentiating an infinite number of terms is an allowed operation (since the series is valid for all x, it is), we obtain the interesting result that we now know *all* the derivatives of $\sin(x)$ at $x = 0$. A much more startling result is the converse, if we know *all* the derivatives of a function at a particular point, we know the function *everywhere* and we know it uniquely.[1] This is the essence of Taylor series, which I will next attempt to prove in a flagrantly nonrigorous manner, i.e., graphically.

Suppose that we know the value of a function of x at a particular value of x, say $y_a = f(x = a)$. (See Figure 10-1.) And we wish to have an approximate value of the function *near* $x = a$. The simplest approximation is to assume that the value of the function remains about the same—i.e., the zeroth-order approximation

$$f(x) \simeq f(a) \qquad \text{if } |x - a| \text{ is small}$$

That is, if we are very close to the point $x = a$, this may not be a bad approximation.

With a bit of thought we can easily improve on this. For the next level of approximation we might assume that the function between a and x is smooth enough to be approximated by a straight line. The slope of the line

---

[1] As with all mathematical statements of this kind, there are some limitations on every-where and uniquely, as we shall see shortly.

Fig. 10-1 The tangent line at the point $x = a$.

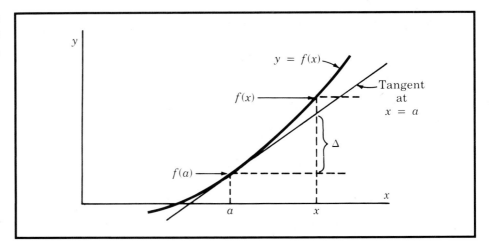

we pick for this approximation would be the same as that of the tangent line at $x = a$. Thus the first-order approximation would be

(10.5)
$$f(x) \simeq f(a) + \Delta \qquad \text{if } |x - a| \text{ is small}$$

where Δ is defined in Figure 10-1. However, recall that the slope of a tangent line at a point is defined to be equal to the derivative at that point, so

(10.6)
$$\begin{array}{l} \text{Slope of} \\ \text{tangent at} \\ x = a \end{array} = \frac{\text{opposite}}{\text{adjacent}} = \frac{\Delta}{x - a} = \left(\frac{df}{dx}\right)\bigg|_{x=a}$$

or

(10.7)
$$\Delta = \left(\frac{df}{dx}\right)\bigg|_{x=a} (x - a)$$

and thus Equation (10.5) becomes

(10.8)
$$f(x) \simeq f(a) + \left(\frac{df}{dx}\right)\bigg|_{x=a} (x - a)$$

The next level of approximation would be to improve on the straight line and assume that the function $f(x)$ between a and x can be approximated by a parabola. This is quite straightforward; however, the algebra becomes somewhat complicated, so I will try a slightly different approach. Consider the function $g(x)$ defined as

$$g(x) = \frac{df(x)}{dx}$$

This function can also be approximated by a relation like Equation (10.8)

$$g(x) \simeq g(a) + \left.\left(\frac{dg}{dx}\right)\right|_{x=a} (x - a) \tag{10.9}$$

We next integrate this equation from $\xi = a$ to $\xi = x$ (replacing the variable x under the integral with ξ). Since $g(a)$ and $(dg/dx)|_{x=a}$ are constants we obtain[2]

$$\int_a^x g(\xi)\, d\xi = \int_a^x \frac{df(\xi)}{d\xi}\, d\xi = f(\xi)\,\Big|_a^x = f(x) - f(a) \tag{10.10}$$

$$\int_a^x g(a)\, d\xi = g(a) \int_a^x d\xi = g(a)(x - a) = \left.\left(\frac{df}{dx}\right)\right|_{x=a} (x - a) \tag{10.11}$$

$$\int_a^x \left.\left(\frac{dg}{dx}\right)\right|_{x=a} (\xi - a)\, d\xi = \left.\left(\frac{dg}{dx}\right)\right|_{x=a} \int_a^x (\xi - a)\, d\xi = \left.\left(\frac{d^2f}{dx^2}\right)\right|_{x=a} \frac{1}{2}(x - a)^2 \tag{10.12}$$

Equation (10.9) then becomes the second-order approximation

$$f(x) \simeq f(a) + \left.\left(\frac{df}{dx}\right)\right|_{x=a} (x - a) + \frac{1}{2} \left.\left(\frac{d^2f}{dx^2}\right)\right|_{x=a} (x - a)^2 \tag{10.13}$$

In order to simplify the equations I will henceforth use the notation

$$f'(a) = \left.\left(\frac{df}{dx}\right)\right|_{x=a}$$

$$f''(a) = \left.\left(\frac{d^2f}{dx^2}\right)\right|_{x=a} \quad \text{etc.}$$

---

[2] In case you have not yet covered integration in your calculus course, I am using the following results concerning the definite integral:

$$\int_a^b \frac{df(x)}{dx}\, dx = [f(b) - f(a)]$$

$$\int_a^b c\, dx = cx\,\Big|_a^b = c(b - a) \quad \text{where } c \text{ is a constant}$$

$$\int_a^b x\, dx = \frac{x^2}{2}\,\Big|_a^b = \frac{1}{2}(b^2 - a^2)$$

$$\int_a^b x^2\, dx = \frac{x^3}{3}\,\Big|_a^b = \frac{1}{3}(b^3 - a^3)$$

$$\int_a^b x^n\, dx = \frac{x^{n+1}}{(n+1)}\,\Big|_a^b = \frac{1}{n+1}(b^{n+1} - a^{n+1})$$

We could continue the procedure of replacing the function $f(x)$ by polynomials of higher and higher order indefinitely, or until we see a pattern emerging. The result would be the Taylor series[3]

(**10.14**)
$$f(x) = f(a) + f'(a)(x - a) + f''(a)\frac{1}{2!}(x - a)^2 + \cdots$$

$$+ f^{[n]}(a)\frac{1}{n!}(x - a)^n + \cdots$$

The main point to emphasize in Equation (10.14) is that this is no longer an approximation, but if expressed as an infinite series the relation is exact and an identity. I will not attempt to prove this last statement, but in light of the way it was derived it does appear plausible. The conclusion is then: *if we know* all *of the derivatives of a function at a single point, we know the function everywhere*. (Again, there are technical qualifications on "everywhere" that will be discussed in Section 10.2.3.) Since the Taylor series expansion defines an algorithm for computing the function, it in turn encompasses the complete meaning of the function.

In general, the smaller the quantity $|(x - a)|$ the fewer the number of terms required to obtain a sufficiently accurate value for $f(x)$. For example, if $(x - a) = h$ and $|h| \ll 1$, then

(**10.15**)
$$f(x) = f(a + h) \simeq f(a) + f'(a)h$$

or solving this equation for $f'(a)$ we obtain

(**10.16**)
$$f'(a) = \left(\frac{df}{dx}\right)\bigg|_{x=a} \simeq \frac{f(a + h) - f(a)}{h}$$

which is just what you would expect.

The special case of Equation (10.14) in which $a = 0$ is called the *Maclaurin series*.

(**10.17**)
$$f(x) = f(0) + f'(0)x + f''(0)\frac{x^2}{2!} + f'''(0)\frac{x^3}{3!} + \cdots + f^{[n]}(0)\frac{x^n}{n!} + \cdots$$

To illustrate the use of Equations (10.14) and (10.17) a number of examples are given in the next section.

10.2.2 Examples of Taylor and Maclaurin Series

To obtain either the Taylor or Maclaurin series expansion for a function we must first compute *all* the derivatives of the function at a point. There are many situations where this formidable-sounding task is actually quite easy. If the function is a polynomial with positive integer powers of x, then even-

---

[3] This equation was introduced by Brook Taylor in 1715.

tually the higher derivatives of the polynomial will all be zero. Consider the following two examples

1. Find the Maclaurin series for $f(x) = x^4 - 8x^3 + 24x^2 - 32x + 16$.

$$f(0) = (x^4 - 8x^3 + 24x^2 - 32x + 16)|_0 = 16 \qquad \text{0th order} = 16$$

$$f'(0) = (4x^3 - 24x^2 + 48x - 32)|_0 \qquad = -32 \quad \text{1st order}$$

$$= \frac{-32}{1}(x - 0) = -32x$$

$$f''(0) = (12x^2 - 48x + 48)|_0 \qquad = +48 \quad \text{2nd order}$$

$$= \frac{48}{2!}(x - 0)^2 = 24x^2$$

$$f'''(0) = (24x - 48)|_0 \qquad = -48 \quad \text{3rd order}$$

$$= \frac{-48}{3!}(x - 0)^3 = -8x^3$$

$$f^{[iv]}(0) = (24)|_0 \qquad = 24 \quad \text{4th order}$$

$$= \frac{24}{4!}(x - 0)^4 = x^4$$

All higher derivatives are zero and thus after inserting these terms into Equation (10.17) we obtain

$$f(x) = x^4 - 8x^3 + 24x^2 - 32x + 16$$

which is exactly what we started with. Notice that since *all* the higher derivatives are zero the infinite series has collapsed into a finite expression, a polynomial. The original series is said to terminate after the fourth-order term. Since we started with a polynomial the result must also be a polynomial and it must be the same polynomial.

2. Find the Taylor series for the same function with $a = 2$. Proceeding in the same manner as in the example above except that all the terms are evaluated at $x = 2$ instead of zero, we obtain the following result:

$$f(2) \quad = 0 \qquad \text{0th order} = 0$$
$$f'(2) \quad = 0 \qquad \text{1st order} = 0$$
$$f''(2) \quad = 0 \qquad \text{2nd order} = 0$$
$$f'''(2) \quad = 0 \qquad \text{3rd order} = 0$$
$$f^{[iv]}(2) = 24 \qquad \text{4th order} = \frac{24}{4!}(x - 2)^4$$

All higher derivatives are zero.

In this case the Taylor series expansion for the polynomial gives the result

$$f(x) = (x - 2)^4$$

which, when multiplied out, is seen to be identical to the original polynomial.

More interesting situations are those that result in nonterminating infinite series. The following three examples are the series expansions for some transcendental functions. A transcendental function is one whose evaluation cannot be reduced to a finite number of arithmetic operations, i.e., its simplest representation must be an infinite series.

Keep in mind that the key to obtaining a series expansion for any function is the ability to evaluate *all* the derivatives of the function at a single point.

1. The Maclaurin series expansion for e^x: The symbol e^x is *defined* by the relation

(**10.18**)
$$\frac{d}{dx} e^x = e^x$$

It should be obvious to you that this single equation defines *all* the derivatives of e^x; thus

$$\frac{d^2}{dx^2}(e^x) = \frac{d}{dx}\left(\frac{de^x}{dx}\right) = \frac{d}{dx}(e^x) = e^x$$

etc., and so all the derivatives of e^x are simply e^x. Furthermore, in the Maclaurin series all the derivatives are evaluated at $x = 0$, where $e^0 = 1$. The Maclaurin series for e^x is then

$$f(x) = f(0) + f'(0)x + f''(0)\frac{x^2}{2!} + f'''(0)\frac{x^3}{3!} + \cdots$$

$$e^x = e^0 + e^0 x + e^0 \frac{x^2}{2!} + e^0 \frac{x^3}{3!} + \cdots$$

(**10.19**)
$$e^x = 1 + x + \frac{x^2}{2!} + \frac{x^3}{3!} + \cdots + \frac{x^n}{n!} + \cdots$$

2. Maclaurin series for hyperbolic functions: We define two functions by the relations:

(**10.20**)
$$\frac{d[\text{sink}(x)]}{dx} = \text{swim}(x)$$

$$\frac{d[\text{swim}(x)]}{dx} = \text{sink}(x) \qquad \textbf{(10.21)}$$

$$\text{sink}(0) = 0 \qquad \textbf{(10.22)}$$

$$\text{swim}(0) = 1$$

To obtain the Maclaurin expansion for the function sink(x) we must first evaluate the derivatives at $x = 0$.

$$\text{sink}(0) = 0$$

$$\text{sink}'(0) = \text{swim}(0) = 1$$

$$\text{sink}''(0) = \text{swim}'(0) = \text{sink}(0) = 0$$

etc.

And thus the Maclaurin series for the function is easily seen to be

$$\text{sink}(x) = x + \frac{x^3}{3!} + \frac{x^5}{5!} + \frac{x^7}{7!} + \cdots \qquad \textbf{(10.23)}$$

Similarly, the series for the companion function swim(x) is found to be

$$\text{swim}(x) = 1 + \frac{x^2}{2!} + \frac{x^4}{4!} + \frac{x^6}{6!} + \cdots \qquad \textbf{(10.24)}$$

The functions sink(x) and swim(x) are actually the same as the hyperbolic functions $\sinh(x)$, $\cosh(x)$, respectively. The mathematically meaningless symbols sink and swim become well-defined functions once we specify their derivatives at a point. It will be shown that the two series expressions are valid for all values of x, and as a consequence we can manipulate the series just as we would ordinary functions. For example, by adding the two series you can show that

$$e^x = \sinh(x) + \cosh(x)$$

3. The Maclaurin series for sin(x): The determination of the series expansion for the sin(x) once again hinges on the evaluation of the derivatives at $x = 0$. These are defined by

$$\frac{d[\sin(x)]}{dx} = \cos(x) \qquad \textbf{(10.25)}$$

$$\frac{d[\cos(x)]}{dx} = -\sin(x) \qquad \textbf{(10.26)}$$

and

$$\sin(0) = 0 \qquad \cos(0) = 1$$

Using these relations you should have no difficulty in verifying the results for the derivatives of the sin(x) [see Equation (10.4)] and then obtaining the result

(10.27)
$$\sin(x) = x - \frac{x^3}{3!} + \frac{x^5}{5!} - \frac{x^7}{7!} + \cdots$$

4. The Taylor series for $f(x) = x^{1/3}$ with $a = 1$. Evaluating the derivatives at $x = 1$ we obtain the following:

$$\begin{aligned}
\text{0th order} \quad & f(1) && = x^{1/3}\big|_0 && = 1 \\[4pt]
\text{1st order} \quad & f'(1) && = \left(\frac{1}{3}x^{-2/3}\right)\bigg|_0 && = \frac{1}{3} \\[4pt]
\text{2nd order} \quad & \frac{1}{2!}f''(1) && = \frac{1}{2}\left(-\frac{2}{9}x^{-5/3}\right)\bigg|_0 && = -\frac{1}{9} \\[4pt]
\text{3rd order} \quad & \frac{1}{3!}f'''(1) && = \frac{1}{6}\left(+\frac{10}{27}x^{-8/3}\right)\bigg|_0 && = \frac{5}{81}
\end{aligned}$$

And so the expansion for $x^{1/3}$ to third order about the point $x = 1$ is

(10.28)
$$f(x) = x^{1/3} \simeq 1 + \frac{1}{3}(x - 1) - \frac{1}{9}(x - 1)^2 + \frac{5}{81}(x - 1)^3 + \cdots$$

10.2.3 Convergence of an Infinite Series

The Maclaurin series, Equation (10.17), could also be written in a somewhat shorter form as

(10.29)
$$f(x) = \sum_{p=0}^{\infty} a_p x^p = a_0 + a_1 x + a_2 x^2 + \cdots$$

where

$$a_p = \frac{1}{p!}\left(\frac{d^p f}{dx^p}\right)\bigg|_0$$

Now if the series terminates—i.e., contains only a finite number of terms,

$$\sum_{p=0}^{n} a_p x^p = a_0 + a_1 x + a_2 x^2 + \cdots + a_n x^n$$

it simply represents a polynomial and is thus obviously a well-defined function for all values of x. However, an infinite series is a different matter. Since it is clearly not possible to add up an infinite number of terms, if the series is to make any sense whatever, somewhere in the series, the terms are going to have to become smaller and eventually approach zero. It may be possible to then approximate the exact value represented by the series to an *arbitrary* degree of accuracy by terminating the summation somewhere in the series. If so the series is said to converge. If not, the series cannot be used to represent any number. We will see that the above series will in some cases converge to a number for any value of x, while in other cases convergence is possible only for a limited range of x. A necessary condition then for a series to converge (i.e., to represent a well-defined number) is that the nth term approach zero as n approaches infinity.

Necessary Condition for Convergence

$$\lim_{n \to \infty} (a_n x^n) \to 0 \qquad\qquad (10.30)$$

Unfortunately, in some circumstances even if this condition is satisfied the series may still not converge. The sufficient condition for the convergence of a series is usually expressed in terms of the *ratio test*. The ratio test examines the ratio of successive terms in the series and requires that eventually each term be smaller in absolute magnitude than the term that preceded it.

Sufficient Condition for Convergence—The Ratio Test

$$\lim_{n \to \infty} \left| \frac{(\text{term})_{n+1}}{(\text{term})_n} \right| < 1 \qquad\qquad (10.31)$$

Even though the terms in a series approach zero, the series may still diverge. The so-called harmonic series

$$1 + \frac{1}{2} + \frac{1}{3} + \frac{1}{4} + \cdots + \frac{1}{n} + \cdots \qquad\qquad (10.32)$$

is the classic example. Obviously the terms will approach zero as $n \to \infty$, yet if you attempt to sum this series you will find that the accumulated sum will slowly grow without limit.

n	Sum of the first n terms of the harmonic series
10	2.928968
100	5.187378
1000	7.485471
10000	9.787606
100000	12.090146

The series fails the ratio test since

$$\text{Ratio} = \left| \frac{n}{(n+1)} \right| \to 1 \qquad \text{as } n \to \infty$$

The terms, though approaching zero, are not decreasing fast enough to result in their accumulation being finite.

Another example is the series

$$1 - 1 + 1 - 1 + 1 - 1 + \cdots$$

This series has a sum that is either zero or one depending on where you stop in the addition. The series clearly does not diverge, but it does not converge either. It fails both tests for convergence and thus cannot represent a well-defined number.

We have used the ratio test in constructing algorithms for numerically summing an infinite series in Section 4.4.3. For example, the ratio of successive terms in the expansion for e^x is given by (see Equation (10.19)):

$$R = \left(\frac{x^{n+1}}{(n+1)!} \right) \left(\frac{n!}{x^n} \right) = \frac{x}{n+1}$$

We see that R approaches 0 as n approaches ∞ regardless of the value of x, so that the expansion is valid and converges for *all* values of x.[4]

The Maclaurin series for the logarithm is found to be (see Problem 10.1)

(10.33)
$$\ln(1+x) = x - \frac{x^2}{2} + \frac{x^3}{3} - \frac{x^4}{4} + \cdots \pm \frac{x^n}{n} + \cdots$$

so that the ratio of the successive terms is

$$R = \left(\frac{n}{n+1} \right) x$$

and as $n \to \infty$, this ratio will approach $1x$. The ratio test then guarantees that the series will converge for values of $|x| < 1$. For positive values of x, the terms in Equation (10.33) alternate in sign and a significant amount of cancellation will occur in the summation, which may in turn result in the convergence of an otherwise divergent series. For the special case of an alternating series, the condition for convergence is simply that the terms approach zero as $n \to \infty$. Thus the series

---

[4] An interesting question is whether the individual terms then satisfy the necessary condition of approaching zero. That is, does $x^n/n! \to 0$ regardless of the value of x? The answer is yes. We have just shown that the series converges for all x, so the individual terms must approach zero.

$$1 - \frac{1}{2} + \frac{1}{3} - \frac{1}{4} + \frac{1}{5} - \cdots \qquad \textbf{(10.34)}$$

has a sum that is finite and equal to the ln(2). Notice that if $x = -1$ is inserted in Equation (10.33) the result is then the negative of the harmonic series. This confirms that $\ln(0) \to -\infty$.

Mathematical convergence of the Taylor or Maclaurin series is of course essential for the series expansion to be valid. A guarantee of convergence, however, is not always enough to someone who wishes to use the series to compute a value for the function. Rapid convergence is most desired for computational purposes. For example, if we use the series for e^x given in Equation (10.19) to calculate e^{15}, the first several terms will be found to progressively increase in size. In fact, since the ratio of successive terms is $x/(n + 1)$, the terms will not even begin to diminish until the fifteenth term. The value of the fifteenth term is 334,864.6. If we continue to add terms until the size of the term is small, say 10^{-3}, or less, the expansion will include 45 terms. This will thus require a great deal of computation and will likely result in considerable round-off error. A more economical procedure would be to evaluate $e^{0.1}$ and then raise this to the 150th power.

There are numerous tricks for accelerating the convergence of a series by grouping terms or replacing the series by an equivalent series that converges faster. These procedures are rather clever and interesting and can be quite useful. However, their discussion here would take us too far afield. The interested student should see *Modern Computing Methods* 2d ed., by van Wijngaarden and published by Philosophical Library, London, 1961.

The Remainder Term

In calculus texts it is shown that the Taylor formula may be written as

$$f(x) = f(a) + f'(a)(x - a) + f''(a)\frac{(x - a)^2}{2!} + \cdots \qquad \textbf{(10.35)}$$

$$+ f^{[n]}(a)\frac{(x - a)^n}{n!} + R_{n+1}(x)$$

where

$$R_{n+1}(x) = f^{[n+1]}(\xi)\frac{(x - a)^{n+1}}{(n + 1)!} \qquad \textbf{(10.36)}$$

and ξ is some (unspecified) value between x and a. This term is called the remainder in Taylor's formula and represents the error incurred when the series is terminated after n terms. Since ξ is unspecified, we cannot determine the value of the remainder precisely, but it is often possible to calculate its maximum value and use this as the truncation error.

For example, suppose that you need a fast algorithm for the cube root of numbers that are close to one. The function $f(x) = x^{1/3}$ could be Taylor-expanded about the point $a = 1$. The result through terms of order 3 was given in Equation (10.28). The truncation error is then the maximum value of the expression

$$(10.37) \qquad \epsilon = \left| \frac{d^4(x^{1/3})}{dx^4} \right|_{\text{max}} \frac{(x-1)^4}{4!} = -\frac{80}{81} \xi^{11/3} \frac{(x-1)^4}{24}$$

Notice that for a specific value of x, Equation (10.35) is valid only for some particular (unknown) value of ξ. In order to determine what value of ξ to use in $R_4(x)$ we must already know the exact value of $x^{1/3}$, which if known, would render the series expansion superfluous. So, in those cases where a knowledge of the truncation error is important, it can be estimated by using the value of ξ that causes the expression to be a maximum. In the present case, that would correspond to using the smallest value of ξ in the range x to 1. These expressions are computed for a variety of x values and presented in Table 10-1.

Error Estimates by Order

If the function $f(x)$ is moderately complicated, it can often be extremely difficult to use the remainder expression to estimate the size of the truncation error. A less accurate but more convenient procedure is to simply make use of the fact that no matter how complicated the remainder term may be, we at least know that it is proportional to $(x - a)^{n+1}$ and that successive terms must diminish in size.

The notation $\mathbb{O}(x - a)^n$ is used to indicate that an expression *is of order* $(x - a)^n$, meaning that the term "varies as" $(x - a)^n$ or "is proportional to" $(x - a)^n$. Thus if a Taylor series is truncated after five terms, we say that the series expression for $f(x)$ "is accurate to $\mathbb{O}(x - a)^6$." The notation when applied to a Taylor series means a bit more than that the remainder term is proportional to $(x - a)^6$, it implies that since the series converges,

$$\mathbb{O}(x - a)^7 < \mathbb{O}(x - a)^6$$

Table 10-1
A comparison of the remainder term and the actual error

		$f(x) = x^{1/3}$		
x	$x^{1/3}$ (from series to 3rd order)	$x^{1/3}$ (exact)	Actual error	Maximum value of remainder $(R_{4,\text{max}})$
0.7	0.8883..	0.8879..	0.0004	0.0012
0.8	0.92840..	0.92832..	0.00008	0.00015
0.9	0.965494..	0.965489..	0.000004	0.000006
0.95	0.9830478..	0.9830476..	0.00000027	0.00000031
1.10	1.032284..	1.032280..	0.0000038	0.0000041

This is of course true if $|x - a| < 1$, but for the terms in the series should also be true even if $|x - a| > 1$.[5]

The expansion for e^x may then be written as

$$e^x = 1 + x + \frac{x^2}{2!} + \mathcal{O}(x^3)$$
(10.38)

denoting that the error in truncating after the x^2 term is of order x^3. From the definition of $\mathcal{O}(x^n)$ it is clear that the following relations are valid:

$$\mathcal{O}(x^3)\mathcal{O}(x^7) = \mathcal{O}(x^{10})$$

$$5x^2\mathcal{O}(x^4) = \mathcal{O}(x^6)$$

$$[\mathcal{O}(x^2)]^3 = \mathcal{O}(x^6)$$

$$\mathcal{O}(x^4) < \mathcal{O}(x^3)$$

The series expansion for $\sin(x)$ could also be written to $\mathcal{O}(x^3)$ as[6]

$$\sin(x) = x + \mathcal{O}(x^3)$$

We can employ both of these series to then obtain the Taylor series for the more complicated function $f(x) = e^{\sin(x)}$

$$e^{\sin(x)} = 1 + [\sin(x)] + \frac{[\sin(x)]^2}{2} + \mathcal{O}\{[\sin(x)]^3\}$$

$$= 1 + [x + \mathcal{O}(x^3)] + \frac{1}{2}[x + \mathcal{O}(x^3)]^2 + \mathcal{O}\{[x + \mathcal{O}(x^3)]^3\}$$

$$= 1 + x + \frac{1}{2}x^2 + \mathcal{O}(x^3)$$
(10.39)

The same expression could also be obtained for $e^{\sin(x)}$ by evaluating the derivatives at $x = 0$ and constructing the Taylor (or Maclaurin) series. Since the Taylor series is a unique representation of a function, a valid series expansion for a function obtained by any means whatsoever must be identical to the Taylor series.

The utility of a series representation for a complex function can be appreciated if you were faced with the task of obtaining a numerical result for the integral

---

[5] To be precise, this may not be true for the first few terms in an expansion or if some of the terms are accidentally zero.

[6] Notice that since there is no x^2 term in the expansion for $\sin(x)$, terminating after the x term will result in a series accurate to $\mathcal{O}(x^3)$.

$$\int_{0.0}^{0.2} e^{\sin(x)}\, dx$$

This integral cannot be done analytically, i.e., expressed in a closed form. However, using Equation (10.39) a numerical answer is easily obtained.

$$\int_{0.0}^{0.2} e^{\sin(x)}\, dx = \int_{0.0}^{0.2} \left[1 + x + \frac{x^2}{2} + \mathcal{O}(x^3) \right] dx$$

$$= \left[x + \frac{x^2}{2} + \frac{x^3}{6} + \mathcal{O}(x^4) \right] \Bigg|_{0.0}^{0.2}$$

$$= 0.221 \pm \mathcal{O}\,|0.0016|$$

A very important consideration when combining two approximate expressions is:

> The accuracy of a combination of two or more approximations is no more accurate than the *least* accurate piece.

Thus if the algorithm to compute e^x were very accurate and time consuming, say to $\mathcal{O}(x^{35})$, while the procedure to obtain $\sin(x)$ were fast and less accurate, say to $\mathcal{O}(x^3)$, then not only would combining the two to compute $e^{\sin(x)}$ be accurate to only $\mathcal{O}(x^3)$, but the lengthy and accurate algorithm for e^x would be wasted; a very inefficient procedure. No part of an algorithm should be excessively accurate if *any* other part of the algorithm will be less precise.

A final point is that it is extremely important in a calculation that you know the accuracy of the numbers at each stage. For example, if an approximation like

$$e^x \simeq 1 + x + \frac{x^2}{2}$$

is used to calculate $e^{0.1112}$ and the computer is then instructed to print the result with an F11.8 format, the machine dutifully complies with

$$1.11738272$$

and if it is not known in advance that the last five digits are meaningless, obvious difficulties could result.

10.2.4   Uses of Taylor Series

The Taylor series formula, Equation (10.14), is useful in the construction of simpler computational algorithms of varying accuracy for much more complicated functions. Just as important, the Taylor series provides a "recipe" for the evaluation of a function, thereby completely specifying the meaning of the function.

The Taylor series is the starting point for much of numerical analysis. For example, frequently a function is known only at a finite number of points. The Taylor formula can be used to fill in the function between points (interpolation) or to predict the value at some subsequent point (extrapolation). In addition, Taylor series are used to construct procedures for numerically differentiating and integrating a function and for the solution of differential equations.

10.3 NUMERICAL DIFFERENTIATION

The definition of a derivative in calculus is based on the idea of a *limit* of a function of a *continuous* variable

$$\frac{df(x)}{dx} = \lim_{\Delta x \to 0} \left| \frac{f(x + \Delta x) - f(x)}{\Delta x} \right| \tag{10.40}$$

and for a variety of functions, this operation can be expressed in terms of simple closed-form expressions. Using this definition equations like

$$\frac{d(x^n)}{dx} = nx^{n-1}$$

$$\frac{d[\sin(x)]}{dx} = \cos(x) \tag{10.41}$$

$$\frac{d(e^{ax})}{dx} = ae^{ax}$$

are derived. However, the result of a computer operation is a number, not a function. So, we must replace all the algebraic rules learned for differentiating various functions with a numerical procedure that will take an arbitrary function and return the *value* of its derivative at a specified point. The procedure could be based on the definition above, but, computationally, the process of a limit is inherently unstable (division by small numbers, subtraction of two nearly equal numbers) and so more well-behaved algorithms must be developed.

10.3.1 The Finite Difference Calculus

The calculus of finite differences employs the fundamental ideas of ordinary calculus up to the point of taking the limit $\Delta x \to 0$. In the finite difference calculus, Δx is treated as a small quantity, but not infinitesimal. Many of the equations we derive will look familiar to you from calculus, the principal distinction being that we must keep track of correction terms proportional to Δx, terms that would vanish in ordinary calculus.

To obtain an approximate expression for the derivative of a function, $f'(x)$, we begin with the Taylor series expansion written as

$$(10.42) \qquad f(x + \Delta x) = f(x) + f'(x)\,\Delta x + f''(x)\frac{\Delta x^2}{2!} + f'''(x)\frac{\Delta x^3}{3!} + \cdots$$

This is a Taylor series expansion of the function about the point x. Formally solving this equation for $f'(x)$, we obtain

$$(10.43) \qquad \begin{aligned} f'(x) &= \left[\frac{f(x + \Delta x) - f(x)}{\Delta x}\right] - \Delta x\left[\frac{f''(x)}{2!} + \frac{f'''(x)}{3!}\Delta x + \cdots\right] \\ &= \left[\frac{f(x + \Delta x) - f(x)}{\Delta x}\right] + \mathbb{O}(\Delta x) \end{aligned}$$

The function is next specified at equally spaced points beginning at $x = a$

$$\begin{aligned} x_0 &= a & f_0 &= f(a) \\ x_1 &= a + \Delta x & f_1 &= f(a + \Delta x) \\ x_2 &= a + 2\,\Delta x & f_2 &= f(a + 2\,\Delta x) \\ &\cdots & &\cdots \\ x_i &= a + i\,\Delta x & f_i &= f(a + i\,\Delta x) \end{aligned}$$

so that at $x = x_i$

$$f'(x_i) = f'_i = \frac{f_{i+1} - f_i}{\Delta x} + \mathbb{O}(\Delta x)$$

Forward and Backward Difference Equations

If we define the *first forward difference* of the function $f(x)$ at x_i as

$$(10.44) \qquad \Delta f_i = f_{i+1} - f_i$$

then the equation for the derivative may be written as

$$(10.45) \qquad f'_i = \frac{\Delta f_i}{\Delta x_i} + \mathbb{O}(\Delta x)$$

This relation states that the derivative at point x_i is approximately equal to the slope of the line connecting (x_i, f_i) and the *next* point (x_{i+1}, f_{i+1}).

A similar equation relating f' to the slope between (x_i, f_i) and the *pre-*

vious point is easily obtained by replacing Δx by $-\Delta x$ in Equations (10.42) and (10.43) to yield

$$f'(x_i) = f'_i = \frac{f(x_i) - f(x_i - \Delta x)}{\Delta x} + \mathcal{O}(\Delta x) \tag{10.46}$$

$$= \frac{f_i - f_{i-1}}{\Delta x} + \mathcal{O}(\Delta x)$$

We then define the *first backward difference* at x_i as

$$\nabla f_i = f_i - f_{i-1} \tag{10.47}$$

and write Equation (10.46) as

$$f'_i = \frac{\nabla f_i}{\Delta x} + \mathcal{O}(\Delta x) \tag{10.48}$$

These two approximations to the first derivative are illustrated in Figure 10-2.

The second forward difference at x_i is defined as

$$\Delta^2 f_i = \Delta(\Delta f_i)$$

$$= \Delta(f_{i+1} - f_i)$$

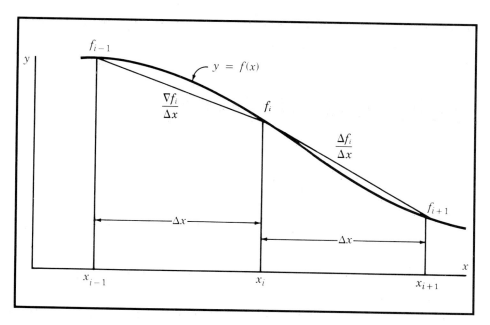

Fig. 10-2 A graphical interpretation of the forward and backward expressions for the first derivative.

$$= \Delta f_i - \Delta f_{i+1} - \Delta f_{i+1} - \Delta f_i$$
$$= (f_{i+2} - f_{i+1}) - (f_{i+1} - f_i)$$

(10.49)
$$= f_i - 2f_{i+1} + f_{i+2}$$

and it is easily shown (See Problem 10.9) that

(10.50)
$$f_i'' = \frac{\Delta^2 f_i}{\Delta x^2} + \mathcal{O}(\Delta x)$$

This can be continued to obtain approximate expressions for the nth derivative in terms of forward differences.

(10.51)
$$f_i^{[n]} = \frac{\Delta^2 f_i}{(\Delta x)^n} + \mathcal{O}(\Delta x)$$

Repeating the procedure for backward differences, we easily obtain

(10.52)
$$\nabla^2 f_i = \nabla(\nabla f_i) =$$
$$= f_i - 2f_{i-1} + f_{i-2}$$

and

(10.53)
$$f_i^{[n]} = \frac{\nabla^n f_i}{(\Delta x)^n} + \mathcal{O}(\Delta x)$$

Central Difference Equations

More symmetrical expressions for numerical derivatives can be derived by combining the equations for forward and backward differences.

$$\delta f_i = \tfrac{1}{2}(\Delta f_i + \nabla f_i)$$
$$= \tfrac{1}{2}[(f_{i+1} - f_i) + (f_i - f_{i-1})]$$

(10.54)
$$= \tfrac{1}{2}(f_{i+1} - f_{i-1})$$

The central difference may be related to the first derivative of $f(x)$ at x_i in a manner similar to that used for forward and backward differences. Rewriting the Taylor series first with Δx and then with $-\Delta x$,

$$f_{i+1} = f(x_i + \Delta x)$$

$$= f(x_i) + f'(x_i)\,\Delta x + f''(x_i)\frac{\Delta x^2}{2} + f'''(x_i)\frac{\Delta x^3}{3!} + \cdots$$

$$= f_i + f_i'\,\Delta x + f_i''\frac{\Delta x^2}{2} + f_i'''\frac{\Delta x^3}{3!} + \cdots$$

$$f_{i-1} = f(x_i - \Delta x)$$

$$= f(x_i) - f'(x_i)\,\Delta x + f''(x_i)\frac{\Delta x^2}{2} - f'''(x_i)\frac{\Delta x^3}{3!} + \cdots$$

$$= f_i - f_i'\,\Delta x + f_i''\frac{\Delta x^2}{2} - f_i'''\frac{\Delta x^3}{3!} + \cdots$$

Subtracting the second equation from the first, the even derivatives cancel and we obtain

$$\frac{1}{2}(f_{i+1} - f_{i-1}) = f_i'\,\Delta x + \Delta x^3\left(\frac{1}{3!}f_i''' + \frac{\Delta x^2}{5!}f_i^{[v]} + \cdots\right) \qquad (10.55)$$

so that

$$f_i' = \frac{\delta f_i}{\Delta x} + \mathcal{O}(\Delta x)^2 \qquad (10.56)$$

You will notice that the central difference expression for the derivative is second-order in Δx and thus is more accurate than either the forward or backward expressions obtained earlier.

The central difference equation for the second derivative can be obtained in a like manner by retaining more terms in the Taylor series. The result is

$$f_i'' = \frac{\delta^2 f_i}{(\Delta x)^2} + \mathcal{O}(\Delta x)^2 \qquad (10.57)$$

where

$$\delta^2 f_i = \tfrac{1}{2}[\Delta^2 f_{i-1} + \nabla^2 f_{i+1}] \qquad (10.58)$$

$$= \tfrac{1}{2}[(f_{i+1} - 2f_i + f_{i-1}) + (f_{i+1} - 2f_i + f_{i-1})]$$

$$= f_{i+1} - 2f_i + f_{i-1}$$

10.3.2 Example of Data Analysis Using Numerical Derivatives

A standard experiment in introductory physics laboratory is to measure the rate of fall of a light spherical object in air. The forces acting on the ball during its fall are gravity and air drag. The functional form of the air drag force is unknown, except that it is known to depend on the velocity. Newton's second law, $F = ma$, then reads

$$a = \frac{d^2 y(t)}{dt^2} = -g + \frac{1}{m}f(v) \qquad (10.59)$$

where $y(t)$ is the distance of fall at time t, g is the gravitational acceleration, m is the mass of the ball, and $f(v)$ is the unknown air drag force. The data from the experiment consist of a table of y vs. t values, evenly spaced at one-fourth of a second. By computing the numerical first derivative of this set, we can estimate the velocity v; the second derivatives will yield the acceleration and thus determine the air drag as a function of *time*. Finally, the tabulated values of v_i and $f(v_i)$ are used to graph $f(v)$ vs. v^2 to test the hypothesis that f is proportional to v^2. The tabulated experimental values and computed first- and second-derivative values (using central differences) are given in Table 10-2 and the graph in Figure 10-3.

10.3.3 Solution of Differential Equations Using Difference Expressions

Although we will not study differential equations in detail until Chapter 15, it is instructive to have at least a glimpse of how difference expressions can be used to solve some common equations numerically.

Again consider the equation defining the motion of an object falling in air. Assuming the air drag is given by an expression like

(10.60)
$$F_{\text{drag}} = \gamma v^2$$

Table 10-2
Numerical first and second derivatives of experimental free-fall data.

i	t_i (sec)	$y(t_i)$ (cm)	$v_i = \dfrac{\delta y_i}{\Delta t}$	$a_i = \dfrac{\delta^2 y_i}{\Delta t^2}$	$g - a_i$
1	0.025	0.75			
2	0.050	1.85	56.0	960.0	20.0
3	0.075	3.55	79.0	880.0	100.0
4	0.100	5.81	101.0	880.0	100.0
5	0.125	8.60	121.2	736.0	244.0
6	0.150	11.9	140.0	768.0	212.0
7	0.175	15.6	156.8	576.0	404.0
8	0.200	19.7	172.0	640.0	340.0
9	0.225	24.2	188.0	640.0	340.0
10	0.250	29.1	202.0	480.0	500.0
11	0.275	34.3	214.0	480.0	500.0
12	0.300	39.8	224.0	320.0	660.0
13	0.325	45.5	234.0	480.0	500.0
14	0.350	51.5	244.0	320.0	660.0
15	0.375	57.7	252.0	320.0	660.0
16	0.400	64.1	259.2	256.0	724.0
17	0.425	70.7	265.0	208.0	772.0
18	0.450	77.4	270.0	192.0	788.0
19	0.475	84.2	274.0	128.0	852.0
20	0.500	91.0	276.8	96.0	884.0
21	0.525	98.0	279.0	80.0	900.0
22	0.550	105.0	280.0	0.0	980.0
23	0.575	112.0			

3. Determine the Taylor series expansions of the following functions:
  a. $32x^5 - 80x^4 + 80x^3 - 40x^2 + 10x - 1$ {with $a = 1/2$}.
  b. $\cos(1 + 2x)$ {with $a = -1/2$}
  c. $\ln(2 + x)$ {with $a = -1$}

4. Determine the maximum value of the remainder term in the series expansion for e^x after including six terms. Use $x = 0.1$ and then $x = 10.0$. Compare this with the difference between the sum of the first six terms of the series for $x^{0.1}$ and e^{10} respectively.

5. Using the Maclaurin series expansion for $\sin(x)$ and $\cos(x)$, show that

$$e^{ix} = \cos(x) + i \sin(x)$$

where $i = \sqrt{-1}$, $i^2 = -1$, $i^3 = -i$, etc.

6. Use the fact that

$$e^x = 1 + x + \mathbb{O}(x^2)$$

and

$$\ln(z) = (z - 1) + \mathbb{O}((z - 1)^2)$$

to determine the series expansion for $\ln(e^x)$ valid to $\mathbb{O}(x^2)$. [Note: The answer is obviously $\ln(e^x) = x$. I want you to go through the algebra.]

7. Use the fact that

$$e^x = 1 + x + \frac{x^2}{2} + \mathbb{O}(x^3)$$

and

$$\ln(z) = (z - 1) - \tfrac{1}{2}(z - 1)^2 + \mathbb{O}[(z - 1)^3]$$

to determine the series expansion for $\ln(e^x)$ valid to $\mathbb{O}(x^3)$.

8. The Maclaurin series for $e^{\sin(x)}$ is

$$e^{\sin(x)} = 1 + x + \frac{x^2}{2} - \frac{x^4}{8} + \mathbb{O}(x^5)$$

  a. Prove this result by using the equations:

$$\frac{d}{dx}(e^{\sin(x)}) = [\cos(x)]e^{\sin(x)}$$

$$\frac{d}{dx}[\cos(x)e^{\sin(x)}] = [\cos^2(x) - \sin(x)]e^{\sin(x)}$$

  b. Obtain the same result directly by using the two series:

$$e^z = 1 + z + \frac{z^2}{2} + \frac{z^3}{3!} + \frac{z^4}{4!} + \mathbb{O}(z^5)$$

and

$$\sin(x) = x - \frac{x^3}{3!} + \mathbb{O}(x^5)$$

9. Use Equation (10.42) to expand $f(x_i + \Delta x)$ and $f(x_i + 2\,\Delta x)$ and then use these equations to prove the result quoted in Equation (10.50).
10. Use Equation (10.50) to replace f'' in Equation (10.43) and thereby obtain the following forward difference result for f' that is accurate to $(\Delta x)^2$.

$$f_i' = \frac{-f_{i+2} + 4f_{i+1} - 3f_i}{2\,\Delta x} + \mathbb{O}(\Delta x)^2$$

11. Using the following data

i	x_i	$f(x_i)$
0	0.0	2.00
1	0.1	2.04
2	0.2	2.20
3	0.3	2.84
4	0.4	5.40
5	0.5	6.68
6	0.6	7.32
7	0.7	7.64
8	0.8	7.80
9	0.9	7.88
10	1.0	7.92

obtain numerical values for f_2', f_5', f_0', f_6', f_6'' that are of order $\mathbb{O}(0.1)^2$. Note: for f_0' you will have to use the results of the previous problem.
12. Obtain the numerical first and second derivatives using the central difference expressions of $f(x) = e^x$ at $x = 0.0, 1.0, 2.0$ that are correct to $\mathbb{O}(0.1)^2$ and compare with the exact answers.

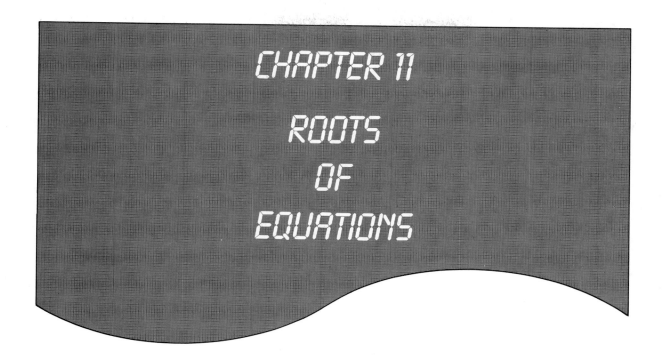

CHAPTER 11

ROOTS

OF

EQUATIONS

11.1 INTRODUCTION

One of the most common tasks in science and engineering is that of finding the roots of equations. That is, given a function $f(x)$, the problem is to find values of x such that $f(x) = 0.0$. Also included in this type of problem is the determination of the points of intersection of two curves. If the curves are represented by functions $f(x)$ and $g(x)$, the intersection points correspond to the roots of the function $F(x) = f(x) - g(x)$.

In addition to their utility, root-solving techniques are important for a number of other reasons. They are easy to understand and usually easy to carry out. Thus with a minimum of instruction you are able to obtain solutions to genuine problems in engineering. Also a vital element in numerical analysis involves an appreciation of what can or cannot be solved and a clear understanding of the accuracy of the answers obtained. Since this comes mostly from experience, it is important that you begin solving numerical problems immediately. Besides, you will find that root-solving problems are fun.

Some examples of the types of functions that are encountered in root-solving problems are

(11.1) $$ax^2 + bx + c = 0$$

(11.2) $$2x^4 - 7x^3 + 4x^2 + 7x - 6 = (x - 1)(x + 1)(x - 2)(2x - 3) = 0$$

(11.3) $$x^5 - 2x^3 - 5x^2 + 2 = 0$$

(11.4) $$\sin^5(x) + \sin^3(x) + 5\cos(x) - 7 = 0$$

(11.5) $$100e^{-x} - \sin(2\pi x) = 0$$

The general quadratic equation, Equation (11.1), can be solved easily and *exactly* by using the quadratic formula:

(11.6)
$$r_1 = \frac{-b + \sqrt{(b^2 - 4ac)}}{2a}$$

$$r_2 = \frac{-b - \sqrt{(b^2 - 4ac)}}{2a}$$

Equation (11.2) can be solved exactly by factoring the polynomial. The roots are then clearly $+1$, -1, $+2$, $+\frac{3}{2}$. However, most polynomials cannot be so easily factored and other more general techniques are required. There are formulas for the exact solution of general cubic or quartic equations, but they are quite cumbersome and are thus seldom used. No exact formula is possible for a polynomial like Equation (11.3) in which the highest power of x is greater than 4. For these polynomials numerical means must generally be used to determine the roots.

You will recall from high school algebra that a polynomial of degree n (i.e., the highest power of x is x^n) has precisely n roots, of which some may be complex numbers and others may be multiple roots. Thus Equation (11.3) has three real roots

$$r_1 = -0.712780744625\ldots$$
$$r_2 = +0.57909844162\ldots$$
$$r_3 = +2.0508836199\ldots$$

and two complex roots

$$r_4 = 0.757225433526 + i(0.57803468208)$$
$$r_5 = 0.757225433526 - i(0.57803468208)$$

The equation

$$x^2 - 2x + 1 = 0$$

can be factored as

$$(x - 1)^2 = 0$$

and has two real roots, both of which happen to be the same value. In this case the root is said to be a multiple root with multiplicity 2.

Equations (11.4) and (11.5) are called *transcendental equations* and represent an entirely different class of functions. Transcendental equations typically involve trigonometric, exponential, or logarithmic functions and cannot be reduced to any polynomial equation in x. Whereas all the roots of any polynomial can be expressed as rational fractions or fractional powers of rational fractions, the roots of transcendental equations cannot. The roots of transcendental equations are frequently nonrepeating decimal fractions like π and are called *transcendental numbers*. These numbers are important to mathematics since they are responsible for the real number system being dense or continuous. The classification of equations as polynomial or transcendental is vital to traditional mathematics; however, the distinction is of less consequence to the computer. In fact, not only is the number system available to the computer not continuous, it is indeed a finite set. At any rate, when finding the roots of equations, the distinction between polynomials and transcendental equations is frequently unnecessary and the same numerical procedures are applied to both. In Section 11.6 a short discussion is given concerning methods that have been devised specifically for finding roots of polynomials. The distinction between the two types of functions is, however, important in other regards. For example, many of the theorems you learned concerning roots of polynomials do not apply to transcendental equations. Thus both Equations (11.4) and (11.5) have an infinite number of real roots.

All of the root-solving techniques discussed in this chapter are of an iterative nature. That is, you specify an initial guess for the root or an interval that is known to contain a root and the various recipes will return an improved guess or a more limited interval. The procedure is then repeated using the new values until a root of desired accuracy is obtained or until the method encounters difficulties and fails. Some of the schemes we will discuss will be guaranteed to find a root eventually but may take considerable computer time to arrive at the answer. Others may converge to a root much faster but are more susceptible to problems of divergence, i.e., they come with no guarantees.

The common ingredient in all root-solving recipes is that potential computational difficulties of any nature are best avoided by mustering as much intelligence as possible in the initial choice of the method used and the accompanying initial guess. This part of the problem is often the most difficult and time consuming and the art involved in numerical analysis consists of balancing off time spent in optimizing the solution of the problem before computation against time spent in correcting unforeseen errors during computation. If it is at all possible, a rough sketch of the function should be done before root solving is attempted. This may be done by using the plotting routine of Section 7.7 or may consist of a table of numbers calculated by the computer and graphed by hand. These graphs are extremely useful to the programmer, not only in estimating the first guess for the root but also in anticipating potential difficulties. If a sketch is not feasible, some method of monitoring the function must be utilized to arrive at some understanding of what the function is doing before the actual computation is initiated. All of this preamble to this chapter is a corollary to the well-known programmer's axiom

G-I / G-O

⟨Garbage In / Garbage Out⟩

11.2 REFINEMENT OF THE BISECTION METHOD

We have already discussed the bisection method in detail in Chapter 4 where it was used as an example of programming techniques. It is a so-called brute-force method and is rarely used, since for almost any problem an alternative method is available which is faster, more accurate, and only slightly more complex. All of the refinements of the bisection method that one might devise are based on attempts to use as much information as is available concerning the behavior of the function at each iteration. In the ordinary bisection method the only feature of the function that is monitored is its sign. Thus if we were searching for roots of the function

$$f(x) = 2e^{-2x} - \sin(\pi x)$$

we would begin the search, as in Chapter 4, by stepping along the x axis and watching for a change in sign of the function.

i	x_i	$f(x_i)$
0	0.0	2.00
1	0.1	1.33
2	0.2	0.75
3	0.3	0.29
4	0.4	−.05

The next step in the bisection procedure is to reduce the step size by half, that is, try $x_5 = 0.35$. However, from the magnitudes of the numbers above we would expect the root to be closer to 0.4 than to 0.3. Thus, by using information about the size of the function in addition to its sign, we may be able to speed up the convergence. In the present case we might interpolate the root to be approximately

$$\left[\frac{0.29 - 0.0}{0.29 - (-0.05)} \right] = \left(\frac{f_3 - 0}{f_3 - f_4} \right) = 0.853$$

of the distance from $x_3 = 0.3$ to $x_4 = 0.4$, or $x_5 = 0.3853$. Continuing in this manner and interpolating at each step, we would obtain the following results:

i	x_i	$f(x_i)$
3	0.30	0.29
4	0.40	$-.05$
5	0.385	$-.0083$
6	0.3823	$-.0013$
7	0.3819	$-.00019$
8	0.38185	$-.000028$
9	0.38184	$-.000004$

Comparing these results with the bisection method applied to a similar function in Section 4.5, we see that the convergence rate for the present method is significantly faster. The next task is to formalize this procedure into a method suitable for a general function.

11.2.1 The Regula Falsi Method

The basic idea in the first refinement of the bisection algorithm is that the new method will be essentially the same as bisection, except that in place of using the midpoint of the interval at each step of the calculation, we use an interpolated value for the root. This is illustrated in Figure 11-1. In the figure a root is known to exist in the interval $(x_1 \leftrightarrow x_3)$, and in the drawing, f_1 is negative while f_3 is positive. The interpolated position of the root is x_2. Since the two triangles ABC and CDE are similar, the lengths of the sides are related by

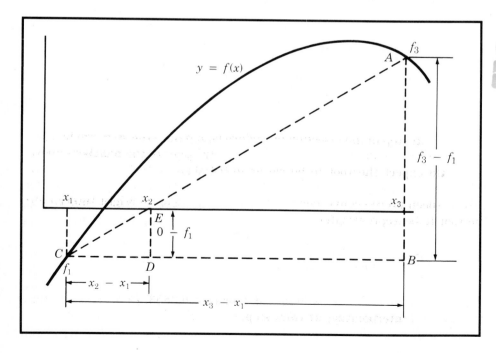

Figure 11-1
Estimating the root by interpolation.

$$\frac{DE}{AB} = \frac{CD}{BC}$$

or

$$\frac{0.0 - f(x_1)}{f(x_3) - f(x_1)} = \frac{x_2 - x_1}{x_3 - x_1}$$

which may be solved for the unknown position x_2 to yield

(11.7)
$$x_2 = x_1 - (x_3 - x_1)\frac{f_1}{f_3 - f_1}$$

This value of x_2 then replaces the midpoint used in the bisection algorithm and the rest of the procedure remains exactly the same. Thus the next step would be to determine whether the actual root is to the left or to the right of x_2. As before,

IF $f_1 * f_2 < 0$ THEN the root is on the left

IF $f_2 * f_3 < 0$ THEN the root is on the right

In the figure the root is to the left of x_2, so the interval used for the next iteration would be

```
X3 = X2
F3 = F2
X2 =                    Use  Equation  (11.7)
F2 = FNC(X2)
```

In other words, to employ this slightly faster algorithm, the only change that has to be made to the previous bisection code is to replace statements of the form

```
X2 = (X1 + X3)/2.
```

by a statement based on Equation (11.7).

This method is still guaranteed to obtain a root eventually and will usually (but not always) converge faster than the conventional bisection algorithm. We do, however, pay a small price. The values of f_1 and f_3 used in Equation (11.7) may be very nearly equal and we could be plagued by round-off errors in their difference. Also, in the bisection algorithm we could predict with some precision the number of iterations required to obtain the root to a desired accuracy. (See Section 4.5.) This is no longer possible if we use the interpolated values and the code *must* now include a check for excessive iterations.

This method illustrates that an almost trivial change in the algorithm which is based on more intelligent monitoring of the function can reap considerable rewards in more rapid convergence. The formal name of the method just described is the *regula falsi method* (the method of false position).

Are there any additional improvements in the basic bisection algorithm that can be easily implemented? To answer this it is necessary to examine in more detail the manner in which the regula falsi method arrives at a solution. This is best done graphically. The calculation begun in Figure 11-1 is continued in Figure 11-2. Notice that in this example, in which the function is concave downward near the root, the value of the left limit of the search interval near the root, x_1, never changes. The actual root always remains in the left segment in each iteration. The right segment of the interval, $x_3 - x_2$, shrinks quite rapidly; but the left segment, $x_2 - x_1$, does not. If the function were concave upward the converse would be true. Thus a drawback in the regula falsi method is that even though the method converges more rapidly to a value of x that results in a 'small' $|f(x)|$, the interval containing the root does *not* diminish significantly.

11.2.2 The Modified Regula Falsi Method

Perhaps the procedure can be made to converge more rapidly if the interval can somehow be made to collapse from both directions. One manner of accomplishing this is demonstrated in Figure 11-3. The idea is as follows:

IF the root is determined to lie in the left segment $x_2 - x_1$
THEN the interpolation line is drawn between the points $(x_1, \frac{1}{2}f_1)$ and (x_2, f_2)
ELSE IF the root is in the right segment, $x_3 - x_2$

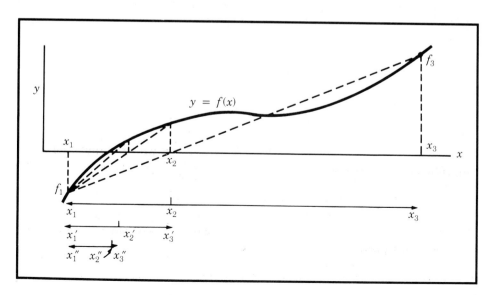

Figure 11-2
A graphical illustration of several iterations of the regula falsi algorithm.

Figure 11-3 A graphical illustration of the Modified Regula falsi method.

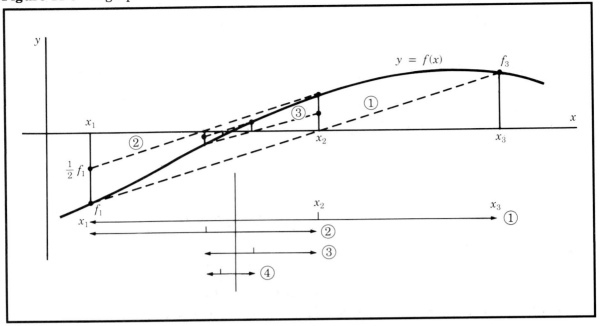

THEN the interpolation line is drawn between the points (x_1, f_1) and $(x_3, \frac{1}{2}f_3)$

Thus the slope of the line is *artificially* reduced. The effect of this is that if the root is in the left of the original interval, it will eventually turn up in the right segment of a later interval and subsequently will alternate between left and right. This last modification to the bisection method in combination with the regula falsi method is known as the *modified regula falsi method,* a very powerful and popular procedure for finding roots of equations. The alterations to the original bisection code of Chapter 4 are quite trivial and are shown in Figure 11-4. A comparison of the rate of convergence of the three methods applied to the function

$$f(x) = 2e^{-2x} - \sin(\pi x)$$

is illustrated Table 11-1.

A slope-reduction factor of one-half was used in constructing the drawing in Figure 11-3. This is an example of what is called a *relaxation factor;* a number used to alter the results of one iteration before inserting into the next. The determination of the optimum relaxation factor is almost always an extremely complex problem in any calculation and is well beyond the scope of this text. However, in this instance a little trial and error shows that a less drastic decrease in the slope will result in improved convergence. Using a reduction factor of 0.9 should be adequate for most problems and this factor was used to generate the values in Table 11-1.

A few comments are in order regarding the Fortran code in Figure 11-4.

```
      SUBROUTINE REGFAL(XA,XC,EPS,IMAX,ROOT,F,ITER)
*
*-- A ROOT OF THE FUNCTION F(X) IS DETERMINED BY THE BISECTION
*-- ALGORITHM OR ITS IMPROVEMENTS. THE MAXIMUM NUMBER OF ITERA-
*-- TIONS PERMITTED IS IMAX. THE CONVERGENCE CRITERION IS EITHER
*-- IF (INTERVAL) < EPS OR IF ABS(F(X)) < EPS. THE ACTUAL NUMBER
*-- OF ITERATIONS IS RETURNED AS ITER.
*-------------------------------------------------------------------
* INITIALIZE INTERVAL AND FUNCTION VALUES
*
      X1 = XA
      X3 = XC
      I  = 0
      F1 = F(X1)
      F3 = F(X3)
      D  = (X3 - X1)
*
*    (BISECTION)                  (REGULA-FALSI)
*  1 X2 = (X1 + X3)/2.   <OR>   X2 = X1 - D * F1/(F3 - F1)
      F2 = F(X2)
*
*-------------------------------------------------------------------
*                    CONVERGENCE TESTS
*
      IF(D .LT. EPS)THEN
*
*                SUCCESS BASED ON INTERVAL
*
          ROOT = X2
          ITER = I
          RETURN
      ELSE IF(ABS(F(X2)) .LT. EPS)THEN
*
*                SUCCESS BASED ON SIZE OF FUNCTION
*
          ROOT = X2
          ITER = I
          RETURN
      ELSE IF(I .GT. IMAX)THEN
*
*                EXCESSIVE ITERATIONS
*
          WRITE(*,10)I,X2,F2
          STOP
      END IF
*-------------------------------------------------------------------
```

Continued

Figure 11-4 *Continued*

```
*                        CHECK FOR CROSSING ON RIGHT OR LEFT
*
     IF(F1 * F2 .LT. 0.0)THEN
*
*                        CROSSING ON LEFT, REDEFINE INTERVAL
*
        X3 = X2
        F3 = F2
*       F1 = F1    (OR FOR MODIFIED REGULA FALSI)      F1 = .9 * F1
     ELSE IF(F2 * F3 .LT. 0.0)THEN
*
*                        CROSSING ON RIGHT
*
        X1 = X2
        F1 = F2
*       F3 = F3    (OR FOR MODIFIED REGULA FALSI)      F3 = .9 * F3
     ELSE
*
*                 NO CROSSING IN EITHER HALF -- ERROR PATH
*
        WRITE(*,*)'NO ROOT IN INTERVAL',X1,X3,'IN STEP',I
        STOP
     END IF
*-------------------------------------------------------------------
*                 ITERATION COMPLETE, PROCEED TO NEXT STEP
*
     D = X3 - X1
     I = I + I
     GO TO 1
*
*-------------------------------------------------------------------
* FORMAT
*
  10 FORMAT(5X,'NO ROOT HAS BEEN FOUND IN ',I4,'ITERATIONS',/,
    +        5X,'THE LATEST VALUES ARE X = ',F10.5,
    +        ' AND F(X) = ',E11.4)
     END
```

1. The function F(X) is evaluated only once per cycle. If the function is quite complicated and therefore costly to compute, this measure of efficiency can be quite attractive, even decisive, in choosing the appropriate method of solution.
2. The code can terminate via four paths:
   a. Two success paths:
      (1) IF $|f(x_2)|$ is small. If we have found a value of x such that $f(x)$ is approximately zero, this value is then an approximate root. Also

i	Bisection x_2	Regula Falsi x_2	Modified Regula Falsi x_2
1	0.35	0.385	0.385
2	0.375	0.3823	0.3820
3	0.3875	0.3819	0.38183
4	0.38125	0.38185	0.381843
5	0.38438	0.381844	0.38184267
6	0.38281	0.381843	0.38184276
7	0.38203	0.3818428	0.38184275
8	0.38164	0.38184275	0.38184275

Table 11-1
The bisection, regula falsi, and modified regula falsi methods applied to $f(x) = 2e^{-2x} - \sin(\pi x)$.

since the algorithm divides by values of $f(x)$, the program should be terminated when division by zero or round-off error is a possibility. This test is appropriate only if the interval fails to collapse, as is the case in the regula falsi method.

(2) IF $|x_3 - x_1|$ is small. The original aim of the program—i.e., to bracket a root—has been achieved. Note, there is no guarantee that this criterion will result in a value of $f(x)$ that is "small." The point is, however, successive iterations have resulted in only small changes in the interval containing the root and so continuing the process is not necessary or productive.

b. Two failure paths

(1) IF the number of iterations is greater than $I_{\max}$—STOP. This test allows the programmer to specify the maximum cost he or she will accept for an attempted solution. Since in the regula falsi and modified regula falsi methods the number of iterations is not predictable, this form of safeguard is essential. Of course it is also a prudent precaution against unforeseen errors in the construction of the problem that could cause the program to cycle forever and not obtain a solution. Statements of this type are required in any program in which there is a danger of infinite looping.

(2) IF the function does not change sign ($f_1 \times f_3 > 0$)—STOP. Since the original interval was known to contain a root, the only way this condition can arise is by error. Usually the error is in the code for the function $f(x)$. That is, you are attempting to find a root of a function different from the one intended.

11.2.3 Comparison of the Algorithms Based on Bisection

In summary the characteristic features of the three methods discussed thus far in this chapter are listed below:

Bisection:
Guaranteed to bracket a root
Interval halved in each iteration
Success based on size of interval

	Predictable number of iterations
Regula falsi:	Slow convergence
	Success based on size of function
	Interval containing root is NOT small
	Faster convergence
	Monitors size of function as well as its sign
	Unpredictable number of iterations
Modified regula falsi:	Success based on size of function or interval
	Faster convergence
	Unpredictable number of iterations

Of the three methods, the modified regula falsi is probably the most efficient for common problems and is the recommended algorithm whenever the only information available is that the function changes sign between x_1 and x_3.

The requirement that the initial search interval be one in which the function changes sign (only once) can occasionally be troublesome. The problem of finding the root of a function like

$$f(x) = x^2 - 2x + 1 = (x - 1)^2$$

is not suited to any of the algorithms based on bisection since the function never changes sign. This difficulty will occur whenever the root of the function is a multiple root of even multiplicity. The method that overcomes some of these limitations is Newton's method, which is discussed in the next section.

11.3 NEWTON'S METHOD FOR ROOT SOLVING

In the previous section we saw that incorporating more information about the behavior of the function into the root-solving algorithm can produce substantial improvements. Newton's method is a further step in this direction—i.e., using as much information as possible in the construction of the method and, not surprisingly, the result is a dramatic improvement in the rate of convergence in most situations. However, as we shall see, Newton's method differs from the earlier procedures in that it does not guarantee that a root will be found in all cases, and sadly, it often will diverge. More on this in Section 11.3.3.

11.3.1 Derivation of Newton's Method

Newton's method (also called the *Newton-Raphson method*) can be derived by starting with the Taylor series for the function $f(x)$ with x_0 being used in place of a [see Equation (10.14)].

$$f(x) = f(x_0) + \left.\frac{df}{dx}\right|_{x=x_0} (x - x_0) + \frac{1}{2!}\left.\frac{d^2f}{dx^2}\right|_{x=x_0} (x - x_0)^2 + \cdots \qquad \textbf{(11.8)}$$

Now if $|x - x_0|$ is small, we need only retain a few terms in the series. To find a root of the function, we seek an x such that $f(x) = 0.0$ or

$$f(x) = 0 = f(x_0) + \left.\frac{df}{dx}\right|_{x_0} (x - x_0) + \frac{1}{2!}\left.\frac{d^2f}{dx^2}\right|_{x_0} (x - x_0)^2 + \cdots \qquad \textbf{(11.9)}$$

If we blindly assume that the desired root x is near the value x_0, then

$$f(x) = 0 \simeq f(x_0) + \left.\frac{df}{dx}\right|_{x_0} (x - x_0) \qquad \textbf{(11.10)}$$

And of course if x is not near x_0 this may not even be approximately true. In Equation (11.10) everything except x (the root) is known and so we can solve for x. Reintroducing the notation

$$f' = \frac{df}{dx}$$

Equation (11.10) becomes

$$-f(x_0) = f'(x_0)(x - x_0)$$

or

$$x = x_0 - \frac{f(x_0)}{f'(x_0)} \qquad \textbf{(11.11)}$$

If our assumption of $|x - x_0|$ being small is valid, then Equation (11.11) will be a good estimate of the actual root of the function. But if $|x - x_0|$ is not small, what have we done? The answer is illustrated in Figure 11-5.

Replacing the function $f(x)$ by the first two terms in its Taylor series is seen to be equivalent to approximating the function by a straight line through the point (x_0, f_0), which has the same slope as the tangent to the curve at that point. Then setting this approximation to $f(x)$ equal to zero, we find the point where the *line* intersects the axis. Thus, as you can see in Figure 11-5, this procedure will not in general give the actual root of $f(x)$. However, the value generated by Equation (11.11) is closer to the actual root than was the starting point x_0. Newton's method then consists of repeating this process. That is, starting from an initial guess for the root of $f(x)$, say x_0, calculate an improved guess x_1 from Equation (11.11)

$$x_1 = x_0 - \frac{f(x_0)}{f'(x_0)}$$

Figure 11-5
Replacing a func-
tion by two terms
of a Taylor series.

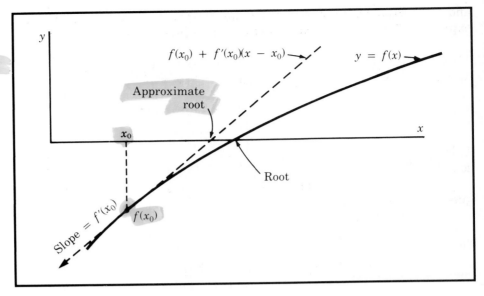

Next use the improved value x_1 for the root in the next cycle to calculate the
second improvement on the root,

$$x_2 = x_1 - \frac{f(x_1)}{f'(x_1)}$$

and so on.

The point to keep in mind is that Newton's method attempts to find a root
of a function $f(x)$ by repeatedly approximating the function by straight lines.
The information content of the method is quite high because we are monitoring at each step not only the value of the function but its slope.

11.3.2 Numerical Examples

Square Roots

The rate of convergence of Newton's method applied to most equations is
quite impressive. For example, the square root of a number can be obtained
in the following manner: Given a number C, we wish to determine a value
of x such that $x = C^{1/2}$; or to phrase the problem in a different way, we wish
to find a root of the equation

$$F(x) = x^2 - C$$

Applying Newton's method to this function, using

$$F'(x) = 2x$$

and an intitial guess of x_0 for the square root, we obtain the following expression for the improved estimate of the square root.

$$x_1 = x_0 - \frac{F(x_0)}{F'(x_0)} = x_0 - \frac{x_0^2 - C}{2x_0}$$

$$= \frac{1}{2}\left(x_0 + \frac{C}{x_0}\right)$$

(11.12)

This equation was used earlier to construct the Fortran code to compute square roots (see Figure 3-10).

To illustrate, we take $C = 111$ with $x_0 = 20$, an obviously poor first guess. Equation (11.12) then generates the following values for $\sqrt{111}$.

Iteration	x	x^2
0	20.0	400.
1	12.78	163.2
2	10.73	115.2
3	10.537	111.04
4	10.53565	111.0000032
5	10.53565375	111.0000000001

Thus five iterations, beginning with a poor first guess, have resulted in an answer correct to nine significant figures.

This procedure can easily be adapted to finding the nth root of a number. I should caution that Newton's method does not always converge as quickly as it did in this example.

The Intersection of Two Functions

As an example of a somewhat more complicated problem utilizing Newton's method, we next solve for the roots of the function

$$f(x) = 100e^{-x} - 5\sin\left(\frac{\pi}{2}x\right) = 0$$

(11.13)

which can also be written as

$$100e^{-x} = 5\sin\left(\frac{\pi}{2}x\right)$$

(11.14)

Thus a root of Equation (11.13) will correspond to the points of intersection of the two functions on the left and right sides of Equation (11.14). The two sides of Equation (11.14) are separately plotted in Figure 11-6, and it is clear that there are an infinite number of intersection points. We must therefore be rather careful in our analysis. The first root appears to be near $x = 4.0$. From what we know about Newton's method we would anticipate problems

Figure 11-6
The points of in-
tersection of
$100e^{-x}$ and
$5 \sin\left(\dfrac{\pi}{2}x\right)$

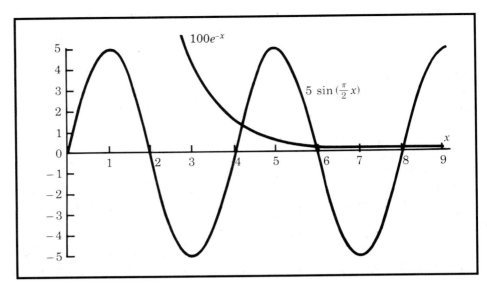

if an initial guess of $x > 5.0$ were chosen. This is because the basic approximation is to replace functions by straight lines and starting at $x > 5.0$ it is
very likely that the procedure would narrow in on one of the many roots
beyond the first. With these considerations made, we begin the calculation
at $x = 4.0$

$$f(x) = 100e^{-x} - 5 \sin\left(\frac{\pi}{2}x\right)$$

(11.15)

$$f'(x) = -100e^{-x} - 5\frac{\pi}{2}\cos\left(\frac{\pi}{2}x\right)$$

$$\Delta x = \frac{f(x)}{f'(x)}$$

(11.16)

$$x_1 = x_0 + \Delta x_0$$

Step	x	f(x)	f'(x)	Δx
0	4.0	1.83	−9.68	+0.189
1	4.189	0.05	−9.03	+0.0058
2	4.19492	0.000086	−9.00	+0.0000096
3	4.1949316	5×10^{-7}	−9.00	$+5 \times 10^{-10}$
4	4.194931571	$<10^{-12}$	$\cdots$	$\cdots$

You are invited to try Newton's method applied to several of the problems in the Problems section. If the function is reasonably simple, it is
instructive and good practice to carry out the calculation on a pocket calculator, especially if your calculator has several storage registers for $f(x), f'(x)$,
and Δx. For more complicated problems, you can use the Fortran subroutine
in Section 11.3.5 or write your own.

11.3.3 Difficulties that May Be Encountered Using Newton's Method

Newton's method is the most popular root-solving technique and it can usually be relied upon to find a root quickly and accurately. However, there are a few potential problems that can cause the method to fail. These are illustrated below:

1. A poor initial guess. If the initial guess x_0 is such that $f'(x_0)$ is small (slope nearly horizontal) the first iteration may be thrown out of the region of interest (see Figure 11-7). Also, if the initial guess is in a region where the function has a local minimum but no root, the method will likely fail (see Figure 11-8).
2. The method will not be able to find a root whenever the derivative at the root is infinite (see Figure 11-9). This situation is rarely encountered and usually ignored in constructing a Fortran code.

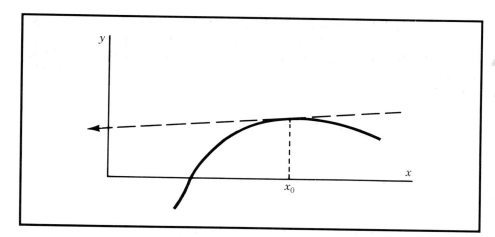

Figure 11-7
A horizontal slope causes Newton's method to fail.

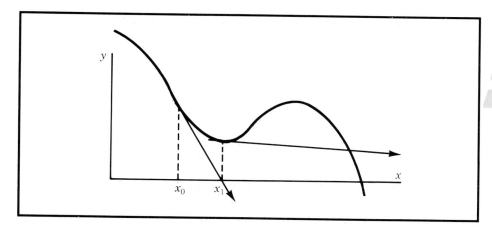

Figure 11-8
Starting Newton's method near a local minimum may cause it to fail.

Figure 11-9
A vertical slope
at a root will
cause Newton's
method to fail.

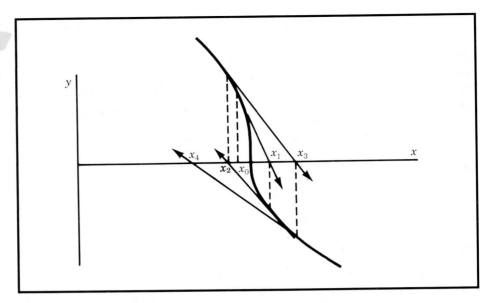

3. The method may have difficulties with multiple roots (see Figure 11-10).
At the position of a multiple root, both $f(x)$ and $f'(x)$ are zero and we would
anticipate that the algorithm would fail in attempting to compute
$\Delta x = -f/f' \to 0/0$.

These problems must be anticipated in writing the Fortran code that
implements Newton's method, and if encountered the program should print
a diagnostic message identifying the problem. The first class of problem is
easily corrected by starting over with a better first guess, perhaps suggested
by a rough sketch of the function. The problem associated with multiple
roots cannot be corrected so easily and requires a special procedure.

Figure 11-10
The function and
its slope are both
zero at a multiple
root.

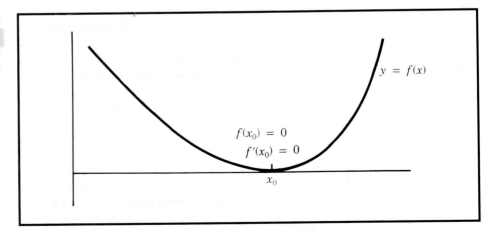

11.3.4 Multiple Roots

We have predicted that Newton's method will fail at a multiple root because of the operation of dividing zero by zero. Of course, dividing anything by zero on the computer is forbidden. However, in mathematics the operation $0/0$ is *not* forbidden; it is simply an *undetermined form*. That is, $0/0$ is neither zero nor infinity. It has no numerical value whatever until it is defined to be a specific value in a particular problem. So perhaps the anticipated problem is not a problem at all. As always, the best way to determine whether or not the problem exists is to carefully carry out a step-by-step calculation.

Consider the function

$$f(x) = (x - 1)^4 \sin(x) \tag{11.17}$$

which has a multiple root of multiplicity 4 at $x = 1.0$. The derivative of the function is

$$f'(x) = 4(x - 1)^3 \sin(x) + (x - 1)^4 \cos(x) \tag{11.18}$$

which is also zero at $x = 1.0$. Applying Newton's method with an initial guess of $x_0 = 0.5$ results in the following:

Step	x	$f(x)$	$f'(x)$	$\Delta x = -f/f'$
0	0.50	0.2996	$-.1849$	0.1620
1	0.66	0.0080	$-.0850$	0.0947
2	0.757	0.0024	$-.0369$	0.0650
3	0.822	0.00074	$-.0159$	0.0465
...	...	...	...	...
24	0.99960	2.2×10^{-13}	-2.2×10^{-9}	0.00010
25	0.99970	7.1×10^{-14}	-9.4×10^{-10}	0.00007

We see, in this example at least, that Newton's method will converge to the correct root, although the rate of convergence is torturously slow. The problem of a possibility of $0/0$ never appeared, since even though $f'(x)$ does approach zero, $f(x)$ does as well and at a faster rate.

In addition to suffering from a slow convergence rate for multiple roots, Newton's method may yield a result that is invalidated by round-off error caused when both f and f' are extremely small. To amend the procedure we begin by noting that if $f(x)$ has a multiple root of multiplicity m at $x = r$, then $f(x)$ can formally be written as

$$f(x) = (x - r)^m g(x) \tag{11.19}$$

Since we as yet do not know the value of r, $g(x)$ is likewise unknown. We can, however, assume that $g(x)$ is *not* zero (or extremely small) at $x = r$. Then applying Newton's method with an initial guess of x_0 near r, we have

$$f(x_0) = (x_0 - r)^m g(x_0)$$

and

$$f'(x_0) = m(x_0 - r)^{m-1} g(x_0) + (x_0 - r)^m g'(x_0)$$

$$= (x_0 - r)^m g(x_0) \left[\frac{m}{x_0 - r} + \frac{g'(x_0)}{g(x_0)} \right]$$

(11.20)
$$= f(x_0) \left[\frac{m}{x_0 - r} + \frac{g'(x_0)}{g(x_0)} \right]$$

The assumptions we have made regarding x_0 and $g(x)$ ensure that the first term in the brackets in Equation (11.20) is much larger than the second. Thus we can approximate this equation as

(11.21)
$$f'(x_0) \simeq f(x_0) \frac{m}{x_0 - r}$$

Solving this for the root r, we obtain

(11.22)
$$r = x_0 - m \frac{f(x_0)}{f'(x_0)}$$

which is almost the same as the original Newton algorithm. The only difference is that for a function with a root of multiplicity m, the replacement $x \rightarrow x - f/f'$ becomes $x \rightarrow x - mf/f'$.

As a test of this procedure, the root of the earlier function in Equation (11.17) is recomputed below. The multiplicity of the root at $x = 1.0$ is 4.

Step	x	f(x)	f'(x)	$\Delta x = -4f/f'$
0	0.500	0.02996	−0.1848	0.6483
1	1.1483	0.000442	0.0121	−0.1459
2	1.00243	2.9×10^{-11}	4.9×10^{-8}	−0.002432
3	1.00000094	6.7×10^{-25}	2.8×10^{-18}	−0.000000944
4	1.0000000000	3.5×10^{-52}	9.9×10^{-39}	-1.4×10^{-13}
5	1	9.7×10^{-107}	1.2×10^{-79}	-3.3×10^{-27}

Obviously the desired convergence rate has been restored with this simple amendment to Newton's method.

11.3.5   The Fortran Code for a Subroutine Implementing Newton's Method for Root Solving

The Fortran code for a subroutine that implements Newton's method for finding a root of a dummy function FNC(X) is given in Figure 11-11. The most important features of the subroutine are:

Figure 11-11 The Fortran code for a subroutine that implements Newton's method for root solving.

```
      SUBROUTINE NEWTON(X,EPS,IMAX,DXMAX,MULT,ROOT,F,DFDX,N)
*--
*-- NEWTON'S ALGORITHM
*--       XNEW = XOLD + DX
*-- WHERE
*--       DX  = -F(XOLD)/DFDX(XOLD)
*-- IS USED TO FIND A ROOT OF THE FUNCTION F(X). ADDITIONALLY,
*-- THE DERIVATIVE OF THE FUNCTION, CALLED DFDX, IS REQUIRED AS
*-- A CODED FUNCTION. THE INITIAL GUESS FOR THE ROOT IS X AND
*-- CONVERGENCE IS ATTAINED WHEN ABS(DX) < EPS. THE ADDITIONAL
*-- PARAMETERS ARE
*--           IMAX   --   THE MAXIMUM NUMBER OF ITERATIONS
*--           DXMAX  --   A LIMIT ON THE SIZE OF COMPUTED DX'S
*--           N      --   THE ACTUAL NUMBER OF ITERATIONS
*--                       (OUTPUT)
*--           MULT   --   THE ASSUMED MULTIPLICITY OF THE
*                         ROOT. (A SIMPLE ROOT HAS MULT = 1)
*--           ROOT   --   THE VALUE OF THE ROOT (OUTPUT)
*--------------------------------------------------------------
* INITIALIZE THE GUESS AND THE FUNCTION VALUES
*
      X1 = X
      I = 0
    1 F1 = F(X1)
      DF = DFDX(X1)
*--------------------------------------------------------------
*                 FAILURE DIAGNOSTICS
*                 CHECK THAT DF IS NOT ZERO
*
      IF(DF .EQ. 0.0)THEN
*
         WRITE(*,10)I,X1,F1
         STOP
*
*                 CHECK FOR EXCESSIVE ITERATIONS
*
      ELSE IF(I .GT. IMAX)THEN
*
         WRITE(*,11)I,X1,F1
         STOP
      END IF
*--------------------------------------------------------------
* COMPUTE IMPROVEMENT IN ROOT ESTIMATE, DX
*
      DX = -MULT * F1/DF
*
*                 CHECK FOR CONVERGENCE OR DIVERGENCE BASED
*                 ON SIZE OF DX
*
      IF(ABS(DX) .GT. DXMAX)THEN
*
*                 DX TOO LARGE, PROBABLY DIVERGING, STOP
*
         WRITE(*,12)I,X1,DX,F1
         STOP
      ELSE IF(I .NE. 0 .AND. ABS(DX) .GT. ABS(DX0))THEN
*
*                 DX IS INCREASING IN SIZE, PRINT WARNING
```

Continued

```
*                    BUT CONTINUE
*
        WRITE(*,13)I,X1,DX,DXO,F1
      END IF
*-------------------------------------------------------------
*              THE ONLY SUCCESS PATH IS IF DX < EPS
*
      IF(ABS(DX) .LT. EPS)THEN
         ROOT = X1
         N = I
         RETURN
      ELSE
         I = I + 1
         DXO = DX
         X1 = X1 + DX
      END IF
      GO TO 1
*-------------------------------------------------------------
* FORMATS
*
   10 FORMAT(5X,'---ERROR IN NEWTON---',/,20X,'IN THE ',I4,
     +       'TH STEP THE DERIVATIVE IS ZERO',/,20X,
     +       'THE CURRENT VALUE OF X = ',F10.4,/,20X,
     +       'AND F(X) = ',E10.3)
*
   11 FORMAT(5X,'---ERROR IN NEWTON---',/,20X,'AFTER ',I4,
     +       ' ITERATIONS CONVERGENCE NOT ACHIEVED',/,20X,
     +       'CURRENT X = ',F10.4,'AND F(X) = ',E10.2)
*
   12 FORMAT(5X,'---ERROR IN NEWTON---,/,20X,' IN THE ',I4,
     +       'TH STEP, DX IS GREATER THAN THE PRESCRIBED LIMIT',/,
     +       20X,'CURRENT X = ',F10.4,' CURRENT DX = ',F10.4,/,
     +       20X,'AND F(X) = ',E10.2)
*
   13 FORMAT(5X,'---WARNING FROM NEWTON---',/,20X,'IN THE ',I4,
     +       'TH STEP, AT X = ',F10.4,/,20X,'THE LATEST DX = ',
     +       E11.4,' IS LARGER THAN THE PREVIOUS DX = ',E11.4,/,
     +       20X,'WHILE F(X) = ',E10.2)
*
      END
```

1. Newton's method requires *two* functions FNC(X) and DFDX(X) be supplied in addition to the subroutine. If the function FNC(X) is quite complicated, its first derivative is most likely much worse and so using this procedure often requires considerable extra time and effort spent in programming the derivative function. In these cases it is probably more convenient to use the modified regula falsi method (if an interval containing a root is known) or the secant method (if only an initial guess for the root is known). The secant method will be discussed in Section 11.5.

2. The presumed multiplicity of the root is M. This will usually be 1, but the alteration discussed in the previous section to accommodate multiple roots is so easily incorporated that this extra parameter is included in the argument list.

3. The subroutine has four failure paths:
   a. IF iteration $> N_{max}$—STOP. Once again, statements of this type are always required in all iterative programs as a safety check to protect against a variety of programming errors. As with all abnormal exits, a diagnostic message is printed that includes the latest values of the variables.
   b. IF f' is identically zero—STOP. As a precaution, before the operation f/f' is attempted, the possibility of $f' = 0$ is checked. If it is zero, the program prints current values and stops. A likely source of the problem is in the coding of the derivative function.
   c. If the first correction to x is larger than a supplied maximum, (IF $|f/f'| > \Delta x_{max}$), it is presumed that the algorithm has jumped out of the region of interest and the program STOPs. Either a better first guess or a larger Δx_{max} should be tried next.
   d. If any correction Δx is *larger* in magnitude than the correction of the previous iteration, a warning statement is printed, and the subroutine RETURNs the current values of the variables. This situation most likely indicates that the process is diverging, but could also be caused by round-off error if Δx is very small.
4. One success path: If the magnitude of a correction ($\Delta x = -f/f'$) is less than the programmer supplied convergence criterion (EPS) the subroutine returns a value of the ROOT, the latest value of the increment DX and the number of iterations required N. We have already seen (Section 11.3.4) that a small value of $|f(x)|$ does not ensure that the root is closely bracketed, so a success path based on the size of the function is not included.

11.4   RATE OF CONVERGENCE[1]

In the problems considered thus far, Newton's method appears to converge faster than the procedures based on the bisection method, which is not surprising as the information content of the Newton algorithm is greater. This observation can be made more precise as follows: If the root of the function is labeled r, then the actual error in the nth iteration, ε_n, would be

$$x_n = r + \varepsilon_n \tag{11.23}$$

and

$$x_{n+1} = r + \varepsilon_{n+1}$$

where

---

[1] This section contains somewhat more advanced material and may be omitted without a loss of continuity.

$$x_{n+1} = x_n + \Delta x_n$$

$$\Delta x_n = -\frac{f(x_n)}{f'(x_n)}$$

and the change in the error in one step would therefore be

(11.24)
$$\varepsilon_{n+1} - \varepsilon_n = (x_{n+1} - x_n) = \Delta x_n = -\frac{f(x_n)}{f'(x_n)}$$

Expanding both $f(x_n)$ and $f'(x_n)$ in a Taylor series we obtain,

(11.25)
$$f(x_n) = f(r + \varepsilon_n) = f(r) + \varepsilon_n f'(r) + \tfrac{1}{2}\varepsilon_n^2 f''(r) + \cdots$$

(11.26)
$$f'(x_n) = f'(r + \varepsilon_n) = f'(r) + \varepsilon_n f''(r) + \tfrac{1}{2}\varepsilon_n^2 f'''(r) + \cdots$$

Since $f(r)$ is zero and ε_n is presumed small, we can approximate Equations (11.25) and (11.26) as

(11.27)
$$f(x_n) \simeq \varepsilon_n f'(r)\left[1 + \frac{1}{2}\varepsilon_n \frac{f''(r)}{f'(r)}\right]$$

(11.28)
$$f'(x_n) \simeq f'(r)\left[1 + \varepsilon_n \frac{f''(r)}{f'(r)}\right]$$

so that Equation (11.24) becomes

(11.29)
$$\varepsilon_{n+1} - \varepsilon_n \simeq = -\varepsilon_n \frac{1 + [\tfrac{1}{2}\varepsilon_n f''(r)/f'(r)]}{1 + [\varepsilon_n f''(r)/f'(r)]}$$

Next, using the expansion $(1 + \alpha)^{-1} = 1 - \alpha - \alpha^2 - \alpha^3 - \cdots$ $(\alpha \ll 1)$, this becomes,

$$\varepsilon_{n+1} - \varepsilon_n = -\varepsilon_n\left[\left(1 + \frac{1}{2}\varepsilon_n \frac{f''(r)}{f'(r)}\right)\left(1 - \varepsilon_n \frac{f''(r)}{f'(r)} - \left[\varepsilon_n \frac{f''(r)}{f'(r)}\right]^2 - \cdots\right)\right]$$

(11.30)
$$\simeq -\varepsilon_n\left[1 - \frac{1}{2}\varepsilon_n \frac{f''(r)}{f'(r)}\right]$$

So that we finally obtain

(11.31)
$$\varepsilon_{n+1} \simeq \frac{1}{2}\varepsilon_n^2 \frac{f''(r)}{f'(r)}$$

or

(11.32)
$$\varepsilon_{n+1} = \mathcal{O}(\varepsilon_n^2)$$

Thus if the error in the nth step is 0.3, the error in the next step should be roughly 0.09. The convergence of Newton's method is then said to be of second order. If you scan the numerical results obtained thus far in this section, you will see that this is more or less satisfied if the root is not a multiple root.

It can similarly be shown that the bisection-based algorithms are first-order convergent, i.e., $\varepsilon_{n+1} \propto \varepsilon_n$. This means that the improvement in each step is by a constant factor.[2]

11.5 THE SECANT METHOD

The principal disadvantage in using Newton's method is that you must supply the code for *two* functions, $f(x)$ and $f'(x)$. Frequently, the task of finding the root of a function will be only an incidental part of a larger problem and it may be inconvenient or distracting to take the time to code a separate function. In these cases you may wish to simply make use of some root-solving subroutine that you have in your personal library that only requires the function $f(x)$ in its argument list. If an interval containing a root is known, the modified regula falsi method would be suitable. If such an interval is not known, or if the faster convergence rate of Newton's method is important, we could still use the basic Newton algorithm but let the computer attempt to compute the derivative numerically. Of course, the computer will only determine approximate values for the derivative which means that some information about the function is being lost and so this procedure will not be quite as rapidly convergent as Newton's method.

If we start with the basic ideas of Newton's method

$$x_1 = x_0 + \Delta x_0$$

$$\Delta x_0 = -\frac{f(x_0)}{f'(x_0)}$$

and use an approximate expression for the derivative,[3]

$$f'(x) \simeq \frac{f(x) - f(x - \Delta x)}{\Delta x} \tag{11.33}$$

we obtain the following:

---

[2] In the ordinary bisection method the interval containing the root is halved in each step, so the error in each iteration is likewise reduced by a factor of $1/2$.

[3] This is the first backward difference expression for the derivative; see Equation (10.46).

$$(11.34) \qquad x_1 = x_0 - \frac{f(x_0)}{f'(x_0)}$$

$$\simeq x_0 - \Delta x_0 \frac{f(x_0)}{f(x_0) - f(x_0 - \Delta x_0)}$$

$$= x_0 + \Delta x_0 \frac{1}{[f(x_0 - \Delta x_0)/f(x_0)] - 1}$$

$$= x_0 + \Delta x_1$$

where

$$(11.35) \qquad \Delta x_1 = \Delta x_0 \left[\frac{f(x_0 - \Delta x_0)}{f(x_0)} - 1 \right]^{-1}$$

The procedure then for using the secant method is

Start with an initial guess for a root, x_0, and a guess for an interval Δx_0 that may contain the root. (Note: It is not required that the root be in the interval $x_0 - \Delta x_0 \leftrightarrow x_0$; however, it is best if the actual root is "not too far" outside this interval.) Expressing the above equations in terms of the left and right ends of the interval, we have

$$x_1 = x_0 - \Delta x$$
$$f_1 = f(x_1)$$
$$x_r = x_0$$
$$1 \quad f_r = f(x_r)$$

Compute $\Delta x = \dfrac{\Delta x_0}{f_1/f_r - 1}$

IF $(|\Delta x| < \varepsilon)$ THEN
        Return with answer $= x_r$
ELSE
        redefine the interval
        $x_1 = x_r$
        $f_1 = f_r$
        $x_r = x_r + \Delta x$
        $\Delta x_0 = \Delta x$
        GO TO 1
END IF

Since the secant method is based on Newton's method it will possess similar divergence problems and similar checks should be built into the Fortran code implementing this procedure. The secant method will likewise exhibit a slow convergence rate to a multiple root and the alterations to Newton's method to accommodate multiple roots could also be added to the secant method and will be found to be just as effective. It is left to the student to construct the Fortran subroutine for this procedure.

11.6 ROOT-SOLVING PROCEDURES FOR POLYNOMIALS[4]

All of the root-solving techniques discussed to this point can be used on any continuous function of a single variable, including polynomials. However, polynomial functions are special since the roots of polynomials must satisfy a variety of conditions that do not apply to transcendental or nonpolynomial functions. Many of these conditions are demonstrated in a high-school algebra course and are simply quoted below without proof.

11.6.1 Properties of the Roots of Polynomials

I. The Number of Roots of a Polynomial An nth-degree polynomial of the form

$$f(x) = a_n x^n + a_{n-1} x^{n-1} + \cdots + a_1 x + a_0 \tag{11.36}$$

where $a_n \neq 0$, has precisely n roots, which may be real or complex, single or multiple, and the complex roots always appear in pairs. That is, if

$$x_+ = a + ib \qquad a, b \text{ real}, i = \sqrt{-1}$$

is a root, then

$$x_- = a - ib$$

is also a root

II. Descartes' Rule of Signs If the number of sign changes of the coefficients of the polynomial is n, then

Positive Real Roots	The number of positive real roots is either n or n minus an even integer.
Negative Real Roots	The number of negative real roots is determined by rewriting the polynomial with $x \to -x$, counting the sign changes in the new polynomial, and applying the rule for positive roots.

For example, the equation

$$f(x) = x^4 - 5x^3 + 5x^2 + 5x - 6 = 0 \tag{11.37}$$

has three sign changes as we read the coefficients across $(+ \;-\; +\; +\; -)$, and thus will have either 3 or 1 real positive roots. The equation with x replaced by $-x$,

---

[4] This section contains somewhat more advanced material and may be omitted without a loss of continuity.

$$f(-x) = x^4 + 5x^3 + 5x^2 - 5x - 6 = 0$$

has only one sign change in the coefficients and so there must be one negative real root. The roots of this polynomial are $+1$, $+2$, $+3$, and -1.

III. Newton's Relations Newton derived a collection of relations between the coefficients of a polynomial and various sums and products of the roots. Two of these relations are

(11.38)
$$\frac{a_{n-1}}{a_n} = -(\text{sum of all roots})$$

(11.39)
$$\frac{a_0}{a_n} = (-1)^n(\text{product of all roots})$$

Thus in Equation (11.37) these relations yield

$$\frac{a_3}{a_4} = -\frac{5}{1} = -(1 + 2 + 3 - 1)$$

and

$$\frac{a_0}{a_4} = -\frac{6}{1} = (-1)^4[(1)(2)(3)(-1)]$$

There have been numerous root-solving techniques devised that employ the above properties of polynomial roots. Every one of these methods is superior to the more general methods discussed thus far in terms of rate of convergence, efficiency of computation, and freedom from divergences. However, they are usually much more complicated, and so in most instances it is preferable to use the slower but more familiar techniques. Occasionally, though, it may be necessary to find the root of a polynomial thousands of times, with the coefficients slightly altered each time. Clearly in such cases, rapid convergence becomes a critical consideration and more exotic, special techniques are called for. One of the simplest, the Birge-Vieta method, is discussed below. For other techniques specially suited to polynomials see *Mathematical Methods for Digital Computers*, A. Ralston and H. S. Wilf, editors, published by John Wiley, New York, 1967.

11.6.2 The Birge-Vieta Method for Roots of Polynomials

The Birge-Vieta method is nothing more than Newton's method using special properties of polynomials to evaluate the function and its first derivative efficiently. The procedure is based on the operation of synthetic division, which, to refresh your memory, is discussed below.

Synthetic Division To apply Newton's method to a polynomial, both the function and its first derivative must be evaluated at the initial estimate of the root x_0. We can write the polynomial $f(x)$ as

$$f(x) = (x - x_0)g(x) + R_1 \qquad (11.40)$$

where R_1 is the remainder of the division of $f(x)$ by $(x - x_0)$. Note that this remainder is equal to $f(x_0)$. Also if $f(x)$ is a polynomial of degree n, $g(x)$ is of degree $n - 1$.

Next, Equation (11.40) is differentiated to yield

$$f'(x) = g(x) + (x - x_0)g'(x) \qquad (11.41)$$

So $f'(x_0) = g(x_0)$. To evaluate $g(x_0)$, we write an equation similar to Equation (11.40).

$$g(x) = (x - x_0)h(x) + R_2 \qquad (11.42)$$

That is, R_2 is the remainder of the division of $g(x)$ by $(x - x_0)$. Thus once the two remainders have been determined,

$$\frac{f(x_0)}{f'(x_0)} = \frac{R_1}{R_2}$$

The remainders will be computed by using synthetic division. Writing the two polynomials in terms of their coefficients, we obtain

$$
\begin{aligned}
f(x) &= a_n x^n + a_{n-1} x^{n-1} + \cdots + a_1 x + a_0 \\
&= (x - x_0)(b_{n-1} x^{n-1} + b_{n-2} x^{n-2} + \cdots + b_1 x + b_0) + R_1 \\
&= b_{n-1} x^n + (b_{n-2} - x_0 b_{n-1}) x^{n-1} + (b_{n-3} - x_0 b_{n-2}) x^{n-2} + \cdots \\
&\qquad\qquad\qquad + (b_0 - x_0 b_1)x + (R_1 - x_0 b_0) \qquad (11.43)
\end{aligned}
$$

Since Equation (11.43) is an identity, true for all x, the coefficients of each power of x may be independently equated; thus

$$
\begin{aligned}
b_{n-1} &= a_n \\
b_{n-2} &= a_{n-1} + x_0 b_{n-1} \\
b_{n-3} &= a_{n-2} + x_0 b_{n-2} \\
\cdots &\quad \cdots \\
b_1 &= a_2 + x_0 b_2 \\
b_0 &= a_1 + x_0 b_1 \\
R_1 &= a_0 + x_0 b_0
\end{aligned}
$$

For example, to obtain the remainder of dividing Equation (11.37) by $(x - 5)$ these relations would yield (Note: $a_4 = 1$, $a_3 = -5$, $a_2 = +5$, $a_1 = +5$, $a_0 = -6$)

$$b_3 = a_4 = 1$$
$$b_2 = (a_3 + x_0 b_3) = [-5 + 5(1)] = 0$$
$$b_1 = (a_2 + x_0 b_2) = [5 + 5(0)] = 5$$
$$b_0 = (a_1 + x_0 b_1) = [5 + 5(5)] = 30$$
$$R_1 = (a_0 + x_0 b_0) = [-6 + 5(30)] = 144$$

Thus $f(5) = R_1 = 144$. All the coefficients b_i in the polynomial $g(x)$ have also been determined so we can divide once more to obtain the second remainder R_2.

$$g(x) = (x - x_0)(c_{n-2}x^{n-2} + c_{n-3}x^{n-3} + \cdots + c_1 x + c_0) + R_2$$
$$c_{n-2} = b_{n-1}$$
$$c_{n-3} = (b_{n-2} + x_0 c_{n-2})$$
$$c_{n-4} = (b_{n-3} + x_0 c_{n-3})$$

etc.

Using the values obtained for the b_i's yields

$$c_2 = b_3 = 1$$
$$c_1 = (b_2 + x_0 c_2) = [0 + 5(1)] = 5$$
$$c_0 = (b_1 + x_0 c_1) = [5 + 5(5)] = 30$$
$$R_2 = (b_0 + x_0 c_0) = [30 + 5(30)] = 180$$

Thus Newton's method would generate the next estimate for the root as

$$x_1 = x_0 - \frac{R_1}{R_2} = 5 - \frac{144}{180} = 4.2$$

The Fortran Code for the Birge-Vieta Method

The algebraic procedure outlined above may appear a bit awkward, but the Fortran code that implements it is amazingly short and efficient.

Assuming that the coefficients of the polynomial $f(x)$ have been stored in an array A(0 : N), the algorithm would be

$x_0 = $ initial guess
$b_{n-1} = a_n$

$$\text{DO } 1 \; i = n - 2, 0, -1$$
$$b_i = a_{i+1} + x_0 b_{i+1}$$
1 CONTINUE
$$R_1 = a_0 + x_0 b_0$$
$$c_{n-2} = b_{n-1}$$
$$\text{DO } 2 \; i = n - 3, 0, -1$$
$$c_i = b_{i+1} + x_0 c_{i+1}$$
2 CONTINUE
$$R_2 = b_0 + x_0 c_0$$

But, a little thought reveals that *all* the b_i's are not needed to compute an individual c_i and so the two loops can be combined.

$$x_0 = \cdots$$
$$b_{n-1} = a_n$$
$$c_{n-2} = b_{n-1}$$
$$\text{DO } 1 \; i = n - 2, 1, -1$$
$$b_i = a_{i+1} + x_0 b_{i+1}$$
$$c_{i-1} = b_i + x_0 c_i$$
1 CONTINUE
$$b_0 = a_1 + x_0 b_1$$
$$R_1 = a_0 + x_0 b_0$$
$$R_2 = b_0 + x_0 c_0$$

Furthermore, none of the coefficients b_i, c_i are needed after R_1 and R_2 are obtained, so it is unnecessary to store them in an array. Thus the final Fortran version of the program segment to compute R_1 and R_2 would simply be

```
      XO  =  ...
      B  =  A(N)
      C  =  B
      DO 1 I  =  N  -  2,  1,  -1
          B  =  A(I + 1)  +  XO*B
          C  =  B           +  XO*C
1     CONTINUE
      B    =  A(1)  +  XO*B
      R1   =  A(0)  +  XO*B
      R2   =  B       +  XO*C
```

Of course, the Birge-Vieta method will require exactly the same number of iterations to converge as would an ordinary Newton's method; the advantage is that in each iteration only elementary arithmetic operations are employed, no exponentiation, and the algorithm will therefore be significantly more efficient in computing each Δx.

11.7   COMPARISON OF ROOT-SOLVING METHODS

To find a root of a function, the first step is to learn as much as possible about the behavior of the function. A graph, if possible, is strongly suggested. This information is then used to select one of the root-solving techniques. Basically there are two classes of algorithms, depending on whether you are starting with an interval containing a root or with an initial estimate of the root. The bisection-based procedures begin with an interval that is known to contain a root and are guaranteed to converge to a prescribed bracketing of the root. Of these methods, the modified regula falsi is the fastest-converging and is recommended.

If only an initial estimate of the root is the starting point, the algorithms based on Newton's method must be used. If the function and its first derivative are not too complicated, the basic Newton method is suggested as the most rapidly converging. Of course, the code must contain safeguards for the several sources of divergence possible in Newton's method along with diagnostic PRINT statements. If the root is presumed to be a multiple root, the algorithm can be easily adapted to incorporate this possibility.

If the function and its first derivative are complicated and coding the derivative function would present a potential source of error, the secant method is suggested. The same safeguards that apply to Newton's method should be built into the secant code.

If the function is a polynomial and an efficient code is essential, the Birge-Vieta method is suggested.

> **A Reminder Concerning EXTERNAL Statements**   If any of the procedures discussed in this chapter are coded in the form of a Fortran subroutine, the references within the subroutine to the function should be to a dummy function—e.g., F(X) or FNC(X). The subroutine is then called from a main program to compute the root of a specific function—e.g., SPEED(T). In the CALL statement, the actual function name (say, SPEED) is used and this name *must* be declared EXTERNAL at the beginning of the program.
>
> ```
>     EXTERNAL SPEED
>          • • •
>     CALL REGFAL(A,B,EPS,IMAX,ANSWER,SPEED)
> ```

Additionally, the root-solving subroutines will be expecting a function with a single variable in its argument list. Your functions should then be constructed in this form with any additional parameters that the function requires passed through a COMMON statement.

PROBLEMS

1. Roughly reproduce the sketch in Figure 11-12 and then graphically apply the regula falsi method for three iterations.
2. Using a pocket calculator, apply the regula falsi procedure for three iterations to the following functions:

    a. $f(x) = xe^{-x^2} - \cos(x)$ $a = 0, b = 2$; exact root = 1.351491185 . . .

    b. $g(x) = x^2 - 2x - 3$ $a = 0, b = 4$; exact root = 3.0
    c. $h(x) = e^x - (1 + x + x^2/2)$ $a = -1, b = 1$; exact root = 0.0
    d. $F(x) = x^3 - 2x - 5$ $a = 1, b = 3$; exact root = 2.0945514815 . . .

    e. $G(x) = 10 \ln(x) - x$ $a = 1, b = 2$; exact root = 1.1183255916 . . .

3. Roughly reproduce Figure 11-12 and then graphically apply the modified regula falsi method for three iterations.
4. Apply the modified regula falsi method to one of the functions of Problem 2 first using a reduction factor of 0.75 and then a factor of 0.9. Comment on the difference in the two calculations.
5. In the figure sketched in Figure 11-13, the exact roots of the function are located at $x = 3.1, 8.0$, and 12.0. In attempting to find the roots of this function what are the probable results of the calculation if:
    a. The initial guess is 5.2 and Newton's method is used?

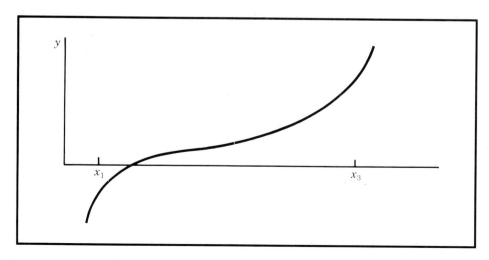

Figure 11-12
The function for Problem 11.1.

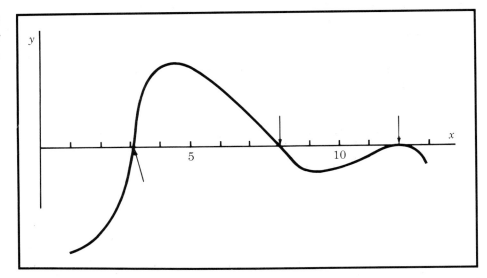

Figure 11-13
The function for
Problem 11.5.

b. The initial guess is 6.2 and Newton's method with a multiplicity factor $M = 2$ is used?

c. The initial guess is 3.0 and Newton's method is used?

d. The regula falsi method with $x_1 = 6.0$ and $x_3 = 12.8$ is used?

e. The secant method is used with an initial guess of $x_0 = 10.0$ and an interval of $\Delta x_0 = 1.0$.

6. The values of the function

$$f(x) = x^3 - 5.5x^2 + 9.68x - 5.324$$

Table 11-2
Tabulated values
of the function in
Problem 11.6

x	f(x)
0.0	−5.324
0.25	−3.23
0.50	−1.64
0.75	−0.74
1.00	−0.14
1.25	+0.14
1.50	+0.20
1.75	+0.13
2.00	+0.04
2.25	+0.003
2.50	+0.13
2.75	+0.50
3.00	+1.22
3.25	+2.37

are tabulated below. The function has one multiple root and one single root.

a. From the tabulated values estimate the vicinity of the *multiple* root. Which is the best method to use to improve the estimate of this root? Explain.

b. Find the multiple root accurate to six significant figures.

7. Show, by using Newton's method, that if x_0 is a guess for the value of the nth root of a number C, then an improved guess is

$$x_0 = \frac{1}{n}\left[(n-1)x_0 + \frac{C}{x_0^{n-1}}\right]$$

(Hint: Show that this problem is the same as finding the root of the equation $f(x) = x^n - C$)

8. In the not-too-distant past mechanical calculators were available that could multiply but not divide. Use Newton's method to devise a scheme that does not employ division to iteratively calculate the inverse of a number C beginning with an initial guess x_0. (The condition on the initial guess is that $(2 - x_0 C)$ be positive.)

9. Given the function $f(x) = x^2 - 2xe^{-x} + e^{-2x}$

a. Start at $x = 0$, step along the x axis in steps of 0.2 until you have determined the vicinity of the root. Then after establishing an initial guess for the root, apply Newton's method for four iterations.

b. In part a you should have concluded that the root was a multiple root. Thus, redo the calculation this time including the modification to Newton's method for a root of multiplicity 2. Is the accuracy improved?

c. Write a program that duplicates the above calculation. That is, the program should step along the axis, determine an initial guess for a root, *and* determine whether the root is likely to be a multiple root. Note: This function will not change sign. Monitor the function with a test like

$$\text{IF}(|f_{\text{new}}| < |f_{\text{old}}|) \text{ THEN}$$

10. Write the Fortran code for a subroutine SECANT which is to find the root of a dummy FNC(X) using the secant method of Section 11.5. The call to the subroutine should be of the form

CALL SECANT(X0,DX0,EPS,IMAX,MULT,ROOT,FNC)

and a value of the ROOT is returned when $|DX| <$ EPS. The code should contain appropriate safeguards.

11. Roughly reproduce the sketch in Figure 11-14 and graphically apply the secant method with an initial guess of $x_0 = 0.6$ and $\Delta x_0 = 0.4$.

12. Apply the secant method to find the root of the function

$$f(x) = e^{-x^2} - \cos(x) \qquad x \text{ is in radians}$$

Figure 11-14
Graphically apply
the secant
method to this
function

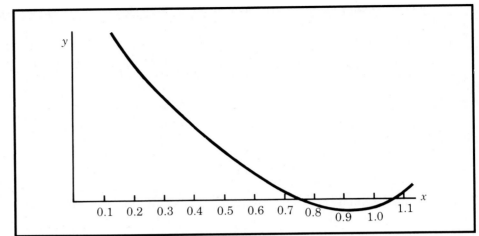

with $x_0 = 1.5$ and $\Delta x_0 = 0.1$. Note the exact root, $1.447414271 \ldots$, is not in the interval x_0 to $x_0 + \Delta x_0$. Make a table of x_0, Δx_0, $f(x_0 - \Delta x_0)$, $f(x_0)$, Δx_1. Carry out three iterations.

13. In this problem you are to estimate the roots of a polynomial without using a calculator or a computer. You may use Newton's relations, the sign rules of Descartes and the values of the functions at $x = 0$ and ± 1,

   a. Determine all four roots of the function $f(x) = x^4 + 6x^3 + 3x^2 - 10x$.

   b. Show that the function $g(x) = 8x^3 + 12x^2 + 14x + 9$ has only one real root and that it is in the interval $x = -1$ to $x = 0$.

   c. Use the value of the derivative of the function $h(x) = x^4 - 2x^3 + 2x^2 - 2x + 1$ at one of the real roots to determine the three remaining roots.

   d. Show that the function $g(x) = x^4 + 7.7x^3 + 39.1x^2 + 14.4x - 13$ has only one positive real root and one negative real root, and that the positive real root is less than one. Also show that the real part of the complex roots is greater than 3.3.

14. Apply the Birge-Vieta method for three iterations to one of the polynomials in the previous problem starting from an appropriate initial guess.

PROGRAMMING ASSIGNMENT V

The Determination of the Diffusion Constant

The diffusion of one fluid into another is a phenomenon that is of great importance in several areas of engineering, especially chemistry and chemical engineering. The rate at which diffusion takes place is governed by the diffusion constant D, which represents the average rate of unit displacement by a fluid particle. One of the most common methods of measuring the diffusion constant is to fill a small capillary tube with one liquid, immerse the tube in a second liquid, and measure the concentration of molecules of one fluid as it diffuses into the other as a function of time. This may be done by labeling the intruder fluid with radioactive isotopes or by simply observing the color change of, for example, ink diffusing into water.

The relationship between the concentration at a later time, $C(t)$, and the initial concentration at time $t = 0$, C_0 is given by the equation

$$\frac{C(t)}{C_0} = \frac{8}{\pi^2} \sum_{k=0}^{\infty} \frac{1}{(2k + 1)^2} \exp\left[-\frac{(2k + 1)^2 \pi^2 D t}{4L^2}\right] \qquad \textbf{(V.1)}$$

where L = length of the capillary tube (m)

   t = time (sec)

Once the concentrations $C(t)$, C_0, are measured, this equation is then solved for the diffusion constant D.

Problem Specifics

Write and execute a computer program that will

1. Read the parameters required by the root-solving routine, namely, EPS,

the convergence criterion; IMAX, the maximum number of iterations; SMALL, criterion for terminating the sum in Equation (IV.1); NMAX, the maximum number of terms that are to be included in a sum; DXMAX, the largest permitted correction in the Newton algorithm.

2. Read the measured ratio of concentrations $C(t)/C_0$, at a time t, the time, the length of the tube L, and the name of the intruder fluid. Echo print with appropriate labels.

3. Code Equation (V.1) as a function of a single variable DIFF(D). The other parameters should be passed to the function via a labeled COMMON statement. The function should sum the series until the absolute value of a term is less than SMALL.

4. Code a second function DDIF(D), which is the first derivative of the function DIFF(D). Recall

$$\frac{d(e^{ax})}{dx} = ae^{ax}$$

so that

(V.2) $$\text{DDIF}(D) = \frac{d[\text{DIFF}(D)]}{dD} = \frac{2t}{L^2} \sum_{k=0}^{\infty} \exp\left[\frac{-(2k+1)^2 \pi^2 Dt}{4L^2}\right]$$

Again you will need a COMMON statement and to terminate the sum when terms are less than SMALL.

5. Code two subroutines NEWTON and REGFAL which implement the Newton and modified regula falsi procedures. The convergence criterion would be on the size of the x increment (here D) or the x interval. Both subroutines should have adequate safeguards.

6. Solve for the root of Equation (V.1) twice, once with the Newton subroutine and next with the modified regula falsi method. For each solution print the root, the number of iterations required, the value of the function at the root.

Suggested Input Data

$$\text{Ratio} = C(t)/C_0 = 0.5$$

$$\text{Time} = t = 43{,}200 \text{ sec}$$

$$L = 0.1 \text{ m}$$

$$I_{\max} = 40$$

$$\text{EPS} = 10^{-13}$$

$$\text{SMALL} = 10^{-7}$$

$$\text{NMAX} = 50$$

$$\Delta x_{\max} = 10^{-6}$$

Initial search interval	$(x_1 = 10^{-8})$ to $(x_3 = 10 \times 10^{-8})$	
Initial guess for root	$x_0 = 3 \times 10^{-8}$	
Name of liquid	= cadmium sulfide	

The complete Fortran code for this problem is given in Figure V-1 and the results are presented in Figure V-2.

Figure V-1 The Fortran program for the calculation of the diffusion constant.

```
      PROGRAM DIFUZE
*--
*-- THIS PROGRAM WILL DETERMINE THE DIFFUSION CONSTANT THAT DES-
*-- CRIBES DIFFUSION OF ONE LIQUID INTO ANOTHER. THE RATIO OF
*-- THE CONCENTRATION OF LIQUIDS IS EQUAL TO AN INFINITE SERIES
*-- THAT INVOLVES THE DIFFUSION CONSTANT. THIS RELATION IS THEN
*-- SOLVED FOR THE DIFFUSION CONSTANT TWICE: FIRST BY NEWTON'S
*-- METHOD AND THEN BY THE MODIFIED REGULA FALSI METHOD.
*-- THE RELATION IS GIVEN IN THE FUNCTION DIFF(D) AND THE DERIV-
*-- ATIVE OF THIS FUNCTION IS DDIF(D). BOTH OF THESE FUNCTIONS
*-- MUST BE DECLARED AS EXTERNAL
*-------------------------------------------------------------------
* VARIABLES
*
      REAL RATIO,T,L,EPS,SMALL,DXMAX,X0,X1,X3,ROOTN,ROOTRF
      INTEGER IMAX,NMAX,MULT,NNEWT,NRF
      CHARACTER*15 NAME
*
      COMMON/PARAM/PI,L,T,RATIO,NMAX,SMALL
      EXTERNAL DIFF,DDIF
*
*          RATIO    --   EXPERIMENTAL RATIO OF CONCENTRATIONS
*          T        --   TIME OF THE MEASUREMENT (SECONDS)
*          L        --   LENGTH OF DIFFUSION TUBE
*          IMAX     --   MAXIMUM NUMBER OF ITERATIONS
*          NMAX     --   MAXIMUM NUMBER OF TERMS IN SUMS
*          EPS      --   CONVERGENCE CRITERION FOR ROOT-SOLVERS
*          SMALL    --   CONVERGENCE CRITERION FOR SUMS
*          MULT     --   MULTIPLICITY OF ROOT (1)
*          DXMAX    --   MAXIMUM SIZE OF DX PERMITTED IN
*                        NEWTON'S METHOD
*          X1,X3    --   INITIAL INTERVAL IN REGULA FALSI
*          X0       --   INITIAL GUESS IN NEWTON METHOD
*          ROOTN    --   ROOT RETURNED BY NEWTON'S METHOD
*          ROOTRF   --   ROOT RETURNED BY MOD. REGULA FALSI
*          NNEWT    --   ACTUAL NUMBER OF ITERATIONS IN NEWTON
*          NRF      --   ACTUAL NUMBER OF ITERATIONS IN MOD.
*                        REGULA FALSI METHOD
*          NAME     --   NAME OF THE DIFFUSING LIQUID
*-------------------------------------------------------------------
```

Continued

```
*  INITIALIZATION
*
      WRITE(*,*)'ENTER INTEGERS FOR IMAX,NMAX'
      READ(*,*)IMAX,NMAX
      WRITE(*,*)'ENTER CONVERGENCE CRITERION EPS,SMALL,DXMAX'
      READ(*,*)EPS,SMALL,DXMAX
      WRITE(*,*)'ENTER INTERVAL AND INITIAL GUESS, X1,X3,X0'
      READ(*,*)X1,X3,X0
      WRITE(*,*)'ENTER VALUES FOR TUBE LENGTH, TIME, ',
     +          'CONCENTRATION RATIO'
      READ(*,*)L,T,RATIO
      WRITE(*,*)'ENTER NAME OF LIQUID'
      READ(*,'(A)')NAME
      MULT = 1
      PI = ACOS(-1.)
*
*               ECHO-PRINT ALL INPUT QUANTITIES
*
      WRITE(*,10)IMAX,EPS,MULT,DXMAX,X0
      WRITE(*,11)IMAX,EPS,X1,X3
      WRITE(*,12)NMAX,SMALL
      WRITE(*,13)NAME,T,L,RATIO
*  COMPUTATION
*
      CALL NEWTON(X0,EPS,IMAX,DXMAX,MULT,ROOTN,DIFF,DDIF,NNEWT)
      CALL REGFAL(X1,X3,EPS,IMAX,ROOTRF,DIFF,NRF)
*
*------------------------------------------------------------------
*  RESULTS
*
      WRITE(*,14)ROOTN,NNEWT
      WRITE(*,15)ROOTRF,NRF
*------------------------------------------------------------------
*  FORMATS
*
   10 FORMAT(//5X,'THE PARAMETERS REQUIRED BY NEWTONS ALGORITHM'
     +        ,/,T10,'MAXIMUM NO. OF ITERATIONS',T40,'= ',I4
     +        ,/,T10,'CONVERGENCE CRITERION',T40,'= ',E8.1
     +        ,/,T10,'MULTIPLICITY OF ROOT',T40,'= ',I2
     +        ,/,T10,'LARGEST PERMITTED DX',T40,'= ',E9.2
     +        ,/,T10,'INITIAL GUESS',T40,'= ',E9.2)
*
   11 FORMAT(//,5X,'THE PARAMETERS REQUIRED BY THE MODIFIED',
     +        ' REGULA FALSI ALGORITHM ARE'
     +        ,/,T10,'MAXIMUM NO. OF ITERATIONS',T40,'= ',I4
     +        ,/,T10,'CONVERGENCE CRITERION',T40,'= ',E8.1
     +        ,/,T10,'INITIAL INTERVAL, ',E9.2,' TO ',E9.2)
*
   12 FORMAT(//,5X,'PARAMETERS REQUIRED TO TERMINATE A SUM'
     +        ,/,T10,'MAXIMUM NUMBER OF TERMS',T40,'= ',I4
     +        ,/,T10,'CUT-OFF WHEN TERM LESS THAN',T40,E8.1)
*
   13 FORMAT(//,5X,'EXPERIMENTAL PARAMETERS',//,
     +        T10,'THE NAME OF THE LIQUID IS',T40,A,//,
     +        T10,'TIME OF THE EXPERIMENT',T40,'= ',F9.0,'SEC'
     +        ,/,T10,'LENGTH OF TUBE',T40,'= ',F8.2,'METERS',//,
     +        T10,'CONCENTRATION RATIO',T40,'= ',F7.4)
*
   14 FORMAT(///,5X,'RESULTS OF THE CALCULATION USING ',
     +        'NEWTONS ALGORITHM',//,
     +        T10,'THE DIFFUSION CONSTANT IS',T40,E14.7,//,
     +        T10,'THE CALCULATION TOOK',T40,I4,' ITERATIONS')
*
```

```
   15 FORMAT(///,5X,'RESULTS OF THE CALCULATION USING ',
     +          'THE MODIFIED REGULA FALSI ALGORITHM',//,
     +          T10,'THE DIFFUSION CONSTANT IS ',T40,E14.7,/,
     +          T10,'THE CALCULATION TOOK',T40,I4,' ITERATIONS')
*
      END
*-----------------------------------------------------------------
      FUNCTION DIFF(X)
      REAL L
      COMMON/PARAM/PI,L,T,RATIO,NMAX,SMALL
      SUM = 0.0
      K = 0
    1 EXPON = (2.*K + 1.) * PI/2./L
      TERM = EXP(-EXPON**2 * X * T)/(2. * K + 1.)**2
*
*              THE SUM IS TERMINATED WHEN THE TERMS
*              ARE LESS THAN THE QUANTITY (SMALL)
*
      IF(ABS(TERM) .GT. SMALL)THEN
        SUM = SUM + TERM
        K = K + 1
*
*              IF THE SUM HAS NOT CONVERGED AFTER
*              NMAX TERMS, THE PROGRAM STOPS
*
        IF(K .GT. NMAX)THEN
          WRITE(*,*)'AFTER ',NMAX,' TERMS, THE SUM IN DIFF',
     +              ' HAS NOT CONVERGED, LATEST X = ',X
          STOP
        ENDIF
        GO TO 1
      ELSE
        SUM = SUM * 8./PI**2
        DIFF = RATIO - SUM
        RETURN
      END IF
      END
******************************************************************************
      SUBROUTINE REGFAL(XA,XC,EPS,IMAX,ROOT,F,ITER)
*
```

See Figure 11-4

```
      END
******************************************************************************
      FUNCTION DDIF(X)
      REAL L
      COMMON/PARAM/PI,L,T,RATIO,NMAX,SMALL
      SUM = 0.0
      K = 0
    1 EXPON = (2. * K + 1.) * PI/2./L
      TERM = EXP(-EXPON**2 * X * T)
*
*              THE SUM IS TERMINATED WHEN THE TERMS
*              ARE LESS THAN THE QUANTITY (SMALL).
*
      IF(ABS(TERM) .GT. SMALL)THEN
        SUM = SUM + TERM
        K = K + 1
*
*              IF THE SUM HAS NOT CONVERGED AFTER NMAX
*              TERMS, THE PROGRAM STOPS.
```

Continued

```
*
      IF(K ,GT, NMAX)THEN
          WRITE(*,*)'AFTER ',NMAX,' TERMS, THE SUM IN DDIF',
     +             ' HAS NOT CONVERGED, LATEST X = ',X
        STOP
      END IF
      GO TO 1
    ELSE
      SUM = SUM * 2, * T/L**2
      DDIF = SUM
      RETURN
    END IF
    END
*************************************************************************
      SUBROUTINE NEWTON(X,EPS,IMAX,DXMAX,MULT,ROOT,F,DFDX,N)
*
              See Figure 11-11

      END
*************************************************************************
```

Figure V-2 The output from the diffusion constant problem.

```
ENTER INTEGERS FOR IMAX,NMAX 40, 50
ENTER CONVERGENCE CRITERION EPS,SMALL,DXMAX 1.E-13, 1.E-7,1.E-6
ENTER INTERVAL AND INITIAL GUESS, X1,X3,X0, 1.E-8, 10.E-8, 3.E-8
ENTER VALUES FOR TUBE LENGTH, TIME,CONCENTRATION RATIO 0.1, 43200,, 0.5
ENTER NAME OF LIQUID CADMIUM SULFIDE

    THE PARAMETERS REQUIRED BY NEWTONS ALGORITHM
        MAXIMUM NO, OF ITERATIONS      =   40
        CONVERGENCE CRITERION          =  .1E-12
        MULTIPLICITY OF ROOT           =  1
        LARGEST PERMITTED DX           =  .10E-05
        INITIAL GUESS                  =  .30E-07

    THE PARAMETERS REQUIRED BY THE MODIFIED REGULA FALSI ALGORITHM ARE
        MAXIMUM NO, OF ITERATIONS      =  40
        CONVERGENCE CRITERION          =  .1E-12
        INITIAL INTERVAL,   .10E-07 TO .10E-06

    PARAMETERS REQUIRED TO TERMINATE A SUM
        MAXIMUM NUMBER OF TERMS        =   50
        CUT-OFF WHEN TERM LESS THAN     .1E-06

    EXPERIMENTAL PARAMETERS

        THE NAME OF THE LIQUID IS     CADMIUM SULFIDE
        TIME OF THE EXPERIMENT        =  43200,SEC
        LENGTH OF TUBE                =   .10METERS
        CONCENTRATION RATIO           =  .5000


    RESULTS OF THE CALCULATION USING NEWTONS ALGORITHM

        THE DIFFUSION CONSTANT IS       .4553952E-07
        THE CALCULATION TOOK            3 ITERATIONS
```

V.2   PROGRAMMING PROBLEMS

Programming Problem A: Civil Engineering and Mechanics: The Buckling of a Tall Mast

A standard, but complex, problem in civil engineering and mechanics is the determination of how tall a mast can be before it will begin to buckle under its own weight. The solution of this problem which is usually covered in an advanced mechanics course,[1] yields the following result.

Defining the following quantities:

L = mast length (m)
Y = Young's modulus of the material (N/m^2). Young's modulus is an experimental value of the ratio of the size of a deformation to the applied force.
λ = mass per unit length of the mast (kg/m)
    (Note: λ = density $\times$ cross-sectional area of the mast)
I_2 = the second area moment of inertia of the mast given as
    $\pi r^4/2$, where r is the radius of the round mast
x = a dimensionless parameter that is related to the above quantities by

$$x = \frac{4}{9} g \frac{\lambda L^3}{Y I_2} \qquad g = 9.8 \text{ m/sec}^2$$

It is found that the mast will just begin to buckle when x has the value corresponding to the smallest positive root of the function

$$F(x) = \sum_{n=0}^{\infty} a_n x^n \tag{V.3}$$

where

$$a_0 = 1 \tag{V.4}$$

$$a_1 = -\frac{3}{4}\left(\frac{1}{2} a_0\right) = -\frac{3}{8}$$

$$a_2 = -\frac{3}{4}\left(\frac{1}{10} a_1\right) = +\frac{9}{320}$$

---

[1] See, for example, S. Timoshenko, *Strength of Materials,* Part I, Van Nostrand, Princeton, N.J., 1955.

$$a_{n+1} = -\frac{3}{4} \frac{1}{(n+1)(3n+2)} a_n$$

The problem is then to find the first root of Equation (V.3), say x_1, and once this value is determined, to specify the maximum lengths of a mast for a variety of materials. The root-solving technique to be used is the secant method, and the program will have to step in small increments of x starting at zero to first determine the vicinity of the root.

Problem Specifics

1. Write the Fortran code for a subroutine SECANT. The subroutine should contain adequate safeguards and should be accessed by a call of the form

    ```
    CALL SECANT(X0,DX0,IMAX,EPS,ROOT,ITER,F)
    ```

    where the answer returned for the root of the function F(X) is ROOT and the actual number of iterations required is ITER.
2. Write the Fortran code for the function in Equation (V.3). The summation should terminate when the absolute value of a term is less than 10^{-6}. The summation algorithm should relate $(\text{Term})_{n+1}$ to $(\text{Term})_n$, and the function should have appropriate safeguards.
3. The input data are given in Table V-1 and should be read from a data file. Assume that all masts have a radius of $r = 0.1$ meter.
4. The output consists of:
    a. The initial guess for x_0, and Δx_0
    b. The computed value of the root, the value of the function at the root, and the number of iterations required.
    c. For each of the materials in Table V-1, list the following
       (1) The name of the material
       (2) The density ρ
       (3) The mass per unit length λ
       (4) Young's modulus Y

Table V-1 Young's modulus and density values for various materials.

Material	Young's Modulus, Y (N/m²)($\times 10^{10}$)	Density, ρ (kg/m³)($\times 10^3$)
Aluminum (cast)	5.6–7.7	2.70
Brass	9.02	8.44
Gold	7.85	19.3
Iron (cast)	8.4–9.8	7.86
Lead	1.5–1.67	11.0
Platinum	16.7	21.4
Steel	20.0	7.83
Tin	3.9–5.39	7.29
Tungsten	35.5	18.8

(5) The second area moment I_2

(6) The maximum height of a mast of this material

Programming Problem B: Mining Engineering: Depth of a Flume

A flume is a simple trough used in mining and various other material-handling operations to transport water and tailings. A rectangular flume is illustrated in Figure V-3.

The rate of flow of a liquid in such a device is given approximately by the Chezy-Manning equation,

$$Q = \frac{1}{\sigma} A R^{2/3} S^{1/2} \tag{V.5}$$

where Q = liquid flow rate in the channel (m³/sec)

σ = channel roughness coefficient

A = cross-sectional area of the channel

R = hydraulic radius (area A divided by the wetted perimeter)

S = slope of the channel (rise over run)

h = depth of the water in the channel (m)

For a rectangular channel, $A = wh$ and $R = wh/(w + 2h)$, so Equation (V.5) can be written as

$$Q = \frac{wh}{\sigma} \left(\frac{wh}{w + 2h} \right)^{2/3} S^{1/2} \tag{V.6}$$

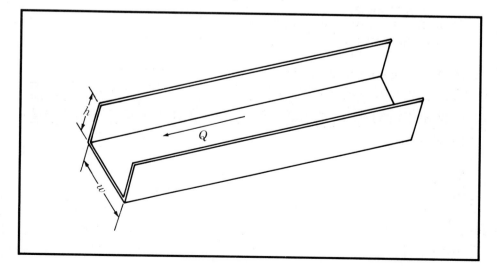

Figure V-3
A rectangular flume for transporting water.

If you cube Equation (V.6) and multiply by $(w + 2h)^2$, a fifth-degree polynomial in h will result.

(V.7)
$$a_5 h^5 + a_2 h^2 + a_1 h + a_0 = 0$$

where

(V.8)
$$a_5 = \frac{1}{\sigma^3} w^5 S^{3/2}$$

$$a_2 = -4Q^3$$

$$a_1 = -4Q^3 w$$

$$a_0 = -Q^3 w^2$$

$$a_4 = 0$$

$$a_3 = 0$$

Thus, once the coefficients in this polynomial are determined, the root of Equation (V.7) can be determined to obtain the appropriate depth to be used in designing the flume.

Problem Specifics

Write a computer program that will:

1. Read the input data (Q, σ, w, S) from a data file and print with appropriate labels. (Use $\sigma = 0.05$ and reasonable values for Q, w, S.)
2. Compute and print the coefficients of the polynomial a_n.
3. Step-in h values starting at $h = 0.0$ in steps of 0.05 m to find the first estimate of the root of Equation (V.7). Print the first estimate of the root.
4. Write a general-purpose subroutine that employs the Birge-Vieta method for obtaining the root of a polynomial of degree n. The subroutine should have appropriate safeguards and should terminate successfully if the root is bracketed by a tolerance of 10^{-5}. The maximum number of iterations in the routine should be 30.
5. Find the root of Equation (V.7) and neatly print the results.

Programming Problem C: General Engineering: Functions Describing Diffusion

Diffusion is a process that is encountered in most areas of science and engineering. It describes the movement of neutrons through a nuclear reactor, the transport of heat through materials, the intrusion of one fluid into an adjacent fluid, the propagation of a disturbance in a line of freeway traffic, and numerous other phenomena. The solution for each case depends on the specifics of the problem, but the mathematical function describing diffusion is always a function that decays exponentially in time and the dependence on the coordinates is a function of the geometry of the problem. A particularly simple geometry is that of a sphere.

Consider the problem of a sphere of radius a which is at an initial temperature of T_0. If the material is characterized by a diffusivity α^2 and it is placed in 0 °C air, the sphere will slowly cool by convection and radiation.[2] If the rate of temperature decrease at the surface is characterized by an experimental constant h, the solution for the temperature at the center of the sphere is

$$T_c = T_0\left(\frac{ah}{\sigma}\right)\sum_{n=1}^{\infty} C_n\, e^{-\beta_n^2 t} \tag{V.9}$$

where

$$\beta_n^2 = \theta_n \frac{\alpha^2}{a^2} \tag{V.10}$$

$$C_n = \frac{4\sin(\theta_n)}{2\theta_n - \sin(2\theta_n)} \tag{V.11}$$

and θ_n is the nth root of the equation

$$\tan(\theta_n) = \frac{1}{1 - (ah/\sigma)}\,\theta_n \tag{V.12}$$

The values of the physical parameters to use in this problem are

$$T_0 = 250\ °C$$
$$\alpha^2 = 1.2 \times 10^{-5}\ \text{m}^2/\text{sec}$$
$$h = 23.0\ \text{W/m}^2\text{-}°C$$
$$\sigma = 46.0\ \text{W/m-}°C$$
$$a = 0.1\ \text{m}$$

and the problem is to determine and tabulate the first 10 roots of Equation (V.12) and then to use Equation (V.9) to compute the the temperature at the center of the sphere for values of time $t = 0$ to $t = 3600$ sec (1 hour) in steps of 60 sec.

Problem Specifics

1. Code a Fortran function subprogram NEWTON,

---

[2] The diffusivity of a material is defined as

$$\alpha^2 = \frac{\text{thermal conductivity}}{(\text{specific heat})(\text{density})} = \frac{\lambda}{C\rho}$$

that will return the root (ROOT) of the arbitrary function $f(x)$. The subprogram will start with an initial guess x_0, and also requires the derivative of $f(x)$, vis. $df\,dx(x)$. The maximum number of iterations is I_{max} and the convergence criterion based on Δx is eps.

2. Since Newton's method will be used to find the roots, you will have to code function subprograms for a function based on Equation (V.12) and a second Fortran function for the derivative. Note, the derivative of the tangent is

$$\frac{d\,(\tan(x))}{dx} = \frac{1}{\cos^2(x)}$$

3. The main program should start with $\theta_1 = 0.1$, step in values of 0.1 until Eq. (V.12) changes sign, then CALL NEWTON to find the first root. The first root is easily found to be near 0.4. You must be extremely careful in searching for the remaining 9 roots. If you continue to step in θ, you will find that the function changes sign as θ crosses $\pi/2$ but does *NOT* go through zero. That is, $\tan(\pi/2) = \infty$ and the function is not continuous. From a sketch of both sides of Eq. (V.12) you can see that the subsequent roots are slightly to the left of multiples of $\pi/2$. For all roots after the first you should begin with the initial guess:

(V.13)
$$\theta_n \simeq \left(n - \frac{1}{2}\right)\pi\left[1 - \frac{1}{(n-1/2)^2\pi^2k^2}\right] \qquad n = 2, 3, \ldots, 9$$

where

$$k = 1 - \left(\frac{ah}{\sigma}\right)$$

4. Once the 10 roots have been computed and neatly printed, the sum in Eq. (V.9) is to be evaluated for each value of time and the value printed and stored in the array TCENTR.

5. Finally, execute a printer-plot of TCENTR vs. time.

Programming Problem D: Mechanical Engineering: Fluid Flow and Implicit Functions

The slow smooth flow of a fluid through a pipe is rather well understood in terms of the basic principles of fluid dynamics. However, as the velocity of flow is increased, a moderately abrupt transition takes place in which the properties of the fluid change from relatively simple to extremely complex. Small eddies are set up in the flow and the friction characterizing the flow increases dramatically. This transition is called the transition from laminar to turbulent flow. Turbulent flow is not understood to this day; in fact, it is called the last unsolved major problem of classical physics.

A quantity that is used to tag the transition from laminar to turbulent flow is called the *Reynold's number,* which for fluid flowing in a smooth pipe is given by

$$R = \frac{rv}{\mu} \tag{V.14}$$

where r is the radius of the pipe, v the velocity of the fluid flow, and μ is the viscosity of the fluid.

The Reynold's number is a dimensionless quantity. For a Reynold's number greater than 1000, turbulent flow is likely to occur. An empirical relation between the coefficient of fluid friction with the pipe c_f and the Reynold's number is

$$\frac{1}{c_f^{1/2}} = 4.04 + 3.94 \ln(Rc_f^{1/2}) \tag{V.15}$$

We wish to make a table of c_f vs. R values. We could easily solve Equation (V.15) for R as a function of c_f; but to solve for c_f as a function of R is quite difficult. Instead, we could specify a value of R and then solve for a root of Equation (V.15). So, the problem is to write a program that will

1. For values of $R = 10^3$ to 10^5 in steps of 5000, solve Equation (V.15) for c_f.
2. You should use Newton's method, which means that you will have to construct the Fortran code for the function represented by Equation (V.15) as well as a function representing the derivative of this equation with respect to c_f. Recall that

$$\frac{d[\ln(ax)]}{dx} = \frac{1}{x}$$

3. The main program should determine an initial guess for the first calculation by stepping in values of c_f, starting at $c_f = 0.001$ in steps of 0.0005, and check for a change in sign of the equation.
4. For each subsequent calculation, the program should use the most recent value of c_f as the initial guess for the next step.
5. Print the values of c_f vs. R neatly in a table.

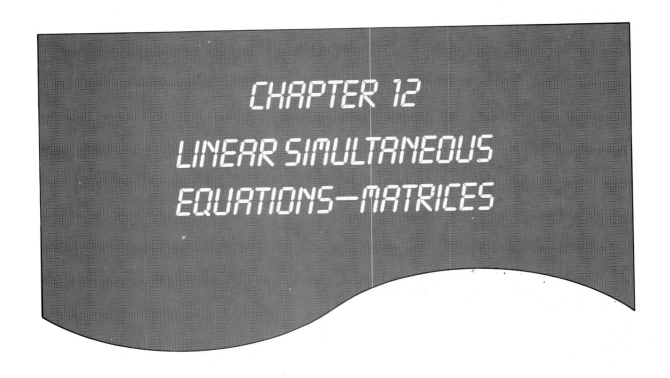

CHAPTER 12
LINEAR SIMULTANEOUS EQUATIONS—MATRICES

12.1 INTRODUCTION

From the earliest days of the computer age it was clear that one type of problem that was particularly well suited to a machine-aided solution was the solution of numerous simultaneous equations in many unknowns. In every real problem, there are numerous variables to consider and changes in any one will affect all the others. If the relationships between all of the variables can be expressed in terms of many equations in which no variable appears with a power higher than one, the problem is then appropriate for the field of mathematics called *linear algebra* or *matrices*. This branch of mathematics was invented long before the computer to simplify the structure of multivariable problems. Coupled with the computer, unimaginably huge problems involving many hundreds of variables have been solved, and the procedures have been extended in some special cases to nonlinear problems or problems involving inequalities in place of equations. The modern advances in this field are important in virtually all areas of engineering and science.

You have already studied the method of solution of two linear equations in two unknowns and perhaps three equations in three unknowns. Beyond that, except in very special circumstances, a solution by hand calculation becomes terribly tedious. To develop machine codes for the more complicated situations, we will, as always, carefully step through the simpler calculation and attempt to generalize the procedures.

The keystone in the development will be the introduction of a new notation to simplify the statement of the problem. This notation is called matrices. I cannot emphasize too strongly the importance that simplifying notations have had in the progress of science, mathematics, and engineering. A notation that makes it possible to distinguish the forest from the trees is essential in most problems.

12.2   THE NOTATION OF MATRICES

The utility of a new notation for handling simultaneous equations is best illustrated by the following common mathematical ploy. We begin by solving a trivial example. Then in successive stages, the example is generalized to accommodate a much broader set of problems. The generalized problem then leads into a variety of new considerations. Here, this will mean the multiplication of matrices and a discussion of determinants.

12.2.1   Square Matrices and Column Vectors

Recall how you would solve two equations in two unknowns. For example,

$$3x - 1y = 7 \tag{12.1}$$
$$2x - 4y = -2 \tag{12.2}$$

One method of attack might involve subtraction of a multiple of one equation from the other with the hope of eliminating one of the variables. Thus multiplying Equation (12.2) by $\frac{3}{2}$, the pair of equations becomes

$$3x - 1y = 7$$
$$3x - 6y = -3 \tag{12.3}$$

Next, replacing Equation (12.3) by Equation (12.3) minus Equation (12.1) yields

$$3x - 1y = 7$$
$$5y = 10 \tag{12.4}$$

and the solution for y is $y = 2$. Substituting this value back into the first equation then determines the solution for x.

$$3x - 1(2) = 7$$
$$3x = 9$$

Thus the solution to the original two equations is the number pair $(x, y) = (3, 2)$.

The reason that such a trivial example has been treated in such detail is that we intend to construct a much more general procedure that is based on the elementary operations just carried out on the simple two equations with two unknowns problem. As a first step in this direction, the original equations are rewritten a bit more formally as

(12.5)
$$a_{11}x_1 + a_{12}x_2 = b_1$$
$$a_{21}x_1 + a_{22}x_2 = b_2$$

where comparison with the earlier pair of equations leads to the assignments

$$\begin{pmatrix} a_{11} & a_{12} \\ a_{21} & a_{22} \end{pmatrix} = \begin{pmatrix} 3 & -1 \\ 2 & -4 \end{pmatrix} \quad \begin{pmatrix} b_1 \\ b_2 \end{pmatrix} = \begin{pmatrix} 7 \\ -2 \end{pmatrix} \quad \begin{pmatrix} x_1 \\ x_2 \end{pmatrix} = \begin{pmatrix} x \\ y \end{pmatrix}$$

Notice that with this notation the two equations can be written

$$\sum_{j=1}^{2} a_{1j}x_j = b_1 \qquad \text{new Equation (12.1)}$$

$$\sum_{j=1}^{2} a_{2j}x_j = b_2 \qquad \text{new Equation (12.2)}$$

Or both equations can even be written simultaneously as

(12.6)
$$\sum_{j=1}^{2} a_{ij}x_j = b_i$$

so that if $i = 1$ is substituted in Equation (12.6), Equation (12.1) is duplicated, and if $i = 2$, Equation (12.2) is duplicated.

For a problem involving only two unknowns, this is rather a waste of time, since the solution was obtained so easily without a new notation. However, for more complicated problems the process of replacing the coefficients in the equations by a single variable name with two subscripts (a_{ij}) and all the variables by a single variable name with a single subscript (x_i) will make a significant difference. Consider a problem involving five equations in five unknowns

(12.7)
$$7v + 2w + 1x - 1y + 5z = 7$$
$$2v + 0w - 4x - 2y + 1z = 2$$
$$0v - 4w + 1x - 6y - 1z = 2$$

$$-3v + 0w + 0x - 2y + 9z = 20$$

$$3v + 3w + 3x + 3y + 3z = 1$$

If we replace the variable names (v, w, x, y, z) with $(x_1, x_2, x_3, x_4, x_5)$ and let the set of coefficients in the problem be collectively called a_{ij} with $i = 1, 5$ and $j = 1, 5$; and the constants on the right-hand side be identified as b_i, $i = 1, 5$; the entire set of equations can be written as

$$\sum_{j=1}^{5} a_{ij}x_j = b_i$$

where the identification of the number sets a_{ij}, b_i are

$$a_{ij}$$

col #					
j	1	2	3	4	5

row #
i

7	2	1	-1	5
2	0	-4	-2	1
0	-4	1	-6	-1
-3	0	0	-2	9
3	3	3	3	3

$$b_i$$

row #
i

7
2
2
20
1

The elements of the square array of numbers a_{ij} are specified by the *row* and *column* of a location in the array. That is the elements of a_{ij} are labeled $a_{row,\ col}$. Thus a_{45} (fourth row, fifth column) is 9. To duplicate, say, the fourth equation in the set of Equations (12.7) from the array of numbers, we use the fourth *rows* of both a_{ij} and b_i to get

$$\sum_{j=1}^{5} a_{4j}x_j = -3x_1 + 0x_2 + 0x_3 - 2x_4 + 9x_5 = 20 \tag{12.8}$$

One of the tedious aspects in writing the set of Equations (12.7) is that the variable names are written repeatedly and unnecessarily. Thus, if it is agreed that the first variable in each equation is always v (or x_1) we could eliminate the variable names from the equation, and the set could be written in block form

$$
\begin{array}{ccccc}
x_1 & x_2 & x_3 & x_4 & x_5
\end{array}
\qquad\qquad b_i
$$

$$
\begin{pmatrix}
7 & 2 & 1 & -1 & 5 \\
2 & 0 & -4 & -2 & 1 \\
0 & -4 & 1 & -6 & -1 \\
-3 & 0 & 0 & -2 & 9 \\
3 & 3 & 3 & 3 & 3
\end{pmatrix}
=
\begin{pmatrix}
7 \\
2 \\
2 \\
20 \\
1
\end{pmatrix}
$$

The set of numbers in the square array on the left, i.e., a_{ij}, is called a *square matrix*. The numbers on the right, b_i, form a *column* matrix,[1] or a *vector*. The variables x_i could also be grouped as a column matrix. In a drastic simplification of the original set of equations, we could symbolically write Equation (12.7) as

(12.9)
$$[A]\mathbf{x} = \mathbf{b}$$

where the symbol $[A]$ is used to represent the entire array a_{ij} and $\mathbf{x}, \mathbf{b}$ are used to represent the column vectors x_i, b_i.

Of course the key to understanding Equation (12.9) as representing the entire set of Equations (12.7) is in the specification of precisely what is meant by the multiplication in Equation (12.9).

12.2.2 Multiplication of Matrices

The multiplication of a square matrix times a column matrix, as in Equation (12.9), is defined as follows: If we take the fourth *row* of the matrix $[A]$ and multiply each element in turn by a corresponding element of the column matrix $\mathbf{x}$, and successively add the products of elements, then the result is equal to the fourth element (or fourth row) of the column matrix $\mathbf{b}$. That is,

$$
\begin{pmatrix}
7 & 2 & 2 & -1 & 5 \\
2 & 0 & -4 & -2 & 1 \\
0 & 4 & 1 & -6 & -1 \\
\boxed{-3 & 0 & 0 & -2 & 9} \\
3 & 3 & 3 & 3 & 3
\end{pmatrix}
\begin{pmatrix}
x_1 \\
x_2 \\
x_3 \\
x_4 \\
x_5
\end{pmatrix}
=
\begin{pmatrix}
7 \\
2 \\
2 \\
\boxed{20} \\
1
\end{pmatrix}
$$

or

---

[1] In general, a matrix is any rectangular array of numbers. The elements of the array are arranged by rows and columns and are enclosed in curved lines.

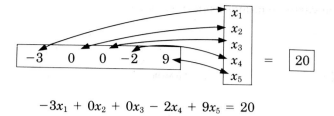

$$-3x_1 + 0x_2 + 0x_3 - 2x_4 + 9x_5 = 20$$

which duplicates the fourth equation of Equations (12.7). The first of Equations (12.7) is duplicated by multiplying element by element and summing the *first* row of $[A]$ by $\mathbf{x}$ and setting the result equal to the *first* element of $\mathbf{b}$. In this way we can reconstruct all of the original equations from the notation $[A]\mathbf{x} = \mathbf{b}$.

This procedure for multiplying a square matrix times a column matrix can easily be generalized to multiplying a square matrix by a square matrix of like size.

$$
\underset{[A]}{\begin{pmatrix} a_{11} & a_{12} & a_{13} \\ a_{21} & a_{22} & a_{23} \\ a_{31} & a_{32} & a_{33} \end{pmatrix}} \cdot \underset{[B]}{\begin{pmatrix} b_{11} & b_{12} & b_{13} \\ b_{21} & b_{22} & b_{23} \\ b_{31} & b_{32} & b_{33} \end{pmatrix}} = \underset{[C]}{\begin{pmatrix} c_{11} & c_{12} & c_{13} \\ c_{21} & c_{22} & c_{23} \\ c_{31} & c_{32} & c_{33} \end{pmatrix}}
\tag{12.10}
$$

Now in Equation (12.9) we obtained the (*i*th row - 1st column) element of $\mathbf{b}$ by multiplying the *i*th row of $[A]$ by the 1st column of $\mathbf{x}$. Of course, in that case the vectors $\mathbf{x}$ and $\mathbf{b}$ have only one column. The generalized multiplication implied in Equation (12.10) could be defined analogously as

$$c_{ij} = (i\text{th row of } [A])\,(j\text{th column of } [B])$$

or

$$
c_{23} = \begin{pmatrix} a_{11} & a_{12} & a_{13} \\ \boxed{a_{21} \quad a_{22} \quad a_{23}} \\ a_{31} & a_{32} & a_{33} \end{pmatrix} \begin{pmatrix} b_{11} & b_{12} & \boxed{b_{13}} \\ b_{21} & b_{22} & \boxed{b_{23}} \\ b_{31} & b_{32} & \boxed{b_{33}} \end{pmatrix}
$$

$$= a_{21}b_{13} + a_{22}b_{23} + a_{23}b_{33} = \sum_{j=1}^{3} a_{2j}b_{j3}$$

Each of the nine elements of the matrix $[C]$ is defined in a similar fashion. All nine equations defining the elements of $[C]$ can be succinctly written as

$$c_{ij} = \sum_{k=1}^{3} a_{ik}b_{kj}
\tag{12.11}$$

Matrix multiplication defined in this manner can obviously be generalized to square matrices of any size.

The following example illustrates the rather surprising fact that matrix multiplication in general is not commutative. Consider the four-square 3 by 3 matrices

$$[A] = \begin{pmatrix} 0 & 0 & 0 \\ 0 & 0 & 1 \\ 0 & 1 & 0 \end{pmatrix} \qquad [B] = \begin{pmatrix} 0 & 0 & -1 \\ 0 & 0 & 0 \\ 1 & 0 & 0 \end{pmatrix}$$

$$[C] = \begin{pmatrix} 0 & -1 & 0 \\ 1 & 0 & 0 \\ 0 & 0 & 0 \end{pmatrix} \qquad [I_3] = \begin{pmatrix} 1 & 0 & 0 \\ 0 & 1 & 0 \\ 0 & 0 & 1 \end{pmatrix}$$

The matrix $[I_3]$ is called the 3 by 3 *identity* matrix and it is easily shown that for any 3 by 3 matrix $[M]$

$$[I_3][M] = [M][I_3] = [M]$$

Identity matrices of arbitrary size are defined in a like manner, and all have the feature that there are ones on their main diagonal (the elements I_{ij} with $i = j$) and all other elements of the matrix are zero.

Next, if we evaluate the following matrix expression

$$[A][B] - [B][A]$$

we obtain

$$\begin{pmatrix} 0 & 0 & 0 \\ 0 & 0 & 1 \\ 0 & -1 & 0 \end{pmatrix} \begin{pmatrix} 0 & 0 & -1 \\ 0 & 0 & 0 \\ 1 & 0 & 0 \end{pmatrix} - \begin{pmatrix} 0 & 0 & -1 \\ 0 & 0 & 0 \\ 1 & 0 & 0 \end{pmatrix} \begin{pmatrix} 0 & 0 & 0 \\ 0 & 0 & 1 \\ 0 & -1 & 0 \end{pmatrix}$$

$$= \begin{pmatrix} 0 & 0 & 0 \\ 1 & 0 & 0 \\ 0 & 0 & 0 \end{pmatrix} - \begin{pmatrix} 0 & 1 & 0 \\ 0 & 0 & 0 \\ 0 & 0 & 0 \end{pmatrix} = \begin{pmatrix} 0 & -1 & 0 \\ 1 & 0 & 0 \\ 0 & 0 & 0 \end{pmatrix} = [C]$$

Since $[A][B] - [B][A]$ does not equal the null matrix (a matrix of like size containing all zeros), matrix multiplication is not in general commutative. It is left to you to show that matrix multiplication is, however, associative—i.e., $([A][B])[C] = [A]([B][C])$.

12.3   DETERMINANTS

All of the preceding discussion was concerned solely with matrix notation for sets of linear equations. We now return to the original problem of solving the equations. In the notation of matrices, the set of equations reads

$$[A]\,\mathbf{x} = \mathbf{b}$$

where $\mathbf{x}$ is the set of unknowns. The solution to this equation is then "obviously"

$$\mathbf{x} = \frac{\mathbf{b}}{[A]}$$

Well, not quite. We have defined multiplication of matrices, but division is quite a bit more difficult. For example, how would the rule prohibiting the division of a number by zero translate into the notation of matrices? We shall return to the problem of division of matrices shortly, but first we refer back to the simple problem of two equations in two unknowns for guidance in obtaining the general solution of the equation $[A]\,\mathbf{x} = \mathbf{b}$.

12.3.1 The Determinant of a 2 by 2 Matrix

Starting with

$$a_{11}x_1 + a_{12}x_2 = b_1 \tag{12.12}$$

$$a_{21}x_1 + a_{22}x_2 = b_2 \tag{12.13}$$

we could solve Equation (12.13) for x_2 and substitute that result into Equation (12.12) to obtain an expression for x_1 alone; x_2 could be found in a like manner. The result would be

$$x_1 = \frac{b_1 a_{22} - b_2 a_{12}}{a_{11} a_{22} - a_{21} a_{12}} \tag{12.14}$$

$$x_2 = \frac{b_2 a_{11} - b_1 a_{12}}{a_{11} a_{22} - a_{21} a_{12}} \tag{12.15}$$

Notice that the solutions for both x_1 and x_2 have the same denominator. This combination of coefficients is called the *determinant* of the 2 by 2 coefficient matrix $[A]$. The notation for a determinant is

$$\det[A] = |A| = \begin{vmatrix} a_{11} & a_{12} \\ a_{21} & a_{22} \end{vmatrix}$$

The determinant of the 2 by 2 matrix $[A]$ is a single number that can be evaluated from the matrix $[A]$ by drawing diagonals and then subtracting the products of elements along each diagonal.

$$\begin{vmatrix} a_{11} & a_{12} \\ a_{21} & a_{22} \end{vmatrix} = \begin{matrix} a_{11} & a_{12} \\ a_{21} & a_{22} \end{matrix} = (a_{11}a_{22}) - (a_{21}a_{12})$$

Clearly, if the determinant of $[A]$ is zero, a unique solution is not possible for x_1 and x_2.

12.3.2 The Determinant of a 3 by 3 Matrix

The entire process is next repeated for three equations in three unknowns, x_1, x_2, x_3. The third equation is solved for x_3 and is then substituted into the first two equations. The second of these is then solved for x_2, which is then substituted into the first. After considerable algebra, the following expressions for the solutions x_1, x_2, x_3 are obtained.

$$(12.16) \qquad x_1 = \frac{b_1(a_{22}a_{33} - a_{23}a_{32}) - b_2(a_{12}a_{33} - a_{13}a_{32}) + b_3(a_{12}a_{23} - a_{13}a_{22})}{a_{11}a_{22}a_{33} + a_{12}a_{23}a_{31} + a_{13}a_{32}a_{21} - a_{11}a_{23}a_{32} - a_{21}a_{12}a_{33} - a_{31}a_{22}a_{13}}$$

$$(12.17) \qquad x_2 = \frac{b_1(a_{23}a_{31} - a_{21}a_{33}) + b_2(a_{11}a_{33} - a_{13}a_{31}) + b_3(a_{13}a_{21} - a_{11}a_{23})}{a_{11}a_{22}a_{33} + a_{12}a_{23}a_{31} + a_{13}a_{32}a_{21} - a_{11}a_{23}a_{32} - a_{21}a_{12}a_{33} - a_{31}a_{22}a_{13}}$$

$$(12.18) \qquad x_3 = \frac{b_1(a_{21}a_{32} - a_{22}a_{31}) + b_2(a_{12}a_{31} - a_{11}a_{32}) + b_3(a_{11}a_{22} - a_{12}a_{21})}{a_{11}a_{22}a_{33} + a_{12}a_{23}a_{31} + a_{13}a_{32}a_{21} - a_{11}a_{23}a_{32} - a_{21}a_{12}a_{33} - a_{31}a_{22}a_{13}}$$

The results of the three equations in three unknowns problem are clearly much more complicated than were the 2 by 2 solutions. The main point to notice in the solutions is the appearance of the same denominator in all three expressions. Once again this combination of coefficients is called the determinant of the matrix $[A]$, where $[A]$ is now a square 3 by 3 matrix.

The determinant of a 3 by 3 matrix may be evaluated by a procedure somewhat like the evaluation of the 2 by 2 determinant. First the matrix is written out in rows and columns. Next the first two columns are duplicated on the right and diagonal lines drawn as shown below. The determinant is then evaluated as the product of elements along the diagonals with terms from parallel diagonals grouped. Finally, the value of the determinant is equal to the difference between the two groups of terms.

$$\det [A] = |A| = \begin{vmatrix} a_{11} & a_{12} & a_{13} \\ a_{21} & a_{22} & a_{23} \\ a_{31} & a_{32} & a_{33} \end{vmatrix} \begin{matrix} a_{11} & a_{12} \\ a_{21} & a_{22} \\ a_{31} & a_{32} \end{matrix}$$

$$(12.19) \qquad = (a_{11}a_{22}a_{33} + a_{12}a_{23}a_{31} + a_{13}a_{21}a_{32})$$

$$- (a_{31}a_{22}a_{13} + a_{32}a_{23}a_{11} + a_{33}a_{21}a_{12})$$

For example,

$$\begin{vmatrix} 1 & 3 & 2 \\ -2 & 1 & -1 \\ 0 & 1 & 4 \end{vmatrix} = \begin{vmatrix} 1 & 3 & 2 \\ -2 & 1 & -1 \\ 0 & 1 & 4 \end{vmatrix} \begin{matrix} 1 & 3 \\ -2 & 1 \\ 0 & 1 \end{matrix}$$

$$= +(4 + 0 - 4) - (0 - 1 - 24)$$

$$= +25$$

12.3.3 The Determinant of an *n* by *n* Matrix

The solution of four simultaneous equations similarly results in expressions for x_1, x_2, x_3, x_4 that are combinations of the coefficients divided by the determinant of the coefficient matrix $[A]$. Unfortunately, there is no simple method of drawing lines to calculate the determinant of a 4 by 4 matrix. To evaluate the determinant of a square matrix of arbitrary size, it is necessary to introduce a quantity called the *cofactor matrix*, which is denoted as $[A^c]$.

The Cofactor Matrix

If a_{ij} is an element of the matrix $[A]$, the *cofactor* of a_{ij}, designated as A^c_{ij}, is defined to be the product of the determinant of what is left of $[A]$ after deleting the *i*th row and *j*th column times the sign $(-1)^{i+j}$. Thus if

$$[A] = \begin{pmatrix} 1 & 3 & 2 \\ -2 & 1 & -1 \\ 0 & 1 & 4 \end{pmatrix}$$

then

$$A^c_{11} = (-1)^2 \begin{pmatrix} \cdots & \cdots & \cdots \\ \cdots & 1 & -1 \\ \cdots & 1 & 4 \end{pmatrix} = +1\,(4 + 1) = 5$$

$$A^c_{23} = (-1)^5 \begin{pmatrix} 1 & 3 & \cdots \\ \cdots & \cdots & \cdots \\ 0 & 1 & \cdots \end{pmatrix} = -1\,(1 - 0) = -1$$

The Determinant as a Sum Over Cofactors

It can be shown[2] that the determinant of a square matrix of arbitrary size is given by the equation

$$\det [A] = |A| = \sum_{j=1}^{n} a_{ij} A^c_{ij} \qquad \text{for any value of } i \qquad\qquad (12.20)$$

---

[2] See C. W. Curtis, *Linear Algebra*, Allyn and Bacon, Boston, 1963; or any textbook on linear algebra.

In Equation (12.20), i may be assigned any value from 1 to n and is usually chosen to be 1 for convenience. Using the matrix above, we find that $A_{11}^c = 5$, $A_{12}^c = 8$, and $A_{13}^c = -2$, so that

$$|A| = a_{11}A_{11}^c + a_{12}A_{12}^c + a_{13}A_{13}^c$$
$$= 1(5) + 3(8) + 2(-2) = 25$$

For example,

$$
\begin{vmatrix}
5 & -3 & 12 & 2 \\
6 & 4 & 8 & 6 \\
3 & -1 & 8 & -1 \\
4 & 2 & 12 & 4
\end{vmatrix}
= ⑤
\begin{pmatrix}
\cdots & \cdots & \cdots \\
4 & 8 & 6 \\
-1 & 8 & -1 \\
2 & 12 & 4
\end{pmatrix}
-
\begin{pmatrix}
\cdots & ③ & \cdots & \cdots \\
6 & \cdots & 8 & 6 \\
3 & \cdots & 8 & -1 \\
4 & \cdots & 12 & 4
\end{pmatrix}
$$

$$
+
\begin{pmatrix}
\cdots & \cdots & ⑫ & \cdots \\
6 & 4 & \cdots & 6 \\
3 & -1 & \cdots & -1 \\
4 & 2 & \cdots & 4
\end{pmatrix}
-
\begin{pmatrix}
\cdots & \cdots & \cdots & ② \\
6 & 4 & 8 & \cdots \\
3 & -1 & 8 & \cdots \\
4 & 2 & 12 & \cdots
\end{pmatrix}
$$

$$= 5(24) - (-3)(160) + 12(-16) - 2(-104) = 616$$

The 4 by 4 determinant is thus expressed as a sum over four 3 by 3 determinants. A 5 by 5 determinant would be written as five 4 by 4 determinants, each in turn written as four 3 by 3 determinants. Clearly, the labor involved in evaluating a determinant increases dramatically with the size of the determinant.

Properties of Determinants

Some useful properties of determinants are listed below without proof.[3]

1. A determinant is identically zero if
   a. All the elements of any one row (or one column) are zero.
   b. The elements of one row are identical to the elements (in the same order) of another row. The same rule applies to columns.
   c. Any one row is proportional to another row. The same rule applies to columns.
2. If all the elements of a row (or column) are multiplied by a constant c the value of the determinant is then multiplied by the same constant.
3. Any two rows (or any two columns) may be interchanged and the value of the determinant merely changes sign.
4. Adding a constant multiple of one row to a different row does not alter the value of the determinant. The same rule applies to columns.
5. Replacing rows by columns, i.e., $a_{ij} \rightarrow a_{ji}$ for all i, j, does not alter the value of the determinant.

---

[3] Each of these properties can be proved by using the expression for a determinant given in Equation (12.20).

Thus, the determinant

$$\begin{vmatrix} 1 & 0 & 1 \\ 3 & 1 & 2 \\ 4 & 1 & 3 \end{vmatrix} -$$

is "obviously" zero. This can be seen by replacing row 3 by $(\text{row}_3) - 1(\text{row}_2)$. This does not alter the value of the determinant and results in

$$\begin{vmatrix} 1 & 0 & 1 \\ 3 & 1 & 2 \\ 1 & 0 & 1 \end{vmatrix}$$

This determinant has two identical rows and is therefore zero.

Finally, how does all of this discussion about determinants relate to the original problem of solving simultaneous equations? Clearly, if the determinant of the coefficient matrix is zero, a solution of the equation $[A]\mathbf{x} = \mathbf{b}$ (probably) does not exist. Additionally, the ability to evaluate determinants of arbitrary size enables us to state the solution to many simultaneous linear equations in terms of an algorithm known as *Cramer's rule*.

12.4 CRAMER'S RULE

If a set of simultaneous linear equations is written in the form

$$[A]\mathbf{x} = \mathbf{b}$$

where $[A]$ is an n by n matrix, $\mathbf{b}$ is a column vector of n elements, and $\mathbf{x}$ is a column vector containing the n unknowns x_i, then the kth element of $\mathbf{x}$ is given by

$$x_k = \frac{|B(k)|}{|A|} \tag{12.21}$$

where $|\ \ |$ denotes a determinant and the matrix $[B(k)]$ is obtained from the matrix $[A]$ by replacing the kth column of $[A]$ by the column vector $\mathbf{b}$. For example,

$$[A]\,\mathbf{x} = \mathbf{b}$$

$$\begin{pmatrix} 3 & 1 & -1 \\ 1 & 2 & 1 \\ -1 & 1 & 4 \end{pmatrix} \begin{pmatrix} x_1 \\ x_2 \\ x_3 \end{pmatrix} = \begin{pmatrix} 2 \\ 3 \\ 9 \end{pmatrix} \tag{12.22}$$

The determinant $|A|$ is easily evaluated to be $|A| = +13$. To evaluate x_1, x_2, and x_3 by Cramer's rule, we must next evaluate the three determinants

$$|B(1)| = \begin{vmatrix} \cancel{3}2 & 1 & -1 \\ \cancel{1}3 & 2 & 1 \\ -\cancel{1}9 & 1 & 4 \end{vmatrix} \qquad |B(2)| = \begin{vmatrix} 3 & \cancel{1}2 & -1 \\ 1 & \cancel{2}3 & 1 \\ -1 & \cancel{1}9 & 4 \end{vmatrix}$$

$$= 26 \qquad\qquad\qquad = -13$$

$$|B(3)| = \begin{vmatrix} 3 & 1 & +\cancel{1}2 \\ 1 & 2 & \cancel{1}3 \\ -1 & 1 & \cancel{1}9 \end{vmatrix}$$

$$= 39$$

Cramer's rule then gives the solution as

$$\begin{pmatrix} x_1 \\ x_2 \\ x_3 \end{pmatrix} = \begin{pmatrix} 2 \\ -1 \\ 3 \end{pmatrix}$$

which can be verified by substituting back into Equation (12.22).

$$3x_1 + 1x_2 - 1x_3 = 3(2) + 1(-1) - 1(3) = 2 = b_1$$
$$1x_1 + 2x_2 + 1x_3 = 1(2) + 2(-1) + 1(3) = 3 = b_2$$
$$-1x_1 + 1x_2 + 4x_3 = -1(2) + 1(-1) + 4(3) = 9 = b_3$$

As a second example, you should obtain the solution to the equations,

$$\begin{pmatrix} 1 & -3 & 1 \\ -3 & 1 & 1 \\ 1 & 1 & -3 \end{pmatrix} \begin{pmatrix} x_1 \\ x_2 \\ x_3 \end{pmatrix} = \begin{pmatrix} 2 \\ 1 \\ 3 \end{pmatrix}$$

The result is

$$\begin{pmatrix} x_1 \\ x_2 \\ x_3 \end{pmatrix} = \begin{pmatrix} -7/4 \\ -2/2 \\ -9/4 \end{pmatrix} = -\frac{1}{4}\begin{pmatrix} 7 \\ 8 \\ 9 \end{pmatrix}$$

Cramer's rule is the most popular method of solution of simultaneous equations in introductory algebra. It is easy to remember and easy to use, provided the number of equations is no larger than three. For larger sets of equations the repeated evaluation of large determinants becomes hopelessly tedious. At this point you may have noticed that the word tedious is a "buzz word" to signal the introduction of a Fortran code to replace the hand calculation. Indeed, Cramer's rule can be coded to handle any number of simultaneous equations. There are two essential elements to such a code: first, a Fortran function, say

```
FUNCTION DET(A,N)
REAL A(N,N)
   ...
   ...
DET = ...
RETURN
END
```

is required to evaluate the determinant of an n by n matrix $[A]$. Such a function is not terribly difficult to construct, but it is not easy either. Second, we must be able to form the matrix $[B(k)]$ by replacing the kth column of $[A]$ by the column vector b, without destroying $[A]$ and then call the function DET(B(K),N). The bookkeeping required to keep track of all the index switching is rather formidable. You might try to write such a code for fun. However, there exists a much more efficient and transparent procedure for solving simultaneous equations which will be discussed in the next section.

The primary reason for bringing up Cramer's rule at all is that it clearly shows that to obtain a solution of the matrix equation $[A]\mathbf{x} = \mathbf{b}$, we must *divide* by the determinant of $[A]$. Thus, if $|A| = 0$, a solution may not exist.

Since the components of the solution vector x_k are determined from

$$x_k = \frac{|B(k)|}{|A|}$$

clearly if $|A| = 0$, the only way a solution can exist is if *all* the determinants $|B(k)|$ are likewise zero. (See Problem 12.6.) This is possible if, for example, the vector $\mathbf{b}$ is proportional to one of the columns of $[A]$. However, for an arbitrary right-hand-side vector, no solution exists for a set of equations with a coefficient matrix $[A]$ which has a determinant equal to zero. The set of equations is then called *singular*.

If $|A| = 0$, the matrix $[A]$ is called *singular*.

Often it is just as bad if $|A|$, even though not zero, is extremely small. In this case the results may be invalidated by round-off errors. We shall return to this situation in more detail in Chapter 16. The set of equations with a coefficient matrix that has a "small" determinant is labeled *ill-conditioned*. An obvious question is "Small compared to what?" One criterion might be to compare $|A|$ with the average of all the elements a_{ij}. If the elements of $[A]$ were typically of the order 10^{-18}, then a determinant of the order 10^{-16} could not be considered small.

So then, when solving a set of simultaneous linear equations, everything rides on the value of $|A|$. We shall shortly see that if $|A| \neq 0$, it is possible to construct a totally different matrix (call it $[A^{-1}]$) such that

$$[A][A^{-1}] = [A^{-1}][A] = [I]$$

where $[I]$ is the identity matrix. This matrix $[A^{-1}]$ is then the multiplicative inverse of the matrix $[A]$ and defines the operation of matrix division mentioned earlier.

Consider once again the set of equations written in matrix form

$$[A]\mathbf{x} = \mathbf{b}$$

If the matrix $[A^{-1}]$ exists and is known, the solution of this equation is then trivial. Simply multiply both sides by $[A^{-1}]$ to obtain

$$[A^{-1}][A]\mathbf{x} = [A^{-1}]\mathbf{b}$$
$$[I]\mathbf{x} = [A^{-1}]\mathbf{b}$$

and the solution vector is then given by the equation,

$$\mathbf{x} = [A^{-1}]\mathbf{b}$$

The operation of matrix division thus consists of determining the matrix $[A^{-1}]$. The procedure for doing this will be a simple extension of the most common method of solving simultaneous equations on a computer, the Gauss-Jordan method.

12.5 THE GAUSS-JORDAN METHOD OF SOLVING SIMULTANEOUS LINEAR EQUATIONS

Perhaps the most straightforward method of solving sets of linear equations is to simply add multiples of one equation to the others in such a way as to introduce zero coefficients in the matrix $[A]$. This is the procedure that we began with at the beginning of this chapter. This process, recast in an extremely systematic algorithm, is known as the *Gauss-Jordan method* and is the most common procedure for obtaining computer solutions to systems of linear simultaneous equations.

12.5.1 Development of the Gauss-Jordan Algorithm

To understand the Gauss-Jordan method in the context of a simple example, I once again return to the solution of the two equations that opened this chapter.

$$3x - 1y = 7 \qquad \text{(equation } \textcircled{1}\text{)}$$
$$2x - 4y = -2 \qquad \text{(equation } \textcircled{2}\text{)}$$

We next wish to replace equation $\textcircled{2}$ by equation $\textcircled{2} + c\textcircled{1}$, where the factor c is chosen in such a way that the terms in, say, x cancel. In order to make the choice of this factor more transparent, we rewrite the two equations, first "normalizing" equation $\textcircled{1}$ by dividing through by the coefficient of x so that the coefficient of x becomes one.

$$x - \frac{1}{3}y = \frac{7}{3} \qquad \textcircled{1'}$$
$$2x - 4y = -2 \qquad \textcircled{2}$$

Next replace equation $\textcircled{2}$ by $(\textcircled{2} - 2\textcircled{1'})$, that is

$$\textcircled{2'} = \textcircled{2} - 2\textcircled{1'}$$
$$= (2x - 4y) - 2\left(x - \frac{y}{3}\right) = (-2) - 2\left(\frac{7}{3}\right)$$
$$= -\frac{10}{3}y \qquad\qquad\qquad = -\frac{20}{3}$$

and the two equations now become

$$x - \frac{1}{3}y = \frac{7}{3} \qquad \textcircled{1'}$$
$$-\frac{10}{3}y = -\frac{20}{3} \qquad \textcircled{2'}$$

Equation $\textcircled{2'}$ is then normalized by dividing through by the coefficient of y to obtain

$$x - \frac{1}{3}y = \frac{7}{3} \quad \textcircled{1'}$$
$$y = 2 \quad \textcircled{2''}$$

The final step consists of replacing equation $\textcircled{1'}$ by $\textcircled{1'} + c\textcircled{2''}$ with c chosen so as to eliminate the coefficient of y. This replacement is clearly $\textcircled{1'} \rightarrow \textcircled{1'} + \frac{1}{3}\textcircled{2''}$. The result is then

$$x + 0 = 3 \quad \textcircled{1''}$$
$$0 + y = 2 \quad \textcircled{2''}$$

This is obviously a very laborious procedure, but it is one that can be quite easily generalized to larger sets of equations. For example, consider the solution of a three equations in three unknowns problem written in matrix form as

$$
\begin{array}{cc}
[A] & \mathbf{b} \\
\begin{pmatrix} 2 & -1 & 3 \\ 1 & -2 & 2 \\ 3 & 2 & -3 \end{pmatrix} & \begin{pmatrix} 9 \\ 3 \\ -2 \end{pmatrix}
\end{array}
$$

The solution vector $\mathbf{x}$ has been omitted since we will only be concerned with operations on the coefficients in the equations.

The procedure starts by writing down side by side the elements of the coefficient matrix and the right-hand-side vector as a so-called augmented matrix. (I will use straight lines to delineate the matrix, since the sequence of operations that follows will proceed vertically down the page.)

First Pass

Step 1   In the first pass the first row is called the *pivot* row and the leftmost element, a_{11}, is called the *pivot element* or simply the pivot. Step 1 consists of normalizing the pivot row (row 1) by dividing all of the elements of that row by the pivot element, $a_{11} = 2$.

$$
\left|\begin{array}{ccc|c}
1 & -1/2 & 1/2 & 9/2 \\
1 & -2 & 2 & 3 \\
3 & 2 & -3 & -2
\end{array}\right|
$$

Step 2   Next, add multiples of the pivot row (here row 1) to every other row in turn with the factor chosen so that the elements of the pivot column (here column 1) become *zero*.

$$
\left|\begin{array}{ccc|c}
1 & -1/2 & 3/2 & 9/2 \\
0 & -3/2 & 1/2 & -3/2 \\
0 & 7/2 & -15/2 & -31/2
\end{array}\right|
\begin{array}{l}
\\
\leftarrow (\text{row } 2) - 1(\text{row } 1) \\
\leftarrow (\text{row } 3) - 3(\text{row } 1)
\end{array}
$$

Second Pass

Step 1   The pivot row is now row 2 and the pivot element is $a_{22} = -3/2$. Normalization of row 2 yields

$$
\left|\begin{array}{ccc|c}
1 & -1/2 & 3/2 & 9/2 \\
0 & 1 & -1/3 & 1 \\
0 & 7/2 & -15/2 & -31/2
\end{array}\right|
$$

Step 2   Add multiples of the pivot row, row 2, to rows 1 and 3 to obtain zeros in the pivot column, i.e., force $a_{12} = a_{32} = 0$.

$$
\left|\begin{array}{ccc|c}
1 & 0 & 4/3 & 5 \\
0 & 1 & -1/3 & 1 \\
0 & 0 & -19/3 & -19
\end{array}\right|
\begin{array}{l}
\leftarrow (\text{row } 1) + \dfrac{1}{2}(\text{row } 2) \\
\\
\leftarrow (\text{row } 3) - \dfrac{7}{2}(\text{row } 2)
\end{array}
$$

Third Pass

Step 1   Normalize row 3 by dividing by $a_{33} = -19/3$.

$$\begin{vmatrix} 1 & 0 & 4/3 \\ 0 & 1 & -1/3 \\ 0 & 0 & 1 \end{vmatrix} \begin{matrix} 5 \\ 1 \\ 3 \end{matrix}$$

and the final step consists of forcing the elements of the present pivot column to be zeros.

$$\begin{vmatrix} 1 & 0 & 0 \\ 0 & 1 & 0 \\ 0 & 0 & 1 \end{vmatrix} \begin{matrix} 1 \\ 2 \\ 3 \end{matrix} \begin{matrix} \leftarrow (\text{row 1}) - 4/3\ (\text{row 3}) \\ \leftarrow (\text{row 2}) + 1/3\ (\text{row 3}) \\ \ \end{matrix}$$

Thus, the original set of equations has become

$$\begin{pmatrix} 1 & 0 & 0 \\ 0 & 1 & 0 \\ 0 & 0 & 1 \end{pmatrix} \begin{pmatrix} x_1 \\ x_2 \\ x_3 \end{pmatrix} = \begin{pmatrix} 1 \\ 2 \\ 3 \end{pmatrix}$$

or simply

$$\begin{pmatrix} x_1 \\ x_2 \\ x_3 \end{pmatrix} = \begin{pmatrix} 1 \\ 2 \\ 3 \end{pmatrix}$$

This procedure, though laborious, is extremely straightforward. You should attempt several problems of this type by hand calculation.

12.5.2   Row Switching

The above algorithm for solution of simultaneous equations is quite clear and it would appear that we are now in a position to construct a Fortran code to implement it. Not quite yet. There is a potential problem. What if the current pivot element is zero or extremely small? Dividing by the pivot will then cause the method to fail. For example, in the solution of the set of equations

$$\begin{pmatrix} 0 & -6 & 9 \\ 7 & 0 & -5 \\ 5 & -8 & 6 \end{pmatrix} \begin{pmatrix} x_1 \\ x_2 \\ x_3 \end{pmatrix} = \begin{pmatrix} 3 \\ 1 \\ 4 \end{pmatrix}$$

the very first pivot is zero and thus row 1 cannot be normalized. The remedy is

If the current pivot element is zero (or very small), switch the position of the entire pivot row with any row *below* it and continue.

Switching the positions of row 1 and row 2 in the above problem yields

$$\begin{pmatrix} 7 & 0 & -5 \\ 0 & -6 & 9 \\ 5 & -8 & 6 \end{pmatrix} \begin{pmatrix} x_1 \\ x_2 \\ x_3 \end{pmatrix} = \begin{pmatrix} 1 \\ 3 \\ 4 \end{pmatrix}$$

Notice that when switching rows, the elements of the right-hand-side vector **b** must be switched as well. Also, notice that the positions of the solution vector x_i *have not* been switched. If you write out the three equations represented by each of the above matrix equations, you will find that the two sets of equations are the same. This means that the ultimate solution of the set of equations by the Gauss-Jordan method will yield the values for x_1, x_2, . . . , in sequence, regardless of whether rows have or have not been switched.

The result of the Gauss-Jordan method applied to the above matrix equation is

$$\begin{vmatrix} 1 & 0 & 0 & 6/17 \\ 0 & 1 & 0 & -1/17 \\ 0 & 0 & 1 & 5/17 \end{vmatrix}$$

The bookkeeping associated with recording all the potential row switching can be quite complex. However, once it has been programmed, a significant improvement can be added to the basic algorithm. Since it is essential to switch rows if the current pivot is extremely small or zero to avoid round-off errors, this would suggest that to improve the accuracy, rows should be switched in *every* pass, bringing the row with the largest element in the pivot column to the current pivot position.[4] This method, with variations, is employed in all "professionally written" Gauss-Jordan codes.

This brings me to a cardinal rule of matrix calculations on a computer. When solving "real" problems involving matrices, you should always try to take advantage of the "canned" matrix routines in the computer library. It is usually a mistake to write your own codes to perform the basic operations of matrix algebra. The reason is that the methods are quite standard and usually independent of the particular problem. This is in contrast with root-solving problems in which the method must be carefully tailored to the

---

[4] The rules for deciding precisely which row (or column) to move into the pivot position are quite complex. This is because any row could be multiplied by, say, 10^{10} without affecting the solution at all, yet it could affect the pivoting strategy. Usually a separate array is used to store the maximum elements of each row individually, and the elements of the pivot column, divided by their corresponding maximum element, are compared when deciding which row to switch. Of course, since rows and not columns represent equations, it would make more sense to move the largest element of an equation to the pivot position, i.e., switch columns. This type of rearrangement does, however, reorder the x_i's. Switching *both* rows and columns to maximize the pivot is rarely employed even though the accuracy would be enhanced.

problem at hand, and thus, it frequently is best to write your own root-solving codes.

One final point: When using the Gauss-Jordan method to obtain a solution of a set of equations, it appears that the solution was obtained without ever dividing by the determinant of the coefficient matrix. Of course, there is an implicit division by $|A|$, but it is hidden somewhere in all the arithmetic. In fact it can be shown that the value of the determinant of the coefficient matrix is equal to the product of the pivot elements. For example, the three pivot elements obtained in the example at the start of this section were $2, -3/2, -19/3$. And the value of the determinant is computed to be 19, which is equal to the product of these pivots. The Fortran code based on the Gauss-Jordan method can therefore easily be adapted to include an additional parameter that returns the value of the determinant of the coefficient matrix $[A]$.

12.5.3 The Fortran Code for the Gauss-Jordan Method

In violation of the rule mentioned above, a short Fortran code to solve simultaneous linear equations using the Gauss-Jordan method is given in Figure 12-1. This code does not include any row switching and is intended mainly to illustrate the basic structure of the algorithm.

The subroutine GAUSS in Figure 12-1 assumes that the coefficient matrix $[A]$ is a square N by N matrix and that it has been previously dimensioned in the calling program as an ND by ND matrix, where $N \leq ND$. This distinction is very important and was discussed earlier in Section 8.3.3.

The code also requires the value of the elements of the right-hand-side vector b_i and returns the elements of the solution vector x_i. Both the coefficient matrix $[A]$ and the right-hand-side vector b_i are destroyed by the subroutine, so if they are needed later in a program, a copy must be made before the subroutine GAUSS is used.

The key section of the code is the line redefining the element A(IROW, ICOL). The effect of this statement is that the element of row IROW that is in the pivot column—i.e., ICOL = IPIV—is replaced by zero. Rewriting this line in an algebraic notation, yields

$$a_{rc} \rightarrow a_{rc} - \frac{a_{rp}a_{pc}}{a_{pp}}$$

where r, c, p, are the indices for the row, column, and pivot counters. Thus, the element in the pivot column, $c = p$ is replaced by

$$a_{rp} \rightarrow a_{rp} - \frac{a_{rp}a_{pp}}{a_{pp}} = 0$$

The determinant, which is the product of the pivot elements, is also returned by the subroutine. This code is quite suitable for most matrix problems provided no zero pivots are encountered. If the matrix $[A]$ is quite

Figure 12-1 The Fortran code for the Gauss-Jordan method

```
      SUBROUTINE GAUSS(A,B,X,ND,N,DET)
*--
*-- GAUSS WILL SOLVE THE EQUATION A * X = B FOR THE SOLUTION
*-- VECTOR X(N) PROVIDED A(N,N) AND B(N) ARE KNOWN AND PROVIDED
*-- NO ZERO PIVOTS ARE ENCOUNTERED. THE ALGORITHM DOES NOT USE
*-- ANY ROW SWITCHING TO MAXIMIZE PIVOTS. ALSO A(N,N) AND B(N)
*-- ARE DESTROYED IN THE PROCESS.
*--
*-- NOTE-- ND IS THE SIZE OF THE ARRAY A AS DIMENSIONED IN THE
*-- CALLING PROGRAM WHILE N IS THE SIZE OF THE ARRAY AS IT IS
*-- USED IN THIS SUBROUTINE. ND MUST BE GREATER THAN OR EQUAL
*-- TO N
*-------------------------------------------------------------
* VARIABLES
*
      REAL A(ND,ND),B(ND),X(ND),DET,PIVOT,FACTOR
      INTEGER ND,N,IPV
*
*              A(ND,ND) -- THE COEFFICIENT MATRIX, DESTROYED
*                          BY GAUSS
*              B(ND)    -- THE RIGHT-HAND-SIDE VECTOR, ALSO
*                          DESTROYED
*              X(ND)    -- THE SOLUTION VECTOR
*              DET      -- THE DETERMINANT OF A IS COMPUTED
*              PIVOT    -- THE CURRENT PIVOT ELEMENT
*              FACTOR   -- A FACTOR USED IN GAUSS ELIMINATION
*              ND       -- SIZE OF ARRAYS AS DIMENSIONED IN
*                          THE CALLING PROGRAM
*              N        -- SIZE OF ARRAYS AS USED IN GAUSS
*              IPV      -- LABELS THE CURRENT PIVOT ROW AND
*                          THE CURRENT PASS NUMBER
*-------------------------------------------------------------
*
*         THE DETERMINANT IS THE PRODUCT OF THE PIVOTS
*
      DET =1.0
*
*         EXECUTE N PASSES, LABELED BY IPV
*
      DO 4 IPV = 1,N
*
*                 IF THE PIVOT IS SMALL THE CODE TERMINATES
*
      IF(ABS(A(IPV,IPV)) .LT. 1.E-6)THEN
         WRITE(*,10)IPV,IPV,A(IPV,IPV)
         STOP
      END IF
      PIVOT = A(IPV,IPV)
      DET = DET * PIVOT
*
*         NORMALIZE THE PIVOT ROW BY DIVIDING ACROSS BY PIVOT
*
      DO 1 J = 1,N
         A(IPV,J) = A(IPV,J)/PIVOT
    1    CONTINUE
      B(IPV) = B(IPV)/PIVOT
*
*         REPLACE ROW-IROW WITH ROW-IROW + FACTOR * (PIVOT-ROW)
*         WITH FACTOR CHOSEN TO GET ZERO IN PIVOT COLUMN
*
```

```
          DO 3 IROW = 1,N
             IF(IROW .NE. IPV)THEN
                FACTOR = A(IROW,IPV)/A(IPV,IPV)
                DO 2 ICOL = 1,N
                   A(IROW,ICOL) = A(IROW,ICOL) -
     +                  FACTOR * A(IPV,ICOL)
  2            CONTINUE
                B(IROW) = B(IROW) - FACTOR * B(IPV)
             END IF
  3      CONTINUE
  4 CONTINUE
*
*        THE SOLUTION VECTOR IS NOW CONTAINED IN THE VECTOR B
*
      DO 5 I = 1,N
         X(I) = B(I)
  5 CONTINUE
*
      RETURN
*---------------------------------------------------------------
* FORMATS
*
  10 FORMAT(//,5X,'---ERROR IN GAUSS---',//,20X,
     +        'A(',I3,',',I3,') = ',E11.4,//,
     +        10X,'IS TOO SMALL.   PROGRAM TERMINATED')
*
      END
```

large, this code is susceptible to significant round-off errors. Of course, the seriousness of round-off error problems also depends on the word length characteristic of your computer. A Gauss-Jordan subroutine that computes the inverse of a matrix and that does employ a limited pivoting strategy is given in Section 12.9.2.

12.6   MATRIX INVERSION BY THE GAUSS-JORDAN METHOD

The inverse of a matrix $[A]$ is a matrix $[A^{-1}]$ that satisfies the equations

$$[A][A^{-1}] = [A^{-1}][A] = [I]$$

Of course, the matrix $[A^{-1}]$ exists only if the determinant of $[A]$ is nonzero. The determination of the inverse of $[A]$ can be achieved by a simple variation of the Gauss-Jordan method of the previous section. The idea is quite simple and is most easily seen via demonstration with a typical 3 by 3 matrix problem. Consider the three independent matrix equations

$$[A]\,\mathbf{x}^{(1)} = \mathbf{b}^{(1)} \tag{12.23}$$

$$[A] \mathbf{x}^{(2)} = \mathbf{b}^{(2)}$$

$$[A] \mathbf{x}^{(3)} = \mathbf{b}^{(3)}$$

in each equation the coefficient matrix $[A]$ is the same, but the three solution vectors $\mathbf{x}^{(i)}$ will be different depending on the choices for the three right-hand-side vectors $\mathbf{b}^{(i)}$. These are next specified as

(12.24)
$$\mathbf{b}^{(1)} = \begin{pmatrix} 1 \\ 0 \\ 0 \end{pmatrix} \quad \mathbf{b}^{(2)} = \begin{pmatrix} 0 \\ 1 \\ 0 \end{pmatrix} \quad \mathbf{b}^{(3)} = \begin{pmatrix} 0 \\ 0 \\ 1 \end{pmatrix}$$

and the three Equations (12.23) are solved by the Gauss-Jordan method for a particular 3 by 3 matrix $[A]$ resulting in values for the solution vectors $\mathbf{x}^i$ that satisfy

$$[A]\begin{pmatrix} x_1^{(1)} \\ x_2^{(1)} \\ x_3^{(1)} \end{pmatrix} = \begin{pmatrix} 1 \\ 0 \\ 0 \end{pmatrix} \quad [A]\begin{pmatrix} x_1^{(2)} \\ x_2^{(2)} \\ x_3^{(2)} \end{pmatrix} = \begin{pmatrix} 0 \\ 1 \\ 0 \end{pmatrix} \quad [A]\begin{pmatrix} x_1^{(3)} \\ x_2^{(3)} \\ x_3^{(3)} \end{pmatrix} = \begin{pmatrix} 0 \\ 0 \\ 1 \end{pmatrix}$$

These three equations are then suggestively grouped as

$$[A]\left(\begin{pmatrix} x_1^{(1)} \\ x_2^{(1)} \\ x_3^{(1)} \end{pmatrix} \begin{pmatrix} x_1^{(2)} \\ x_2^{(2)} \\ x_3^{(2)} \end{pmatrix} \begin{pmatrix} x_1^{(3)} \\ x_2^{(3)} \\ x_3^{(3)} \end{pmatrix} \right) = \left(\begin{pmatrix} 1 \\ 0 \\ 0 \end{pmatrix} \begin{pmatrix} 0 \\ 1 \\ 0 \end{pmatrix} \begin{pmatrix} 0 \\ 0 \\ 1 \end{pmatrix} \right)$$

But the square array on the right is the identity matrix I_3, and thus the square array on the left must be the inverse of matrix $[A]$. That is, the solution of Equations (12.23) with the choices Equations (12.24) for the vectors $\mathbf{b}^{(i)}$ generates three solution vectors $\mathbf{x}^{(i)}$, which are the respective *columns* of the inverse matrix. This means that the inverse of an n by n matrix can be obtained by n applications of the Gauss-Jordan method with the right-hand-side vectors $\mathbf{b}^{(i)}$ chosen to be n component generalizations of Equations (12.24).

Moreover, the elements of the coefficient matrix determine the numerical operations of the Gauss-Jordan, and since the matrix $[A]$ is the same for all n equations, a little thoughtful contemplation suggests that *all n* computations could be executed *simultaneously*. This is demonstrated below for a 3 by 3 matrix.

First the matrix $[A]$ to be inverted and the identity matrix of $[I]$ of like size are written side by side. For example,

$$\left| \begin{array}{ccc|ccc} 2 & -1 & 0 & 1 & 0 & 0 \\ -1 & 2 & -1 & 0 & 1 & 0 \\ 0 & -1 & 2 & 0 & 0 & 1 \end{array} \right|$$

Next the Gauss-Jordan method is carried out as before with the addition that when replacing rows, all the elements of a row in both $[A]$ and in $[I]$ are affected.

First Pass

Step 1
$$\left[\begin{array}{ccc|ccc} 1 & -1/2 & 0 & 1/2 & 0 & 0 \\ -1 & 2 & -1 & 0 & 1 & 0 \\ 0 & -1 & 2 & 0 & 0 & 1 \end{array}\right] \leftarrow \text{Normalize pivot row}$$

Step 2
$$\left[\begin{array}{ccc|ccc} 1 & -1/2 & 0 & 1/2 & 0 & 0 \\ 0 & 3/2 & -1 & 1/2 & 1 & 0 \\ 0 & -1 & 2 & 0 & 0 & 1 \end{array}\right] \begin{array}{l} \leftarrow \text{Replace row 2 by} \\ \text{row 2 + row 1} \end{array}$$

Second Pass

Step 1
$$\left[\begin{array}{ccc|ccc} 1 & -1/2 & 0 & 1/2 & 0 & 0 \\ 0 & 1 & -2/3 & 1/3 & 2/3 & 0 \\ 0 & -1 & 2 & 0 & 0 & 1 \end{array}\right] \leftarrow \text{Normalize pivot row}$$

Step 2
$$\left[\begin{array}{ccc|ccc} 1 & 0 & -1/3 & 2/3 & 1/3 & 0 \\ 0 & 1 & -2/3 & 1/3 & 2/3 & 0 \\ 0 & 0 & 4/3 & 1/3 & 2/3 & 1 \end{array}\right] \begin{array}{l} \leftarrow (\text{row 1}) + (1/2)(\text{row 2}) \\ \\ \leftarrow (\text{row 3}) + (\text{row 2}) \end{array}$$

Third Pass

Step 1
$$\left[\begin{array}{ccc|ccc} 1 & 0 & -1/3 & 2/3 & 1/3 & 0 \\ 0 & 1 & -2/3 & 1/3 & 2/3 & 0 \\ 0 & 0 & 1 & 1/4 & 1/2 & 3/4 \end{array}\right] \leftarrow \text{Normalize pivot row}$$

Step 2
$$\left[\begin{array}{ccc|ccc} 1 & 0 & 0 & 3/4 & 1/2 & 1/4 \\ 0 & 1 & 0 & 1/2 & 1 & 1/2 \\ 0 & 0 & 1 & 1/4 & 1/2 & 3/4 \end{array}\right] \begin{array}{l} \leftarrow (\text{row 1}) + (1/3)(\text{row 3}) \\ \leftarrow (\text{row 2}) + (2/3)(\text{row 3}) \end{array}$$

The contention is then that the matrix on the right in the last step is the inverse of the original matrix; i.e.,[5]

$$[A^{-1}]\begin{pmatrix} 3/4 & 1/2 & 1/4 \\ 1/2 & 1 & 1/2 \\ 1/4 & 1/2 & 3/4 \end{pmatrix} = \frac{1}{4}\begin{pmatrix} 3 & 2 & 1 \\ 2 & 4 & 2 \\ 1 & 2 & 3 \end{pmatrix}$$

To verify this we simply multiply $[A][A^{-1}]$ to obtain

$$[A][A^{-1}] = \frac{1}{4}\begin{pmatrix} 2 & -1 & 0 \\ -1 & 2 & -1 \\ 0 & -1 & 2 \end{pmatrix}\begin{pmatrix} 3 & 2 & 1 \\ 2 & 4 & 2 \\ 1 & 2 & 3 \end{pmatrix}$$

---

[5] The multiplication of a matrix by a simple number as in $c[A]$ is defined to mean that every element of the matrix is to be multiplied by the number c.

The product of these two matrices is itself a matrix which I will call $[C]$. For example, the row 1, column 1 element of $[C]$ is obtained by multiplying row 1 of $[A]$ by column 1 of $[A^{-1}]$ element by element and summing:

$$c_{11} = \frac{1}{4}[2 \quad -1 \quad 0]\begin{pmatrix} 3 \\ 2 \\ 1 \end{pmatrix}$$

$$= \frac{1}{4}[2(3) + (-1)(2) + 0(1)] = 1$$

In a like manner the nine elements of the product are found to be

$$[A][A^{-1}] = \begin{pmatrix} 1 & 0 & 0 \\ 0 & 1 & 0 \\ 0 & 0 & 1 \end{pmatrix}$$

Once the inverse of the matrix $[A]$ is known, the solution of the set of equations

(12.25)
$$\begin{array}{ccc} [A] & \mathbf{x} & = & \mathbf{b} \end{array}$$
$$\begin{pmatrix} 2 & -1 & 0 \\ -1 & 2 & -1 \\ 0 & -1 & 2 \end{pmatrix}\begin{pmatrix} x_1 \\ x_2 \\ x_3 \end{pmatrix} = \begin{pmatrix} 1 \\ 2 \\ 3 \end{pmatrix}$$

is simply given by

(12.26)
$$\begin{array}{ccc} \mathbf{x} & = & [A^{-1}] & \mathbf{b} \end{array}$$
$$\begin{pmatrix} x_1 \\ x_2 \\ x_3 \end{pmatrix} = \frac{1}{4}\begin{pmatrix} 3 & 2 & 1 \\ 2 & 4 & 2 \\ 1 & 2 & 3 \end{pmatrix}\begin{pmatrix} 1 \\ 2 \\ 3 \end{pmatrix} = \frac{1}{4}\begin{pmatrix} 3+4+3 \\ 2+8+6 \\ 2+4+9 \end{pmatrix} = \begin{pmatrix} 5/2 \\ 4 \\ 7/2 \end{pmatrix}$$

Notice that if the original set of equations is altered by changing only the right-hand-side vector, the same inverse matrix may be used to obtain the solution. Thus

$$\begin{array}{ccc} [A] & \mathbf{x} & = & \mathbf{c} \end{array}$$
$$\begin{pmatrix} 2 & -1 & 0 \\ -1 & 2 & -1 \\ 0 & -1 & 2 \end{pmatrix}\begin{pmatrix} x_1 \\ x_2 \\ x_3 \end{pmatrix} = \begin{pmatrix} 1 \\ 1 \\ 1 \end{pmatrix}$$

has a solution vector $\mathbf{x}$

$$\begin{array}{ccc} \mathbf{x} & = & [A^{-1}] & \mathbf{c} \end{array}$$
$$\begin{pmatrix} x_1 \\ x_2 \\ x_3 \end{pmatrix} = \frac{1}{4}\begin{pmatrix} 3 & 2 & 1 \\ 2 & 4 & 2 \\ 1 & 2 & 3 \end{pmatrix}\begin{pmatrix} 1 \\ 1 \\ 1 \end{pmatrix} = \begin{pmatrix} 3/2 \\ 2 \\ 3/2 \end{pmatrix}$$

This is a rather common situation in engineering and science problems. The coefficient matrix $[A]$ remains constant and the equations are solved for a variety of right-hand-side vectors **b**. The code for a subroutine MINV that computes the inverse of an n by n matrix is given in Section 12.9.2.

12.7 RELATIVE SPEED AND ACCURACY OF THE VARIOUS MATRIX ALGORITHMS

We have seen that a 5 by 5 determinant can be evaluated by expanding in terms of its five cofactor determinants, each a 4 by 4 determinant. This suggests that the evaluation of a single nth order determinant requires $\mathcal{O}n!$ multiplications.[6] Therefore a solution of n simultaneous linear equations using Cramer's rule will require $\mathcal{O}(n + 1)!$ multiplications. So, if you have a Fortran code that will solve five equations in five unknowns using Cramer's rule with an execution cost of 10 cents, the bill for solving 10 equations would be roughly $5,000 and since round-off errors accumulate with each arithmetic operation, it is very likely that the numbers obtained will be incorrect. The solution of large numbers of equations by Cramer's rule is clearly impractical.

This situation is rather typical of all tasks that require the solution of simultaneous equations on a computer. The number of arithmetic operations required to obtain a solution grows very rapidly with the number of equations n, with a corresponding growth in the execution time costs, memory costs, and round-off error accumulation.

A careful analysis of the Gauss-Jordan method[7] reveals that the method requires roughly $n^3/3$ multiplications. Thus, for this method the cost comparison between the $n = 5$ and $n = 10$ cases would be a modest increase of from 10 cents to 80 cents.

Efficient codes for obtaining the inverse of a matrix using the Gauss-Jordan method require only about three times the total number of arithmetic operations needed to obtain a single solution vector. Thus if a solution is required for more than a few right-hand-side vectors, it may be prudent to solve for the inverse matrix directly. Moreover, the only sure way to test for round-off errors in the method requires the calculation of $[A^{-1}]$.

In the solution of a matrix equation of order n by the Gauss-Jordan method, where n is 100 or greater, round-off error will be a serious concern that cannot be ignored. For example, solving 100 equations on a computer with eight-figure accuracy, will yield results that are at best accurate to only two significant figures. The programmer may then be forced to use double-

---

[6] Since addition is ordinarily much faster on a computer, I will only consider multiplication and division to obtain order-of-magnitude execution time estimates.

[7] K. S. Kunz, *Numerical Analysis*, McGraw-Hill, New York, 1957.

precision variables, which will drive up the execution cost significantly. A second alternative is to employ an iterative solution procedure, such as the Gauss-Siedel method described in the next section. Errors in one step of an iterative method are usually corrected in the next step, and so round-off errors are rarely a concern. Unfortunately, this advantage is frequently offset by a slow convergence rate, as we shall see.

The severity of round-off error problems in a Gauss-Jordan calculation can be determined by computing the inverse of the coefficient matrix $[A^{-1}]$, then performing the multiplication $[A][A^{-1}]$ and examining the product, which should be the identity matrix. If any off-diagonal term is significantly different from zero or any diagonal term is significantly different from one, the reason is probably due to round-off error.

12.8 ITERATIVE TECHNIQUES FOR SOLVING SIMULTANEOUS EQUATIONS

The matrices that are encountered in science and engineering problems can almost always be categorized as belonging to one of two types: (1) small to moderately large *dense* matrices, or (2) large and *sparse* matrices.

A sparse matrix is one in which most of the elements are zeros. Such matrices are frequently encountered in certain methods of solving differential equations. Often a sparse matrix will consist of diagonal elements plus nonzero elements only to the immediate left or right of the main diagonal, such as

$$(12.27) \qquad [C] = \begin{pmatrix} 4 & -1 & 0 & 0 & 0 \\ -1 & 4 & -1 & 0 & 0 \\ 0 & -1 & 4 & -1 & 0 \\ 0 & 0 & -1 & 4 & -1 \\ 0 & 0 & 0 & -1 & 4 \end{pmatrix}$$

This matrix is called a *banded* matrix as it has two "bands" of -1's on either side of the main diagonal. Sparse banded matrices that arise in physical problems can often be truly enormous; the order being thousands or even hundreds of thousands. Solving such a set of equations by the Gauss-Jordan method would not only be very likely impossible due to round-off error and storage considerations, it would be extremely inefficient as well. The procedure would spend an inordinate amount of time multiplying by zeros. The Gauss-Jordan method is only suitable for relatively small ($n \leq 100$) matrices that contain few zeros (i.e., dense). Alternative procedures must be developed for the remaining class of matrices. To minimize the danger of round-off errors, an iterative procedure would seem to be a likely candidate.

12.8.1 The Gauss-Siedel Iterative Procedure

A popular iterative technique, much like the method of successive substitution used to find roots of equations, is the Gauss-Siedel iteration method. The method is quite simple and is most easily illustrated by means of an example. The matrix equation

$$[A]\mathbf{x} = \mathbf{b}$$

where $[A]$ is a square matrix of order 3 is shorthand for the three equations

$$a_{11}x_1 + a_{12}x_2 + a_{13}x_3 = b_1 \tag{12.28}$$

$$a_{21}x_1 + a_{22}x_2 + a_{32}x_3 = b_2 \tag{12.29}$$

$$a_{31}x_1 + a_{32}x_2 + a_{33}x_3 = b_3 \tag{12.30}$$

If *none* of the diagonal elements of the coefficient matrix $[A]$ are zero, we can formally solve Equation (12.28) for x_1, Equation (12.29) for x_2, and Equation (12.30) for x_3 to obtain

$$x_1 = \frac{b_1 - a_{12}x_2 - a_{13}x_3}{a_{11}} \tag{12.31}$$

$$x_2 = \frac{b_2 - a_{21}x_1 - a_{23}x_3}{a_{22}} \tag{12.32}$$

$$x_3 = \frac{b_3 - a_{31}x_1 - a_{32}x_2}{a_{33}} \tag{12.33}$$

Of course, this is not much of a solution, since to obtain values for x_1, x_2, x_3 on the left, we need to know the values of x_1, x_2, x_3 on the right. However, it does suggest the next best thing, a solution by iteration.

We begin with an initial guess for the unknowns, say $x_1^{(0)}$, $x_2^{(0)}$, $x_3^{(0)}$, and using these values in the expressions on the right, compute a new set of values, $x_1^{(1)}$, $x_2^{(1)}$, $x_3^{(1)}$.[8] This procedure is then continued until the difference between successive solution vectors is sufficiently small.

The Gauss-Siedel method is a minor variation of this scheme that requires less storage and usually will converge more rapidly. The idea is to always use the most recently computed values for the variables. Thus once $x_1^{(1)}$ has been computed, this value is used in the next equation for x_2^1 in place of $x_2^{(0)}$, etc.

---

[8] The procedure of using one set of x_i's as an initial guess and then holding these values fixed while a second set is computed is known as *fixed-point* or *Jacobi iteration*. It is less efficient than the Gauss-Siedel technique that follows and is important mainly in the theoretical analysis of convergence proofs.

(12.34)
$$x_1^{(1)} = \frac{b_1 - a_{12}x_2^{(0)} - a_{13}x_3^{(0)}}{a_{11}}$$

(12.35)
$$x_2^{(1)} = \frac{b_2 - a_{21}x_1^{(1)} - a_{23}x_3^{(0)}}{a_{22}}$$

(12.36)
$$x_3^{(1)} = \frac{b_3 - a_{31}x_1^{(1)} - a_{32}x_2^{(1)}}{a_{33}}$$

Notice that there is never a need to store both the old and the new values of the components of the solution vector. Once an element of the vector **x** is computed, it is subsequently used in all equations that follow. Thus only one storage location is required for each element. The Fortran statements that implement these operations would be

```
X(1) = (B(1) - A(1,2) * X(2) - A(1,3) * X(3))/A(1,1)

X(2) = (B(2) - A(2,1) * X(1) - A(2,3) * X(3))/A(2,2)

X(3) = (B(3) - A(3,1) * X(1) - A(3,2) * X(2))/A(3,3)
```

For an arbitrary number of equations these statements would be rewritten in terms of DO loops.

12.8.2 Convergence

The proof of the convergence of a multivariable iterative procedure is beyond the scope of this text, but the result is very simple:

> If the coefficient matrix is *diagonally dominant*, the Gauss-Siedel iteration procedure is *guaranteed* to converge for *any* initial guess for the solution vector.

Of course, the better the initial guess, the more rapidly the method will converge.

A diagonally dominant matrix is one in which the magnitude of the element on the diagonal in each row is larger than the sum of the magnitudes of all the other elements in that row. That is, for each $i = 1, n$,

$$|a_{ii}| > \sum_{\text{all } j \neq i} |a_{ij}|$$

If the matrix does not meet this rather stringent definition of diagonal dominance, the Gauss-Siedel method may still converge, particularly if the largest elements of the matrix are located on the diagonal. In other words, the requirement that the matrix be diagonally dominant is a sufficient condition for convergence, but it is not a necessary condition.

If a set of equations does not possess diagonal dominance in its present form, it is frequently possible to rearrange the set so that the coefficient matrix is diagonally dominant. For example, if the Gauss-Siedel method is applied to the set of equations (see also Problem 12.15),

$$\begin{pmatrix} 1 & 4 & 1 \\ 4 & 1 & 0 \\ 0 & 1 & 4 \end{pmatrix} \begin{pmatrix} x_1 \\ x_2 \\ x_3 \end{pmatrix} = \begin{pmatrix} 2 \\ 1 \\ 3 \end{pmatrix} \tag{12.37}$$

the method will diverge for any initial guess not equal to the exact solution. However, interchanging the first and second rows yields

$$\begin{pmatrix} 4 & 1 & 0 \\ 1 & 4 & 1 \\ 0 & 1 & 4 \end{pmatrix} \begin{pmatrix} x_1 \\ x_2 \\ x_3 \end{pmatrix} = \begin{pmatrix} 1 \\ 2 \\ 3 \end{pmatrix} \tag{12.38}$$

which is obviously diagonally dominant and thus convergence is assured. The most common criterion to use in deciding whether or not a sufficiently accurate solution vector has been attained is to test the percentage change in each component of x from one iteration to the next. That is, defining

$$\Delta_i = |x_{i,\text{new}} - x_{i,\text{old}}|/x_{i,\text{old}}$$

the test could be that *every* Δ_i be less than some small quantity ε; or a less stringent test might be that the average of all the Δ_i's be less than ε. In some cases, only a few of the many variables have important physical significance and the convergence test may then be written to check successive changes in only those variables.

12.8.3 The Fortran Code for an Iterative Gauss-Siedel Subroutine

The Fortran code for a Gauss-Siedel algorithm applied to N linear simultaneous equations is given in Figure 12-2. The subroutine contains the following features:

1. The coefficient matrix is assumed to be a square N by N matrix that is dimensioned as an ND by ND matrix in the calling program. As was mentioned earlier in connection with the Gauss-Jordan subroutine, N must be less than or equal to ND.
2. It is assumed that the first N elements of the solution vector X are supplied in the call as the initial guess.
3. The subroutine first checks for diagonal dominance. If the matrix is not diagonally dominant, a warning message is printed.
4. If any of the diagonal elements of the coefficient matrix are zero, the subroutine prints a diagnostic and stops.

Figure 12-2 A subroutine implementing the Gauss-Siedel method.

```
      SUBROUTINE GAUSDL(A,B,ND,N,X,IMAX,EPS,ISTOP)
*--
*--   GAUSDL is a Gauss-Siedel iteration algorithm to solve the
*--   matrix eq. [A]*X = B. The maximum number of iterations is
*--   IMAX and a successful termination is achieved when the
*--   successive fractional changes in ALL the X-s are less than
*--   EPS. The number of equations is N and the starting values
*--   for the X-s are assumed equal to the values initially con-
*--   tained in the array X when the subroutine is called. ISTOP
*--   is a success flag, (ISTOP = 1 => Success, = 0 => Failure).
*-------------------------------------------------------------
* Variables
*--
      REAL A(ND,ND),B(ND),X(ND),EPS,RMSDV,XOLD,DEV
      INTEGER N,ND,IMAX,IPASS,ISTOP
*--
*--         A(ND,ND)  --  The coefficient matrix dimensioned as
*--                       ND by ND in the calling program
*--         B(ND)     --  The right-hand-side vector
*--         X(ND)     --  The solution vector. As input, it
*--                       contains the initial guess
*--         EPS       --  Convergence criterion. Successful if
*--                       ALL fractional changes in X < EPS
*--         IMAX      --  The limiting number of iterations
*--         XOLD      --  The previous value of X(I)
*--         DEV       --  The fractional change in X(I)
*--         RMSDEV    --  Root-Mean-Square deviation in the X-s
*--         IPASS     --  The iteration counter
*--         ISTOP     --  The Success(1)/Failure(0) flag
*-------------------------------------------------------------
*--
*--         First check whether A is diagonally dominant.
*--
      DO 2 IROW = 1,N
            SUMAIJ = 0.0
            DO 1 ICOL = 1,N
                  IF(ICOL .NE. IROW)THEN
                        SUMAIJ = SUMAIJ + ABS(A(IROW,ICOL))
                  END IF
1           CONTINUE
            IF(ABS(A(IROW,IROW)) .LT. SUMAIJ)THEN
                  WRITE(*,10)IROW
            END IF
2     CONTINUE
*-------------------------------------------------------------
* Initialization
*--
      IPASS = 1
3     ISTOP = 1
      RMSDEV = 0.0
*-------------------------------------------------------------
*-------------------------------------------------------------
* Computation
*--
*--         Solve Eq. No. IEQ for X(ieq).
*--
      DO 5 IEQ = 1,N
```

```
*--
                    XOLD = X(IEQ)
                    SUM = 0.0
                    DO 4 J = 1,N
                            IF(J .NE. IEQ)THEN
                                    SUM = SUM + A(IEQ,J)*X(J)
*--
*--                                 Check for zero diagonal element.
*--
                            ELSE IF(A(IEQ,IEQ) .EQ. 0.)THEN
                                    WRITE(*,11)IEQ,IEQ
                                    STOP
                            END IF
    4               CONTINUE
                    X(IEQ) = (B(IEQ) - SUM)/A(IEQ,IEQ)
                    DEV = (X(IEQ) - XOLD)/XOLD
*--
*--                     If any of the deviations are greater than
*--                     EPS success has not yet been achieved.
*--
                    IF(ABS(DEV) .GT. EPS)ISTOP = 0
                    RMSDV = RMSDV + DEV*DEV
    5       CONTINUE
*--
*--                 Iteration No. IPASS is complete. Test for
*--                 success or continue.
*--
            IPASS = IPASS + 1
            RMSDV = RMSDV/N
            RMSDV = SQRT(RMSDV)
*--
*--                 Excessive iterations check
*--
            IF(IPASS .GT. IMAX)THEN
                    WRITE(*,12)IPASS,RMSDV
                    WRITE(*,13)(X(I),I=1,N)
            ELSE IF(ISTOP .EQ. 1) THEN
*--
*--                 If ISTOP = 1 through all eqs. success achieved
*--
            RETURN
            ELSE
*--
*--                 Otherwise continue with the next iteration
*--
            GO TO 3
            END IF
*------------------------------------------------------------------
* Formats
*--
   10   FORMAT(5X,'--WARNING FROM GAUSDL--',//,10X,'ROW ',I4,
     +          'IS NOT DIAGONALLY DOMINANT. PROGRAM CONTINUES')
*--
   11   FORMAT(5X,'--ERROR IN GAUSDL--',//,10X,
     +          'THE DIAGONAL ELEMENT A(',I4,',',I4,') IS ZERO',//,
     +          10X,'PROGRAM TERMINATED')
*--
   12   FORMAT(5X,'--GAUSDL UNSUCCESSFUL--',//,10X,'AFTER ',
     +          I4,' ITERATIONS THE CALCULATION HAS NOT CONVERGED',
     +          //,10X,'THE LATEST RMS DEVIATION = ',F10.4,//,
     +          10X,'THE LATEST VALUES FOR THE SOLUTION VECTOR ARE')
```

Continued

5. The convergence criterion is that *all* of the percentage changes in the components of the solution vector must be less than a programmer supplied quantity EPS.
6. The maximum number of iterations is limited to IMAX. In the likely event that the procedure has not converged in IMAX iterations, the subroutine prints the average percentage change in the components of X and a warning message, and stops.

This Fortran code is used in the example calculation of the next section.

12.8.4 A Numerical Example of the Gauss-Siedel Method

The Gauss-Siedel algorithm applied to the diagonally dominant set of Equations (12.38) with an initial guess of zero for all the components of **x** results in the values in Table 12-1.

The results of the same calculation on the same set of equations except not arranged in a diagonally dominant form is given in Table 12-2. After only a few iterations it is clear that the calculation is diverging.

Table 12-1 Results of Gauss-Siedel iteration if the coefficient matrix is diagonally dominant.

i	x_1	x_2	x_3	Average Δ_i
0	0.00	0.00	0.00	
1	0.25	0.44	0.64	0.44
2	0.14	0.30	0.674	0.13
3	0.174	0.288	0.6780	0.018
4	0.1780	0.2860	0.6785	0.0023
5	0.17850	0.28575	0.67856	0.00027
6	0.17856	0.28572	0.678570	0.000034
7	0.178570	0.285715	0.6785713	0.000006
	. . .	. . .	. . .	
∞	5/28	2/7	19/28	

Table 12-2 The Gauss-Siedel method applied to a nondiagonally dominant matrix.

i	x_1	x_2	x_3
0	0.0	0.0	0.0
1	2.0	−7.0	2.5
2	27.5	−109.0	28.0
3	410.0	−1639.0	410.5
4	6147.5	−24589.0	6148.0

12.9 MISCELLANEOUS FORTRAN CODES RELATING TO MATRICES

12.9.1 The Product of Two Square Matrices

If $[A]$ and $[B]$ are square matrices of order n, the elements of the product matrix $[C] = [A][B]$ are given by the equation

$$c_{ij} = \sum_{k=1}^{n} a_{ik} b_{kj} \qquad (12.39)$$

A subroutine that computes and returns the product matrix is given in Figure 12-3.

12.9.2 A Fortran Subroutine to Compute the Inverse of a Matrix

The scientific software library of your computing center will have stored on a disk file an efficient and accurate subroutine to compute the inverse of a

```
      SUBROUTINE PROD(A,B,C,N,ND)
      REAL A(ND,ND),B(ND,ND),C(ND,ND)
*
*
*               the three matrices are of size n by n
*               and are dimensioned in the main program
*               as ND by ND
*
*
*               for all rows and columns of C
*               execute the sum
*
      DO 2 I = 1,N
      DO 2 J = 1,N

         C(I,J) = 0.0
         DO 1 K = 1,N

            C(I,J) = C(I,J) + A(I,K) * B(K,J)

1        CONTINUE
2     CONTINUE
      RETURN
      END
```

Figure 12-3 A subroutine for multiplying two matrices.

matrix and I suggest you seek out the instructions required to access that code. In the unlikely event that such a code is not available, a less efficient code that employs only a limited pivoting strategy is given in Figure 12-4. This code was constructed to be easy to read and should give satisfactory results for most matrices of modest size.

Figure 12-4 A subroutine to compute the inverse of a matrix.

```
      SUBROUTINE MINV(A,AINV,ND,N,DET)
*--
*-- MINV COMPUTES THE INVERSE OF THE SQUARE N BY N MATRIX A. THE
*-- MATRIX IS DESTROYED IN THE PROCESS. THE DETERMINANT IS ALSO
*-- CALCULATED AND RETURNED AS DET. IF DET IS ZERO, THE CALCU-
*-- LATION IS TERMINATED AND A DIAGNOSTIC STATEMENT PRINTED. THE
*-- INVERSE OF THE MATRIX A IS RETURNED IN THE MATRIX AINV.
*--
*--    A STANDARD GAUSS-JORDAN ELIMINATION ALGORITHM IS USED. THE
*-- ROWS ARE REARRANGED IN EACH PASS TO USE THE MAXIMUM AVAILABLE
*-- PIVOT. HOWEVER, NO ADDITIONAL ATTEMPT TO IMPROVE EFFICIENCY,
*-- ACCURACY, OR TO MINIMIZE STORAGE IS INCLUDED (E.G., SWITCHING
*-- COLUMNS AS WELL). THE MAIN PURPOSE IS TO CONSTRUCT A CODE
*-- THAT IS READABLE FOR A NOVICE.
*------------------------------------------------------------------
* VARIABLES
*
      REAL A(ND,ND),AINV(ND,ND),DET
      INTEGER ND,N,IPASS
*
*          A(ND,ND)     --  THE MATRIX WHOSE INVERSE IS DESIRED.
*                           IT IS DIMENSIONED AS ND BY ND IN THE
*                           CALLING PROGRAM AND IS OF SIZE N BY
*                           N HERE
*          AINV(ND,ND)  --  RETURNED AS THE INVERSE OF A. ALSO
*                           DIMENSIONED AS ND BY ND
*          DET          --  THE COMPUTED DETERMINANT OF A.
*          ND           --  THE DIMENSION SIZE OF THE ARRAYS.
*          N            --  THE ACTUAL SIZE (.LE. ND)
*          IPASS        --  LABELS THE CURRENT PIVOT ROW.
*------------------------------------------------------------------
* INITIALIZATION
*
      DET = 1.0
*
*                    INITIALLY STORE THE IDENTITY MATRIX IN AINV
*                    AFTER THE LAST PASS, THIS WILL BE REPLACED BY
*                    THE INVERSE OF A.
*
      DO 1 I = 1,N
      DO 1 J = 1,N
        IF(I .EQ. J)THEN
           AINV(I,I) = 1.0
        ELSE
           AINV(I,J) = 0.0
        END IF
    1 CONTINUE
*------------------------------------------------------------------
* COMPUTATION
*
*                    THE CURRENT PIVOT ROW IS LABELED IPASS.
*
      DO 9 IPASS = 1,N
```

```
*
*                      FOR EACH PASS, FIRST FIND THE MAXIMUM ELEMENT
*                      IN THE PIVOT COLUMN
*
         IMX = IPASS
         DO 2 IROW = IPASS,N
            IF(ABS(A(IROW,IPASS)) .GT. ABS(A(IMX,IPASS)))THEN
               IMX = IROW
            END IF
   2     CONTINUE
*
*                      INTERCHANGE THE ELEMENTS OF ROW IPASS AND
*                      ROW IMX IN BOTH A AND AINV
*
         IF(IMX .NE. IPASS)THEN
            DO 3 ICOL = 1,N
*
               TEMP = AINV(IPASS,ICOL)
               AINV(IPASS,ICOL) = AINV(IMX,ICOL)
               AINV(IMX,ICOL)   = TEMP
*
               IF(ICOL .GE. IPASS)THEN
*
                  TEMP = A(IPASS,ICOL)
                  A(IPASS,ICOL) = A(IMX,ICOL)
                  A(IMX,ICOL)   = TEMP
*
               END IF
   3        CONTINUE
         END IF
*
*
*
*                      THE CURRENT PIVOT IS NOW A(IPASS,IPASS).
*
         PIVOT = A(IPASS,IPASS)
*
*                      THE DETERMINANT IS THE PRODUCT OF THE
*                      PIVOT ELEMENTS.
*
         DET = DET * PIVOT
*
*                      IF THE DETERMINANT IS ZERO, THE MATRIX IS
*                      SINGULAR. THE CALCULATION STOPS AND A
*                      DIAGNOSTIC MESSAGE IS PRINTED.
*
         IF(DET .EQ. 0.0)THEN
            WRITE(*,10)
            STOP
         END IF
*
*                      STEP 1 CONSISTS IN NORMALIZING THE PIVOT ROW
*                      BY DIVIDING ACROSS BY THE CURRENT PIVOT.
*
         DO 6 ICOL = 1,N
*
            AINV(IPASS,ICOL) = AINV(IPASS,ICOL)/PIVOT
            IF(ICOL .GE. IPASS)THEN
               A(IPASS,ICOL) = A(IPASS,ICOL)/PIVOT
            END IF
*
   6     CONTINUE
*
```

Continued

```
*                    STEP TWO CONSISTS IN REPLACING EACH ROW BY THE
*                    ROW PLUS A MULTIPLE OF THE PIVOT ROW WITH THE
*                    FACTOR CHOSEN SO THAT THE ELEMENT OF A IN THE
*                    PIVOT COLUMN IS ZERO.
*
         DO 8 IROW = 1,N
*
           IF(IROW .NE. IPASS)THEN
*
*                    SET THE FACTOR FOR THIS ROW.
*
               FACTOR = A(IROW,IPASS)
           END IF
*
*                    REPLACE ALL ELEMENTS (INCLUDING AINV) OF THIS ROW.
*
           DO 7 ICOL = 1,N
*
             IF(IROW .NE. IPASS)THEN
               AINV(IROW,ICOL) = AINV(IROW,ICOL) -
     +              FACTOR*AINV(IPASS,ICOL)
               A(IROW,ICOL)    = A(IROW,ICOL)    -
     +              FACTOR*A(IPASS,ICOL)
             END IF
*
   7         CONTINUE
*
   8     CONTINUE
*
   9 CONTINUE
*
      RETURN
*-------------------------------------------------------------
* FORMAT
*
  10 FORMAT(5X,'---ERROR IN MINV--- THE MATRIX IS SINGULAR',/,
     +        10X,'PROGRAM TERMINATED')
      END
```

PROBLEMS

1. Given the two matrices

$$[A] = \begin{pmatrix} 1 & -1 & 1 \\ -1 & 1 & -1 \\ 1 & -1 & 1 \end{pmatrix} \quad [B] = \begin{pmatrix} 0 & 1 & 1 \\ -1 & 0 & 1 \\ -1 & -1 & 0 \end{pmatrix}$$

evaluate the following
a. $[A] + [B]$

b. $[A]^2$, i.e., $[A][A]$

c. $[A][B] - [B][A]$

2. Given the two matrices

$$[A] = \begin{pmatrix} 0 & -2 & 1 \\ -2 & 1 & -2 \\ 1 & -2 & 0 \end{pmatrix} \quad [B] = \begin{pmatrix} -4 & -2 & 3 \\ -2 & -1 & -2 \\ 3 & -2 & -4 \end{pmatrix}$$

a. Evaluate $[A][B]$

b. From the result of part a, determine $[B^{-1}]$

c. Using the result for $[B^{-1}]$, solve the equation $[B]\mathbf{x} = \mathbf{b}$ where $\mathbf{b}$ is given below. Verify that the solution is correct.

$$\mathbf{b} = \begin{pmatrix} 1 \\ -3 \\ 1 \end{pmatrix}$$

3. Evaluate the following determinants:

a. $\begin{vmatrix} 1 & 2 \\ 2 & 3 \end{vmatrix}$ **b.** $\begin{vmatrix} 1 & 0 & 1 \\ 0 & 1 & 2 \\ 1 & 2 & 3 \end{vmatrix}$ **c.** $\begin{vmatrix} 1 & 0 & 0 & 2 \\ 0 & 1 & 0 & 1 \\ 0 & 0 & 1 & 2 \\ 2 & 1 & 2 & 3 \end{vmatrix}$

4. The following determinants are all zero. Justify this statement without explicitly evaluating each determinant.

a. $\begin{vmatrix} 1 & 2 \\ 2 & 4 \end{vmatrix}$ **b.** $\begin{vmatrix} 1 & 2 & 3 \\ 3 & 2 & 1 \\ 4 & 4 & 4 \end{vmatrix}$ **c.** $\begin{vmatrix} 1 & 0 & 1 & 0 \\ 0 & 1 & 0 & 1 \\ 1 & 1 & -1 & -1 \\ 2 & -1 & 1 & -2 \end{vmatrix}$ ~~determinant not zero~~

5. Solve the matrix equation

$$\begin{pmatrix} 0 & 4 & 4 \\ -4 & 0 & 4 \\ -4 & -4 & 1 \end{pmatrix} \begin{pmatrix} x_1 \\ x_2 \\ x_3 \end{pmatrix} = \begin{pmatrix} 4 \\ 4 \\ 1 \end{pmatrix}$$

by using Cramer's rule. Verify your solution.

6. The matrix

$$[A] = \begin{pmatrix} 0 & 2 & 2 \\ -2 & 0 & 2 \\ -2 & -2 & 0 \end{pmatrix}$$

is singular (i.e., $|A| = 0$). Use Cramer's rule to determine the value of α for which there is a solution of the equation $[A]\mathbf{x} = \mathbf{b}$, where

$$\mathbf{b} = \begin{pmatrix} 2 \\ 2 \\ \alpha \end{pmatrix}$$

For this value of α is the solution *unique*?

7. Solve the following matrix equations by Gauss-Jordan elimination. Verify the solution.

a. $\begin{pmatrix} 1 & 2 & 0 \\ 2 & 1 & 2 \\ 0 & 2 & 1 \end{pmatrix} \begin{pmatrix} x_1 \\ x_2 \\ x_3 \end{pmatrix} = \begin{pmatrix} 1 \\ 7 \\ -1 \end{pmatrix}$

b. $\begin{pmatrix} 5 & -1 & 5 \\ 0 & 2 & 0 \\ -5 & 3 & -15 \end{pmatrix} \begin{pmatrix} x_1 \\ x_2 \\ x_3 \end{pmatrix} = \begin{pmatrix} 1 \\ -2 \\ 7 \end{pmatrix}$

c. $\begin{pmatrix} 2 & 0 & 1 \\ 1 & 0 & 1 \\ 0 & -2 & 0 \end{pmatrix} \begin{pmatrix} x_1 \\ x_2 \\ x_3 \end{pmatrix} = \begin{pmatrix} 2 \\ 2 \\ 4 \end{pmatrix}$ Beware of zero pivots!

8. Determine the inverse matrix of each of the matrices below by using the method of Gauss-Jordan elimination.

a. $\begin{pmatrix} 3 & 0 & 1 \\ 0 & 5 & 0 \\ -1 & 1 & -1 \end{pmatrix}$ b. $\begin{pmatrix} 1 & 1 & 1 & 1 \\ 0 & 1 & 1 & 1 \\ 0 & 0 & 1 & 1 \\ 0 & 0 & 0 & 1 \end{pmatrix}$ c. $\begin{pmatrix} 2 & 0 & 1 \\ 1 & 0 & 1 \\ 0 & -2 & 0 \end{pmatrix}$

9. Write the Fortran code for a subroutine CHECK(A, N, EPS) that will determine whether or not an n by n matrix $[A]$ is the identity matrix. If the test is affirmative, the subroutine will print a verification and return. If the test fails, a diagnostic is printed and the routine will stop. The form of the test is to verify that for all elements of the matrix $[A]$,

for nondiagonal elements, $(i \neq j)$: $|a_{ij}| < \text{EPS}$

for diagonal elements, $(i = j)$: $|a_{ii} - 1| < \text{EPS}$

10. Construct the Fortran code for a function subprogram MAXCOL (A, N, IPV, K) that will scan the kth column of the n by n matrix $[A]$ from the IPV row on down and will return the *row* number of the maximum element. For example, if the matrix $[A]$ is

$$[A] = \begin{pmatrix} 3 & 1 & 6 \\ 0 & 5 & 1 \\ 4 & 2 & 2 \end{pmatrix}$$

then MAXCOL(A, 3, 2, 2) would return a value of 2. The maximum element of the second column is 5, which is in row 2.

11. Design a Fortran subroutine SWITCH(A, B, N, I1, I2) that will interchange the contents of rows i_1 and i_2 of the n by n matrix $[A]$ and the column vector **b**.

12. Using the subprograms of the two previous problems:
  a. Rewrite the Fortran code for the subroutine GAUSS of Figure 12-1 to switch rows to maximize the pivot element for each pass.
  b. Test your routine by finding the solutions to the matrix equations of Problem 12.7.

13. Rewrite the Fortran code for the subroutine GAUSS of Figure 12-1 so that the subroutine will compute the inverse of a matrix $[A]$. The subroutine will return the elements of the inverse in the array $[B]$, and the matrix $[A]$ will be destroyed in the process. Do *not* attempt row switching to maximize pivots; if the current pivot is "small," stop.

14. Using the subprograms of Problems 12.10 and 12.11, construct the Fortran code for a subroutine MINV based on the Gauss-Jordan routine of Figure 12-1 that computes the inverse of a matrix $[A]$. The elements of the inverse are returned in an array **b**, the matrix $[A]$ will be destroyed in the process, and the code *should* employ row switching to maximize the pivot in each pass.

15. Solve the matrix equation below by the Gauss-Siedel iteration procedure,
  a. Do not switch rows to obtain diagonal dominance. Continue for at least five iterations. Does the solution appear to be converging?
  b. Interchange rows to achieve diagonal dominance and redo the calculation. For both calculations use the same initial guess for the solution vector.

$$\begin{pmatrix} 1 & 4 & 1 \\ 1 & 1 & 4 \\ 4 & 1 & 1 \end{pmatrix} \begin{pmatrix} x_1 \\ x_2 \\ x_3 \end{pmatrix} = \begin{pmatrix} 1 \\ -1 \\ 0 \end{pmatrix}$$

16. Construct a Fortran function that will examine an n by n matrix and will return the value 1 if the matrix is diagonally dominant and the value 0 if it is not.

17. Design a Fortran subroutine that will attempt in a single pass to rearrange the rows of a nondiagonally dominant matrix to bring it into a diagonally dominant form. Use the subprograms of Problems 10 and 11. (It may not be possible to bring a matrix into a diagonally dominant form in a single pass.)

18. Solve the following set of *nonlinear* equations by a Gauss-Siedel procedure. (Note: Diagonal dominance does not guarantee convergence of nonlinear equations.)

$$4x - y^2 - z^2 = 3$$
$$-x + 4y^2 - z = 2$$
$$-x - y - 4z = 1$$

Start with an initial guess of $x = y = z = 0$ and continue for four or five iterations.

19. **a.** Using the Gauss-Siedel subroutine, solve the equation below which contains a banded coefficient matrix of order 50. Start with an initial guess for the solution vector of all zeros.

$$\begin{pmatrix} 8 & -2 & 1 & 0 & \cdots & \cdots & \cdots & 0 \\ -2 & 8 & -2 & 1 & 0 & \cdots & \cdots & 0 \\ 1 & -2 & 8 & -2 & 1 & 0 & \cdots & 0 \\ 0 & 1 & -2 & 8 & -2 & 1 & \cdots & 0 \\ \cdots & \cdots & \cdots & \cdots & \cdots & \cdots & \cdots & \cdots \\ \cdots & \cdots & \cdots & \cdots & \cdots & \cdots & \cdots & \cdots \\ \cdots & \cdots & 1 & -2 & 8 & -2 & 1 & 0 \\ \cdots & \cdots & 0 & 1 & -2 & 8 & -2 & 1 \\ \cdots & \cdots & 0 & 0 & 1 & -2 & 8 & -2 \\ \cdots & \cdots & \cdots & 0 & 0 & 1 & -2 & 8 \end{pmatrix} \begin{pmatrix} x_1 \\ x_2 \\ x_3 \\ x_4 \\ \cdots \\ \cdots \\ x_{47} \\ x_{48} \\ x_{49} \\ x_{50} \end{pmatrix} = \begin{pmatrix} 1 \\ 1 \\ 1 \\ 1 \\ 1 \\ 1 \\ 1 \\ 1 \\ 1 \\ 1 \end{pmatrix}$$

b. Since the matrix contains a great many zeros, the general Gauss-Siedel subroutine is not very efficient. Construct a more compact program by solving the equations directly as

$$x_1 = (1 + 2x_2 - x_3)/8$$

$$x_2 = [1 + 2(x_3 + x_1) - x_4]/8$$

$$\vdots$$

$$x_i = [1 + 2(x_{i-1} + x_{i+1}) - (x_{i-2} + x_{i+2})]/8 \qquad \text{for } i = 3, 48$$

$$\vdots$$

$$x_{49} = [1 + 2(x_{48} + x_{50}) - x_{47}]/8$$

$$x_{50} = (1 + 2x_{49} - x_{48})/8$$

using DO loops in an obvious manner. Compare the execution times for the two solutions.

PROGRAMMING ASSIGNMENT VI

Civil Engineering: Fluid Flow through a Plumbing Network

When designing a system for transporting fluid from one point to another, the engineer is frequently faced with the task of incorporating a new pipe into an existing and complicated maze of pipes, pumps, and valves. Adding an additional pipe anywhere in the system will change the rate of fluid flow in all pipes in the system in a complicated way. However, in a simple modeling of the network, the relationships between the flows in the different parts of the system can be represented by a set of linear equations which are then solved using the methods of Chapter 12. The ideas used to establish these equations are really quite simple. They are

Rule 1:

The Junction Equation: At a junction of two or more pipes, the amount of fluid flowing into the junction must equal the amount of fluid flowing out of the junction. This rule is a statement of the conservation of matter. Thus, for the junction below

$$Q_1 = Q_2 + Q_3 + Q_4$$

437

Rule 2:
Linear Pressure Drop: The pressure drop a fluid experiences when flowing through a pipe is due to the friction with the walls of the pipe. The fluid flow is classified as either turbulent or laminar. Turbulent flow is extremely complicated and will not be treated in this problem. (Unfortunately, almost all flow in pipes is turbulent and thus this problem may not be an adequate model of the network.) Laminar flow is very slow, even flow through the pipe. For this case the pressure drop across a length of pipe is given by the equation

(VI.1)
$$\Delta P = \frac{8\eta L}{\pi R^4} Q = KQ$$

where
Q = flow rate (m³/sec)

L = pipe length (m)

R = pipe radius (m)

η = fluid viscosity (kg/sec-m)

ΔP = pressure drop (N/m²)

K = effective resistance (kg/sec-m⁴)

Rule 3:
The Loop Equation: If the total pressure drop is computed as the sum of the pressure drops of pipes connected in a series, then the pressure drop around any closed loop must be zero. (Note: When traversing a pipe *against* the direction of flow, the pressure across

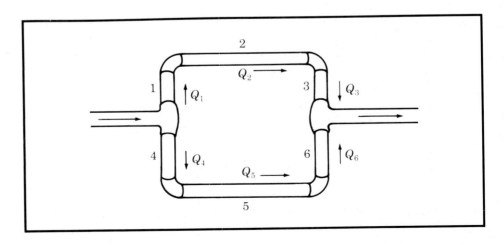

the length of pipe will increase, i.e., the pressure drop ΔP is negative.)

Thus around the loop containing pipes 1 through 6 and in the direction of the fluid flow as drawn, we have

$$\Delta P_1 + \Delta P_2 + \Delta P_3 - \Delta P_4 - \Delta P_5 - \Delta P_6 = 0$$

While rule 1 states

$$Q_1 = Q_2 = Q_3$$
$$Q_4 = Q_5 = Q_6$$
$$Q_{\text{in}} = Q_{\text{out}} = Q_1 + Q_4 = Q_3 + Q_6$$

And from rule 2, we have

$$(K_1 + K_2 + K_3)Q_1 = (K_4 + K_5 + K_6)Q_2$$

which may easily be solved to obtain Q_1 in terms of Q_{in} and the pipe resistances.

The purpose of this problem is to apply these rules to compute the flow rates in the very complicated pipe network shown in Figure VI-1.

In Figure VI-1 the following conditions apply:

1. The resistance of a pipe is $K = (8\eta L)/(\pi R^4)$
2. The pressure drop across a pipe in the direction of the fluid flow is $\Delta P = KQ$
3. The pressure at the main pump starts out equal to P_0.
4. The pressure at an open tap is zero.

The problem is analyzed by first writing junction equations for all the junctions labeled A through I on the Figure.

Junction	Junction equation
A	$Q_1 - Q_2 - Q_3 = 0$
B	$Q_2 - Q_4 - Q_{16} = 0$
C	$Q_{16} - Q_5 - Q_{17} = 0$
D	$Q_{17} - Q_6 - Q_{18} = 0$
E	$Q_3 + Q_{18} - Q_7 = 0$
F	$Q_4 - Q_9 - Q_8 = 0$
G	$Q_5 - Q_{11} - Q_{10} = 0$
H	$Q_6 - Q_{13} - Q_{12} = 0$
I	$Q_7 - Q_{15} - Q_{14} = 0$

We have thus far 9 equations in 18 unknowns (the Q_i). Nine more equations are therefore required for a solution. These are supplied by rule 3 applied to nine arbitrary but independent loops.

Figure VI-1 A schematic of a complicated plumbing network.

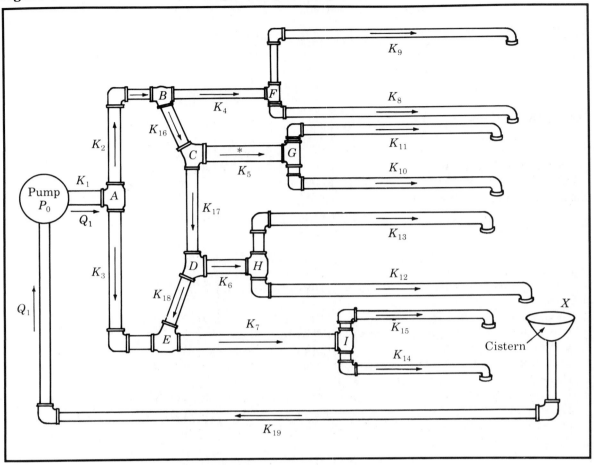

Loop	Equation
ABCDEA	$\Delta P_2 + \Delta P_{16} + \Delta P_{17} + \Delta P_{18} - \Delta P_3 = 0$
	$K_2 Q_2 + K_{16} Q_{16} + K_{17} Q_{17} + K_{18} Q_{18} - K_3 Q_3 = 0$
FXF	$\Delta P_9 - \Delta P_8 = 0$
	$K_9 Q_9 - K_8 Q_8 = 0$
GXG	$\Delta P_{11} - \Delta P_{10} = 0$
	$K_{11} Q_{11} - K_{10} Q_{10} = 0$
HXH	$\Delta P_{13} - \Delta P_{12} = 0$
	$K_{13} Q_{13} - K_{12} Q_{12} = 0$
IXI	$\Delta P_{15} - \Delta P_{14} = 0$
	$K_{15} Q_{15} - K_{14} Q_{14} = 0$
BFXGCB	$\Delta P_4 + \Delta P_9 - \Delta P_{10} - \Delta P_5 - \Delta P_{16} = 0$
	$K_4 Q_4 + K_9 Q_9 - K_{10} Q_{10} - K_5 Q_5 - K Q_{16} = 0$

CGXHDC
$$\Delta P_5 + \Delta P_{11} - \Delta P_{12} - \Delta P_6 - \Delta P_{17} = 0$$
$$K_5 Q_5 + K_{11} Q_{11} - K_{12} Q_{12} - K_6 Q_6 - K_{17} Q_{17} = 0$$

DHXIED
$$\Delta P_6 + \Delta P_{13} - \Delta P_{14} - \Delta P_7 - \Delta P_{18} = 0$$
$$K_6 Q_6 + K_{13} Q_{13} - K_{14} Q_{14} - K_7 Q_7 - K_{18} Q_{18} = 0$$

$P_0 AEIXP_0$
$$\Delta P_1 + \Delta P_3 + \Delta P_7 + \Delta P_{14} + \Delta P_{19} = P_0$$
$$(K_1 + K_{19})Q_1 + K_3 Q_3 + K_7 Q_7 + K_{14} Q_{14} = P_0$$

Notice that the last equation does not equal zero because there is a pump (i.e., a source of pressure increase) within the loop. We now have 18 equations in 18 unknowns and can proceed to fomulate the problem in a matrix form suitable for computer solution. If the equations are written in the form $[A]\mathbf{Q} = \mathbf{b}$, the resulting coefficient matrix is shown in Figure VI-2 and the right-hand-side vector, $\mathbf{b}$ has components, $b_i = 0$ for $i = 1$ to 17 and $b_{18} = P_0$.

Problem Specifics

1. Construct a data file that contains the fluid viscosity η, the pressure head at the pump P_0, and the lengths L_i and radii R_i, of the 19 pipes in the problem. The main program should then read all these quantities, compute the effective resistances for the pipes K_i, and print in a neat form. (Note: K_i should not be an integer variable.)
2. Use a data statement to initially "zero" the entire coefficient matrix. Then assign values to the nonzero elements. Note that although it is not standard Fortran 77, some compilers permit multiple assignments on one line; for example,

$$A(1, 1) = A(2, 2) = A(5, 3) = A(6, 4) = 1$$

3. Form a copy of the coefficient matrix.
4. Use the subroutine MINV to compute the inverse of the matrix $[A]$.
5. Compute $[A][A^{-1}]$ and have the program check that it is the identity matrix within a tolerance EPS $= 10^{-6}$.
6. Solve for the flow rates Q_i by using the inverse matrix.
7. Print in a neat form the matrix $[A]$, the determinant of $[A]$, the inverse matrix $[A^{-1}]$, and the solution for the flow rates.
   Note: If the numbers for the flow rate turn out to be negative, this means that the direction of flow is opposite to that assumed in the figure.

Additional Problem   (to be solved by hand using the computed values for the inverse matrix): Since the computed flow in pipes 10 and 11 is weak, perhaps a helper pump is needed. If the helper pump were placed in pipe 5 at the point indicated by an asterisk on Figure VI-1, find the *new* flow rate in pipe 15. (Hint: This change alters *only* the fifteenth and sixteenth equa-

Figure VI-2 The coefficient matrix for the plumbing network problem (all blank entries are zero).

	1	2	3	4	5	6	7	8	9	10	11	12	13	14	15	16	17	18
1	1	-1	-1															
2		1		-1												-1		
3					-1											1	-1	
4						-1											1	-1
5			1	1	1													1
6							-1	-1	-1									
7					1	1				-1	-1							
8							1					-1	-1					
9														-1	-1			
10		K_2	$-K_3$															
11								K_8	$-K_9$									
12										$-K_{10}$	K_{11}							
13												$-K_{12}$	K_{13}					
14														$-K_{14}$	K_{15}			
15									K_9	$-K_{10}$						$-K_{16}$		
16					K_5	$-K_6$					K_{11}	$-K_{12}$					$-K_{17}$	
17						K_6	$-K_7$						K_{13}	$-K_{14}$				$-K_{18}$
18	$K_1+ K_{19}$		K_3				K_7							K_{14}				

tions of the set. Rewrite these two equations and see how the overall matrix equations are affected. The solution should then be clear.)

The solution for this problem is given in Figures VI-3 and VI-4.

The solution for this problem is given in Figures VI-3 and VI-4.

```
      PROGRAM PLUMB
*--
*-- This program computes the rate of flow of fluid through a
*-- complicated network of pipes and pumps. There are 18 equations in
*-- 18 unknown flow rates which are written in matrix form. The
*-- coefficient matrix is [A] and a copy of this matrix is needed as
*-- the subroutine (MINV) that computes the inverse also destroys
*-- [A]. The effective resistances of each of the pipes are stored
*-- in the array K(). The pressure from the main pump is P0. The
*-- inverse of [A] is computed and stored in [AINV]. The product
*-- of [A] with its inverse is computed and compared with the identity
*-- to determine the effect of round-off errors.
*-------------------------------------------------------------------
* Variables
*--
      PARAMETER (AA = -1.)
      REAL A(18,18),ACOPY(18,18),AINV(18,18),B(18),Q(18),K(19),
     +     R(19),L(19),P0,VISCOS,DET
      INTEGER N
*--
*--          A(,)     --  The Coefficient Matrix
*--          ACOPY(,)--  A Copy of [A]
*--          AINV(,)  --  The Inverse of Matrix [A]
*--          B()      --  The Right-Hand-Side Vector
*--          Q()      --  The Solution Vector Containing Flow Rates
*--          L()      --  The Lengths of the Pipes
*--          R()      --  The Radii of the Pipes
*--          K()      --  Effective Resistances of the Pipes
*--          P0       --  The Pressure Head of the Main Pump
*--          VISCOS   --  The Fluid Viscosity
*--          DET      --  The Determinant of [A]
*--          N        --  The Size of the Matrices (Here 18)
*--          AA       --  A Constant (-1.) used in filling A()
*-------------------------------------------------------------------
* Initialization
*--
      DATA ((A(I,J),J=1,18),I=1,18)/324*0.0/
      DATA (B(I),I=1,18)/18*0.0/
*--          Since A() has so many plus and minus ones, the
*--          easiest way to assign these values is via a
*--          DATA statement.
*--
      DATA A(1,1), A(2,2), A(3,16),A(4,17),A(5,3), A(5,18),
     +     A(6,4), A(7,5), A(8,6), A(9,7)/10*1.0/
*
      DATA A(1,2), A(1,3), A(2,4), A(2,16),A(3,5), A(3,17),
     +     A(4,6), A(4,18),A(5,7), A(6,8), A(6,9), A(7,10),
     +     A(7,11),A(8,12),A(8,13),A(9,14),A(9,15)/17*AA/
*
      N = 18
      PI = ACOS(-1.)
*--
*--          Read the data file for the values of
*--          the pipe lengths and radii
*--
```

Continued

Continued

Figure VI-3
The Fortran code for the solution of the sample problem.

```
            OPEN(21,FILE='PIPES')
            REWIND 21
            READ(21,*)PO,VISCOS
            READ(21,*)(R(I),I=1,19)
            READ(21,*)(L(I),I=1,19)
*--
*--              Compute individual pipe effective resistances
*--
            DO 1 I = 1,19
                    K(I) = 8. * VISCOS * L(I)/(PI * R(I)**4)
    1       CONTINUE
*--
*--              Since the range of values of the elements of the
*--              coefficient matrix is so extreme, scale down the
*--              rows containing the K's. This does not alter the eqs.
*--
            DO 2 I = 1,19
                    K(I) = K(I)/10000.
    2       CONTINUE
            PO = PO/10000.
*--
*--              Print the input parameters of the problem
*--
            WRITE(*,23)PO,VISCOS
            WRITE(*,24)(I,R(I),L(I),K(I),I = 1,19)
*--
*--              Reassign all the nonzero elements of [A]
*--
            A(10,2)  =   K(2)
            A(10,3)  =  -K(3)
            A(18,3)  =   K(3)
            A(15,4)  =   K(4)
            A(15,5)  =  -K(5)
            A(16,5)  =   K(5)
            A(16,6)  =  -K(6)
            A(17,6)  =   K(6)
            A(17,7)  =  -K(7)
            A(18,7)  =   K(7)
            A(11,8)  =   K(8)
            A(11,9)  =  -K(9)
            A(15,9)  =   K(9)
            A(12,10) =  -K(10)
            A(15,10) =  -K(10)
            A(12,11) =   K(11)
            A(16,11) =   K(11)
            A(13,12) =  -K(12)
            A(16,12) =  -K(12)
            A(13,13) =   K(13)
            A(17,13) =   K(13)
            A(14,14) =  -K(14)
            A(17,14) =  -K(14)
            A(18,14) =   K(14)
            A(14,15) =   K(15)
            A(10,16) =   K(16)
            A(15,16) =  -K(16)
            A(10,17) =   K(17)
            A(16,17) =  -K(17)
            A(10,18) =   K(18)
            A(17,18) =  -K(18)
            A(18,1)  =   K(1) + K(19)
*--
            B(18)    =   PO
*--
```

```
*--              Form a copy of the coefficient matrix
*--
        DO 3 I = 1,N
        DO 3 J = 1,N
              ACOPY(I,J) = A(I,J)
   3    CONTINUE
*--
*--              Call the subroutine MINV to compute the inverse
*--
        CALL MINV(A,AINV,18,N,DET)
*--
*--              Check that the determinant is not too small
*--
        IF(ABS(DET) .LT. 1.E-6)THEN
              WRITE(*,*)'MATRIX ILL-CONDITIONED DETERMINANT = ',DET
              WRITE(*,*)'PROGRAM TERMINATED'
              STOP
        END IF
*--
*--              Check that [AINV] * [ACOPY] = Identity
*--              (Store the product in [A] since it has been destroyed)
*--
        DO 5 I = 1,N
        DO 5 J = 1,N
              A(I,J) = 0.0
              DO 4 M = 1,N
                    A(I,J) = A(I,J) + AINV(I,M)*ACOPY(M,J)
   4          CONTINUE
   5    CONTINUE
*--
*--              Next scan the product to verify that it has 1's on
*--              the diagonal and zeros elsewhere
*--
        DO 6 I = 1,N
        DO 6 J = 1,N
              IF(I .EQ. J)THEN
                    IF(ABS(A(I,I)-1.) .GT. 1.E-6)THEN
                          WRITE(*,26),I,I,A(I,I)
                          STOP
                    END IF
              ELSE
                    IF(ABS(A(I,J)) .GT. 1.E-6)THEN
                          WRITE(*,26),I,J,A(I,J)
                          STOP
                    END IF
              END IF
   6    CONTINUE
*--
*--              Compute the solution vector for the flow rates
*--
        DO 8 I = 1,N
              Q(I) = 0.0
              DO 7 M = 1,N
                    Q(I) = Q(I) + AINV(I,M) * B(M)
   7          CONTINUE
   8    CONTINUE
*--
*--              Finally, print the matrices [A], [AINV], and the
*--              solution for the flow rates.
*--
        WRITE(*,27)(I,I = 1,18)
        DO 9 I = 1,N
              WRITE(*,28)I,(ACOPY(I,J),J = 1,N)
```

Continued

```
    9     CONTINUE
          WRITE(*,29)(I,I = 1,N)
          DO 10 I = 1,N
                  WRITE(*,281)I,(AINV(I,J),J = 1,N)
   10     CONTINUE
          WRITE(*,30)(I,I = 1,N),(B(J),J = 1,N)
          WRITE(*,31)(I,I = 1,9),(Q(J),J = 1,9)
          WRITE(*,32)(I,I = 10,N),(Q(J),J = 10,N)
*-------------------------------------------------------------------
* Formats
*--
   23     FORMAT(//,5X,'THE RESULTS OF THE CALCULATION OF THE FLOW',
          +        ' RATES',//,10X,'PRESSURE HEAD AT MAIN PUMP',T40,
          +        '=',E9.2,' NT/M2',//,10X,'LIQUID VISCOSITY',T40,
          +        '=',E9.2,///,10X,'PIPE PARAMETERS',//,15X,'PIPE NO.',
          +        T25,'RADIUS',T35,'LENGTH',T45,'EFFECTIVE',/,
          +        T27,'(M)',T36,'(M)',T45,'RESISTANCE (SCALED)')
*--
   24     FORMAT(T18,I2,T25,F5.2, T35,F5.1,T47,F10.2)
   25     FORMAT(//,'THE DETERMINANT OF THE COEFFICIENT MATRIX = ',
          +        E11.4)
   26     FORMAT(/,5X,'--WARNING--',//,10X,'THE PRODUCT A*AINV SHOULD',
          +        ' BE THE IDENTITY MATRIX',//,10X,'BUT THE ELEMENT',/
          +        ,10X,'A(',I2,',',I2,') = ',F12.9)
*--
   27     FORMAT(//,5X,'THE COEFFICIENT MATRIX',//,
          +        4X,18(2X,I2,1X),/)
   28     FORMAT(1X,I2,1X,18F5.1)
  281     FORMAT(1X,I2,1X,18(F4.2,1X))
*--
   29     FORMAT(/,4X,'THE INVERSE OF THE COEFFICIENT MATRIX',//,
          +        4X,18(2X,I2,1X),/)
   30     FORMAT(/,4X,'THE RIGHT-HAND-SIDE VECTOR',/,
          +        4X,18(2X,I2,1X),//,4X,18F5.2,/)
   31     FORMAT(/,4X,'THE SOLUTION FOR THE FLOW RATES',//,
          +        4X,9(4X,I2,4X),/,4X,9(F9.5,1X),/)
   32     FORMAT(/,5X,9(4X,I2,4X),/,4X,9(F9.5,1X),/)
*--
          END
*-------------------------------------------------------------------
          SUBROUTINE MINV(A,AINV,ND,N,DET)
```

Table VI-1 The Parameters for the pipes of the sample problem.

Pipe No.	1	2	3	4	5	6	7	8	9	10
R (m)	0.12	0.08	0.08	0.06	0.06	0.06	0.06	0.02	0.02	0.02
L (m)	200.	200.	100.	50.	100.	30.	10.	20.	15.	15.

$\eta = 0.001\,\text{Pa-sec}$
$P_0 = 4 \times 10^4\ \text{N/m}^2 = 4 \times 10^4\ \text{Pa}$

Pipe No.	11	12	13	14	15	16	17	18	19
R (m)	0.02	0.03	0.03	0.02	0.02	0.06	0.08	0.08	0.24
L (m)	8.	5.	30.	20.	18.	40.	140.	80.	125.

Figure VI-4 The output of the sample problem.

```
THE RESULTS OF THE CALCULATION OF THE FLOW RATES

    PRESSURE HEAD AT MAIN PUMP   = 0.40E+01 NT/M2
    LIQUID VISCOSITY             = 0.10E-02

    PIPE PARAMETERS
        PIPE NO.   RADIUS    LENGTH    EFFECTIVE
                    (M)       (M)      RESISTANCE (SCALED)
            1       0.12     200.0        0.25
            2       0.08     200.0        1.24
            3       0.08     100.0        0.62
            4       0.06      50.0        0.98
            5       0.06     100.0        1.96
            6       0.06      30.0        0.59
            7       0.06      10.0        0.20
            8       0.02      20.0       31.83
            9       0.02      15.0       23.87
           10       0.02      15.0       23.87
           11       0.02       8.0       12.73
           12       0.03       5.0        1.57
           13       0.03      30.0        9.43
           14       0.02      20.0       31.83
           15       0.02      18.0       28.65
           16       0.06      40.0        0.79
           17       0.08     140.0        0.87
           18       0.08      80.0        0.50
           19       0.24     125.0        0.01
```

THE COEFFICIENT MATRIX

	1	2	3	4	5	6	7	8	9	10	11	12	13	14	15	16	17	18
1	1.0	-1.0	-1.0	0.0	0.0	0.0	0.0	0.0	0.0	0.0	0.0	0.0	0.0	0.0	0.0	0.0	0.0	0.0
2	0.0	1.0	0.0	-1.0	0.0	0.0	0.0	0.0	0.0	0.0	0.0	0.0	0.0	0.0	0.0	-1.0	0.0	0.0
3	0.0	0.0	0.0	0.0	-1.0	0.0	0.0	0.0	0.0	0.0	0.0	0.0	0.0	0.0	0.0	1.0	-1.0	0.0
4	0.0	0.0	0.0	0.0	0.0	-1.0	0.0	0.0	0.0	0.0	0.0	0.0	0.0	0.0	0.0	0.0	1.0	-1.0
5	0.0	0.0	1.0	0.0	0.0	0.0	-1.0	0.0	0.0	0.0	0.0	0.0	0.0	0.0	0.0	0.0	0.0	1.0
6	0.0	0.0	0.0	1.0	0.0	0.0	0.0	-1.0	-1.0	0.0	0.0	0.0	0.0	0.0	0.0	0.0	0.0	0.0
7	0.0	0.0	0.0	0.0	1.0	0.0	0.0	0.0	0.0	-1.0	-1.0	0.0	0.0	0.0	0.0	0.0	0.0	0.0
8	0.0	0.0	0.0	0.0	0.0	1.0	0.0	0.0	0.0	0.0	0.0	-1.0	-1.0	0.0	0.0	0.0	0.0	0.0
9	0.0	0.0	0.0	0.0	0.0	0.0	1.0	0.0	0.0	0.0	0.0	0.0	0.0	-1.0	-1.0	0.0	0.0	0.0
10	0.0	1.2	-0.6	0.0	0.0	0.0	0.0	0.0	0.0	0.0	0.0	0.0	0.0	0.0	0.0	0.8	0.9	0.5
11	0.0	0.0	0.0	0.0	0.0	0.0	0.0	31.8	-23.9	0.0	0.0	0.0	0.0	0.0	0.0	0.0	0.0	0.0
12	0.0	0.0	0.0	0.0	0.0	0.0	0.0	0.0	0.0	-23.9	12.7	0.0	0.0	0.0	0.0	0.0	0.0	0.0
13	0.0	0.0	0.0	0.0	0.0	0.0	0.0	0.0	0.0	0.0	0.0	-1.6	9.4	0.0	0.0	0.0	0.0	0.0
14	0.0	0.0	0.0	0.0	0.0	0.0	0.0	0.0	0.0	0.0	0.0	0.0	0.0	-31.8	28.6	0.0	0.0	0.0
15	0.0	0.0	0.0	1.0	-2.0	0.0	0.0	0.0	23.9	-23.9	0.0	0.0	0.0	0.0	0.0	-0.8	0.0	0.0
16	0.0	0.0	0.0	0.0	2.0	-0.6	0.0	0.0	0.0	0.0	12.7	-1.6	0.0	0.0	0.0	0.0	-0.9	0.0
17	0.0	0.0	0.0	0.0	0.0	0.6	-0.2	0.0	0.0	0.0	0.0	0.0	9.4	-31.8	0.0	0.0	0.0	-0.5
18	0.3	0.0	0.6	0.0	0.0	0.0	0.2	0.0	0.0	0.0	0.0	0.0	0.0	31.8	0.0	0.0	0.0	0.0

Continued

THE INVERSE OF THE COEFFICIENT MATRIX

	1	2	3	4	5	6	7	8	9	10	11	12	13	14	15	16	17	18
1	.89	.70	.61	.57	.70	.65	.50	.40	.69	.15	.02	-.07	-.36	.02	.05	.11	.40	.45
2	-.04	.57	.35	.14	.06	.53	.29	.10	.06	.31	.02	-.05	-.14	.00	.04	.07	.15	.15
3	-.08	.13	.26	.43	.64	.12	.21	.30	.63	-.16	.00	-.02	-.22	.02	.01	.03	.26	.30
4	-.01	-.06	-.04	-.02	-.02	.88	-.03	-.02	-.02	.04	.03	-.06	-.05	.00	.06	.06	.05	.05
5	-.02	-.06	-.09	-.04	-.03	-.05	.74	-.03	-.03	.03	.00	-.03	-.07	.00	.00	.08	.06	.06
6	-.08	-.17	-.24	-.33	-.21	-.16	-.19	.47	-.21	.07	.00	.02	-.26	-.01	-.01	-.03	.31	.30
7	-.01	-.02	-.02	-.03	-.04	-.02	-.02	-.02	.95	.00	.00	.00	.02	.03	.00	.00	-.02	.05
8	-.01	-.03	-.02	-.01	-.01	-.05	-.01	-.01	-.01	.02	.03	-.03	-.02	.00	.03	.03	.02	.02
9	-.01	-.03	-.02	-.01	-.01	-.07	-.02	-.01	-.01	.02	.00	-.04	-.03	.00	.04	.03	.03	.03
10	-.01	-.02	-.03	-.02	-.01	-.02	-.09	-.01	-.01	.01	.00	-.04	-.02	.00	.00	.03	.02	.02
11	-.01	-.04	-.06	-.03	-.02	-.04	-.17	-.02	-.02	.02	.00	.01	-.04	.00	.00	.06	.04	.04
12	-.06	-.14	-.20	-.28	-.18	-.13	-.16	-.46	-.18	.06	.00	.02	-.31	-.01	-.01	-.03	.27	.25
13	-.01	-.02	-.03	-.05	-.03	-.02	-.03	-.08	-.03	.01	.00	.00	.05	.00	.00	.00	.04	.04
14	-.01	-.01	-.01	-.01	-.02	-.01	-.01	-.01	-.02	.00	.00	.00	.01	.00	.00	.00	-.01	.02
15	-.01	-.01	-.01	-.01	-.02	-.01	-.01	-.01	-.03	.00	.00	.00	.01	.03	.00	.00	-.01	.02
16	-.03	-.37	.39	.17	.08	-.34	.32	.12	.08	.28	-.01	.01	-.09	.00	-.03	.01	.10	.10
17	-.01	-.31	-.52	.21	.11	-.29	-.42	.15	.11	.24	-.01	.04	-.02	.00	-.02	-.07	.04	.04
18	.06	-.14	-.28	-.46	.32	-.13	-.23	-.32	.32	.17	.00	.02	.24	.01	-.01	-.04	-.27	-.25

THE RIGHT HAND SIDE VECTOR

1	2	3	4	5	6	7	8	9	10	11	12	13	14	15	16	17	18
0.00	0.00	0.00	0.00	0.00	0.00	0.00	0.00	0.00	0.00	0.00	0.00	0.00	0.00	0.00	0.00	0.00	4.00

THE SOLUTION FOR THE FLOW RATES

1	2	3	4	5	6	7	8	9
1.79977	0.60870	1.19107	0.19036	0.23908	1.18701	0.18333	0.08158	0.10878

10	11	12	13	14	15	16	17	18
0.08316	0.15592	1.01743	0.16957	0.08684	0.09649	0.41835	0.17927	-1.00774

VI.2 PROGRAMMING PROBLEMS

Programming Problem A: Civil Engineering: A Model of a Stress Calculation for a Bridge

Large computer programs are used in civil engineering to compute the stresses in the supporting elements of a bridge. This is usually an extremely difficult problem since the effect of a load on the bridge and the weight of the bridge itself are transmitted to all elements of the bridge and result in a complicated interconnection of stress relations. However, by making enough simplifying assumptions the problem can be made tractable and employs only the simple essentials of statics that were learned in introductory physics. The bridge design considered here is a seven-element plane truss shown in Figure VI-5.

Each element or strut is assumed to be weightless and all are of length L. They are connected by frictionless pins. There is a load P on the bridge a

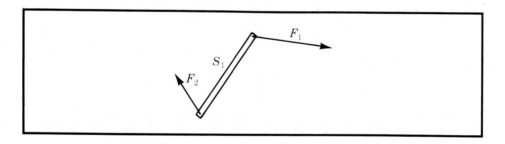

Figure VI-5 A
seven-element
plane truss.

distance x from the midpoint. To analyze the problem, we must draw a force
diagram for each strut and require

$$\sum F_x = 0 \qquad \sum F_y = 0 \qquad \sum \text{torques} = 0$$

Since all the struts are weightless, the forces on each strut (except S_7) act at
the ends only. For example, the force diagram for strut S_1 is

By requiring that the sum of the forces equal zero and the sum of the torques
equal zero, we see that $|F_1| = |F_2|$ *and* that the direction of the force must be
parallel to the strut. Thus the force diagram for all struts except S_7 is simply

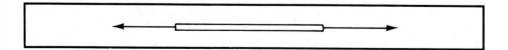

The diagram for S_7 is

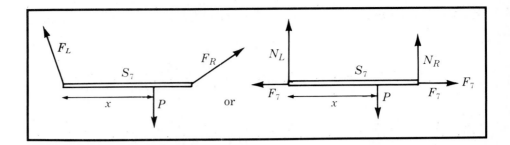

where the forces F_L and F_R have been written in terms of components perpendicular to the beam (N_L, N_R) and parallel to the beam, F_7. Since the sum of the torques on the strut is zero, we have

$$N_L = \left(1 - \frac{x}{L}\right)P$$

$$N_R = \frac{x}{L}P$$

Next, the forces on the struts can be either compressive or stretching. If they are *all* drawn as stretching forces, then if the calculation results in a force that is actually compressive, the computed value of the force will be negative.

The forces acting on the five pins must likewise be evaluated using force diagrams. The force of a strut on a pin is the negative of the force of the pin on the strut. If the forces exerted by the bridge supports are labeled as σ_L, σ_R, the resulting five force diagrams are drawn below.

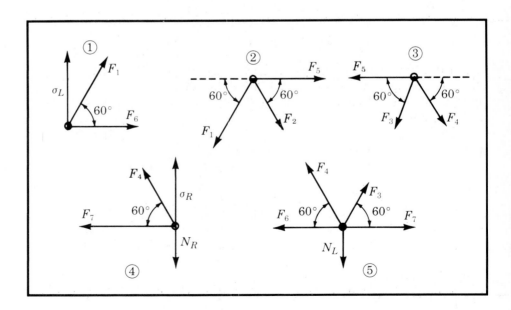

Finally, since the torque on the whole bridge is zero, we obtain the relations

$$(2L)\sigma_L = (L - x)P$$

$$\sigma_L = \frac{1}{2}\left(1 - \frac{x}{L}\right)P$$

Writing out the x and y equations for the five force diagrams we obtain the following equations: (Recall that $\cos(60°) = \frac{1}{2}$, $\sin(60°) = \sqrt{3}/2$.)

1. $F_1 + 2F_6 \qquad\qquad = 0$
2. $F_1 \qquad\qquad\qquad = -S(x, P) \qquad S(x, P) = \frac{1}{\sqrt{3}}\left(1 - \frac{x}{L}\right)P$
3. $F_1 + F_2 \qquad\qquad = 0$
4. $F_1 - F_2 - 2F_5 \quad\ = 0$
5. $F_3 + F_4 \qquad\qquad = 0$
6. $F_3 - F_4 + 2F_5 \quad\ = 0$
7. $F_2 - F_3 + 2F_6 - 2F_7 = 0 \qquad$ We only need seven equations.

These equations may be written in matrix form as

$$
\begin{matrix}
[A] & \mathbf{F} & = & \mathbf{b}_0
\end{matrix}
$$

$$
\begin{pmatrix}
1 & 0 & 0 & 0 & 0 & 2 & 0 \\
1 & 0 & 0 & 0 & 0 & 0 & 0 \\
1 & 1 & 0 & 0 & 0 & 0 & 0 \\
1 & -1 & 0 & 0 & -2 & 0 & 0 \\
0 & 0 & 1 & 1 & 0 & 0 & 0 \\
0 & 0 & 1 & -1 & 2 & 0 & 0 \\
0 & 1 & -1 & 0 & 0 & 2 & -2
\end{pmatrix}
\begin{pmatrix}
F_1 \\ F_2 \\ F_3 \\ F_4 \\ F_5 \\ F_6 \\ F_7
\end{pmatrix}
=
\begin{pmatrix}
0 \\ -S(x, P) \\ 0 \\ 0 \\ 0 \\ 0 \\ 0
\end{pmatrix}
$$

The problem is then to solve this equation for the forces on the struts.

In a more realistic analysis of the problem, the struts have a weight. This of course complicates the problem considerably. However, in many circumstances the complications appear only in the vector $\mathbf{b}$ and the coefficient matrix remains the same. The right-hand-side vector you should use for this problem is

$$
\mathbf{b} = \mathbf{b}_0 +
\begin{pmatrix}
-1 \\ 6 \\ -5 \\ 2 \\ 1 \\ 8 \\ 4
\end{pmatrix}
$$

where $P = 50$. The units of the elements of the vector $\mathbf{b}$ are 10^4 N. The equations are to be solved for $x/L = 0., 0.1, \ldots, 1.0$.

Problem Specifics

The main program for this problem should:

1. Read the elements of the vector, the load P, and the length L (use $L = 10$ m).
2. Set all the elements of $[A]$ to zero with a DATA statement, then redefine the nonzero elements. Also, since $[A]$ will be destroyed when its inverse is computed, a copy should be made.
3. Use the subroutine MINV or a library subroutine to compute the inverse of the matrix $[A]$ and evaluate $[A][A^{-1}]$.
4. Check that $[A][A^{-1}]$ is indeed the identity matrix.
5. Neatly print $\mathbf{b}$, $[A]$, $[A^{-1}]$, $|A|$, and the product $[A][A^{-1}]$.
6. Solve for the forces for $x/L = 0., 0.1, \ldots, 1.0$ and print the results.
7. Determine which of the load positions used results in the maximum stress on strut 5.

Programming Problem B: Electrical Engineering: The Currents in an Electrical Network

Electrical engineers frequently spend a good bit of their time solving network problems using Kirchoff's laws. Sounds impressive. However, the truth is that anyone can do the most complicated of linear network problems with a knowledge of matrix algebra and after a few minutes instruction in the theory of electrical networks. Consider the network illustrated in Figure VI-6.

In the figure the cube has a resistor on each of its 12 edges. The resistors are of known values R_i, $i = 1$ to 12. The eight corners are labeled a through

Figure VI-6 An electrical network consisting of resistors on the edges of a cube.

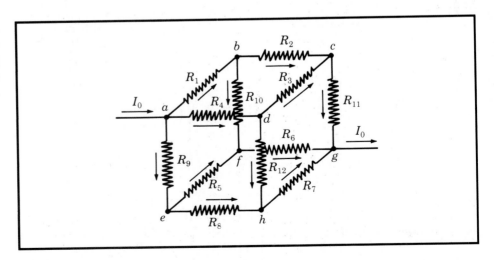

h. A known current I_0 flows into corner *a*. It then divides among the various wires and eventually flows out again at corner *g*. The assumed direction of the current in each edge is indicated by arrows.

The currents along each edge, I_i, $i = 1$ to 12, are not known and the problem is to solve for them. We will thus need 12 equations. These equations are supplied by Kirchoff's laws, which read

1. **Junction Law:** The sum of all current flowing into a corner must equal the sum of the currents flowing out of the corner (conservation of current).
2. **Ohm's Law:** The voltage drop across a resistor R_i (in the direction of the assumed current) is given by the product $V = I_i R_i$. The voltage against the direction of current increases, i.e., a negative voltage drop.
3. **Closed-Loop Rule:** The sum of the voltage drops around a closed loop must be zero. That is, the voltage at a point (the start of a loop) must equal the voltage at the same point (the end of the loop).

For example, the first rule applied to the currents flowing into corner *b* yields

$$I_1 = I_2 + I_{10} \qquad \text{corner } b$$

And the sum of the voltage drops around the loop labeled *abcda* is

$$V_{ab} + V_{bc} + V_{cd} + V_{da} = 0 \qquad abcda$$

But $V_{ad} = -V_{da} = I_4 R_4$, $V_{ab} = I_1 R_1$, etc. Thus, using Ohm's law, this relation can be written

$$I_1 R_1 + I_2 R_2 - I_4 R_4 - I_3 R_3 = 0 \qquad abcda$$

These rules are next applied to the cube network to obtain the 12 necessary equations. First the junction rule is applied to seven of the eight corners[1] resulting in

$$
\begin{array}{ll}
(a) & I_0 = I_1 + I_4 + I_9 \\
(b) & I_1 = I_2 + I_{10} \\
(c) & I_{11} = I_2 + I_3 \\
(d) & I_4 = I_{12} + I_3 \\
(e) & I_9 = I_5 + I_8 \\
(f) & I_6 = I_5 + I_{10} \\
(g) & I_0 = I_6 + I_7 + I_{11}
\end{array}
$$

[1] Applying the junction rule to the full eight corners would result in an additional equation that would simply be a combination of some of the previous seven. That is, the equations would not be independent. Try it and see.

The five additional equations that are required are obtained by considering any five loops.

$$abcda \qquad I_1R_1 + I_2R_2 - I_4R_4 - I_3R_3 = 0$$

$$abfea \qquad I_1R_1 + I_{10}R_{10} - I_9R_9 - I_5R_5 = 0$$

$$efghe \qquad I_5R_5 + I_6R_6 - I_8R_8 - I_7R_7 = 0$$

$$adhea \qquad I_4R_4 + I_{12}R_{12} - I_9R_9 - I_8R_8 = 0$$

$$bcgfb \qquad I_2R_2 + I_{11}R_{11} - I_{10}R_{10} - I_6R_6 = 0$$

These 12 equations in the 12 unknowns, I_i, and the known quantities, I_0 and the resistances R_i are next written in matrix form as

$$
\begin{pmatrix}
1 & 0 & 0 & 1 & 0 & 0 & 0 & 0 & 1 & 0 & 0 & 0 \\
-1 & 1 & 0 & 0 & 0 & 0 & 0 & 0 & 0 & 1 & 0 & 0 \\
0 & 1 & 1 & 0 & 0 & 0 & 0 & 0 & 0 & 0 & -1 & 0 \\
0 & 0 & -1 & 1 & 0 & 0 & 0 & 0 & 0 & 0 & 0 & -1 \\
0 & 0 & 0 & 0 & 1 & 0 & 0 & 1 & -1 & 0 & 0 & 0 \\
0 & 0 & 0 & 0 & -1 & 1 & 0 & 0 & 0 & -1 & 0 & 0 \\
0 & 0 & 0 & 0 & 0 & 1 & 1 & 0 & 0 & 0 & 1 & 0 \\
R_1 & 0 & 0 & 0 & -R_5 & 0 & 0 & 0 & -R_9 & -R_{10} & 0 & 0 \\
R_1 & R_2 & -R_3 & -R_4 & 0 & 0 & 0 & 0 & 0 & 0 & 0 & 0 \\
0 & 0 & 0 & 0 & R_5 & R_6 & -R_7 & -R_8 & 0 & 0 & 0 & 0 \\
0 & 0 & 0 & R_4 & 0 & 0 & 0 & -R_8 & -R_9 & 0 & 0 & R_{12} \\
0 & R_2 & 0 & 0 & 0 & -R_6 & 0 & 0 & 0 & -R_{10} & R_{11} & 0
\end{pmatrix}
\begin{pmatrix}
I_1 \\ I_2 \\ I_3 \\ I_4 \\ I_5 \\ I_6 \\ I_7 \\ I_8 \\ I_9 \\ I_{10} \\ I_{11} \\ I_{12}
\end{pmatrix}
=
\begin{pmatrix}
I_0 \\ 0 \\ 0 \\ 0 \\ 0 \\ 0 \\ I_0 \\ 0 \\ 0 \\ 0 \\ 0 \\ 0
\end{pmatrix}
$$

The resistances on the edges of the cube have the values listed below for the three cases to be considered. All resistances are in units of 1000 Ω.

Case 1 $R_i = 3.0$ for all $i = 1, 12$

Case 2 $R_1 = 1, R_2 = 2, \ldots , R_{11} = 11, R_{12} = 12$

Case 3 $R_{10} = R_{12} = 1000$, the remaining $R_i = 1$

Also, use $I_0 = 10^{-3}$ A.

Problem Specifics

The main program in your solution should

1. Use a DATA statement to set the coefficient matrix $[A]$ equal to zero and then redefine the nonzero elements. Also, since the matrix $[A]$ will be destroyed when the inverse is computed, form a copy of this matrix.

2. For each of the three cases compute the inverse matrix $[A^{-1}]$, the determinant $|A|$, and the product $[A][A^{-1}]$.
3. Check that the product $[A][A^{-1}]$ is the identity.
4. Solve for the currents in each resistor.
5. Neatly print $[A]$, $[A^{-1}]$, $[A][A^{-1}]$, $|A|$, R_i, I_0, and the solutions for the currents I_i.

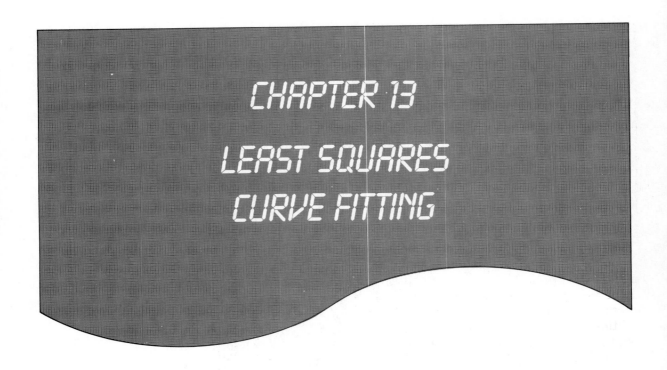

CHAPTER 13
LEAST SQUARES
CURVE FITTING

13.1   INTRODUCTION

We have all done laboratory experiments that result in lengthy tables of data. These data are than plotted on graph paper and from the appearance of the resulting curves we were supposed to arrive at some wise conclusions. As an example, consider the typical freshman physics lab experiment of dropping a ball in air and measuring the distance it falls as a function of the time elapsed from the point of release. The data are collected as a set of points (y_i, t_i), where y_i is the distance the ball has fallen at the time t_i. If the data are graphed as y_i vs. t_i^2, the result may be similar to that shown in Figure 13-1.

The estimated errors in t^2 are indicated by ⊢⊙⊣ and the estimated errors in the y values are indicated by ⌽. A line has been drawn through the data points and the conclusion might be: "within error, the data are consistent with the assumption that $y \propto t^2$." That is, a straight line fit to the data seems valid. However, there are numerous lines that could have been drawn, all going more or less through the data. So which is the best line? In addition, there appears to be a slight waviness to the data. Might not some function other than a straight line provide a better fit to the experimental points? Clearly the principal criterion that is being imposed when a line is sketched

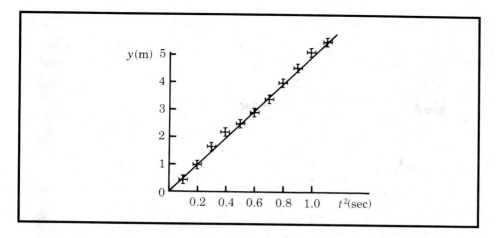

Figure 13-1 The distance fallen as a function of time squared.

through the data is that both the number of points that do not fit on the line and the size of the discrepancies of those away from the line be a minimum. To be more precise, consider the set of three points and the possible straight-line fits to these points illustrated in Figure 13-2. The magnitudes of the vertical distances of the three points to line A are (d_1, d_2, d_3) while (d_1', d_2', d_3') are the vertical distances to line B. Line A would be judged a better fit since the sum $(d_1 + d_2 + d_3)$ is less than $(d_1' + d_2' + d_3')$. The line of best fit would then be defined as the one that minimized the sum of the magnitudes of the deviations.[1]

13.2   THE PRINCIPLE OF LEAST SQUARES ANALYSIS

To implement the above ideas we begin with the following:

1. The results of an experiment in the form of data pairs (x_i, y_i) that are to be graphed on a two-dimensional plot of y vs. x.

---

[1] It has probably occurred to you that it would perhaps be more reasonable to use perpendicular distances, as drawn below, than vertical distances.

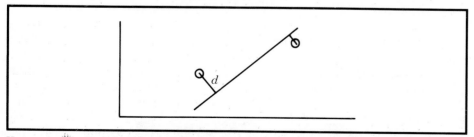

However, such an analysis loses whatever advantages it may have in accuracy to the increased complexity of the resulting algebra.

Figure 13-2
Vertical deviations from two lines.

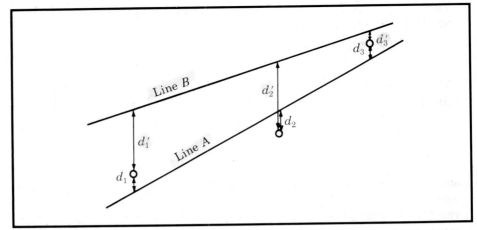

2. We also have an idea of how the results should appear. That is, the functional dependence of y on x [viz., $y(x)$] is suggested by some external considerations. The function that is used to attempt a fit to the data is known as the model.

If the data points are labeled as $(x_{i,\text{exp}}, y_{i,\text{exp}})$, then the difference between the data and the model is

For the data: Given a *particular* measured value of $x_{i,\text{exp}}$, the corresponding value of y is $y_{i,\text{exp}}$.

For the model: Given *any* x, in particular $x_{i,\text{exp}}$, the corresponding model value of y is $y(x_{i,\text{exp}})$

To put it concisely,

$y(x_{i,\text{exp}})$ is what the quantity *should be* (the model)

$y_{i,\text{exp}}$ is what the quantity *is* (experimental value)

It is the difference between these two that is to be minimized. The deviation of the model from the data for the ith point is defined as

(13.1)
$$d_i = y(x_{i,\text{exp}}) - y_{i,\text{exp}}$$

Since the sign of d_i is not important, we next define a function E which is the sum of the squares of the deviations of the N data points.

(13.2)
$$E = \sum_{i=1}^{N} d_i^2 = \sum_{i=1}^{N} \left[y(x_{i,\text{exp}}) - y_{i,\text{exp}} \right]^2$$

The next step is to select the model. The simplest model is to assume a linear relation between x and y.

$$y(x_{i,\text{exp}}) = a_0 + a_1 x_{i,\text{exp}} \qquad \text{linear model} \qquad (13.3)$$

This expression is then inserted into Equation (13.2) and the task is then to minimize the function

$$E = \sum_{i=1}^{N} (a_0 + a_1 x_{i,\text{exp}} - y_{i,\text{exp}})^2 \qquad (13.4)$$

to obtain the best line. Minimize with respect to what? Recall that we want to vary the *line* to obtain a minimum value for E and thus the parameters to vary are the slope (a_1) and the intercept (a_0) of the line. This means that E is a function of the two variables a_0, and a_1 (*not x, y*). Also, a function of two variables is represented by a surface in space rather than a curve.

13.3 MINIMUM OR MAXIMUM OF A FUNCTION OF TWO VARIABLES

A local minimum or maximum of a function of a single variable $f(x)$ is a point on the curve of f vs. x at which the tangent line has zero slope. To determine the point of extremum (minimum or maximum) we simply find a value of x such that $df/dx = 0$ (see Figure 13-3).

To find the extremum of a function of two variables $F(x, y)$, we must find a point on the surface where the slopes of *all* possible tangent lines drawn

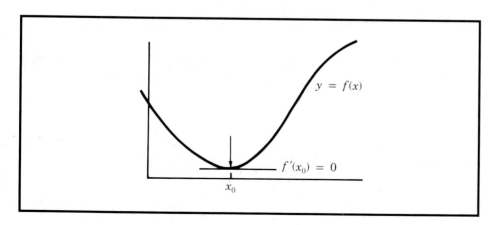

Figure 13-3
Local extremum of a function of a single variable.

$y = f(x)$

$f'(x_0) = 0$

x_0

Figure 13-4
The surface
$z = F(x, y)$ is cut
by the plane
$y = y_c$.

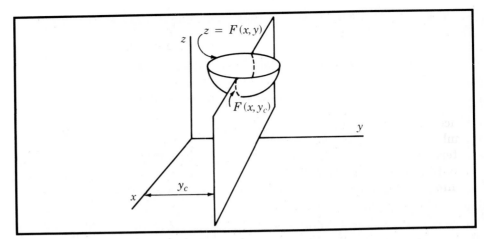

at that point have zero slope. In other words, the tangent plane at the point
of an extremum must be parallel to the xy plane (see Figure 13-4).

The problem is how to determine the point on the surface that has a
horizontal tangent plane. One way to proceed is to consider just one variable
at a time. For a fixed value of y, say $y = y_c = $ constant, $F(x, y_c)$ is then a
function of a single variable x. This is represented in Figure 13-4 by the
dashed curve resulting from the cut through the surface by the plane $y = y_c$.
The slope of the tangent *line* to the dashed curve is then $dF(x, y_c)/dx$ and the
extremum on this curve is obtained by finding a value of x such that

$$\frac{dF(x, y_c)}{dx} = 0$$

Notice that this equation is an equation in one variable x and the constant y_c. If we choose a different value y_c, a different dashed curve results and
a different value for the extremum will be obtained. We next introduce a new
type of derivative, the *partial derivative*.

$$\frac{\partial F(x, y)}{\partial x} = \begin{array}{l} \text{The ordinary derivative of } F(x, y) \text{ with} \\ \text{respect to } x, \textit{ but } y \text{ is treated} \\ \text{as if it were just another constant.} \end{array}$$

Thus if $F(x, y) = 3x^2y + y^3$, then

$$\frac{\partial F}{\partial x} = 6xy \qquad \frac{\partial F}{\partial y} = 3x^2 + 3y^2$$

Using this definition we can then express the condition that the slopes
of tangent lines in both the x and y directions be simultaneously zero as

$$\frac{\partial F(x, y)}{\partial x} = 0 \qquad \text{zero slope in the}$$
$$x \text{ direction for a given } y$$

$$\frac{\partial F(x, y)}{\partial y} = 0 \qquad \text{zero slope in the}$$
$$y \text{ direction for a given } x$$

Since the slopes in both the x and y directions are zero, the slope of any combination of these two directions is also zero, and thus these conditions determine the point of a horizontal tangent plane. Solving both of these equations simultaneously for the unknowns x and y will determine the minimum or maximum point of a function of two variables.[2]

13.4   MINIMIZATION OF THE SUM OF THE SQUARED DEVIATIONS

The sum of the squares of the deviations of the data points from a straight line is given in Equation (13.4). The function E is a function of the two variables a_1, the slope of the line, and a_0, the intercept. To determine the minimum of $E(a_0, a_1)$, the two equations

$$\frac{\partial E(a_0, a_1)}{\partial a_0} = 0 \qquad \frac{\partial E(a_0, a_1)}{\partial a_1} = 0$$

must be solved simultaneously for the values a_0, a_1.

To apply the first of these equations to the function of Equation (13.4)

$$E(a_0, a_1) = \sum_{i=1}^{N} (a_0 + a_1 x_{i,\text{exp}} - y_{i,\text{exp}})^2$$

we will need the following properties of the derivative:

1. $\dfrac{d}{dx}\Sigma(\ ) = \Sigma \dfrac{d}{dx}(\ )$

2. $\dfrac{d}{dx}(\ )^2 = 2(\ )\dfrac{d}{dx}(\ )$

---

[2] Additionally, there is the possibility that the equations will specify a "saddle point," i.e., a maximum along the x direction and a minimum along the y direction, or vice versa. This possibility is ordinarily rather remote in physical problems and will be ignored.

$$3. \quad \frac{\partial}{\partial a_0}(a_0) = 1$$

$$4. \quad \frac{\partial}{\partial a_1}(a_1 x_{i, \exp}) = x_{i, \exp}$$

We thus obtain

(13.5)
$$\frac{\partial E(a_0, a_1)}{\partial a_0} = \sum_{i=1}^{N} \frac{\partial}{\partial a_0}(a_0 + a_1 x_{i, \exp} - y_{i, \exp})^2$$
$$= 2 \sum_{i=1}^{N} (a_0 + a_1 x_{i, \exp} - y_{i, \exp}) \frac{\partial a_0}{\partial a_0} = 0$$

Next the notation of Equation (13.5) is simplified by using the following:

(13.6)
$$\sum_{i=1}^{N} a_0 = \underbrace{(a_0 + a_0 + \cdots + a_0)}_{N \text{ terms}} = N a_0$$

(13.7)
$$\sum_{i=1}^{N} a_1 x_{i, \exp} = a_1 \sum_{i=1}^{N} x_{i, \exp} \equiv a_1 \Sigma x$$

(13.8)
$$\sum_{i=1}^{N} y_{i, \exp} \equiv \Sigma y$$

Thus the first condition for the minimum may be written as

(13.9)
$$(N) a_0 + (\Sigma x) a_1 = \Sigma y$$

The second of the conditions for the minimum of $E(a_0, a_1)$ is handled in similar manner.

(13.10)
$$\frac{\partial E(a_0, a_1)}{\partial a_1} = \sum_{i=1}^{N} \frac{\partial}{\partial a_1}(a_0 + a_1 x_{i, \exp} - y_{i, \exp})^2$$
$$= 2 \sum_{i=1}^{N} (a_0 + a_1 x_{i, \exp} - y_{i, \exp}) \frac{\partial(a_1 x_{i, \exp})}{\partial a_1}$$
$$= 2 \sum_{i=1}^{N} [a_0 x_{i, \exp} + a_1 (x_{i, \exp})^2 - x_{i, \exp} y_{i, \exp}] = 0$$

which may be written more concisely as

(13.11)
$$(\Sigma x) a_0 + (\Sigma x^2) a_1 = \Sigma xy$$

where I have used the definitions:

(13.12)
$$\sum_{i=1}^{N} (x_{i, \exp})^2 \equiv \Sigma x^2$$

$$\sum_{i=1}^{N} (x_{i,\,exp})(y_{i,\,exp}) = \Sigma xy \qquad (13.13)$$

The two simultaneous equations, Equations (13.9) and (13.11), are linear in the unknowns a_0 and a_1 and can be written in matrix form as

$$[A] \quad \mathbf{a} \;=\; \mathbf{c} \qquad (13.14)$$

$$\begin{pmatrix} N & \Sigma x \\ \Sigma x & \Sigma x^2 \end{pmatrix} \begin{pmatrix} a_0 \\ a_1 \end{pmatrix} = \begin{pmatrix} \Sigma y \\ \Sigma xy \end{pmatrix}$$

This matrix equation can be solved by using the Gauss-Jordan method of Chapter 12. The solution will yield the values for the coefficients a_0 and a_1 which then specify the least squares best-fit line.

$$y(x) = a_0 + a_1 x$$

However, since the problem involves only two equations in two unknowns, the general procedures of Chapter 12 are rather an overkill and the equations are more conveniently solved by hand. When solving these two equations by hand, it is common to rewrite the problem and its solution in terms of average values of the data elements defined in the following way:

$$\langle x \rangle = \text{average of } x\text{'s} = \frac{\Sigma x}{N}$$

$$\langle y \rangle = \frac{\Sigma y}{N}$$

$$\langle xy \rangle = \frac{\Sigma xy}{N} \qquad (13.15)$$

$$\langle x^2 \rangle = \frac{\Sigma x^2}{N}$$

and also define

$$D_{xx} = \langle x^2 \rangle - \langle x \rangle \langle x \rangle \qquad (13.16)$$

$$D_{xy} = \langle xy \rangle - \langle x \rangle \langle y \rangle \qquad (13.17)$$

The solution of Equation (13.14) by Cramer's rule yields

$$a_1 = \text{slope} = \frac{D_{xy}}{D_{xx}} \qquad (13.18)$$

$$a_0 = \text{intercept} = \langle y \rangle - a_1 \langle x \rangle \qquad (13.19)$$

13.4.1 Example of Least Squares Best-Fit Line

The data listed in Table 13-1 are used to compute the line that minimizes the squares of the deviations from the line. From these data we obtain the following:

Table 13-1
Data used in a
linear least
squares fit.

i	1	2	3	4	5	6	7	8	9	10
$x_{i,\,exp}$	−0.3	0.4	1.1	1.4	3.3	5.0	5.2	7.1	9.2	13.
$y_{i,\,exp}$	0.2	2.0	3.1	4.0	7.0	11.	13.	14.5	20.	29.

$$\Sigma x = 45.4 \qquad \Sigma y = 103.8$$
$$\Sigma x^2 = 370.4 \qquad \Sigma xy = 819.4$$
$$\langle x \rangle = 4.54 \qquad \langle y \rangle = 10.38$$
$$\langle x^2 \rangle = 37.04 \qquad \langle xy \rangle = 81.94$$
$$D_{xx} = 16.43 \qquad D_{xy} = 34.81$$
$$a_1 = \text{slope} = 2.119 \qquad a_0 = \text{intercept} = 0.7598$$

The best-fit line is then

$$y(x) = 0.7598 + 2.119x$$

and the model prediction for $x = 13.0$ (the last experimental x value) is $y(13.0) = 28.31$ compared with the actual experimental value of 29.0

13.4.2 Least Squares Fit of an Exponential Function

Frequently a theory will suggest a model other than a straight line as the best interpretation of the data. A common functional form for the model is the exponential function.

(13.20)
$$F(t) = \alpha e^{\beta t}$$

In this equation the dependent variable is F and the independent variable is t. If this expression for the model is inserted into Equation (13.4) and the derivatives with respect to the two parameters α and β are set equal to zero, the resulting equations are

$$\frac{\partial E(\alpha, \beta)}{\partial \alpha} = 2 \sum_{i=1}^{N} e^{\beta t_i}(\alpha e^{\beta t_i} - F_i) = 0 \tag{13.21}$$

$$\frac{\partial E(\alpha, \beta)}{\partial \beta} = 2\alpha t_i \sum_{i=1}^{N} e^{\beta t_i}(\alpha e^{\beta t_i} - F_i) = 0 \tag{13.22}$$

These are two equations in two unknowns but they are *nonlinear* equations in the variables α and β and therefore cannot be written in matrix form. The procedures of Chapter 12 are thus of no help in solving the equations. Nonlinear problems are almost always extremely difficult to solve.

A different approach is to attempt a change of variables to a model that is *linear* in the new parameters. In the present instance this is easily accomplished by taking the natural logarithm of Equation (13.20).

$$\begin{aligned} \ln(F) &= \ln(\alpha e^{\beta t}) \\ &= \ln(\alpha) + \ln(e^{\beta t}) \tag{13.23} \\ &= \ln(\alpha) + \beta t \end{aligned}$$

We next introduce two variables (X, Y) in place of (t, F) and two parameters (a_0, a_1) in place of (α, β) defined by the relations:

$$X = t \qquad Y = \ln(F) \tag{13.24}$$

$$a_0 = \ln(\alpha) \qquad a_1 = \beta \tag{13.25}$$

In terms of these variables, Equation (13.23) becomes

$$Y(X) = a_0 + a_1 X \tag{13.26}$$

and the ordinary linear least squares analysis may then be applied to the problem.

In summary, if an exponential model, $F(t) = \alpha e^{\beta t}$, is to be used to interpret the set of data points (t_i, F_i) the data set is first replaced by the data set (X_i, Y_i), where the relation between (t, F) and (X, Y) is given in Equations (13.24). Next, the ordinary linear least squares analysis is applied to the set (X_i, Y_i) and the parameters a_0 and a_1 are computed. Finally, the original parameters, α, β, are calculated from the known values of a_0, a_1 by using Equations (13.25). Specifically,

$$\alpha = e^{a_0} \qquad \beta = a_1 \tag{13.27}$$

Of course, the result of this analysis is a set of parameters that minimizes the squared deviations of $\ln(F)$ from $\ln(\text{data})$. This is ordinarily a satisfactory approximation to the more difficult problem of minimizing the squared deviations of F directly. Several problems of this type can be found in the Problems Section.

13.5 LEAST SQUARES FIT OF A POLYNOMIAL

Next consider the problem of fitting a parabola to a data set by means of the least squares approach. In this case the model is a general quadratic of the form,

(13.28)
$$y(x) = a_0 + a_1x + a_2x^2$$

Inserting this function into the expression for the sum of the squared deviations, Equation (13.2), yields,

(13.29)
$$E(a_0, a_1, a_2) = \sum_{i=1}^{N} [a_0 + a_1x_{i,\,\text{exp}} + a_2(x_{i,\,\text{exp}})^2 - y_{i,\,\text{exp}}]^2$$

Notice that E is now a function of three variables, a_0, a_1, and a_2, and the minimization criterion is then the set of equations

(13.30)
$$\frac{\partial E}{\partial a_0} = 0 \qquad \frac{\partial E}{\partial a_1} = 0 \qquad \frac{\partial E}{\partial a_2} = 0$$

Evaluating these three derivatives, setting them equal to zero, and simplifying the equations yields the following set of three equations:

$$Na_0 + (\Sigma x)a_1 + (\Sigma x^2)a_2 = \Sigma y$$
$$(\Sigma x)a_0 + (\Sigma x^2)a_1 + (\Sigma x^3)a_2 = \Sigma xy$$
$$(\Sigma x^2)a_0 + (\Sigma x^3)a_1 + (\Sigma x^4)a_2 = \Sigma x^2y$$

which can be written in matrix form as

(13.31)
$$\begin{pmatrix} N & \Sigma x & \Sigma x^2 \\ \Sigma x & \Sigma x^2 & \Sigma x^3 \\ \Sigma x^2 & \Sigma x^3 & \Sigma x^4 \end{pmatrix} \begin{pmatrix} a_0 \\ a_1 \\ a_2 \end{pmatrix} = \begin{pmatrix} \Sigma y \\ \Sigma xy \\ \Sigma x^2y \end{pmatrix}$$

The coefficients of the parabola are of course calculated by using the techniques of Chapter 12, once all of the sums that appear in the coefficient matrix and the right-hand-side vector have been evaluated. Again, each of the sums involve only experimental quantities and all are from $i = 1$ to $i = N$.

The least squares procedure can easily be generalized to handle the problem of fitting a polynomial of degree n to the data. Thus, if the model function is

(13.32)
$$y(x) = a_0 + a_1x + a_2x^2 + \cdots + a_nx^n = \sum_{i=0}^{n} a_ix^i$$

the coefficients of the polynomial are determined by solving the matrix equation

$$\begin{pmatrix} N & \Sigma x & \Sigma x^2 & \cdots & \Sigma x^n \\ \Sigma x & \Sigma x^2 & \Sigma x^3 & \cdots & \Sigma x^{n+1} \\ \Sigma x^2 & \Sigma x^3 & \Sigma x^4 & \cdots & \Sigma x^{n+2} \\ \cdots & \cdots & \cdots & \cdots & \cdots \\ \Sigma x^n & \Sigma x^{n+1} & \Sigma x^{n+2} & \cdots & \Sigma x^{2n} \end{pmatrix} \begin{pmatrix} a_0 \\ a_1 \\ a_2 \\ \cdots \\ a_n \end{pmatrix} = \begin{pmatrix} \Sigma y \\ \Sigma xy \\ \Sigma x^2 y \\ \cdots \\ \Sigma x^n y \end{pmatrix} \qquad (13.33)$$

13.5.1 Example of a Polynomial Least Squares Fit to Data

The data listed in Table 13-2 will be used to obtain first a linear least squares fit. This calculation will then be followed by a calculation of the best-fit parabola to the data. For the linear fit ($n = 1$), Equation (13.33) becomes

$$\begin{pmatrix} N & \Sigma x \\ \Sigma x & \Sigma x^2 \end{pmatrix} \begin{pmatrix} a_0 \\ a_1 \end{pmatrix} = \begin{pmatrix} \Sigma y \\ \Sigma xy \end{pmatrix}$$

$$\begin{pmatrix} 9 & 18 \\ 18 & 51 \end{pmatrix} \begin{pmatrix} a_0 \\ a_1 \end{pmatrix} = \begin{pmatrix} 208.6 \\ 565.45 \end{pmatrix}$$

Solution of this matrix equation yields

$$\begin{pmatrix} a_0 \\ a_1 \end{pmatrix} = \begin{pmatrix} 3.411 \\ 9.883 \end{pmatrix}$$

and thus the best-fit line to the data is

$$y(x) = 3.411 + 9.883x$$

To fit a parabola to the data we again use Equation (13.33) with $n = 2$.

$$\begin{pmatrix} N & \Sigma x & \Sigma x^2 \\ \Sigma x & \Sigma x^2 & \Sigma x^3 \\ \Sigma x^2 & \Sigma x^3 & \Sigma x^4 \end{pmatrix} \begin{pmatrix} a_0 \\ a_1 \\ a_2 \end{pmatrix} = \begin{pmatrix} \Sigma y \\ \Sigma xy \\ \Sigma x^2 y \end{pmatrix}$$

$$\begin{pmatrix} 9 & 18 & 51 \\ 18 & 51 & 162 \\ 51 & 162 & 548.25 \end{pmatrix} \begin{pmatrix} a_0 \\ a_1 \\ a_2 \end{pmatrix} = \begin{pmatrix} 208.6 \\ 565.45 \\ 1790.82 \end{pmatrix}$$

i	1	2	3	4	5	6	7	8	9
$x_{i,\,exp}$	0.0	0.5	1.0	1.5	2.0	2.5	3.0	3.5	4.0
$y_{i,\,exp}$	4.90	8.50	14.2	17.0	22.0	26.0	32.0	39.0	45.0

Table 13-2
Data used in a linear and a quadratic least squares fit.

The solution for a_0, a_1, a_2 is obtained by either the Gauss-Jordan method or Cramer's rule and yields

$$\begin{pmatrix} a_0 \\ a_1 \\ a_2 \end{pmatrix} = \begin{pmatrix} 5.321 \\ 6.609 \\ 0.819 \end{pmatrix}$$

and the best-fit parabola is then

$$y(x) = 5.321 + 6.609x + 0.819x^2$$

The least squares best-fit line and parabola are compared with the data in Figure 13-5. From the figure it appears that the parabolic fit is slightly better. If the calculation were continued, you would find that the fit of a cubic function to the data would be better still and an eighth-degree polynomial would fit the data exactly. The reason for this is that the eighth-degree polynomial contains nine unknown parameters $(a_i, i = 0, 8)$ which are determined by using the nine data points. This is analogous to nine equations in nine unknowns and the parameters can be uniquely determined without resorting to a least squares procedure.

So it would seem that the best procedure is to fit N data points with a polynomial of degree $n = N - 1$. The resulting least squares fit would be exact, but in what sense would it be a valid interpretation of the data? The answer to this question is usually found deep in advanced statistics courses. However, it is important that we have at least a cursory understanding of this situation if we are to draw any conclusions from the results of a least squares fit of a polynomial to experimental data.

Figure 13-5
Comparison of a best-fit line and parabola with the data.

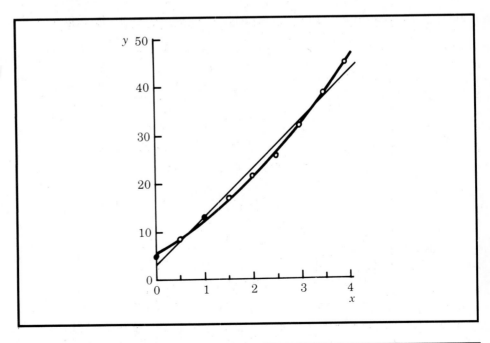

To decide whether a least squares straight line is an adequate fit to the data, some information is required concerning the experimental errors in the data. Experimental errors are often indicated on a graph by error bars, ϕ , or by following the data item by the magnitude of the estimated error preceded by a $\pm$ sign. Thus the experimental value of y could be represented as 17.32 ± 0.07, indicating that the actual value of y could be anywhere in the range 17.23 to 17.39. In the discussion that follows, it is assumed that the errors are in the dependent variable (y) only and that the independent variable (x) values are exact.

First I begin with a few commonsense ideas regarding validity of fit and error bars. In Figure 13-6 I have drawn three possible curve fits to the data. Clearly the line is a poor fit to the data, whereas the parabola appears to be an adequate fit. That is, within error, the parabola roughly goes through all the data points. The third curve, which exactly fits the data, is certainly not justified by the data. We cannot assume that the actual values of y are at the center of the error bars. Any value of y within the range of the error bar is just as acceptable as another. Forcing the model function to fit the y values exactly has introduced numerous wiggles in the curve that are unlikely to be representative of the actual physical phenomena. The third curve thus *overfits* to data.

Another common situation, especially in introductory laboratory courses, is for students to overestimate the size of the experimental error in order to ensure that the data, within error, fall on a straight line. Thus an

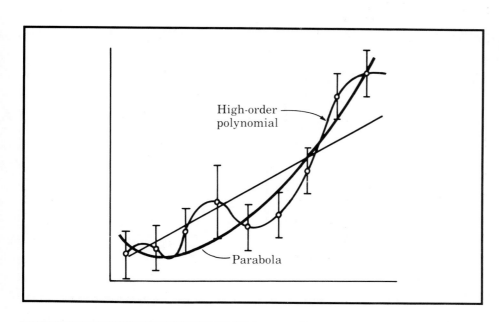

Figure 13-6
Three possible curve fits to experimental data.

High-order polynomial

Parabola

instructor presented with the results in Figure 13-7 would immediately conclude that the indicated error bars are quite wrong. The instructor expects to see scatter of the data about the straight line and the size of the scatter should be approximately the same as the size of the error. Since the data are very nearly linear the actual experimental error is probably quite small.

The essential idea then in determining whether a particular functional fit to the data is poor, adequate, or an overfit is to compare the deviations of the curve from the actual data with the size of the experimental error. The deviations of the data from the curve (i.e., the scatter) is expected to be the same order of magnitude as the experimental error. We next define a quantity called χ^2 (chi-squared) by the equation

$$(13.34) \qquad \chi^2 = \sum_{i=1}^{N} \frac{[y(x_{i,\text{exp}}) - y_{i,\text{exp}}]^2}{(\Delta y_{i,\text{exp}})^2}$$

where $y(x_{i,\text{exp}})$ is the best-fit model function evaluated at the experimental value of $x = x_{i,\text{exp}}$, then $y_{i,\text{exp}}$ is the measured value of y and $\Delta y_{i,\text{exp}}$ is the magnitude of the error in the value of $y_{i,\text{exp}}$. The sum is over all N data points. Since each term in the sum is expected to be of order 1, the computed value of χ^2 should be of order N. Thus if χ^2 is much greater than N, the deviations from the curve are larger than predicted by the error bars and the curve is therefore judged to be a poor fit. If χ^2 is much less than N, indicating deviations much smaller than the anticipated scatter, the curve is possibly an overfit (or the errors are wrong).

A goal of statistics courses is to restate the above much more precisely and to define what is meant by "much greater than ," and "much less than." For the present, I will attempt to firm up these ideas only slightly.

First consider the situation of fitting a line to only two data points. Since two points uniquely determine a line, the deviations are then zero and $\chi^2 = 0$, not 2. Similarly three points determine a parabola, four a cubic, etc. It would thus appear that the hypothesis that $\chi^2 \approx N$ should be amended to

Figure 13-7 An example of erroneously large error bars.

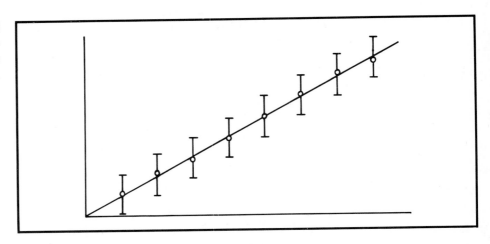

$\chi^2 \simeq N - g$, where g is the number of parameters in the model function. To summarize, if

$$\chi^2 \begin{cases} \gg (N - g) \rightarrow \text{poor fit} \\ \sim (N - g) \rightarrow \text{adequate fit} \\ \ll (N - g) \rightarrow \text{over fit} \end{cases}$$

13.7 THE FORTRAN CODE FOR A POLYNOMIAL LEAST SQUARES CURVE FIT

The code to fit a polynomial of degree n to a set of data points must first assemble the square coefficient matrix and the right-hand-side vector given in Equation (13.33). The solution for the coefficients of the polynomial is then obtained by the standard Gauss-Jordan techniques of Chapter 12. Frequently least squares curve fitting is but a single part of a larger analysis of the data and so the Fortran code in Figure 13-8 is written in the form of a subroutine.

In the subroutine the N experimental data pairs are assumed to be stored in the arrays X, Y. The number of parameters in the fitted polynomial is NP. Thus NP = 2 is a linear fit, NP = 3, a parabola, etc. The coefficient matrix of Equation (13.33) is a square matrix of size NP by NP of the form

$$\begin{pmatrix} N & D(1) & D(2) & D(3) & \cdots & D(NP-1) \\ D(1) & D(2) & D(3) & D(4) & \cdots & D(NP) \\ D(2) & D(3) & D(4) & D(5) & \cdots & D(NP+1) \\ D(3) & D(4) & D(5) & D(6) & \cdots & D(NP+2) \\ \cdots & \cdots & \cdots & \cdots & \cdots & \cdots \\ D(NP-1) & D(NP) & D(NP-1) & \cdots & D(2NP-2) & D(2NP-1) \end{pmatrix}$$

where

$$D(k) = \sum_{i=1}^{N} (x_{i,\text{exp}})^k \qquad (13.35)$$

The right-hand-side vector is of the form

$$B = \begin{pmatrix} B(1) \\ B(2) \\ \cdots \\ \cdots \\ B(NP) \end{pmatrix}$$

where

$$B(k) = \sum_{i=1}^{N} (y_{i,\text{exp}})(x_{i,\text{exp}})^{k-1} \qquad (13.36)$$

Figure 13-8
The Fortran code
for a least
squares poly-
nomial fit to
data.

```
        SUBROUTINE LSTSQR(X,Y,NDATA,A,NP,ICHI,DY)
*--
*--     THE ARRAYS X(NDATA), Y(NDATA) ARE INPUT TO THE SUBROUTINE
*--     AND CONTAIN THE EXPERIMENTAL DATA.
*--
*--     THE ARRAY A(NP) IS THE PRIMARY OUTPUT AND CONTAINS THE COEF-
*--     FICIENTS OF THE BEST-FIT POLYNOMIAL OF DEGREE NP - 1. THE LEAST
*--     SQUARES BEST-FIT POLYNOMIAL IS OF THE FORM
*--
*--         Y(X) = A(O) + A(1) * X + ... + A(NP) * X**(NP - 1)
*--
*--     AND IS WRITTEN AS A SEPARATE SUBFUNCTION. (SEE FIGURE 13-9.)
*--
*--     ALSO, IF ICHI = 1, A VALUE OF CHI-SQUARED IS COMPUTED AND IS
*--     PRINTED. TO COMPUTE CHI-SQUARED, THE EXPERIMENTAL ERRORS FOR
*--     EACH OF THE Y VALUES ARE REQUIRED AND ARE SUPPLIED IN THE
*--     ARRAY DP(NDATA). IF ALL THE ERRORS ARE THE SAME AND EQUAL TO
*--     Z, SAY, SIMPLY ASSIGN DY(1) = -Z. THE SUBROUTINE WILL THEN
*--     USE THE VALUE +Z FOR ALL ERRORS.
*--
*--     THE SUBROUTINE REQUIRES A SEPARATE MATRIX-INVERTING SUB-
*--     ROUTINE AND WE USE HERE THE ROUTINE MINV OF CHAPTER 12. THE
*--     HIGHEST-DEGREE POLYNOMIAL THAT CAN BE HANDLED IS NP = 10.
*--
*--     THE COEFFICIENT MATRIX IS OF THE FORM
*--
*--     NDATA     D(1)      D(2)      D(3)    ...     ...      D(NP)
*--
*--      D(1)     D(2)      D(3)      D(4)    ...     ...     D(NP+1)
*--
*--      D(2)     D(3)      D(4)      D(5)    ...     ...     D(NP+2)
*--
*--      ...      ...       ...       ...     ...     ...       ...
*--
*--     D(NP)   D(NP+1)  D(NP+2)     ...      ...     ...     D(2NP)
*--
*--     WHERE
*--
*--                 D(N)  =  SUM< X(I)**N >
*-------------------------------------------------------------------
* VARIABLES
*
        REAL X(NDATA),Y(NDATA),AC(11,11),AINV(11,11),B(11),CHI2,
     +    D(20),DET,DY(NDATA),A(0:NP)
        INTEGER NDATA,NP
*
*                  X(),Y()   --  THE EXPERIMENTAL DATA (INPUT)
*                  AC()      --  THE COEFFICIENT MATRIX (SEE ABOVE)
*                  AINV()    --  INVERSE OF AC()
*                  B()       --  THE RIGHT-HAND-SIDE VECTOR OF THE
*                                FORM SUM< X**N * Y >
*                  D()       --  ELEMENTS OF AC() (SEE ABOVE)
*                  DY()      --  EXP. ERRORS IN Y VALUES (INPUT)
*                  DET       --  DETERMINANT OF AC()
*                  NDATA     --  NUMBER OF DATA POINTS (INPUT)
*                  NP        --  DEGREE OF POLYNOMIAL FIT (INPUT)
*                  CHI2      --  CHI-SQUARED COEFFICIENT OF FIT
*                                FOR AN ADEQUATE FIT = NDATA - NP - 1
*-------------------------------------------------------------------
* INITIALIZATION
*
*                  FIRST FILL IN THE ARRAY D()
*
```

```
      DO 2 K = 1,2*NP
        D(K) = 0.
        DO 1 I = 1,NDATA
          D(K) = D(K) + X(I)**K
  1     CONTINUE
  2 CONTINUE
*
*                   NEXT ASSIGN VALUES TO THE ELEMENTS OF THE
*                   COEFFICIENT MATRIX, NOTING
*                   AC(ROW,COL) = D(ROW + COL - 2)
*
      AC(1,1) = NDATA
      DO 3 I = 1,NP + 1
      DO 3 J = 1,NP + 1
        K = I + J - 2
        IF(K .NE. 0)THEN
          AC(I,J) = D(K)
        END IF
  3 CONTINUE
*
*                   THE RIGHT-HAND-SIDE VECTOR IS OF THE FORM
*                   B(K) = SUM< X(I)**(K - 1) * Y >
*
      DO 5 K = 1,NP + 1
        B(K) = 0.0
        DO 4 I = 1,NDATA
          IF(K .EQ. 1)THEN
            TERM = Y(I)
          ELSE
            TERM = Y(I) * X(I)**(K - 1)
          END IF
          B(K) = B(K) + TERM
  4     CONTINUE
  5 CONTINUE
*---------------------------------------------------------------------
* COMPUTATION
*
*                   SOLVE THE MATRIX EQUATION BY FINDING THE INVERSE
*
      CALL MINV(AC,AINV,11,NP + 1,DET)
*
*                   IF THE DETERMINANT IS ZERO - STOP, IF VERY
*                   SMALL, PRINT A WARNING.
*
      IF(DET .EQ. 0.0)THEN
        WRITE(*,10)DET
        STOP
      ELSE IF(ABS(DET) .LT. 1.E-8)THEN
        WRITE(*,11)DET
      END IF
*
*                   THE COEFFICIENTS OF BEST-FIT POLYNOMIAL ARE THEN
*                   A() = AINV() * B()
*
      DO 7 I = 1,NP + 1
        A(I - 1) = 0.0
        DO 6 J = 1,NP + 1
          A(I - 1) = A(I - 1) + AINV(I,J) * B(J)
  6     CONTINUE
  7 CONTINUE
*
```

Continued

```
*                   IF NO CHI-SQUARED CALCULATION IS REQUIRED RETURN
*
      IF(ICHI .NE. 1)RETURN
*
*------------------------------------------------------------------
* COMPUTATION OF CHI-SQUARED
*
      IF(DY(1) .LT. 0.0)THEN
         E = -DY(1)
         DO 8 I = 1,NDATA
            DY(I) = E
    8    CONTINUE
      END IF
*                   THE THEORETICAL VALUE OF Y() IS GIVEN BY THE
*                   BEST-FIT POLYNOMIAL YTHEO().
*
      CHI2 = 0.0
      DO 9 I = 1,NDATA
         CHI2 = CHI2 + (YTHEO(X(I),NP - 1,A) - Y(I))**2/DY(I)**2
    9 CONTINUE
*
      WRITE(*,12)CHI2,NDATA - NP - 1
      RETURN
*------------------------------------------------------------------
* FORMATS
*
   10 FORMAT(//,T10,'*****ERROR IN LSTSQR*****',/,T10,
     +        'THE COEFFICIENT MATRIX IS SINGULAR',//,T10,
     +        'THE DETERMINANT = ',E10.3,//,T10,
     +        'PROGRAM TERMINATED')
*
   11 FORMAT(//,T10,'******WARNING FROM LSTSQR******',/,T10,
     +        'THE COEFFICIENT MATRIX IS ILL-CONDITIONED',//,T10,
     +        'THE DETERMINANT = ',E10.3,//,T10,'PROGRAM CONTINUES'
     +        ,' BUT BEWARE OF ROUND-OFF ERRORS.')
*
   12 FORMAT(//,T10,'THE COMPUTED CHI-SQUARED FOR THIS FIT IS ',
     +        //,T20,F10.5,//,T10,'WHILE AN ADEQUATE FIT SHOULD HAVE'
     +        //,T20,I3)
      END
```

The first task of the subroutine is then to construct the elements of the arrays $D(K)$, $B(K)$. The elements of the matrix $[A]$ are then expressed in terms of the array D by noting that the matrix elements along the diagonals are all identical. Thus $A_{14} = A_{23} = A_{32} = A_{41} = D(3)$, or in general

$$A_{ij} = D(i + j - 2) \quad \text{and} \quad A_{11} = N$$

The polynomial that is constructed from the coefficients that are returned by the subroutine is given in Figure 13-9.

Figure 13-9
Fortran code for
the best-fit poly-
nomial.

```
        FUNCTION YTHEO(Z,N,C)
*
*--   YTHEO IS THE THEORY OR MODEL FIT TO THE DATA.  IT IS IN THE
*--   FORM OF A POLYNOMIAL IN Z OF DEGREE N.  THE COEFFICIENTS OF
*--   THE POLYNOMIAL, C(I), ARE COMPUTED BY THE SUBROUTINE LSTSQR.
*-------------------------------------------------------------
*
        REAL C(0:N),Z,SUM
*
        SUM = C(0)
        DO 1 I = 1,N
           SUM = SUM + C(I) * Z**I
    1   CONTINUE
        YTHEO = SUM
*
        RETURN
        END
```

13.8   AN EXAMPLE OF A LEAST SQUARES POLYNOMIAL FIT

As an example of curve fitting to experimental data, consider the following freshman laboratory experiment. The experiment consisted of measuring the cooling curve of an initially hot shiny copper cylinder—i.e., measurements of temperature vs. time. The hypothesis is that the graph of $(T - T_0)$ vs. time should be approximately exponential, where T_0 is the known room temperature. The independent variable is t (time in minutes). The model function is thus

$$(T(t) - T_0) = \alpha e^{\beta t} \tag{13.37}$$

As was done in Section 13.4.2, to apply a *linear* least squares analysis we must change variables by defining

$$y_{i,\exp} = \ln(T_i - T_0) \qquad x_{i,\exp} = t_i$$
$$a_0 = \ln(\alpha) \qquad\qquad a_1 = \beta \tag{13.38}$$

Taking the logarithm of Equation (13.37), the hypothesis now reads,

$$y_{i,\exp} = a_0 + a_1 x_{i,\exp}$$

Computing the coefficients a_0, a_1, then, is equivalent to fitting a straight line to $\ln(T - T_0)$. This process will be extended to next successively fitting a parabola, a cubic, etc. to $\ln(T - T_0)$.

To determine which polynomial fit is most appropriate to the data we require information on the magnitude of the errors for each value of $y_{i,\text{exp}}$. It is known that the experimental error in each of the temperature measurements is approximately $\Delta T \simeq 0.8\ °C$. The errors in the corresponding values of y are determined by

$$y \pm \Delta y = \ln(T \pm \Delta T)$$

$$= \ln\left[T\left(1 \pm \frac{\Delta T}{T} \right) \right]$$

(13.39)
$$= [\ln(T)] + \left[\ln\left(1 \pm \frac{\Delta T}{T} \right) \right]$$

thus

(13.40)
$$\pm \Delta y = \ln\left(1 \pm \frac{\Delta T}{T} \right)$$

Table 13-3
Experimental cooling curve data.

i	t_i (min)	$(T_i - T_0)$ (°C)	$y_{i,\text{exp}}$ $[\ln(T_i - T_0)]$
1	0.01	178.0	5.182
2	1.0	173.4	5.156
3	2.0	169.4	5.132
4	3.0	165.0	5.106
5	4.0	160.8	5.080
6	5.0	157.0	5.056
7	6.0	153.3	5.032
8	7.0	149.9	5.010
9	8.0	146.0	4.984
10	9.0	142.8	4.961
11	10.0	139.7	4.939
12	11.0	135.8	4.911
13	12.0	133.0	4.890
14	13.0	130.6	4.872
15	14.0	127.6	4.849
16	15.0	124.1	4.821
17	16.0	121.2	4.797
18	17.0	118.3	4.773
19	18.0	115.5	4.749
20	23.0	105.5	4.659
21	28.0	94.8	4.552
22	33.0	85.0	4.443
23	38.0	76.4	4.336
24	48.0	61.1	4.113
25	53.0	55.2	4.011
26	58.0	50.0	3.912
27	63.0	45.2	3.811

But $\Delta T/T$ is much less than 1 and so Equation (13.40) may be approximated by (see also Equation 10.33)

$$\pm \Delta y = \ln\left(1 \pm \frac{\Delta T}{T}\right)$$

$$\simeq \pm \frac{\Delta T}{T} \qquad\qquad (13.41)$$

thus

$$\Delta y = \frac{\Delta T}{T} = \frac{0.8}{T}$$

The experimental data are listed in Table 13-3. The results of a series of polynomial fits

$$y_{\text{model}} = a_0 + a_1 x + a_2 x^2 + \cdots + a_n x^n$$

are given in Table 13-4 where χ^2 is also computed for each polynomial fit. From the values of χ^2 we would infer that the quadratic fit is the most appropriate.

Table 13-4   Results of a succession of polynomial fits to the cooling curve data. The number of parameters in the model function is labeled g.

g	$(N-g)$	χ^2	a_0	a_1	a_2	a_3	a_4	a_5
2	25	94.93	5.16	-0.022				
3	24	24.53	5.17	-0.024	3.8×10^{-5}			
4	23	10.52	5.18	-0.025	9.9×10^{-5}	-7.9×10^{-7}		
5	22	7.84	5.18	-0.026	3.0×10^{-4}	-6.2×10^{-6}	4.5×10^{-8}	
6	21	6.19	5.18	-0.026	1.5×10^{-4}	8.5×10^{-7}	-8.7×10^{-8}	8.6×10^{-10}

13.9   LIMITATIONS OF THE LEAST SQUARES PROCEDURE

13.9.1   Caution: The Least Squares Problem May Be Ill-Conditioned

The underlying premise of a least squares fit to experimental data is that the data can be summarized by a relatively smooth model function that is linear in the parameters; i.e., a polynomial of modest degree. With large computers available, it is tempting to fit polynomials of higher and higher degree so as to improve the fit. Such an exercise is quite risky. Not only will a polynomial of high degree induce spurious wiggles in the curve if forced through the data, the least squares analysis becomes ill-conditioned for large n, the degree of the model polynomial, resulting in rapidly escalating round-off errors. This can be seen as follows.

The elements of the coefficient matrix in Equation (13.33) are of the form Σx^k, where $k = 1, \ldots, 2n$. To obtain a rough estimate of these terms we assume that the N x values are equally spaced between 0 and 1. Then if N is large, $dx \simeq 1/N$ or

(13.42)
$$\Sigma x_i^k \simeq \int_0^1 x^k (N\,dx) = N\frac{x^{k+1}}{k+1}\Big|_0^1 = \frac{N}{k+1}$$

Thus the matrix in Equation (13.33) is approximately

$$[A] = \begin{pmatrix} N & \dfrac{N}{2} & \dfrac{N}{3} & \cdots & \dfrac{N}{n+1} \\[2ex] \dfrac{N}{2} & \dfrac{N}{3} & \dfrac{N}{4} & \cdots & \dfrac{N}{n+2} \\[2ex] \dfrac{N}{3} & \dfrac{N}{4} & \dfrac{N}{5} & \cdots & \dfrac{N}{n+3} \\[2ex] \cdots & \cdots & \cdots & \cdots & \cdots \\[2ex] \dfrac{N}{n+1} & \dfrac{N}{n+2} & \dfrac{N}{n+3} & \cdots & \dfrac{N}{2n+1} \end{pmatrix}$$

and the determinant of $[A]$ is

$$|A| = N^{n+1} \begin{vmatrix} 1 & \dfrac{1}{2} & \dfrac{1}{3} & \cdots & \dfrac{1}{n+1} \\[2ex] \dfrac{1}{2} & \dfrac{1}{3} & \dfrac{1}{4} & \cdots & \dfrac{1}{n+2} \\[2ex] \dfrac{1}{3} & \dfrac{1}{4} & \dfrac{1}{5} & \cdots & \dfrac{1}{n+3} \\[2ex] \cdots & \cdots & \cdots & \cdots & \cdots \\[2ex] \dfrac{1}{n+1} & \dfrac{1}{n+2} & \dfrac{1}{n+3} & \cdots & \dfrac{1}{2n+1} \end{vmatrix}$$

The common factor N^{n+1} in each term of the determinant of $[A]$ can be a very large number depending on N, but the remaining determinant, which is independent of the number of points, is a very rapidly diminishing function of n, the degree of fit. Some values of this determinant are given below.

n	Determinant
0	1.0
1	0.0823
2	0.000463
3	1.653×10^{-7}

4	3.75×10^{-12}
5	5.37×10^{-18}
6	4.84×10^{-25}
7	2.74×10^{-33}
8	9.72×10^{-43}
9	2.17×10^{-53}

Clearly a least squares fit of a polynomial of even modest degree may involve the solution of a matrix equation in which the coefficient matrix is ill-conditioned. There are thus compelling reasons for not pushing a least squares analysis beyond a third- or fourth-degree polynomial.

13.9.2 Nonlinear Least Squares Analysis

Very frequently nature is unwilling to generate data that can be nicely summarized by simple polynomials or exponentials. For example, the model function suggested by a theory may be nonlinear in its parameters and not readily rewritten as linear by a change of variables, such as

$$y(x) = \alpha \sin(\beta t)$$

An expression like this can be inserted in the equation for $E(\alpha, \beta)$ [Equation (13.2)] and the derivatives with respect to α and β computed to find the minimum of the squared deviations. Since these equations are nonlinear in α and β, a completely different approach must be developed for their solution. The procedures of Chapter 11 were conceived to solve iteratively *one* nonlinear equation in one unknown. These algorithms can be extended to solve iteratively several simultaneous equations in several unknowns. The idea, not surprisingly, is to start with a Taylor series expansion of a function of two or more variables. Unfortunately, this topic is beyond the scope of this book. If you are interested you can find a moderately light-weight discussion in R. H. Pennington, *Computer Methods and Numerical Analysis*, Macmillan, Toronto, 1970.

The least squares analysis of this chapter is based on the idea of optimizing the fit of model functions that are expressed in terms of polynomials of varying degree. A different approach is to rephrase the discussion, replacing a model function

$$y_{model}(x) = a_0 + a_1 x + \cdots + a_n x^n$$

with a model function of the form

$$y_{model}(x) = a_0 g_0(x) + a_1 g_1(x) + \cdots + a_n g_n(x)$$

where the functions $g_n(x)$ are a special class of so-called orthogonal functions. This analysis, while not complicated, requires a detour into the study of orthogonal functions and will not be considered here. (An example of fitting with one class of orthogonal functions can be found in programming assignment VIII-B.)

13.10 CUBIC SPLINE FITS[3]

Often it is best to abandon the attempt to use least squares analysis to fit a simple function to complex data and simply "connect the dots" by drawing a smooth curve through the data using a French curve or a draftsman's spline (a flexible elastic bar). This is especially true if the points are not experimental values but are simply representative points of a physical structure such as an airplane wing. If we want the computer to duplicate the work of a draftsman, the prime concern is that the function smoothly pass through each of the points with a minimum of intermediate wiggles. The exact nature of the function is unimportant. This process is obviously very important in computer graphics applications.

The most common procedure is to fit each segment of two points $(x_i \leftrightarrow x_{i+1})$ with a cubic that passes through both points and then connect all of the segments into a smooth curve. Thus if the combined fitting curve is called $F(x)$, then $F(x)$ is represented by n segments $[f_i(x), i = 0, n - 1]$ each of which can be written as

(13.43)
$$f_i(x) = a_{0i} + a_{1i}(x - x_i) + a_{2i}(x - x_i)^2 + a_{3i}(x - x_i)^3$$

for $x_i \leq x \leq x_{i+1}$ and $i = 0, n - 1$

Each of the segments contains four parameters that must be determined by imposing four conditions on each segment. Two of these are obviously that the function segment must pass through the points (x_i, y_i), (x_{i+1}, y_{i+1}),

$$y_i = F(x_i) = f_i(x_i) = a_{0,i}$$
$$y_{i+1} = F(x_{i+1}) = f_i(x_{i+1}) = a_{0,i} + a_{1,i}\Delta x_i + a_{2,i}\Delta x_i^2 + a_{3,i}\Delta x_i^3$$

where I have defined

$$\Delta x_i = (x_{i+1} - x_i) \qquad \text{for } i = 0, \ldots, n - 1$$

Two additional conditions are required. These will be requirements on the "smoothness" of the overall function at the connections (knots) between the segments. Mathematically the conditions will be that the slopes of two adjoining segments must match at the knots at each end.

---

[3] This section contains more advanced material and may be omitted without a loss of continuity.

$$f'_{i-1}(x_i) = f'_i(x_i) \qquad \text{for } i = 1, n \qquad\qquad (13.44)$$

$$f'_i(x_{i+1}) = f'_{i+1}(x_{i+1}) \qquad \text{for } i = 0, n-1$$

These relations are illustrated graphically in Figure 13-10.

Applying these four conditions to determine the coefficients of the cubic is straightforward but involves considerable algebra as the latter two conditions have introduced adjoining segments (along with their coefficients) into the problem. The details of the solution for the coefficients is given in M. H. Schultz, *Spline Analysis*, Prentice-Hall, Englewood Cliffs, N.J., 1973. The results are given below.

$$a_{0,i} = y_i \qquad\qquad (13.45)$$

$$a_{1,i} = Z_i \qquad\qquad (13.46)$$

$$a_{2,i} = \frac{y_{i+1} - y_i}{\Delta x_i^2} - \frac{Z_i}{\Delta x_i} - a_{3,i}\Delta x_i \qquad\qquad (13.47)$$

$$a_{3,i} = \frac{Z_{i+1} + Z_i}{(\Delta x_i)^2} - 2\frac{y_{i+1} - y_i}{(\Delta x_i)^3} \qquad\qquad (13.48)$$

where Z_i is the derivative of the function at the point x_i (i.e., y'_i). If the values of the derivative of the fitting function are known, the coefficients of the cubic segments can be readily computed from the above equations.

Ordinarily the derivative of the fitting function is not known at each point and the data consist of only the pairs (x_i, y_i). For such cases a *separate* computation must be carried out to first obtain the Z_i, $i = 0, \ldots, n$. Since

Figure 13-10 The combined fitting function $F(x)$ is a combination of smoothly joined cubic segments.

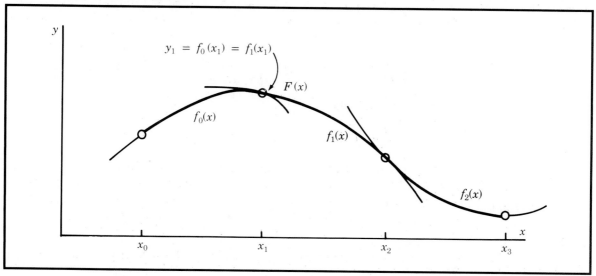

there are $n + 1$ unknown quantities Z_i, we will require $n + 1$ additional conditions. Most of these can be supplied by requiring that the second derivative of each segment match the adjoining segments at the knots; i.e.,

$$(13.49) \qquad F''(x_i) = f''_{i-1}(x_i) = f''_i(x_i) \qquad \text{for } i = 1, \ldots, n$$

Two additional requirements are

$$(13.50) \qquad \begin{aligned} F''(x_0) &= f''_0(x_0) = 0 \\ F''(x_n) &= f''_{n-1}(x_n) = 0 \end{aligned}$$

which are equivalent to allowing the draftsman's spline to be free and straight at both ends of the curve.

Applying the conditions of Equation (13.49) to our cubic segments yields

$$(13.51) \qquad 2a_{2,i-1} + 6a_{3,i-1}\Delta x_{i-1} = 2a_{2,i} \qquad i = 1, \ldots, n$$

Inserting the earlier expressions for the coefficients and after simplifying (again the details are in Schultz, op. cit.) we obtain,

$$(13.52) \qquad \begin{aligned} \Delta x_i Z_{i-1} &+ 2(\Delta x_{i-1} + \Delta x_i)Z_i + \Delta x_{i-1} Z_{i+1} \\ &= 3\left[(y_{i-1} - y_i)\frac{\Delta x_i}{\Delta x_{i-1}} + (y_{i+1} - y_i)\frac{\Delta x_{i-1}}{\Delta x_i} \right] \end{aligned}$$

for $i = 1, \ldots, n - 1$

These are $n - 1$ relations in the $n + 1$ unknowns Z_i, $i = 0, \ldots, n$. The two relations in Equations (13.50) are used to specify Z_0 and Z_n.

$$(13.53) \qquad Z_0 = \frac{3}{2}\left(\frac{y_1 - y_0}{\Delta x_0}\right) - \frac{1}{2}Z_1$$

$$(13.54) \qquad Z_n = \frac{3}{2}\left(\frac{y_n - y_{n-1}}{\Delta x_{n-1}}\right) - \frac{1}{2}Z_{n-1}$$

The equations simplify considerably for equally spaced points, $\Delta x_i = d$, for all i. Equation (13.52) may then be written

$$(13.55) \qquad Z_i = \frac{1}{4}[3(h_i + h_{i-1}) - (Z_{i-1} - Z_{i+1})] \qquad \text{for } i = 1, \ldots, n - 1$$

and Equations (13.53) and (13.54) become

$$(13.56) \qquad Z_0 = \tfrac{1}{2}(3h_0 - Z_1)$$

$$(13.57) \qquad Z_n = \tfrac{1}{2}(3h_{n-1} - Z_{n-1})$$

where

$$h_i = \frac{y_{i+1} - y_i}{d}$$

Equation (13.55) is written in a form suitable for a Gauss-Siedel iterative solution. The Fortran code to solve these equations is given in Figure 13-11. This code can easily be generalized to accommodate unevenly spaced data points.

Once the quantities Z_i have been computed we can return to Equations (13.46) to (13.49), compute the entire set of coefficients of the cubic segments and have the computer graph the function.

As an example, this procedure is applied to the wildly oscillating set of points shown in Figure 13-12.

```
      SUBROUTINE SPLINE(X0,XN,Y,N,EPS,KMAX,A)
*--
*-- SPLINE COMPUTES THE COEFFICIENTS OF THE CUBIC SEGMENTS, A()
*-- TO FIT THE N + 1 DATA POINTS Y() OVER THE INTERVAL X0 TO XN.
*-- THE DATA IS ASSUMED TO BE EQUALLY SPACED.
*--
*-- THE COMPUTATION REQUIRES THE DETERMINATION OF THE FIRST
*-- DERIVATIVES OF THE FITTING FUNCTION AT EACH POINT. THIS IS
*-- ACCOMPLISHED BY A GAUSS-SIEDEL ITERATION PROCEDURE STARTING
*-- WITH A CENTRAL DIFFERENCE APPROXIMATION AS THE INITIAL
*-- GUESS FOR THE DERIVATIVES.
*--
*-- THE GAUSS-SIEDEL SOLUTION IS TERMINATED SUCCESSFULLY WHEN
*-- THE RMS DEVIATION OF THE SET OF VALUES FOR THE DERIVATIVES
*-- Z() FROM THE PREVIOUS SET IS LESS THAN THE USER SUPPLIED
*-- EPS. THE SUBROUTINE THEN COMPUTES THE COEFFICIENTS A() AND
*-- RETURNS.
*--
*-- THE SOLUTION FAILS IF NOT SUCCESSFUL IN KMAX ITERATIONS.
*-- THE MAXIMUM NUMBER OF DATA POINTS THE CODE CAN HANDLE IS 50.
*------------------------------------------------------------
* VARIABLES
*
      REAL X0,XN,Y(0:N),Z(0:49),A(0:3,0:N),H(0:49),DX,SUM,TERM,
     +     EPS
      INTEGER N,KMAX
*
*            X0,XN -- THE X INTERVAL FROM X0 TO XN
*            Y()   -- THE EQUALLY SPACED DATA POINTS
*            DX    -- THE X SPACING OF THE DATA POINTS
*            N     -- THE NO. OF DATA POINTS IS N + 1
*            EPS   -- CONVERGENCE CRITERION ON THE RMS DEV-
*                     IATION OF THE Z() FROM ONE ITERATION
*                     TO THE NEXT
*            Z()   -- THE FIRST DERIVATIVES OF THE CUBIC
*                     SEGMENTS AT THE DATA POSITIONS. THE
*                     MAIN PART OF THE SUBROUTINE CONCERNS
*                     THE SOLUTION FOR THESE QUANTITIES.
*            KMAX  -- MAXIMUM NUMBER OF ITERATIONS ALLOWED
*            H()   -- THE SECANT SEGMENTS (Y(+1) - Y(I))/DX
*            A()   -- THE COMPUTED COEFFICIENTS OF THE CUBIC
*                     SEGMENTS. A(K,I) IS THE COEFFICIENT OF
*                     X**K IN THE I-TH SEGMENT. THE I-TH
*                     SEGMENT RUNS FROM X(I) TO X(I + 1).
*------------------------------------------------------------
```

Figure 13-11
A cubic spline fit to nonsmooth data.

Continued

```
*  INITIALIZATION AND INITIAL GUESS FOR Z()
*
      DX = (XN - X0)/N
*
*                   WE USE CENTRAL DIFFERENCE EXPRESSION FOR THE Z()
*                   AT ALL INTERIOR POINTS. AT LEFT AND RIGHT ENDS,
*                   USE FORWARD OR BACKWARD DIFFERENCES RESPECTIVELY
*
*                   ALSO USE THIS LOOP TO COMPUTE THE H()'S
*
      Z(N) = (-3. * Y(N) + 4. * Y(N - 1) - Y(N-2))/2./DX
      Z(0) = (-3. * Y(0) + 4. * Y(1)   - Y(2)  )/2./DX
      H(0) = (Y(1) - Y(0))/DX
      DO 1 I = 1,N - 1
         Z(I) = (Y(I + 1) - Y(I - 1))/2./DX
         H(I) = (Y(I + 1) - Y(I))/DX
    1 CONTINUE
*-------------------------------------------------------------
* THE GAUSS-SIEDEL SOLUTION FOR THE Z()'S
*
      K = 0
*
*                   TOP OF THE G-S ITERATION LOOP
*
   99 SUM = 0.0
*
*                   SOLVE THE N + 1 EQS. FOR THE Z(I) AND ALSO LET
*                   TERM = (ZNEW(I)-ZOLD(I))**2, SUM IS THEN THE
*                   RMS DEVIATION FROM ONE ITERATION TO THE NEXT
      DO 2 I = 0,N
         IF(I .EQ. 0)THEN
            TERM = Z(0)
            Z(0) = 0.5*(3.*H(0) - Z(1))
            TERM = (TERM - Z(0))**2
         ELSE IF(I .EQ. N)THEN
            TERM = Z(N)
            Z(N) = 0.5*(3.*H(N - 1) - Z(N - 1))
            TERM = (TERM - Z(N))**2
         ELSE
            TERM = Z(I)
            Z(I) = 0.25*(3.*H(I) - Z(I-1) - Z(I + 1))
            TERM = (TERM - Z(I))**2
         END IF
         SUM = SUM + TERM
    2 CONTINUE
*
      SUM = SQRT(SUM/N)
*
*                   TEST FOR CONVERGENCE
*
      IF(SUM .GT. EPS)THEN
*
*                   NOT YET CONVERGED, INCREMENT K AND TEST FOR
*                   EXCESSIVE ITERATIONS.
*
         K = K + 1
         IF(K .GT. KMAX)THEN
            WRITE(*,10)SUM,(Z(I),I = 0,N)
            STOP
         END IF
```

```
*
*                    LOOP BACK FOR NEXT ITERATION
*
            GO TO 99
        END IF
*------------------------------------------------------------------
*                 THE Z()'S HAVE BEEN SUCCESSFULLY COMPUTED, THE
*                 THE COEFFICIENTS A() ARE NOW EASILY COMPUTED
*
        DO 4 I = 0,N - 1
*
            A(0,I) = Y(I)
*
            A(1,I) = Z(I)
*
            A(3,I) = (Z(I + 1) + Z(I) - 2.*H(I))/DX**2
*
            A(2,I) = (H(I) - Z(I))/DX - A(3,I)*DX
      4 CONTINUE
*------------------------------------------------------------------
* FORMATS
*
    10 FORMAT(///,T10,'*****ERROR IN SPLINE*****',//,T15
      +       ,'THE CALCULATION HAS NOT CONVERGED',//,T15,
      +       'THE LATEST RMS DEVIATION IS = ',E10.4,//,T10,
      +       'AND THE LAST SET OF Z()S WAS',//,(2X,7E10.3))
*
        RETURN
        END
------------------------------------------------------------------
        FUNCTION YSPLIN(X,A,B,N,C)
*
*    THE FUNCTION COMPUTES THE MODEL VALUE OF Y FOR THE I-TH
*    CUBIC SEGMENT USING THE COEFFICIENTS OF THE CUBIC SEGMENTS
*    COMPUTED IN THE SUBROUTINE SPLINE.  (I .E. C(K,I))
*
        REAL X,XI,YSPLIN,A,B,C(0:3,0:N)
        INTEGER N
*
        DX = (B - A)/N
*
*                 THE I-TH SEGMENT IS DETERMINED AS
*
        I = (X - A)/DX
*
*                 BUT BE CAREFUL, IF X = B => I = N - 1
*
        IF(X .EQ. B)I = N - 1
*
*                 THE SEGMENT BEGINS AT XI
*
        XI = A + I * DX
        YSPLIN = C(0,I)
        DO 1 K = 1,3
           IF(X - XI .NE. 0.0)THEN
              YSPLIN = YSPLIN + C(K,I) * (X - XI)**K
           END IF
      1 CONTINUE
        RETURN
        END
```

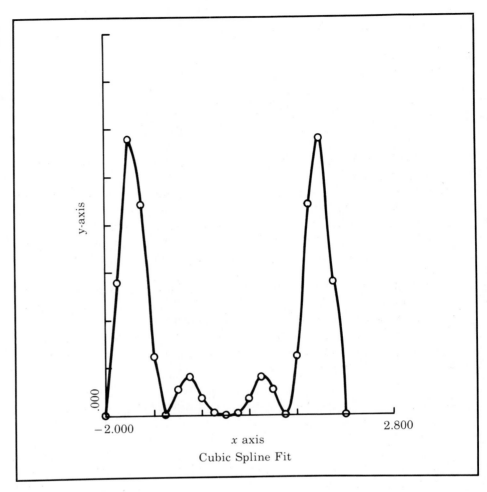

Figure 13-12 A cubic spline fit to nonsmooth data.

PROBLEMS

1. Determine the value of d that minimizes the sum of the squared deviations from the numbers (4, 3, 6, 1, 2) and then evaluate the minimum sum of the squared deviations

$$E = (4 - d)^2 + (3 - d)^2 + (6 - d)^2 + (1 - d)^2 + (2 - d)^2$$

Verify that with this value of d the sum of the deviations (not squared) is zero.

2. Evaluate the following partial derivatives:

   a. $\dfrac{\partial}{\partial a}(a^2 b + 4xe^a)$

   b. $\dfrac{\partial}{\partial c}\left[\sum_{i=1}^{N}(c^2 x_i^2 - y_i)\right]$

c. $\dfrac{\partial}{\partial b}\left\{\displaystyle\sum_{i=1}^{N}\left[y(x_i)-y_i\right]^2\right\}$ where $y(x_i)=e^{bx_i}$

3. For the data set

i	1	2	3	4	5	6
x_i	1.0	2.0	3.0	4.0	5.0	6.0
y_i	0.0	3.0	2.0	5.0	4.0	7.0

a. Determine the intercept (a_0) and the slope (a_1) of the least squares best-fit line.

b. Plot the data on graph paper, draw the best-fit line by eye, and then draw the least squares line $y(x)=a_0+a_1x$.

c. Explain why the two lines differ by such a large amount.

d. Which line do you think is the more accurate—i.e., which results in the smaller deviations. (Be careful in defining what is meant by deviations.)

e. Interchange the x and y values in the table and determine the least squares line $(x=b_0+b_1y)$ once more. Explain why the latest line is not the same as the previous least squares line.

4. Fit the data below first to a straight line and then to a parabola. For each case compute the resulting value of the minimum of the sum of the squared deviations—i.e., Equation (13.2).

i	1	2	3	4	5	6	7	8
x_i	−2.0	−1.0	0.0	1.0	2.0	3.0	4.0	5.0
y_i	−33.0	−24.0	−15.0	−3.0	10.0	24.0	39.0	55.0

5. The amount of a particular radioactive element decreases with time according to the equation $N(t)=N_0e^{-\lambda t}$ where $N(t)$ is the number of atoms left at time t if the original number at $t=0$ is N_0. The decay constant is λ. The half-life of the decay is defined to be $\tau=\ln(2)/\lambda$. The data below have been measured for a particular type of radioactive hydrogen atom. Fit the data to an equation of the form $N(t)=ae^{\beta t}$ and determine the half-life and the original number of atoms present.

i	1	2	3	4	5
t (months)	0.0	10.0	20.0	40.0	80.0
N	1.41×10^{18}	1.35×10^{18}	1.29×10^{18}	1.17×10^{18}	9.72×10^{17}

6. Fit the data below to an equation of the form $y=ax^\beta$. (Hint: Take the logarithm of this equation to suggest a linear model.)

i	1	2	3	4	5	6
x_i	1.0	2.0	3.0	4.0	5.0	6.0
y_i	1.0	3.3	7.2	13.0	20.0	28.0

Once you have obtained the best-fit values of α and β compare the theoretical results with the data.

7. According to the Stefan-Boltzmann law, the total energy radiated per second, R, from a hot object varies as the absolute temperature to the fourth power according to

$$R = \sigma(T^4 - T_0^4)$$

where T_0 is the room temperature (K) and σ is called the Stefan-Boltzmann constant. From the data below determine a value for σ by fitting a line $y = a_0 + a_1x$ to the data where $y_i = R_i$ and $x_i = T_i^4$. The accepted value of σ is $\sigma = 5.670 \pm 0.003 \times 10^{-8}$ W/m^2 = K^4.

i	1	2	3	4	5	6
T	300.0	350.0	400.0	450.0	500.0	550.0
R	40.0	430.0	1050.0	1920.0	3150.0	4750.0

8. Fit a line, a parabola, and a cubic to the data below and for each fit compute χ^2 using an error in each of the y values of $\Delta y \approx \pm 0.5$. What is your conclusion?

i	1	2	3	4
x_i	0.0	0.5	1.0	2.0
y_i	3.6	5.0	7.4	13.6

9. Graph the data below, including error bars, and fit the following functional form selecting the most appropriate from the values of chi-squared determined for each. Plot each of the three theoretical curves.

i	1	2	3	4	5
x_i	0.0	0.5	1.0	1.5	2.0
y_i	3.4	6.0	13.3	25.7	51.5
Δy_i	± 0.4	± 0.5	± 0.5	± 0.7	± 0.9

10. The purpose of this problem is to carry out the procedures for fitting a cubic spline by a hand calculation through three equally spaced points. The three points are

i	0	1	2
x_i	−2	1	4
y_i	15	3	9

Thus $d = x_{i+1} - x_i = 3$ and $h_0 = (y_1 - y_0)/d = -4$, $h_1 = (y_2 - y_1)/d = 2$.

   a. Write Equations (13.55) to (13.57) in matrix form and solve for the quantities Z_i. You should get:

$$\begin{pmatrix} Z_0 \\ Z_1 \\ Z_2 \end{pmatrix} = \frac{1}{4} \begin{pmatrix} 5h_0 - h_1 \\ 2h_0 + 2h_1 \\ -h_0 + 5h_1 \end{pmatrix} = \begin{pmatrix} -9/2 \\ -1 \\ 3/2 \end{pmatrix}$$

b. Use these values and Equations (13.45) to (13.48) to compute the coefficients of the *two* cubics drawn between the adjacent pairs of points. You should obtain

$$f_0(x) = y_0 + \frac{(x - x_0)}{4d}(-5y_0 + 6y_1 - y_2) + \frac{(x - x_0)^3}{4d^2}(y_0 - 2y_1 + y_2)$$

$$= \tfrac{1}{6}(x^3 + 6x^2 - 21x + 32)$$

$$f_1(x) = y_1 + \frac{(x - x_1)}{2d}(y_2 - y_0) + \frac{3(x - x_1)^2}{4d^2}(y_2 - 2y_1 + y_0)$$

$$- \frac{(x - x_1)^3}{4d^3}(y_2 - 2y_1 + y_0)$$

$$= \tfrac{1}{6}(-x^3 + 12x^2 - 27x + 34)$$

11. Determine the cubic spline fit through just *two* points (x_0, y_0), (x_1, y_1).
   a. First, using Equations (13.55) to (13.57), show that $Z_0 = Z_1 = h_0 = (y_1 - y_0)/(x_1 - x_0)$.
   b. Then, by using Equations (13.45) to (13.48), determine the coefficients of the cubic and show that the "cubic" is simply a straight line:

$$y(x) = y_0 + h_0(x - x_0)$$

PROGRAMMING ASSIGNMENT VII

VII.1   SAMPLE PROGRAM

Empirical Heat Capacities of Gases

The specific heat of a substance is a measure of the heat energy that must be added in order to raise the temperature of one kilogram of the substance 1 K. If the proportionality constant relating heat added (ΔQ) to increase in temperature (ΔT) is measured at a constant pressure, the result is called c_p, the specific heat at a constant pressure.

$$c_p = \frac{\Delta Q}{\Delta T}$$

The measured values of the specific heat of all common gases have been extensively tabulated and are of vital concern to the engineer when designing any apparatus or system that deals with heat transfer in gases. Both mechanical engineers (e.g., combustion, heat transfer) and chemical engineers (thermodynamics of chemical processes in gases) use tables of c_p vs. T in their work.

It is usually more convenient to have on hand a simple equation that summarizes limited portions of the tables. It has been found that the following equation quite accurately duplicates the actual c_p values for some gases.

(VII-1)
$$c_p(T) = a + bT + cT^2 + \frac{d}{T^2}$$

490

The temperature T is in Kelvin and the four parameters, a, b, c, d, are determined by a best fit of the equation to the experimental values. Notice that this model function, because of the d/T^2 term, is not a polynomial fit. This fact can be easily rectified by a change of variables. Multiplying Equation (VII.1) by T^2 suggests the change of variables $y(T) \rightarrow T^2 c_p(T)$, or

$$y(T) = d + aT^2 + bT^3 + cT^4 \tag{VII.2}$$

This equation is now a polynomial (minus a linear term) that is to be fit to the data. How do we incorporate the missing term in the model function into our theory? There is no shortcut. Equation (VII.2) is inserted into the equation for the sum of the squared deviations, Equation (13.2)

$$E(d, a, b, c) = \sum_{i=1}^{N} [(d + aT_i^2 + bT_i^3 + cT_i^4) - (T_i^2 c_{p,i})] \tag{VII.3}$$

The condition for a minimum of this function is that the four equations

$$\frac{\partial E}{\partial d} = 0 \qquad \frac{\partial E}{\partial a} = 0 \qquad \frac{\partial E}{\partial b} = 0 \qquad \frac{\partial E}{\partial c} = 0$$

are solved simultaneously. By evaluating these derivatives and simplifying the resulting equations in a manner similar to that in Chapter 12, we easily obtain the following matrix equation for the coefficients

$$\begin{pmatrix} N & \Sigma T^2 & \Sigma T^3 & \Sigma T^4 \\ \Sigma T^2 & \Sigma T^4 & \Sigma T^5 & \Sigma T^6 \\ \Sigma T^3 & \Sigma T^5 & \Sigma T^6 & \Sigma T^7 \\ \Sigma T^4 & \Sigma T^6 & \Sigma T^7 & \Sigma T^8 \end{pmatrix} \begin{pmatrix} d \\ a \\ b \\ c \end{pmatrix} = \begin{pmatrix} \Sigma c_p T^2 \\ \Sigma c_p T^4 \\ \Sigma c_p T^5 \\ \Sigma c_p T^6 \end{pmatrix} \tag{VII.4}$$

The problem then is to use the values of c_p vs. T in Table VII-1 to compute the sums in Equation (VII.4) and then to solve the matrix equation for the parameters a, b, c, d. Since the matrix differs somewhat from the ordinary least squares polynomial fit, the subroutine LSTSQR of Chapter 12 will have to be amended.

If the experimental errors in the c_p values are $\Delta c_p = \pm 3$ J/kg-K, compute χ^2 and comment on the validity of the overall fit to the data.

Duplicate the entire calculation, this time first adding $+\Delta c_p$ to the first, third, fifth, etc. c_p values and $-\Delta c_p$ to the second, fourth, sixth, etc. c_p values. The resulting change in the parameters should give some indication of the sensitivity of the parameters to the experimental error in c_p.

Sample Program Solution

The Fortran code for the solution of this problem is given In Figure VII-1. The required alterations to the subroutine LSTSQR are trivial enough that this subroutine is not listed. The results of the program are given in Figure VII-2.

Table VII-1 Specific heat vs. temperature for carbon dioxide. The pressure is constant at 7.0×10^5 N/m^2. The error in the c_p values is ± 15 J/kg-K.

i	T (°C)	c_p (J/kg-K)
1	170.	1101.
2	225.	1110.
3	275.	1123.
4	330.	1136.
5	390.	1153.
6	445.	1170.
7	500.	1185.
8	555.	1200.
9	610.	1216.
10	670.	1230.
11	725.	1243.
12	775.	1256.
13	830.	1268.
14	1100.	1318.
15	1390.	1354.
16	1670.	1373.

Figure VII-1
Main program for sample problem VII.

```
      PROGRAM SEVEN
*--
*--   THIS PROGRAM EXECUTES A LEAST SQUARES BEST-FIT CALCULATION
*--   OF A MODEL FUNCTION OF THE FORM
*--
*--       CP(T) = A + B * T + C * T**2 + D/T**2
*--
*--   TO THE EXPERIMENTAL SPECIFIC HEAT VALUES FOR A GAS OVER A
*--   BROAD RANGE OF TEMPERATURES BUT AT A CONSTANT PRESSURE.
*--   MULTIPLYING THE MODEL FUNCTION BY T**2 YIELDS A POLYNOMIAL
*--   OF DEGREE FOUR BUT MISSING THE LINEAR TERM. THE SUBROUTINE
*--   LSTSQR IS ALTERED TO ADJUST TO THIS CHANGE.
*--
*--   ADDITIONALLY, THE EXPERIMENTAL ERROR IN THE DATA, DC, IS USED
*--   TO COMPUTE CHI-SQUARED TO TEST THE VALIDITY OF THE MODEL FIT
*--
*--   FINALLY, EACH DATA POINT IS ALTERED BY C(T) => C(T) +/- DC
*--   AND THE ENTIRE CALCULATION IS REPEATED TO DETERMINE THE
*--   EFFECT OF EXPERIMENTAL ERROR ON THE PARAMETER VALUES.
*--
*--------------------------------------------------------------
* VARIABLES
*
      REAL T(20),CP(20),Y(20),DC,DY(20),AC(4,4),CHI2,COEF(0:3),
     +    P0,A,B,C,D
      INTEGER NDATA,KRUN
      CHARACTER NAME*15
```

```
*                     T()     --   TEMPERATURE (DEG-K) (INPUT DATA)
*                     CP()    --   SPECIFIC HEAT AT CONSTANT PRESSURE
*                                   (J/KG/DEG-K) (INPUT DATA)
*                     Y()     --   T**2 TIMES THE CP() VALUES
*                     DC      --   CONSTANT ERROR IN THE CP VALUES
*                     DY()    --   ERROR IN Y(), = DC * T**2
*                     PO      --   PRESSURE AT WHICH DATA TAKEN(N/M**2)
*                     AC()    --   THE COEFFICIENT MATRIX OF THE LEAST
*                                   SQUARES ANALYSIS
*                     COEF()--    COEFFICIENTS OF THE BEST-FIT POLYN.
*                     A,B,    --   THE SAME AS COEF(), MORE FAMILIAR
*                     C,D          NAMES FOR THE PARAMETERS.
*                     NDATA --    NUMBER OF DATA POINTS
*                     KRUN  --    THE CALCULATION IS EXECUTED TWICE,
*                                   KRUN = 0,1
*                     NAME  --    NAME (A15) OF THE GAS
*------------------------------------------------------------------
* INITIALIZATION
*
*                     READ THE EXPERIMENTAL VALUES FROM A DATA FILE
*
      OPEN(21,FILE = 'DATA7')
      REWIND 21
      OPEN(22,FILE = 'RESULT')
*
      READ(21,10)PO,DC,NAME
      DO 1 I = 1,50
         READ(21,11,END = 2)T(I),CP(I)
    1 CONTINUE
    2 NDATA = I - 1
*
*                     NEATLY ECHO PRINT THE DATA
*
      WRITE(22,12)NAME,PO,DC
      DO 3 I = 1,NDATA
         WRITE(22,13)I,T(I),CP(I)
    3 CONTINUE
*------------------------------------------------------------------
* COMPUTATION
*
*                     FILL IN THE Y-ARRAY AND THE ERROR ARRAY
*                     AND CONVERT TEMPERATURE TO KELVIN
*
      DO 4 I = 1,NDATA
         T(I) = T(I) + 273.16
         Y(I) = CP(I) * T(I)**2
         DY(I) = DC * T(I)**2
    4 CONTINUE
*
*
*                     CALL THE AMENDED SUBROUTINE LSTSQR TO COMPUTE
*                     THE COEFFICIENTS OF THE MODEL POLYNOMIAL.
*
      KRUN = 0
    5 CALL LSTSQR(T,Y,NDATA,COEF,3,1,DY,CHI2)
*
*                     PRINT RESULTS FOR PRIMARY CALCULATION
*
      IF(KRUN .EQ. 0)THEN
```

Continued

```
                KRUN = KRUN + 1
                WRITE(22,14)CHI2,NDATA - 5
                A = COEF(1)
                B = COEF(2)
                C = COEF(3)
                D = COEF(0)
                WRITE(22,15)A,B,C,D
*
*                    ALTER THE DATA AND REPEAT THE CALCULATION
*
                DO 6 I = 1,NDATA
                   IF(I/2 * 2 .EQ. I)THEN
                      Y(I) = Y(I) - DY(I)
                   ELSE
                      Y(I) = Y(I) + DY(I)
                   END IF
       6        CONTINUE
                GO TO 5
            ELSE
*
*                    AFTER THE SECOND CALCULATION CHECK THE
*                    FRACTIONAL CHANGES IN THE PARAMETERS.
*
                WRITE(22,16)
                WRITE(22,14)CHI2,NDATA - 5
                WRITE(22,15)COEF(1),COEF(2),COEF(3),COEF(0)
                A = ABS( (A - COEF(1))/A )
                B = ABS( (B - COEF(2))/B )
                C = ABS( (C - COEF(3))/C )
                D = ABS( (D - COEF(0))/D )
                WRITE(22,17)A,B,C,D
            END IF
            STOP
*----------------------------------------------------------------
* FORMATS
*
   10 FORMAT(2E10.3,A15)
*
   11 FORMAT(F5.1,E10.3)
*
   12 FORMAT(///,T5,'A CALCULATION OF THE PARAMETERS IN AN ',
      +        'EMPIRICAL FORMULA FOR',//,T5,
      +        'THE SPECIFIC HEAT OF ',A,///,T5,
      +        'THE DATA IS AT A CONSTANT PRESSURE OF',E9.2,' NT/M2',
      +        //,T5,'THE EXPERIMENTAL ERROR IN THE CP VALUES IS ',
      +        E9.2,' J/KG/DEG-K',///,T5,'THE DATA CONSISTS OF',//,
      +        T15,'I',T20,'TEMP',T26,'SPECIFIC HEAT',/,
      +        T20,'(K)',T26,' (J/KG/DEG-K)',/)
*
   13 FORMAT(T14,I2,T20,F6.1,T30,E10.4)
*
   14 FORMAT(//,T5,'THIS CALCULATION HAS A CHI-SQUARED OF',//,
      +        T20,E12.5,//,T5,
      +        'AN ADEQUATE FIT WILL HAVE A VALUE OF',//,T22,I2)
*
   15 FORMAT(///,T5,'THE RESULTS FOR THE PARAMETERS ARE',///,
      +        T10,'A',T25,'B',T40,'C',T55,'D',//,T6,4(E10.4,5X))
*
   16 FORMAT(////,T5,'THE CALCULATION IS NOW REPEATED WITH THE'
      +        ,' DATA ALTERED BY',//,T5,'ALTERNATELY ADDING OR ',
      +        'SUBTRACTING THE ERROR',/)
*
   17 FORMAT(///,T5,'THE FRACTIONAL CHANGES IN THE PARAMETERS'
```

```
      +     ,' ARE THEN',//,
      +     T10,'A',T25,'B',T40,'C',T55,'D',/,T6,4(F8.3,7X))
*
      END
```

A CALCULATION OF THE PARAMETERS IN AN EMPIRICAL FORMULA FOR
THE SPECIFIC HEAT OF CARBON DIOXIDE

THE DATA IS AT A CONSTANT PRESSURE OF .70E+06 NT/M2

THE EXPERIMENTAL ERROR IN THE CP VALUES IS   .30E+01 J/KG/DEG-K

THE DATA CONSISTS OF

I	TEMP (C)	SPECIFIC HEAT (J/KG/DEG-K)
1	170.0	.1101E+04
2	225.0	.1110E+04
3	275.0	.1123E+04
4	330.0	.1136E+04
5	390.0	.1153E+04
6	445.0	.1170E+04
7	500.0	.1185E+04
8	555.0	.1200E+04
9	610.0	.1216E+04
10	670.0	.1230E+04
11	725.0	.1243E+04
12	775.0	.1256E+04
13	830.0	.1268E+04
14	1100.0	.1318E+04
15	1390.0	.1354E+04
16	1670.0	.1373E+04

THIS CALCULATION HAS A CHI-SQUARED OF
          .73531E+01
AN ADEQUATE FIT WILL HAVE A VALUE OF
          11

THE RESULTS FOR THE PARAMETERS ARE

A	B	C	D
.8831E+03	.4664E+00	-.1107E-03	.5113E+07

THE CALCULATION IS NOW REPEATED WITH THE DATA ALTERED BY
ALTERNATELY ADDING OR SUBTRACTING THE ERROR

THIS CALCULATION HAS A CHI-SQUARED OF
          .17925E+02

Continued

Figure VII-2
Output of the curve fit to gaseous specific heats.

```
AN ADEQUATE FIT WILL HAVE A VALUE OF
                  11

THE RESULTS FOR THE PARAMETERS ARE

       A              B              C              D
   .8424E+03      .5183E+00     -.1277E-03     .1066E+08

THE FRACTIONAL CHANGES IN THE PARAMETERS ARE THEN

       A              B              C              D
    .046           .111           .154          1.086
```

VII.2 PROGRAMMING PROBLEMS

Programming Problem A: Aerodynamics: Free Fall in Air

Several times in earlier examples we have made use of the results of a relatively simple experiment, that of measuring the distance of fall vs. time for an object released in air. Typically, the trajectory is photographed while illuminated by a rapidly flashing light. The positions of the images on the film are then used to determine the distance of fall at regular time intervals. The results for one run of such an experiment are given in Table VII-2 and are graphed in Figure VII-3.

From the graph it can be seen that the functional dependence of position on time is rather complicated. The data start out parabolic in appearance and end up being very nearly a straight line. The straight-line portion of the curve is a result of the ball reaching its terminal velocity. That is, dy/dt = constant. If we attempt to fit a polynomial to this curve by a least squares analysis, neither a parabola nor a line will be suitable over the entire range of data. The apparent solution is to use a parabolic fit over the first part and a straight-line fit over the last part. The problem is then where to make the break. This can be determined in the following way.

There are 33 data points. Fit the first six with a parabola and determine the coefficients a_0, a_1, a_2 [see Equation (13.33)]. Then fit the final $33 - 6 = 27$ points with a straight line and determine the coefficients of the line b_0, b_1. Print all the coefficients along with the sum of the squared deviations,

(VII.5)
$$E_6 = \sum_{i=1}^{6} [(a_0 + a_1 t_i + a_2 t_i^2) - y_i]^2 + \sum_{i=7}^{33} [(b_0 + b_1 t_i) - y_i]^2$$

Table VII-2 Fall distance vs. time for a styrofoam ball.

Index	t_i (sec)	y_i (cm)
1	0.2650	16.55
2	0.2900	18.85
3	0.3150	21.68
4	0.3400	25.00
5	0.3650	28.90
6	0.3900	33.36
7	0.4150	36.07
8	0.4400	43.06
9	0.4650	48.51
10	0.4900	54.30
11	0.5150	60.29
12	0.5400	66.53
13	0.5650	73.26
14	0.5900	80.69
15	0.6150	87.12
16	0.6400	94.15
17	0.6650	101.60
18	0.6900	109.00
19	0.7150	116.60
20	0.7400	124.40
21	0.7650	132.20
22	0.7900	140.10
23	0.8150	148.10
24	0.8400	156.20
25	0.8650	164.30
26	0.8900	172.40
27	0.9150	180.60
28	0.9400	189.70
29	0.9650	197.90
30	0.9900	206.00
31	1.0150	214.20
32	1.0400	223.30
33	1.0650	231.50

Next repeat the calculation with the break at point number 7. That is, fit the first 7 points with a parabola and the last 26 with a line. Continue this up to a break point at point number 22. The calculation with the smallest value of E gives the best fit by this method.

Finally, for the overall optimum fit, print the terminal velocity.

Problem Specifics

1. Create a data file containing the experimental values.
2. For NC (cut point) = 7 to 22
   a. Construct the matrices

Figure VII-3
Fall distance vs. time.

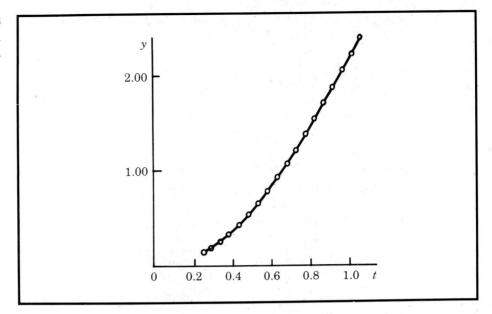

and the right-hand-side vectors

$$\mathbf{c} = \begin{pmatrix} \Sigma y \\ \Sigma ty \\ \Sigma t^2 y \end{pmatrix} \qquad \mathbf{d} = \begin{pmatrix} \Sigma' y \\ \Sigma' ty \end{pmatrix}$$

where

$$\Sigma \equiv \sum_{i=1}^{NC} \qquad \Sigma' \equiv \sum_{i=NC+1}^{N}$$

b. Solve the two matrix equations by using the matrix subroutine MINV of Chapter 12. Store the coefficients of the parabola and the line for this value of NC [e.g., A(I,NC),B(I,NC)].

c. Evaluate E(NC) for this value of NC.

3. Determine the overall minimum of the set of values E(NC). Print a neat table of E(NC),A(I,NC),B(I,NC) for NC = 7, 22. Tag the optimum value in the table with a label OPTIMUM FIT.

4. Use the best-fit coefficients a_i, b_i to determine the velocity (dy/dt) and the acceleration (d^2y/dt^2), and print a table of $y_{i,\,exp}$, $y_{i,\,theory}$, vel_i, acc_i for $i = 1, 33$.

Programming Problem B: Record Times for the Mile Run

Very frequently in least squares data fitting, the assumed model function, $y(x)$, cannot be forced to resemble a straight line or a polynomial by a change of variables. As a result, the equations that determine the minimum of the squared deviations are nonlinear in the parameters and an interative procedure must be used in place of the ordinary matrix techniques.

For example, the record times for the mile are listed in Table VII-3 and graphed in Figure VII-4.

From the graph it appears that the record times are decreasing in an exponential fashion, but the curve is not asymptotic to zero as t approaches infinity but rather approaches a fixed number somewhat below 4 min. Thus we might attempt to fit the data to a model equation of the form

$$R(t) = R_0(1 + e^{-\alpha t}) \tag{VII.6}$$

where $R(t)$ is the record time, t is the year measured from 1865, and the parameters are R_0, the asymptote, and the decay constant α. For large values of t the expression approaches R_0, which we expect to be ≈ 4 min. Since Equation (VII.6) will result in nonlinear equations for R_0 and α, an alternate method of solution must be developed.

If we define

$$y = \ln\left[\frac{R(t)}{R_0} - 1\right] \tag{VII.7}$$

Equation (VII.6) may be written as

$$y = -\alpha t \tag{VII.8}$$

i	Year	Time	i	Year	Time	i	Year	Time
1	1865	4:36.5	14	1913	4:14.1	27	1957	3:57.5
2	1868	4:29.0	15	1915	4:12.6	28	1958	3:54.5
3	1869	4:28.9	16	1923	4:10.4	29	1962	3:54.4
4	1874	4:26.0	17	1931	4:09.2	30	1964	3:54.1
5	1875	4:24.5	18	1933	4:07.6	31	1965	3:53.6
6	1880	4:23.2	19	1934	4:06.8	32	1966	3:51.3
7	1882	4:21.4	20	1937	4:06.4	33	1967	3:51.3
8	1882	4:19.4	21	1942	4:06.2	34	1975	3:49.5
9	1884	4:18.2	22	1943	4:04.6	35	1979	3:49.0
10	1894	4:18.1	23	1944	4:01.6	36	1980	3:48.8
11	1895	4:17.0	24	1945	4:01.4	37	1981	3:47.3
12	1911	4:15.4	25	1954	3:59.4			
13	1913	4:14.6	26	1954	3:58.0			

Table VII-3
Record times for the mile run over the last century.

Figure VII-4
The decrease in
the record time
for the mile run
in the last
century.

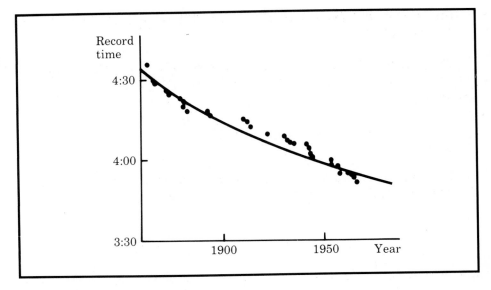

Inserting this model function into the expression for $E(R_0, \alpha)$, the sum of the squared deviations, yields

(VII.9)
$$E = \sum_{i=1}^{n}(\alpha t_i + y_i)^2$$

which is to be minimized by solving $\partial E / \partial \alpha = 0$ for the value of α. [Note: The values of y_i, computed from Equation (VII.7) are all negative.] The result is

(VII.10)
$$\alpha = -\frac{\Sigma \, ty}{\Sigma \, t^2}$$

Unfortunately, to carry out the summations we need to first know the values of R_0 to be used in Equation (VII.7). This suggests the following iterative procedure:

1. Read the data $[t_i, R(t_i)]$, compute the set of values y_i from Equation (VII.7) and neatly print in a table.
2. Choose an initial guess for R_0. Note that since the logarithm of a negative number is undefined, Equation (VII.7) requires that R_0 be smaller than the minimum value of $R(t)$ in the data.
3. Determine α from Equation (VII.10).
4. Compute a *new* value of R_0 by using Equation (VII.6). For example,

(VII.11)
$$R_{0,\text{new}} = \frac{1}{N} \sum_{i=1}^{n} \frac{R(t_i)}{1 + e^{-\alpha t_i}}$$

---

5. If the change in R_0 is less than 10^{-5} stop, otherwise return to the second step and repeat.

The output of the program should consist of values for α, R_0, the number of iterations required, and the final value for the root-mean-square deviation defined as

$$\sigma = \left(\frac{E}{N-1}\right)^{1/2}$$

Finally, use the computed values of α and R_0 to determine the precise day and time that the time of 3:40 will be recorded.[1]

---

[1] The times in Table VII-3 are given as minutes:seconds. All the times used in computation must be converted to decimal minutes, while all times that are printed should be converted to the form minutes:seconds.

CHAPTER 14
NUMERICAL INTEGRATION

14.1 INTRODUCTION

The integration of a function of a single variable can be thought of as either the opposite of differentiation—i.e., the antiderivative— or as the area under a curve. The former is ordinarily discussed in depth in a calculus course. We shall concentrate here on the second approach.

The interpretation[1] of the integral

$$I = \int_a^b f(x) \, dx$$

as the area under the curve of f vs. x from $x = a$ to $x = $ b (see Figure 14-1) lends itself so naturally to numerical computation that the most effective way to understand the process of integration is to learn the numerical approach first and later have these ideas reinforced by the more formal concepts of the antiderivative.

---

[1] This interpretation defines regions where the function falls below the x axis to have *negative* area. Thus the area "under" the sine function from $\theta = 0$ to $\theta = 2\pi$ is zero.

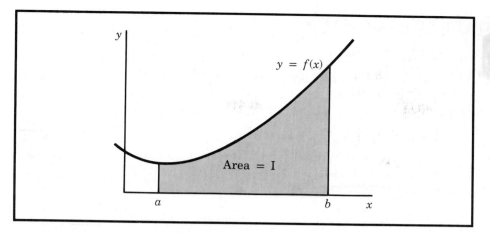

Figure 14-1
The integral as
an area under a
curve.

Another reason for studying numerical integration at this stage is that it is a so-called stable process; it almost always works. Contrast this with numerical differentiation studied in Chapter 10 and defined by a relation like

$$\frac{df}{dx} = \lim_{\Delta x \to 0} \left[\frac{f(x + \Delta x) - f(x)}{\Delta x} \right]$$

Clearly, as we attempt to evaluate this expression for smaller and smaller values of Δx, the problems of round-off error (subtracting numbers of about the same magnitude) and division by zero will complicate the computation for even the simplest functions. Numerical integration, on the other hand, consists of expressing the area as the sum of areas of smaller segments, a procedure that is relatively safe from such computational difficulties.

Finally, it is unfortunately true that many, perhaps most, of the integrals that occur in actual engineering or science problems cannot be expressed in any closed form. For example, an integral as innocent appearing as

$$I = \int_{b}^{a} e^{-x^2} \, dx$$

is of this type and the only way that it can be evaluated is numerically. To formally integrate a function—i.e., to obtain a closed expression for the answer—quite often takes considerable training and experience. There are dozens of "tricks" that must be learned and understood. The procedures of numerical integration are in contrast rather few in number, all rather easy to understand and remember.

14.2 THE TRAPEZOIDAL RULE

An approximation to the area under a complicated curve is obtained by assuming that the function can be replaced by simpler functions over a limited range. A straight line, the simplest approximation to a function, is the first to be considered and leads to what is called the *trapezoidal rule*.

The area under the curve $f(x)$ from $x = a$ to $x = b$ is approximated by the area beneath a straight line drawn between the points (x_a, f_a) and (x_b, f_b) (see Figure 14-2). The shaded area is then the approximation to the integral and is the area of a trapezoid, which is

$$I = \text{(average value of } f \text{ over interval)(width of interval)}$$

or

(14.1)
$$I = \tfrac{1}{2}(f_a + f_b)(b - a) \equiv T_0$$

This is the trapezoidal rule for one panel, identified as T_0.

14.2.1 The Formula for the Trapezoidal Rule for *n* Panels

To improve the accuracy of the approximation to the area under a curve the interval is next divided in half and the function approximated by straight-line segments over each half. The area in this case is approximated by the area of two trapezoids (see Figure 14-3).

$$I \simeq T_1 = [\tfrac{1}{2}(f_a + f_1)\,\Delta x_1] + [\tfrac{1}{2}(f_1 + f_b)\,\Delta x_1]$$

Figure 14-2
Approximating the area under a curve by a single trapezoid.

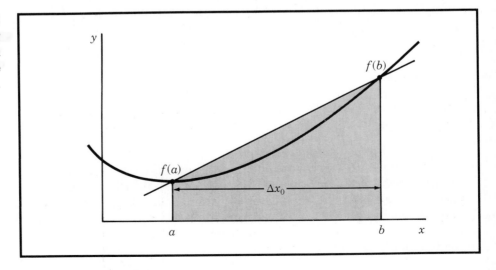

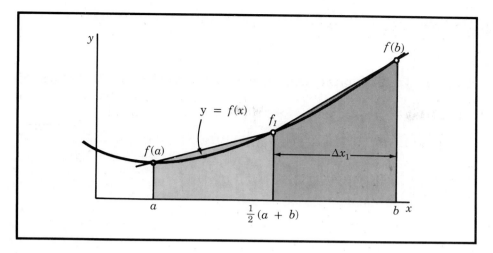

Figure 14-3 A two-panel approximation to the area.

or

$$T_1 = \frac{\Delta x_1}{2}(f_a + 2f_1 + f_b)$$ (14.2)

where

$$\Delta x_1 = \frac{(b - a)}{2}$$

$$f_1 = f(x = a + \Delta x_1)$$

Notice that when adding the areas of the trapezoids, the sides at f_a and f_b are sides of only the first and last trapezoid, while the side at f_1 is a side of two trapezoids and thus "counts twice," explaining the factor of 2 in Equation (14.2).

Furthermore, the two-panel approximation, T_1, can be related to the earlier one-panel result, T_0, as

$$T_1 = \frac{T_0}{2} + \Delta x_1 f_1$$ (14.3)

To increase the accuracy further, the interval is simply subdivided into a larger number of panels. The result for n panels is clearly

$$I \simeq T_n = \frac{1}{2}\Delta x_n \left(f_a + 2\sum_{i=1}^{n-1} f_i + f_b \right)$$ (14.4)

where $\Delta x_n = (b - a)/n$ and f_i is the function evaluated at all the interior points,

$$f_i = f(x = a + i\,\Delta x_n)$$ (14.5)

14.2   THE TRAPEZOIDAL RULE   505

The reason for the extra factor of 2 in Equation (14.4) is the same as in the two-panel example.

14.2.2   An Alternate Form of the Trapezoidal Rule Equation

Equation (14.4) was derived assuming that the widths of all the panels are the same and equal to Δx_n. This is not required in the derivation, and the equation can easily be generalized to a partition of the interval into unequal panels of width Δx_i, $i = 1, \ldots, n - 1$. However, for reasons to be explained a bit later, I will not only restrict the panel widths to be equal but the number of panels to be a power of 2—i.e.,

$$n = 2^k$$

The number of panels is n, the order of the calculation will be called k, and the corresponding trapezoidal rule approximation will be labeled as T_k. Thus T_0 is the result for $n = 2^0 = 1$ panel. The situation for $k = 2$ or $2^2 = 4$ panels is illustrated in Figure 14-4. In the figure, the width of a panel is $\Delta x_2 = (b - a)/2^2$ and the value of the $k = 2$ trapezoidal rule approximation is

(14.6)
$$T_2 = \frac{\Delta x_2}{2}[f_a + 2f(a + \Delta x_2) + 2f(a + 2\,\Delta x_2) + 2f(a + 3\,\Delta x_2) + f_b]$$

However, since $2\,\Delta x_2 = \Delta x_1$ we see that

(14.7)
$$f(a + 2\,\Delta x_2) = f(a + \Delta x_1)$$

and $f(a + \Delta x_1)$ was already determined in the previous calculation of T_1 [Equation (14.3)]. The point is, once a particular-order trapezoidal rule ap-

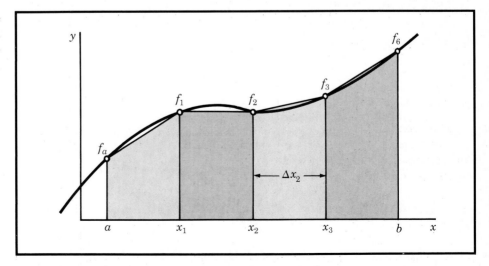

Figure 14-4
The four-panel trapezoidal approximation, T_2.

proximation has been computed, to proceed to the next-order trapezoidal rule approximation the only new information that is required is the evaluation of the function at the *midpoints* of the current intervals. This is of course true only if the number of panels is successively doubled in each stage.

To exploit this fact further, Equation (14.2) and (14.7) can be used to rewrite Equation (14.6) in the form

$$T_2 = \frac{\Delta x_1}{4}[f_a + 2f(a + \Delta x_1) + f_b] + \Delta x_2[f(a + \Delta x_2) + f(a + 3 \Delta x_2)]$$

$$= \frac{T_1}{2} + \Delta x_2[f(a + \Delta x_2) + f(a + 3 \Delta x_2)]$$

(14.8)

This can easily be generalized to yield

$$T_k = \frac{1}{2}T_{k-1} + \Delta x_k \sum_{\substack{i=1 \\ \text{odd only}}}^{n-1} f(a + i \Delta x_k)$$

(14.9)

where

$$\Delta x_k = \frac{b - a}{2^k}$$

The procedure for using Equation (14.9) to approximate an integral by the trapezoidal rule is

1. Compute T_0 by using Equation (14.1)
2. Repeatedly apply Equation (14.9) for $k = 1, 2, \ldots$ until sufficient accuracy is obtained.

14.2.3 An Example of a Trapezoidal Rule Calculation

To illustrate the ideas of this section, consider the integral

$$I = \int_1^2 \left(\frac{1}{x}\right) dx$$

The function $f(x) = 1/x$ can of course be integrated analytically to give $\ln(x)$ and since $\ln(1) = 0$, the value of the integral is $\ln(2) = 0.69314718$. The trapezoidal rule approximation to the integral with $b = 2$ and $a = 1$ begins with Equation (14.1) to obtain T_0.

$$T_0 = \frac{1}{2}\left(\frac{1}{1} + \frac{1}{2}\right)(2 - 1) = 0.75$$

Repeated use of Equation (14.9) then yields

$$k = 1 \qquad \Delta x_1 = \tfrac{1}{2}$$

$$T_1 = \frac{T_0}{2} + \frac{1}{2}\left[f\left(1 + \frac{1}{2}\right)\right] = \frac{0.75}{2} + \frac{1}{2}\left(\frac{1}{1.5}\right)$$

$$= 0.708333$$

$$k = 2 \qquad \Delta x_2 = \tfrac{1}{4}$$

$$T_2 = \frac{T_1}{2} + \frac{1}{4}\left(\frac{1}{1.25} + \frac{1}{1.75}\right)$$

$$= 0.6970238$$

$$k = 3 \qquad \Delta x_3 = \tfrac{1}{8}$$

$$T_3 = \frac{T_2}{2} + \frac{1}{8}\left(\frac{1}{1.125} + \frac{1}{1.375} + \frac{1}{1.625} + \frac{1}{1.875}\right)$$

$$= 0.69412185$$

Continuing the calculation through $k = 5$ yields

k	T_k
0	0.75
1	0.70833
2	0.69702
3	0.69412
4	0.69339
5	0.693208
. . .	. . .
exact	0.693147 . . .

The convergence of the computed values of the trapezoidal rule is not particularly fast, but the method is quite simple.

14.3 SIMPSON'S RULE APPROXIMATION FOR AN INTEGRAL

The trapezoidal rule is based on approximating the function by straight line segments. To improve the accuracy and the convergence rate of the method, an obvious direction to take would be to approximate the function by parabolic segments in place of straight lines. That is, use the next term in a Taylor series expansion of the function. This idea results in an approximation for the integral known as Simpson's rule, the simplest example of

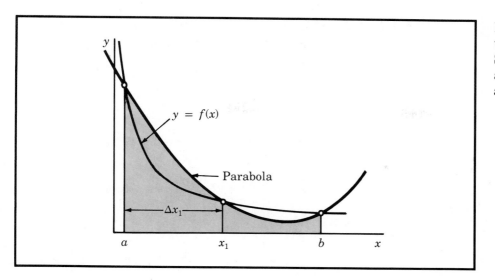

Figure 14-5   A two-panel Simpson's rule approximation to an integral.

which is illustrated in Figure 14-5. To uniquely specify a parabola requires three points, and so the lowest-order Simpson's rule has two panels.

To proceed, we need to know the area under a parabola drawn through three points. Note that the corresponding step in the derivation of the trapezoidal rule was trivial: the area under a line through two points is simply $\Delta x (f_a + f_b)/2$. Here, we must first derive the expression for the area under a parabola.

14.3.1   The Area Under a Parabola Drawn Through Three Points

A general parabola can be written as

$$y_2(x) = c_0 + c_1 x + c_2 x^2 \tag{14.10}$$

The area under the parabola from $x = a$ to $x = b$ is then

$$
\begin{aligned}
A_2 = \int_a^b y_2(x)\, dx &= c_0(b - a) + c_1 \frac{(b^2 - a^2)}{2} + c_2 \frac{(b^3 - a^3)}{3} \\[2mm]
&= c_0(b - a) + c_1 \frac{(b - a)(b + a)}{2} \\[2mm]
&\quad + c_2 \frac{(b - a)(b^2 + ab + a^2)}{3} \\[2mm]
&= \left(\frac{b - a}{6} \right) [6c_0 + 3c_1(b + a) + 2c_2(b^2 + ab + a^2)]
\end{aligned}
\tag{14.11}
$$

To simplify this result, consider the following:

$$y_2(x = a) + 4y_2\left(x = \frac{a+b}{2}\right) + y_2(x = b) = c_0 + c_1a + c_2a^2$$

(14.12)

$$+ 4c_0 + 2c_1(a+b) + c_2(a+b)^2$$
$$+ c_0 + c_1b + c_2b^2$$
$$= 6c_0 + 3c_1(a+b) + 2c_2(a^2 + ab + b^2)$$

By comparing Equations (14.11) and (14.12), the area under a parabola may be written as

(14.13)

$$A_2 = \frac{1}{3}\left(\frac{b-a}{2}\right)\left[y_2(a) + 4y_2\left(\frac{a+b}{2}\right) + y_2(b)\right]$$

Thus the area under a general parabola over the interval $x = a$ to $x = b$ can be expressed in terms of the value of the parabola at the left and right ends and at the midpoint of the interval. Equation (14.13) is then the starting point of the derivation of Simpson's rule in the same way that Equation (14.1) is the basis of the trapezoidal rule derivation.

14.3.2   Derivation of the Simpson's Rule Approximation

If the curve $f(x)$ drawn in Figure 14-5 is approximated by a parabola drawn through the three points f_a, f_b, the value of $f(x)$ at the midpoint of the interval, f_{mid}, the first-order Simpson's rule approximation is obtained.

$$k = 1 \qquad n = 2^1 \text{ panels} \qquad \Delta x_1 = \frac{b-a}{2}$$

(14.14)

$$S_1 = \tfrac{1}{3}\,\Delta x_1[f_a + 4f(a + \Delta x_1) + f_b]$$

The next level of approximation is to halve the interval width and partition the interval into four panels, as shown in Figure 14-6. The area under the function $f(x)$ is then approximated as the area under the two parabolas drawn through the two sets of points (f_a, f_1, f_2) and (f_2, f_3, f_b). Since the area under a single parabola is given by Equation (14.13), the area under the two parabolas is

$$S_2 = \tfrac{1}{3}\,\Delta x_2[(f_a + 4f_1 + f_2) + (f_2 + 4f_3 + f_b)]$$

(14.15)

$$= \tfrac{1}{3}\,\Delta x_2[f_a + 4(f_1 + f_3) + 2f_2 + f_b]$$

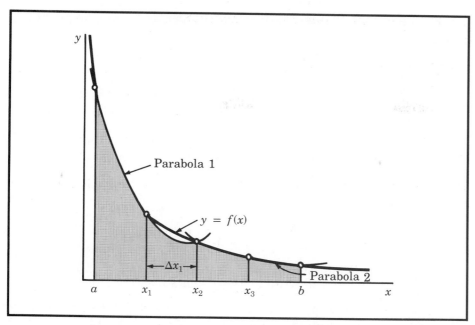

Figure 14-6 A second-order Simpson's rule approximation is the area under two parabolas.

where

$$\Delta x_2 = \frac{b - a}{2^2}$$

and

$$f_i = f(x = a + i\,\Delta x_2)$$

This procedure can be extended to 8, 16, 32, etc. panels. The result is a rather simple generalization of Equation (14.15) and for $n = 2^k$ panels is:

$$S_k = \frac{1}{3}\Delta x_k \Big[f_a + 4 \sum_{\substack{i=1 \\ \text{odd only}}}^{n-1} f(a + i\,\Delta x_k) + 2 \sum_{\substack{i=2 \\ \text{even only}}}^{n-2} f(a + i\,\Delta x_k) + f_b \Big] \qquad (14.16)$$

where

$$\Delta x_k = \frac{b - a}{2^k}$$

Equation (14.16) is an extremely popular method of evaluating integrals of functions that are rather smooth, and rightly so. As we shall see in Section 14.3.4, Simpson's rule converges quite nicely in most instances and it is rather easy to use. Also, Equation (14.16) can easily be adapted to handle an odd number of unevenly spaced points and is the most common method for estimating the integral of experimentally obtained data.

14.3.3 The Relationship between Simpson's Rule and the Trapezoidal Rule

Both the trapezoidal rule [Equation (14.9)] and Simpson's rule [Equation (14.15)] employ the values of the function evaluated at the same points and thus the two formulas should be related. If we collect the relevant equations for $k = 0$ and 1, we have

$$T_0 = \frac{1}{2} \Delta x_0 (f_a + f_b)$$

$$T_1 = \frac{T_0}{2} + \Delta x_1 f_1$$

$$S_1 = \frac{1}{3} \Delta x_1 [f_a + 4f_1 + f_b]$$

Since $\Delta x_0 = 2 \Delta x_1$, we can write the last equation as

$$S_1 = \frac{\Delta x_0}{6} (f_a + f_b) + \frac{4}{3} \Delta x_1 f_1$$

$$= \frac{1}{3} T_0 + \frac{4}{3} \left(T_1 - \frac{1}{2} T_0 \right)$$

or

(14.17)
$$S_1 = T_1 + \frac{T_1 - T_0}{3}$$

For $k = 2$ the equations are

$$T_1 = \Delta x_2 (f_a + 2f_2 + f_b)$$
$$T_2 = \tfrac{1}{2} \Delta x_2 [f_a + 2(f_1 + f_2 + f_3) + f_b]$$
$$S_2 = \tfrac{1}{3} \Delta x_2 [f_a + 4(f_1 + f_3) + 2f_2 + f_b]$$

where $f_i = f(x = a + i \Delta x_2)$.

Using these expressions you can easily verify that

(14.18)
$$S_2 = T_2 + \frac{T_2 - T_1}{3}$$

In fact, using the general expressions for T_k [Equation (14.9)] and for S_k [Equation (14.16)] this result can be generalized to

(14.19)
$$S_k = T_k + \frac{T_k - T_{k-1}}{3}$$

This important result provides a convenient alternative method of obtaining the results of Simpson's rule: First compute the trapezoidal rule values through order k, then use Equation (14.19) to generate the Simpson's rule values likewise through order k. Notice that by this method once the trapezoidal rule values are obtained, the function itself is not evaluated at any additional points.

14.3.4 An Example of Simpson's Rule as an Approximation to an Integral

We will again consider the integral

$$I = \int_1^2 \frac{1}{x}\,dx$$

Using Equation (14.16) first for $k = 1$ yields,

$$k = 1 \qquad n = 2^1 = 2 \qquad \Delta x_1 = \frac{b - a}{2} = \frac{1}{2}$$

$$S_1 = \frac{1}{3}\left(\frac{1}{2}\right)\left[1 + 4\left(\frac{1}{1.5}\right) + \frac{1}{2}\right]$$

$$= 0.6944444$$

Repeating for $k = 2$,

$$k = 2 \qquad n = 2^2 = 4 \qquad \Delta x_2 = \frac{1}{4}$$

$$S_2 = \frac{1}{3}\left(\frac{1}{4}\right)\left[1 + 4\left(\frac{1}{1.25} + \frac{1}{1.75}\right) + 2\left(\frac{1}{1.5}\right) + \frac{1}{2}\right]$$

$$= 0.69325397$$

Continuing the calculation we obtain the values listed in Table 14-1. For comparison, I have also included the results for the same integral obtained in the previous section by the trapezoidal rule. Clearly, Simpson's rule converges much faster than the trapezoidal rule, at least for this example.

The Simpson's rule values could also have been computed directly from the trapezoidal rule numbers by using Equation (14.19). For example,

$$S_2 = \frac{1}{2}(0.69702) + \frac{(0.69702) - (0.70833)}{3}$$

$$= 0.69325$$

Table 14-1 The trapezoidal and Simpson's rule results for the integral $I = \int_1^2 dx/x$.

Order k	No. of panels n	T_k	S_k
0	1	0.75	—
1	2	0.7083	0.6944
2	4	0.69702	0.69325
3	8	0.69412	0.69315
4	16	0.69339	0.6931466
5	32	0.693208	0.6931473
6	64	0.693162	0.6931472

14.4 BEYOND SIMPSON'S RULE

For the next level of integration algorithm, the function $f(x)$ could be approximated by a cubic or higher-degree interpolating polynomial over segments of the interval $a - b$. For example, a fourth-order polynomial, $y_4(x)$, can be fit through the points associated with a four-panel partition ($k = 2$, $n = 2^2$) of the interval and the integral $\int f(x)\, dx$ can be approximately replaced with $\int y_4(x)\, dx$. For eight panels, two fourth-degree segments are used, and so on. The resulting equation that follows from this procedure is called Cote's rule for the approximate value of $\int f(x)\, dx$. Cote's rule is similar to, but more complicated than, the equations for the trapezoidal and Simpson's rule. (See Problem 14.9.) I will not include the equation for Cote's rule here, as I have grander things in mind.

If the partitioning of the interval proceeds as before into 2, 4, 8, . . . panels, the values of the function that enter Cote's rule will be the same set that was used in both Simpson's and the trapezoidal rule. It should then be possible to relate the Cote's calculation to the previous estimates in a manner similar to Equation(14.19). This is in fact possible, and, if the Cote's kth-order result is labeled as C_k, yields,

(14.20)
$$C_k = S_k + \frac{S_k - S_{k-1}}{15}$$

Thus once a table of Simpson's rule values have been determined, the improved Cote's rule results can easily be computed. For example, a third column can be added to the values in Table 14-1 in the evaluation of the integral

$$I = \int_1^2 \frac{1}{x} dx = \ln(2) = 0.6931471806\ldots$$

The Cote's rule values are an improvement over the Simpson's rule and the trapezoidal rule estimates. The easiest way to obtain the more accurate Cote's rule results is to first generate a table of trapezoidal rule estimates through order k, then use Equation (14.19) to determine the Simpson's rule values, and then apply (Equation (14.20) to generate the Cote's rule numbers.

Order k	No. of panels n	T_k	S_k	C_k
0	1	0.75	—	—
1	2	0.7083	0.6944	—
2	4	0.69702	0.69325	0.69317
3	8	0.69412	0.693154	0.693149
4	16	0.69339	0.693146	0.6931472
5	32	0.693208	0.69314721	0.693147181
6	64	0.693162	0.6931471842	0.69314718054
			Exact	0.6931471806. . .

Table 14-2 A column of Cote's rule values is added to Table 14-1.

You can probably see the pattern emerging in this analysis. The next step would be to fit the eight-panel partition with an eighth-degree polynomial, $y_8(x)$, approximate the area under the curve $f(x)$ by the area under successively more and more polynomial segments and label the kth-order such approximation as, say, D_k. Finally, this higher-degree estimate is related to the previous area estimates C_k, S_k, and T_k. The result of this formidable but straightforward exercise is that the higher-degree approximations D_k are related to the Cote's rule results by

$$D_k = C_k + \frac{C_k - C_{k-1}}{63}$$

(14.21)

The limit suggested by the sequence of integration algorithms

$$T_k \rightarrow S_k \rightarrow C_k \rightarrow D_k \rightarrow \ldots$$

is known as *Romberg integration*[2] or Richardson extrapolation to the limit.

14.5 ROMBERG INTEGRATION

The first step in unifying the previous numerical integration algorithms is to define a new notation, T_k^m, where the subscript k labels the order of the

---

[2] The proof of the Romberg algorithm, however, follows a quite different path. See S. Kuo, *Computer Applications of Numerical Methods,* Addison-Wesley, Reading, Mass., 1972.

approximation (n = no. of panels = 2^k) and m will now identify the *level* of the integration algorithm, i.e.,

$$m = 0 \quad \text{(trapezoidal rule)}$$

$$T_0^0 = T_0$$

$$T_1^0 = T_1$$

$$\cdots$$

$$T_k^0 = T_k$$

$$m = 1 \quad \text{(Simpson's rule)}$$

$$T_k^1 = S_k$$

$$m = 2 \quad \text{(Cote's rule)}$$

$$T_k^2 = C_k$$

$$m = 3$$

$$T_k^3 = D_k$$

etc.

Equations (14.19), (14.20), and (14.21) rewritten in terms of these quantities become

$$T_k^1 = T_k^0 + \frac{1}{3}(T_k^0 - T_{k-1}^0)$$

$$T_k^2 = T_k^1 + \frac{1}{15}(T_k^1 - T_{k-1}^1)$$

$$T_k^3 = T_k^2 + \frac{1}{63}(T_k^2 - T_{k-1}^2)$$

The generalization of these results leads to the equation for the Romberg algorithm:

(14.22)
$$T_k^{m+1} = T_k^m + \frac{T_k^m - T_{k-1}^m}{4^{m+1} - 1}$$

The importance of this equation lies in the fact that, under normal conditions, quite accurate results may be obtained for the integral of a reasonably smooth[3] function with little more work than is applied in obtaining the trapezoidal rule estimates.

---

[3] By "smooth" is meant that the function must be continuous over the interval and all of its derivatives must be finite in that interval; i.e., the function must be expandable as a Taylor series in this region.

14.5.1 Constructing Romberg Tables

The procedure is to start with the one-panel trapezoidal rule value

$$T_0 \to T_0^0 = \tfrac{1}{2}(b - a)(f_a + f_b)$$

then increase the *order* of the calculation (increment k from 0 to 1) by using Equation (14.9)

$$T_k = \frac{1}{2} T_{k-1} + \Delta x_k \sum_{\substack{i=1 \\ \text{odd only}}}^{n-1} f(a + i\,\Delta x_k)$$

Next increase the *level* of the algorithm (i.e., from trapezoidal to Simpson's) by using Equation(14.22). These ideas can be collected together in the form of a triangular table

$$
\begin{array}{llll}
T_0 \\
T_1 & S_1 \\
T_2 & S_2 & C_2 \\
T_3 & S_3 & C_3 & D_3 \\
T_4 & S_4 & C_4 & D_4 & \cdots
\end{array}
$$

or in terms of the symbols T_k^m,

m $\diagdown$	0	1	2	3	4
k					
0	T_0^0				
1	T_1^0	T_1^1			
2	T_2^0	T_2^1	T_2^2		
3	T_3^0	T_3^1	T_3^2	T_3^3	
4	T_4^0	T_4^1	T_4^2	T_4^3	T_4^4

An increase in accuracy is achieved by increasing the number of panels (stepping down in the triangle) or by increasing the level of the algorithm (stepping across horizontally in the triangle). The chief advantage of the method is that the function is evaluated only in obtaining the elements of the first column, the trapezoidal rule results.

14.5.2 Convergence and Accuracy

The Romberg procedure is terminated when the numbers along the diagonal of the triangle no longer change significantly. To be more precise we must analyze the algorithm more carefully for potential problems. In the determination of the first set of trapezoidal rule elements, only addition and subtraction of terms is involved, and so we expect the potential for round-off error problems is minimal. However, when determining the higher-level approximations, subtraction of numbers of like size occurs (i.e., $T_k^m - T_{k-1}^m$) and round-off error will eventually limit the accuracy of these terms. It is essential that we have some sort of indicator that will tell us when this is occurring. To this end we rewrite Equation (14.22) in a slightly different form for two values of k,

$$(4^{m+1} - 1)T_k^{m+1} = 4^{m+1} T_k^m - T_{k-1}^m$$
$$(4^{m+1} - 1)T_{k-1}^{m+1} = 4^{m+1} T_{k-1}^m - T_{k-2}^m$$

and subtract.

(14.23) $$4^{m+1}(T_k^m - T_{k-1}^m) - (T_{k-1}^m - T_{k-2}^m) = (4^{m+1} - 1)(T_k^{m+1} - T_{k-1}^{m+1})$$

Since the terms on the right side of Equation (14.23) correspond to a higher level of approximation, we expect the right side of the equation to approach zero. We next define

(14.24) $$R_k^m = \frac{1}{4^{m+1}} \frac{T_{k-1}^m - T_{k-2}^m}{T_k^m - T_{k-1}^m}$$

and from Equation (14.23), R_k^m should approach the limit

$$R_k^m \to 1$$

Notice that three values of T_k^m are required to determine each R_k^m.

Clearly the quantity R_k^m is extremely susceptible to round-off error problems when successive calculations of T_k^m are nearly the same. A satisfactory flag of a problem is when R_k^m begins to differ significantly from 1.

Formulas exist that give estimates of the magnitude of the errors involved in all of the integration algorithms discussed thus far. All of these error estimates require that the third, fourth, or higher derivatives of the function be evaluated on the interval and that the maximum value of this derivative on the interval be estimated. This is usually a difficult task and requires much more effort than simply allowing the computer to run longer, keeping an eye out for round-off errors and divergences. The error estimate equations are of importance particularly in convergence proofs but are rarely used in actual computations.

14.5.3 An Example Calculation Using the Romberg Algorithm

As an example of the Romberg method we return to the integral

$$I = \int_1^2 \frac{1}{x}\, dx = \ln(2) = 0.6931471806\ldots$$

Table 14-3 The results of a Romberg integration of $\int_1^2 dx/x$.

k \ m	0	1	2	3	4
			T_k^m		
0	0.75				
1	0.70833	0.694444			
2	0.6970238	0.6932540	0.69317460		
3	0.69412185	0.69315453	0.693147901	0.693147478	
4	0.69339120	0.693147653	0.693147194	0.693147183	0.6931471808
5	0.693208208	0.693147210	0.6931471808	0.6931471806	0.6931471806
6	0.693162439	0.693147182	0.6931471805	0.6931471806	0.6931471806

The results through $m = 4$ are listed in Table 14-3.

The values of the quantities R_k^m defined by Equation (14.24) are listed in Table 14-4. Notice that in this instance the presence of a divergent value for the error flag R_k^m does not indicate a failure of the calculation but rather marks a limit beyond which accuracy will not increase with further computation. Thus continuing the calculation beyond the $k = 6, m = 3$ step does not add to the accuracy of the result.

14.5.4   A Fortran Code for Romberg Integration

The Fortran code for a function subprogram that employs the Romberg algorithm to approximate the integral of a function is given in Figure 14-7. The function follows the procedure used in the previous section in obtaining the numbers in Tables 14-3 and 14-4.

First, the one-panel (zeroth-order) trapezoidal rule value is computed. Next, Equation (14.9) is used to compute the next-order trapezoidal rule approximation that is one step down the first column of the triangle. After incrementing the order by $k \to k + 1$, Equation (14.22) is used to step across from the first column ($m = 0$) to the diagonal column ($m = k$). If two successive elements along the diagonal of the triangular Romberg table differ by

Table 14-1   The quantities R_k^m monitor round-off error in the previous Romberg table.

k \ m	0	1	2	3	4
			R_k^m		
0	—				
1	—	—			
2	0.921	—	—		
3	0.974	0.748	—	—	
4	0.993	0.904	0.590	—	—
5	0.998	0.971	0.818	0.460	—
6	1.000	0.991	0.941	∞	∞

Figure 14-7
The Fortran code
for a function
that implements
the Romberg
integration
algorithm.

```
        FUNCTION ROMBRG(F,A,B,KMX,EPS,IPRNT)
*--
*-- ROMBERG INTEGRATES THE FUNCTION F(X) FROM X = A TO X = B. THE
*-- ELEMENTS OF THE ROMBERG TABLE ARE STORED IN T(K,M), WHERE
*-- K DENOTES THE ORDER OF THE CALCULATION AND M THE LEVEL OF
*-- THE APPROXIMATION, I.E., THE NUMBER OF PANELS, N = 2**K,
*-- WHILE M = 0 => TRAPEZOIDAL RULE, M = 1 => SIMPSON'S RULE, ETC.
*--
*-- THE CALCULATION IS TERMINATED SUCCESSFULLY WHEN SUCCESSIVE
*-- DIAGONAL ELEMENTS DIFFER BY LESS THAN THE USER-SUPPLIED
*-- CONVERGENCE CRITERION EPS.
*--
*-- ROUND-OFF ERROR IS MONITORED BY COMPUTING THE QUANTITY
*-- R(K,M) WHICH SHOULD BE CLOSE TO ONE. IF IT DIFFERS SIG-
*-- NIFICANTLY FROM I, THE COMPUTATION IS HALTED, A DIAG-
*-- NOSTIC IS PRINTED AND THE MOST RECENT VALUE RETURNED.
*--
*-- THE CALCULATION IS CONTINUED THROUGH A MAXIMUM ORDER K = KMX,
*-- SUPPLIED BY THE USER. IF THE DESIRED ACCURACY IS NOT
*-- ACHIEVED AFTER ORDER KMX, A DIAGNOSTIC IS PRINTED AND THE
*-- LATEST, MOST ACCURATE VALUE RETURNED.
*--
*-- THE COMPLETE ROMBERG TABLE AND THE TABLE OF THE ROUND-OFF
*-- ERROR FLAGS ARE PRINTED BEFORE ANY RETURN OR STOP IF THE
*-- ARGUMENT LIST PARAMETER IPRNT HAS THE VALUE 1.
*-------------------------------------------------------------------
* VARIABLES
*
        REAL T(0:15,0:15),R(0:15,0:15),DX,A,B,EPS,SUM
        INTEGER K,M,NPTS,KMX,IPRNT
*
*               A,B    --  THE ITEGRATION INTERVAL
*               EPS    --  CONVERGENCE CRITERION
*               T( )   --  THE ELEMENTS OF THE ROMBERG TABLE
*               R( )   --  THE TABLE OF ROUND-OFF ERROR FLAGS
*               K      --  THE CURRENT ORDER OF THE CALC.
*               M      --  THE CURRENT LEVEL OF THE CALC.
*               KMX    --  THE MAXIMUM-ORDER CALC.
*               NPTS   --  CURRENT NUMBER OF SAMPLING POINTS
*               SUM    --  SUM OF INTERIOR FUNCTION VALUES
*               IPRNT  --  PRINT FLAG, IF 1 PRINT TABLES
*-------------------------------------------------------------------
*
*               FIRST COMPUTE THE ZEROTH ORDER/ONE PANEL
*               TRAPEZOIDAL RULE VALUE
*
        K = 0
        DX = (B - A)
        T(0,0) = 0.5 * DX * (F(A) + F(B))
*
*               COMPUTE THE NEXT-ORDER TRAPEZOIDAL RULE VALUE,
*               I.E., STEP DOWN IN THE 1ST COL. OF THE TABLE
*               BY HALVING THE INTERVALS AND DOUBLING THE
*               NUMBER OF POINTS, NPTS
*
      1 K = K + 1
        NPTS = 2**K
        DX = DX/2.
*
*               SUM THE FUNCTION AT ALL ODD POINTS, I.E., THE
*               MIDPOINTS OF THE PREVIOUS CALCULATION
```

```
*
      SUM = 0.0
      DO 2 I = 1,NPTS - 1,2
         SUM = SUM + F(A + I*DX)
    2 CONTINUE
*
*                    THE NEXT-ORDER TRAPEZOIDAL RULE IS GIVEN BY
*
      T(K,0) = T(K - 1,0)/2. + DX * SUM
*
*                    NEXT STEP ACROSS THE TABLE, M = 1, 2, ..., K
*
      DO 3 M = 0,K - 1
         T(K,M+1) = T(K,M) + (T(K,M)-T(K-1,M))/(4.**(M+1)-1.)
*
*                    ADDITIONALLY, COMPUTE THE ROUND-OFF ERROR
*                    FLAGS WHERE POSSIBLE. (THREE ELEMENTS OF A
*                    COLUMN OF THE T(K,M) TABLE ARE REQUIRED.)
*
         IF(K .GE. 2 .AND. M .LE. K - 2)THEN
            R(K,M) = (T(K-1,M)-T(K-2,M))/(T(K,M)-T(K-1,M))/4.**(M+1)
*
         END IF
*
*                    THE CALCULATION SHOULD BE TERMINATED IF
*                    R(K,M) DIFFERS SIGNIFICANTLY FROM ONE.
*
         IF(ABS(R(K,M) - 1.0) .GT. 0.75)THEN
            WRITE(*,10)R(K,M),T(K - 1,K - 1)
            IF(IPRNT .EQ. 1)GO TO 5
            ROMBRG = T(K - 1,K - 1)
            RETURN
         END IF
      END IF
*
    3 CONTINUE
*
*                    THE TABLE IS COMPLETE THROUGH ORDER K. NEXT
*                    TEST FOR CONVERGENCE.
*
      IF(ABS(T(K,K) - T(K - 1,K - 1)) .LT. EPS)THEN
         ROMBERG = T(K,K)
         IF(IPRNT .EQ. 1)GO TO 5
         RETURN
*
*                    IF K < KMX, INCREMENT K AND REPEAT.
*
      ELSE IF(K .LT. KMX)THEN
         GO TO 1
      ELSE
*
*                    THE CALCULATION HAS FAILED TO OBTAIN A SUF-
*                    FICIENTLY ACCURATE VALUE. PRINT A WARNING
*                    AND RETURN WITH THE BEST RESULT SO FAR.
*
      WRITE(*,11)KMX,T(K,K),T(K - 1,K - 1)
      ROMBRG = T(K,K)
      IF(IPRNT .EQ. 1)GO TO 5
      RETURN
```

Continued

```
      END IF
*----------------------------------------------------------------
* OUTPUT ROMBERG TABLE
*
    5 CONTINUE
*
      WRITE(*,12)(I,I = 0,K)
      DO 6 I = 0,K
         WRITE(*,13)I,(T(I,M),M = 0,I)
    6 CONTINUE
*
*                    AND THE TABLE OF THE QUANTITIES R(K,M)
*
      WRITE(*,14)(I,I = 0,K)
      DO 7 I = 2,K
         WRITE(*,15)I,(R(I,M),M = 0,I - 2)
    7 CONTINUE
      ROMBERG = T(K,K)
      RETURN
*----------------------------------------------------------------
* FORMATS
*
   10 FORMAT(T20,'******WARNING FROM ROMBERG******',/,
     +        T20,'ROUND-OFF ERROR FLAG          = ',F9.5,/,
     +        T20,'MOST RECENT DIAG. ROMBERG TERM = ',E12.6,/,
     +        T20,'CALCULATION HALTED AND THIS VALUE RETURNED')
*
   11 FORMAT(T20,'******WARNING FROM ROMBERG******',/,
     +        T20,'THROUGH ORDER ',I2,' THE REQUIRED ACCURACY',/,
     +        T20,'COULD NOT BE ACHIEVED. THE LATEST VALUE',/,
     +        T20,'RETURNED TO CALLING PROGRAM WAS = ',E12.6,/,
     +        T20,'AND THE PREVIOUS VALUE IN TABLE IS = ',E12.6)
*
   12 FORMAT(///,T10,'THE ROMBERG TABLE',//,T5,'LEVEL =>',/,
     +        1X,'ORDER',//,1X,9(6X,I2,6X))
*
   13 FORMAT(1X,I2,1X,9(F13.9,1X))
*
   14 FORMAT(///,T10,'THE TABLE OF THE ROUND-OFF ERROR FLAGS',///,
     +        T10,'LEVEL =>',//,1X,'ORDER',//,4X,15(3X,I2,3X))
*
   15 FORMAT(1X,I2,1X,15(F7.4,1X))
*
      END
```

less than the user supplied tolerance, EPS, the function returns with the most recent and most accurate value for the integral.

Additionally, the round-off error flags R_k^m are also computed and can be used to monitor the progress of the calculation and pinpoint the onset of the loss of accuracy.

14.6 BEYOND ROMBERG

All numerical integration techniques, and for that matter most numerical procedures of any kind, are based on the following idea: a complicated function may be approximated over a small enough interval by polynomials of varying degree and then the differentiation, integration, or whatever operation on the original function is replaced by the same operation on the simpler polynomial. The procedures of numerical integration that we have discussed thus far, the trapezoidal rule, Simpson's rule, and Romberg integration are examples of this. Romberg integration is the theoretical optimum procedure that can be applied to an arbitrary smooth function over a finite interval that contains no singularities (points where the function approaches infinity) *provided* that the calculation is restricted to *evenly* spaced points. If the constraint of evenly spaced points is removed, a new class of numerical integration algorithms may be developed, known collectively as *Gauss quadrature algorithms*. (Quadrature is the technical name for numerical integration.)

14.6.1   A Derivation of a Simple Gauss Quadrature Procedure

Each of the various numerical integration methods we have seen—e.g., trapezoidal, Simpson's, Cote's—approximate the integral $\int f(x)\, dx$ by a sum of function evaluations at equally spaced points multiplied by so-called weight factors ω_i.

$$\int_a^b f(x)\, dx \simeq \sum_{i=0}^{n} \omega_i f(x_i) \qquad (14.25)$$

where $x_i = a + i\,\Delta x_k$, and the weights are specified by the particular type of integration algorithm. For example, the trapezoidal rule has a set of weights $\omega_i = \frac{1}{2}(1, 2, 2, \ldots, 2, 2, 1)\,\Delta x$, i.e.,

$$\int_a^b f(x)\, dx \simeq \Delta x_k \frac{1}{2}(f_0 + 2f_1 + 2f_2 + \cdots + 2f_{n-1} + f_n) \qquad \text{Trapezoidal}$$

while the set of weights for Simpson's rule is $\omega_i = \frac{1}{3}(1, 4, 2, 4, \ldots, 2, 4, 2, 4, 1)\,\Delta x$, i.e.,

$$\int_a^b f(x)\, dx \simeq \Delta x_k \frac{1}{3}(f_0 + 4f_1 + 2f_2 + \cdots + 4f_{n-1} + f_n) \qquad \text{Simpson's}$$

The set of multiplicative weight factors were determined by fitting successively higher-degree polynomials to segments of the function.

The great mathematician and scientist Carl Friedrich Gauss suggested that the accuracy of the computational algorithm could be significantly improved if the positions of the function evaluations as well as the set of weight factors were left as parameters to be determined by optimizing the overall accuracy. By this he meant that the procedure should be *exact* when applied to polynomials of as high degree as possible. If the approximation employs function evaluations at the points $x_0, x_1, \ldots, x_n$, the procedure has $2n + 2$ parameters to be determined (the x_i and the factors ω_i). Since a general polynomial of degree N has $N + 1$ coefficients, the Gauss procedure with $n + 1$ points is required to be exact for any polynomial of degree $N = 2n + 1$ or less.

The Gauss quadrature algorithms are usually stated in terms of integrals over the interval -1 to $+1$. Thus, the remaining task is to determine the parameters $\omega_0, \omega_1, \ldots, \omega_n : x_0, x_1, \ldots x_n$ such that the expression

$$\textbf{(14.26)} \qquad \int_{-1}^{1} f(x) \, dx \simeq \omega_0 f(x_0) + \omega_1 f(x_1) + \cdots + \omega_n f(x_n)$$

is of optimum accuracy in the sense discussed above.

For example, for $n = 1$, the parameters $\omega_0, \omega_1, x_0, x_1$ in the first-order approximation,

$$\textbf{(14.27)} \qquad \int_{-1}^{1} f(x) \, dx \simeq \omega_0 f(x_0) + \omega_1 f(x_1)$$

are to be determined by requiring that Equation (14.27) is exact whenever $f(x)$ is a polynomial of degree 3 or less. Applying this condition successively to the functions $1, x, x^2, x^3$, results in the following four relations:

$$\int_{-1}^{1} 1 \, dx = 2 = \omega_0 + \omega_1$$

$$\int_{-1}^{1} x \, dx = 0 = \omega_0 x_0 + \omega_1 x_1$$

$$\int_{-1}^{1} x^2 \, dx = \frac{2}{3} = \omega_0 x_0^2 + \omega_1 x_1^2$$

$$\textbf{(14.28)} \qquad \int_{-1}^{1} x^2 \, dx = 0 = \omega_0 x_0^3 + \omega_1 x_1^3$$

These four equations are *nonlinear* in the four parameters and can be solved in the following way: The second and fourth of the relations can be written as

$$\begin{pmatrix} x_0 & x_1 \\ x_0^3 & x_1^3 \end{pmatrix} \begin{pmatrix} \omega_0 \\ \omega_1 \end{pmatrix} = 0$$

Since the trivial solution ($\omega_0 = \omega_1 = 0$) is not what we are after, this equation requires that the determinant of the 2 by 2 matrix be zero—i.e.,

$$x_0 x_1^3 - x_1 x_0^3 = 0$$

and if $x_0 \neq 0$, $x_1 \neq 0$,

$$x_1^2 - x_1^2 = 0$$

or

$$x_1 = \pm x_0$$

Since the solution $x_1 = x_0$ implies only one sampling point, which would contradict the original assumption of two distinct points, we conclude that $x_0 = -x_1$. Also, the second of the four equations then requires that $\omega_0 = \omega_1$. Inserting this information into the remaining equations (the first and third) finally yields

$$\omega_0 + \omega_1 = 2 \rightarrow \omega_0 = \omega_1 = 1$$

$$\omega_0 x_0^3 + \omega_1 x_1^3 = \frac{2}{3} \rightarrow x_1 = -x_0 = \frac{1}{\sqrt{3}}$$

and Equation (14.27) now reads

$$\int_{-1}^{1} f(x)\, dx \simeq f\left(x = \frac{-1}{\sqrt{3}}\right) + f\left(x = +\frac{1}{\sqrt{3}}\right) \qquad \textbf{(14.29)}$$

You should verify that this remarkably simple approximation does indeed give the exact result for the integral of any polynomial of degree 3 or less.

If the function $f(x)$ is not a polynomial of degree 3 or less, the result of the first-order Gauss quadrature expression, Equation (14.29), will only be an approximation to the actual integral. The accuracy of the approximation will depend on how much the function $f(x)$ resembles polynomials of degree 3 or less. For example, consider the integral

$$I = \int_{-1}^{1} \cos(x)\, dx = [\sin(x)]|_{-1}^{1} = 1.6829 \ldots$$

The Gauss approximation to this integral is

$$I \simeq \cos\left(-\frac{1}{\sqrt{3}}\right) + \cos\left(\frac{1}{\sqrt{3}}\right) = 1.6758$$

14.6.2   Higher-Order Gauss Quadrature Procedures

To improve the accuracy of the approximation given in Equation (14.27), the number of sampling points is increased from 2 to 3, 4, ... For each choice of n, the number of points, the weight factors ω_i, and the position of the sampling points x_i, must be determined by requiring that the approximation be exact for polynomials of degree $N \leqslant 2n + 1$. These have been determined and tabulated for $n = 2$ through 95.[4] An abbreviated table of the weights and sampling points for several values of n is given in Table 14-5.

---

[4] M. Abramowitz and I. Stegun, *Handbook of Mathematical Functions*, Nat. Bur. reprint, Dover, New York, 1965.

Table 14-5 Sampling points and weight factors for Gauss quadratures. $I = \int_{-1}^{1} f(x)\, dx \simeq \sum_{i=0}^{n} \omega_i f(x_i)$

n	i	x_i	ω_i
2	0	−0.5773502692	1.0000000000
	1	0.5773502692	1.0000000000
3	0	−0.7745966692	0.5555555556
	1	0.0	0.8888888889
	2	0.7745966692	0.5555555556
5	0	−0.9061798459	0.2369268850
	1	−0.5384693101	0.4786286705
	2	0.0	0.5688888889
	3–4	(See note below.)	
10	0	−0.9739065285	0.0666713443
	1	−0.8650633667	0.1494513492
	2	−0.6794095683	0.2190863625
	3	−0.4333953941	0.2692667193
	4	−0.1488743390	0.2955242247
	5–9	(See note below.)	
20	0	−0.9931285992	0.0176140071
	1	−0.9639719273	0.0406014298
	2	−0.9122344283	0.0626720483
	3	−0.8391169718	0.0832767416
	4	−0.7463319065	0.1019301198
	5	−0.6360536807	0.1181945320
	6	−0.5108670020	0.1316886384
	7	−0.3737060887	0.1420961093
	8	−0.2277858511	0.1491729865
	9	−0.0765265211	0.1527533871
	10–19	(See note below.)	

Note: The sampling points are symmetrically placed about zero, so $x_{n-k-1} = x_k$. Also the weight factors for symmetrically placed points are the same, so $\omega_{n-k-1} = \omega_k$.

14.6.3 Applying the Gauss Quadrature to Integrals with a Range Other Than −1 to +1

For integrals that are over an x range that differs from −1 to +1, a change of variables must first be effected before the Gauss quadrature procedures of the previous section can be employed. For example, if the integral is from a to b,

$$I = \int_a^b f(x)\, dx$$

the change of variable would be

$$x = \left(\frac{b-a}{2}\right)\xi + \left(\frac{b+a}{2}\right)$$

(14.30)

so that when $\xi = 1$, $x = b$, and when $\xi = -1$, $x = a$.

The idea then is first to transform the variable x to ξ and the integral is then replaced by an integral from -1 to $+1$ in ξ. For example, the integral

$$I = \int_0^2 \sin(x)\, dx$$

is first rewritten in terms of ξ defined by the transformation,

$$x = \xi + 1$$
$$dx = d\xi$$

to give

$$I = \int_{-1}^1 \sin(\xi + 1)\, d\xi$$

This integral may then be numerically integrated by the Gauss quadrature procedure using the weights and sampling points given in Table 14-5. The result for the $n = 5$ point calculation is then

$$I \simeq 0.237[\sin(0.906 + 1) + \sin(-0.906 + 1)]$$
$$+ 0.479[\sin(0.538 + 1) + \sin(-0.538 + 1)]$$
$$+ 0.569 \sin(1)$$
$$= 1.4161467 \quad \text{exact answer} = 1.0 - \cos(2) = 1.4161468.$$

14.7 WHAT IF THE INTEGRATION INTERVAL IS INFINITE?

It is very likely that you will often find it necessary to obtain a numerical value for an integral of the form

$$I = \int_a^\infty f(x)\, dx$$

Obviously for this expression to have meaning the value of the integral on the right must be finite, which in turn means that the function $f(x)$ must become infinitesimal for large x. This is analogous to the situation we faced when evaluating infinite summations in Chapter 6. To obtain an answer we proceed similarly, integrating far enough out along the x axis until we are satisfied that the remainder of the integral will contribute only an insignificant amount.

If the integrand $f(x)$ is largest near the beginning of the interval, one procedure is to break the interval $[a$ to $\infty]$ into *four* parts, say,

(14.31)
$$I = \int_a^\gamma f(x) \, dx + \int_\gamma^{5\gamma} f(x) \, dx + \int_{5\gamma}^{25\gamma} f(x) \, dx + \int_{25\gamma}^\infty f(x) \, dx$$

$$= I_1 + I_2 + I_3 + I_4$$

The value of γ is chosen so that the interval $[a$ to $\gamma]$ contains the dominant part of the integral; i.e., the region where $f(x)$ is the largest. If the following sequence of inequalities is satisfied,

$$I_1 \gg I_2 \gg I_3$$

and I_3 is very small, we are quite probably justified in neglecting the last term, I_4, which cannot be integrated numerically anyway. The first three integrals can be approximately integrated by any of the methods discussed thus far in this chapter.

14.7.1 An Example of an Integral over an Infinite Range in x

Consider the following integral,

$$I = \int_0^\infty x^2 e^{-x^2} \, dx$$

This integral can be found in tables of definite integrals and the result is $\sqrt{\pi}/4$. The integrand is tabulated below for various values of x.

x	$f(x) = x^2 e^{-x^2}$
0.0	0.0
0.5	0.195
1.0	0.368
1.5	0.237
2.0	0.073
4.0	0.000002
8.0	1.03×10^{-26}

Since the integrand falls to zero so rapidly beyond $x = 2.0$, we might try a partition like the following:

$$\int_0^\infty x^2 e^{-x^2} \, dx = \int_0^2 + \int_2^6 + \int_6^{18} + \int_{18}^\infty$$

$$= I_1 + I_2 + I_3 + I_4$$

$$= 0.422725056486 + 0.020388560464 + 1.2 \times 10^{-26} + ?$$

$$= 0.4431136169 \qquad \text{exact} = 0.443113463. . .$$

The above integrals were evaluated using a ten-point Gauss quadrature and the numerical values for the weights and sampling points found in Table 14-5.

14.7.2 Asymptotic Replacements

A procedure somewhat similar to that of the previous section is to approximate the integrand by a simpler function for the portion of the integral where x is large. For example, consider the function

$$f(x) = \frac{x^2}{e^x - 1}$$

and the integral,

$$I = \int_0^\infty f(x) \, dx$$

First, since $e^0 = 1$, it may appear that the integrand diverges near the origin. However, using the series expression for e^x (viz., $e^x = 1 + x + \cdots$), we see that $f(x = 0) = 0.5$ [5]

Second, for very large values of x, $e^x \gg 1$, and therefore it is a good approximation to replace $f(x)$ in this region by the simpler expression

$$f(x) \rightarrow x^2 e^{-x} \qquad \text{for large } x$$

and this expression can be integrated *analytically*. Since $e^{10} = 22026.5$ the approximation

$$I = \int_0^\infty \frac{x^2}{e^x - 1} \, dx$$

$$\approx \int_0^{10} \frac{x^2}{e^x - 1} \, dx + \int_{10}^\infty x^2 e^{-x} \, dx$$

$$= I_1 + I_2$$

------

[5] In a situation such as this it would be prudent to include in the Fortran code for the function $f(x)$ a statement of the form

```
IF(X .EQ. 0.0)F = 0.0
```

rather than attempt to compute a value that may result in 0.0/0.0

should be valid to better than five significant figures. The first integral is done numerically; the second can be done analytically. The results, again using a ten-point Gauss quadrature, are

$$I_1 = 2.3985748995$$

$$I_2 = 0.0055387914$$

$$I \simeq I_1 + I_2 = 2.40411369$$

Numerous other techniques, such as change of variables, can be developed to handle integrals with infinite limits. Most of these tricks are acquired through experience and will not be discussed here.

14.8 SINGULARITIES IN THE INTEGRAND

As odd as it may seem, even though a function is infinite for some value of x, the area under the function over an interval containing this point may still be finite. The integral

$$I = \int_0^1 \frac{dx}{(1 - x^2)^{1/2}}$$

is such an integral.

Obviously, the computer will be unable to obtain a value for this integral since the integrand approaches infinity as $x \to 1$. The standard procedure is to rewrite the integral in a form that eliminates the singularity by changing variables.[6] For example, if we make the replacement

$$x \to \sin(\theta)$$

$$dx \to \cos(\theta)\, d\theta$$

$$1 - x^2 \to \cos^2(\theta)$$

and when

$$x = 0 \to \theta = 0$$

$$x = 1 \to \theta = \pi/2$$

-----

[6] A caution: It may not be possible to avoid the singularity by any change in variables. This usually indicates that the integral is itself divergent (i.e., infinite). This can be verified by replacing the integrand by its asymptotic form near the singular point and integrating the simpler expression over the interval containing the point. If the simpler integral still diverges, the original integral does as well.

The above integral may be written as

$$I = \int_0^{\pi/2} \frac{\cos(\theta)\, d\theta}{\cos(\theta)} = \frac{\pi}{2}$$

I repeat, these change-of-variable tricks come mostly from experience and are not an appropriate concern of an elementary text.

14.9 DOUBLE INTEGRALS

14.9.1 The Interpretation of a Double Integral

Occasionally the solution of a problem in engineering or science will require the evaluation of a double integral of the form

$$I = \int_a^b dy \int_c^d dx\, f(x, y) \tag{14.32}$$

For example, the total force of a stream on the side of a dam is a sum of the pressure at a point on the dam times an infinitesimal area element, summed over the entire area of the dam. If the height of the dam is h and the width is w, the total force is then

$$\text{force} = \int_0^h dy \int_0^w dx\, P(x, y) \tag{14.33}$$

The procedure for evaluating a double integral is to first evaluate the innermost integral [in Equation (14.32) this is the integral over dx]. The result of this first integration is then a function of y. That is,

$$I = \int_a^b dy \int_c^d dx\, f(x, y) = \int_c^b dy\, g(y) \tag{14.34}$$

where

$$g(y) = \int_c^d dx\, f(x, y)$$

For example, the pressure on the dam is a function of position and is given by

$$P(x, y) = \rho g (h - y)$$

Figure 14-8
The force on the
infinitesimal area
element $dx\, dy$ is
$P(x, y)\, dx\, dy$.

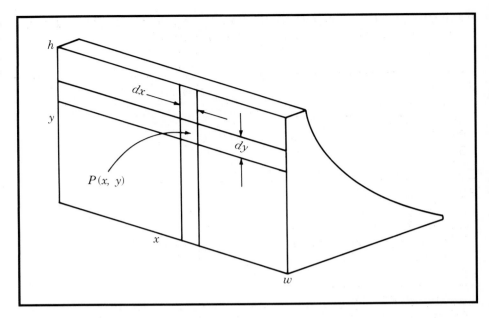

where ρ is the density of water (10^3 kg/m^3) and g is the gravitational acceleration (9.8 m/sec^2). The first integral then yields, for a dam with vertical sides[7]

(14.35)

$$g(y) = \int_0^w dx\, [\rho g(h - y)] = \rho g(h - y)x\,\big|_0^w$$

$$= \rho g w(h - y)$$

and the total force is then

(14.36)

$$\text{force} = \int_0^h dy\, \rho g w(h - y)$$

$$= \rho g w(hy - \tfrac{1}{2}y^2]\,\big|_0^h$$

$$= \tfrac{1}{2}\rho g w h^2$$

14.9.2 The Fortran Code To Evaluate Double Integrals

To construct a Fortran Code for the evaluation of a double integral, the programmer would simply mimic the actions of the previous section. As-

---

[7] The integration limits of the inner integral may themselves be function of the outer variable. Thus, if the sides of the stream are not vertical, the width of the dam will not be a constant but will be a function of the height above the stream bottom.

suming that we have an adequate function subprogram[8] to evaluate a single integral of a function, the code might be as follows:

```
PROGRAM MAIN              This code
 EXTERNAL G               contains an
 ANS = GAUSQD(G,0.,1.,10) execution time
 PRINT *,'ANS = ',ANS     error.
 STOP
END
```

```
FUNCTION G(Y)
 COMMON/Y/YY
 EXTERNAL FF
 G = GAUSQD(FF,0.,1.,10)
 RETURN
END
```

$$g(y) = \int_0^1 dx\, ff(x)$$

```
FUNCTION FF(X)
 COMMON/Y/Y
 FF = F(X,Y)
 RETURN
END
```

```
FUNCTION F(X,Y)
 F = ...
 RETURN
END
```

```
FUNCTION GAUSQD(FNC,A,B,K)
 ...
 RETURN
END
```

Notice that since the function subprogram GAUSQD expects a function of a *single* variable, the function $f(x,y)$ is finessed into appearing as such a function by introducing the function FF(X) and passing the value of the variable y through a COMMON block.

The logical structure of this code is perfectly valid; however, if you attempt to execute the program, it will fail. The fault is not with the logic of the program, it is in the basic structure of Fortran itself. Fortran forbids one subprogram from calling itself either directly or indirectly. In our program, the first reference to the subprogram GAUSQD in the main program

---

[8] I will use a function subprogram GAUSQD(F,A,B,K) that employs the weights and sampling points of Table 14-5 to approximate numerically the integral of $f(x)$ from $x = a$ to $x = b$ using k sampling points. We could just as well have used the function ROMBRG of Figure 14-7.

will in turn reference the function G(Y) which will then itself call GAUSQD. Thus, GAUSQD is in effect referencing GAUSQD, which is not allowed. You may wish to attempt to execute this program; but be warned, tracing the ultimate error in the execution of the program is extremely difficult. This is an example of one of the most subtle errors in Fortran, especially troublesome owing to the fact that the problem lies in the language itself.

Not surprisingly, there is no easy solution to the problem. The function GAUSQD must not reference the function GAUSQD. Two distinct functions must be used. One remedy might simply be to use two identical copies of the function and then rename them GAUSQD and GAUSQF. Once these changes are made, the program is found to execute quite smoothly.

14.10 CONCLUSION

There are several important topics in numerical integration that have not been mentioned in this chapter. One of these is how to integrate highly oscillatory functions. Special techniques have been developed to handle such functions, but they are rather specialized and beyond the scope of this text. Also, there are several variations to the Gauss quadrature procedure we have discussed to accommodate functions that resemble quantities other than polynomials. Again, these procedures are somewhat specialized and not of sufficient importance to include here.

However, I do not want to give you the impression that the material of this chapter is merely an introduction to the topic. The procedures and algorithms detailed here are suitable for the vast majority of the problems that you will encounter. Most professional engineers and scientists include the methods of this chapter among their skills; only a small percentage need (or know) more.

PROBLEMS

1. Evaluate the integrals below by using the trapezoidal rule in the following way:
   a. Evaluate T_0 for one panel by using Equation (14.1).
   b. Compute T_1 using the value of T_0 and Equation (14.9).
   c. Continue the calculation through T_4.
   Collect your results in the form of a table. (Be careful, errors in one step will carry over into the next.)

		Exact result
a.	$\int_0^8 x^2\,dx$	$170\frac{2}{3}$

b. $\displaystyle\int_0^8 x^4\,dx$ 6553.6

c. $\displaystyle\int_0^1 xe^{-x}\,dx$ $1 - 2/e = 0.2642411175.\,.\,.$

d. $\displaystyle\int_0^{\pi/2} x\sin(x)\,dx$ 1.0

e. $\displaystyle\int_0^1 (1 + x^2)^{3/2}\,dx$ $1.567951962.\,.\,.$

f. $\displaystyle\int_0^1 e^{-x^2}\,dx$ $0.74682404.\,.\,.$

2. Calculate the two-panel and the four-panel Simpson's rule results, S_1, S_2, for the same integrals attempted in the above problem using Equation (14.16).
3. Calculate S_1 through S_4 for the integrals attempted in Problem 14.1 using the trapezoidal rule results and Equation (14.19).
4. Complete the entire Romberg table for the integrals attempted in Problem 14.1 using the trapezoidal rule values and Equation (14.22).
5. From any of the Romberg tables you constructed in the previous problem, compute a table of round-off error flags, R_k^m, by using Equation (14.24).
6. Evaluate each of the integrals below by the method of Section 14.7. After selecting an appropriate partition of the x axis, compute the integral segments numerically using (1) the Romberg algorithm with $k = 3$, (2) the Gauss quadrature procedure with three-point sampling.

Exact result

a. $\displaystyle\int_0^{\infty} xe^{-x}\,dx$ 1.0

b. $\displaystyle\int_0^{\infty} x^2 e^{-x}\cos(x)\,dx$ $-\frac{1}{2}$

c. $\displaystyle\int_0^{\infty} xe^{-x}\sin(x)\,dx$ $+\frac{1}{2}$

7. Use the fact that for large values of x the integrand of the integral below can be approximated by a simpler function and that part of the integral may then be done in closed form, and the remaining part may be done numerically. Choose the cut point carefully.

$$\int_0^{\infty} \frac{dx}{(e^x + x)}$$

8. The integral

$$\int_0^1 \ln(x)\,dx$$

has a singularity as $x \to 0$. Find the change of variables that enables you to rewrite this integral as

$$-\int_0^\infty \xi e^{-\xi}\, d\xi$$

which may then be integrated by the methods of the previous problem.

9. A function $f(x)$ can be approximated by a fourth-degree polynomial

$$y_4(x) = c_0 + c_1(x - a) + c_2(x - a)^2 + c_3(x - a)^3 + c_4(x - a)^4$$

with the coefficients of c_i chosen so that the function and the polynomial are equal at the five equally spaced points: $x_0 = a$, $x_1 = a + \Delta x_2$, $x_2 = a + 2\,\Delta x_2$, $x_3 = a + 3\,\Delta x_2$, $x_4 = b$. That is, $y_4(a) = f_0 = f(a)$, $y_4(x = a + \Delta x_2) = f_1 = f(x = a + \Delta x_2)$, etc., where $\Delta x_2 = (b - a)/2^2$. The integral of $f(x)$ over this interval is then approximated by the integral of the fourth-degree polynomial.

a. Show that the area under the polynomial is

$$\int_a^b f(x)\, dx \simeq \frac{2\,\Delta x_2}{45}(7f_0 + 32f_1 + 12f_2 + 32f_3 + f_4)$$

This is then the next higher approximation to the integral beyond Simpson's rule—i.e., Cote's rule for C_2.

b. Explicitly write out the Simpson's rule approximations S_1, S_2 and show that $C_2 = (16S_2 - S_1)/15$, which is the Romberg algorithm for improving the Simpson's rule values.

10. Write a subroutine GAUSQD that will approximate an integral using a ten-point sampling. Use the sampling points and weight factors given in Table 14-5. Test this subroutine by evaluating the integrals of Problem 14.1.

11. Using a suitable root-solving subroutine and the subroutine GAUSQD of the previous problem, return to Problem 8.21 and complete the problem by finding the root of the given function. This function has one positive root near $x = 0.631607$.

PROGRAMMING ASSIGNMENT VIII

Mechanical Engineering: Conductive Heat Losses

The analysis of heating losses through various types of insulation has become a very important problem in the last decade. The equation that describes heat flow through a material is

$$Q(x,y) = -\gamma \frac{\partial T(x, y, z)}{\partial z}\bigg|_{z=h} \tag{VIII.1}$$

where $Q(x, y)$ = the rate of heat flow through the xy plane at the point (x, y) (the units are J/sec-m^2)

γ = the heat conductivity of the material (assumed to be constant)

$T(x, y, z)$ = the temperature (°C) as a function of position

$\dfrac{\partial T}{\partial z}\bigg|_{z=h}$ = the partial derivative of T with respect to z, then evaluated at $z = h$

Equation (VIII.1) represents the heat flowing at a point in the z direction. The net heat flowing through an infinitesimal area $dx\, dy$ is $dH = Q(x, y)\, dx\, dy$. To find the total heat flowing through an extended surface, we divide the surface into infinitesimal $dx\, dy$ and sum or integrate over all infinitesimal areas. In other words, perform the double integral

$$H = \int_a^b dy \int_c^d dx\, Q(x, y) \tag{VIII.2}$$

Equation (VIII.2) can be arranged as in Section 14.9 as

Figure VIII-7
The infinites-
imal areas are
first summed in
the x direction.

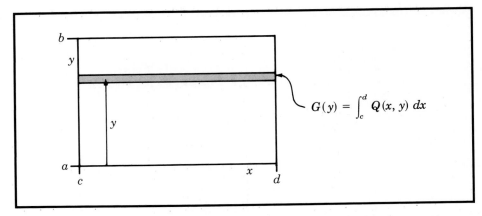

$$H = \int_a^b \int_c^d Q(x, y) \, dx \, dy$$

(VIII.3)

$$= \int_a^b G(y) \, dy$$

where

$$G(y) = \int_c^d Q(x, y) \, dx$$

That is, the first or inner integral results in a function $G(y)$ which is then integrated over y between the limits $y = a$ to $y = b$ (see Figure VIII-1).

Problem

A four-room structure with equal-size rooms (x_0 by y_0) is sketched in Figure VIII-2. There is one radiator for each room at the indicated positions $\{R(i) = [R_x(i), R_y(i)]$ for $i = 1, 4\}$.

The positions of the four radiators are

No.	x position $R_x(i)/x_0$	y position $R_y(i)/y_0$
1	0	$+\frac{1}{2}$
2	0	$+\frac{1}{2}$
3	$-\frac{1}{2}$	$-\frac{1}{2}$
4	$+\frac{1}{2}$	$-\frac{1}{2}$

By measurement, the temperature in each room is found to be

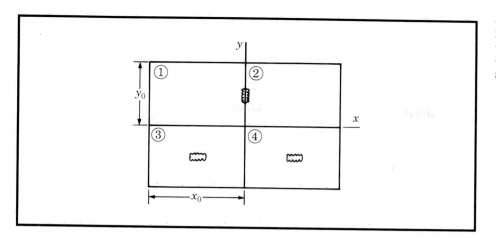

Figure VIII-2
Heat flow in
a four-room
structure.

$$T_i(x, y, z) \qquad \text{(VIII.4)}$$

$$= \frac{T_0}{2 \ln(2)} \left(1 + \exp\left\{ -\frac{[x - R_x(i)]^2}{x_0^2} - \frac{[y - R_y(i)]^2}{y_0^2} \right\} \right) \ln\left(3 - \frac{z}{h} \right)$$

for rooms $i = 1, 4$.

Furthermore, the height of each room is $z = h$ and the insulation for the roof of each room is different.

Room no.	Roof insulation
1	Wood
2	Brick
3	Slate
4	Asbestos

The problem is to find the heat flowing per second through the roofs of each room.

Details

1. Evaluate $\partial T/\partial z|_{z=h}$ for each room using

$$\frac{d}{dz} \ln(az + b) = \frac{a}{az + b}$$

and multiply by the appropriate heat conductivity γ to obtain $Q(x, y)$.

2. Construct the Fortran subprogram Q(X, Y) that will return the value of the heat flow at the point (x, y). The additional parameters required by the function should be passed via a COMMON block.

3. Use the function ROMBRG (see Figure 14-7) to evaluate integrals. As described in Section 14.9, you will have to load two complete and identical copies of this function in your complete program and then rename one of them. This is necessary to avoid having the function ROMBRG indirectly referencing ROMBRG when evaluating a double integral.

4. When using ROMBRG to evaluate the inner integral in Equation (VIII.3), the integrand function must be a function of a single variable, not $Q(x, y)$. This can be accomplished by introducing a function (QQ(x)) defined as

```
FUNCTION QQ(X)
COMMON/Y/Y
QQ = Q(X,Y)
RETURN
END
```

5. The main program should read a data file containing the input data and neatly echo print. Then integrate Equation (VIII.1) over the coordinates of each room.

6. It is instructive to also keep track of how many times the function Q(X, Y) is called in the complete evaluation of the double integral. Add a counter to the function Q(X, Y) that will contain this information. Run the complete program using KMAX = 6 and then 8, where KMAX is the maximum order of the Romberg integration.

7. Print all the computed results for the two computations and compare the results.

Input Data

$$T_0 = 20 \text{ °C} \qquad x_0 = 6.5 \text{ m}$$
$$y_0 = 4.2 \text{ m}$$
$$h = 3.0 \text{ m}$$

γ_1 (wood)   = 0.385 W/m°C

γ_2 (brick)   = 0.584

γ_3 (slate)   = 1.966

γ_4 (asbestos) = 0.0795

EPS = 10^{-6} KMAX = 6, 8

Sample Problem—Solution

Using Equations (VIII.1) and VIII.4), we obtain the following for the heat flow through the roofs of each room:

$$Q(x, y) = \frac{\gamma_i T_0}{4h \ln(2)} \left(1 + \exp\left\{ -\frac{[x - R_x(i)]^2}{x_0^2} - \frac{[y - R_y(i)]^2}{y_0^2} \right\} \right)$$ **(VIII.5)**

The complete code for the program is given in Figure VIII-3 and the computed results are shown in Figure VIII-4. Especially noteworthy is the use of COMMON blocks and EXTERNAL statements in this program.

```
       PROGRAM MAINE
*--
*--
*-- THIS PROGRAM PERFORMS A DOUBLE INTEGRAL OVER THE HEAT
*-- FLOWING THROUGH THE CEILINGS OF A FOUR-ROOM STRUCTURE WITH
*-- DIFFERENT INSULATION IN EACH ROOM. THE MOST INTERESTING
*-- FEATURE IS THE MANNER IN WHICH A FORTRAN PROGRAM CAN BE
*-- WRITTEN TO EXECUTE A DOUBLE INTEGRAL. THE CALCULATION IS
*-- REPEATED TWICE WITH DIFFERENT VALUES OF KMAX, THE MAXIMUM
*-- ORDER OF A ROMBERG INTEGRATION, TO DETERMINE THE ACCURACY
*-- OF THE CALCULATION.
*-------------------------------------------------------------------
*-- VARIABLES
*--
       REAL GAMMA ,RX ,RY ,X0 ,Y0 ,H ,T0 ,EPS ,HEAT(4) ,
     +     A ,B ,C ,D
       INTEGER ICALL ,KMAX ,IROOM
       CHARACTER ROOF(4)*8
*--
*--            VARIABLE              DESCRIPTION          IN
*--            NAME                                       BLOCK
*--            --------              -----------------    --------
*--            GAMMA()    --    THE ROOF HEAT CONDUCTIVITIES  /PARAM/
*--            RX() ,RY()--    RADIATOR POSITIONS        /PARAM/
*--            X0 ,Y0 ,H  --    ROOM DIMENSIONS          /PARAM/
*--            T0         --    A CONSTANT TEMPERATURE    /PARAM/
*--            ICALL      --    A COUNTER TO DETERMINE THE  /ICALL/
*--                             NUMBER OF TIMES Q() IS CALLED
*--            EPS        --    THE CONVERGENCE CRITERION  /ROMBRG/
*--                             USED BY ROMBERG FUNCTIONS
*--            KMAX       --    THE MAXIMUM ORDER OF THE   /ROMBRG/
*--                             ROMBERG INTEGRATIONS
*--            A ,B       --    THE LIMITS OF THE INTEGRATION
*--            C ,D             IN THE Y AND X DIRECTIONS
*--            IPRNT      --    A PRINT PARAMETER IN THE
*--                             ROMBERG FUNCTIONS (USE = 0)
*--            HEAT()     --    THE COMPUTED HEAT FLOWING THROUGH
*--                             THE CEILINGS OF EACH ROOM
*--            IROOM      --    A COUNTER THAT SPECIFIES  /IROOM/
*--                             EACH ROOM
*-------------------------------------------------------------------
```

Continued

Figure VIII-3
The Fortran code for the conductive heat-loss problem.

```
*--    COMMON BLOCKS
*--
       COMMON/PARAM/GAMMA(4),RX(4),RY(4),XO,YO,H,TO
       COMMON/ROMBRG/KMAX,EPS,IPRNT,A,B,C,D
       COMMON/ICALL/ICALL
       COMMON/IROOM/IROOM
*------------------------------------------------------------------
*--
*--             THE OUTER INTEGRAL OVER Y IS OVER THE FUNCTION
*--             G(Y) WHICH MUST BE DECLARED EXTERNAL.
*--
       EXTERNAL G
*------------------------------------------------------------------
*--    INITIALIZATION
*--
       OPEN(57,FILE='DATA8')
       REWIND 57
       READ(57,'(4A8)')(ROOF(J),J=1,4)
       READ(57,*)(GAMMA(J),J=1,4)
       READ(57,*)(RX(K),RY(K),K=1,4)
       READ(57,*)XO,YO,H
       READ(57,*)TO,EPS
       WRITE(*,20)
       WRITE(*,21)(J,J = 1,4),(ROOF(K),K = 1,4),(GAMMA(M),M = 1,4)
       WRITE(*,22)XO,YO,H,TO
       WRITE(*,23)(J,J = 1,4),(RX(K),K = 1,4),(RY(M),M = 1,4)
       WRITE(*,24)EPS
       IPRNT = 0
*------------------------------------------------------------------
*--
*--             TWO COMPLETE CALCULATIONS ARE PERFORMED FOR
*--             DIFFERENT VALUES OF KMAX
*--
       DO 2 KMAX = 6,8,2
          ICALL = 0
*--
*--             INTEGRATE OVER THE FOUR ROOMS INDIVIDUALLY
*--
          DO 1 IROOM = 1,4
*--
*--             SPECIFY THE INTEGRATION LIMITS FOR THE
*--             CURRENT ROOM
*--
             IF(IROOM .EQ. 1)THEN
                A = 0.0
                B = YO
                C = -XO
                D = 0.0
             ELSE IF(IROOM .EQ. 2)THEN
                A = 0.0
                B = YO
                C = 0.0
                D = XO
             ELSE IF(IROOM .EQ. 3)THEN
                A = -YO
                B = 0.0
                C = -XO
                D = 0.0
             ELSE
                A = -YO
                B = 0.0
                C = 0.0
                D = XO
             END IF
```

542   PROGRAMMING ASSIGNMENT VIII

```
*--
*--               THE OUTER INTEGRAL OVER Y IS ACCOMPLISHED BY
*--               USING THE SECOND COPY OF THE ROMBERG FUNCTION
*--               TO INTEGRATE OVER THE FUNCTION G(Y)
*--
              HEAT(IROOM) = ROMBRG2(G,A,B,KMAX,EPS,IPRNT)
    1     CONTINUE
*--
*--           FOR THIS VALUE OF KMAX ALL FOUR ROOMS HAVE BEEN
*--           INTEGRATED. PRINT THE RESULTS.
*--
          WRITE(*,25)KMAX,(J,J = 1,4),(HEAT(K),K = 1,4)
          WRITE(*,26)ICALL
    2 CONTINUE
*--
*--
      STOP 'PROGRAM COMPLETED'
*------------------------------------------------------------------------
*--   FORMATS
*--
   20 FORMAT(///,T5,'THE RESULTS OF THE DOUBLE INTEGRAL OVER',/,
      +        T5,'THE FOUR-ROOM STRUCTURE',//,
      +        T7,'THE INPUT PARAMETERS ARE',//)
*--
   21 FORMAT(T10,'ROOM',T27,'-',T34,I1,T44,I1,T53,I1,T62,I1,/,
      +        T10,'ROOF MATERIAL',T27,'-',T32,4(1X,A8),/,
      +        T10,'CONDUCTIVITY' ,T27,'-',T32,4(2X,F6.4,1X),//)
*--
   22 FORMAT(//,T10,'THE FOUR ROOMS ARE OF IDENTICAL SIZE',//,
      +        T15,'LENGTH ',T25,'= ',F5.2,' METERS',/,
      +        T15,'WIDTH'  ,T25,'= ',F5.2,' METERS',/,
      +        T15,'HEIGHT' ,T25,'= ',F5.2,' METERS',//,
      +        T15,'THE TEMPERATURE CONSTANT = ',F5.2,' OC')
*--
   23 FORMAT(//,T10,'THE POSITIONS OF THE RADIATORS IN EACH ROOM',
      +        //,T15,'ROOM',T25,'-',T32,I1,T38,I1,T44,I1,T50,I1,/,
      +        T15,'X-POS.',T25,'-',T30,4(1X,F4.2,1X),/,
      +        T15,'Y-POS.',T25,'-',T30,4(1X,F4.2,1X))
*--
   24 FORMAT(//,T10,'THE CONVERGENCE CRITERION FOR THE ROMBERG',//,
      +        T10,'INTEGRATIONS IS EPS = ',E9.2)
*--
   25 FORMAT(//,T5,'THE RESULTS OF THE CALCULATION FOR KMAX = ',I2
      +        ,//,T10,'ROOM',T25,'-',4(4X,I2,4X),/,
      +            T10,'HEAT FLOW',T25,'-',4(1X,E9.2))
*--
   26 FORMAT(//,T10,'THE TOTAL NUMBER OF TIMES THAT THE FUNCTION',//,
      +        T10,'Q(X,Y) WAS CALLED WAS ',I6,' TIMES.')
      END
*------------------------------------------------------------------------
*------------------------------------------------------------------------
      FUNCTION Q(X,Y,I)
*--
*--   THIS FUNCTION RETURNS THE HEAT FLOWING THROUGH THE CEILINGS
*--   OF A FOUR-ROOM STRUCTURE. THE ROOMS ARE LABELED BY I AND
*--   THE HEAT FLOW IS EVALUATED AT A POSITION <X,Y>. THE ROOM
*--   DIMENSIONS, CONDUCTIVITIES, AND RADIATOR POSITIONS ARE
*--   PASSED TO THE FUNCTION THROUGH COMMON BLOCKS. TO IS A
*--   TEMPERATURE CONSTANT.
*------------------------------------------------------------------------
*--
      REAL GAMMA,RX,RY,XO,YO,H,TO,CONST,EXPON
```

Continued

```
      INTEGER ICALL
      COMMON/PARAM/GAMMA(4),RX(4),RY(4),X0,Y0,H,T0
      COMMON/ICALL/ICALL
*-------------------------------------------------------------------
*--
      CONST = GAMMA(I)*T0/(4.*H*LOG(2.))
      EXPON = (X - RX(I))**2/X0**2 + (Y - RY(I))**2/Y0**2
      Q = CONST*(1. + EXP(-EXPON))
      ICALL = ICALL + 1
      RETURN
      END
*-------------------------------------------------------------------
*-------------------------------------------------------------------
      FUNCTION QQ(X)
*--
*--   THIS FUNCTION IS MERELY THE FUNCTION Q(X,Y,IROOM)
*--   WRITTEN AS A FUNCTION OF A SINGLE ARGUMENT. THE OTHER
*--   TWO PARAMETERS IN THE ARGUMENT LIST OF Q() ARE PASSED
*--   THROUGH A COMMON BLOCK.
*-------------------------------------------------------------------
*--
      COMMON/Y/Y
      COMMON/IROOM/IROOM
      QQ = Q(X,Y,IROOM)
      RETURN
      END
*-------------------------------------------------------------------
*-------------------------------------------------------------------
      FUNCTION G(Y)
*--
*--   THE FUNCTION G(Y) IS THE INTEGRAL OF Q(X,Y,I) OVER X FROM
*--   X = C TO X = D. THE INTEGRATION IS DONE BY CALLING THE FIRST
*--   COPY OF THE ROMBERG FUNCTION <RMBRG1>. THE LIMITS FOR THE
*--   ROMBERG INTEGRATION ARE PASSED THROUGH THE COMMON BLOCK
*--   /ROMBRG/. SINCE THE ROMBERG ROUTINE EXPECTS A FUNCTION OF
*--   A SINGLE ARGUMENT, THE ACTUAL INTEGRATION IS OVER THE
*--   FUNCTION QQ(X). <SEE ABOVE FUNCTION.>
*-------------------------------------------------------------------
      COMMON/Y/YY
      COMMON/IROOM/I
      COMMON/ROMBRG/KMAX,EPS,IPRNT,A,B,C,D
      EXTERNAL QQ
*-------------------------------------------------------------------
*--
      YY = Y
      G = RMBRG1(QQ,C,D,KMAX,EPS,IPRNT)
      RETURN
      END
*-------------------------------------------------------------------
*-------------------------------------------------------------------
      FUNCTION RMBRG1(F,A,B,KMX,EPS,IPRNT)
*--
```

```
THE RESULTS OF THE DOUBLE INTEGRAL OVER
THE FOUR-ROOM STRUCTURE

     THE INPUT PARAMETERS ARE

        ROOM              -    1        2        3        4
        ROOF MATERIAL     -   WOOD    BRICK    SLATE   ASBESTOS
        CONDUCTIVITY      -   .3850   .5840   1.9660   .0795


        THE FOUR ROOMS ARE OF IDENTICAL SIZE

             LENGTH   =  6.50 METERS
             WIDTH    =  4.50 METERS
             HEIGHT   =  3.00 METERS

        THE TEMPERATURE CONSTANT = 20.00 OC

     THE POSITIONS OF THE RADIATORS IN EACH ROOM

        ROOM       -     1    2    3    4
        X-POS.     -   .00  .00 -.50  .50
        Y-POS.     -   .50  .50 -.50 -.50


     THE CONVERGENCE CRITERION FOR THE ROMBERG
     INTEGRATIONS IS EPS =   .10E-05

THE RESULTS OF THE CALCULATION FOR KMAX =  6
        ROOM             -    1        2        3        4
        HEAT FLOW        -  .43E+02  .66E+02  .23E+03  .92E+01


     THE TOTAL NUMBER OF TIMES THAT THE FUNCTION
     Q(X,Y) WAS CALLED WAS  1396 TIMES.

THE RESULTS OF THE CALCULATION FOR KMAX =  8
        ROOM             -    1        2        3        4
        HEAT FLOW        -  .43E+02  .66E+02  .23E+03  .92E+01


     THE TOTAL NUMBER OF TIMES THAT THE FUNCTION
     Q(X,Y) WAS CALLED WAS   1396 TIMES.
  STOP   PROGRAM COMPLETED
```

Figure VIII-4
The computed results of the conductive heat-loss program.

VIII.2 PROGRAMMING PROBLEMS

Programming Problem A: Mechanical/Aeronautical Engineering: The Shear Force on an Airplane Wing

Introduction An airplane wing is acted upon by a wide variety of loads and each must be carefully analyzed to determine the safety and performance of the wing. The net shear force at the base of the wing is the total upward force of the wing on the body or fuselage of the plane. This force in turn is a sum of all upward forces on the wing itself. These depend in a rather complicated manner on the physical properties of the wing and other parameters concerned with flight such as air speed.

The simplified wing structure to be used in this problem is illustrated in Figure VIII-5. The net shear force at the base of the wing is the sum of the upward pressure on the point (x, y) times the infinitesimal area $dx\, dy$, summed over the entire area of the wing.

(VIII.6)
$$S = \int_0^L dx \int_{e_b}^{e_f} P(x, y)\, dy$$

where L is the length of the wing, e_f is the leading (front) edge of the wing, and e_b is the trailing (back) edge of the wing.

The inner integral over y results in a function of x only, so the stress S could also be expressed as

Figure VIII-5
The top and side views of an airplane wing.

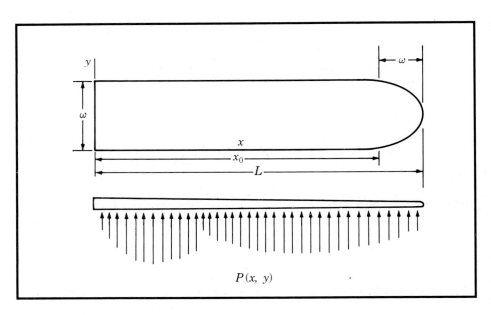

$$S = \int_0^L W(x)\, dx \qquad \text{(VIII.7)}$$

where

$$W(x) = \int_{e_b(x)}^{e_f(x)} P(x,\, y)\, dy$$

Notice that unlike the example problem the integration over the inner variable (here y) is not between constant limits. As you can see from Figure VIII-5, the y integration slice extends from the back edge to the front edge and both of these are themselves functions of x.

Problem

If the wing width is ω and if we define $x_0 = L - \omega$, the equations for the front and back edges of the wing are

$$
\begin{aligned}
e_f(x) &= \omega && \text{if } 0 \le x \le x_0 && \text{(VIII.8)} \\
&= \frac{\omega}{3}\left\{ 1 + 2\left[1 - \left(\frac{x - x_0}{\omega} \right)^2 \right]^{1/2} \right\} && \text{if } x_0 \le x \le L
\end{aligned}
$$

$$
\begin{aligned}
e_b(x) &= 0 && \text{if } 0 \le x \le x_0 && \text{(VIII.9)} \\
&= \frac{\omega}{3}\left\{ 1 - \left[1 - \left(\frac{x - x_0}{\omega} \right)^2 \right]^{1/2} \right\} && \text{if } x_0 \le x \le L
\end{aligned}
$$

The wing is subject to the following upward pressure at a point $(x,\, y)$

$$0 \le x \le \frac{L}{3} \qquad\qquad P(x,\, y) = 2 + 1.85\frac{x}{L} + 1.95\left(\frac{y}{\omega}\right)^{1/2} \qquad \text{(VIII.10)}$$

$$\frac{L}{3} < x \le \frac{2}{3}L$$

$$P(x,\, y) = 2 + 0.60 \sin\left(\frac{3\pi x^2}{L^2}\right) + 0.1 \cos\left(\frac{3\pi y^2}{\omega^2}\right) \qquad \text{(VIII.11)}$$

$$\frac{2}{3}L < x \le L$$

$$P(x,\, y) = 1.69(1 - e^{-x/L} + 0.45e^{-y/\omega}) \qquad \text{(VIII.12)}$$

Details

Your program should evaluate the double integral for the shear stress on the fuselage in the following manner.

1. The main program will integrate the function $G(x)$ [Equation (VIII.7)] from $x = 0$ to $x = L$ using the Romberg algorithm with a convergence criterion EPS and a maximum order KMAX.
2. The function $G(x)$ will integrate a function PX(Y) from $y = e_b(x)$ to $y = e_f(x)$ also using the Romberg algorithm; however, the reference to the integration subprogram must be to a renamed second copy of the function ROMBRG. (See the sample program.)
3. The function PX(Y) is simply the function $P(x, y)$ written as a function of a single variable, e.g.,

```
FUNCTION PX(Y)
  COMMON/X/X
  PX = P(X,Y)
  RETURN
END
```

4. In addition, the complete program will contain function subprograms for the functions $e_f(x)$, $e_b(x)$, $P(x, y)$, and two copies with different names of the Romberg code.
5. Be very careful in assembling this program, paying special attention to the numerous COMMON blocks and EXTERNAL statements that are required.
6. As a point of interest, your program should also print the total number of times the function $P(x, y)$ was referenced. Use a counter that is initialized in the main program, passed to $P(x, y)$ via a COMMON block, and incremented in $P(x, y)$.

Input Parameters

Use the following values in your program:

$$L = 16.25 \text{ m}$$

$$\omega = 2.2 \text{ m}$$

$$EPS = 10^{-6} \text{ (convergence criterion in ROMBRG)}$$

$$KMAX = 8 \text{ (maximum order of Romberg algorithm)}$$

Programming Problem B: Curve Fitting with Legendre Polynomials

Frequently one is faced with the task of fitting a set of data to a given curve. If you wish to fit to polynomials, the least squares procedures of Chapter 13 are quite adequate; however, it is sometimes preferable to fit to a different class of functions. For example, the functions listed below are called Legendre polynomials and are defined for $-1 \le x \le +1$.

$$P_0(x) = 1$$
$$P_1(x) = x$$
$$P_2(x) = \tfrac{1}{2}(3x^2 - 1)$$
$$P_3(x) = \tfrac{1}{2}(5x^3 - 3x)$$
$$P_4(x) = \tfrac{1}{8}(35x^4 - 30x^2 + 3)$$
$$P_5(x) = \tfrac{1}{8}(63x^5 - 70x^3 + 15x)$$
$$\cdots$$

$$P_{m+1}(x) = \frac{2m+1}{m+1}xP_m - \frac{m}{m+1}P_{m-1}$$

The idea then is to express an arbitrary function of x over the interval $-1 \le x \le +1$ as an expansion in these P_m functions.

$$f(x) = \sum_{m=0}^{N} a_m P_m(x) \qquad \textbf{(VIII.13)}$$

where the coefficients in the expansion are a_m and are yet to be determined.
The advantage in expanding in Legendre polynomials is that these functions were designed to satisfy the following orthogonality condition:

$$\int_{-1}^{1} P_m(x)P_{m'}(x)\ dx \begin{cases} = 0 & \text{if } m \neq m' \\ = \dfrac{2}{2m+1} & \text{if } m = m' \end{cases} \qquad \textbf{(VIII.14)}$$

For example,

$$\int_{-1}^{1} P_2(x)P_1(x)\ dx = \int_{-1}^{1} \frac{x}{2}(3x^2 - 1)\ dx$$

$$= \left(\frac{3}{8}x^4 - \frac{1}{4}x^2 \right)\Bigg|_{-1}^{1} = 0$$

$$\int_{-1}^{1} P_2(x)P_2(x) \, dx = \int_{-1}^{1} \frac{1}{4}(3x^2 - 1)^2 \, dx$$

$$= \frac{1}{4} \int_{-1}^{1} (9x^4 - 6x^2 + 1) \, dx$$

$$= \frac{1}{4}\left(\frac{9}{5}x^5 - 2x^3 + x\right)\Big|_{-1}^{1}$$

$$= \frac{1}{4}\left(\frac{18}{5} - 4 + 2\right) = \frac{2}{5}$$

We can use this fact to solve Equation (VIII.13) for the unknown coefficients in the expansion, a_m. First multiply both sides of Equation (VIII.13) by $P_{m'}(x)$ and then integrate over x from -1 to $+1$.

(VIII.15)
$$\int_{-1}^{1} P_{m'}(x)f(x) \, dx = \sum_{m=0}^{N} a_m \int_{-1}^{1} P_m(x)P_{m'}(x) \, dx$$

Now, because of the orthogonality property of the P_m's, *every* term in the sum over m on the right is zero *except* the single term when $m = m'$. Thus,

$$\int_{-1}^{1} f(x)P_{m'}(x) \, dx = a_{m'}\frac{2}{2m' + 1}$$

or since m' was an arbitrary value, the coefficients can be expressed as

(VIII.16)
$$a_m = \frac{2m + 1}{2} \int_{-1}^{1} f(x)P_m(x) \, dx$$

Thus fitting the expansion to a function consists in the evaluation of the integrals for the coefficients a_m.

Problem

Listed in Table VIII-1 is a set of 33 equally spaced data points $[x_i, f_{exp}(x_i), i = 1, 33]$. Use the Romberg integration algorithm and the expressions for $P_m(x)$ given above to evaluate the coefficients a_m for $m = 0, 5$ by integrating Equation (VIII.16). In ROMBRG use KMAX = 5; i.e., $2^5 = 32$ panels.
    Your program should

1. Print the computed values of the coefficients a_m, $m = 0, 5$
2. Print a table of values of i, x_i, $f_{exp}(x_i)$, $f_{model}(x_i)$, where $f_{model}(x)$ is obtained from Equation VIII.13).
3. Calculate and print the root-mean-square deviation, defined as

(VIII.17)
$$\sigma^2 = \frac{1}{32} \sum_{i=1}^{33} [f_{exp}(x_i) - f_{model}(x_i)]^2$$

---

i	x_i	$f_{exp}(x_i)$	i	x_i	$f_{exp}(x_i)$
1	−1.0000	0.630	18	0.0625	4.080
2	−0.9375	0.910	19	0.1250	5.800
3	−0.8750	1.310	20	0.1875	5.060
4	−0.8175	1.870	21	0.2500	3.600
5	−0.7500	2.460	22	0.3125	2.260
6	−0.6875	3.160	23	0.3750	1.320
7	−0.6250	3.690	24	0.4375	0.770
8	−0.5625	3.870	25	0.5000	0.370
9	−0.5000	3.570	26	0.5625	0.260
10	−0.4375	2.600	27	0.6250	0.180
11	−0.3750	1.100	28	0.6875	0.110
12	−0.3125	−0.770	29	0.7500	0.008
13	−0.2500	−2.460	30	0.8175	0.006
14	−0.1875	−3.210	31	0.8750	0.005
15	−0.1250	−2.760	32	0.9375	0.004
16	−0.0625	−0.960	33	1.0000	0.003
17	0.0000	1.950			

Table VIII-1
Experimental data to be fit to Legendre polynomials.

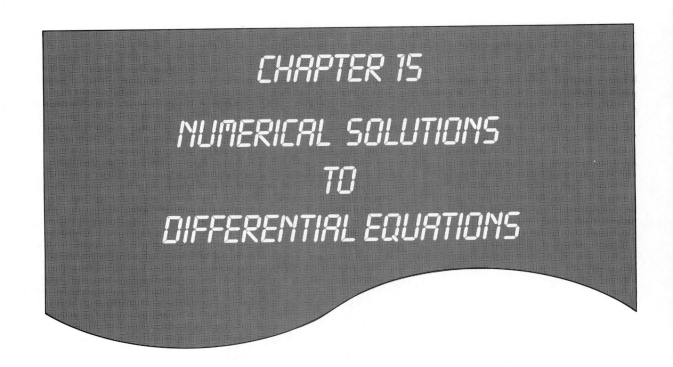

CHAPTER 15

NUMERICAL SOLUTIONS TO DIFFERENTIAL EQUATIONS

15.1 INTRODUCTION

The solution of differential equations is not an appropriate topic for an elementary text. With that said, allow me to attempt to justify why the material of this chapter is worth your time, effort, and attention. First of all, the solution of differential equations by numerical methods is where the action is. Not only are a vast number of problems in engineering and science expressible in terms of differential equations, but the numerical procedures for their solution on a computer are presently under active development to improve both their accuracy and their efficiency. These modern methods are far too complex to be of interest to us here. However, I believe the more standard procedures, sufficiently distilled, can be understood by a novice. The material of this chapter is intended merely as an introduction; I hope you will see a more thorough discussion in later courses in numerical analysis. This is to be contrasted with all of the topics previously covered in this text in which a serious description of the modern methods used by practicing engineers and scientists was given.

The second and more important reason for risking your confusion and frustration is that the best way to understand what a differential equation is and what is meant by a solution to a differential equation is to learn how to solve one by numerical means. The situation with respect to the analytical integration of differential equations is even worse than that of the integration of functions. There seems to be an endless parade of procedures and tricks that must be learned for a large variety of situations. By contrast, numerical methods work for a very large class of functions, often yielding good results even when you might expect them to fail.

15.2   THE MEANING OF A DIFFERENTIAL EQUATION

Any equation that relates an independent variable, say x, a dependent variable $y(x)$, and the first derivative $y'(x) = dy/dx$ is called a *first-order differential equation*. Thus any first-order differential equation can be written formally as

$$F(x, y, y') = 0 \tag{15.1}$$

The solution of a differential equation consists in finding a *function $y(x)$* such that the above equation is satisfied. This is quite a bit different from finding the root of an equation; that is, to find a single value of x such that $f(x) = 0$. A few examples of differential equations and their solutions follow.

15.2.1   Examples of Differential Equations and Their Solution

1. The simplest differential equation is

$$y'(x) = \frac{dy(x)}{dx} = 0$$

and the solution, by inspection, is

$$y(x) = \text{constant} \qquad \langle any\ constant \rangle$$

The proposed solution is verified as correct by differentiating and inserting back into the original differential equation.

2. An equation that is not quite so trivial is

$$y' + ax = 0 \tag{15.2}$$

This equation is commonly solved by writing $y' = dy/dx$ so that

$$dy + ax \, dx = 0$$

$$\int dy = -a \int x \, dx$$

(15.3)
$$y(x) = -\frac{a}{2}x^2 + \text{constant}$$

Again you can verify that this is a solution of Equation (15.2) by differentiating. You should take special note of the fact that we have solved Equation (15.2) not for a single value of y but for a complete function $y(x)$, and the function we obtained is a valid solution for *any* value of the undetermined constant.

The appropriate value of the constant for a particular problem can only be determined by some additional information expressed in terms of boundary conditions. For example, we may be given the value of y for a particular value of x, say $y(x = 6) = 0$. Then using the general form of the solution we can use this information to determine the value of the unknown constant.

$$y(x = 6) = 0 = -\frac{a}{2}(6^2) + \text{constant}$$

or

$$\text{constant} = 18a$$

Thus the solution for this equation plus the particular auxiliary condition is

$$y(x) = -\frac{a}{2}x^2 + 18a$$

3. Moving on to more complicated first-order differential equations, the difficulty in obtaining closed-form expressions for the solution $y(x)$ increases dramatically. In fact the arbitrary first-order differential equation generally has no closed-form solution and the only alternative then is a numerical solution in the form of a table of values of x and $y(x)$. For example, the innocent-looking equation

$$F(x, \, y, \, y') = (y')^2 + y \sin(x) = 0$$

has no closed-form solution.

A second-order differential equation is one similar to Equation (15.1) but which contains, in general, the second as well as the first derivative of $y(x)$,

(15.4)
$$F(x, \, y, \, y', \, y'') = 0$$

Higher-order differential equations are defined analogously.

15.2.2 Examples of Physical Phenomena Described by Differential Equations

A great many problems in all fields of science and engineering are expressible in terms of relations between the rates of change of the variables. A few examples are

1. The melting rate of a snowball is roughly proportional to its surface area. That is,

$$\frac{d(\text{volume})}{dt} \propto \text{surface} \tag{15.5}$$

And since for a sphere

$$V = \tfrac{4}{3}\pi r^3 \qquad S = 4\pi r^2$$

we have

$$S = (36\pi)^{1/3} V^{2/3}$$

and the proportionality in Equation (15.5) may be expressed as

$$\frac{dV}{dt} = -kV^{2/3} \tag{15.6}$$

The proportionality constant is chosen to be negative since the volume decreases with time. This equation can be integrated by grouping the V terms on one side of the equation and the t terms on the other.

$$\int \frac{dV}{V^{2/3}} = -k \int dt$$

Using the relation $\int x^c \, dx = x^{c+1}/(c+1)$, the solution is then

$$3V^{1/3} = -kt + C_0$$

where C_1 is an as yet undetermined constant. If we are told that at time $t = 0$ the volume is known to be $V(t = 0) = V_0$, the constant C_0 must have the value $C_0 = 3(V_0)^{1/3}$, so that

$$V(t) = (V_0^{1/3} - \tfrac{1}{3}kt)^3$$

and the snowball disappears $(V \to 0)$ when $t = 3V_0^{1/3}/k$ sec.
2. Radioactive decay: If there are N radioactive atoms in a sample at time t, the number of decays expected per second at that time is proportional

to the number of such atoms present. Thus the number of radioactive atoms at time t, $N(t)$, decreases by an amount dN/dt where

$$\frac{dN(t)}{dt} \propto N(t)$$

or

$$\frac{dN(t)}{dt} = -kN(t)$$

where once again the proportionality constant is chosen to be negative since $N(t)$ is decreasing. The solution is obtained as before by arranging the different variables on opposite sides of the equation and integrating:

$$\int \frac{dN}{N} = -k \int dt$$

$$\ln(N) = -kt + C$$

since $e^{\ln(N)} = N$, we obtain

$$N = e^C e^{-kt}$$

The integration constant C could be specified by, for example, the additional information that at time $t = 0$ the number of radioactive atoms is known to be $N(t = 0) = N_0$, or

$$N(t) = N_0 e^{-kt}$$

3. Simple Harmonic Motion: In mechanics, problems are expressed in terms of forces and since $F = ma$, where the acceleration a is the second derivative of position with respect to time, d^2x/dt^2, these problems amount to solving a second-order differential equation. Of course, most forces encountered in the real world are extremely complicated. However, if x is small we can use a Maclaurin series approximation for $F(x)$ and write

$$F(x) \simeq F_0 - kx + \cdot \; \cdot \; \cdot$$

where F_0 and k are constants. The term F_0 is ordinarily ignored since it represents a constant force and can only add uninteresting constant acceleration motion. The equation $F = ma$ then results in

(15.7)
$$m\frac{d^2x}{dt^2} \simeq -kx$$

This is a second-order differential equation; i.e., it depends on the variables (t, x, x', x''). The analytical solution of this equation is

$$x(t) = C_1 \sin\left(\sqrt{\frac{k}{m}}\, t\right) + C_2 \cos\left(\sqrt{\frac{k}{m}}\, t\right)$$

where C_1, C_2 are as yet undetermined integration constants. Notice that since a second-order equation must be integrated twice to obtain a solution, there are two constants of integration.

You can verify that this is indeed the solution to the original differential equation by differentiating twice and plugging back into Equation (15.7).

Second-order differential equations are generally much more difficult to solve and obtain closed-form expressions for the solutions than are first-order equations. However, we can always reduce a higher-order differential equation to a series or set of first-order equations by introducing superfluous variables in the following manner. If we introduce the variable v, the velocity, by the relation $v = dx/dt$ and then note that $a = dv/dt$, the second-order equation, Equation (15.7), may be expressed as two first-order equations:

$$m\frac{dv}{dt} = -kx$$

$$\frac{dx}{dt} = v$$

The introduction of the new variable v has indeed reduced the single second-order equation to two first-order equations, but these equations are *coupled*; that is, they cannot be solved independently. The same variables appear in both equations. However, if we have a tried-and-true method of solving first-order equations, it may not be difficult to adapt this method to equations of any order by the above procedure.

The main objective, then, of this chapter is to explain the various methods that can be used to obtain solutions to first-order differential equations. Any such equation can be written in the form

$$\frac{dy(x)}{dx} = f(x, y) \tag{15.8}$$

15.3   A NOTE ON COMPUTATIONAL ERRORS: A QUESTION OF TRADE-OFFS

The procedures of this chapter are intended to obtain approximate numerical solutions to Equation (15.8) in the form of a table of values of y corresponding to values of x in some interval $a \leq x \leq b$. Though the details of one algorithm may differ substantially from another, the underlying idea to all the methods is to partition the x interval into a finite number of points, x_i, then, knowing the value of y at some starting value of x, say $y(x_0) = y_0$, the value of the dependent variable y at the next x value is computed by some approximation procedure. This is repeated for all the x values in the partitioned interval. That is, knowing (x_i, y_i) + approximation algorithm $\rightarrow [x_{i+1}, y_{i+1}]$. Clearly the smaller the step size, the more accurate will be the computed values of successive y values. The computational errors in such methods are of three types:

Discretization Errors: If the step size from x_i to x_{i+1}, i.e., Δx_i, were allowed to approach zero, all of the algorithms would be exact. Unfortunately this is not possible since an infinitesimal step size implies an infinite number of steps required to span the x interval. The fact that the step size we use in a numerical algorithm is not truly infinitesimal will generate errors in each step. These errors can often be estimated theoretically to be say $\mathbb{O}(\Delta x)^2$ or $\mathbb{O}(\Delta x)^3$, etc. Alternatively, the accuracy of the calculation can be monitored by noting the changes in the computed results when the step size is reduced from Δx_i to $\frac{1}{2}\Delta x_i$. Reducing the step size will improve the theoretical accuracy of the results at the expense of more steps and consequently more arithmetic operations.

Truncation Errors: One method that can be used to get from point y_i to y_{i+1} is to assume that the function $y(x)$ can be approximated by a straight line over the interval x_i to x_{i+1}. This would correspond to retaining only the first two terms in a Taylor expansion of the function $y(x)$. This approximation may be adequate if the function is smooth enough and if the step size is small enough. Truncation errors can be reduced by improving the basic approximation for the function—e.g., by including quadratic terms. In general this will result in an algorithm that is more complicated and that requires more arithmetic operations per cycle.

Round-Off Errors: Every arithmetic operation involving real numbers executed by the computer results in a loss of accuracy due to the finite nature of the computer word. If the basic computer word is ten digits or so, the loss of the last digit is inconsequential in one multiplication or addition. However, if the computation requires tens or hundreds of millions of arithmetic operations to obtain a result, round-off error becomes a serious concern and will often invalidate a result even though it is based on perfectly sound analytical procedures. The *more* arithmetic there is to be done in an algorithm, the *greater* will be the associated round-off error. Thus round-off error will in general *increase* with a smaller step size or with an improved higher-order algorithm.

In developing a numerical solution to a differential equation we must keep the various types of computation errors in mind. For all procedures there is an *optimum* step size which minimizes the overall error. That is, either a larger or a smaller step size will result in an increase in the overall numerical error. This will be discussed in more detail in Chapter 16.

15.4   EULER'S METHOD

Numerical procedures for solving the differential equation $y' = f(x, y)$ are classified as either one-step or multistep algorithms. A one-step method will use the most recently computed value for y at the position x_n—i.e., y_n—and values of the function $f(x, y)$ evaluated at this point or possibly at points in the following interval x_n to $x_n + \Delta x$ to estimate the next value of y; i.e., y_{n+1}. A multistep algorithm uses the current value of y_n plus one or more previously computed values from preceding steps. Not surprisingly, the multistep methods are typically more accurate and more efficient than the one-step methods. But a price is paid in that the algorithms are generally much more complicated to code, and also since information from several previous steps is required, these methods are difficult to start. We will deal almost exclusively in this chapter with single-step algorithms; however, a short discussion of a relatively simple multistep procedure will be discussed in Section 15.7.

The simplest of the one-step methods is called Euler's method and is based on the definition of the derivative.

$$\frac{dy}{dx} \simeq \frac{y(x + \Delta x) - y(x)}{\Delta x}$$

In all that follows, $y(x_i)$ will denote the exact value of the solution at the position x_i and y_i will be the computed value. Since Δx is finite, the above equation is equivalent to the first two terms of a Taylor series expansion

$$y(x_i + \Delta x) \simeq y(x_i) + \frac{dy}{dx} \Delta x$$

and since the original differential equation reads $dy/dx = f(x, y)$, we arrive at the computational algorithm

$$y_{i+1} = y_i + f_i \, \Delta x \tag{15.9}$$

where f_i represents the function $f(x, y)$ evaluated at the point (x_i, y_i). Euler's method is illustrated graphically in Figure 15-1.

Just as in Chapter 10 where Taylor series were described, Equation (15.9) simply replaces the function $y(x)$ at the point x_i by a straight line with the same slope as the tangent line at that point. If this is not a particularly good approximation (e.g., if Δx is not small enough or if $y(x)$ is rapidly

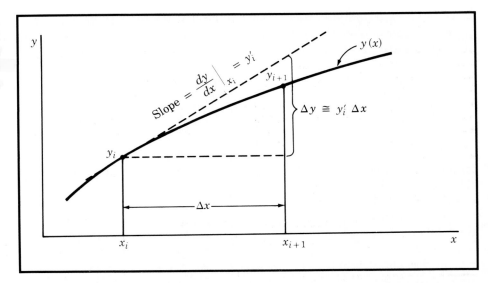

Figure 15-1
Euler's method
for computing the
step from y_i to
y_{i+1}.

changing), then the calculated value for y_{i+1} will not be very accurate. The subsequent point, y_{i+2}, which depends upon the values calculated for y_{i+1}, will of course be even worse. The error will accumulate for subsequent points. Despite the obvious inadequacies of Euler's method, its compelling simplicity makes it quite useful as a starting point for the development of more sophisticated procedures for solving differential equations. Even though Euler's method is rarely used in a serious solution of a problem, the Fortran code implementing the method is given in the next section and is applied to several example differential equations in order to better understand the shortcomings of the procedure and to suggest improvements.

15.4.1 The Fortran Code for Euler's Method

A Fortran code to solve the differential equation $y' = f(x, y)$ by using the approximation of Equation (15.9) would require the following:

1. A function subprogram F(X, Y) for the derivative $y' = f(x, y)$.
2. A specified interval $a \le x \le b$ and the number of subdivisions N of this interval. That is, $\Delta x = (b - a)/N$.
3. The *starting* value of $y(x)$. That is, $y(x = a) = y_0$.

The code is quite simple and is given in Figure 15-2. The accuracy of the code could be tested by doubling the value of N and monitoring the change in the computed values. This procedure may require excessive computer time and expense and additionally it should be remembered that the finer-grain calculation can be used to judge the accuracy of the course-grain results but tells us nothing about the accuracy of the fine-grain calculation itself.

From Equation (15.9) it is evident that the truncation error in a single

```
      SUBROUTINE EULER(X,Y,N,A,B,F)
*--
*--  Euler integrates the differential equation Y' = F(X,Y) using
*--  the Euler stepping method. The interval is X = A to X = B
*--  and a total of N steps is computed. The step size is
*--  DX = (B - A)/N and it is assumed that the starting value of Y,
*--  i.e., Y(0), has already been stored in the array Y.
*--  The function subprogram F(X,Y) must be user-supplied.
*-----------------------------------------------------------------
      REAL X(0:N),Y(0:N),A,B,DX
*
      X(0) = A
      DX = (B - A)/N
      DO 1 I = 0,N - 1
         X(I + 1) = X(I) + DX
         Y(I + 1) = Y(I) + F(X(I),Y(I)) * DX
1     CONTINUE
      RETURN
      END
```

Figure 15-2
The Fortran code for Euler's method.

step of Euler's method is proportional to $(\Delta x)^2$, the next term in the Taylor series. After completing the N steps in the interval, the accumulated error will be of order $\mathbb{O}(N(\Delta x)^2)$. Since $\Delta x = (b - a)/N$, the total accumulated error incurred in Euler's method will be of order $\mathbb{O}(\Delta x)$; that is, the error in the procedure is linear in Δx; the method is a so-called first-order procedure.

15.4.2 Example Calculations Using Euler's Method

As an example of the application of Euler's method I have tabulated the results for the simple test equation

$$y' = +y(x) \quad \text{and} \quad y(x = 0) = 1.0 \tag{15.10}$$

The analytical solution to this differential equation is $y(x) = e^x$. The results of the Euler integration for a variety of step sizes are presented in Table 15-1.

Also included in Table 15-1 and positioned below each of the computed numbers is the fractional difference between the computed values and the exact analytical result, i.e., $\delta_i = |y_i - y(x_i)|/y(x_i)$. You will notice that as the step size is diminished by a factor of 10, the fractional error also decreases by about the same factor. In addition the accumulated error after marching across the entire interval is roughly $\frac{1}{2}\Delta x$. Both of these observations are consistent with our prediction that Euler's method is a first-order procedure in Δx.

The above example yielded a very smooth and simple function over the interval $x = 0$ to $x = 1$ and yet it required on the order of 10,000 steps to obtain satisfactory results. Since the error in the calculation decreased uniformly with a decrease in the step size, we can conclude that the source of the

Table 15-1 The computed solutions to $y' = +y$ using Euler's method are compared with the exact solution $y(x) = e^x$.

X	N = 10	N = 100	N = 1000	N = 10000	EXACT
.0	1.0000000000	1.0000000000	1.0000000000	1.0000000000	1.0000000000
.1	1.1000000000 .00468	1.1046221254 .00050	1.1051156977 .00005	1.1051653926 .00000	1.1051709181
.2	1.2100000000 .00934	1.2201900399 .00099	1.2212807053 .00010	1.2213905450 .00001	1.2214027582
.3	1.3310000000 .01397	1.3478489153 .00149	1.3496564788 .00015	1.3498385612 .00001	1.3498588076
.4	1.4641000000 .01858	1.4888637336 .00198	1.4915265613 .00020	1.4917948635 .00002	1.4918246976
.5	1.6105100000 .02318	1.6446318218 .00248	1.6483094164 .00025	1.6486800560 .00002	1.6487212707
.6	1.7715610000 .02775	1.8166966986 .00298	1.8215726108 .00030	1.8220641413 .00003	1.8221188004
.7	1.948717100 .03230	2.0067633684 .00347	2.0130484867 .00035	2.0136822321 .00003	2.0137527075
.8	2.1435888100 .03682	2.2167152172 .00397	2.2246514829 .00040	2.2254519146 .00004	2.2255409285
.9	2.3579476910 .04133	2.4486326746 .00446	2.4584972757 .00045	2.4594924390 .00004	2.4596031112
1.0	2.5937424601 .04582	2.7048138294 .00495	2.7169239322 .00050	2.7181459269 .00005	2.7182818285

error is not round-off error but is rather a reflection of the inadequacies of the basic algorithm. If the solution were more rapidly varying over the interval, an even smaller step size would be required. Eventually, reducing the step size to achieve satisfactory accuracy will be offset by the growth in the round-off errors due to the increased amount of arithmetic. Even more important, if the function appearing on the right of the differential equation were much more complicated, calling this function tens of thousands of times can be quite expensive. Improvements in Euler's method are urgently needed.

15.5 IMPROVEMENTS TO EULER'S METHOD

The simplest and most direct improvements to Euler's method are based on the following observation:

In Euler's approximate algorithm for estimating the next value of y (i.e., y_{i+1}) the function is approximated by a straight line with the same slope as the tangent to the curve at the *left* end of the interval. As is illustrated in Figure 15-3, it is usually the case that much better results would be obtained if, instead, the slope of the tangent drawn at the *middle* of the interval were used for the approximating straight line.

Figure 15-3 Approximating the function $y(x)$ by a straight line using the slope at the midpoint of the interval.

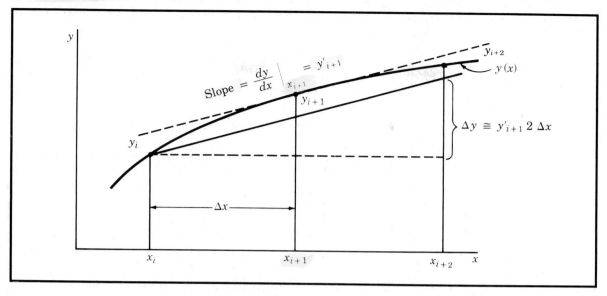

This idea is the basis of the two modifications to Euler's method known as (1) modified Euler's method and (2) improved Euler's method. Both of the new methods use an algorithm of the form

$$y_{i+1} = y_i + f_{i+1/2} \, \Delta x \qquad\qquad (15.11)$$

where $f_{i+1/2}$ represents the slope of the function $y(x)$ at the midpoint of the interval x_i to x_{i+1}. The two methods differ in how this slope is estimated.

15.5.1 The Modified Euler Method

Equation (15.11) can also be used to step from the current position (x_i, y_i) to (x_{i+2}, y_{i+2}) using the midpoint (x_{i+1}, y_{i+1}) to compute the slope of the approximating line.

$$y_{i+2} = y_i + f_{i+1}(2 \, \Delta x) \qquad\qquad (15.12)$$

where $f_{i+1} = f(x_{i+1}, y_{i+1})$. The procedure is then quite simple. Knowing the starting value of y, i.e., y_0, *and* the first computed value, y_1, the algorithm then successively computes

$$y_2 = y_0 \quad + f_1(2 \, \Delta x) \quad f_1 = f(x_1, y_1)$$
$$y_3 = y_1 \quad + f_2(2 \, \Delta x) \quad f_2 = f(x_2, y_2)$$
$$\cdots \quad \cdots \quad \cdots$$
$$y_n = y_{n-2} + f_{n-1}(2 \, \Delta x)$$

It can be shown that the accumulated error, not including round-off error, in this method is proportional to $(\Delta x)^2$; that is, the modified Euler method is a second-order method. This procedure is also known as the *midpoint method*.

Of course to start the march across the interval we need to determine the first computed value of y. (It is assumed that the initial value y_0 has been given in the statement of the problem.) This could be estimated by using the basic Euler's method,

$$y_1 = y_0 + f_0 \, \Delta x$$

However, if the entire algorithm is to be an improvement over the basic Euler's method, it is important that *every* step, including the first, be an improvement. The errors in the first step will propagate through all succeeding steps. Thus we must seek a first step that is a second-order approximation. One suggestion is to simply apply the basic Euler algorithm twice to obtain y_1 and then proceed thereafter with the procedure given in Equation (15.12).

More specifically, we use the slope at x_0—i.e., f_0—to first estimate the first computed y value, y_1. (This is Euler's method.)

$$(\Delta y)_a = f(x_0, y_0) \, \Delta x$$
$$y_1 \simeq y_0 + (\Delta y)_a$$

This estimate of y_1 can then be used to compute $f_1 = f(x_1, y_1)$, which is then used to compute a second approximation for y_1.

$$(\Delta y)_b = f_1 \, \Delta x$$

The two estimates for the first increment in y, $(\Delta y)_a, (\Delta y)_b$, are next averaged and y_1 is recomputed,

$$\Delta y = \tfrac{1}{2}[(\Delta y)_a + (\Delta y)_b]$$

This procedure is illustrated graphically in Figure 15-4.

The Fortran Code for the Modified Euler Procedure

The Fortran code for a subroutine that implements the algorithm of Equation (15.12) plus the averaging process for the first step is given in Figure 15-5.

This subroutine will ordinarily yield better results than the simple Euler method and at significantly less cost. There are, however, situations when even the simple Euler method will yield more accurate results. Example calculations for both cases are given in the next section.

Figure 15-4 The average of the slope on the left and on the right sides of the first interval is used in the first step of modified Euler's method.

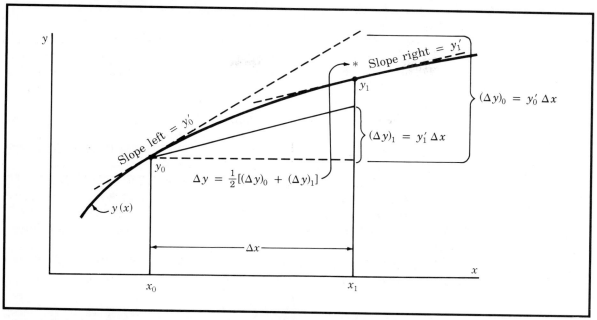

```
SUBROUTINE MIDPT(X,Y,N,A,B,F)
*--
*--    MIDPT integrates the differential equation Y' = F(X,Y)
*--    using the modified Euler algorithm. The initial value
*--    of Y(0) is assumed to already have been stored in the
*--    array Y(). The interval is X = A to X = B and the step
*--    size is (B - A)/N. The simple Euler method is applied
*--    twice to the first step and thereafter every other Y
*--    value is computed using the slope at the intermediate
*--    point. The function F(X,Y) is user-supplied.
*-----------------------------------------------------------
* VARIABLES
*
       REAL X(0:N),Y(0:N),A,B,DX
*
*-----------------------------------------------------------
* COMPUTATION
*
       DX = (B - A)/N
       X(0) = A
       X(1) = A + DX
*
*
*              To start the procedure the first Y value is
*              computed twice using Euler's method and then
*              averaging the two results
*
```

Figure 15-5
A subroutine for the modified Euler method.

Continued

```
                   DY1 = F(X(0),Y(0)) * DX
                   Y(1)= Y(0) + DY1
                   DY2 = F(X(1),Y(1)) * DX
                   Y(1)= Y(0) + .5 * (DY1 + DY2)
*
*
                   DO 1 I = 0,N-2
                       X(I + 2) = X(I) + 2. * DX
                       Y(I + 2) = Y(I) + F(X(I + 1),Y(I+1)) * 2. * DX
        1          CONTINUE
*
                   RETURN
                   END
```

Table 15-2
A comparison of
the Euler method
and the modified
Euler method ap-
plied to the equa-
tion $y' = +y$.

```
THE INTEGRATION IS FROM X = .00 TO 1.00

FOR X = .00 EXACT = 1.00000000          FOR X = .80 EXACT = 2.22554093

            EULER      MODIFIED                     EULER      MODIFIED

N =   10  1.00000000  1.00000000     N =   10  2.14358881  2.22259974
           .0000000    .0000000                 .0368235    .0013216

N =  100  1.00000000  1.00000000     N =  100  2.21671522  2.22551126
           .0000000    .0000000                 .0039656    .0000133

N = 1000  1.00000000  1.00000000     N = 1000  2.22465148  2.22554063
           .0000000    .0000000                 .0003997    .0000001

  FOR X = .20 EXACT = 1.22140276       FOR X = 1.00 EXACT = 2.71828183

            EULER      MODIFIED                     EULER      MODIFIED

N =   10  1.21000000  1.22100000     N =   10  2.59374246  2.71378988
           .0093358    .0003298                 .0458155    .0016525

N =  100  1.22019004  1.22139869     N =  100  2.70481383  2.71823653
           .0009929    .0000033                 .0049546    .0000167

N = 1000  1.22128071  1.22140272     N = 1000  2.71692393  2.71828138
           .0000999    .0000000                 .0004995    .0000002
```

Example Calculations Using the Modified Euler Method

The differential equation

$$y' = +y(x) \quad \text{and} \quad y(x = 0) = 1.0$$

is once again solved numerically, this time using the subroutine of Figure
15-5. The results are compared with the previous Euler method results in
Table 15-2. Notice that for every calculation the modified Euler method is
significantly more accurate.

As a second example, consider the differential equation

(15.13)
$$y' = \frac{1}{x^2} - \frac{y}{x} - y^2 \quad \text{and} \quad y(x = 1) = -1$$

This rather formidable-looking equation was designed to have the simple solution $y = -1/x$, as can easily be verified by substitution. The results of a numerical solution by both the simple Euler method and the modified Euler method are presented in Table 15-3.

The results for this example are rather poor for both calculations. The primary reason for this is that the solution ($y(x) = -1/x$) is a decreasing function, and thus for moderately large x the error terms will be of the same magnitude as the function $y(x)$. By decreasing the step size, the discretization error can be reduced. By progressing from a simple Euler algorithm to the modified Euler procedure (i.e., from a linear to a quadratic method in Δx) the truncation error is reduced.

15.5.2 The Improved Euler Algorithm

An alternative suggestion for improving the basic Euler method is to approximate the slope at the middle of the interval by the *average* of the slopes at the left and right sides of the interval. This is precisely what was done in computing the first step of the modified Euler method. The improved Euler algorithm reads

$$y_{i+1} = y_i + \tfrac{1}{2}(f_i + f_{i+1})\, \Delta x \qquad\qquad (15.14)$$

Table 15-3 Comparison of Euler and modified Euler results for the equation $y' = 1/x^2 - y/x - y^2$ and $y(1) = -1$.

THE INTEGRATION IS FROM X = 1.0 TO 11

FOR X = 1.0 EXACT = -1.0000000	EULER	MODIFIED
N = 10	-1.0000000	-1.0000000
	.0000	.0000
N = 100	-1.0000000	-1.0000000
	.0000	.0000
N = 1000	-1.0000000	-1.0000000
	.0000	.0000

FOR X = 5.0 EXACT = -.2000000	EULER	MODIFIED
N = 10	.1776138	-.2651459
	1.8881	.3257
N = 100	-.0769110	-.2084852
	.6154	.8424
N = 1000	-.1840351	-.2001201
	.0798	.0006

FOR X = 9.0 EXACT = -.1111111	EULER	MODIFIED
N = 10	.1032026	-.1871329
	1.9288	.6842
N = 100	.0215046	-.1269421
	1.1935	.1425
N = 1000	-.0845526	-.1113275
	.2390	.0019

FOR X = 3.0 EXACT = -.3333333	EULER	MODIFIED
N = 10	.2500000	-.4062500
	1.7500	.2188
N = 100	-.2453290	-.3384588
	.2640	.0154
N = 1000	-.3237991	-.3334048
	.0286	.0002

FOR X = 7.0 EXACT = -.1428571	EULER	MODIFIED
N = 10	.1305678	-.2095577
	1.9140	.4669
N = 100	-.0085789	-.1548795
	.9399	.0842
N = 1000	-.1212161	-.1430254
	.1515	.0012

FOR X = 11.0 EXACT = -.0909091	EULER	MODIFIED
N = 10	.0853582	-.1852320
	1.9389	1.0376
N = 100	.0345174	-.1109209
	1.3797	.2201
N = 1000	-.0602343	-.0911737
	.3374	.0029

If the function $f(x, y)$ happens to be a function of x *only*, this approximation is equivalent to integrating the equation $y' = f(x)$ by the trapezoidal rule.

Notice that since f_{i+1} depends upon y_{i+1}, Equation (15.14) cannot be solved directly for y_{i+1}. This form of equation for y_{i+1} is commonly called a *closed-type* formula since it cannot be used directly to step from one point to the next. The equations that do permit a direct stepping from point x_i to the point x_{i+1} are designated *open* formulas [see Equations (15.9) and (15.12)]. Equation (15.14) could of course be solved by iteration by guessing a value of y_{i+1} to be inserted on the right and then using Equation (15.14) to compute an improved value. However, since this equation is itself only a somewhat rough approximation, an accurate determination of y_{i+1} by this means is not warranted. Instead, we will simply carry out what amounts to a one-time iteration by first estimating y_{i+1} via the Euler method and then using Equation (15.14) to improve the estimate. The improved Euler algorithm is then for $i = 0, n - 1$,

$$f_i = f(x_i, y_i)$$
$$y_{i+1} = y_i + f_i \, \Delta x$$
$$f_{i+1} = f(x_{i+1}, y_{i+1})$$
$$y_{i+1} = y_i + \tfrac{1}{2}(f_i + f_{i+1}) \, \Delta x$$

This algorithm is a one-step procedure. That is, to proceed from point x_i to the next point we require only the values of x and y at the point x_i. You may have noticed that the modified Euler, or midpoint, method is a multistep process. To compute the value of y_{i+2} we required both the values y_i and y_{i+1}. As we shall see, multistep procedures are often more accurate and simpler to use (once they are started) than are single-step procedures, but they are much more susceptible to problems associated with instability of the solution. That is, in some solutions the error will be found to grow exponentially as the solution is marched out, or the computed values will be found to change wildly with only an infinitesimal change in the initial conditions.

Numerical Examples of the Improved Euler Method

In Table 15-4 the computed results for the differential equation $y' = -y$ with $y(x = 0) = 1$ are compared using the three methods developed thus far in this chapter. In this particular example, the midpoint method appears to be unstable. That is, the errors seem to be growing exponentially. The improved Euler method, on the other hand, has generated rather accurate values for a variety of step sizes. You should not infer from these results that one method is superior to another for all cases. The solution of differential equations is even more idiosyncratic than is the solution for roots of equations. The mode of solution should in every case be suited to the problem at

Table 15-4 The solutions of $y' = -y$, $y(0) = 1$ by the simple Euler, modified Euler, and improved Euler methods are compared.

THE INTEGRATION IS FROM X = .0 TO 10.0

FOR X = .0 EXACT = 1.00000000

		EULER	MODIFIED	IMPROVED
N =	10	1.0000000 .00000	1.0000000 .00000	1.0000000 .00000
N =	100	1.0000000 .00000	1.0000000 .00000	1.0000000 .00000
N =	1000	1.0000000 .00000	1.0000000 .00000	1.0000000 .00000

FOR X = 2.0 EXACT = .13533528

		EULER	MODIFIED	IMPROVED
N =	10	.0000000 1.00000	.0000000 1.00000	.2500000 .84726
N =	100	.1215767 .10166	.1357404 .00299	.1358225 .00360
N =	1000	.1339797 .01002	.1353398 .00003	.1353398 .00003

FOR X = 4.0 EXACT = .01831564

		EULER	MODIFIED	IMPROVED
N =	10	.0000000 1.00000	-1.0000000 55.59815	.0625000 2.41238
N =	100	.0147809 .19299	.0181021 .01166	.0184477 .00721
N =	1000	.0179506 .01993	.0183168 .00006	.0183169 .00007

FOR X = 6.0 EXACT = .00247875

		EULER	MODIFIED	IMPROVED
N =	10	.0000000 1.00000	-6.0000000 2421.57276	.0156250 5.30357
N =	100	.0017970 .27503	.0000318 .98715	.0025056 .01084
N =	1000	.0024050 .02975	.0024787 .00000	.0024790 .00010

FOR X = 8.0 EXACT = .00033546

		EULER	MODIFIED	IMPROVED
N =	10	.0000000 1.00000	-35.0000000 *********	.0039063 10.64437
N =	100	.0002185 .34874	-.0178632 54.24953	.0003403 .01448
N =	1000	.0003222 .03947	.0003336 .00542	.0003355 .00013

FOR X = 10.0 EXACT = .00004540

		EULER	MODIFIED	IMPROVED
N =	10	.0000000 1.00000	-204.0000000 *********	.0009766 20.51022
N =	100	.0000266 .41495	-.1340125 2952.82202	.0000462 .01813
N =	1000	.0000432 .04909	.0000316 .30298	.0000454 .00017

hand. Precisely how this is accomplished is learned primarily from experience, from trial and error, and of course by understanding the principles behind and the limitations inherent in each of the algorithms.

15.6 THE METHOD OF RUNGE-KUTTA

The elementary refinements of the basic Euler method were based on the idea that using the average slope of the tangent over an interval to extrapolate a function to the next point should result in greater accuracy. The method of Runge-Kutta carries this a bit further. The slope that is used in the linear extrapolation is taken to be a *weighted* average of the slope at the left end of the interval and some intermediate point. Thus the algorithm reads

(15.15)
$$y_{i+1} = y_i + f_{\text{ave}} \, \Delta x$$

where f_{ave} is determined by the equation

(15.16)
$$f_{\text{ave}} = af_i + bf_{i'}$$

where a, b are the "weights" and f_i is the function evaluated at the point x_i while $f_{i'}$ is the function evaluated at some intermediate point defined as

(15.17)
$$f_{i'} = f(x_i + \alpha \, \Delta x, \, y_i + \beta f_i \, \Delta x)$$

where the two parameters α, β specify the position of the intermediate point.

Runge and Kutta used this form of the algorithm with the four parameters chosen to optimize the accuracy of the computed result. The parameters are not totally free parameters. By expanding the function $f(x, y)$ in a Taylor series expansion (in two variables!) they were able to obtain the following constraint equations on the parameters.

(15.18)
$$a + b = 1$$
$$\alpha b = \beta b = \tfrac{1}{2}$$

These are three equations in the four unknown parameters and thus there is still some freedom in how the parameters are chosen. The particular choice of modified Euler parameters

$$a = 0 \qquad b = 1 \qquad \alpha = \beta = \tfrac{1}{2}$$

will result in an algorithm that is identical to the modified Euler method discussed earlier. And the choice of improved Euler parameters

$$a = b = \tfrac{1}{2} \qquad \alpha = \beta = 1$$

yields the improved Euler algorithm.

Both of these computational algorithms are known as second-order Runge-Kutta procedures, meaning that the accumulated truncation error is proportional to $(\Delta x)^2$ in either method.

15.6.1 Fourth-Order Runge-Kutta Algorithm

By including more sampling points in the interval, the basic Runge-Kutta method can be improved to a procedure that has an accumulated truncation error proportional to $(\Delta x)^4$—i.e., a fourth-order method. The determination of the many parameters is once again partially given by comparing with a two-variable Taylor series expansion and involves considerable algebra. The results are simply quoted below.

$$y_{i+1} = y_i + \tfrac{1}{6}[\Delta y_0 + 2\,\Delta y_1 + 2\,\Delta y_2 + \Delta y_3] \qquad (15.19)$$

where

$$
\begin{aligned}
\Delta y_0 &= f(x_i, y_i)\,\Delta x \\
\Delta y_1 &= f(x_i + \tfrac{1}{2}\,\Delta x, y_i + \tfrac{1}{2}\,\Delta y_0)\,\Delta x \\
\Delta y_2 &= f(x_i + \tfrac{1}{2}\,\Delta x, y_i + \tfrac{1}{2}\,\Delta y_1)\,\Delta x \\
\Delta y_3 &= f(x_{i+1}, y_i + \Delta y_2)\,\Delta x
\end{aligned}
\qquad (15.20)
$$

You can easily show that for the special case where the function $f(x, y)$ is a function of x *only*, the above procedure amounts to an integration of $\int f(x)\,dx$ by the Simpson's rule approximation. That is,

$$y_{i+1} = y_i + \frac{\Delta x/2}{3}\left[f(x_i) + 4f\left(x_i + \frac{\Delta x}{2}\right) + f(x_{i+1})\right] \qquad (15.21)$$

The classical fourth-order Runge-Kutta algorithm is by far the most popular method for obtaining numerical solutions to differential equations. It is very easy to code, and except for especially perverse differential equations, is very stable and accurate. The method is self-starting and the step size can easily be adjusted in the middle of a calculation to accommodate a function that is rapidly varying. There are other, more modern, methods that are somewhat more difficult to code but which are occasionally preferred over the Runge-Kutta methods since they require fewer function evaluations and are thus a bit more efficient.

15.6.2 Numerical Comparison of the Fourth-Order Runge-Kutta Method with the Previous Methods for the Test Equation y′ = −y

The solution of the differential equation

$$y' = -y \quad \text{and} \quad y(0) = 1 \qquad (15.22)$$

is $y(x) = e^{-x}$. As x increases the solution decreases exponentially while the accumulated errors wil be monotonically increasing, eventually becoming larger than the function itself. This particular equation should then be a sensitive test of the stability of the various methods. The equation is solved over the interval $x = 0$ to $x = 10$ for a variety of step sizes and by the three basic procedures covered thus far: modified Euler, improved Euler, and fourth-order Runge-Kutta. The results are presented in Table 15-5. Once again the fractional errors in the computed values are listed just below, and from these numbers we can determine that the fourth-order Runge-Kutta method is indeed fourth-order, that improved Euler is second-order, and that modified Euler appears to be unstable for this case.

Table 15-5
Modified Euler, improved Euler, and fourth-order Runge-Kutta methods are compared for the test equation $y' = -y$.

THE INTEGRATION IS FROM X = .0 TO 10.0

FOR X = .0 EXACT = 1.00000000

	MODIFIED EULER	IMPROVED EULER	RUNGE-KUTTA
N = 10	1.0000000000	1.0000000000	1.0000000000
	.00000000	.00000000	.00000000
N = 100	1.0000000000	1.0000000000	1.0000000000
	.00000000	.00000000	.00000000
N = 1000	1.0000000000	1.0000000000	1.0000000000
	.00000000	.00000000	.00000000

FOR X = 2.0 EXACT = .13533528

	MODIFIED EULER	IMPROVED EULER	RUNGE-KUTTA
N = 10	.0000000000	.2500000000	.1406250000
	1.00000000	.84726402	.03908601
N = 100	.1357403965	.1358224575	.1353355284
	.00299340	.00359976	.00000181
N = 1000	.1353397898	.1353398285	.1353352833
	.00003330	.00003358	.00000000

FOR X = 4.0 EXACT = .01831564

	MODIFIED EULER	IMPROVED EULER	RUNGE-KUTTA
N = 10	-1.0000000000	.0625000000	.0197753906
	55.59815003	2.41238438	.07969974
N = 100	.0181020924	.0184477400	.0183157053
	.01165924	.00721247	.00000362
N = 1000	.0183168258	.0183168692	.0183156389
	.00006480	.00006717	.00000000

FOR X = 6.0 EXACT = .00247875

	MODIFIED EULER	IMPROVED EULER	RUNGE-KUTTA
N = 10	-6.0000000000	.0156250000	.0027809143
	2421.57276096	5.30357490	.12190090
N = 100	.0000318472	.0025056174	.0024787656
	.98715192	.01083820	.00000544

| N = 1000 | .0024787480 | .0024790019 | .0024787522 |
| | .00000170 | .00010076 | .00000000 |

FOR X = 8.0 EXACT = .00033546

	MODIFIED EULER	IMPROVED EULER	RUNGE-KUTTA
N = 10	-35.0000000000	.0039062500	.0003910661
	**************	10.64436714	.16575154
N = 100	-.0178632268	.0003403191	.0003354651
	54.24952867	.01447697	.00000725
N = 1000	.0003336447	.0003355077	.0003354626
	.00541921	.00013435	.00000000

FOR X = 10.0 EXACT = .00004540

	MODIFIED EULER	IMPROVED EULER	RUNGE-KUTTA
N = 10	-204.0000000000	.0009765625	.0000549937
	**************	20.51022050	.21131612
N = 100	-.1340125124	.0000462230	.0000454003
	2952.82201958	.01812884	.00000906
N = 1000	.0000316446	.0000454076	.0000453999
	.30298210	.00016794	.00000000

15.7   PREDICTOR-CORRECTOR METHODS

Consider once again the two equations,

1. Modified Euler (open-type equation)

$$y_{i+1} = y_{i-1} + f_i\, 2\, \Delta x \tag{15.23}$$

2. Improved Euler (closed-type equation)

$$y_{i+1} = y_i + \tfrac{1}{2}(f_i + f_{i+1})\, \Delta x \tag{15.24}$$

Both equations are second-order in Δx. These two equations can be combined into a very popular modern procedure for solving differential equations called the *predictor-corrector method*. The idea is quite simple. First, the predictor equation, Equation (15.23), is used to estimate a value for y_{i+1}. Next, this value is inserted into the right side of Equation (15.24) which is then *iterated* once or twice to improve the value of y_{i+1}.

Ordinarily, predictor-corrector methods will employ two equations similar to those above but of higher accuracy. A common choice introduced by Milne,[1] is given below without a proof.

1. Predictor equation (Milne method)

(**15.25**)
$$y_{i+1} = y_{i-3} + \tfrac{4}{3} \Delta x (2f_i - f_{i-1} + 2f_{i-2})$$

2. Corrector equation (Milne method)

(**15.26**)
$$y_{i+1} = \tfrac{1}{3} \Delta x (f_{i+1} + 4f_i + f_{i-1})$$

You will notice that predictor-corrector methods will be difficult to start. For example, to use the Milne method, the initial point y_0 and the first three computed values, y_1, y_2, y_3, will be required before the predictor equation can be used. This will complicate the Fortran code somewhat.

15.8   SECOND-ORDER DIFFERENTIAL EQUATIONS

As discussed previously in Section 15.2 a second-order differential equation like Newton's second law, $F = m \, d^2y/dt^2$, can be rewritten as two coupled first-order equations by introducing the superfluous variable $v = dy/dt$.

(**15.27**)
$$m \frac{dv}{dt} = F(t, y, v)$$
$$\frac{dv}{dt} = v$$

These two equations can then be solved by any of the methods we have developed for first-order equations. However, we must carefully rewrite any of the algorithms that we have chosen to solve the equations so that both equations are solved *simultaneously*. That is, in the above example, for each time step $t_i \rightarrow t_{i+1}$, both a new value of y_{i+1} and a new v_{i+1} are computed.

Of course, to start the calculation initial values of *both* y and v will be required. If both of the dependent variables (y, v) are specified at the *same*

---

[1] See W. E. Milne, *Numerical Calculus*, Princeton University Press, Princeton, N.J., 1949. The predictor equation was obtained by fitting a cubic (four parameters) through the points $(f_{i-3}, f_{i-2}, f_{i-1}, f_i)$ and then integrating,

$$\int_{x_{i-3}}^{x_{i+1}} y' \, dx = y_{i+1} - y_{i-3} = \int f(x, y) \, dx \simeq \int (\text{cubic}) \, dx$$

Clearly the corrector equation is based on a similar integration using Simpson's rule [see Equation (14.14)].

value of the independent variable t, the problem is called an *initial-value problem*.[2] For *any* other form of the specifications for y and v the problem is called a *boundary-value* problem. The typical starting conditions for an initial-value problem are $y(t = 0) = y_0$, $v(t = 0) = v_0$, while examples of specifications for a boundary-value problem might be $[y(t = 0) = y_0,$ $v(t = 10) = v_{10}]$ or $[y(t = 0) = y_a, y(t = 10) = y_b]$. In general, numerical solutions to boundary-value problems are substantially more difficult to obtain than are the solutions to a corresponding initial-value problem. In this section we will be concerned exclusively with initial-value problems, procedures for solving boundary-value problems will be discussed in Section 15.9.

Returning to the two coupled Equations (15.27), they can be written in a more general notation as

$$\frac{dy_a(t)}{dt} = f_a(t, y_a, y_b)$$
$$\frac{dy_b(t)}{dt} = f_b(t, y_a, y_b) \tag{15.28}$$

where $y_a = y$, $y_b = v$, and $f_a(t, y_a, y_b) = (1/m)F(t, y, v)$, $f_b(t, y_a, y_b) = v$. If we have in hand a satisfactory procedure for solving the equation $y' = f(t, y)$, say the subroutine MIDPT of Figure 15-5, it is then a straightforward exercise to adapt this code to solving both of Equations (15.28) simultaneously.

15.8.1 The Fortran Code to Solve Two Simultaneous Differential Equations Using the Midpoint Method

The Fortran code for a subroutine MIDPT2 that will solve Equations (15.28) is given in Figure 15-6. It is assumed that the starting values of both of the dependent variables y_a and y_b have already been stored in the arrays YA, YB. Also the user-written functions f_a, f_b must be supplied elsewhere in the assembled program.

15.8.2 Examples of Solutions of Coupled Differential Equations

In this section the subroutine of Figure 15-6 is used to solve two problems involving coupled differential equations. The first example is a continuation of the $F = ma$ problem.

---

[2] Even if we specify both $v(t)$ and $y(t)$ at the *end* of the time interval the problem is still classified as an initial-value problem. In this case the solution is obtained by using a negative time step and marching backward across the interval.

Figure 15-6
The midpoint method is used to solve two coupled equations.

```
SUBROUTINE MIDPT2(X,YA,YB,N,A,B,FA,FB)
REAL X(0:N),YA(0:N),YB(0:N),A,B,DX
INTEGER N
X(0) = A
DX = (B - A)/N
X(1) = A + DX
DYA1 = FA(X(0),YA(0),YB(0)) * DX
DYB1 = FB(X(0),YA(0),YB(0)) * DX
YA(1) = YA(0) + DYA1
YB(1) = YB(0) + DYB1
DYA2 = FA(X(1),YA(1),YB(1)) * DX
YA(1) = YA(0) + .5 * (DYA1 + DYA2)
DYB2 = FB(X(1),YA(1),YB(1)) * DX
YB(1) = YB(0) + .5 * (DYB1 + DYB2)

DO 1 I = 0,N - 2
   X(I + 2) = X(I) + 2. * DX
   YA(I + 2) = YA(I) + FA(X(I + 1),YA(I + 1),YB(I + 1)) * DX * 2.
   YB(I + 2) = YB(I) + FB(X(I + 1),YA(I + 1),YB(I + 1)) * DX * 2.
1 CONTINUE
RETURN
END
```

The Position vs. Time of a Projectile, Including Air Drag

If an object is thrown straight up, the trajectory is determined by solving Newton's second law, $F = ma$, where the force on the object is given as

(15.29)
$$F = -mg - \lambda v^2 \quad \text{if } v > 0$$
$$= -mg + \lambda v^2 \quad \text{if } v < 0$$

That is, the air drag force λv^2 is always directed opposite to the direction of the velocity.

The initial conditions for an object that is thrown straight up are

$$y_a(0) = y(t = 0) = y_0$$
$$y_b(0) = v(t = 0) = v_0$$

For this problem we will use $y_0 = 0$, $v_0 = 20$ m/sec, and the coefficient of the drag force will be taken as $\lambda = 0.1$ kg/m. The two functions that must be supplied are then

$$f_a(t, y_a, y_b) = a = \frac{1}{m}F = -g - \frac{v}{|v|}\frac{\lambda}{m}v^2$$
$$f_b(t, y_a, y_b) = v = y_b$$

Figure 15-7 The computed trajectory of an object thrown straight up and subject to air drag.

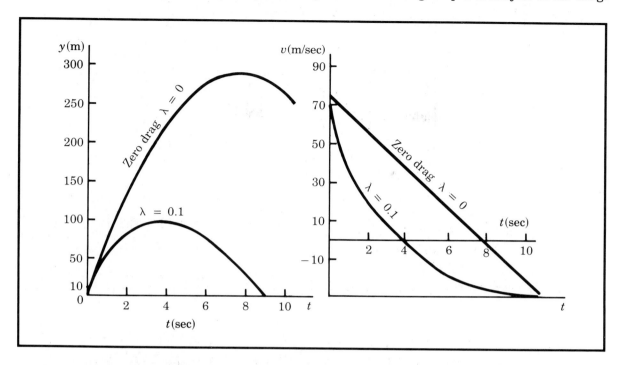

The results of the calculation over the time interval $t = 0$ to $t = 10$ sec are shown in Figure 15-7.

Before leaving this example I should point out the significance of what has been done. A large fraction of the problems of engineering and science are expressed in terms of the forces acting between atoms, or support beams, or machine parts, or any number of other possibilities. The computer code to solve the equation $F = ma$ frees engineers and scientists from the less productive labor of finding solutions to an equation and enables them to spend more time on the "loftier" ideas concerning the principles or assumptions involved in setting up the problem.

Coupled Differential Equations: The Predator-Prey Problem

In the previous example, a second-order differential equation was rewritten as two *coupled* first-order equations. This is not the only way that coupled equations can arise. Frequently a physical problem will be specified in terms of numerous variables and a variety of relations among the variables. Often the relations are differential equations. One example of a problem of this type is the predator-prey problem.

The predator-prey problem is an attempt to understand how two or more species compete with each other in a limited environment with limited resources. This is a very complicated problem, and as with all complicated problems in science and engineering, we begin by replacing the original problem, which we cannot solve, by a simpler but similar one that we can solve. In solving the easier problem we usually gain some information that will lead to the next refinement of the model.

First, we consider a single species, say foxes, in an infinite environment, with an instant maturation period. If we start with more than two foxes, the rate of increase of the population is likely to be proportional to the number of foxes now present.

$$\frac{dN_f}{dt} \propto N_f$$

or

(15.30)
$$\frac{dN_f}{dt} = G_f N_f$$

where G_f is the growth rate of the fox population. This is the same equation that was used to describe radioactive decay in Section 14.2. Since G_f is positive, the solution is a growing exponential.

(15.31)
$$N_f(t) = N_0 e^{G_f t}$$

If the environment is finite—e.g., an island— we might expect that there is a maximum number of foxes that can be supported, M_f. This could be included in the model as

(15.32)
$$\frac{dN_f}{dt} = G_f N_f(t)\left[1 - \frac{N_f(t)}{M_f}\right]$$

so that the growth rate approaches zero as the population approaches the limit of the population, M_f. The solution of this differential equation is sketched at the top of page 579. Notice, there are problems with the model already. You might expect the population to first overshoot the maximum before some foxes begin to die off. That is, we expect to see some oscillations at the top of the curve of $N_f(t)$ vs. t. I will leave this refinement out just now; perhaps you can think of a way of including it later.

The next refinement is to introduce a second species (rabbits) to the environment. An equation similar to Equation (15.32) will describe the population of the rabbits. At this point the populations are controlled by two uncoupled equations that can be solved independently. Of course the rabbit and fox populations are not independent; there is a competition between the two species. To put it bluntly, the fox population will benefit at the expense of the rabbit population. A new competition term must be added to the equations for both N_f and N_r.

The competition term will reflect the idea that the growth rate of each

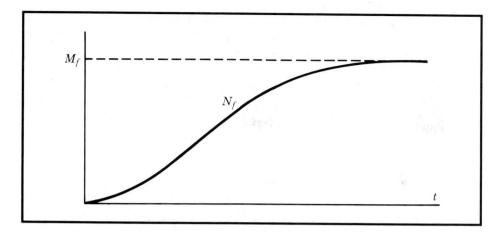

species will depend upon the likelihood of two members of different species meeting. That is, the term will be proportional to the product $N_f N_r$. The equations for the growth rates now read

$$\frac{dN_f}{dt} = G_f N_f \left(1 - \frac{N_f}{M_f}\right) + A_f N_f N_r \tag{15.33}$$

$$\frac{dN_r}{dt} = G_r N_r \left(1 - \frac{N_r}{M_r}\right) + A_r N_f N_r \tag{15.34}$$

If the coefficient A is positive, the species will benefit from the encounter (i.e., foxes eat rabbits), and conversely, if the coefficient is negative. The two equations above describing the populations of competing species are known as the *Lotka-Volterra equations*.

Before solving these two equations, I will add one more simple refinement. Since the fox population depends heavily on the rabbits for food, but not the reverse, we would expect this to be reflected in the maximum number of foxes. As a hypothesis

$$\text{If } N_r > 10 N_f \quad \text{then } M_f = M_f$$

$$\text{If } N_r \leq 10 N_f \quad \text{then } M_f \to \frac{1}{2}\left[1 + \exp\left(1 - \frac{10 N_f}{N_r}\right)\right] M_f \tag{15.35}$$

Finally, some of each species will be fortunate enough to avoid starvation and being eaten and will die a natural death after a normal life span. That is, there will be a decrease in the population now, at time t, which will be proportional to the number of the species alive at time $t - t_0$, where t_0 is the life span of the species.

There are numerous additional refinements you could add to this model, but let us proceed directly to the numerical solution. I will ignore the correction due to the finite life span, because it makes the Fortran code rather long.

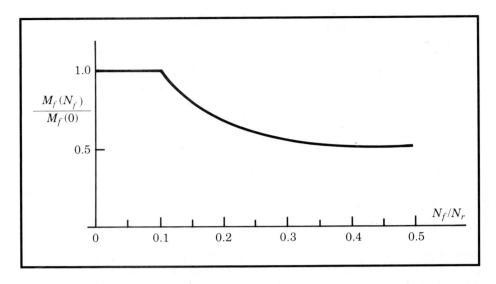

The Fortran code to solve Equations (15.33) and (15.34) used the subroutine MIDPT2 of Figure 15-6. All that is additionally required is the code for the main calling program, the two function subprograms for the derivative functions, and some reasonable estimates for all of the parameters. The Fortran code for the derivative functions is given in Figure 15-8. The values used for the parameters are given in Figure 15-9 and the populations of both species are graphed versus time in Figure 15-10.

Of course in actual situations the comparison of computed results with experiment is very difficult, since there are seldom only two species and the factors controlling the populations are much more numerous, complicated, and perhaps poorly understood than those discussed here. However, Equations (15.33) and (15.34) are a start, and building from these, extremely complicated "world population forecasting" codes have been constructed. Their validity is of course no better than the assumptions that were built into the code, as is also the case in the rabbit-fox problem.

The two example calculations of this section illustrate how two very dissimilar problems can be cast in terms of coupled first-order differential equations and can be solved by almost identical means. However, these examples are inadequate to convey to you the enormous variety of problems in all branches of science and engineering that can also be cast in a similar form and solved by the methods of this chapter. This is an extremely important concept that I cannot allow to slip by unnoticed.

The primary reason for the tremendous progress in the physical sciences and engineering in the last several centuries is that we have learned to express problems in terms of tightly phrased mathematical equations and these equations are then solved or manipulated in place of the original phenomena. The solution of the abstract equations, once done, understood, and tested, then is used to understand the original problem and any other physical phenomena that can be phrased in a mathematically similar structure. The trick is to be sufficiently fluent in mathematics to recognize two

```
      FUNCTION DFOXDT(R,F,T)
      COMMON/FOX/GF,AF,XF
*
*
*        GF   --   the growth rate of the foxes
*        AF   --   competition coef. for foxes with rabbits
*        XF   --   maximum number of foxes
*        R    --   current number of rabbits
*        F    --   current number of foxes
*        T    --   current time
*        XXF  --   adjusted maximum number of foxes
*
      XXF = XF
      IF(R .LE. 10. * F)XXF = .5 * XF * (1. + EXP(1. - 10. * F/R))
      DFOXDT = GF * F * (1. - F/XXF) + AF * R * F
      RETURN
      END
*
*

      FUNCTION DRABDT(R,F,T)
*
      COMMON/RAB/GR,AR,XR
*
*        GR   --   growth rate for rabbits
*        AR   --   competition coef. for rabbits with foxes
*        XR   --   maximum number of rabbits
*
      DRABDT = GR * R * (1. - R/XR) + AR * R * F
      RETURN
      END
```

Figure 15-8
The Fortran code for the two derivative functions in the Lotka-Volterra equations.

```
A SOLUTION OF TWO COUPLED DIFFERENTIAL EQUATIONS
       THE PREDATOR-PREY PROBLEM
            (RABBITS-FOXES)

THE CALCULATION EXTENDS FROM
     T =      .00 DAYS TO
     T = 250.00 DAYS

     THE INITIAL POPULATIONS ARE

          RABBITS -   10.
          FOXES   -    4.

     PARAMETERS

                           RABBITS       FOXES
          GROWTH RATE         .05          .02
          COMPETITION RATE  -.0004        .0001
          MAX. POPULATION  4000.00       250.00
```

Figure 15-9
The parameters used in the solution of the Lotka-Volterra equations.

Figure 15-10
The rabbit and
fox populations
as a function of
time.

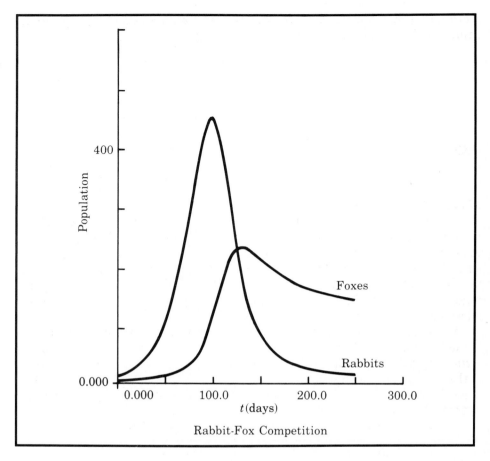

Rabbit-Fox Competition

dissimilar problems as being mathematically similar. Newton's second law and the competition of rabbits and foxes appear totally unrelated, yet both can be expressed in terms of second-order differential equations and solved by identical means. To a scientist or engineer, once the phenomena are approximately described in terms of equations, understanding the phenomena reduces to a tested recipe for the solution of the equations. These phenomena and any other that are described by similar equations are then understood completely, within the limitations of the assumptions that went into setting up the problem, with the solution of the equations. In short, coding a problem for solution on the computer is a true test of your understanding of the problem.

15.9   BOUNDARY-VALUE PROBLEMS

The solutions of coupled differential equations given to this point have been concerned with initial-value problems only. Boundary-value problems are usually much more difficult. You will recall that a boundary-value problem is ordinarily one in which the additional constraints are specified at *different* values of the independent variable. For example,

$$\frac{dv}{dt} = \frac{1}{m}F(t, y, v)$$

$$\frac{dy}{dt} = v$$

with

$$y(t = 0) = y_0 \qquad y(t = T) = y_T$$

where T is a given constant.

The initial-value problem started with the values for y_0, v_0 and then proceeded to step along the t axis computing successive values of y_i, v_i along the way. In the problem above we have a dilemma: we have no starting value for v. We might try guessing a value for v_0, then march across the t interval to $t = T$ and finally check whether $y(t = T)$ is indeed equal to the given condition y_T. In the likely event that it is not, we would alter the original guess for v_0 and start over.

If all this sounds vaguely familiar, rather like root-solving, it was intended so, for in this case we are searching for a single number, the *missing initial condition* v_0. Thus the task is to phrase the current problem in terms of the root-solving techniques of Chapter 11. Remember that the "variable" is v_0. Therefore, the function whose root we seek must be zero for a value of v_0 that ultimately results in $y(t = T) = y_T$.

First recall the structure of the subroutine MIDPT2.

```
SUBROUTINE MIDPT2 (T,YA,YB,N,A,B,FA,FB)
COMMON/INITL/TO,YAO,YBO
REAL T(0:N),YA(0:N),YB(0:N)
```

and next consider the following rather odd function.

```
FUNCTION F(X)
 COMMON/INITL/TO,YAO,YBO
 COMMON/ENDPT/N,YAF          YAF is the given end-
                            point of the first function ya.

 EXTERNAL FA,FB

 REAL T(0:100),YA(0:100),YB(0:100)
*
 YBO = X
*
 CALL MIDPT2(T,YA,YB,N,A,B,FA,FB)
*
 F = YA(N) - YAF
 RETURN
 END
```

This function is *zero* when the boundary condition is satisfied—i.e., $y_a(t = T) = y_T$—and the independent variable is $y_b(0)$ or in our case, v_0. All that remains is to use an appropriate root-solving subroutine, say the secant method, to solve the problem. You are I am sure aware that the solution will require solving the entire initial-value problem perhaps hundreds of times. That is, each call to the function F(X) solves a complete initial-value problem. There are, thankfully, more efficient means in existence for some problems, but for moderately small problems and if the computer time is not excessive, the above method is adequate.

This procedure for solving boundary-value problems is called *shooting*, in an obvious analogy to trajectory problems. Most other methods for solving boundary-value problems are handled in a similar fashion—that is, converting the problem into a search for the equivalent initial-value problem.

15.10 CONCLUSION

As was mentioned in the introduction, the discussion in this chapter is definitely not state-of-the-art numerical methods; yet it should be sufficient for solving the majority of differential equations that you will encounter. The fancier methods of solving differential equations will no doubt be discussed later in your career. Actually, to solve differential equations more carefully than we have done here requires more than just fancier methods. A detailed understanding of the growth of numerical errors in a computation; some knowledge of whether a particular method applied to a specific equation is stable or unstable—that is, if we reduce the step size does the error increase; a feeling for choosing the appropriate procedure for a particular equation that minimizes the error, maximizes the accuracy, and the efficiency, and uses the smallest storage are of prime concern to an advanced course in numerical solutions of differential equations. A few relatively readable texts are listed in the References.

PROBLEMS

1. Solve the following differential equations by arranging the terms in each variable on opposite sides of the equation using $y' = dy/dx$ into a form

$$M(x)\ dx = N(y)\ dy$$

and integrating. In each case determine the value of the integration constant by imposing the extra condition. Verify that your solution is indeed a solution of the original equation.

a. $y'y = x$ $\qquad\qquad\qquad$ $y(2) = 4$

b. $xy' = 2y$ $\qquad\qquad\qquad$ $y(2) = 4$

c. $y' = 2y$ $\qquad\qquad\qquad$ $y(0) = 1$

d. $L\dfrac{dI(t)}{dt} + RI(t) = 0$ $\qquad$ $I(0) = 2$ $\qquad$ $L = 0.001, R = 50$

e. $N(t) = k\dfrac{dN(t)}{dt}$ $\qquad\qquad$ $N(0) = N_0$ $\qquad$ $k = $ constant

2. Replace the following differential equations by two (or more) first-order differential equations by introducing new variables. Be sure to rewrite the extra conditions in terms of the new variables.

   a. The equation describing the oscillations in time of the charge $Q(t)$ on the plates of a capacitor placed in an electric circuit containing the capacitor (capacitance, C) and a coil (inductance, L) is

$$L\frac{d^2Q(t)}{d^2t} + \frac{1}{C}Q(t) = 0 \qquad Q(0) = Q_0, \quad \frac{dQ}{dt}\bigg|_{t=0} = 0$$

   b. The equation for the steady-state heat conduction through a large flat slab with a temperature-dependent heat conductivity ($\lambda = \lambda_0 + \alpha T$) is given below. The solution describes the temperature $T(x)$ as a function of x through the slab.

$$\frac{d}{dx}\left[(\lambda_0 + \alpha T)\frac{dT}{dx}\right] = 0 \qquad T(0) = 5, \frac{dT}{dx}\bigg|_{x=0} = 1$$

   c. The equations

$$a_x = \frac{d^2x}{dt^2} = -k\frac{x}{r^3}$$

$$a_y = \frac{d^2y}{dt^2} = -k\frac{v}{r^3}$$

   with

$$r = (x^2 + y^2)^{1/2} \qquad \text{and} \qquad k = Gm_1$$

   determine the orbital motion of one object about another when the force acting between the two is the gravitational force. The constant G is the gravitational force strength (6.6720×10^{-11} N-m^2/kg^2) and m_1, m_2 are the masses of the two objects. The initial conditions are

$$x(0) = -2.0 \times 10^7 \text{ m} \qquad \left.\frac{dx}{dt}\right|_0 = 0$$

$$y(0) = 0 \qquad\qquad \left.\frac{dy}{dt}\right|_0 = 5000 \text{ m/sec}$$

$$m_1 = m_{\text{earth}} \qquad\qquad m_2 = 10 \text{ kg}$$

$$= 5.97 \times 10^{24} \text{ kg}$$

3. Solve the following equations with the help of a calculator using Euler's method. Carry out five steps using the indicated step size and compare with the exact solution.

Equation	Initial condition	Δx	Exact solution
a. $y' = -y/x$	$y(1) = 1.0$	0.1	$y(x) = 1/x$
*b. $y' = -y^2$	$y(1) = 1.0$	0.1	$y(x) = 1/x$
c. $y' = -y/x$	$y(1) = 1.0$	-0.1	$y(x) = 1/x$
d. $y' = x + y$	$y(0) = 0$	0.4	$y(x) = e^x - 1 - x$

4. Solve the differential equations of the previous problem using the modified Euler method.
5. Solve the differential equation $y' = -y$ using the modified Euler method as in Table 15-4, using a step size of 0.10. However, start the calculation at $x = 6.0$ and use $y(6.0) = 0.002478752$. Notice how the solution ultimately begins to alternate in sign. (This will depend on the word length of your calculator or computer.)
6. Show that the two choices for the parameters a, b, α, β given in Section 15.6 do indeed result in algorithms identical to the modified and improved Euler methods, respectively.
7. (a) Write a Fortran subroutine MIDPT4 that will handle four simultaneous coupled differential equations. (b) Test this code by solving Problem 15.2c. (Use $N = 1000$ and integrate from $t_0 = 0$ to $t_f = 50,000$ sec.)
8. Carry out one step in detail using the fourth-order Runge-Kutta algorithm of Section 15.6.1 applied to the initial-value problem

$$y' = \left(\frac{y}{x}\right) + 2\left(\frac{y}{x}\right)^2 \qquad y(1) = -\frac{1}{2} \qquad y_{\text{exact}} = -\frac{x}{2 + 2\ln(x)}$$

Use a step size of $\Delta x = 0.1$ and compare with the exact solution.
9. (a) Write a general-purpose Fortran subroutine to implement the fourth-order Runge-Kutta algorithm of Section 15.6.1. (b) Test the code by solving the differential equation

$$y' = 4x - 2\frac{y}{x} \qquad y(1) = 1 \qquad y_{\text{exact}} = x^2$$

and compare with the exact result.

10. Alter the rabbit-fox problem to account for the natural death of both species, as described in Section 15.8.2.

11. Apply the predictor-corrector method using Equations (15.23) and (15.24) and carry out two steps applied to the equation

$$y' = -2xy^2 \qquad y(1) = 1 \qquad y_{\text{exact}} = \frac{1}{x^2}$$

Start with a step size of $\Delta x = 0.01$, compute y_0 and y_1 from the exact solution, and use these values and the predictor equation, (15.23), to estimate y_2. Then apply the corrector equation, (15.24), twice to improve the estimate of y_2. Then move on to calculate y_3.

12. Solve the previous problem using the predictor-corrector method of Milne [Equations (15.25) and (15.26)].

13. Write a complete Fortran program to implement the predictor corrector method using Equations (15.23) and (15.24). The main program should use an appropriate method to first compute y_1 in order to get the procedure started and then call a subroutine to apply the predictor-corrector equations and obtain a solution. Test the code on the equation given in Problem 15.11.

14. Write a complete Fortran program to implement the predictor-corrector method using the Milne equations, (15.25) and (15.26). The main program should use an appropriate method (fourth-order Runge-Kutta) to first compute y_1, y_2, y_3 in order to get the procedure started and then call a subroutine MILNE to apply the predictor-corrector equations and obtain a solution. Test the code on the equation given in Problem 15.11.

15. The differential equation describing heat conduction in Problem 15.2b is specified as an initial-value problem. It is more common to specify the temperature at two points on the slab and solve the differential equation to obtain $T(x)$ for the remaining x values. The conditions then might be

$$T(0) = T_0 = 0 \qquad T(x = 10) = T_{10} = 100$$

With these conditions the equation becomes a boundary-value problem. Set up the Fortran code that will use the subroutine MIDPT2 of Figure 15-6 and a root-solver, say SECANT, to obtain the solution of the differential equation in the manner of Section 15.9.

CHAPTER 16

ERROR ANALYSIS

16.1 INTRODUCTION

Conventionally, a discussion of error analysis precedes the study of the various numerical methods we have covered to this point. However, there are several compelling reasons for postponing this particular topic till last. First, particularly for the novice, it is important to develop a feel for how numerical procedures work and acquire experience in correcting computational problems as they arise before attacking the complicated and subtle job of predicting and verifying the accuracy of a calculation.

But perhaps just as important is the impression most students have that error analysis is terribly tedious and boring. The description of significant figures and round-off error, which is usually first encountered in a freshman physics laboratory, is quite often felt to be a rather monotonous, even painful, experience. Instead of taking advantage of the enthusiasm of novices and their desire to involve themselves in some laboratory work, a detour into a study of all the things that can go wrong in analyzing data often is less productive than the instructor had hoped. After the experiment is finished or after a calculation has been completed is certainly not the appropriate time to begin to be concerned about experimental or numerical errors, but it most definitely is a point at which those errors can be better appreciated.

At this stage of your study of numerical methods I am sure you would agree that the importance of a valid estimate of the total errors involved in a numerical solution cannot be overstressed. Frequently the error estimate itself is more valuable than the actual answer. If your computed results are to be of any value whatsoever, you must be able to justify your confidence in them by some manner of validity check. Of course there is no way to be 100 percent sure of any result, but the prudent engineer will have carried out every reasonable test before submitting a solution to a problem and the estimate of the uncertainty of the results should always be part of the solution.

The numerical error in a computation has been an incidental concern in most of the example programs to this point. We are aware of the deleterious effects that a finite computer word length can have on a variety of calculations. And we have seen that retaining too few terms in a Taylor series when approximating a function can often invalidate a calculation. The purpose of this chapter is to summarize these error considerations and, where possible, to suggest remedies.

The study of errors in numerical computation is a vast and complex field which is seldom studied in isolation and is usually tacked onto the analysis of individual problems. The discussion in this chapter is by no means complete; however, it should be adequate to at least begin an error analysis of the problems you face in the future.

16.2   A REVIEW OF DEFINITIONS RELATING TO ERROR ANALYSIS

16.2.1   Significant Figures

The numbers used in mathematics are exact. For example,

$$\tfrac{5}{7} = 0.714285714285714 \ldots$$

$$\pi = 3.1415926536 \ldots$$

$$e = 2.7182818285 \ldots$$

where . . . indicates that the number continues indefinitely either by repeating a pattern of digits (714285 in the case of $\tfrac{5}{7}$) or by never repeating any such pattern as in the case of e and π. The numbers used to represent physical quantities are never exact. A number that represents a measured physical quantity is also used to reflect the quality of the measurement itself. For example, measuring the temperature with a common household thermometer can at best result in a determination of the temperature to $\pm \tfrac{1}{2}$ °C. A measured temperature could be 27.5 °C, indicating that the measurement has determined three figures with some uncertainty in the last digit. The same temperature measured by a more accurate laboratory thermometer may result in a value of 27.500 °C, indicating that in this measurement five digits have been determined with a presumed error in the last digit. The first measurement has three significant figures and the second has five. Explicitly writing trailing zeros on a quantity usually means that these zeros are intended to be significant figures. On the other hand, *leading* zeros are never counted as significant figures. A standard convention for indicating how many digits are of significance in a measured quantity is to write the numbers in scientific notation—e.g., 2.75×10^1 and 2.7500×10^1 for the two measured temperatures.

Next, if the temperatures are converted to Kelvin by adding 273.16, the second measurement of the temperature would be written as 3.0066×10^2, again indicating five significant digits. This number would not, however, be a realistic representation of the less accurate measurement. After all, simply converting from Celsius to Kelvin cannot increase the accuracy or the number of significant digits in the result. To reflect the three-figure accuracy of the measured quantity the result is *rounded* to 3.01×10^2 K.

Furthermore, when two numbers are combined in the arithmetic operation of multiplication or division, the result cannot have more significant figures than *any* of the numbers that enter into the expression. This of course means that the result will at best have the same number of significant digits as the *least* accurate number used. Numerical constants that are part of an arithmetic expression will be assumed to have an infinite number of significant digits or at least the number corresponding to the word length of the computer.

16.2.2   Relative and Absolute Error

If the error in a temperature measurement is ±0.5 °C out of a measured value of 27.5 °C, the result is then represented as $T = 27.5 \pm 0.5$ °C. The error in the measurement has the units of temperature and is called the *absolute* error. Another way to express the size of the error in the measured value is to indicate the size of the error relative to the actual measured value. This may be done as a fraction as $|\Delta T|/T = 0.5/27.5 = 0.02$ and is then called the *fractional* or *relative* error. Another common usage is to express this result as a percentage, say 2 percent, indicating that the temperature measurement is correct to 2 parts in 100. Also, notice that since there is only *one* significant figure in the absolute error (0.5 °C) it would be inconsistent to retain more in the relative error.

Addition of Errors as a Result of Arithmetic Operations

When adding (or subtracting) two numbers, both of which have experimental errors, the *absolute* error of the result is the *sum* of the *absolute* errors of each of the original numbers.

$$T_1 = 27.5 \pm 0.5 \ °C$$

$$T_2 = 36.445 \pm 0.005 \ °C$$

$$T_1 + T_2 = 63.945 \pm 0.505 \ °C = 63.9 \pm 0.5 \ °C$$

A digital position in a result of addition or subtraction is a significant figure *only* if the same digital position is a significant figure in *all* of the terms involved. Thus, even though T_2 has significant digits in the 10^{-3} position, the result of adding or subtracting T_1 is rounded to the 10^{-1} position since this number contains significant digits only to the tenths position.

The same absolute error results from a subtraction.

$$T_2 - T_1 = 8.945 \pm 0.505 \ °C = 8.9 \pm 0.5 \ °C$$

Notice that even though the less accurate number has three significant figures, the result of the subtraction has only two. This is because the error is in the first digit after the decimal and representing the result as 8.94 would incorrectly suggest significance to the last digit. This is an important example of how significant figures can be lost as a result of subtracting two numbers of like size.

When multiplying (or dividing) two numbers, both of which have experimental errors, the *relative* error of the result is the *sum* of the *relative* errors of each of the original numbers.

You can easily see this result by symbolically writing the product of two numbers as

$$(T_1 \pm \Delta T_1)(T_2 \pm \Delta T_2) = \left[T_1\left(1 \pm \frac{\Delta T_1}{T_1}\right)\right]\left[T_2\left(1 \pm \frac{\Delta T_2}{T_2}\right)\right]$$

$$= (T_1 T_2)\left[1 \pm \left(\frac{\Delta T_1}{T_1} + \frac{\Delta T_2}{T_2}\right) + \frac{\Delta T_1 \Delta T_2}{T_1 T_2}\right]$$

Since the last term in the brackets is much smaller that the first two terms, the relative error in the product can be identified as $(\Delta T_1/T_1 + \Delta T_2/T_2)$. Thus

$$(27.5 \pm 2\%)(27.500 \pm 0.02\%) = 756.25 \pm 2.02\% = 756 \pm 2\%$$

The Error in a Function $f(x \pm \Delta x)$

If we assume that the error Δx in a number x is much smaller than the number, an arbitrary function of $x \pm \Delta x$ may then be expanded in a Taylor series as

$$f(x \pm \Delta x) \simeq f(x) \pm f'(x) \, \Delta x + \cdots$$

Thus the error in the function is roughly $f'(x) \, \Delta x$. For example, if a number plus its error is represented as $T + \Delta T$, then the corresponding absolute error in the logarithm of the number is[1]

$$\ln(T + \Delta T) = \ln(T) + \Delta[\ln(T)] = \ln(T) + \frac{1}{T} \Delta T$$

i.e., the *absolute* error in the logarithm of a number is the same as the relative error in that number. (We have seen this result before in Section 13.8.) Similarly, the error in $(T + \Delta T)^4$ is $4T^3 \Delta T$.

Finally, all of the considerations of error in numbers referred to experimental error. But the numbers used in computations are likewise only approximate values limited by the word length of the computer and so each of the concerns that are allotted to experimental values must simultaneously be given to all computed quantities as well.

16.3 TYPES OF ERROR

The types of errors present in most computations can be separated into four classes:

Experimental
Error: Measurement error present in all data that is submitted for analysis. The numerical methods used to analyze the data may have the effect of amplifying or diminishing the experimental error.

Round-Off
Error: Caused by the finite word length of the computer and, except for being much smaller, has the same characteristics as experimental error.

Discretization
Error: Basically, the result of using calculus equations that assume $\Delta x \to 0$, while the smallest Δx used in the calculation is finite. These errors will diminish as $\Delta x \to 0$.

Truncation
Errors: Usually refer to the approximation of a function by a straight line or a parabola over a limited interval. As with discretization errors, if the interval is reduced, the errors should decrease. Also, the errors can be reduced by in-

---

[1] Recall that the derivative of the logarithm is

$$\frac{d}{dT} \ln(T) = \frac{1}{T}$$

creasing the level of the approximation by, for example, replacing a linear approximation by a parabolic approximation.

We have encountered each of these errors at various points in this text. Here, I will concentrate on each type individually and try to show how to recognize impending problems and perhaps how to minimize them.

16.4   ROUND-OFF ERRORS

Ordinarily, the easiest error to spot and one that can be the most troublesome is round-off error. Typically, problems with round-off error are caused by a dramatic loss of significant figures when either (1) numbers of similar size are subtracted, or when (2) an elementary arithmetic operation is repeated hundreds of thousands of times, each time the round-off error accumulating inexorably.

16.4.1   A Calculation of π

One of the earliest calculations of π was done by Archimedes who compared the (unknown) circumference of a circle with the (known) circumference of a regular polygon inscribed within the circle. If the circle has a unit radius and a square is inscribed within the circle, as drawn in Figure 16-1, the length of one side of the square is[2]

$$S = 2 \sin\left(\frac{\pi}{4}\right) = 2\left(\frac{1}{\sqrt{2}}\right) = \sqrt{2} \qquad (16.1)$$

Thus, the circumference is $4S = 4\sqrt{2}$. This is then the first approximation for the circumference of the unit circle (i.e., 2π). If we next label this approximation for π as the kth-order approximation, p_k, where the number of sides of the inscribed polygon is $n = 2^k$, then

$$p_k = \frac{n}{2}[2 \sin(\theta_k)] = 2^k \sin(\theta_k) \qquad (16.2)$$

where the angle is given by $\theta_k = \pi/n = \pi/2^k$.

---

[2] Of course, Archimedes did not have trigonometric functions or square roots available to him. His calculation is all the more impressive for this reason.

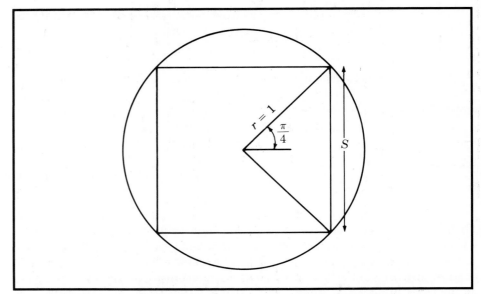

Figure 16.1 A square is inscribed within a unit circle.

Doubling the number of sides—i.e., $k \to k + 1$ then yields

(16.3)
$$p_{k+1} = 2(2^k) \sin(\tfrac{1}{2} \theta_k) \qquad {}^*$$

Equations (16.2) and (16.3) can be related using the trigonometric identity

(16.4)
$$\sin^2\left(\frac{\theta}{2}\right) = \frac{1}{2}[1 - \cos(\theta)]$$

$$= \frac{1}{2}\{1 - [1 - \sin^2(\theta)]^{1/2}\}$$

which then yields

(16.5)
$$p_{k+1} = \sqrt{2}(2^k)\left\{1 - \left[1 - \left(\frac{p_k}{2^k}\right)^2\right]^{1/2}\right\}^{1/2}$$

Starting with $k = 2$, $p_2 = 2\sqrt{2}$, we can apply this equation repeatedly to obtain ever-improved estimates for π by using inscribed polygons with ever more sides. Thus for $k = 3$ (8 sides) we obtain

$$p_3 = \sqrt{2}(4)\left\{1 - \left[1 - \left(\frac{2\sqrt{2}}{4}\right)^2\right]^{1/2}\right\}^{1/2}$$

$$= \sqrt{2}(4)\left[1 - \frac{1}{\sqrt{2}}\right]^{1/2}$$

$$= 3.0614675 \ldots$$

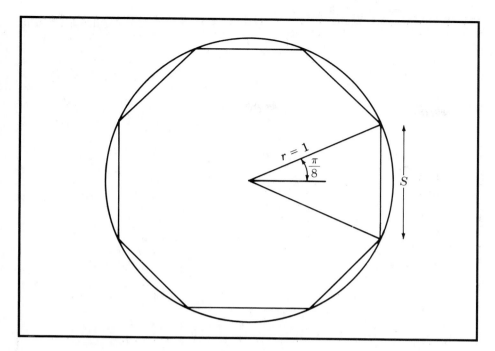

Figure 16-2
Doubling the number of sides improves the approximation for π.

Using a pocket calculator it is relatively easy to generate the higher approximations for π that are listed in Table 16-1. If we assume that we do not know the correct value of π, we can use the most recently computed value in the table to estimate the accuracy of the previous table entry. Thus the third calculation ($k = 4$) suggests that at best only the first three digits of the $k = 3$ calculation are significant and the rest can be discarded. The digits that are so judged are overprinted with a dash.

The calculation then proceeds quite nicely for the next several steps with the estimated accuracy increasing in every step until the $k = 12$ calculation. In this step the computed value seems to suggest that fewer digits are correct than were correct in the previous step. This turn of events continues, each successive calculation being less accurate than the previous one, until a very strange thing happens in steps 14, 15, and 16. The computed value remains the same for 10 digits out of 11 for three steps. Should we quit here and proudly publish a new value for π accurate to 10 figures?[3] Perhaps not, since the same thing happens at a different value in steps 17 and 18. Thereafter the calculation falls apart completely.

Notice that the most accurate value occurs in step 11, the last step before the onset of the strange behavior. By carefully monitoring the progress of the calculation in each step we would avoid the embarrassment of incorrectly reporting a result as accurate to 10 figures only to learn that 7 of the 10

---

[3] This odd feature will occur on most computing devices; where depends on the computer word length and the procedures for executing the arithmetic operations.

Table 16-1
A calculation of π
using Equation
(16.3).

k	n	p_k
2	4	2.8284271248
3	8	3.0614674589
4	16	3.1214451525
5	32	3.1365484904
6	64	3.1403311479
7	128	3.1412772578
8	256	3.1415137813
9	512	3.1415737570
10	1024	3.1415862735
11	2048	3.1415946179
12	4096	3.1416613714
13	8192	3.1419288372
14	16384	3.1429961472
15	32768	3.1429961471
16	65536	3.1429961472
17	131072	3.2105951957
18	262144	3.2105951957
19	524288	3.707276324
20	1048576	7.414552684

figures are in error. Unfortunately, this example illustrates a situation that is more common than it should be. Every day, in technical papers, numbers are reported that are the result of extensive computation and frequently many of these values are slightly to grossly in error and in both cases outside the stated error estimates.

If there is any hint that round-off errors are affecting the results in a serious way, the calculation should be repeated using a slightly different starting position or step size.

16.4.2 The Causes of Round-Off Error

The characteristic indicator of the onset of round-off error problems is an *increase* in the inaccuracy after successive iterations or after a decrease in the step size. The absence of such an indicator is not a guarantee of no serious round-off error problems, of course, but in most cases this test, if applied with caution, will suffice. Since round-off errors are always present, it would be best to estimate their effects both before and after the calculation. Unfortunately, this is rarely possible or practical. Since round-off errors are essentially a growth of a random "noise" in a calculation, statistical models are often used to estimate the progress of round-off errors through a calculation. These models are frequently quite successful and interesting; however, they are beyond the scope of this text. Unless your program costs many hundreds or thousands of dollars for each computer run, it is usually most cost-effective to simply run the program more than once with different parameters and watch for anomalous features in the results. Of course the best advice is to always thoroughly understand the computational algorithm and to use common sense.

The prime candidate for a source of round-off error problems is a calculation that involves repeated subtraction of numbers of comparable size. For example, the Romberg integration algorithm of Chapter 13 used the equation

$$T_k^{m+1} = T_k^m + \frac{(T_k^m - T_{k-1}^m)}{(4^{m+1} - 1)}$$

to repeatedly improve the estimate of an integral. The two quantities in the term $(T_k^m - T_{k-1}^m)$ are possibly very close together and their difference will then suffer serious round-off error problems. This was monitored by the quantity R_k^m of Equation 13.24. However, the main term in the above equation is T_k^m, which is ordinarily much larger than the correction term and thus the accuracy of the calculation is only marginally affected. The result is therefore limited by round-off errors but is not in danger of being destroyed by them.

Another situation that can lead to problems concerns the addition of very small terms to a not-so-small sum. This was illustrated in Problem 2.3, where it was pointed out that on any computing device there is a small number, EPS, for which the arithmetic statement

$$1.0 + \text{EPS} \rightarrow 1.0$$

is true. For example, on a computer with only a six-digit word length, if the value for TERM were carefully calculated as 3.14159×10^{-4}, the result of $1.0 + \text{TERM}$ would be simply 1.00031 and most of the accuracy of the calculation has been lost. This is especially common in the solution of differential equations. The basic operation consists of computing a correction term, $y' \Delta x$, and then adding this small term to the current y value to obtain the next value of y.

$$y_{i+1} = y_i + y_i' \Delta x$$

This is then repeated hundreds or thousands of times to obtain the complete solution. In each step much of the accuracy of the correction term is lost, and then to compound the problem the new, less accurate value of y is used in the next step. It may be surprising that any numerical solutions to differential equations are possible at all. Of course most calculations do work and yield accurate results, and even in those cases where the validity of the calculation is in jeopardy due to round-off error the problems can usually be greatly reduced by a simple modification of the code that we will discuss in Section 16.4.4.

16.4.3 A Theoretical Investigation of the Growth of Round-Off Error in the Solution of a Differential Equation

For some differential equations it is possible to determine theoretically the manner of growth of the round-off error in the solution. For example, consider the equation for which the modified Euler method of Section 15.5 produced such poor results,

$$y' = -y \qquad \text{with } y(x = 0) = 1$$

which has the analytic solution $y(x) = e^{-x}$—i.e., simple exponential decay.

The solution via the modified Euler method is obtained by applying the equation

$$\begin{aligned}(16.6) \qquad y_{i+2} &= y_i + y'_{i+1}\, 2\,\Delta x \\ &= y_i - y_{i+1}\, 2\,\Delta x \end{aligned}$$

Next we attempt to determine the affect of round-off errors in the application of this equation. To make things simple, I will assume that round-off error appears in the first step only and then propagates through the solution. We can simulate this by assuming that the original specification of the condition at $y(x = 0)$ is slightly in error due to round-off or other problems. That is, in place of $y(x = 0) = 1$ we will begin the problem with $y(x = 0) = 1 + \delta$, where δ will represent the slight error in the starting value. The computed values based on this initial condition will be slightly different from the values obtained by starting with $y(x = 0) = 1$ and will be designated as y_i^*. Put another way, with round-off error included, we are actually solving the equation

$$(16.7) \qquad y_{i+2}^* = y_i^* - y_{i+1}^*\, 2\,\Delta x \qquad \text{with } y_0^* = 1 + \delta$$

Defining the difference between the y_i^* values and the true values y_i as

$$(16.8) \qquad \varepsilon_i = y_i^* - y_i$$

an equation can be obtained that governs the growth of the error ε_i by subtracting Equation (16.6) from Equation (16.7) to yield

$$(16.9) \qquad \varepsilon_{i+2} = \varepsilon_i - \varepsilon_{i+1}\, 2\,\Delta x \qquad \text{with } \varepsilon_0 = \delta$$

Notice that this equation is of exactly the same form as Equation (16.6), and as we already know the solution to that equation is $y(x) = e^{-x}$, we might guess that a solution to Equation (16.9) is by analogy

$$(16.10) \qquad \varepsilon_i \propto e^{-x_i}$$

This can be verified as a solution of Equation (16.9) in the limit of infinitesimal Δx as follows: let $x = x_i$, then $x_{i+2} = x + 2\,\Delta x$, so

$$\varepsilon_{i+2} \propto e^{-(x+2\Delta x)} = e^{-x}e^{-2\Delta x}$$

$$\cong e^{-x}(1 - 2\,\Delta x)$$

while the right hand side of Equation (16.9) becomes

$$\varepsilon_i - \varepsilon_{i+1}2\,\Delta x \propto e^{-x} - 2\,\Delta x e^{-(x+\Delta x)} = e^{-x}(1 - 2\,\Delta x\,e^{-\Delta x})$$

$$\cong e^{-x}[1 - 2\,\Delta x\,(1 - \Delta x)]$$

$$\cong e^{-x}(1 - 2\,\Delta x)$$

where I have used the approximation $e^{-2\Delta x} \simeq 1 - 2\Delta x$ in the last step.

However, $\varepsilon_i = e^{-x_i}$ is not the only solution to this equation. After a bit of trial and error, you would find that a second function that also satisfies Equation (16.9) is

$$\varepsilon_i = (-1)^i e^{+x_i} \tag{16.11}$$

Again, this expression may be verified as a solution by plugging into Equation (16.9) and showing that the equation is satisfied for small Δx.

The complete solution to Equation (16.9) is then any linear combination of the two solutions, Equations (16.10) and (16.11).

$$\varepsilon_i = c_1 e^{-x_i} + c_2(-1)^i e^{+x_i} \tag{16.12}$$

To determine the two unknown constants we use the extra information of the initial condition—i.e., $\varepsilon_0 = \delta$. This is one condition to determine the two constants, c_1, c_2, and so an additional equation is required. For this we might assume that the error after the first step is approximately the same value—i.e., $\varepsilon_1 = \delta$. These two conditions then lead to the following equations for the constants:

$$\varepsilon_0 = c_0 + c_1 = \delta$$

$$\varepsilon_1 = c_1 e^{-\Delta x} - c_1 e^{+\Delta x} = \delta$$

or in matrix form

$$\begin{pmatrix} 1 & 1 \\ e^{-\Delta x} & -e^{\Delta x} \end{pmatrix} \begin{pmatrix} c_1 \\ c_2 \end{pmatrix} = \begin{pmatrix} \delta \\ \delta \end{pmatrix} \tag{16.13}$$

which can be solved by Cramer's rule to yield

$$c_1 = \delta \frac{e^{\Delta x} - 1}{e^{\Delta x} + e^{-\Delta x}} \qquad \cong \frac{\delta\,\Delta x}{2} \tag{16.14}$$

$$c_2 = \delta \frac{1 - e^{-\Delta x}}{e^{\Delta x} + e^{-\Delta x}} \cong \frac{\delta \Delta x}{2}$$

and so the solution for the growth of the error of the differential equation is

(16.15)
$$\varepsilon_i = \frac{\delta \Delta x}{2} \left[e^{-x_i} + (-1)^i e^{+x_i} \right]$$

Now let us examine this result. The first term in the brackets represents normal exponential decay and results from the fact that ε_i satisfies the same equation as y_i, Equation (16.6), which in turn was a result of the original differential equation $y' = -y$. The second term in the brackets is called a "parasitic" solution since it does *not* satisfy the original differential equation though it is a solution of the difference equation, Equation (16.6). This term *grows* exponentially with increasing x while the function $y(x)$ is simultaneously decreasing. Thus, even though the coefficient $\delta \Delta x$ multiplying the positive exponential is very small, the error term will likely grow to exceed the diminishing value of $y(x)$. Also, a signature of these error terms is that they are expected to alternate in sign from term to term due to the $(-1)^i$.

The same analysis applied to the equation $y' = +y$ generates an error term similar to Equation (16.15). However, in this case the round-off errors are *not* expected to present problems. (See Problem 15.5.)

Admittedly, the above discussion is not completely rigorous and perhaps less than totally convincing.[4] Yet even approximate theoretical predictions of the growth of error in a numerical solution to an arbitrary differential equation are usually not possible. The reason is that it is not always so easy to obtain a form for the parasitic solution. Thus, in the final appraisal, I can give no recipe for the estimation of round-off errors in a general problem. You must use your own common sense, solve the problem more than once, be knowledgeable about the instabilities inherent in the algorithm you are using, and be ever watchful for suspicious anomalous features in the computed results.

16.4.4 Suggestions to Minimize Round-Off Errors

If it is clear to you that the accuracy of your calculation can be adversely affected by round-off error, there are a few remedies that you can try. First, attempt to locate the part of the code that is the major source of the problem.

---

[4] The fact that the actual computed results in Chapter 15 do indeed exhibit errors that grow exponentially and that alternate in sign is convincing circumstantial evidence of the validity of the basic approximation of assuming round-off error in the initial assignment $y(x = 0) = 1 + \delta$.

You should look for repeated operations that either subtract numbers of like size or add small numbers to not-so-small numbers. That is, operations like

$$(T_{k+1} - T_k) \qquad \text{or} \qquad \sum_{1}^{1000} \frac{1}{i^3}$$

are very likely to result in a loss of significant figures.

A suggestion I gave earlier to partially rectify the problem in the summation example is to sum the terms in reverse order. This will have the effect of accumulating the smallest terms first into a value that is comparable to the magnitude of the larger earlier terms in the sum, thereby avoiding the possibility of encountering operations of the type $1 + \text{EPS} \to 1$.

Unfortunately this trick is usually of little use in reducing the round-off error in a differential equation. The solution proceeds by adding very small terms to not-so-small terms as in

$$y_{i+1} = y_i + y_i' \Delta x$$

but the value of y_{i+1} is required for the next step, so we cannot simply add up the small terms $y_i' \Delta x$ separately. You could declare all the variables required in the calculation to be double-precision, however this will frequently result in prohibitive execution costs.[5] An intermediate approach that is found to be extremely effective and efficient is:

1. Compute the small correction terms $y_i' \Delta x$ in ordinary single-precision arithmetic.
2. Execute the summation of (current term) + (correction term) using a temporary double-precision variable. For example,

```
DOUBLE PRECISION ONE
    . . .           . . .
EPS = 1.E-8
ONE = 1.D+00
ONE = ONE + EPS
```

The major computation time in a code usually involves the calculation of the correction term, say EPS, and the only use of double-precision arithmetic is then in the one line employing mixed-mode addition (real + double precision). This improvement is so easily implemented and is so effective in reducing round-off error that it is strongly suggested that you include it in every program that repeatedly adds small terms to not-so-small terms.

Similar tricks can be employed to reduce the loss of significant figures resulting from subtraction of numbers of like size and still retain an efficient

---

[5] With some compilers double-precision arithmetic is a factor of 8 slower than the same arithmetic operations carried out on ordinary single-precision numbers.

program, but the prescription is not as clear and these problems must be resolved on a case-by-case basis.

16.5 APPROXIMATION ERRORS: DISCRETIZATION AND TRUNCATION

To compute an exact value for e^x, or for any other transcendental function, requires an infinite number of elementary arithmetic operations, or equivalently, summing an infinite number of terms in the series

$$e^x = 1 + x + \frac{x^2}{2!} + \frac{x^3}{3!} + \cdots$$

Anything short of an infinite number of terms will lead to errors, called *truncation errors*. This is a special case of the general situation wherein a function $f(x)$ is first written in terms of its Taylor series

$$f(x) = f(a) + f'(a)(x - a) + \frac{1}{2!}f''(a)(x - a)^2 + \cdots$$

and the series is then truncated after a finite number of terms.

As we know, this approximation is the cornerstone of most of numerical analysis. For example, when evaluating the value of the integral of a function $f(x)$ via the trapezoidal rule, the function is replaced by straight line segments over limited intervals. This is of course equivalent to retaining only the first two terms in the Taylor series. Simpson's rule integration replaces the function with parabolic segments, a better approximation corresponding to retaining an additional term in the series. Thus, for a given step size Δx, Simpson's rule should give more accurate results.

We can obtain more accurate trapezoidal rule results by reducing the step size (discretization error), and in the limit $\Delta x \to 0$, the trapezoidal rule will return exact answers for most functions. However, that is calculus, not numerical analysis. On a computer, as the panel width is reduced, the total number of computational operations is increased, and with them the round-off error. Thus the discretization error and the round-off error are in competition. As the panel width Δx is successively decreased, the accuracy of the calculation will increase for a while but must eventually decrease when the round-off error begins to dominate. This suggests that there is an *optimum* panel width for each problem that will minimize the *overall* error. This is demonstrated in Table 16-2 where the results of a Simpson's rule and a trapezoidal rule calculation are compared. Notice that in this case the most accurate values ultimately obtained by each method are the same. However, Simpson's rule reaches this value much more quickly.

Table 16-2
A comparison of
the failure point
of the trapezoidal
rule and
Simpson's rule
applied to an in-
tegral.

		$I = \dfrac{2\sqrt{2}}{\pi} \displaystyle\int_0^1 \dfrac{1 + x^2}{1 + x^4}\, dx = 1.0$	
Order	Number of panels	Trapezoidal rule	Simpson's rule
1	2	0.9797560126	1.0062358975
2	4	0.9952501804	1.0004149079
3	8	0.9988240451	1.0000153035
4	16	0.9997067153	1.0000009537
5	32	0.9999267384	1.0000000745
6	64	0.9999817312	1.0000000298
7	128	0.9999954253	1.0000000149
8	256	0.9999988452	1.0000000149
9	512	0.9999997467	0.9999999851
10	1024	1.0000000298	1.0000000149
11	2048	1.0000000149	1.0000000745
12	4096	1.0000000596	1.0000000149
13	8192	1.0000000447	0.9999999851
14	16384	1.0000000596	0.9999998808

As a general rule, the higher the level of the approximation algorithm, the more accurate *and* the more efficient the resulting computer code. However, this must be balanced against the time and effort of coding and debugging the problem. Most of us would ordinarily opt for the simpler solution and merely let the computer run longer to achieve the desired accuracy. But as we have just seen, this may not always be possible due to the accumulation of round-off error. In such cases, we have no choice but to resort to a fancier, higher-lever algorithm. Of course, in those situations in which a high-level approximation can be used with very little additional effort, as in Romberg integration, it is almost unforgivable to use a very coarse algorithm such as the trapezoidal rule. You should notice that one of the best and most efficient means of reducing the effects of round-off errors is to improve the level of the approximation algorithm. This is perhaps best illustrated in the solution of differential equations.

I mentioned earlier that truncation errors are introduced into a solution whenever the Taylor series representing a function is terminated after a few terms. Euler's method, which is based on the approximation

$$y_{i+1} \simeq y_i + y_i' \, \Delta x$$

is clearly a lowest-order method. The improved or modified Euler methods can be shown to be equivalent to using the approximation

$$y_{i+1} \simeq y_i + y_i' \, \Delta x + \tfrac{1}{2} y_i'' \, \Delta x^2$$

and as we have seen yield consistently better results than the ordinary Euler method.

Again, the fancier numerical methods are not just a matter of esthetics; depending upon the computer and the problem, they are quite often essential in obtaining a solution.

16.6   EXPERIMENTAL ERRORS

Many of the calculations you will do in the future will involve either the analysis of experimental data or the comparison of model calculations with experimental numbers. Since each and every measurement includes unavoidable errors, this is yet another source of error to be considered. Of course, experimental errors, unlike round-off error and approximation errors, are something over which numerical analysis has very little control. The minimization of the experimental errors is of prime concern to the experimental scientist or engineer, but as we shall see, the uncertainties in measured quantities are also critically important to the person who wishes to use those numbers in a calculation. It is absolutely essential that anyone using numbers resulting from measurements be aware of the quality of those experimental numbers. There are any number of numerical analysis algorithms that will normally proceed smoothly and without problems to an accurate solution but collapse completely when even small experimental errors are introduced. A very instructive example of this is found in the solution of linear algebraic equations.

16.6.1   Amplification of Experimental Errors in Ill-Conditioned Matrix Equations

In the discussion of Cramer's rule in Section 11.3 you were told that a pivotal ingredient in the solution of the matrix equation $[A]\mathbf{x} = \mathbf{b}$ is the evaluation of the determinant of the coefficient matrix $[A]$. If the determinant $|A|$ is zero then ordinarily no solution is possible; and if $|A| = $ small, the solution may be suspect. In this section we will investigate more carefully the consequences of ill-conditioned equations.

In order to make the discussion as simple as possible we will consider first only two equations in two unknowns. The extension to larger sets of equations is straightforward. We begin with the following equations:

(**16.16**)
$$x + 0.8y = 0.2$$
$$2x + 1.6y = 0.5$$

or

(**16.17**)
$$\begin{pmatrix} 1.0 & 0.8 \\ 2.0 & 1.5 \end{pmatrix} \begin{pmatrix} x \\ y \end{pmatrix} = \begin{pmatrix} 0.2 \\ 0.5 \end{pmatrix}$$
$$[A] \qquad \mathbf{x} \quad = \quad \mathbf{b}$$

The determinant of the coefficient matrix is $|A| = -0.1$ which, for our purposes, will be considered to be small. Nonetheless, since $|A| \neq 0$ a solution of the equation can be obtained either by the Gauss-Jordan technique or by Cramer's rule. The result is

$$\begin{pmatrix} x \\ y \end{pmatrix} = \begin{pmatrix} 1.0 \\ -1.0 \end{pmatrix} \tag{16.18}$$

Next consider the consequences of small experimental errors in the numbers in the right-hand-side vector $\mathbf{b}$. For example, if the uncertainty in $\mathbf{b}$ were 1 percent, then the acceptable range in the elements of $\mathbf{b}$ would be

$$\mathbf{b} \pm \Delta\mathbf{b} = \begin{pmatrix} 0.2 \\ 0.5 \end{pmatrix} \pm \begin{pmatrix} 0.0020 \\ 0.0050 \end{pmatrix} = \begin{pmatrix} 0.198 & \longleftrightarrow & 0.202 \\ 0.495 & \longleftrightarrow & 0.505 \end{pmatrix} \tag{16.19}$$

If we next solve Equation (16.17) using Equation (16.19) as the right-hand-side vector and use the complete range of $\mathbf{b}$ values that are given, the result is a range of values for the solution vector.

$$\begin{pmatrix} x \\ y \end{pmatrix} = \begin{pmatrix} 0.93 & \longleftrightarrow & 1.07 \\ -0.91 & \longleftrightarrow & -1.09 \end{pmatrix} = \begin{pmatrix} 1.00 \\ -1.00 \end{pmatrix} \pm \begin{pmatrix} 0.07 \\ 0.09 \end{pmatrix} \tag{16.20}$$

Another way to express this result is to solve the matrix equation

$$[A]\mathbf{x} = \mathbf{b} \pm \Delta\mathbf{b}$$

directly as

$$\mathbf{x} = [A^{-1}](\mathbf{b} \pm \Delta\mathbf{b})$$

Inserting the inverse of the coefficient matrix, which is easily computed, we obtain

$$\begin{pmatrix} -15 & 8 \\ 20 & -10 \end{pmatrix} \left[\begin{pmatrix} 0.20 \\ 0.45 \end{pmatrix} + \begin{pmatrix} \pm 0.002 \\ \pm 0.005 \end{pmatrix} \right] = \begin{pmatrix} 1 \\ -1 \end{pmatrix} + \begin{pmatrix} -15 & 8 \\ 20 & -10 \end{pmatrix} \begin{pmatrix} \pm 0.002 \\ \pm 0.005 \end{pmatrix} \tag{16.21}$$

Special care must be employed when the second term in Equation (16.21) is evaluated. If the *same* sign is used for both of the elements of $\Delta\mathbf{b}$ the result will be ± 0.1 for the error in both elements of the solution vector. However, there is no reason to assume that the errors in b_1 and b_2 are related; thus the proper procedure is to evaluate the product not as

$$\sum_{j=1}^{2} A_{ij}^{-1} b_j$$

but rather as

$$\sum_{j=1}^{2} |A_{ij}^{-1} b_j|$$

That is, in the worst possible case, the errors all add in the same direction. The result is then the same as obtained in Equation (16.20).

The most important feature of this example is the fact that a small 1 percent error in **b** has been amplified into a 7 percent error in x and a 9 percent error in y. If there were also uncertainties in the elements of $[A]$ or if $|A|$ were smaller still, the results would be even worse. To see how this has come about, the same problem is solved once more, graphically.

The two equations

$$x + 0.8y = 0.2$$
$$2y + 1.5y = 0.5$$

can be written as

(**16.22**) $$y = -\frac{5}{4}x + \frac{1}{4}$$

(**16.23**) $$y = -\frac{4}{3}x + \frac{1}{3}$$

The intersection of these two lines then determines the single point (x, y) that is simultaneously a solution of both equations. This is shown in Figure 16-3 to the point $(1, -1)$.

Figure 16-3
The solution of two simultaneous equations corresponds to the point of intersection of the two curves.

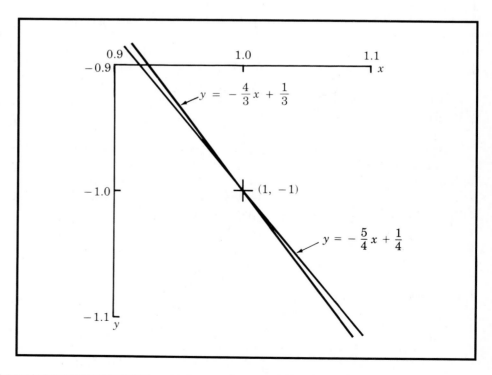

To include the uncertainties in the elements of **b** in the graphical solution, Equation (16.22), for example, would be replaced by

$$y = -\frac{5}{4}x + \left(\frac{1}{4} \pm \frac{1}{400}\right) \tag{16.24}$$

That is, the "thin" line, Equation (16.22) is replaced by a "broad" line that is bounded by

$$y = -\frac{5}{4}x + \frac{101}{400}$$

and

$$y = -\frac{5}{4}x + \frac{99}{400}$$

Following the same procedure for the second of the two equations and once again obtaining the solutions by graphing the two lines now with the error included, results in the plot of Figure 16-4.

The intersection of the two lines is now represented by the thin diamond-shaped region extending roughly from $(x = 0.93, y = -0.91)$ to $(x = 1.07,$

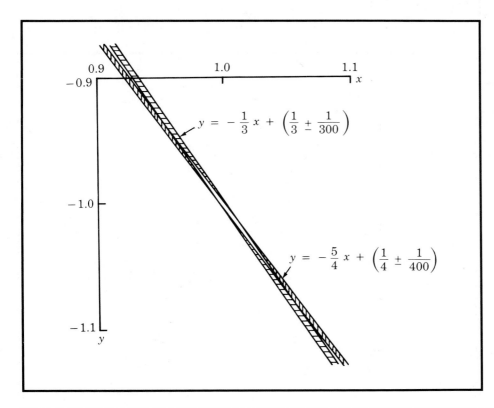

Figure 16-4
The intersection of two lines with error results in an extended region of permissible solutions.

$y = -1.09$). The reason for the amplification of the 1 percent error in b into a 7 to 9 percent error in the solution is now clear. The two equations are very nearly parallel. This is indicated by the small value of the determinant of the coefficient matrix. If the two lines were precisely parallel, one would be simply a multiple of the other with a different intercept (b value) and the determinant would be exactly zero. If the determinant were relatively large, this would suggest that the two lines are approximately perpendicular and therefore the band of values in the intersection region would be much smaller, indicating a well-defined solution. Including round-off errors in the solution will of course only compound the difficulties of solving ill-conditioned problems.

So far we have only considered the possibility of experimental errors in the right-hand-side vector. If there are also errors in the coefficient matrix, the situation can be much worse. Returning to the original equation,

$$\begin{pmatrix} 1 & 0.8 \\ 2 & 1.5 \end{pmatrix} \begin{pmatrix} x \\ y \end{pmatrix} = \begin{pmatrix} 0.2 \\ 0.5 \end{pmatrix}$$
$$[A] \quad \mathbf{x} \quad = \quad \mathbf{b}$$

you can easily show that if there is a 1 percent error in the elements of $[A]$, the error in the determinant $|A|$ is then 62 percent. Since $|A|$ is required in the solution, the final results will be almost meaningless.

The consequences of experimental error in other areas of numerical analysis can be equally dramatic. Keep in mind that experimental error behaves exactly like round-off error except it is ordinarily much larger. Experimental error in the initial conditions of a differential equation can very quickly grow in successive steps to swamp the solution.

16.7 CONCLUSION

I have postponed this discussion of numerical errors until now for fear of frightening you. You should not get the impression from all this worry about errors that all or most of your calculations are doomed to yield meaningless results or that you must spend 90 percent of your time ferreting out sources of round-off error and devising clever procedures to minimize the amplification of experimental errors. Most computers carry a sufficient number of significant figures and most of the procedures described in this text are sufficiently accurate so that your programs will work smoothly and accurately in the majority of cases. Of course, at each stage in the solution of a problem you should be aware of the potential difficulties that may arise and have some ideas regarding their correction. The problems associated with the various forms of numerical errors are always lurking in the dark corners of a program, and when they do finally appear is when the engineer or scientist really begins to earn his or her pay.

After considerable experience in numerical analysis you may even find the study of error considerations to be interesting—but that is the proper province of a later course in numerical methods.

APPENDIX   SUMMARY OF FORTRAN STATEMENTS AND GRAMMAR RULES

The information contained in this appendix is intended for quick reference. A detailed account of most of the items listed can be found in the text as indicated. For the sake of completeness, several Fortran statements are included here that are not described in the text. These are denoted by asterisks.

In this Appendix I have used the following notation:

[. . .]   indicates an optional part of a statement
⟨ . . . ⟩   a list or numerical value that is to be supplied by the programmer.
CAPITALS   Fortran statements

Fortran statements are entered in columns 7 through 72. Blanks are ignored. A line beginning with a "∗" or a "C" in column 1 is ignored by the compiler and is treated as a comment. Any character other than "blank" or zero in column 6 indicates that this line is a continuation of the previous Fortran line. Some Fortran statements may be given an identifying statement number of 1 to 5 digits in columns 1 through 5.

A.1 PROCEDURE STATEMENTS

Statement	Comment
PROGRAM ⟨name⟩ [p.41]	Defines the program name that is used as an entry point for the program execution. If omitted, the compiler assigns a name.
SUBROUTINE ⟨name⟩ [arg. list] [pp.245–246]	The symbolic name defines the main entry point. The subroutine name is not to be assigned a value. The optional argument list contains dummy variable names that can be variables, arrays, dummy procedure names, or alternate return addresses of the form ∗⟨stmt. no.⟩. Multiple ENTRYs and alternate RETURNs are permitted.
FUNCTION ⟨name⟩ ([arg. list]) [p.254]	The symbolic name defines the main en-

try point. If the type of the function is specified (e.g., REAL FUNCTION ⟨name⟩), the name must not appear in a type statement. The name must be assigned a value before any RETURN. Control is back to the referencing program unit when a RETURN or an END statement is encountered. Multiple ENTRY points are permitted, but alternate RETURNs are not.

Statement Functions [pp.105–107, 244]	A user-defined, single statement computation that is valid only within the program unit containing the definition. It is a nonexecutable statement. The argument list may not contain an array or a function name. The statement function name must not appear in an INTRINSIC or EXTERNAL statement.
(*)BLOCK DATA [name]	A nonexecutable subprogram unit that is used to initialize variables in COMMON blocks by means of one or more DATA statements. It may contain specification statements but may not contain any executable Fortran statements.
END	All Fortran procedures must have END as their last line. No procedure may reference itself either directly or indirectly.

Argument Lists

Statement	Comment
Actual Arguments: [pp.108, 245]	Arguments that appear in the "call" to the subprogram. They can be variable names, expressions, array names or elements. They cannot contain a statement function name.
Dummy Arguments: [pp.108, 245]	Arguments that appear in the definition of a subprogram. They are associated with the actual arguments when the subprogram is referenced and when it returns. Dummy arguments that refer to arrays must be dimensioned within

the subprogram to a size less than or equal to the actual dimensioning. The association with actual arguments is by position in the list, and both the total number and types of variables in both lists must agree. If the dummy argument list contains a procedure name, it must be available at the time of the call. The subprogram must not redefine a dummy argument that is a constant, a name of a function, an expression using operators, or any expression enclosed in parentheses.

A.2   SPECIFICATION STATEMENTS

Type Declaration Statements

Statement	Comment
INTEGER ⟨name list⟩ [p.32]	Used to define the names of variables, arrays, functions, or dummy procedures to be of type INTEGER. The names in the name list must be separated by commas.
REAL ⟨name list⟩ [p.32]	Similar to INTEGER, used to define names to be of type REAL.
CHARACTER[*s], ⟨name[*s_1], . . . ⟩ [pp.39–40]	Defines a variable, array, function, or dummy procedure to be of type CHARACTER. If the optional [*s] is present, each of the elements of the name list is of length s, where s is a positive (unsigned) constant or an asterisk enclosed in parentheses. The latter is used in subprograms for the assigning of dummy argument names to have whatever length the associated actual argument has at the time of the call. Alternately, each name in the name list can be assigned different lengths by using the form ⟨name⟩*s_1, where s_1 is the length of the string and satisfies the

same rules as does s. The string lengths (s, s_1) may be variable names only if the variable has been initialized in a previous PARAMETER statement and is enclosed in parentheses.

DOUBLE PRECISION ⟨name list⟩
[pp.286–288]

Similar to INTEGER and REAL. Used to define names to be of type DOUBLE PRECISION.

COMPLEX ⟨name list⟩
[pp.288–289]

Similar to INTEGER and REAL. Used to define names to be of type COMPLEX. COMPLEX numbers consist of two real numbers corresponding to the real and imaginary parts. Thus if C is complex, an assignment statement would be

```
C = (3,0,4,0)
```

and SQRT(C) would return the complex result

```
SQRT(C) → (2,0,1,0)
```

LOGICAL ⟨name list⟩
[pp.289–290]

Similar to INTEGER and REAL. Used to define names to be of type LOGICAL. LOGICAL variables can have only two values, namely,

```
,TRUE,      ,FALSE,
```

(The periods are part of the value.) Thus if X is of type LOGICAL, the expression

```
X = 4 ,GT, 7
```

assigns a value of .FALSE. to X.

IMPLICIT ⟨type⟩ (a_1-a_2)
[pp.290–291]

Used to override or augment the default typing. ⟨type⟩ is any of the above six variable types and a_1, a_2, are single letters. The IMPLICIT statement must precede all statement specifications except PARAMETER. Explicit typing overrides an IMPLICIT specification.

Other Specification Statements

Statement	Comment
PARAMETER (⟨name⟩=⟨exp⟩, . . .) [pp.293–294]	Assigns a symbolic name to a constant. ⟨exp⟩ is a constant expression (can be of type CHARACTER). Any variable name in the expression must have been previously defined in a PARAMETER statement. The parentheses may contain more than one assignment. Variables in one PARAMETER statement may not be redefined in another. Variables initialized in PARAMETER statements may be used in a DATA statement but not in a FORMAT statement.
DATA ⟨name list⟩/ ⟨value list⟩/ [,⟨name list⟩/⟨value list⟩/ . . .] [pp.292–293]	Used to initialize variables, arrays, array elements, and substrings at compilation time. DATA statements are nonexecutable and must appear after other specification statements and should appear before the first executable statement. The same name should not appear in two DATA name lists. The values in the value list are assigned, one-to-one, to the elements of the name list which should agree in type and must agree in total number of elements. The name list may contain an array name and an implied DO loop (or nested loops) of the form: (A(I),I=ILO,IHI,ISTEP). The values in the limits of the implied DO and in the value list must be constants or named constants defined in a PARAMETER statement. The values in the value list may be repeated by preceding by a positive (unsigned) integer or named integer constant (defined in a PARAMETER statement). Variables in blank COMMON cannot be assigned values with a DATA statement.
DIMENSION ⟨array name⟩(n_d [,n_d, . . .]) [pp.180–182]	Designates a name as an array name and defines the subscript bounds. More than one array can be declared in a sin-

gle DIMENSION statement. The form of the subscript bound definition, n_d, is either one of the forms

i_{top} limits are 1, 2, . . . , i_{top}; $i_{top} > 0$

$i_{bot} : i_{top}$ limits are i_{bot}, $i_{bot} + 1$, . . . , i_{top}

If only the upper bound (i_{top}) is given, the default value for i_{bot} is 1. The bounds must be integers or integer expressions. In the initial dimensioning, the bounds must be integer constants; while in subsequent dimensioning (in subprograms) the bounds can be dummy integer variables or expressions.

EXTERNAL ⟨proc. name⟩
[pp.268–269]

Used to define a name as representing a user-written, externally defined, subprogram, procedure, or dummy procedure name. More than one name can be declared external in a single EXTERNAL statement. The purpose of the EXTERNAL statement is to allow the name to appear as an actual argument in an argument list. If an intrinsic function name is entered in an EXTERNAL ⟨proc. name⟩ list, the name then refers to a user-written function and the library function can no longer be referenced.

INTRINSIC ⟨func. name⟩
[pp.268–269]

Similar to EXTERNAL, but applies to library functions. All intrinsic function names that appear as actual arguments in an argument list must be declared INTRINSIC. A function cannot be declared both intrinsic and external. Type conversion functions (e.g., FLOAT, IFIX) and min/max functions (e.g., MIN, MAX) cannot be used as actual arguments.

COMMON [/blockname/] ⟨name list⟩
[pp.276–278]

Stores all the variables in name list together in a block of memory which can be given a block name. These variables may then be accessed by different program units without using argument lists. As with argument lists, elements in the name list are assigned values by position. Two program units that share data via COMMON blocks must have a COMMON statement with the same block name (or unnamed) and be of identical lengths. More than one block name may be defined in a single COMMON statement. The block name may also be used as a variable name without conflict. If any variable in a COMMON block is of type CHARACTER, then *all* variables in the block must be of type CHARACTER. Entries in a labeled COMMON block can be initially defined via a DATA statement in BLOCK-DATA subprogram only. The variables in blank COMMON are automatically saved upon return from a subprogram, while those in labeled COMMON *may* not be. (They are saved if the labeled COMMON in the subprogram also appears in the main program.)

(*)EQUIVALENCE (⟨name list⟩)

Provides for the sharing of the same memory locations by two or more variables, arrays, array elements, or character substrings. When coupled with COMMON statements, the effect of EQUIVALENCE statements can be extremely complex, and use of this statement is not recommended.

SAVE [⟨name list⟩]
[p.271]

Preserves the value of variables in a subprogram after a RETURN has been executed. The value of the variable may then be referenced in a subsequent call to the subprogram. Dummy variable names, names in a COMMON block, and procedure names must not appear in the name list. A SAVE statement with no name list will SAVE *all* allowable variables in the subprogram.

(*)ENTRY ⟨entry name⟩[(arg. list)]

In addition to the main entry point of a

subprogram (the top), the ENTRY statement may be used to begin the subprogram execution anywhere except within a DO loop or an IF-THEN-END IF block. The subprogram is initiated at the alternate entry point by replacing the subprogram name by ⟨entry name⟩ in the referencing line. The argument list in the entry statement should be similar to the argument list in the subprogram definition. ENTRY statements are often used to skip repetitive computations or assignments in a subprogram, such as

```
PROGRAM MANE
   ...      ...
CALL XX(A,M)
   ...      ...
CALL XXMID(B,N)
   ...      ...
END
SUBROUTINE XX(C,L)
DIMENSION C(L)
DO 1 I = 1,L
1 C(I) = 0.0
ENTRY XXMID(C,L)
C(5) = ...
   ...      ...
END
```

A.3   ASSIGNMENT AND PROGRAM CONTROL STATEMENTS

Statement
Assignment Statement:
⟨var. name⟩ = ⟨exp.⟩
[p.39]

Comment
Where ⟨var. name⟩ is the name of a variable or array element. If the expression ⟨exp.⟩ on the right is arithmetic, it is first evaluated according to the hierarchy rules and the type of the dominant variable type, then converted to the type of ⟨var. name⟩ and then as-

signed to ⟨var. name⟩. If the expression is of type CHARACTER, the variable name must also be of type CHARACTER and if the string lengths differ the expression is either padded with blanks to the right or truncated on the right to match the length of ⟨var. name⟩. If ⟨var. name⟩ is of type LOGICAL, then the expression must have a value of either .TRUE. or .FALSE. Multiple assignments of the form A = B = C = D = 5. are not standard Fortran 77.

(∗)ASSIGN ⟨stmt. no.⟩ TO ⟨name⟩

In this statement, ⟨stmt. no.⟩ is the statement number of an executable statement or a FORMAT statement, and ⟨name⟩ is the name of an integer variable. This statement is used in conjunction with the ASSIGNED GO TO statement or with WRITE(5, ⟨name⟩). . . statements and in general is not recommended.

END
[p.47]

Used to mark the end of a compilation unit. The END statement can have a statement number. If during execution of the main program, the program flow branches to, or encounters, an END statement, the program terminates. The same situation in a subprogram will result in a RETURN. Both are considered poor style.

STOP [tag]
[pp.13, 47]

The STOP statement terminates the execution of the program wherever it is encountered in a program or subprogram and the word "STOP" is displayed in the day file or on the terminal screen. The optional [tag] can be a positive integer (of five digits or less) or a character string constant and will be displayed along with STOP. Example,

```
STOP 'SUCCESSFUL RUN -
              JOB TERMINATED'
STOP 97
```

A program may have more than one STOP statement.

(*)PAUSE [tag]	Similar to the STOP statement. This statement causes the program execution to be interrupted and the word "PAUSE" followed by the optional [tag] to be displayed. If the program is being run in batch mode, only the operator at the console can cause the program to continue. In interactive mode, the user enters either "DROP" to terminate or "GO" to continue. Use of this statement is not recommended.

A.4 FLOW-CONTROL STATEMENTS

Statement	Comment
RETURN [exp.] [p.246]	A RETURN statement causes the termination of a subprogram procedure and the return to the referencing program or subprogram. RETURN statements may only appear in subprograms and each subprogram may have more than one RETURN. If the optional alternate return address expression [exp] is omitted, the procedure returns to the next statement in the referencing program unit; the normal situation.
(*)Alternate RETURN	An alternate RETURN (from subroutines only) is effected by including an integer or integer expression following RETURN *and* a sequence of asterisks in the defining subroutine argument list which will function as dummy address labels and will be associated with the actual statement numbers in the referencing call. Thus RETURN 3 will cause a return to the statement number in the third position in the actual argument list. The statement numbers in the actual argument list must refer to executable statements and be preceded by single asterisks.

```
                        PROGRAM MANE
                         ...      ...
                        CALL CAL(A,B,*1,*3,*7)
                        STOP
                         ...      ...
                     3  C = A + B
                         ...      ...
                     1  C = A - B
                         ...      ...
                     7  C = A/B
                         ...      ...
                        END
                        SUBROUTINE CAL(S,T,*,*,*)
                         ...      ...
                        RETURN 3    ⟨causes return
                                     to stmt. 7⟩
                         ...      ...
                        RETURN      ⟨normal
                                     return,
                                     executes the
                                     STOP⟩
                        END
```

CALL ⟨subname⟩ [(arg. list)]
[p.246]

Initiates a transfer of control to the sub-routine named ⟨subname⟩. The argument list contains actual arguments that may be constants, expressions, variable names, array names or elements, procedure names, or an alternate return address in the form *⟨stmt. no.⟩.

CONTINUE
[pp.76, 190]

The CONTINUE statement is an executable statement that performs no operation and may be placed anywhere among the executable statements. It is most commonly used as the terminus of DO loops. The CONTINUE statement should have a statement number.

GO TO Statements

Statement
GO TO ⟨stmt. no.⟩
[pp.25, 96]

Comment
Unconditional GO TO: Simply transfers control to the statement labeled with

---

〈stmt. no.〉, which must be an integer constant, not a variable name, and correspond to an existing executable statement anywhere in the same program or subprogram. When possible, use of the GO TO should be avoided and replaced with structured Fortran.

GO TO (〈stmt. no. list〉), 〈exp.〉
[p.87]

Computed GO TO: The statement number list contains labels of existing executable statements, and 〈exp.〉 is an integer or integer expression. If 〈exp.〉 is 1, control transfers to the statement identified by the first number in the list; if 〈exp.〉 is 2, to the second; etc. If 〈exp.〉 is less than 1 or greater than the number of labels in the list, execution continues with the next line of the program after the GO TO.

(*)GO TO 〈ivar〉, [(〈stmt. no. list〉)]

Assigned GO TO: The integer variable 〈ivar〉 must have been previously assigned a value by an ASSIGN TO statement. The statement then acts much like the unconditional GO TO if the statement number list is not present and like the computed GO TO if it is. Use of this statement should be avoided.

IF Statements

Statement	Comment

IF(〈arith. exp.〉) s_-, s_0, s_+
[p.88]

Arithmetic IF: The arithmetic expression is evaluated and if negative, zero, or positive control is transferred to the executable statement labeled by the statement number s_-, s_0, or s_+, respectively.

IF(〈log. exp.〉) 〈exec. stmt.〉
[p.86]

Logical IF: The logical expression 〈log. exp.〉 is evaluated, and if true, the executable Fortran statement 〈exec. stmt.〉 is executed, otherwise the program continues with the next line after the IF. The executable statement ⟨exec. stmt.⟩ cannot be a DO, IF, ELSE, ELSE IF, END, or END IF statement.

Block IF Statements

Statement	Comment
IF(⟨log. exp.⟩)THEN [p.60]	If the logical expression ⟨log. exp.⟩ is true, then the program execution continues with the next line; otherwise the control branches to the next ELSE or ELSE IF statement if present, or to the END IF, the terminus of the block, if an ELSE or ELSE IF is not present.
ELSE [p.67]	Marks the beginning of the alternate (false) path of an IF(. . .)THEN or an ELSE IF(. . .)THEN statement. The ELSE statement should not have a statement number.
ELSE IF(⟨log. exp.⟩)THEN [p.70]	The operation of this statement is the same as the IF(. . .)THEN statement, however, it can only be reached by an evaluation of ⟨false⟩ in a previous IF(. . .)THEN or ELSE IF(. . .)THEN statement. ELSE and ELSE IF statements must be placed within a corresponding IF(. . .)THEN - END IF block. Block IF structures can be nested. That is, one block IF structure may contain another only if the entire second block IF is contained within the first. It is permitted to branch to a block IF statement, but not permitted to branch to any statement within a block. Each block IF structure can contain several ELSE IF statements but only a single ELSE statement which must follow all the ELSE IFs in the structure.
END IF [p.60]	Marks the end of an IF(. . .)THEN structure. The END IF statement should not have a statement number. (It is not permitted to GO TO ⟨ENDIF⟩.)

Each IF(. . .)THEN must have a corresponding END IF statement. If the program flow arrives at an END IF statement, the program continues with the next line of the program.

DO-loop Structures

Statement	Comment
DO $\langle$stmt. no.$\rangle$ $a_c = b_{low}, b_{high}$ [,b_{step}] [p.189ff]	Marks the beginning of a block of statements that are executed with the value of the counter variable, a_c, set equal to the initial limit, b_{low}, and then the entire block is repeated with a_c assigned the value $b_{low} + b_{step}$ (or $b_{low} + 1$ if the optional b_{step} is omitted). This is repeated until the counter variable exceeds the final limit, b_{high}. The program then continues with the line following the loop terminator. The loop terminator is an executable statement with statement number $\langle$stmt. no.$\rangle$ which occurs after the related DO statement and which is not an IF, GO TO, RETURN, STOP, END, ELSE, or another DO. CONTINUE statements are always recommended as DO terminators. The DO-loop limits, $b_{low}, b_{high}, b_{step}$, are numerical constants, variables, or expressions that are converted to the type of the counter a_c before execution of the loop. Generally, a DO loop will execute zero times if $b_{low} > b_{high}$ (if $b_{step} > 0$ or omitted) or if $b_{low} < b_{high}$ and b_{step} is negative. If the loop executes zero times, the counter variable has the value of b_{low}. Transfer out of a loop before completion is permitted and the value of a_c will be its most recent value. Branching into a DO loop that has not yet been initiated is forbidden; however, branching out and then back in is permitted provided the counter variable has not been redefined. This, however, is strongly discouraged.
Nested Loops [p.78]	DO loops can be nested provided one loop is totally contained within the

other. Nested loops may share the same terminal line. Branching to a shared terminal statement from an inner loop does not constitute branching out of the inner loop. If a block IF contains a DO loop, the loop must be completely contained within the block.

A.5 FORTRAN FILE DIRECTIVE STATEMENTS

Statement
OPEN(⟨arg. list⟩)
[pp.129–131]

Comment
The OPEN statement is used to assign a unit number to an already existing file, to a newly created file, or to alter some properties of existing files. The extensive options permitted in the argument list are explained in Section 4.6.2. The most common use is to permit a program to access a separate data file or to write output on a disk-stored file. The shortened form is then

```
OPEN(13,FILE='DATAFL',STATUS='OLD')
OPEN(14,FILE='RESULTS',STATUS='NEW')
```

The unit number can be a positive integer (of three digits or less) or an integer constant name initialized in a parameter statement. When a program begins execution, the input and output files are automatically connected to the program and need not be opened. These files may be specified by using an asterisk in place of the unit number in I/O statements.

CLOSE(⟨arg. list⟩)
[pp.131–132]

The CLOSE statement is used to disconnect a file from a unit number enabling that unit to be connected to a different file. The most common form is

```
CLOSE(<unit no.>)
  or
CLOSE(UNIT=<unit no.>)
```

Any file that has been previously opened with a status other than "SCRATCH" (i.e., either "OLD" or "NEW") will automatically be retained on the system after a CLOSE. To disconnect *and* delete the file from the system, the option STATUS = "DELETE" is included in the argument list. SCRATCH files are always automatically deleted upon termination of a program. Also, the system will automatically CLOSE all connected files upon program termination, so this statement is often unnecessary.

(∗)INQUIRE(⟨arg. list⟩)

Fortran 77 permits the user to ascertain the present attributes of a file by means of the INQUIRE statement. This statement is generally used to avoid errors in opening a file or in reading or writing a file. The options available in the argument list are very extensive and it is suggested that if you think you have need for this statement, a detailed account can be found in Balfour and Marwich or in Wagener listed in the references.

REWIND([UNIT=]⟨unit no.⟩)
[pp.131–132]

The REWIND statement positions a file to the beginning of the file. The file must have been previously opened and assigned a ⟨unit no.⟩. A shortened form is

```
REWIND <unit no.>
```
⟨no parentheses needed⟩

The ⟨unit no.⟩ is a positive integer (of three digits or less) or an integer constant initialized in a PARAMETER statement.

(∗)BACKSPACE ([UNIT=]⟨unit no.⟩)

Similar to REWIND, except the file is only backspaced one record (usually one line). Only sequential files can be backspaced.

(∗)ENDFILE([UNIT =]⟨unit no.⟩)

The END FILE statement puts an end-of-file mark on the file connected to ⟨unit no.⟩. This is useful when constructing a data file and the "END =" option in the READ statement is anticipated. Only sequential files can be marked with an end-of-file.

A.6 INPUT/OUTPUT STATEMENTS

Input/Output Lists

The I/O list (designated in what follows as either ⟨in list⟩ or ⟨out list⟩) is that part of an I/O statement in which the elements to be read or written are specified along with their ordering. The elements of an input list may be variables, array names, or elements, or these items enclosed in an implied DO loop. The elements of an output list may additionally include constants, arithmetic expressions, character string constants, or references to functions, provided the functions themselves neither cause I/O operations nor alter other elements of the list. A character string constant is a string enclosed in apostrophes—e.g., 'THE ANSWER IS'. The appearance of the name only of an array in either an input or an output list will cause the entire array to be read or written in the order in which it is stored. An implied DO loop in an I/O list is treated as a single element of the list. (For a more detailed description of implied DO loops see Section 6.5.)

Statement	Comment
READ([UNIT=]⟨unit no.⟩,⟨format⟩[,ERR=⟨err-sl⟩][,END=⟨end-sl⟩])⟨in list⟩ [p.139]	The only essential specifications in the READ statement are the input unit number ⟨unit no.⟩ and the format specification ⟨format⟩ that specifies the arrangement of the items in the input list ⟨in list⟩. The unit number may refer to any opened file or may be replaced by an asterisk which is the default specification for file INPUT. The optional specifications, ERR = ⟨err-sl⟩ will cause a transfer to the statement labeled by statement number ⟨err-sl⟩ if an error is encountered during the read and END = ⟨end-sl⟩ will do similarly if an end-of-file mark is encountered. Examples,

```
READ(5,3)X
```
Read from file 5 according to format 3, the value of X.

```
READ(*,3,ERR=9)Y
```
Read X from file INPUT according to format 3; if error, branch to statement 9.

Additionally, the format specification ⟨format⟩ may be either the statement number of an existing FORMAT statement, a set of format specifications enclosed in parentheses and delimited fore and aft by apostrophes, as

```
'(1X,F5.3,/,10X,I5)'
```

or it may simply be a single asterisk, in which case the variables are read without format as list-directed input. List-directed input data elements are separated by commas. Example,

```
READ(*,*)X
```
Reads X from file INPUT without a format.

Statement	Comment

WRITE([UNIT=]⟨unit no.⟩,⟨format⟩[,ERR=⟨err-sl⟩])⟨out-list⟩
[p.139]
The meaning of the specifications are the same as in the READ statement except that replacing the ⟨unit no.⟩ by an asterisk will cause the output to be written to the file OUTPUT. A shortened form of this statement is

```
PRINT <format>,<out list>
e.g.
PRINT 6,X     Print X according
to format 6
PRINT *,X Print X without
format specifications
```

If the ⟨format⟩ = '*' option is used, the elements of the ⟨out list⟩ are written in a format controlled by the compiler.

⟨stmt. no.⟩ FORMAT (⟨format spec. list⟩)
[p.140ff]
A FORMAT statement is nonexecutable, must have a statement number, and can appear anywhere within a program unit. The format specification list is a sequence of editing specifications

separated by commas and of the form

$$[n]\langle\text{edit-rep.}\rangle$$
$$\langle\text{edit-nonrep.}\rangle$$
$$[n](\text{format spec. list})$$

where $[n]$ is an optional positive (unsigned) integer repeat constant, $\langle\text{edit-rep.}\rangle$ is a repeatable edit specification, $\langle\text{edit-nonrep.}\rangle$ is a nonrepeatable edit specification, and the last form is a multiple of an entire format specification sublist. For a description of the more common edit specifications see Chapter 5.

REFERENCES

Fortran 77 References

American National Standards Institute: *American National Standard Fortran X3.9-1978* (this is the standard of Fortran-77.), 1430 Broadway, New York.

Balfour, A., and D. H. Marwick: *Programming in Standard Fortran 77*, North Holland, New York, 1979. A comprehensive listing of all features of Fortran-77.

Kernighan, B., and P. J. Plauger: *The Elements of Programming Style*, McGraw-Hill, New York, 1974.

Merchant, Michael J.: *Fortran-77, Language and Style*, Wadsworth, Belmont, Cal., 1981. A comprehensive treatment of Fortran 77 from a nonengineering perspective.

Wagener, Jerold L.: *Fortran 77*, John Wiley, New York, 1980. Contains a more extensive description of the application of data files.

Numerical Methods References

Abramowitz, M., and I. Stegun (eds.): Handbook of *Mathematical Functions with Formulas, Graphs, and Mathematical Tables*, National Bureau of Standards (reprinted by Dover, New York, 1964).

Acton, F. S.: *Numerical Methods That Work*, Harper & Row, New York, 1970.

Cheney, W., and D. Kincaid: *Numerical Mathematics and Computing,* Brooks/Cole, Monterey, Cal., 1980.

Collatz, L. *The Numerical Treatment of Differential Equations,* 3rd ed., Springer-Verlag, Berlin, 1966.

Conte, S. D., and C. deBoor: *Elementary Numerical Analysis,* McGraw-Hill, New York, 1972.

Hornbeck, R. W.: *Numerical Methods,* Quantum, New York, 1975.

Milne, W. E.: *Numerical Solution of Differential Equations,* John Wiley, New York, 1953.

Pennington, R. H.: *Introductory Computer Methods and Numerical Analysis,* 2nd ed., Macmillan, London, 1970.

Ralston, A.: *A First Course in Numerical Analysis,* McGraw-Hill, New York, 1965.

Schultz, M. H.: *Spline Analysis,* Prentice-Hall, Englewood Cliffs, N.J., 1973.

Southworth, R. W., and S. L. DeLeeuw: *Digital Computation and Numerical Methods,* McGraw-Hill, New York, 1965.

Wilkinson, J. H.: *Rounding Errors in Algebraic Processes,* Prentice-Hall, Englewood Cliffs, N.J., 1963.

ANSWERS AND SOLUTIONS TO ODD-NUMBERED PROBLEMS

Chapter 1

1. a) $(11)_{10} = 2 \times 5 + 1$
$\quad\quad\quad\quad \llcorner = 2 \times 2 + 1$
$\quad\quad\quad\quad\quad\quad \llcorner = 2 \times 1 + 0$
$\quad\quad\quad\quad\quad\quad\quad\quad \llcorner = 2 \times 0 + 1$

$\quad\quad = (1011)_2$

c) $(100)_{10} = (1100100)_2$

e) $(12.625)_{10}$: $\quad (12)_{10} = (1100)_2$

$\quad\quad\quad .625 \times 2 = 1 + .25$
$\quad\quad\quad .25 \quad \times 2 = 0 + .5$
$\quad\quad\quad .5 \quad\ \times 2 = 1 + 0$
$\quad\quad\quad (.625)_{10} = (.101)_2$
$\quad (12.625)_{10} = (1100.101)_2$

f) $(0.1)_{10}$: $\quad .1 \times 2 = 0 + .2$
$\quad\quad\quad\quad .2 \times 2 = 0 + .4$
$\quad\quad\quad\quad .4 \times 2 = 0 + .8$
$\quad\quad\quad\quad .8 \times 2 = 1 + .6$
$\quad\quad\quad\quad .6 \times 2 = 1 + .2$
$\quad\quad\quad\quad .2 \times 2 = 0 + .4$
$\quad\quad\quad\quad .4 \times 2 = 0 + .8$
$\quad\quad\quad\quad .8 \times 2 = 1 + .6$
$\quad\quad\quad\quad\quad\quad \cdots\quad\quad\quad \cdots$
$\quad (0.1)_{10} = (.00011001100110011\ldots)_2$

3. a) $\quad 1011 \quad\quad\quad\quad 11$
$\quad\ \underline{+\ 11} \quad \rightarrow \quad \underline{+3}$
$\quad\ \overline{(1110)_2} \quad\quad\quad \overline{(14)_{10}}$

b) $\quad 1010 \quad\quad\quad\quad 10$
$\quad\ \underline{-\ 11} \quad \rightarrow \quad \underline{-3}$
$\quad\ \overline{(111)_2} \quad\quad\quad\ \overline{(7)_{10}}$

5. Faced with an arrangement of two unequal rows of markers, the winning move is to remove markers from the longer row until the remaining two rows are of equal length. The opponent's move must remove this symmetry. Your next move restores it—i.e., results in rows of equal length. Finally, your next to last move results in

$$X$$
$$X$$

which obviously leads to a win.

The idea is to keep the number of counters in each *column* even. Extending this to more than two rows, the basic idea of preserving a pattern from one move to the next remains. The final winning pattern above can also be described in terms of the base-two number of markers in each row.

$$X\ (0001)_2$$
$$X\ (0001)_2$$

The signature of this pattern is that the ones or zeros in each *column* of the base-two representation of the numbers add to an even number (here 0 or 2). *Any* alteration of a single row, even empty rows, will result in at least one of the columns being odd.

Chapter 2

1. a) $[(2.^{1/2})^2 - 2.]$ evaluated on a variety of computing devices yields:

CDC-CYBER computer	DEC-20 computer	TI calc.
0.0	2.980E−8	−1.9E−9

while $[(3.^{1/2})^2 - 3.]$ yields:

−1.421E−14	0.0	−2.5E−9

The approximate number of significant figures is then:

14	8	9

b) Executing the INTEGER program yields the following results:

$$\text{CDC-CYBER} - I_{max} = 100\ 000\ 000\ 000\ 000$$
$$\text{DEC-20} - I_{max} = 1\ 000\ 000\ 000$$

3. a) $\quad 1000.00$
$\quad\ \underline{+\quad .00999999}$
$\quad = 1000.00\underline{999999}$ ⟨Assuming the computer does not round the result.⟩ Thus, EPS = .00999999.

b) If EPS = 0.0001 and forgetting for a moment that the computer does binary, not decimal arithmetic, the first 100,000,000 terms add to 100.000. Adding .0001 to this number does not change the sum. (100.000 + .0001 = 100.) Thus the 10^8 terms will add to 100.

c) $10^8 \times 10^{-4} = 10^4 = 10,000.$

5. a) ERROR, no commas

   b) ERROR, no decimal point allowed in exponent

   c) OK, but base should have decimal point

   d) OK, mixed-mode replacement

e) OK

f) ERROR, 6XA not valid variable name

g) OK

h) ERROR, two arithmetic operators cannot touch, ⟨**−⟩

i) ERROR, cannot take square root of negative 3.

j) OK, result = 1.

k) OK, mixed-mode replacement

l) OK, but does nothing

7. a) 3.　　b) 4　　c) 0
　 d) 4.　　e) 1　　f) 1.5
　 g) 9　　 h) 5　　i) 4.5
　 j) 27.　 k) 1

9. a) X*Y/(Z + 1)
   b) X**(N + 1)
   c) X**(1./2.) or X**.5
   d) ACOS(ABS(LOG(X))) ⟨note three right parentheses⟩
   e) (X**A)**B or X**(A*B)

Chapter 3

1. a) THEN must be on same line as IF(. . .)
   b) OK
   c) OK, but note the first two tests are mutually exclusive—i.e., there is no possibility of executing the PRINT.

3. a) ERROR, must GO TO a statement number, not a name.
   b) OK
   c) OK
   d) ERROR, A = 0. does not have a value of true or false. The expression should be A .EQ. 0.
   e) ERROR, both sides of .AND. must be either true or false. Expression should read

   ```
   X .EQ. 1.5 .AND. Y .EQ. 1.5
   ```

   f) OK, but odd logic
   g) ERROR, the conditional result of a logical IF must be an executable statement,

   ```
   IF(A .EQ. 0.)A = 0.
   ```

   Note, this statement will not alter A.
   h) ERROR, the executable statement following the IF test must not be another IF test.
   i) OK, assuming the variables GE and LE have values.
   j) OK, assuming the variable EQ has a value.

k) OK

5. a) True; b) True; c) False

7. Using the features of integer arithmetic, the program can be constructed from

```
INTEGER N
READ *, N
IF((N/2)*2 .EQ. N)THEN
    N is divisible by 2 and is even
ELSE
    N is odd
END IF
```

9. The conditions that must be satisfied if four lengths a, b, c, d are to form a polygon are:

$$a \leq b + c + d$$
$$b \leq a + c + d$$
$$c \leq a + b + d$$
$$d \leq a + b + c$$

```
    PROGRAM POLYGON
    REAL A,B,C,D
    READ *,A,B,C,D
*      a) Test four conditions
    IF(A.LE.B+C+D .AND.B .LE. A+C+D .AND.
   + C.LE.A+B+D .AND. D .LE. A+B+C)THEN
       PRINT *,A,B,C,D,'CAN FORM A POLYGON'
    ELSE
       PRINT *,A,B,C,D,'CAN NOT FORM POLYGON'
    END IF
*      b) Next test for equal sides
    IF(A .EQ. C .AND. B .EQ. D)THEN
       PRINT *,'A RECTANGLE IS POSSIBLE'
       IF(A .EQ. B)THEN
       PRINT *,'WHICH IS A SQUARE'
       END IF
    ELSE
        PRINT *,'RECTANGLE NOT POSSIBLE'
    END IF
    STOP
    END
```

11. The results for the functions given in the problem are:

```
IMAX = 25, DXMAX = 0.8,
EPS = 1.E-5, X0 = 0.8
```

a) $x_1 = [\ln(3/x)]^{1/2}$,　$x = 1.032683$
   after 14 iterations
   $x_1 = 3e^{-x^2}$, diverges after one iteration

b) $x_1 = [7 - 5x^3]^{1/10}$, diverges after one step negative base to real
   $x_1 = [(7 - x^{10})/5]^{1/3}$, excessive iterations last $x = 1.0347$

13.
```
   PROGRAM PRIME
   INTEGER N,P
   PRINT *,'ENTER A POTENTIAL PRIME, N'
```

```
READ *,N
IF((N/2)*2 ,EQ, N)THEN
    PRINT *,N,'IS NOT PRIME'
    PRINT *,'IT IS AN EVEN NUMBER'
END IF
P = 3
1 IF((N/P)*P ,EQ, N)THEN
    PRINT *,N,' IS NOT PRIME'
    PRINT *,'IT IS DIVISIBLE BY ',P
    STOP
ELSE
    P = P + 2
    IF(P ,GE, SQRT(N + 1,))THEN
       PRINT *,N,' IS PRIME'
       STOP
    ELSE
       GO TO 1
    END IF
END IF
END
```

Chapter 4

1. a) `F(X) = 3,*X*X + X - 1,`
b) `G(X,A,B,C) = A*X*X + B*X + C`
c) `H(X,A) = EXP(-A*X) + LOG(SIN(ACOS(-1,)*X))`
d) `INDEX(I,J) = 3*I + 2*J`

3.
```
PROGRAM SUMS
INTEGER I,IMAX
REAL    ANSWER,TERM,EPS
IMAX = 100
EPS = 1,E-6
I   = 0
    ANSWER = 0,         ⟨problems a–e⟩
           = 1,         ⟨problem f⟩
    TERM   = 1,         ⟨problems a,b,c,e⟩
           = 0,25       ⟨problem d⟩
           = 4,/3,      ⟨problem f⟩
*
  1 ANSWER = ANSWER + TERM      ⟨problems a–e⟩
           = ANSWER * TERM      ⟨problem f⟩
    IF(ABS(TERM) ,LT, EPS)THEN  ⟨problems a–e⟩
    IF(ABS(TERM-1,) , , ,       ⟨problem f⟩
       PRINT *,'ANSWER = ',ANSWER
       STOP
    END IF
    I = I + 1
    IF(I ,GT, IMAX)THEN
       PRINT *,'NO RESULT IN ',I,' STEPS'
       STOP
    END IF
    TERM = 1,/I**2                      (a)
         = (-1,)**(I+1)/(2,*I-1,)       (b)
         = TERM/2,                      (c)
         = TERM/4,                      (d)
         = TERM/I                       (e)
         =(2,*I)**2/(2,*I-1,)/(2,*I+1,) (f)
```

```
GO TO 1
END
```

5. The equation can be written as

$$r^2 + r - 1 = 0$$

which, from the quadratic equation, has roots $(\sqrt{5} - 1)/2, -(\sqrt{5} + 1)/2$.

7.
```
PROGRAM NUMBRS
INTEGER I
REAL T,DT,X,Y,VX,VY,G
G = 9,8
VX = 10,5
VY = 51,0
DT = 0,1
OPEN(22,FILE = 'DATA22',STATUS = 'NEW')
WRITE(22,*)DT, ',' ,VX, ',' ,VY
I = 1
1 T = I*DT
X = VX*T
Y = VY*T - (G/2,)*T*T
WRITE(22,*)T, ',' ,X, ',' ,Y
I = I + 1
IF(I ,LE, 100)THEN
    GO TO 1
ELSE
    CLOSE 22
    STOP
END IF
STOP
END
```
```
*********************************************
PROGRAM READAT
INTEGER I
REAL    T,DT,X,VX,Y,VY
OPEN(35,FILE = 'DATA22',STATUS = 'OLD')
REWIND 35
READ(35,*)DT,VX,VY
PRINT *,'DT = ',DT,' VX = ',VX,' VY = ',VY
I = 1
PRINT *,'I      T       X        Y'
1 READ(35,*)T,X,Y
PRINT *,I,T,X,Y
I = I + 1
IF(I ,LE, 100)THEN
    GO TO 1
ELSE
    PRINT *,'END OF DATA FILE'
    STOP
END IF
END
```

9.
```
PROGRAM MAX
INTEGER I,IMAX
REAL    X0,X1,DX,F0,F1
F(X) = ⟨statement function for f(x)⟩
PRINT *,'ENTER STARTING X AND STEP SIZE'
```

```
      READ  *,X,DX
      PRINT *,'ENTER MAXIMUM NUMBER OF STEPS'
      READ  *,IMAX
      I = 0
      XO = X
      FO = F(XO)
  1  X1 = XO + DX
      F1 = F(X1)
      I  = I + 1
      IF(I .GT. IMAX)THEN
          PRINT *,'IN THE RANGE ',X,' TO ',X1
          PRINT *,'THE MAXIMUM OF F(X) IS AT ',
     +          'F(',X1,') = ',F1
          STOP
      END IF
      IF(FO .GT. F1)THEN
        DX = -DX/2.
      ELSE IF(F1 .EQ. FO)THEN
        PRINT *,'THE FUNCTION IS THE SAME',
     +          ' AT X = ',XO,' AND X = ',X1
        PRINT *,'PROGRAM STOPS WITH I = ',I
        STOP
      END IF
        XO = X1
        FO = F1
        GO TO 1
      END
```

Chapter 5

1. a)

Method 1:   `READ *, . . . ⟨defaults to file INPUT⟩`

or

Method 2:   `OPEN(12,FILE = 'INPUT')`
`READ(12,*) . . .`

`READ(*,*) . . .`

b)

Method 1:   `READ(*,*,END = . . .)`

Method 2:   insert a trailing data line that can be used as a flag.

```
READ(*,*)ID,Q1,Q2, . . .
IF(ID .LT. 0)THEN
```
⟨End of data⟩

c) `PRINT '(1X,F9.6)',EXP(ACOS(-1.)`

d) Most compilers will not inform you if a FORMAT statement is not referenced in the program.

e) The format specifications T, /, and ' cannot be repeated by preceding with an integer.

f) Examples of when replacing WRITE by READ will result in a compilation error.

`READ(*,*,END = . . .) → WRITE(*,*,END = . . .)`

⟨There is no End-of-File check with a WRITE statement.⟩

`READ 12,A,B,C → WRITE 12,A,B,C`

⟨The correct form of the shortened WRITE statement is PRINT 12, A,B,C.⟩

g) No, FORMAT statements are not executable.

3. a) ERROR. The integer IY is read with an F4.1 format. This will result in an incorrect assignment.

b) ERROR. The REAL variable Y is read with an I5 format and the integer IX is read with an F5.1. If Y contains a decimal point, this will result in an execution time error.

c) No error, but FORMAT 3 is used twice.

d) ERROR. The FORMAT is too wide. This is an execution time error.

e) OK. Note, the entire FORMAT is not used.

f) OK

5. a) OK, results in three lines of output.

b) OK

c) OK

d) ERROR. The FORMAT partially overwrites the values for A and B, and the values for C and D. Three lines are printed.

e) OK

f) OK, however, the zero and the second + sign are not displayed.

g) ERROR. The real quantity A is assigned to an 'A' format.

h) OK. No value for C will be printed. The FORMAT statement is only partially used.

7.
```
col.          1    1    2    2    3
    1...5....0....5....0....5....0
a) ϦϦ1.ϦϦ2.00.3ϦϦϦϦ2ϦϦϦϦ3
b) ϦϦϦϦ    .1E+01    .2E+01
   Ϧ3
c) ϦϦ     .1E+01    2
   ϦϦ     .2E+01    3
   ϦϦ     .3E+00
d)   1.0 = X
e) ϦϦϦϦϦϦϦ
      1.
   ϦϦϦϦϦϦϦ
      2.
   ϦϦϦϦϦϦϦ
      0.
f) ϦϦ 0.*****
g) 1.0***    2
   2.0---    3
h) ϦϦϦϦ    .333E+00    .300E+01  ⟨the last number
                           will be small and machine dependent⟩
```

9. a)
```
PRINT '(1X,F10.5)',X,Y,X + Y
```
b)
```
PRINT '(1X,A,F10.5)','X = ',X,'Y = ',Y
```

11.
```
PROGRAM METALS
CHARACTER METAL*10
INTEGER   STEP
REAL      TEMP
OPEN(27,FILE = 'MTLDTA')
REWIND 27
I = 0
WRITE(*,10)
1 READ(27,11,END = 99)METAL,TEMP
   I = I + 1
   WRITE(*,12)I,METAL,TEMP
   IF(TEMP .GT. 1400.)THEN
      WRITE(*,13)'TOO HIGH'
   ELSE IF(TEMP .LT. 600.)THEN
      WRITE(*,13)'TOO LOW'
   END IF
   GO TO 1
99 STOP
10 FORMAT(T4,'      METAL    MELTING',/,
   +       T4,'NUMBER TYPE      TEMP. ',/,
   +       T4,'----   -----    -------')
11 FORMAT(A10,F6.0)
12 FORMAT(T6,I2,3X,A10,1X,F6.1)
13 FORMAT('+',T28,A)
   END
```

13.
```
PROGRAM PERFEC
INTEGER I, ITEST
REAL XI
I = 2
WRITE(*,9)
1 XI = I
WRITE(*,10)I
ITEST = SQRT(XI) + .000001
```
⟨A small number is added to SQRT to avoid truncation of a real number like 1.99999999 . . . .⟩
```
IF(ITEST**2 .EQ. I)THEN
   WRITE(*,11)ITEST
END IF
ITEST = XI**(1./3.) + .000001
IF(ITEST**3 .EQ. I)THEN
   WRITE(*,12)ITEST
END IF
I = I + 1
IF(I .LE. 100)THEN
   GO TO 1
ELSE
   STOP
END IF
9 FORMAT('1',T10,'LIST OF THE INTEGERS')
10 FORMAT(T20,I3)
11 FORMAT('+',T25,'IS THE SQUARE OF ',I4)
12 FORMAT('+'T46,'IS THE CUBE OF ',I4)
   END
```

15. a)
```
1 FORMAT(T10,' MM      MM ',/,
  +       T10,' MMM    MMM ',/,
```

```
  +       T10,' MM M    M MM ',/,
  +       T10,' MM M  M  M MM ',/,
  +       T10,' MM  M M  M MM ',/,
  +       T10,' MM   M M   MM ',/,
  +       T10,'MMMM    M  MMMM')
```

c)
```
   PROGRAM ADDER
   CHARACTER RESPNS*3
   INTEGER   I
   REAL      X, SUM
   PRINT *,'DO YOU WISH TO COMPUTE A SUM'
   PRINT *,'ENTER YES OR NO'
   READ'(A)'RESPNS
   IF(RESPNS .EQ. 'YES')THEN
      WRITE(*,*)'ENTREES'
      I = 0
      SUM = 0.0
      PRINT *,'ENTER THE TEN NUMBERS ONE'
   +         ' AT A TIME USING F10.5'
1     PRINT *,'ENTER NUMBER NOW'
      READ(*,'(F10.5)')X
      WRITE(*,'(T13,F8.4)')X
      I = I + 1
      SUM = SUM + X
      IF(I .LT. 10)THEN
         GO TO 1
      ELSE
         WRITE(*,11)SUM
      END IF
   END IF
   STOP
11 FORMAT('+',8X,'+',/,T12,9('-'),/,1X,
   +       'TOTAL = ',E12.4)
   END
```

Chapter 6

1. a) ERROR. This was probably intended as B(5000). It will be interpreted as B(5,0) and an array cannot be specified as having zero positions for a subscript.

b) OK, but the array will reserve $9^7 \sim 5$ million computer words. This is very likely beyond the capacity of your computer's main memory.

c) ERROR. Executable statements may not precede dimension statements.

d) ERROR. The variable name INTEGERI has 8 characters. This was probably intended as

```
INTEGER I(50)
REAL    X(25)
```

e) ERROR. Only integers may be used to specify subscript bounds.

f) ERROR. Variable names cannot be used to specify subscript bounds.

g) ERROR. Even if A is of type CHARACTER,

the expression (1:2) following the specification of the subscript bound has no meaning. This may have been intended as A(5,1:2), which is the same as A(5,2).

h) OK

i) OK

j) OK. That is, A(0) is an integer.

k) OK. However, it is bad style to use the name REAL as a variable.

l) OK. Same comment as above.

m) ERROR. The order must be lower bound:upper bound, i.e., (−7:−5).

3.

```
PROGRAM GRIDS
INTEGER IZ(0:20,0:20),IX,IY
REAL     Z(0:20,0:20),X,Y,ZMAX,ZMIN
F(X,Y) = EXP(X-Y)*SIN(5.*X)*COS(2.*Y)
DO 1 IX = 0,20
DO 1 IY = 0,20
   X = IX/10.
   Y = IY/10.
   Z(IX,IY) = F(X,Y)
1  CONTINUE
ZMAX = Z(0,0)
ZMIN = Z(0,0)
DO 2 IX = 0,20
DO 2 IY = 0,20
   IF(Z(IX,IY) .LT. ZMIN)ZMIN = Z(IX,IY)
   IF(Z(IX,IY) .GT. ZMAX)ZMAX = Z(IX,IY)
2  CONTINUE
DO 3 IX = 0,20
DO 3 IY = 0,20
   IZ(IX,IY) = 10.*(Z(IX,IY) - ZMIN)/
  +              (ZMAX - ZMIN)
3  CONTINUE
DO 4 IY = 20,0,-1
   Y = IY/10.
   WRITE(*,10)Y,(Z(IX,IY),IX = 0,20)
4  CONTINUE
WRITE(*,11)(IX/10.,IX = 0,20,5)
STOP
10 FORMAT('1',T3,F3.1,T9,21(1X,I1,1X))
11 FORMAT(T9,5(F3.1,12X))
END
```

5.

```
PROGRAM SUMS
INTEGER I,IMAX
REAL     ANSWER,TERM,EPS
IMAX = 100
EPS  = 1.E-6
   ANSWER = 0.       ⟨probs.  a–e⟩
        = 1.         ⟨prob.  f⟩
   TERM  = 1.        ⟨probs.  a,b,c,e⟩
        = 0.25       ⟨prob.  d⟩
        = 4./3.      ⟨prob.  f⟩
DO 1 I = 1,IMAX
```

```
   ANSWER = ANSWER + TERM          ⟨probs.  a–e⟩
          = ANSWER * TERM          ⟨prob.  f⟩
   IF(ABS(TERM) .LT. EPS)THEN      ⟨probs.  a–e⟩
      (ABS(TERM-1.)...             ⟨prob.  f⟩
      PRINT *,'ANSWER = ',ANSWER
      STOP
   END IF
   TERM = 1./I**2                          (a)
        = (-1.)**(I + 1)/(2.*I - 1.)       (b)
        = TERM/2.                          (c)
        = TERM/4.                          (d)
        = TERM/I                           (e)
        = (2.*I)**2/(2.*I - 1.)/(2.*I + 1.) (f)
1  CONTINUE
PRINT *,'NO RESULT IN ',IMAX,' STEPS'
STOP
END
```

7. a)
```
   SUM = 0.0
   DO 1 I = 1,10
      SUM = SUM + A(I)*X(I)
1  CONTINUE
```
b)
```
   DO 2 I = 1,10
      T(I) = 0.0
      DO 1 J = 1,10
         T(I) = T(I) + A(I,J)*X(J)
1     CONTINUE
2  CONTINUE
```
c)
```
   DO 2 I = 1,10
   DO 2 J = 1,10
      C(I,J) = 0.0
      DO 1 K = 1,10
         C(I,J) = C(I,J) + A(I,K)*B(K,J)
1     CONTINUE
2  CONTINUE
```

9. The array K_{ij} contains the following integers:

i \ j	0	1	2	3	4
0	0	1	2	3	4
1	10	11	12	13	14
2	20	21	22	23	24
3	30	31	32	33	34
4	40	41	42	43	44

a) ⊮ 1 2 3 4

b) ⊮⊮ 11 12 13 14 21
⊮⊮ 22 23 24 31 32
⊮⊮ 33 34 41 42 43
⊮⊮ 44

c) ⊮⊮⊮⊮⊮   0   1   2   3   4
⊮⊮0⊮⊮   0   1   2   3   4
⊮⊮1⊮⊮ 10 11 12 13 14
⊮⊮2⊮⊮ 20 21 22 23 24
⊮⊮3⊮⊮ 30 31 32 33 34
⊮⊮4⊮⊮ 40 41 42 43 44

d) ⊮⊮   0   1   2   3   4
⊮⊮ 11 12 13 14 22
⊮⊮ 23 24 33 34 44

e)
```
ʙʙ 40 30 20 10 0
ʙʙ 41 31 21 11 1
ʙʙ 42 32 22 12 2
ʙʙ 43 33 23 13 3
ʙʙ 44 34 24 14 4
```
f)
```
ʙʙ  0  1  2  3  4
ʙʙ 11 12 13 14
ʙʙ 22 23 24
ʙʙ 33 34
ʙʙ 44
```
g)
```
 0  1  2  3  4
   11 12 13 14
      22 23 24
         33 34
            44
```

Chapter 7

1. a) ʙA
   b) ʙ12345
   c) ʙAʙʙʙʙ
   d) ʙA
   e) ʙ45
   f) ʙAʙʙʙʙ
   g) ʙ12345
   h) ʙA4512
   i) ʙ1
      ʙ2
      ʙ3
      ʙ4
      ʙ5
   j) ʙA1234
   k) ʙ1234512345

3.
```
PROGRAM FOG
CHARACTER LINE*80
INTEGER NSNTC,NWORD,LEFTWD,RGHTWD,
+                    LEFTSN,RGHTSN
NSNTC = 0
NWORD = 0
LEFTSN = 1
1 READ(*,'(A)',END = 99)LINE
LEFTWD = 1
```
⟨LEFTWD is the position of the left end of the current word. LEFTSN is the position of the left end of the current sentence.⟩
```
3 RGHTSN = INDEX(LINE(LEFTSN:),'. ')
  IF(RGHTSN .NE. 0)THEN
     NSNTC = NSNTC + 1
     LEFTSN = RGHTSN + 1
     GO TO 3
  END IF
2 RGHTWD = INDEX(LINE(LEFTWD:),' ')
  IF(RGHTWD .EQ. LEFTWRD + 1)THEN
     GO TO 1
  ELSE
     NWORD = NWORD + 1
```

```
     LEFTWD = RGHTWD + 1
     GO TO 2
  END IF
GO TO 1
99 PRINT *,'FOG FACTORS'
PRINT *,'NUMBER OF WORDS = ',NWORD
PRINT *,'NUMBER OF SENTENCES = ',NSNTC
STOP
END
```

5.
```
CHARACTER LINE*50, NUMB*8
1 READ(*,'(A)',END = 99)LINE
  MATCH1 = INDEX(LINE,'JONES, JAMES')
  IF(MATCH1 .NE. 0)THEN
     I      = MATCH1 + 12
     MATCH2 = INDEX(LINE(I:),'JENNINGS')
     IF(MATCH2 .NE. 0)THEN
        NPOS = INDEX(LINE,'-')
        NUMB = LINE(NPOS-3:NPOS + 4)
        WRITE(*,'(A,A)')'NO. = ',NUMB
        STOP
     ELSE
     GO TO 1
     END IF
     END IF
     GO TO 1
99 WRITE(*,*)'NOT IN PHONE BOOK'
STOP
END
```

7. Simply replace MIN by MAX and .LT. by .GT.

9.
```
DO 2 I = 1,N - 1      ⟨I is the top element
                       in current comparison
                       set.⟩
   FLAG = 'OFF'
   DO 1 J = N,I + 1,-1  ⟨Compare pairs of
                         remaining set
                         starting at the
                         bottom.⟩
      IF(A(J) .LT. A(J - 1))THEN
                         ⟨If out of order,
                          exchange.⟩
         TEMP = A(J)
         A(J) = A(J - 1)
         A(J - 1) = TEMP
         FLAG = 'ON '
      END IF
1     CONTINUE
      IF(FLAG .EQ. 'OFF')THEN
         GO TO 3
      END IF
2  CONTINUE
3  CONTINUE
```
11.
```
PROGRAM BUBBLE
CHARACTER FLAG*3
INTEGER   INDX(1000),I,N,J,TEMP
REAL      A(1000)
READ(*,*,END = 99)(A(I),I = 1,1000)
```

```
 99  N = I - 1
     DO 1 I = 1,N
         INDX(I) = I
  1  CONTINUE
     DO 3 I = N,2,-1
         FLAG = 'OFF'
         DO 2 J = 1,I-1
           IF(A(INDX(J)) .GT. A(INDX(J + 1))THEN
               TEMP        = INDX(J)
               INDX(J)     = INDX(J + 1)
               INDX(J + 1) = TEMP
               FLAG        = 'ON '
           END IF
  2      CONTINUE
         IF(FLAG .EQ. 'OFF')THEN
             GO TO 4
         END IF
  3  CONTINUE
  4  CONTINUE
```

13.
```
     PROGRAM PLOT2
     CHARACTER*1 LINE(0:60)
     INTEGER    ISTAR,IPLUS,IX,N
     REAL       X(0:25),Y(0:25,2),XSTEP,
    +           YMAX,YMIN,SCALE,Z,F1,F2
     F1(Z) = ...
     F2(Z) = ...
     N = 25
     BLANK = ' '
     STAR  = '*'
     PLUS  = '+'
     READ(*,*)XLO,XHI
     XSTEP = (XHI - XLO)/(N - 1.)
     DO 1 I = 0,N
         X(I) = I*XSTEP
         Y(I,1) = F1(X(I))
         Y(I,2) = F2(X(I))
  1  CONTINUE
     YMAX = Y(0,1)
     YMIN = Y(0,1)
     DO 2 I = 0,N
     DO 2 K = 1,2
         IF(Y(I,K) .LT. YMIN)YMIN = Y(I,K)
         IF(Y(I,K) .GT. YMAX)YMAX = Y(I,K)
  2  CONTINUE
     SCALE = YMAX - YMIN
     DO 3 I = 0,60
         LINE(I) = ' '
  3  CONTINUE
     WRITE(*,12)
     DO 4 IX = 0,25
         ISTAR = (Y(IX,1) - YMIN)/SCALE * 60,
         IPLUS = (Y(IX,2) - YMIN)/SCALE * 60,
         LINE(ISTAR) = '*'
         LINE(IPLUS) = '+'
         WRITE(*,11)X(IX),Y(IX,1),Y(IX,2),
    +               (LINE(I),I = 0,60)
         LINE(ISTAR) = ' '
         LINE(IPLUS) = ' '
  4  CONTINUE
     STOP
Formats
     END
```

15. A page plot of the function $e^{-x/3}\sin(\pi x/2)$

Chapter 8

1.
```
READ(*,*)X,Y
CALL LENGTH(X,Y,R)
PRINT *,'THE POINT (',X,',',Y,') IS'
IF((R .LT. 3.) .AND. (R .GT. 1.))THEN
    PRINT *,'BETWEEN THE CIRCLES'
ELSE
    PRINT *,'NOT BETWEEN THE CIRCLES'
END IF
```

3. a) Note: A Fortran function must have an argument list; however, the actual list may be empty; for example,

```
FUNCTION DBUG()
SAVE ICALL
DATA ICALL/0/
PRINT *,'IN THIS DEBUGGING RUN THE PRO',
+       'GRAM GOT TO THE ',ICALL,'TH CALL'
+       ' OF THE FUNCTION DBUG'
ICALL = ICALL + 1
DBUG = 1.
RETURN
END
```

b) In all reasonable uses of a function subprogram it is expected that the function will either return to the calling program or will stop.

c) i. yes, ii. yes, iii. no, iv. yes, v. yes.

5.
```
SUBROUTINE MATPRD(A,B,C,N,M)
REAL A(N,N),B(N,N),C(N,N)
DO 7 I = 1,M
DO 7 J = 1,M
   C(I,J) = 0.0
   DO 3 K = 1,M
      C(I,J) = C(I,J) + A(I,K)*B(K,J)
3      CONTINUE
4   CONTINUE
RETURN
END
```

7. a)
```
   SUBROUTINE INPUT(FILE,NAME,INIT,ID,
+          CLASS,SEX,SAT,COLL,GPA,N)
   CHARACTER NAME(8000)*10,INIT(8000)*1,
+          FILE*6,SEX(8000)*1
   INTEGER   ID(8000),CLASS(8000),
+          SAT(2,8000),COLL(8000)
   REAL      GPA(2,8000)
   OPEN(21,FILE = FILE,STATUS = 'OLD')
   REWIND 21
   I = 1
1  READ(21,10,END = 99)NAME(I),INIT(I),
+          ID(I),CLASS(I),SEX(I),SAT(1,I),
+          SAT(2,I),COLL(I),(GPA(L,I),L=1,2)
   I = I + 1
   GO TO 1
99 N = I - 1
   CLOSE 21
   PRINT *,'THE FILE ',FILE,' CONTAINS ',
+     INFORMATION ON ',N,' STUDENTS'
   RETURN
10 FORMAT(A10,A1,I9,I2,A1,2I3,I1,2F4.2)
   END
```

9. The program solution to this problem is quite long but easy to construct. Each of the constants a–f and the variables x, y are declared to be integer arrays with the first element representing the numerator and the second the denominator of the rational fraction. For example, if $a = 1/2$, then $A(1) = 1$,

$A(2) = 2$. The arithmetic required in the equations for the solutions x, y must be written explicitly in terms of subfunctions to multiply and subtract fractions. Finally, after the numerator and denominator of x and y are obtained, they are reduced to lowest terms by using the function IGCD to divide out the greatest common factor in the numerator and the denominator.

11. Replace the line

$$IC = 2.*C + 1$$

by

$$IC = 2.*C - 1$$

13. a) ERROR. An arithmetic operation $(I + 1)$ cannot appear in the definition line of a subroutine.

b) OK, if the position in which $I + 1$ appears is used only as input to the subroutine.

c) ERROR. Parentheses are not allowed within the argument list of the definition line of a subroutine or function.

d) OK

e) ERROR. The name of the function is not assigned a value before the return.

f) ERROR. The name of a subroutine cannot be assigned a value.

15. a)
```
FUNCTION POLY(X,N,C)
INTEGER N
REAL     X,C(0:N),SUM,POLY
SUM = C(0)
DO 1 I = 1,N
   SUM = SUM + C(I)*X**I
1 CONTINUE
POLY = SUM
RETURN
END
```

b)
```
FUNCTION POLYB(X,N,C)
INTEGER N
REAL     X,C(0:N),SUM,POLYB
SUM = C(N)
DO 1 I = N,1,-1
   SUM = SUM*X + C(I - 1)
1 CONTINUE
POLYB = SUM
RETURN
END
```

17.
```
FUNCTION CUBRT(X)
REAL CUBRT,C,X
   C = ABS(X)**(1./3.)
   IF(X .LT. 0.)C = -C
CUBRT = C
RETURN
END
```

19. The result of the calculation is:

```
THE MAXIMUM SURFACE SEPARATION IS
          11009.22 MILES
BETWEEN RIO DE JANEIRO AND VLADIVOSTOK
```

21.

```
PROGRAM SOLVE
REAL GUESS,ANSWER,G
EXTERNAL G
 GUESS = 1.0
 CALL ROOT(GUESS,ANSWER,G)
 PRINT *,'THE ROOT IS ',ANSWER
 STOP
END
FUNCTION G(X)
REAL X,ARGMT,G,PI
EXTERNAL ARGMT
 PI = ACOS(-1.)
 G = 5.*EXP(-2.*X**2) - SIN(PI*X/2.)
+                 + XINTGL(0.,X,ARGMT)
RETURN
END
FUNCTION ARGMT(T)
 ARGMT = (4.*T**2 - 5.)*EXP(-T**2)
RETURN
END
SUBROUTINE ROOT(A,ANSWER,F)
     ...         ...
END
FUNCTION XINTGL(A,B,FNC)
  ...         ...
END
```

Chapter 9

1. a) FALSE, but variables assigned values in a PA-RAMETER statement may only be used after the PARAMETER statement. Thus

```
REAL A(N)
PARAMETER (N = 12)
```

would be an error.

b) False

c) True

d) False

e) False

f) False

3.

```
PROGRAM CSQRT
COMPLEX GUESS, C
REAL DIFF,EPS
INTEGER I,IMAX
IMAX = 30
EPS = 1.E-6
PRINT *,'ENTER A COMPLEX NUMBER WHOSE ',
+        'SQUARE ROOT IS DESIRED'
READ *,C
I = 0
```

```
  PRINT *,'ENTER A GUESS FOR THE SQUARE ',
+        ' ROOT. THE GUESS MUST HAVE ',
+        'A NONZERO IMAGINARY PART'
  READ *,GUESS
1 DIFF = ABS(GUESS*GUESS - C)
  IF(DIFF .LT. EPS)THEN
    PRINT *,'THE SQUARE ROOT OF ',C,' IS'
+       ,X1,' AFTER ',I,' ITERATIONS'
    STOP
  ELSE
    I = I + 1
    IF(I .GT. IMAX)THEN
      PRINT *,'EXCESSIVE ITERATIONS'
      STOP
    END IF
    GUESS = .5*(GUESS + C/GUESS)
    GO TO 1
  END IF
END
```

5. For $I = -1$ and $I = 0$, D has the value ⟨false⟩ while E is ⟨true⟩. So the statement

```
THE ORDER OF AND/OR MAKES
A DIFFERENCE FOR
F .AND. F .OR. T
```

is printed twice.

7. a) ERROR. Only arithmetic expressions involving constants, not intrinsic functions, are allowed in a PARAMETER statement.

b) OK

c) ERROR. Variables assigned values in a PARAMETER statement cannot be used in place of statement numbers.

d) OK

e) OK

f) OK

Chapter 10

1. a) $f(x) = (2x - 1)^5$
$$= -1 + 10x - 4x^2 + 80x^3 - 80x^4 + 32x^5$$

b) $f(x) = e^{2x}$
$$= 1 + (2x) + (2x)^2/2! + (2x)^3/3! + \cdots$$

c) $f(x) = \cos(1 + 2x)$

⟨Define $C_1 = \cos(1)$, $S_1 = \sin(1)$⟩

$$\cos(1 + 2x) = C_1 - S_1(2x) - C_1\frac{(2x)^2}{2!}$$
$$+ S_1\frac{(2x)^3}{3!} + C_1\frac{(2x)^4}{4!} - \cdots$$

Note this can also be written as

$$\cos(1 + 2x) = C_1[1 - \frac{(2x)^2}{2!} + \frac{(2x)^4}{4!} - \cdots]$$

$$- S_1[(2x) - \frac{(2x)^3}{3!} + \frac{(2x)^5}{5!} + \cdots]$$

$$= C_1 \cos(2x) - S_1 \sin(2x)$$

$$= \cos(1) \cos(2x) - \sin(1) \sin(2x)$$

d) $f(x) = (1 - x)^{1/2}$

$$= 1 - \frac{x}{2} - \frac{x^2}{8} - \frac{x^3}{16} - \frac{5x^4}{128} - \frac{7x^5}{256} - \cdots$$

e) $f(x) = \ln(1 + x)$

$$= x - \frac{x^2}{2} + \frac{x^3}{3} - \frac{x^5}{5} + \frac{x^7}{7} + \cdots$$

$$+ \frac{x^n}{n} + \cdots$$

The ratio of successive terms is

$$(\text{term})_{n+1}/(\text{term})_n = -x \frac{n}{n + 1}$$

3. The Taylor Series

$$f(x) = f_a + f_a'(x - a) + f_a'' \frac{(x - a)^2}{2!} + \cdots$$

a) $f(x) = 32x^5 - 80x^4 + 80x^3 - 40x^2 + 10x - 1$

$$= 0 + 0 + 0 + 0 + 0 + 3840(x - \tfrac{1}{2})^5/5!$$

$$= 32(x - \tfrac{1}{2})^5$$

b) $f(x) = \cos(1 + 2x)$, $a = -1/2$

$$f(x) = 1 - [2(x + \tfrac{1}{2})]^2/2! + [2(x + \tfrac{1}{2})]^4/4!$$

$$+ \cdots$$

$$= 1 - (2x + 1)^2/2! + (2x + 1)^4/4! + \cdots$$

c) $f(x) = \ln(2 + x)$, $a = -1$

$$f(x) = (x + 1) - (x + 1)^2/2 + (x + 1)^3/3 - \cdots$$

5. The Maclaurin series for e^x with x replaced by (ix) is

$$e^{ix} = 1 + (ix) + (ix)^2/2! + (ix)^3/3! + \cdots$$

$$= 1 + ix - x^2/2! - ix^3/3! + x^4/4!$$

$$+ ix^5/5! - x^6/6! - \cdots$$

$$= [1 - \frac{x^2}{2!} + \frac{x^4}{4!} - \cdots]$$

$$+ i[x - \frac{x^3}{3!} + \frac{x^5}{5!} - \cdots]$$

$$= \cos(x) + i \sin(x)$$

7. The same problem as Problem 10-6 except more terms are retained in the approximations.

$$\ln(e^x) = (e^x - 1) - \frac{1}{2}(e^x - 1)^2 + \mathcal{O}(e^x - 1)^3$$

$$(e^x - 1) = x + \frac{x^2}{2} + \mathcal{O}(x^3)$$

$$(e^x - 1)^2 = \left[x + \frac{x^2}{2} + \mathcal{O}(x^3) \right]^2$$

$$= x^2 + \mathcal{O}(x^3)$$

$$(e^x - 1)^3 = \mathcal{O}(x^3)$$

So

$$\ln(e^x) = x + \frac{x^2}{2} + \mathcal{O}(x^3) - \frac{1}{2}x^2 + \mathcal{O}(x^3)$$

$$= x + \mathcal{O}(x^3)$$

11. Using Equation 10.56 for f_i' when $i > 1$, and the result of the previous problem for f_0', and Equation 10.58 for f_i'', we obtain the following results.

i	x_i	f_i	f_i'	f_i''
0	0.0	2.00	-0.20	-------
1	0.1	2.04	1.00	12.0
2	0.2	2.20	4.00	48.0
3	0.3	2.84	16.00	192.0
4	0.4	5.40	19.20	-128.0
5	0.5	6.68	9.60	-64.0
6	0.6	7.32	4.80	-32.0
7	0.7	7.64	2.40	-16.0
8	0.8	7.80	1.20	-8.0
9	0.9	7.88	0.60	-4.0
10	1.0	7.92	------	-------

Chapter 11

1.

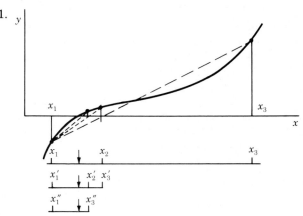

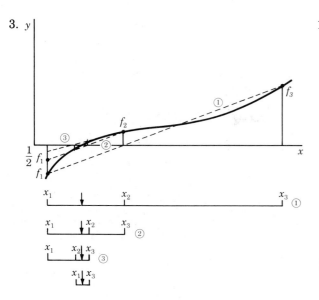

3.

11.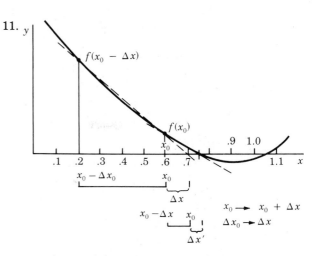

5. a) Will converge to the root at 12.0.
   b) Will converge to the root at 12.0.
   c) It is likely that the root at 3.1 will be found. However, the tangent at $x = 3.1$ is very nearly vertical and the method may diverge.
   d) The root at $x = 8.0$ will be found.
   e) If the secant is drawn between points at x_0 and $(x_0 - \Delta x_0)$, the method will diverge.
      If the secant is drawn between points at x_0 and $(x_0 + \Delta x_0)$, the method will converge to the root at $x = 12.0$.

7. Finding the nth root of a number C is obviously the same as finding an x such that $f(x) = x^n - C = 0.0$. Applying Newton's method to this function, we easily obtain the result in the problem.

9. a) Starting at $x = 0$ and stepping in units of $\Delta x = 0.2$, an apparent root is found near $x = 0.6$. Newton's method with this as an initial guess yields a value of 0.569 ± 0.001 after four iterations.
   b) Using a multiplicity factor of MULT = 2 in Newton's method greatly accelerates the convergence. The same calculation after two iterations yields 0.567143 ± 0.0000001

13. a) $f(x) = x^4 + 6x^3 + 3x^2 - 10x$
    $= x(x^3 + 6x^2 + 3x - 10) = xg(x)$

   Obviously one root of $f(x)$ is $x = 0$. The function $g(x)$ has one positive real root and either two or zero negative real roots. Also, $g(-1) = -8$, $g(0) = -10$, $g(1) = 0$. So the positive root is $x = 1$. If the remaining roots are labeled $-r_3$, $-r_4$, Newton's relations give the conditions

   $$6/1 = -(1 - r_3 - r_4), \quad -10/1 = (-1)^3(r_3 r_4)$$

   or $r_3 + r_4 = 7$, and $r_3 r_4 = 10$. The solution is clearly $r_3 = 2$, $r_4 = 5$. The four roots of $f(x)$ are then $-5, -2, 0, 1$.

   b) $g(x) = 8x^3 + 12x^2 + 14x + 9$. The number of positive real roots is zero, the number of negative real roots is either three or one. Also, $g(-1) = -1$, $g(0) = +9$. Thus, one real root is in the interval -1 to 0. The remaining two roots are labeled as $-r_2$, $-r_3$ and, for the moment, are assumed to be real. Newton's relations yield

   $$12/8 = -(-r_1 - r_2 - r_3), \quad 9/8 = (-1)^3(-r_1 r_2 r_3)$$

   where $0 < r_1 < 1$. So,

   $$\frac{1}{3} < r_2 + r_3 < \frac{4}{3}, \quad (r_2 r_3) > \frac{9}{8}$$

   The maximum of the product of the two numbers occurs when $r_2 = r_3$. But this would imply $r_2 < 2/3$, so that the product cannot be greater than $9/8$. This contradiction then requires that the two remaining roots be complex.

   c) Since both $h(x)$ and $h'(x)$ are zero at $x = 1$, this

is a multiple root (multiplicity two). The solution for the remaining two roots is similar to part a) and the result is that the roots are 1, 1, i, $-i$.

d) The solution is similar to part b).

Chapter 12

1. a) $\begin{pmatrix} 1 & 0 & 2 \\ -2 & 1 & 0 \\ 0 & -2 & 1 \end{pmatrix}$ b) $\begin{pmatrix} 3 & -3 & 3 \\ -3 & 3 & -3 \\ 3 & -3 & 3 \end{pmatrix}$

c) $\begin{pmatrix} 0 & 0 & 0 \\ 0 & 0 & 0 \\ 0 & 0 & 0 \end{pmatrix}$

3. a) -1; b) -2; c) -6

5. $(x_1, x_2, x_3) = (0, 0, 1)$

7. a) $(x_1, x_2, x_3) = (3, -1, 1)$
   b) $(x_1, x_2, x_3) = (1, -1, -1)$
   c) $(x_1, x_2, x_3) = (0, -2, 2)$

9.
```
   SUBROUTINE CHECK(A,N,EPS)
   REAL A(N,N)
   DO 1 I = 1,N
   DO 1 J = 1,N
       IF(I .EQ. J)THEN
           IF(ABS(A(I,J)-1.) .GT. EPS)THEN
               PRINT*,'THE DIAGONAL TERM ',
  +              'A(',I,',',J,') = ',A(I,J)
               STOP
           END IF
       ELSE
           IF(ABS(A(I,J)) .GT. EPS)THEN
               PRINT*,'THE NON-DIAGONAL ',
  +              'TERM A(',I,',',J,') = ',
  +              A(I,J)
               STOP
           END IF
       END IF
 1 CONTINUE
   PRINT *,'WITHIN ',EPS,' THE MATRIX IS',
  +     ,' EQUAL TO THE IDENTITY MATRIX'
   RETURN
   END
```

11.
```
   SUBROUTINE SWITCH(A,B,N,I1,I2)
   INTEGER N,I1,I2
   REAL  A(N,N) ,B(N),TEMP
   TEMP = B(I1)
   B(I1) = B(I2)
   B(I2) = TEMP
   DO 1 I = 1,N
       TEMP    = A(I1,I)
       A(I1,I) = A(I2,I)
       A(I2,I) = TEMP
```

```
 1   CONTINUE
     RETURN
     END
```

13. Replace the right-hand-side vector B( ) by an identity matrix B( ). To be more specific, replace the definition line by

```
        SUBROUTINE GAUSS(A,B,ND,N,DET)
```

add a DO loop initializing B( ):

```
     REAL B(ND,ND)
        ...        ...
     B(N,N) = 1.0
     DO 50 I = 1,N - 1
        B(I,I) = 1.0
        DO 49 J = I + 1,N
            B(I,J) = 0.0
            B(J,I) = 0.0
49      CONTINUE
50   CONTINUE
```

Alter the section of step-1 that divides by the pivot element as

```
     DO 1 J = 1,N
        A(IPV,J) = A(IPV,J)/PIVOT
        B(IPV,J) = B(IPV,J)/PIVOT
1    CONTINUE
```

and the section of step-2 that replaces row-IROW by row-IROW plus a multiple of the pivot row—i.e., the DO 2 loop.

```
     DO 2 ICOL = 1,N
        A(IROW,ICOL) = A(IROW,ICOL) -
  +             FACTOR*A(IPV,ICOL)
        B(IROW,ICOL) = B(IROW,ICOL) -
  +             FACTOR*B(IPV,ICOL)
2       CONTINUE
```

Finally, delete the DO 5 loop entirely. The inverse of the matrix A will be contained in the matrix B.

15. a) With the equations written in a non-diagonally dominant form, the solution is found to quickly diverge.
    b) Moving the third equation to the top brings the system into a diagonally dominant form. The solution then converges, though slowly, to the solution $(x_1, x_2, x_3) = (0, 1/3, -1/3)$.

17.
```
     SUBROUTINE RERANG(A,B,N)
     REAL A(N,N),B(N),SUM
     INTEGER ROW,COL,NEWRO
     DO 2 ROW = 1,N
```
⟨Check for diagonal dominance from this row on down.⟩
```
        SUM = 0.0
        DO 1 COL = 1,N
```

```
        IF(ROW .NE. COL)THEN
            SUM = SUM + ABS(A(ROW,COL))
        END IF
1     CONTINUE
      IF(ABS(A(ROW,ROW)) .LT. SUM)THEN
```
⟨This row is nondiagonally dominant. Unless it is the last row, find one below to switch with.⟩
```
        IF(ROW .EQ. N)THEN
          PRINT *,'THE LAST ROW IS BAD',
 +             ' AND CAN NOT BE FIXED.'
          STOP
        END IF
        NEWRO = MAXCOL(A,N,ROW,ROW)
        CALL SWITCH(A,B,N,NEWRO,ROW)
      END IF
2     CONTINUE
      RETURN
      END
```

19. Solving the fifty-one equations by the Gauss-Siedel procedure yields a solution after about ten iterations. The values obtained for the unknowns are

x_1	x_2	x_3	x_4	x_5
0.14959	0.18500	0.17330	0.16578	0.16653

x_6	x_7	x_8	x_9	x_{10}
0.16653	0.16678	0.16671	0.16666	0.16666

x_{11}	x_{12}	x_{13}	x_{14}	x_{15}
0.16666	0.16667	0.16667	0.16667	0.16667

etc. The elements of the solution are related by $x_i = x_{51-i}$.

Chapter 13

1. The minimum of the function $E(d)$ is obtained at a value of $d_{\min} = 16/5$. The value of $E(d_{\min})$ is then zero.

3. The line that minimizes the deviations in the y direction is then given by

$$y_1(x) = a_1x + b_1$$

with

$$a_1 = \frac{41}{35}, \; b_1 = -3/5$$

Interchanging the x- and y-values and repeating the calculation is equivalent to finding the line that now minimizes the deviations in the x direction,

$$x_2(y) = a_2y + b_2$$

where

$$a_2 = \frac{41}{59}, \; b_2 = 63/59$$

Rewriting the second equation as $y_2(x)$, the equations for the two best-fit lines are

$$y_1(x) = \frac{41}{35}x - \frac{3}{5}$$

$$y_2(x) = \frac{59}{41}x - \frac{63}{41}$$

These two lines are compared with the data on the sketch that follows. Notice that the two lines are substantially different, indicating that minimizing the deviations in the x direction can yield results quite different from those obtained by minimizing deviations in the y direction.

Also included on the sketch is a best by-eye fit to the data. This line differs substantially from either of the two earlier lines. This is because a best by-eye fit will tend to minimize the *perpendicular* deviations of the data from the line. In the present case I would judge the best by-eye fit to be superior to either of the least-squares fits.

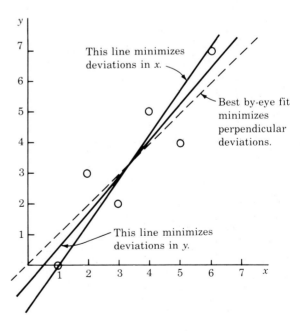

5. The model function $N(t) = N_0 e^{-\lambda t}$ is linearized by taking the logarithm of both sides of the equation to yield

$$y(t) = at + b$$
$$= \ln[N(t)]$$
$$= \ln[N_0 e^{-\lambda t}] = -\lambda t + \ln(N_0)$$

A least-squares analysis to obtain a and b yields $a = -4.67654$, $b = 41.7922$, and these in turn determine the values of λ and N_0 to be

$$\lambda = -a = 4.6765, \quad N_0 = e^b = 1.413\text{E}+18$$

7. The Stefan-Boltzman law is used as the model function. To linearize this equation we make the identifications

$$y(x) = ax + b$$
$$= R(T) = \sigma(T^4 - T_0^4)$$

Thus

$$y(x) = R(T), \quad x = T^4, \quad a = \sigma, \quad b = -\sigma T_0^4$$

The result of the least-squares analysis for a and b is

$$a = 5.657\text{E} - 8 = \sigma, \quad b = -407.9845 = -\sigma T_0^4$$

$$T_0 = [407.9845/\sigma]^{1/4} = 291.4\text{K} = 18.24°\text{C}$$

i	T_i	R_i	$R_{\text{model}}(T_i)$
1	300.	40.	50.26
2	350.	430.	440.96
3	400.	1050.	1040.28
4	450.	1920.	1911.86
5	500.	3150.	3127.83
6	550.	4750.	4768.80

9. Linear, quadratic, and exponential fits to the data yield.

Linear fit $(y_1(x) = a_0 + a_1 x)$,

$$a_0 = -3.200$$
$$a_1 = 23.180$$

Quadratic fit $(y_2(x) = b_0 + b_1 x + b_2 x^2)$

$$b_0 = 4.24571$$
$$b_1 = -6.40286$$
$$b_2 = 14.77143$$

Exponential fit $(y_3(x) = \alpha e^{\beta x})$

Let $Y(X) = c_0 + c_1 X$
$$= \ln[y(x)] = \beta x + \ln(\alpha)$$

So, $Y_i = \ln(y_i)$, $X_i = x_i$, $\beta = c_1$, $\ln(\alpha) = c_0$. The results for c_0, c_1 are then

$$c_1 = 1.37807, \quad c_0 = 1.18021$$
$$\alpha = e^{c_0} = 3.25504, \quad \beta = c_1 = 1.37806$$

The three model fits are compared with the data in the following table. Beneath each computed value is the deviation from the data point.

i	x_i	y_i	Linear $y_1(x_i)$	Quadratic $y_2(x_i)$	Expon. $y_3(x_i)$
1	0.0	3.4	-3.200	+4.2462	+3.255
			$\langle-6.60\rangle$	$\langle+0.846\rangle$	$\langle-0.145\rangle$
2	0.5	6.0	8.390	4.7371	6.483
			$\langle+2.390\rangle$	$\langle-1.263\rangle$	$\langle+0.483\rangle$
3	1.0	13.3	19.980	12.6143	12.914
			$\langle+6.680\rangle$	$\langle-0.6857\rangle$	$\langle-0.386\rangle$
4	1.5	25.7	31.570	27.8770	25.721
			$\langle+5.870\rangle$	$\langle+2.1770\rangle$	$\langle+0.021\rangle$
5	2.0	51.5	43.160	50.5261	51.231
			$\langle-8.340\rangle$	$\langle-0.9739\rangle$	$\langle-0.269\rangle$
Sum of squared deviations			197.907	8.4689	0.476
Chi-squared			629.77	23.58	1.75

Thus the only adequate fit of the three is the exponential fit.

11. For a cubic drawn through just two points, $i = 0$ only, $d = (x_1 - x_0)$, and $h_0 = h = (y_1 - y_0)$

a) The Z_i values are determined first by using Equations 13.55–57.

$$Z_0 = \frac{1}{2}(3h - Z_1), \quad Z_1 = \frac{1}{2}(3h - Z_0)$$

which can be solved to yield $Z_0 = Z_1 = h$.

b) Next, Equations 13.45–48 are used to determine the four coefficients of the cubic function drawn through the two points. (Note, $i = 0$ for all equations.)

$$a_{00} = y_0$$

$$a_{10} = Z_0 = h = (y_1 - y_0)/(x_1 - x_0)$$

$$a_{30}d^2 = (Z_0 + Z_1) - 2h = 2h - 2h = 0$$

$$a_{20}d = h - Z_0 - a_{30}d^2 = h - h - 0 = 0$$

Thus the equation for the cubic is

$$f(x) = a_{00} + a_{10}(x - x_0) + a_{20}(x - x_0)^2 + a_{30}(x - x_0)^3$$

$$= y_0 + \frac{y_1 - y_0}{x_1 - x_0}(x - x_0)$$

which is obviously just a straight line drawn through the two points (x_0, y_0) and (x_1, y_1).

Chapter 14

1. a) Evaluate $T_0 = \frac{1}{2}\Delta x_0(f_a + f_b)$,

   b) $T_1 = \frac{T_0}{2} + \Delta x_1 f(a + \Delta x_1)$, and

   c) $T_k = \frac{1}{2}T_{k-1} + \Delta x_k \sum_{\substack{i=1 \\ i=\text{odd only}}}^{n-1} f(a + \Delta x_k)$

for the functions and intervals given.

	T_0	T_1	T_2	T_3	T_4
i	256.0	192.0	176.0	172.0	171.0
ii	16384.0	9216.0	7232.0	6724.0	6597.0
iii	0.18393	0.24360	0.25904	0.26293	0.26392
iv	1.23370	1.05303	1.01295	1.00322	1.00080
v	1.91421	1.65588	1.59002	1.57347	1.56933
vi	1.68393	0.73137	0.74298	0.74587	0.74658

3. The Simpson rule values can be computed directly from the trapezoidal rule numbers using the relation

$$S_{k+1} = T_{k+1} + (T_{k+1} - T_k)/3$$

The results for the functions of Problem 14-1 are

	S_1	S_2	S_3	S_4
i	$170\frac{2}{3}$	$170\frac{2}{3}$	$170\frac{2}{3}$	$170\frac{2}{3}$
ii	$6826\frac{2}{3}$	$6570\frac{2}{3}$	$6554\frac{2}{3}$	$6553\frac{2}{3}$
iii	0.26349	0.26419	0.26424	0.26424
iv	0.99281	0.99959	0.99998	1.00000
v	1.56977	1.56808	1.56796	1.56795
vi	0.74718	0.74686	0.74683	0.74682

5. The tables of the round-off error monitors, R_k^m, given by Equation 14.24 for each of the functions in Problem 14-1 follow.

i) $f(x) = x^2$, $a = 0$, $b = 8$
   $R_2^0 = 1.0$, the rest are 0/0.

ii) $f(x) = x^4$, $a = 0$, $b = 8$

k	R_k^0	R_k^1
2	0.903	
3	0.976	1.000

iii) $f(x) = xe^{-x}$, $a = 0$, $b = 1$

k	R_k^0	R_k^1	R_k^2
2	0.9659		
3	0.9912	0.9646	
4	0.9978	0.9909	0.9672

iv) $f(x) = x\sin(x)$, $a = 0$, $b = \pi/2$

k	R_k^0	R_k^1	R_k^2
2	1.1270		
3	1.0296	1.1050	
4	1.0073	1.0246	1.0933

v) $f(x) = (1 + x^2)^{3/2}$, $a = 0$, $b = 1$

k	R_k^0	R_k^1	R_k^3
2	0.9807		
3	0.9951	0.9785	
4	0.9988	1.0040	-1.3409

vi) $f(x) = e^{-x^2}$, $a = 0$, $b = 1$

k	R_k^0	R_k^1	R_k^2
2	1.0210		
3	1.0076	0.6943	
4	1.0019	0.9815	4.0638

7. The integrand $(e^x + x)^{-1}$ approaches e^{-x} for large x. To see how accurate such a replacement might be, we first construct a table of both quantities as a function of x.

x	$(e^x + x)^{-1}$	e^{-x}
0.0	1.000000	1.000000
1.0	0.268941	0.367879
2.0	0.106507	0.135335
4.0	0.017065	0.018316
8.0	0.000335	0.000335

Thus the approximation

$$\int_0^\infty \frac{dx}{(e^x + x)} \approx \int_0^9 \frac{dx}{(e^x + x)} + \int_9^\infty e^{-x}dx$$

should be accurate to about five significant figures. The first integral must be done numerically. I chose to use Gauss Quadrature with $k = 10$ sampling points. The result for the first integral is

$$I_1 = 0.806160570$$

The second integral can be done analytically and the

result is

$$I_2 = e^{-9} = 0.00012341$$

So the approximate value of the integral is

$$I \simeq 0.806284$$

11. We wish to find the root of the function in Problem 8-21. That is,

$$g(x) = 5e^{-2x^2} - \sin(\pi x/2) + \int_0^x (4t^2 - 5) \, dt$$

The root is known to be near 0.6316. Since the derivative of this function appears to be quite complicated, we chose to use the secant method to find the root. (I will use $\Delta x_0 = 0.1$.) In addition we will use the subroutine GAUSQD of the previous problem to handle the integral. The Fortran program is outlined as follows:

```
PROGRAM MAIN
REAL G, X0,DX0,ROOT
INTEGER IMAX
EXTERNAL G
X0 = 0.6316
DX0 = 0.1
IMAX = 20
EPS = 1.E-8
CALL SECANT(X0,DX0,IMAX,EPS,ROOT,G)
PRINT *,'THE ROOT IS ',ROOT
STOP
END
*******************************************
FUNCTION G(X)
REAL X,PI,XINTGL
PARAMETER (PI = 3.1415926)
EXTERNAL ARG
XINTGL = GAUSQD(0.,X,ARG)
G = 5.*EXP(-X**2) - SIN(PI*X/2.)
+                  + XINTGL
RETURN
END
*******************************************
FUNCTION ARG(T)
ARG = (4.*T*T - 5.)*EXP(-T*T)
RETURN
END
*******************************************
SUBROUTINE GAUSQD(A,B,F)
   ...
END
*******************************************
SUBROUTINE SECANT(X0,DX0,IMX,EPS,R,F)
   ...
END
*******************************************
```

Chapter 15

1. a) $y(x) = x$ b) $y(x) = x^2$
   c) $y(x) = e^{2x}$ d) $I(t) = 2e^{-50000t}$
   e) $N(t) = N_0 e^{t/k}$

3. Euler's method applied to a variety of differential equations.

a) $y' = -y/x$, $y(1) = 1.0$, $\Delta x = +0.1$

   ⟨exact solution, $y(x) = 1/x$⟩

i	x_i	$y(x_i)$ exact	$y(x_i)$ Euler	Fractional difference
0	1.0	1.000000000	1.000000000	0.00000
1	1.1	0.909090909	0.900000000	0.01000
2	1.2	0.833333333	0.818181818	0.01818
3	1.3	0.769230769	0.750000000	0.02500
4	1.4	0.714285714	0.692307692	0.03077
5	1.5	0.666666667	0.642857143	0.03571
6	1.6	0.625000000	0.600000000	0.04000
7	1.7	0.588235294	0.562500000	0.04375
8	1.8	0.555555556	0.529411765	0.04706
9	1.9	0.526315789	0.500000000	0.05000
10	2.0	0.500000000	0.473684211	0.05263

b) $y' = -y^2$, $y(1) = 1.0$, $\Delta x = 0.1$

   ⟨exact solution, $y(x) = 1/x$⟩

i	x_i	$y(x_i)$ exact	$y(x_i)$ Euler	Fractional difference
0	1.0	1.000000000	1.000000000	0.00000
1	1.1	0.909090909	0.900000000	0.01000
2	1.2	0.833333333	0.819000000	0.01728
3	1.3	0.769230769	0.751923900	0.02250
4	1.4	0.714285714	0.695384945	0.02646
5	1.5	0.666666667	0.647028923	0.02946
6	1.6	0.625000000	0.605164280	0.03174
7	1.7	0.588235294	0.568541899	0.03348
8	1.8	0.555555556	0.536217910	0.03481
9	1.9	0.526315789	0.507464946	0.03582
10	2.0	0.500000000	0.481712878	0.03657

c) $y' = -y/x$, $y(1) = 1.0$, $\Delta x = -0.1$

⟨exact solution, $y(x) = 1/x$⟩

i	x_i	$y(x_i)$ exact	$y(x_i)$ Euler	Fractional difference
0	1.0	1.000000000	1.000000000	0.00000
1	0.9	1.111111111	1.100000000	0.01000
2	0.8	1.250000000	1.222222222	0.02222
3	0.7	1.428571429	1.375000000	0.03750
4	0.6	1.666666667	1.571428571	0.05714
5	0.5	2.000000000	1.833333333	0.08333
6	0.4	2.500000000	2.200000000	0.12000
7	0.3	3.333333333	2.750000000	0.17500
8	0.2	5.000000000	3.666666667	0.26667
9	0.1	10.000000000	5.500000000	0.45000
10	0.0	∞	11.000000000	---

d) $y' = x + y$, $y(0) = 0$, $\Delta x = 0.4$

⟨exact solution, $y(x) = e^x - 1 - x$⟩

i	x_i	$y(x_i)$ exact	$y(x_i)$ Euler	Fractional difference
0	0.0	0.000000000	0.000000000	-----
1	0.4	0.091824698	0.000000000	1.0000
2	0.8	0.425540928	0.160000000	0.6240
3	1.2	1.120116923	0.544000000	0.5143
4	1.6	2.353032424	1.241600000	0.4723
5	2.0	4.389056099	2.378240000	0.4581
6	2.4	7.623176381	4.129536000	0.4583
7	2.8	12.644646771	6.741350400	0.4669
8	3.2	20.332530197	10.55789056	0.4807
9	3.6	31.998234444	16.06104678	0.4981
10	4.0	49.598150033	23.92546550	0.5176

5. Solving the equation $y' = -y$ starting at $x = 6.0$ with $\Delta x = 0.1$ yields the following results on a CDC-CYBER computer.

⟨exact solution, $y(x) = e^{-x}$⟩

i	x_i	$y(x_i)$ exact	$y(x_i)$ Midpoint	Fractional difference
0	6.0	0.002478752	0.002478752	-----
1	6.1	0.002242868	0.002243271	0.000180
...	...	...	...	...
34	9.4	0.000082724	0.000082736	0.000138
35	9.5	0.000074852	0.000075793	0.012577
36	9.6	0.000067729	0.000067577	-0.002242
37	9.7	0.000061283	0.000062278	0.016226
38	9.8	0.000055452	0.000055122	-0.005956
39	9.9	0.000050175	0.000051254	0.021503
40	10.0	0.000045400	0.000044871	-0.011659

This computer has an exceptionally long word length (~14 digits) and it therefore takes a great many steps for the round-off error to sufficiently accumulate to cause a problem. Once the problem occurs at about step 36, the fractional error will continue to alternate in sign. This is characteristic of the midpoint method.

7. A Fortran subroutine MIDPT4 to handle four simultaneous coupled differential equations follows.

```
      SUBROUTINE MIDPT4(X,Y,N,A,B,F)
      REAL X(0:N),Y(0:N),A,B,DX,F,
     +    YY(4),DY1(4),DY2(4)
      INTEGER I,J,K,N
      DX = (B - A)/N
      X(0) = A
      X(1) = A + DX
*
*        <We use the array YY to hold
*        the current (I) values of Y>
*
      DO 1 I = 1,4
        YY(I) = Y(0,I)
1     CONTINUE
*
*        <The initial half-step>
*
      DO 2 I = 1,4
        DY1(I) = F(X(0),YY,I)*DX
        YY(I)  = Y(0,I) + DY1(I)
        DY2(I) = F(X(1),YY,I)*DX
        Y(1,I) = Y(0,I) + .5*(DY1(I) + DY2(I))
2     CONTINUE
*
*        <Next use every other point>
*
      DO 5 K = 0,N - 2
        X(K + 2) = X(K) + 2.*DX
        DO 4 I = 1,4
          DO 3 J = 1,4
            YY(J) = Y(K + 1,J)
3         CONTINUE
          Y(K + 2,I) = Y(K,I) + F(X(K + 1),YY,I)
     +                 *2.*DX
4       CONTINUE
5     CONTINUE
      RETURN
      END
**************************************************
```

The function that follows will incorporate the four differential equations for the orbit problem. (See also Problem 15-2c.)

i) $f_1 = v_x \left(\text{i.e., } \dfrac{dy_1}{dt} = y_3 \right)$

ii) $f_2 = v_y \left(\text{i.e., } \dfrac{dy_2}{dt} = y_4 \right)$

iii) $f_3 = -k\dfrac{x}{r^3} \left(\text{i.e., } \dfrac{dy_3}{dt} = -k\dfrac{y_1}{(y_1^2 + y_2^2)^{3/2}} \right.$

iv) $f_4 = -k\dfrac{y}{r^3}$ $\left(\text{i.e., }\dfrac{dy_4}{dt} = -k\dfrac{y_2}{(y_1^2 + y_2^2)^{3/2}},\text{ where}\right.$

$k = 3.863E15$

```
   FUNCTION F(X,Y,I)
*
*      <This function will handle the four
*      separate eqs. depending on the value
*      of I.>
*
   REAL X,Y(4)
   INTEGER I
   COMMON/CONSTS/C
*
   GO TO (1,2,3,4),I
1      F = Y(3)
          RETURN
2      F = Y(4)
          RETURN
3      F = -C*Y(1)/(Y(1)**2 + Y(2)**2)**1.5
          RETURN
4      F = -C*Y(2)/(Y(1)**2 + Y(2)**2)**1.5
          RETURN
   END
```

Executing these subprograms with the initial conditions $x_0 = -2.0E7$, $y_0 = 0$, $v_x(0) = 0$, $v_y(0) = 5000.0$, will result in an elliptical orbit around the earth. The results of the calculation are listed below for times $t = 0$ to $t = t_f = 5.E4$ seconds in steps of 50 seconds. (Only every hundredth line is listed.) As a check on the accuracy of the code, the current value of the energy (potential plus kinetic) is also listed. This should remain constant.

i	t_i	x_i	y_i	Energy
0	0.0	$-2.00E+7$	0.0	$-7.42E+6$
100	5000.0	$-9.41E+6$	$2.07E+7$	$-7.42E+6$
200	10000.0	$9.99E+6$	$2.58E+7$	$-7.42E+6$
300	15000.0	$2.54E+7$	$1.87E+7$	$-7.42E+6$
400	20000.0	$3.31E+7$	$5.60E+6$	$-7.42E+6$
500	25000.0	$3.20E+7$	$-9.05E+6$	$-7.42E+6$
600	30000.0	$2.24E+7$	$-2.12E+7$	$-7.43E+6$
700	35000.0	$5.39E+6$	$-2.59E+7$	$-7.43E+6$
800	40000.0	$-1.35E+7$	$-1.69E+7$	$-7.43E+6$
900	45000.0	$-1.93E+7$	$5.96E+6$	$-7.41E+6$
10^3	50000.0	$-4.85E+6$	$2.34E+7$	$-7.40E+6$

9. a) A subroutine implementing the 4th order Runge-Kutta algorithm is given below.

```
   SUBROUTINE RK4(X,Y,N,A,B,F)
   INTEGER N
   REAL X(0:N),Y(0:N),A,B,DX,DY,F,
   +     DY0,DY1,DY2,DY3,XX,YY
   DX = (B - A)/N
   X(0) = A
   DO 1 I = 0,N - 1
     X(I + 1) = X(I) + DX
     DY0      = F(X(I),Y(I))*DX
     XX       = X(I) + DX
     YY       = Y(I) + DY0
     DY1      = F(XX,YY)*DX
     YY       = Y(I) + .5*DT1
     DY2      = F(XX,YY)*DX
     YY       = Y(I) + DY2
     DY3      = F(X(I + 1),YY)*DX
     DY       = (DY0 + 2.*DY1 + 2.*DY2 + DY3)/6.
     Y(I + 1) = Y(I) + DY
1  CONTINUE
   RETURN
   END
```

b) Applying this algorithm to the equation

$$y' = 4x - 2\frac{y}{x}, \; y(1) = 1, \; y_{\text{exact}}(x) = x^2$$

over the interval $x = 1$ to $x = 11$ yields the results tabulated here.

For N = 100 points

i	x_i	$y(x_i)$ exact	$y(x_i)$ Runge-Kutta	Fractional difference
0	1.0	1.00	1.000000	0.00000
10	2.0	4.00	4.080303	0.02008
20	3.0	9.00	9.131916	0.01466
30	4.0	16.00	16.178945	0.01118
40	5.0	25.00	25.224606	0.00898
50	6.0	36.00	36.269719	0.00749
60	7.0	49.00	49.314570	0.00642
70	8.0	64.00	64.359281	0.00561
80	9.0	81.00	81.403909	0.00499
90	10.0	100.00	100.448486	0.00448
100	11.0	121.00	121.493028	0.00408

For $N = 1000$ points

i	x_i	$y(x_i)$ exact	$y(x_i)$ Runge-Kutta	Fractional difference
0	1.0	1.00	1.000000	0.00000
100	2.0	4.00	4.007805	0.00195
200	3.0	9.00	9.012876	0.00143
300	4.0	16.00	16.017541	0.00110
400	5.0	25.00	25.022087	0.00088
500	6.0	36.00	36.026587	0.00074
600	7.0	49.00	49.031065	0.00063
700	8.0	64.00	64.035531	0.00056
800	9.0	81.00	81.039990	0.00049
900	10.0	100.00	100.044445	0.00044
1000	11.0	121.00	121.048898	0.00040

11. The lowest-order predictor-corrector method applied to the equation

$$y' = -2xy^2, \; y(1) = 1, \; \Delta x = 0.01$$
$$\langle \text{exact solution, } y(x) = 1/x^2 \rangle$$

for two steps yields the following results. (Note, to get the procedure started, we need the value of y_1. Here, we will use the exact solution to obtain y_1.)

$$x_0 = 1.0, \; y_0 = 1.0$$
$$x_1 = 1.01, \; y_1 = 0.98029605$$

Step 1 ($i = 1$)

$$x_2 = x_1 + \Delta x = 1.02$$

Predictor equation

$$y_2 = y_0 + 2\Delta x f(x_1, y_1)$$
$$= 1.0 + 0.02(-1.941180)$$
$$= 0.9611764$$

Corrector equation

$$y_2 = y_1 + \Delta x[f_1 + f(x_2, y_2)]/2$$
$$= 0.9802960 + 0.005[-1.941180 - 1.884675]$$
$$= 0.9611668$$

Repeat this twice more

$$y_2 = 0.9802960 + 0.005[-1.941180 - 1.884637]$$
$$= 0.9611670$$
$$y_2 = 0.9802960 + 0.005[-1.941180 - 1.884638]$$
$$= 0.9611670$$

$$\langle \text{exact value} = 0.9611688..\rangle$$

Step 2 ($i = 2$)

$$x_3 = x_2 + \Delta x = 1.03$$

Predictor equation

$$y_3 = y_1 + 2\Delta x f(x_2, y_2)$$
$$= 0.9802960 + 0.02(-1.884638)$$
$$= 0.9234744$$

Corrector equation

$$y_3 = y_2 + \Delta x[f_2 + f(x_3, y_3)]/2$$
$$= 0.9429600 + 0.005[-1.884638 - 1.756778]$$
$$= 0.9425853$$

Repeat this twice more

$$y_3 = 0.9429600 + 0.005[-1.884638 - 1.831697]$$
$$= 0.9425853$$

$$y_3 = 0.9429600 + 0.005[-1.884638 - 1.830242]$$
$$= 0.9425926$$

$$\langle \text{exact value} = 0.9425959..\rangle$$

13. A Fortran code implementing the lowest-order predictor-corrector method.

```
PROGRAM PC1
PARAMETER (N = 100)
INTEGER N,ITER
REAL X(0:N),Y(0:N),F,YEX,XX,YY,
     DY1,DY2,DY,DX,FD
F(XX,YY) = -2.*XX*YY**2
YEX(XX)  = 1./XX**2
*
*    YEX() is the exact solution
*
X(0) = 1.0
Y(0) = 1.0
DX   = 0.01
X(1) = X(0) + DX
*
*    <We use the initial half-step method
*    to get Y(1), which is needed in the
*    predictor equation.>
*
YY   = Y(0)
DY1  = F(X(0),YY)*DX
YY   = Y(0) + DY1
DY2  = F(X(1),YY)*DX
DY   = 0.5*(DY1 + DY2)
Y(1) = YY + DY
*
WRITE(*,12)0,X(0),Y(0),Y(0),0,0
DO 2 I = 1,N-1
   X(I+1) = X(I) + DX
*
*    <Predictor equation>
*
   Y(I+1) = Y(I-1) + 2.*DX*
+           F(X(I),Y(I))
*
*    <Corrector equation applied
```

```
*          four times>
*
         DO 1 ITER = 1,4
           YY = Y(I+1)
           XX = X(I+1)
           Y(I+1) = Y(I) + 0.5*DX*
  +               (F(X(I),Y(I)) + F(XX,YY))
  1      CONTINUE
         IF((I+1)/(N/10)*(N/10).EQ.I+1)THEN
           FD = (Y(I+1)-YEX(XX))/YEX(XX)
           WRITE(*,12)I+1,XX,YEX(XX),
  +                   Y(I+1),FD
         END IF

  2 CONTINUE
    STOP
*
 12 FORMAT(2X,I4,2X,F5.2,2(2X,F9.6),
  +         2X,F8.5)
    END
```

The program above solves the differential equation of Problem 15-11. The tabulated results follow.

$$y' = -2xy^2, \ y(1) = 1.0, \ \Delta x = +0.01$$

$$\langle \text{exact solution}, \ y(x) = 1/x^2 \rangle$$

i	x_i	$y(x_i)$ exact	$y(x_i)$ Predictor -corrector	Fractional difference
0	1.0	1.0000000	1.0000000	0.00000
10	1.1	0.8264462	0.8264346	−0.000014
20	1.2	0.6944444	0.6944228	−0.000024
30	1.3	0.5917158	0.5916983	−0.000030
40	1.4	0.5102039	0.5101871	−0.000033
50	1.5	0.4444444	0.4444288	−0.000035
60	1.6	0.3906248	0.3906160	−0.000036
70	1.7	0.3460206	0.3460083	−0.000036
80	1.8	0.3086418	0.3086309	−0.000035
90	1.9	0.2770082	0.2769986	−0.000035
100	2.0	0.2500000	0.2499914	−0.000034

15. Solve the differential equation

$$\frac{d}{dx}\left[(\lambda_0 + \alpha T)\frac{dT}{dx}\right] = 0, \ T(0) = 0., \ T(10) = 100.$$

by a shooting procedure. We first rewrite this second order, nonlinear (nonlinear in T) differential equation as two coupled first-order equations by introducing the variables $y_1(x) = T(x)$, and $y_2(x) = \dfrac{dT}{dx} = y_1'$.

$$\frac{d}{dx}\left[(\lambda_0 + \alpha y_1)y_2\right] = 0, \ y_1(0) = 0, \ y_1(10) = 100$$

Differentiating, we obtain

$$\alpha y_2^2 + (\lambda_0 + \alpha y_1)y_2' = 0$$

Thus, the two first-order differential equations for y_1 and y_2 are

$$y_1' = y_2 \qquad\qquad y_1(0) = 0$$
$$y_2' = -\frac{\alpha y_2^2}{(\lambda_0 + \alpha y_1)} \qquad y_2(0) = ?$$

and

$$y_1(10) = 100$$

Since the starting value of y_2 is not known, the most important part of the problem amounts to a search for the value of $y_2(0)$ that will result in a final value of $y_1(10) = 100$. That is, this boundary-value problem must first be transformed into an equivalent initial-value problem by finding the missing initial condition.

Before beginning the search, note that even though this is a nonlinear second-order equation, its analytic solution is relatively easy to obtain. From the structure of the equation we have that

$$[(\lambda_0 + \alpha y_1)y_1'] = C_1 = \text{constant}$$

Solving this first-order equation and using the two boundary conditions on y_1, the exact analytic solution is found to be

$$y_1 = T(x) = \frac{\lambda_0}{\alpha}\left\{\left[1 + 20\frac{\alpha}{\lambda_0}\left(1 + 50\frac{\alpha}{\lambda_0}\right)x\right]^{\frac{1}{2}} - 1\right\}$$

The derivative of this equation gives the analytical expression for y_2.

$$y_2 = 10\left(1 + 50\frac{\alpha}{\lambda_0}\right)\left[1 + 20\frac{\alpha}{\lambda_0}\left(1 + 50\frac{\alpha}{\lambda_0}\right)x\right]^{\frac{1}{2}}$$

Using the values $\lambda_0 = 100$, $\alpha = 1$, these become (exact solution)

$$y_1(x) = 100\left[\left(1 + \frac{3x}{10}\right)^{\frac{1}{2}} - 1\right]$$

$$y_2(x) = 15\left(1 + \frac{3x}{10}\right)^{-\frac{1}{2}}$$

Thus the exact value for the missing initial condition is $y_2(0) = 15$.

Since Δy_1 is 100 over a range $\Delta x = 10$, we chose as the initial guess for $y_2(0)$ the value $\Delta y_1/\Delta x = 10$. This is then used in a SECANT subroutine to find the root of a function that will be zero when $y_1(x = 10) = 100$. The structure of the Fortran code is given below.

```
PROGRAM SHOOT
REAL X0,Y10,Y20,Y1F,XF,LAMDA,ALPHA,
+      GUESS,DGESS,ROOT,G
INTEGER ITER
COMMON/INITAL/Y10,Y20
COMMON/ENDPT/N,Y1F,XF
COMMON/CNSTS/LAMDA,ALPHA
EXTERNAL G
N      = 100
LAMDA = 100,
ALPHA =   1,
X0    =   0,
XF    =  10,
Y10   =   0,
Y1F   = 100,
GESS  =  10,
DGESS =   0,5
CALL SECANT(GESS,DGESS,25,1,E-4,ROOT,
+            ITER,G)
PRINT *,'AFTER ',ITER,' ITERATIONS',
PRINT *,'THE COMPUTED VALUE FOR THE'
PRINT *,'MISSING INITIAL CONDITION IS'
PRINT *,'     Y2(0) = ',ROOT
STOP
END
*******************************************
FUNCTION G(Z)
COMMON/INITAL/Y10,Y20
COMMON/ENDPT/N,Y1F,XF
EXTERNAL F1,F2
REAL X(0:100),Y1(0:100),Y2(0:100),Z
*
Y20   = Z
Y1(0) = Y10
Y2(0) = Y20
CALL MIDPT2(X,Y1,Y2,N,0,,XF,F1,F2)
*
G = Y1(N) - Y1F
*
RETURN
END
*******************************************
FUNCTION F1(X,Y1,Y2)
  F1 = Y2
RETURN
END
*******************************************
FUNCTION F2(X,Y1,Y2)
COMMON/CNSTS/LAMDA,ALPHA
REAL LAMDA
  F2 = -ALPHA*Y2**2/(LAMDA + ALPHA*Y1)
RETURN
END
*******************************************
```

```
SUBROUTINE SECANT(X0,DX0,IMAX,EPS,
+                  ROOT,ITER,G)
     ...                    ...
END
*******************************************
SUBROUTINE MIDPT2(X,Y1,Y2,N,
+                 A,B,F1,F2)
     ...                    ...
END
*******************************************
```

The result of this program for the missing end condition is

```
AFTER 5 ITERATIONS
THE COMPUTED VALUE FOR THE
MISSING INITIAL CONDITION IS
Y2(0) = 14,9995
```

INDEX

A-format, 205
Absolute error, 590
Access option in OPEN statement, 131
ACOS(X), 46, 49, 299
Actual arguments, 108, 611
Aeronautical engineering, 303–304, pro-
    gramming problems VII-A (496),
    VIII-A (546)
Algorithm, 3, 56
Alphanumeric variables, 150
Alternate entry point, 617
Alternate return, 619
.AND. , 61–62
Antiderivative, 502
Apostrophe
    within a character constant, 30
    as a string delimiter, 148
Approximation errors, 602–603
Archimedes, 593
Argument list
    of a function, 254
    of a statement function, 106, 108
    of a subroutine, 245–246
Arguments
    actual, 611
    dummy, 612
Arithmetic
    hierarchy of operations, 36
    IF statement, 88, 621
    INTEGER, 35
    operators, 10, 34
    REAL, 35
    rules for expressions, 34
Arithmetic-logic unit (ALU), 7
Array, 181
    as an element of an argument list, 252–
        254
    bounds on indices, 183–184
    input/output, 188
    internal storage, 187–188
    variable dimensions, 252
ASIN(X), 299
ASSIGN TO statement, 618
Assigned GO TO, 621
Assignment
    of CHARACTER variables, 39
    operator, 39
    statement, 39, 617–618
Asterisk, used
    as a default for input/output device unit,
        129, 139
    to implement list-directed input/output,
        127, 129
Asymptotic replacements, 529–530
ATAN(X), 299
Automatic positioning of Fortran lines, 17

BACKSPACE statement, 625
Backward difference equations, 339–340
Banded matrix, 422
Batch processing, 11
Beattie-Bridgeman equation of state, 240
Binary
    representation of numbers, 4
    numbers and the game of Nim, 25

Binomial expansion, 198
Birge-Vieta method, 374–378
    Fortran code for, 376–378
Bisection method, 119–124
    algorithm, 122
    convergence rate, 371
    Fortran code for, 125, 249–251, 355–356
    -like algorithms, comparison of, 357–358
    refinements, 350–358
Bits, 5
Blank
    COMMON, 277
    option in OPEN statement, 130–131
    used to separate values in list-directed
        input/output, 50
Block DATA, 611
Block IF statement, see logical IF
Boundary value problems, 575, 583–584
Bubble sort, 212–213
    Fortran code for, 213
Buckling of a tall mast, programming
    problem V-A, (389)
Bytes, 5

Cache memory, 6
CALL statement, 246, 620
Carburization, programming problem II-A,
    169
Carriage control, 152–153
Cathode-ray tube (CRT), 12
Central difference equations, 340–341
Central processing unit (CPU), 7–8
CHAR(I), 209, 300
CHARACTER
    assignment statement, 39–40
    constants, 30
    function, 255
    set, 22
    substring, 180
    type statement, 33, 612
    variables, 203ff
    variables, comparison of, 204, 209
    variables, input/output of, 148ff
Chemical engineering, 161, sample problem
    V (383), programming problems II-
    C (174), III-C (240), IV-C (315)
Chezy-Manning equation, 391
Chi-square, 470–471
Civil Engineering, 102, sample problems
    I (93), VI (437), programming prob-
    lems V-A (389), VI-A (448)
CLOSE statement, 131–132, 624
Closed-type difference equations, 568
CMPLX(X), 300
Cofactor, 405
Combinatorial, 198
Comment lines, 14–15
COMMON, 276–278, 379, 616
    blank, 277
    labeled, 277
    variables in both DATA and, 292
Compilation, 10
Compilation error, 22, 32
Compiler, 10
COMPLEX

numbers, 289
    input/output, 289
    type statement, 288–289, 613
Compound interest and loan payments, 78
Compressibility of gases, 240–242
Computation block, 85
Computed GO TO, 87, 621
Computer
    languages, 11
    operating principles, 4ff
    word, 6
Concatenation, 208
Condon, E. U., 315
Conduction of heat, 99, 238, 537
Conductivity, thermal, 100
Constant
    CHARACTER, 30
    COMPLEX, 289
    DOUBLE PRECISION, 286
    LOGICAL, 289
    named, 293
    REAL, 28
    REAL with an exponent, 29
Continuation field, 13
CONTINUE statement, 76, 190, 620
Contour plotting, 201, 218–219
    Fortran code for, 221–224
Control unit, 7
Convection, 100, 238
Convergence
    of bisection method, 123, 371
    of Gauss-Siedel method, 424–425
    of Newton's method, 369–371
    of Romberg integration, 517
    of a series, 116, 330ff
        accelerated, 333
        necessary condition for, 331
        sufficient condition for, 331
Cooling curves, programming problem III-
    B (237ff)
COS(X), 46, 299
Cote's rule, 514, 536
Coupled differential equations, 557, 574–
    583
    Fortran code for, 575–576
Cramer's rule, 407–410
    speed of, 421
Critical point, 175
Cubic spline fits, 480–486
    Fortran code for, 483–485

D-format, 287
Data analysis using numerical derivative,
    341–344
Data files, 124–134
    creating, 132
    direct access (DAM), 130
    sequential access (SAM), 129
DATA statement, 292–293, 614
    block, 611
Dayfile, 23
Debugging, 22
Decision structures, 59ff
Default typing, 31
    of function names, 255

of statement functions, 106
Dense matrix, 422
Descartes' rule of signs, 373–374
Determinant, 402–407
Determinant, properties of, 406
Diagonal dominance, 424
Diagnostic prints, 228
   in the bisection method, 124, 356–357
   in Gauss-Siedel method, 425, 428
   in Newton's method, 363–364, 369
Difference equations, see finite difference
   equations
Differential equations, 342–344, 552ff
Differentiation, numerical, 337ff
Diffusion constant, 170, 383
Diffusion of temperature, 169ff, 393ff
DIMENSION statement, 180ff, 615
   combining with COMMON, 277
   combining with type statements, 181
Diode, 172
Direct access method (DAM) files, 130
Discretization errors, 558, 592, 602–603
Disk, magnetic, 6, 129
Disk files, see data files
Divergence
   of an infinite series, 331
   of an integral, 530
DO loop, 189ff, 623
   implied, 194ff
   nested, 78, 192–193
   terminators, 189, 623
   transfer in and out, 623
DoWhile structure in extended Fortran, 71,
   73, 74, 296–298
Dominance levels for data types, 38, 287
Double integrals, 531–534
   Fortran code for, 533, 541–544
DOUBLE PRECISION
   input/output, 287
   statement, 286–288, 613
   to minimize round-off error, 601
Drag, 341, 576
Dummy arguments, 108, 246, 248, 612
   protecting, 248

E-format, 144–145
Echo print, 43, 86, 142
Editing programs, 12
Electrical engineering, 171–172, program-
   ming problems III-A (235), VI-B (452)
ELSE statement, 67, 622
   as terminator of a DO loop, 189
ELSE IF statement, 70, 622
   as terminator of a DO loop, 189
END option in READ/WRITE statements,
   155
END statement, 47, 246, 611, 618
   as terminator of a DO loop, 189
End Do in extended Fortran, 71, 73, 296–
   298
END IF statement, 60, 622
ENDFILE statement, 625
END-OF-FILE flags, 119, 134, 154
ENTRY statement, 617
.EQ. , 61
EQUIVALENCE statement, 616
.EQV. , 290
ERF(X), 170
Error
   absolute, 590
   analysis, 588ff

bars and validity of fit, 469–470
compilation, 22
   translating algebra to Fortran, 52
   misspelling variable names, 291
   using CHARACTER variables in
     arithmetic expressions, 41
computational, 557–559
discretization, 556, 592, 602–603
estimates by order, 334
in Euler's method, 561
execution, 23, 47
   array index out of bounds, 183
   floating point overflow, 275–276
   in formatted input/output, 143
   noninitialized variables, 47, 113
experimental, 589, 592
experimental, amplification of, 603–608
fractional, 590
function, Efr(x), 170
in a function, 591
option in OPEN statements, 130
option in READ/WRITE statements, 155
relative, 590
in Romberg integration, 517
round-off, 233, 287, 556, 592–602
   causes of, 596
   growth of, in differential equations,
     598–600
   in matrix problems, 422
   minimizing, 600–602
   syntax, 22
   truncation, 334, 556, 592, 602–603
Euler's method, 559–569, 603
   Fortran code for, 560–561
Exchange sort, see selection sort
Execution error, see error, execution
EXP(X), 45, 299
Experimental error, see error, experimental
Explicit typing, 32
Exponentiation (**), 44–45
Exponentiation, successive, 36
Expression
   arithmetic, 34
   character, 208
   logical, 60
   mixed mode, 38
Extended Fortran, 296
EXTERNAL statement, 268–270, 378, 615
Extremum of a function, 459

F-format, 140–142
Factorial, 115, 226
   Fortran code for, 191
Failure path, 85
.FALSE. , 61, 289, 613
False position, method of, see Regula Falsi
   method
File, 14, see also data file
File specifier in OPEN statements, 130
Finite difference calculus, 337ff
First backward difference, 339, 371
First forward difference, 338
First order differential equations, 553
Fixed point iteration, 423, see also succes-
   sive substitution
Fixed point numbers, 28, see also INTEGER
Floating point
   numbers, 28, 140, see also REAL
   overflow, 275–276
Flow control statements, 619–623
   CALL, 246, 620

CONTINUE, 76, 190, 620
DO, 78, 189ff, 194ff, 623
ELSE, 67, 622
ELSE IF, 70, 622
GO TO, 19, 75, 87, 620–621
IF, 60, 64, 86, 88, 621–622
RETURN, 246, 619
Flowchart, 56–58
   examples, 57, 58, 69, 72, 74, 79, 83
   symbols, 57
Fluid flow, 93, 394, 437
Fluidized bed reactor, 315
Force diagram, 449–450
FORMAT
   of a Fortran line, 13–14, 610
   input/output errors, 143
   statement, 140ff, 627
   statement, repeated use of, 154
   specifications, apostrophe, 148
   specifications, Aw, 150–152, 204–205
   specifications, Dw.d, 287
   specifications, Ew.d, 144–145
   specifications, Fw.d, 140–142
   specifications, Iw, 142–143
   specifications, nX, 145–146
   specifications, repeatable, 147
   specifications, slash (/), 146
   specifications, Tn, TLn, TRn, 147
Fortran
   first installation, 10
   format of lines, 13, 610
   limitations, 3
Forward difference equations, 338–340
Fractional error, 590
FUNCTION, 254ff, 611
   argument list, 254
   statement-, 105–107, 244, 611

Gas separation, 162ff
Gauss, Carl Friedrich, 523
Gauss-Jordan method, 410–421
   Fortran code for, 415–417
   for matrix inversion, 417–421
   speed of, 421
Gauss quadrature, 523–527
Gauss-Siedel method, 422–429
   convergence, 424–425
   for cubic spline fits, 483
   Fortran code for, 425–429
.GE. , 61
Generic intrinsic functions, 298
GO TO
   computed, 87, 621
   as terminator of DO statements, 189
   unconditional, 19, 75, 620
Graphics plotter, 242
Graphing on the printer, 216ff
Greatest common factor (GCF), 257–260
.GT. , 61

Hardware, 8
Harmonic motion, 262–267, 556–557
Harmonic series, 331
Heat capacity, 490, see also specific heat
Heat transfer, 99, 312ff, 537
Hierarchy rule
   of arithmetic operations, 36–38
   for order of .AND. and .OR. , 62
Higher-level languages, 11
Hollerith, 148
Hyperbolic functions, 299, 328

I-format, 142–143
ICHAR( ), 210, 300
Ideal gas, 174
Identification field, 14
Identity matrix, 402
IF, see logical or arithmetic IF
IF-THEN statements, 621–622
Ill-conditioned matrix, 409, 604
   causing amplification of errors, 603–608
   and least squares curve fitting, 477–479
IMPLICIT type statement, 290–291, 614
Implied DO loop, 194ff
   within a DATA statement, 292, 615
Improved Euler's method, 567–569
   as part of predictor-corrector method, 573
Indefinite values, 47, 113
Indentation of DO and IF blocks, 60, 192
INDEX(sl,s), 207, 300
Industrial engineering, 228–229, sample
   problem III (229)
Infinite limits and numerical integration,
   527–529
Infinite series, 135, 196ff
Initial value problems, 575
Initialization
   block, 85
   of an array, 191, 292
   of variables during compilation, 291–294
Input/output statements, 625–627
   READ, 19, 42, 127, 139, 626–627
   WRITE, 127, 139, 627
   PRINT, 18, 30, 139
   and implied DO loop, 194ff
Input/output device number, 128
INQUIRE statement, 625
Installment loans, 78; Fortran code, 81
Insulation of steam pipes, 99ff
INT(X), 300
INTEGER
   constants, 28
   type specification statement, 32, 612
Integration, numerical, 502ff
   and infinite limits, 527–529
   of a function of two variables, 531–534
   of singular functions
Interactive processing, 11, 12
Interpolation and the Regula Falsi method,
   351
Interval-halving, see bisection method
INTRINSIC statement, 268–269, 615
Intrinsic functions, 45–46, 299–300, name
   conflict with user-written functions,
   107
Inverse matrix, 410
   computed by Gauss-Jordan method, 417–
   421
   Fortran code for 429–432
Iterative
   loop structures, 78–84
   solutions to differential equations, 573
   solutions of matrix equations, 422–427

Jacobi iteration, 423
Job control language (JCL), 12
Junction equation
   in fluid flow, 437
   in electrical networks, 453

Kirchoff's laws, 452–453

Labeled COMMON, 277, 616
Laminar, 395
.LE. , 61
Least squares, 456ff
   as an ill-conditioned problem, 477–479
   exponential, 464–465
   Fortran code for, 471–475
   line, 463–464
   nonlinear, 499
   polynomial, 466–468
Legendre polynomials, curve fitting with,
   549
LEN(ch), 207, 300
Library functions, see intrinsic functions
Limit, 337
Line numbers, 16
Linear simultaneous equations, see matrix
   equations
List-directed input/output, 50–51, 127, 139,
   148
   of complex numbers, 290
Load map, 23
Locally defined variables, 271
LOG(X), 45, 299
LOG10(X), 261, 299
LOGICAL
   block IF structure, 60ff, 622
   combinational operators, 61
   constants, 289
   expressions, 60
   IF statement, 86, 621
   type statement, 289–290, 613
   variables, 61
Loop equation
   in electrical networks, 453
   in fluid flow, 438
Loop structures, 71ff
   flowchart example, 74
   iterative, 78
   repetitive, 76
Lotka-Volterra equations, 579
.LT. , 61

Machine language, 10
Maclaurin series, 326
Main memory, 4–6
Main program name, 41, see also
   PROGRAM
Materials engineering, 168–169, programming problem II-A (169)
Matrix (linear simultaneous equations),
   396ff
   banded, 422
   column, 400
   comparison of numerical algorithms, 421–
   422
   dense, 400
   identity, 402
   ill-conditioned, 409
   inverse, 410
      computed by Gauss-Jordan method,
      417–421
      Fortran code for, 429–432
   multiplication, 279, 400–402
      Fortran code for, 429
   notation, 397–400
   null, 402
   printing, 200
   singular, 409

sparse, 422
square, 400
MAX( ), 299
Maximum/minimum, see minimum/max-
   imum
Measurement error, 589, see also error,
   experimental
Mechanical engineering, 99, sample problem VIII (537), programming problems III-B (237), IV-A (312), V-D
   (394), VIII-A (546)
Melting rate, 555
Memory
   main, 4–6
   preset to zero, 113
Metallurgical engineering, see materials
   engineering
Midpoint method, see modified Euler's
   method
Milne, W. E., 574, predictor-corrector
   equations, 574
MIN( ), 299
Minimum
   of squared deviations, 461–463
   repair costs, sample problem III (229)
Minimum/maximum
   algorithm, 109
   and horizontal tangent lines, 112
   exam scores, Fortran code, 118
   of an array, 199
Mining engineering, programming problem
   V-B (391)
Mixed mode
   expressions, 38
   replacement, 40–41
MOD(X,Y), 299
Mode conversion, 40–41, 300
Model function in least squares fitting, 458
Modified Euler's method, 563–567
   Fortran code for, 564–566
   in predictor-corrector method, 573
Modified Regula Falsi method, 353–357
   Fortran code for, 355, 356
Multiple assignments, 441
Multiple roots, 348, in Newton's method,
   365–366

Name
   conflict with intrinsic function, 107
   of data file, 130
   of Fortran variables, 31–33
   of FUNCTION, 255
   of main program, 41
   of statement function, 106
   of SUBROUTINE, 245–246
Named constants, 293
Necessary condition for convergence of infinite series, 331
Nested
   block IF structures, 68
   DO loops, 192–193, 623
   loops, 78, 98
Network
   electrical, programming problem VI-B
   (452)
   plumbing, sample problem VI (437)
Newton's algorithm for square roots, 78,
   297, 360–361
   Fortran code for, 84

Newton's method, 358ff
  convergence rate, 369–371
  Fortran code for, 366–368
  problems with, 363–364
Newton's relations for roots of polynomials, 374
Newton-Raphson method, see Newton's method
Nim, 25, programming problem IV-B (315)
NINT(X), 300
Nonexecutable statement, 30, 140
Nonlinear equations, 524
Nonrepeatable edit descriptors, 147
.NOT. , 61
Null matrix, 402
Numerical differentiation, 337ff
Numerical integration, 502ff

Object code, 10
Ohm's law, 453
One-step methods, 559
OPEN statement, 129–131
Optimum
  panel width, 602
  step size, 559
.OR. , 61–62
Order
  of Euler's method, 561
  of modified Euler's method, 564
  of Runge-Kutta method, 571
Ordering of Fortran statements, 295
Orthogonal functions, 480
Overfit to data, 469
Overprinting, 153
Overwriting constants, 251
Oxygen deficiency of a polluted stream, programming problem I-B (102)

Parabola, area beneath, 509
PARAMETER statement, 293–294, 614
Parasitic solution, 600
Parentheses in arithmetic expressions, 36
Partial derivative, 460
PAUSE statement, 618
Pivot element, 412
Pivot element and row switching, 413–415
Plotting, 216ff
  contour, 201, 218–224
  Fortran code for, 216ff, 221–224, 263–267
Pointer, 199, 214
Poisson distribution function, 271
Polynomials
  orthogonal, 480
  roots of, 373–378
Precedence, see hierarchy
Predator-prey problem, 577–582
Predictor-corrector methods, 573–574
Pressure, in a pipe, 93ff; on a dam, 532–533
Prime number, 201
PRINT, 18, 30, 139
Probability theory, 272
Procedure statements, 610–612
  BLOCK DATA, 611
  FUNCTION, 254ff, 611
  Statement function, 105–107, 244, 611
  SUBROUTINE, 245ff, 610

PROGRAM statement, 41, 610
Programming style, 85
Prompt, 41
Pseudocode, 59
Pseudocode examples, 79, 82, 110, 134

Quadratic equation, 67, 348
Queuing theory, 231

Radian to degree, Fortran code, 66
Random access memory (RAM), 6
Ratio test, 116, 331
READ, 19, 127, 139, 626
READ, list-directed, 42
REAL
  constants, 28
  constants with exponents, 29
  type statement, 32, 612
  variables as DO loop indices, 190
REAL(X), 300
Record times for the mile run, programming problem VII-B (499)
Referencing
  an array element, 181
  recursive, 533
  statement functions, 106
Regula Falsi method, 351–353
  Fortran code for, 355–356
  modified, 353–357
Relational operators, 60–61
Relative error, 590
Relaxation factor, 354
Remainder
  in synthetic division, 375
  term, in a Taylor series, 333–334
Repair costs, minimizing, sample problem III (229)
Repeatable format specifications, 147
Resonant circuit, programming problem III-A (235)
RETURN statement, 246, 619
RETURN statement, alternate, 619
REWIND statement, 131–132, 625
Reynold's number, 94, 395
Richardson extrapolation, 515
Rocket trajectory, sample problem IV (304)
Romberg method of integration, 515–522
  convergence, 517
  equation, 516
  Fortran code for, 519–522
Roots of equations, 347ff
  bisection technique, 119–124
  comparison of methods, 378
  multiple, 348
Round-off error, 287, 333, 556, 592–602
  causes, 596
  growth in solutions to differential equations, 598–600
  in matrix problems, 422
  minimizing, 600–602
Rounding
  Fortran code for, 261
  of nonsignificant digits, 590
  when printing, 141
Runge-Kutta method, 569–573
  fourth order, 571
  second order, 570

Saddle point, 461
SAVE statement, 271–275, 616
Secant method, 371–372
Second order differential equations, 554
Secondary memory, 6
Selection sort, 211–212
  Fortran code for, 215
Sequential access method (SAM) files, 129
Series, see also Taylor series
  alternating, 332
  convergence, 331
  harmonic, 331
  summation, 119ff, 135, 197
  summation using INTEGER arithmetic, 257
Shear force, programming problem VIII-A (546)
Shooting, 584
Significant figures, 589–592, loss of, 601
Simpson's rule, 507–514, 523, 602–603
  equation, 511
  relation to fourth Runge-Kutta method, 571
  relation to trapezoidal rule, 512
SIN(X), 46, 299
Singular
  function, integration of, 530
  matrix, 409
Slash(/) format, 146
Software, 8
Sorting, 210ff
  bubble sort, 212–213
  selection, sort, 211–212
  with a pointer, 214
Source code, 10, 23
Sparse matrix, 422
Special characters in Fortran, 22
Specific heat, sample problem VII (490)
Specification statements, 32, 612–616
  CHARACTER, 33, 612
  COMMON, 276–278, 379, 616
  COMPLEX, 288–289, 613
  DATA, 292–293, 614
  DIMENSION, 180ff, 615
  DOUBLE PRECISION, 286–288, 613
  ENTRY, 617
  EQUIVALENCE, 616
  EXTERNAL, 268–270, 378, 615
  IMPLICIT, 290–291, 614
  INTEGER, 32, 612
  INTRINSIC, 268–269, 615
  LOGICAL, 289–290, 613
  PARAMETER, 293–294, 614
  REAL, 32, 612
  SAVE, 271–272, 616
Speed of sound, 77
Spline fits, see cubic spline fits
SQRT(X), 46, 299
Standard deviation, 183
Statement function, 105–107, 244, 611
Status option in OPEN statements, 130–131
Stefan-Boltzmann law, 488
STOP statement, 13, 47, 618
  as terminator of a DO loop, 189
Stress on bridge elements, programming problem VI-A (448)
String length, 33
Structured programming, 86, 188
Style, programming, 85, 182, 188

SUBROUTINE statement, 245ff, 610
   arguments, 245–246
   CALL, 246
   name, 245–246
Subscripts, array, 180
Substring of a CHARACTER string, 205
Success path, 85
Successive substitutions, 91, 318
Sufficient condition, 331
Summation
   algebraic notation, 114, 180
   algorithms, 113–119
   and the DO loop, 190
   finite, 114
   Fortran code for, 114–115, 117–118
   infinite, 115
Syntax error, 22
Synthetic division, 375–376

T-format, 147
TAN(X), 299
Taylor, Brook, 326
Taylor series, 322ff
   convergence, 330–331
   remainder term, 333–334
Terminator statement of a DO loop, 189
Top-down programming, 244

Trailer data line, 77, 153–155
Trajectory of a satellite, 585
Transcendental
   equations, 349
   functions, 120, 328
   numbers, 321
Trapezoidal rule, 504ff, 523, 602
   iterative algorithm, 506
.TRUE. , 61, 289, 613
Truncation
   error, 334, 556, 592, 602–603
   in INTEGER division, 35
   of REAL numbers, 35
Turbulence, 395
Type declaration statements, 612–614
   CHARACTER, 33, 612
   COMPLEX, 288–289, 613
   DOUBLE PRECISION, 286–288, 613
   IMPLICIT, 290–291, 614
   INTEGER, 32, 612
   LOGICAL, 289–290, 613
   REAL, 32, 612

Unconditional GO TO, 19, 75, 620
Unit specifier in OPEN statements, 129–130
Unstable differential equation, 572

Validity of fit, 469–470
Van der Waal's equation, 174, parameters, 177
Variable
   dictionary, 85
   names, 31
Vector
   column matrix, 400
   multiplication, 282
Velocity of water waves, 49
Vertical spacing of output, 152–153
Viscosity, 94
Very large scale integrated circuit (VLSIC), 5

Weight factors for Gauss quadrature, 523, 526
Word length, 29, 35, 276
WRITE statement, 127, 139, 627

X-format, 145–146

Young's modulus, 389–390

Statement	Comment

(*)BACKSPACE ⟨unit no.⟩   Not used in this text.

(*)INQUIRE(⟨arg. list⟩)   Not used in this text.

(*)ENDFILE(⟨unit no.⟩)   Not used in this text.

INPUT/OUTPUT STATEMENTS

READ(⟨unit no.⟩,⟨format no.⟩,[options],⟨in-list⟩)
READ ⟨format no.⟩,⟨in-list⟩
READ *,⟨in-list⟩   List-directed READ.

WRITE(⟨unit no.⟩,⟨format no.⟩,[options],⟨out-list⟩)
PRINT ⟨format no.⟩,⟨out-list⟩
PRINT *,⟨out-list⟩   List-directed PRINT.

FORMAT(⟨format spec. list⟩)   I/O editing specifications.

THE ORDER OF FORTRAN STATEMENTS

PROGRAM/SUBROUTINE/FUNCTION				Comments
IMPLICIT		PARAMETER	FORMAT	
Type Specifications (REAL, INTEGER, etc.)				
Other Specifications DIMENSION/COMMON/EXTERNAL/INTRINSIC/				
Statement functions				
All executable statements	DATA			
END				